Building Brands Directly

Building Brands Directly

Creating Business Value from Customer Relationships

Stewart Pearson

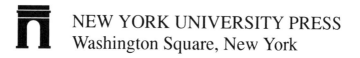

NEW YORK UNIVERSITY PRESS
Washington Square, New York

First published in the U.S.A. in 1996 by
NEW YORK UNIVERSITY PRESS
Washington Square
New York, N.Y. 10003

Library of Congress Cataloging-in-Publication Data
Pearson, Stewart.
Building brands directly : creating business value from customer
relationships / Stewart Pearson.
p.   cm.
Includes bibliographical references (p.   ) and index.
ISBN 0–8147–6618–8
1. Direct marketing.   2. Advertising, Direct mail.   3. Customer
relations.   4. Brand name products—Marketing.   I. Title.
HF5415.126.P4   1996
658.8'4—dc20   95–22869
                                                      CIP

Printed in Great Britain

For my father,
Alec B. Pearson

Contents

. . . .

List of Figures

List of Tables

Acknowledgements

My special thanks to Mitch Stockton and Drayton Bird, who made me think.

And to everyone who exchanged their ideas, in particular Paul Ashby, Tony Dale, Michael Herbert, Penny Harris, Derek Holder, Melanie Howard, Jo Howard-Brown, Karen Lee, John Lomer, Andy May, Denise O'Dwyer and Brian Thomas.

And to Stella Pearson, Bill and Helen Nicoll, and Lalage Sadler for their welcome and patience.

And T.L.

Introduction

I have written this book for those who own and manage brands, those who advise them and those who are studying to be the brand stewards of the future.

The most valuable asset of any company is its customer base. I have found that most companies achieve no more than one-third of the potential profit that customers would contribute, if only they were asked. This book shows you how to realise the commerical value of your customer relationships. You will discover how to put the philosophy of customer focus into practice, and how to motivate more customers to seek a closer association with your brand and exchange more value with your company.

My purpose is to invite you to look at your marketing from a new perspective. To add a new dimension to your brand. To look at your organisation through new eyes. And to look at your accounts and balance sheet on a new basis.

The new perspective is that of your customers. The new dimension is the relationship. The new eyes are those of your staff. The value of your business is the financial value of your customers.

Successful companies know the value of a customer. This knowledge becomes a touchstone, shared by everyone, guiding everything they do. Almost every company claims to give priority to its customers. Do they behave as if they do? *Do you?*

I use six tests of 'customer honesty'. The answers help me to measure a company's commitment to its customers and its prospects for growth.

I have worked with a small number of companies that know how to do these things well. I will share their secrets with you.

I began my career in 1975, with the *Reader's Digest*, work-

The Customer Honesty Tests

---

1 The 'Thank You' Test
When a customer buys, how do you say 'thank you'?

2 The 'Recognition' Test
On meeting regular customers, how do your staff recognise them?

3 The 'Listening' Test
How do you seek out your customers, and find out what they want?

4 The 'Learning' Test
How do you know what will make customers buy more from you?

5 The 'Retention' Test
How do you make sure you keep your existing customers?

6 The 'Loyalty' Test
How do your know what your customers will buy next – and from whom?

---

ing in database and marketing management. The *Reader's Digest* is intensely private: its secrets are well-guarded, and its business is not well understood. With Ogilvy & Mather Direct I worked with American Express and Rank Xerox, amongst others. American Express charges for a service that the competition generally provides free, or at significantly lower cost. The American Express card thrives. Rank Xerox competes successfully against Japanese manufacturing innovation at its most aggressive.

The big issues faced by every business – Competitive Advantage, Quality Management, Customer Service and Information Technology – are all concerned with re-engineering the business towards the customer. But too much time in business is spent determining how to be more efficient today, and too little time building for the future. It is the responsibility of marketing to build a future of change and growth. In its first editorial of 1995 the *Financial Times* quoted Professor Gary Hamel of the London Business School, who argued that European management must make growth its *'overwhelming obsession'*.[1]

The capacity for growth lies within two groups of people: your customers and your staff. Others have written about how to raise the performance of an organisation by releasing the potential of its people. My theme is: building brands and financial value from customer relationships.

For most organisations, the potential that lies within customer relationships is untapped. Marketing can realise this potential, but not if regarded as a function, department or specialist activity. Marketing is the responsibility of everyone – from the board of directors through to the front-line staff. And building brands is the major role of marketing.

Brands are important – a vital source of value to the businesses that own them. But long-established brand leaders are under threat everywhere. Ownership of a well-established, leading brand once guaranteed a steady flow of earnings. Now lower entry barriers and technology costs are ushering in new competition that threatens to wipe out these earnings, overnight.

Owning a strong brand once guaranteed what marketers described as 'brand loyalty.' Consumers bought the brand regularly. The brand's share of its market was stable. Advertising had largely been responsible for building the brand. I have worked with many leading consumer brands – including Coca-Cola, Marlboro and Heinz. I have learned how to retain customers and how to revitalise brands. I have attended many market research interviews: consumers understand and still appreciate the leading brands, but they buy less and less of them. Consumers understand and enjoy brand advertising, but they are not involved with it.

The idea of going direct to consumers to involve them is not new. Direct marketing has been recognised as an aspect of marketing since the 1970s. Although alluring as a concept, direct marketing is not well established, and not yet respectable. To some, direct marketing is junk mail. To others it is mail order. But direct marketing is growing: in Europe the expenditure on direct marketing has been estimated at 27 billion ECU in 1992 (at a growth rate of 8% p.a.) against media advertising of 37.4 billion ECU (forecast to decline over the next five years).[2]

Those with vested interests – advertising agencies in particular – seek to deny this growth. They regard direct marketing as a medium of communication, and measure it as direct mail. But direct marketing offers a completely fresh perspective on business, that encompasses communication and distribution, advertising and sales, customer service and public relations, information technology and human resources.

New language is needed to break down the barriers. Business management is concerned with investment, earnings, strategy and growth. Marketers focus on share, positioning, brands and values. Meanwhile, direct marketers talk about database, targeting, response and sales.

What I call relationship management reconciles these different views. Marketing can revitalise brands by building direct relationships with customers. Realising the potential value of customers is *the* strategic business objective.

STEWART PEARSON
3 January 1995

Your questions or comments are most welcome. Please write to me at:
Stewart Pearson
Chief Operating Officer
FCB Direct Worldwide
150 E 42nd Street
New York 10017 – 5612

Notes

1. 'A Business Resolution', *Financial Times* (London), (2 January 1995).
2. 'An Examination of the Statistics', The European Direct Marketing Association (Brussels) (June 1993).

PART I: STRATEGY

A TIME FOR CHANGE 1

'Marketing is critically ill, but more vital than ever'

The Value of Marketing – The Failure of Marketing – The Value of a Brand – The Threats to Brands – The New Customer – The Value of Advertising – The Potential Value of Direct Marketing – From Direct Marketing to Relationship Management – Testing the Value of a Brand – Summary

The Value of Marketing

Marketing has always promised more to business than it has delivered.

In *the* marketing textbook, *Marketing Management,* Philip Kotler defines marketing as: '. . . the social process by which individuals and groups achieve what they need and want through creating and exchanging products and values with others'.[1] Kotler's definition has four key truths. As a *social* process, marketing is concerned with relationships between people, and companies are defined by people as well as products. *Individuals and groups* in society differ, and so marketing must satisfy the widest variety of needs and wants. Satisfaction is achieved through *exchange*, which is a two-way process between individuals and companies. And the exchange involves *values*, not just physical products.

According to the classical theory of the market economy, many producers are in competition for many consumers. Price is the balancing mechanism. If supply exceeds demand prices fall, and if demand exceeds supply prices rise. Supply and demand adjust to the point at which the desire of producers to sell equals the desire of consumers to buy. The adjustment happens because – in theory – both sides have perfect *information*. Producers know what consumers need and want, and consumers know what products are available.

Profit is the difference between the cost to the producer and the price the consumer is willing to pay. The price that balances supply and demand maximises the total profit achieved by producers and the total value gained by consumers. The greater the value to consumers, the higher the price they are willing to pay, and so the higher the producers' profits.

Based on the exchange of money in competitive markets, the capitalist system of markets has succeeded where the only alternative – central planning – has failed. At university in London, I studied Marxist economics, from which central planning grew, specialising in the USSR and China under communism. At the centre of the system in both countries was a state planning function which set prices and matched consumers to producers. In '*The Soviet Economic System*', Alec Nove describes the mission of the planners as 'the maximum satisfaction of the needs of members of the society, and of society as a whole'.[2]

There was no market and no marketing because, if producers and consumers behaved as planners directed, they did not need any information. In theory, the central planners had all the information necessary to run the economy. In practice, the task of collecting and managing so much information was impossible.

Marketing *is* vital, because it communicates the information that producers and consumers require to maximise their satisfaction.

The Failure of Marketing

The theory of marketing is simple. Producers collect information about consumers and create products to meet their needs. They communicate, or advertise, to inform consumers about the availability and features of their products.

But the practice of marketing does not follow the theory. Marketers have forgotten these key truths in Kotler's definition:

— Marketing is about relationships between people

— Individuals and groups differ in their needs and wants

— Marketing involves an exchange of information between producer and consumer

— Values are as important as products.

Marketers have forgotten that marketing starts with the consumer, and most marketers are remote from their consumers. Most companies sell through complex distribution channels: geographically dispersed sales forces, agents and retailers. Most transactions by consumers are conducted out of the control of producers whose products reach consumers through multiple retail chains or independent outlets. Staff in most companies never have direct contact with the consumers who buy their products.

Most companies create products and services to meet the wants and needs of the largest possible mass market, rather than for individuals or groups.

The exchange of products and values between producer and consumer is largely in one direction: companies communicate information and values, consumers reply by paying money.

Stanley Marcus, founder of the US department store chain Neiman Marcus, famously said that consumers are statistics but customers are people. Because marketing is the development of relationships with individuals and groups, I use the term 'customer' rather than consumer throughout this book.

Forty years ago, in *The Practice of Management*, Peter Drucker argued the importance of marketing in terms of customers: 'There is only one valid definition of business purpose: to create a customer . . . Because of its purpose to create a customer, any business has two – and only two –

basic functions: marketing and innovation.'[3] Yet in most companies marketing has been relegated to the second division of management. Its responsibilities are narrow, usually limited to external communication to customers. Manufacturing tells marketing what to sell. Distribution is managed by operations or logistics. Sales and service meet the customer. Pricing decisions are controlled by finance.

Marketing at the Crossroads, a study by Coopers & Lybrand, highlights the gulf between how marketing sees its own importance and the more sceptical views of business management. One manager summarises the general belief that 'marketing is increasingly living a lie in my organisation'. The survey concludes: 'Marketing as a discipline is more vital than ever, marketing as a department is increasingly failing to match up to expectations. The marketing department is critically ill; only urgent treatment will enable it to fulfil the role that is now clearly staked out in the minds of top management.'[4]

The marginalisation of marketing is reflected in the careers of marketers and the composition of boardrooms. Most companies are managed by people with *professional* financial, manufacturing and engineering backgrounds. Few marketers become business managers: Colin Marshall at British Airways and George Bull at Grand Metropolitan are notable exceptions.

Marketing lacks credibility because it is rarely accountable. The contribution of marketing to financial performance is not well understood, and the effects of marketing are not rigorously measured. When marketing is evaluated the traditional measures are current sales, market share and brand awareness. Marketing is not measured on long-term financial return and shareholder value, the ultimate yardsticks of business performance.

In accounting, the practice is to treat marketing budgets as current expenditure. The effectiveness with which marketing budgets are spent is rarely scrutinised and the returns are rarely analysed. Contrast the treatment of marketing spend with investment in fixed assets. Capital expenditure is evaluated on the basis of long-term return on investment, and even modest capital budgets are rigorously analysed. In most companies, marketing is simply not part of the investment planning process.

The Japanese economy has been the success story of the last forty years. With reference to Drucker's definition of the purpose of business, the Japanese achievement is usually attributed to innovation rather than to marketing. Paul Kennedy, in *Preparing for the Twenty First Century*, refers to 'the extraordinary successes of Japan in recent decades in the fields of invention, design, manufacturing, and finance'.[5] Like most commentators, he makes no re-ference to Japanese marketing prowess, because marketing theory and education are dominated by US and British thinking. New York and London take great pride, for example, in their leadership in the creation of advertising. Yet it is indisputable that Japanese companies understand that marketing is an investment – and that US and British companies do not.

The difference is that Japanese business strategy builds market share as the basis for long-term profits, while Anglo-Saxon companies see profitability as a platform from which to build market share.

Japanese marketers have different time horizons, planning investment as much in the creation and development of markets as in manufacturing innovation. They enter a market, accept initial losses, but reap the rewards of volume and the economies of scale as volume builds. Historically, they have entered markets at the low end and then moved upmarket along with their customers.

Japanese marketing has different priorities. In Japan and most of continental Europe, a company is perceived as a community within society, with responsibilities to three groups: shareholders, customers and employees. In the US and Britain, the interests of shareholders have priority over those of customers and employees. Michel Albert, president of one of France's largest insurance companies, describes in *Capitalism Against Capitalism*[6] how this imbalance handicaps US and British companies. He reports how dividends from profits in the US and Britain are sacrosanct – they have been as high as 50 per cent for IBM and 60 per cent for Xerox – and limit the funds available for investment in innovation and marketing.

The low rate of capital investment in the US and Britain is frequently reported, but equally disastrous is the lack of investment in marketing. The lack of investment takes two forms: inadequate attention is paid to *internal* marketing, to build employee skills and motivation; and inadequate investment is made in *external* marketing, to build the company's brands and customer relationships.

The Value of a Brand

The concept of the *brand* lies at the heart of marketing theory and practice.

A brand is a combination of *features* (what the product is), customer *benefits* (what needs and wants the product meets) and *values* (what the customer associates with the product). A brand is created when marketing adds *values* to a product, and in the process *differentiates* it from other products with similar features and benefits.

By value, I mean the worth or contribution to profit of an activity such as marketing, or an entity such as a brand. By values, I mean the perceptions of a product, and beliefs about the product, that make consumers want to associate with it and buy it. Values make a brand, and as a result a brand has added value.

Brands are a short cut in communication: the values offered by brands are often summarised by simple advertising themes.

Pepsi drinkers are encouraged to see themselves as members of the Pepsi Generation. For decades, Pepsi has competed against the much larger Coca-Cola brand by targeting heavy-consuming young cola drinkers.

The American Express cardmember expects recognition and service superior to that offered to the average credit card holder, and recognition is at the heart of the long-running strapline 'The American Express Card. That will do nicely.' Recently the advertising theme has become

'Membership has its benefits' to reflect how American Express has maintained its differentiation by increasing the range of the services and privileges available to cardmembers.

Owning a Volkswagen is associated with dependability – 'If only everything in life was as reliable as a Volkswagen.' According to Volkswagen's UK agency BMP DDB Needham, consistent communication of this message has generated £30 million profit over three years in the UK, for an advertising spend of £10.9 million.[7]

Volkswagen illustrates why it is better to compete on values than on benefits. The Volkswagen brand value is dependability. Volvo advertising, in contrast, emphasises a product benefit – safety. A product benefit is easier to emulate than a brand value. Many car manufacturers now advertise the same safety benefit, reducing the differentiation of the Volvo brand and the perceived value of owning a Volvo.

The British Airways (BA) passenger has confidence in arriving on time and in comfort with 'The World's Favourite Airline'. The bold corporate advertising demonstrates BA's values: above all, a commitment to bringing people together from all around the world. In the early 1980s, BA transformed its image and performance by making customer service its priority. Its corporate mission, 'To fly to serve', embraces all points of contact with customers – before and after travel, as well as during flights.

The airline market illustrates why it is better to compete on values than on features. BA does not claim to be the biggest airline in passenger miles, so an advertising claim to carry more passengers from US rival Delta may be true, but it is still irrelevant. How we think about BA is what matters, and this is determined by our experiences of the airline.

The process of *branding* associates values with the name of a product or company, and customers choose a brand because they relate to or associate with its values. To the manufacturer of the brand, values are a source of competitive advantage – as much so as innovation in manufacturing or distribution.

Brands play a vital role in the market economy. To make efficient choices amongst alternative products, customers need information, and brands communicate information in a shorthand summary. The features, benefits and values they offer are immediately recognised and carry guarantees of quality: customers know what to expect. Brands simplify customer decision-making and make economic behaviour more efficient. Customer decision-making is a mix of the rational and the emotional: customers choose the brands with which they associate and which they perceive will offer them quality, innovation and value for money.

Traditionally, the leading brands bestrode and dominated their markets. Customers paid more for them than for unbranded alternatives, assuring higher margins for brand owners. The profits generated by brands were reinvested in innovation and marketing to enable them to retain market leadership.

Brands are usually considered to be intangibles. One measure of brand value is the size of the price premium that the brand commands. To calculate a brand's value, its earnings are compared with those of equivalent unbranded products. But few companies value their brands on their balance sheets. The practice is controversial and some of the results surprising – in the 1994 *Financial World* survey of brands, the value of the IBM brand was reported as negative.[8]

Brands have value. In an acquisition, a company with a strong brand can command a price many times its asset value.

—   In the biggest leveraged buy-out of the 1980s, a group of investors raised over $25 billion to buy RJR Nabisco. They were not investing in factories or plants, but in the revenue streams assured by the Nabisco food brands and the RJ Reynolds tobacco brands.

—   Philip Morris bought General Foods and Kraft to acquire leading brands, like Maxwell House coffee and Philadelphia cheese. Similarly, Nestlé bought Rowntree to acquire leading brands like Kit Kat and Yorkie.

Philip Morris and Nestlé both calculated that it was cheaper to acquire existing brands than to build their own.

Brands are important in every business sector. Software company Borland bought Ashton-Tate principally for its Dbase brand of database software. The price paid by BMW for Rover was controversial, because most British observers did not believe that BMW was paying enough for the Rover name and famous badges like MG and Triumph, which were perceived to be valuable, even though no current models carried them. The value of a powerful brand can long outlive its product.

The Threats to Brands

Established brands are threatened as never before, by a new and hostile marketing environment. In a rare leader on marketing *The Economist* reported: 'all over the world look-alike competitors are elbowing aside brands that have been famous for so long some owners have been reckless enough to name a generation after them'.[9]

The new competition consists of:

 (i)   retailer private label

 (ii) specialist retail category killers

(iii) service manufacturers

(iv) direct marketers.

In consumer markets, the fiercest new competition comes from retailer private label products, which are taking a growing share in many categories. The trend is most advanced in the UK, where private label share exceeds 30 per cent in most supermarkets, is over 50 per cent in the largest, Sainsbury's, and is 100 per cent in Marks & Spencer. The trend is most visible for everyday, low price goods, but private label is also emerging in more expensive, high technology categories like consumer electronics, photography and computers.

Private label products are copycats. They reproduce

the features and benefits of brands, and add the values associated with the retailer's brand. Retailers need invest little in research, do not need to market each product separately, have guaranteed distribution, and can compete at lower prices.

The early private label products did not match brands for quality. But brands have not maintained their differentiation, squeezed as they are between increasing marketing costs and declining margins. Private label has narrowed the gap – partly because many brand manufacturers make private label products for retailers, and customers know this. Brands are still perceived to offer more value, but their commanding position has been undermined.

According to *Financial World* the two biggest brands in the world are Coca-Cola and Marlboro, and in 1993 *Financial World* reported Marlboro as the leader. But Marlboro has been in decline for some years, with its share of the US cigarette market falling from a high of 30 per cent to 22 per cent. Smokers were increasingly unwilling to pay Marlboro's price premium. On Marlboro Friday, 2 April 1993, Philip Morris cut the brand's price and accepted lower profits as the cost of rebuilding market share. Instantly, Philip Morris' market capitalisation fell 23 per cent.

Marlboro's strategy was almost Japanese. By the following summer, market share had recovered, back to almost 30 per cent. But the company's market capitalisation had not re-covered: the financial markets were unimpressed, and the architect of Marlboro Friday, chief executive Michael Miles, was out of a job. There are few better examples of the failure of the financial markets to support the creation of long-term value.

Marlboro was losing share to lower priced brands and to private label. But multiple retailers, responsible for the growth in private label, confront other forms of new com-petition. In many retail sectors, specialist retail category killers like Toys 'R' Us, Staples, PC World, and the ware-house clubs like Costco, offer wide selections of goods at low prices. They spend little on their sites or their mer-chandising and compete at prices even lower than the multiples.

The third form of new competition applies manufacturing principles to the service sector, to deliver standardised, quality-controlled products and an assured level of customer service. Examples are the fast food chains, like McDonald's and Pizza Hut, and the low priced hotel chains, like Novotel and Accor.

The fourth form of new competition sells direct, and is exemplified by Dell Computer and DirectLine Insurance in the UK. Dell calls itself a 'manu-tailer'[10] – it manufactures all its PCs to order. Dell's growth is founded on a standard of customer service that established manufacturers cannot match through their dealer networks and sales forces. DirectLine has used technology to reduce price and enhance service in the general insurance market. The long-established leaders in the UK insurance market were highly vulnerable to attack. Relying on antiquated distribution systems, their failure has been double: to build their own brands, and to develop direct links to their customers.

The common advantage enjoyed by the new competition is ownership of the *customer interface*. In every market power resides with whomever is in direct contact with the customer.

Competition creates choice, and choice changes customer behaviour. The effect of the Thatcher government's legislation in the 1980s was to create new competition in new areas – notably financial services, telecommunications, gas, electricity and water. In the 1990s, competition is intensifying in many markets, from publishing to petrol, and competition can attack even the most well-established brands from *any* direction.

In 1994 Coca-Cola overtook Marlboro as *Financial World's* most valuable brand. Coca-Cola has fought the Cola Wars with Pepsi for decades, but the new competition in cola comes from a little known Canadian company, the Cott Corporation. On Coca-Cola Monday, Sainsbury's launched its private label Classic Cola in partnership with Cott, taking a 60 per cent share in its own stores and a 15 per cent share of the total cola market in just one week. Coca-Cola's share in Sainsbury's fell from 63 to 33 per cent, and Pepsi's from 18 to 6 per cent. So much for Coca-Cola brand value and customer loyalty. As the chairman of Sainsbury's says: 'For the first time a cola has been found that is as good as Coca-Cola. That is a new situation for Coke.'[11]

The next competitor to confront Coca-Cola and Pepsi is Virgin, originally a music label, now an airline as well. Virgin is so confident of the strength of its brand that it is moving into radio, PCs and vodka, as well as cola.

The New Customer

Demography, education, diversity, competition and recession have changed the customer decision-making process in general, and brand choice in particular.

Customers are more questioning and less trusting. They want more choice and better information about the products they consume. They are more demanding, and seek products and services that are designed to meet their needs as individuals. Aware of the increased choices on offer, they expect to be rewarded for their custom. Constrained by a reduction in disposable income, they seek better value for their money.

In researching a wide range of markets, I have found a consistent pattern. Established brand values are still well appreciated, but they no longer govern consumer choice. Even where they do, brand values command a smaller price premium. Customers set the terms: they decide what they want and demand it at a low price. Customers increasingly *direct* producers.

So marketing strategy must satisfy customer-directed values at low prices. Continuous tracking of customers and innovation to meet changing customer demands are essential for survival.

In the early 1990s, computer manufacturer Compaq lost share as lower priced competition matched its product quality. Compaq responded successfully with manufacturing innovation that allowed it to compete on price and at the same time to regain leadership in quality. Simultaneously, Compaq changed its marketing strategy: previously it sold only through 3000 independent dealers, now it does business through over 30 000 outlets – any channel that customers want to use, including direct.

When innovation is based purely on product it can be matched quickly, as Europe's Soap Wars demonstrate. Unilever seemed to gain an advantage with the relaunch of Persil and Omo Power. But Procter & Gamble was only months behind with its own reformulation, and Unilever gained no long-term advantage.

So innovation based on marketing is vital. Traditional marketing is under pressure to justify its business role, and at the same time it faces a new, dynamic and hostile environment. Marketing is ill-equipped for this new environment. For example, the traditional marketing approach to new brands is fraught with risk, as Kotler reports: 'The new product failure rate was 40 per cent for consumer products, 20 per cent for industrial products, and 18 per cent for services.'[12] Most surveys of new product launches put the failure rate considerably higher.

New brands can be launched into the new environment, but successes are rare. Unilever built washing powder Radion by promoting a new benefit, the removal of odour from clothes. Grand Metropolitan developed Häagen-Dazs by targeting ice cream to a new market segment, young adults. And marketing can still revitalise brands: for example, Lucozade, formerly a health drink for hypochondriacs, is now advertised successfully by associating it with new sporting values.

But the marketing response to the new competition and the new customer is inhibited by lack of investment. Worse, traditional marketing is increasingly ineffective. General advertising in broadcast media, the weapon that built today's famous brands, is rusty. Even some of its largest users fear that advertising as we know it today may become obsolete.

The Value of Advertising

Today's famous brands were created by mass marketing and built primarily by television advertising. The link between television and advertising is close – in the heyday of the commercial television networks, marketers built brands by reaching a mass television audience at low cost. Television *is* a powerful and involving medium, with advertising often superior to programming in scripting and production quality. As result, television advertising is enjoyed and appreciated, and much of it is engaging, entertaining and compelling. It can communicate powerfully the features, benefits and values that motivate customer choice.

But television advertising is becoming less effective. More channels mean smaller audiences, lower entry costs, more advertisers, higher media costs and lower production values.

A report on viewing habits of television advertising, commissioned by the Newspaper Publishers' Association, dramatises the decline in consumer involvement with television advertising: 'The combined ad loss due to set changes, movements and inattention is 68.5 per cent. In other words, because viewers change channels, switch off the TV, leave the room, and look elsewhere, more than two-thirds of the advertising that they would have seen is lost.'[13]

The increase in marketing messages and promises has two effects. Customers filter out messages they perceive as irrelevant. And marketers have to work harder than ever to be credible. The Henley Centre's 1994 survey, *Planning for Social Change*, reveals the decline in television's credibility: 41 per cent said that television had become a little or lot worse, and only 11 per cent felt it had improved a little or a lot.[14]

Advertising is less involving and advertisers less trusted. One symptom of a lack of trust and a search for credibility was a spate of US advertising in 1994 associating brands with truth, led by American Express with its 'True Grace' credit card, and AT&T with services like 'True Voice' and benefits like 'True Rewards'.

Procter & Gamble is one of the world's largest advertisers, yet in May 1994 P&G Chief Executive Ed Artz endorsed a vision of the future without mass television advertising – reported by *Advertising Age* as 'Advertising's Grave New World'.[15] In this vision of the future, television will become *narrowcast*, with a multitude of channels reaching finely targeted audiences.

Artz envisaged three consequences. Advertising will be *integrated*. To engage the consumer more closely, advertising will be more tightly matched to the programming of the selected channel. Advertising will be *interactive*. To increase the value of the contact, the customer will be *invited to* make a direct response to the advertiser. Advertising will be *targeted*, to individual households. The database developed from customer contact will be used to match future messages to meet customer interests.

Artz endorsed a vision of '500 channel' television. The trends point in this direction, although few believe the number of channels will be so high. The share of the three networks NBC, ABC and CBS in the US fell in three decades from above 90 per cent to just above 60 per cent, losing share to local stations and to cable. Although their share has recently stabilised, it is likely that in the late 1990s a number of new networks led by Rupert Murdoch's Fox will further fragment the television audience. In Europe, the number of television channels grew from 70 in 1980 to 157 in 1993.

With more channels reaching smaller audiences, the entry costs of television have fallen, and so have the production values of programming and advertising. The result – as any TV viewer in the US will corroborate – is *junk television*. These trends are rarely admitted. Advertising is continued as before, even when the budget delivers less impact, amongst a smaller audience, at higher cost, within a lower quality environment. Advertising is rarely held to account, with few companies planning and measuring the long-term effects of their expenditure.

Sales promotion has taken an increasing share of the marketing budget, at the expense of advertising, because promotion can achieve a measurable increase in short-term sales, which advertising cannot. Like advertising, however, the long-term effects of sales promotions are poorly measured. There is tension between the short-term effects of promotion and the long-term effects of advertising. This results in confusion and in-fighting within the marketing community. Advertising agencies castigate their clients for promotions that increase sales but damage brand values. They exhort marketers to return to the glory days of big brand-building media campaigns. Sales promotion specialists deride the effectiveness of advertising and seduce marketers with the promise of an immediate boost to sales.

To *integrate* advertising and promotion makes sense. But integration is more a buzz-word than an established practice. As I will show, marketing has lacked a strategy for integration and the tools to combine the best of the disciplines. Moreover, the structure of marketing departments, with specialists responsible for each activity, militates against integration.

There *is* one area of marketing that is growing quickly, and which is being adopted by leading organisations in all sectors. Although he did not use the term, Ed Artz's vision is of a *direct marketing* world. At the Spring 1993 Direct Marketing Association conference in New Orleans, a spokesperson for Procter & Gamble was more specific about the four forces driving the company's interest in direct marketing.

(i) Advertising media costs are rising. As channels proliferate and audiences fragment, the costs per contact of the traditional, general media are rising. Meanwhile, the costs of data management, direct mail and telephone contact are falling.

(ii) Advertising effectiveness is reducing. There are more media and more advertisers. With more media reaching smaller audiences, the entry cost to advertising has fallen. With fiercer competition in more sectors of business, there are more advertisers, and the resulting clutter makes each message harder to put over, and less likely to be received. Direct contact with customers can have higher impact.

(iii) There is as much clutter in promotion as in advertising. Consumers are educated to expect a deal, to buy when the product is on offer. Brand values become less important. The objective of a promotion is to increase sales, but the quality of sales matters more than the quantity.

Only sales from certain customers represent incremental revenue. Only involvement in certain promotions changes the long-term behaviour of the customers.

(iv) Price discounting is reducing brand profitability. It erodes the price premium, reduces the perceived value, and damages the profit stream on which the future development of the brand depends. The result is a decline in the funds available for product innovation and advertising investment. Marketing needs to find new ways of justifying its role.

The Potential Value of Direct Marketing

The best definition of direct marketing is by the editor of *Direct Marketing* magazine: 'Direct marketing is an integrated system of marketing that uses one or more advertising media to effect a measurable response and/or transaction at any location, with this activity stored on database.'[16]

Direct marketing offers marketers, advertisers and business managers a new perspective, and a new opportunity. By adopting a direct marketing strategy, *marketers* can find more efficient and effective ways of using their budgets. By analysing their customers from a direct marketing perspective, *advertisers* can find a new weapon to build and sustain their brands. By thinking about customers and staff as assets, *business managers* can invest in them both and develop new revenue streams.

Direct marketing makes efficient use of marketing budgets because it is *targeted*. Customers are identified as *individuals*. Marketing captures *data* about individual customers and stores it on a *database*. Targeting from the database means that the right message can be sent to the right customer at the right time, motivating the customer to buy at the right place. Wastage is minimised. Direct marketing is effective because it is *powerful* and *personal*.

But direct marketing is not well understood. Most direct mail, for example, is poorly conceived and executed. As a result, it is neglected and derided by traditional marketers, and when it is used badly by them their customers call it *junk*.

Even so, consumers do read direct mail – and respond to it. A direct mail package can command the reader's attention for minutes. The presentation can be visually arresting and emotionally involving. The information contained can be involving and helpful. Direct mail is an interactive medium, the first of the many envisaged by P&G's Artz, because it prompts customer response. Direct marketing uses direct mail, direct response advertising, and the telephone as an outbound and inbound medium. But direct marketing also uses the Internet, interactive television, fax-on-demand, and smart cards that are automatically read and updated at the point of sale.

On the basis of cost per customer contact, direct marketing is more expensive than traditional advertising – but it is targeted, and the impact of a direct message to the customer is greater than the effect of watching television or reading a newspaper. On the basis of cost per *effective* contact, direct marketing can even be a cheaper way of reaching small audiences. Devoting a proportion of any marketing budget to direct marketing can create better returns than from relying exclusively on traditional advertising. The impact can surpass television, as Elida Gibbs found in marketing a line extension to its Impulse brand: *the peak for spontaneous awareness of the new product was almost three times as high when direct mail was added to the media plan.*

Direct marketing *is* more accountable because it can be controlled, tested and measured, and investment can be planned against increased sales and against the long-term value of the customer relationships created. Direct marketers have long known some basic truths new to many companies. For example, most companies find that it costs less to sell to an existing customer than to a new prospect. In my experience, the cost differential ranges from 4 to 16.

Here are two ways for any company to generate more sales and profits:

(i) Redirect marketing spend towards targeted media, starting with direct mail.

(ii) Redirect marketing spend towards existing customers, away from prospects.

From Direct Marketing to Relationship Management

Direct marketing is an efficient and effective system for communicating to customers. But direct marketing is more than just communication. It is one of a number of developments in business that have a common goal: to bring the company closer to its customers.

An organisation depends fundamentally on its customers – as Levitt states in *The Marketing Imagination*: 'the purpose of business is to make and keep a customer'.[17] Power in business resides with the owner of the customer interface, yet most companies have no experience of controlling their customers or managing their customer interface. Every company now needs to consider the potential of direct relationships with individual customers, and a process in required to manage relationships. My definition of this process is: 'Relationship management is a social process which harnesses the skills and resources of an organisation to exchange more products, values and information at all points of contact with customers.' This develops Kotler's original definition of marketing in three ways. I emphasise the importance of investing in the skills and resources of the organisation, because I believe that these will become the major sources of competitive advantage in the future. To the exchange of products and values, I add information, because knowledge about customers will be essential to win and retain their custom. And I see every customer contact as an opportunity to exchange more value.

By creating more contacts with the customer, a company can engage the customer in a relationship. By developing the relationship, the company can motivate more purchase of the brand and of its other brands. A customer relationship is both a private advertising medium and an individual distribution channel.

Brands can compete through the relationships they build with their customers as well as through product features, benefits and values. With less differentiated products and more cluttered advertising media, it becomes increasingly difficult to compete on features, benefits and values. The service element of a product increases, and the quality of service becomes important in differentiating brand and company.

Direct marketing is often described as *database* marketing. But customers are people, and people buy from people. The staff in a company exchange products and values with customers, and the staff deliver service. Relationship management recognises both customers and staff as assets. Investment in these assets creates new value and new streams of revenues and profits. With a relationship perspective, a company's responsibilities to its shareholders, customers and staff are complementary, not conflicting.

The productivity of people is the greatest challenge facing management. From a macroeconomic viewpoint, unemployment is the greatest social problem facing governments. Relationship management provides a framework for companies to evaluate the returns from greater investments in people by getting them closer to their customers. With the growth in customer contact centres, telephone is set to become a major new source of employment: in 1993 there were an estimated 365 000 customer contact centres in the US, averaging seven staff and representing over 2 million jobs, and the forecast is that telephone employment will be over 8 million by 2001.

By adopting relationship management, companies can invest more in customers *and* employees at the same time as they create new value for shareholders.

Testing the Value of a Brand

The evaluation of the effect of changes in the marketplace should not be left to financial analysts. It is the responsibility of marketing to test the influence of the different effects on the value of a brand.

I use these eight tests as a framework for developing a relationship management strategy:

Tests of the New Marketing Environment

Test 1

New competition:	Increase in the number of competitors
New customer:	Willing to consider alternatives to established brands
Test:	What are the alternative brands purchased by your customers or considered by them?

Test 2

New competition:	New forms of competitor, from new sectors and markets
New customer:	Questioning of company values and mission
Test:	What do your customers want to know from you about the products and services you provide?

Test 3

New competition:	Innovation and lower prices
New customer:	Searching for higher value for money
Test:	How much more can you charge for your brand against your competitors?

Test 4

New competition:	New forms of distribution
New customer:	Changing place and time of purchase
Test:	Where, when and how would your customers prefer to buy?

Test 5

| New competition: | Customisation of product and service |
| New customer: | Behaving individually |

| Test: | How many different types of customer do you have? |

Test 6

| New competition: | Higher service levels |
| New customer: | Expecting more of the seller |

| Test: | What are your customer expectations of service? |

Test 7

| New competition: | Increased advertising clutter |
| New customer: | Resistant to advertising |

| Test: | What is the cost per effective contact of advertising to your most important customers? |

Test 8

| New competition: | Increased offers and promotions |
| New customer: | Responds to good offers from anywhere |

| Test: | What is the long term effect on their custom from respondents to your promotions? |

Summary

Marketing is failing to deliver results, and advertising is declining in effectiveness. New competition and new customer behaviour demand new strategies to revitalise brands.

Direct marketing is an alternative to traditional advertising because it is powerful and personal. But, in every market, power resides with the owner of the customer interface, and the challenge to every company is to build direct re-lationships with customers. Relationship management is the new process which builds brands by building in concert customer relationships and employee motivation.

SUCCESSFUL BUSINESS MODELS 2

'. . . it pays to advertise. You could see the results'

Mail Order and the Origins of Relationship Management –
Reader's Digest and the Direct Model – The Membership Model
and the Development of Customer Relationships – American
Express and the Membership Model – The Customer/Channel
Management Model – The Customer/Channel Management
Model in Action: The Car Industry – Summary: The Critical
Success Factors of Relationship Management

Mail Order and the Origins of Relationship Management

Relationships with customers are individual and private. Marketing to the individual makes fewer headlines than television and is less well understood. It is instructive to analyse companies that are expert in managing their customer interface, to understand their business models and their critical success factors.

I see relationship management as the synthesis of two contrasting historical approaches to marketing: brand management and mail order. Relationship strategy is a logical development of brand management, applied to the individual customer instead of the mass market. Relationship tactics are based on best practice in mail order, a marketing and distribution system considerably older than either brand management or multiple retailing.

24

Mail order developed in the US over a hundred years ago to deliver products to a geographically dispersed population. The large distances and undeveloped retail networks created the need to reach customers directly. Department store chain Sears began in mail order, selling a complete range of clothing and household goods to the inhabitants of frontier towns, even delivering house-building kits. Many of the first consumer brands were built through mail order, and the early copywriters honed their skills on mail order. In 1905, one of the first, John Kennedy, defined advertising as 'salesmanship in print', and was promptly hired by Albert Lasker to write for the first advertising agency, Lord & Thomas.

In mail order, direct mail was both the marketing medium and the distribution channel – the method of communicating and of delivering products to customers. Mail order developed two relationship management tools:

(i) The catalogue, which became the virtual store of the mail order merchant, displaying and promoting the full range of merchandise

(ii) The customer list, which held names, addresses and transaction histories.

In Europe, a mail order catalogue industry developed along similar lines to the US. The European counterparts to Sears were the big book catalogues of Great Universal Stores in Britain, La Redoute in France and Quelle in Germany. Mail order companies used agents to sell products on to a group of customers, with the agent receiving a commission on sales. Agents, mainly housewives, sold to neighbours and friends to supplement their household incomes. One agent recruited a number of customers, a pointer to the relationship future.

The customer base was downmarket, and sales were encouraged by credit terms and long repayment periods. Catalogue marketers became experts in the management and control of credit, and still generate significant revenue by providing credit control systems to the retail and financial sectors.

The development of multiple retailing and the increasing numbers of working women have resulted in a decline in the number of agents. Most catalogue customers are now personal shoppers, whose credit needs are met by plastic cards and other forms of loan. Sears closed its catalogue business in the early 1990s and all over the world the big book catalogues are in decline.

But mail order as a segment is growing at a rate faster than retail sales. In the US, specialist catalogues like Lands' End (adult fashion) and Hanna Andersson (children's wear) have developed profitable customer franchises by tightly defining their target audiences and product portfolios. In Europe, specialist catalogues are also emerging: in the UK, the Next Directory has proved that a quality catalogue distribution channel can complement a national retail chain. Lands' End, by its successful entry into the UK market, is demonstrating the potential for international marketing through mail order.

The largest catalogue marketer in Europe, Germany's Quelle, foresees a future in which the large catalogue survives but becomes increasingly individualised for each household, and distributed on new electronic formats.[1]

Increasingly, companies sell to customers directly, by-passing agents, sales forces and retailers. Consumer and business buyers are gaining experience of shopping directly, for products as varied as fashion, insurance and computers. Mail order has become a mainstream distribution channel, which I call the Direct Model.

The Direct Model can work in three ways.

—   An exclusive method of selling: there are no sales forces or retailers
—   A channel specific to certain products or services, for example peripherals and supplies for a computer manufacturer
—   A channel complementary to an existing retail distri-bution network, to reach a wider market that does not buy in retail.

The computing industry illustrates the three types. Dell Computer grew by selling PCs to end-users, bypassing the traditional dealer network. Dell flirted with retail in the early 1990s but withdrew, disliking the loss of control over the customer interface to which it had grown accustomed and at which it is the master. Other computer manufacturers, like Digital, only sell low end products and supplies direct, and still market their mainstream products through a sales force and authorised dealers. IBM claims that it can now sell any product direct, and is testing direct contact with customers through on-line networks and the Internet.

Food companies are testing the three approaches. In the US, the Kraft General Foods premium coffee brand, Gevalia, is sold direct to the customer and is not available in retail. Babyfood brands sold in retail, like Gerber, are offering advice and additional services directly over the telephone. Carnation has tested direct delivery of a pet food brand, Perform.

The Direct Model ensures control of the customer interface. There is no need to find distributors and share margin with them. There is no investment in an owned sales channel and no competition for support from an independent dealer channel. Going direct shortens the time to market and improves control of finance and cashflow, and of marketing. With control comes the ability to test, measure and improve all aspects of marketing effectiveness. When the effectiveness of all marketing expenditure can be measured accurately, the value of marketing is demonstrable. Direct response advertisers place their budgets in media guaranteed to produce acceptable returns. It is no coincidence that direct response advertising is growing alongside the fragmentation of media: narrowcast television channels, radio stations and specialist magazines. Direct response advertising increasingly funds these new media.

The most famous employee of the Lord & Thomas agency, Claude Hopkins, wrote about the early days of advertising in his book *Scientific Advertising*: 'It was mail order which demonstrated to sceptical advertisers that it really paid to advertise; you could see the results.'[2]

The Direct Model is *not* a lower cost method of marketing. The percentage of revenue typically allocated to marketing in the Direct Model can exceed 20 per cent, high compared to retail. But the leverage – the sales effect of increased marketing spend – can also be very high. When I was Marketing Manager of *Reader's Digest* Music, we increased profits by significantly increasing the percentage of revenue invested in marketing.

Managers with no experience of the Direct Model find the scale of marketing budgets and the leverage of marketing spends difficult to understand.

Application of the Direct Model is evolving quickly and new technology is an important driver. Home shopping is increasingly conducted on-line, and business supplies are increasingly ordered through electronic data interchange (EDI). Many UK catalogues take up to 90 per cent of their orders over the telephone, and in France the Minitel videotex system, which is in 6 million homes and most businesses, contributes one-third of catalogue orders. In the US there is growing direct response advertising on the major on-line services: CompuServe, Prodigy, GEnie, Delphi, America Online and Apple's eWorld. To develop its understanding of the potential of these new media, PC Flowers, which delivers flowers and gifts in the US, has made itself accessible through on-line networks, videotex, personal digital assistants, and interactive kiosks in retail shopping sites.

The Direct Model used to be considered an alternative to retailing, yet it can complement retailing by offering the customer greater choice and convenience. Catalogues can drive new customers into retail outlets and generate incremental sales from existing retail shoppers. The Next Directory closely complements the Next shops – they sell similar ranges, with the catalogues issued in advance to test demand by product.

Reader's Digest and the Direct Model

Mail order is the delivery channel of many publishers, most notably of the *Reader's Digest* Association. The *Reader's Digest* became the most successful magazine in the world by selling monthly subscriptions by direct mail. Even today, news-stand sales are only a small proportion of its total circulation.

The *Reader's Digest* is the only mass market magazine to survive worldwide. It has over 100 million readers and is published in eighteen languages (the most recent is a Polish edition). Less well known is that the company sells 56 million books, 9 million music collections and 4 million videos each year. These other products contribute 70 per cent of worldwide revenues. The company grew these product lines by marketing them to its magazine subscribers: in the US alone the company sends 400 million messages to customers each year and receives 300 million responses.[3]

The *Reader's Digest* sets *the* standard of excellence for the Direct Model, with five factors critical to success.

Reader's Digest business model

(i) A steady, high volume supply of new customers is recruited cost effectively.

(ii) A stream of additional products and services is targeted to the customer base to increase customer spend.

(iii) A rigorously structured programme of research keeps the company in touch with customer preferences, and guides a new product development programme which rarely produces a failure.

(iv) A continuous programme of testing, coordinated worldwide, makes marketing, creative and promotion ever more effective and profitable.

(v) Investment in information technology is made primarily to meet marketing needs and is justified on the basis of marketing effectiveness.

Reader's Digest maintains a guaranteed circulation base and invests continuously in new subscribers. The magazine generates earnings from annual subscriptions and advertising, and the profit from marketing the other product lines to the magazine subscribers funds the continuing investment in the magazine circulation. The other product lines would not be as profitable without the magazine customer base as a receptive market. So the magazine and the other products could not exist without each other.

Analyses of product line profitability or a single accounting period are ultimately meaningless: long-term customer profitability matters more than annual accounts by product line.

New products are designed through a programme of research and testing. This is conducted among samples from the best customer segment, not in the general market, ensuring that the product concepts that win in research are those that will definitely be bought by existing customers.

A *Reader's Digest* new product research and test programme

Step One   Questionnaires invite customers to rank possible new product concepts in order of their attractiveness.

Step Two   Solus questionnaires about the higher ranking concepts probe more deeply into their desirable features and perceived benefits, to confirm new product design.

Step Three   New product promotion material is created and mailed to customers to measure their response to the material and to estimate their demand for the product ahead of production.

Step Four   A small run of the product is produced, and key marketing variables – creative, offer, price and promotion – are tested live to confirm the most effective marketing plan and most accurate forecast of demand.

Step Five   The product launch is accompanied by further tests to improve future marketing of the product.

Reader's Digest controls its test marketing rigorously and achieves *an almost 100 per cent new product success rate*. It collects information from research and testing to maximise the profitability of each new product. Production plans benefit from accurate sales forecasts based on testing. When I became marketing manager responsible for music collections I inherited a new product concept, 'The Sensational Seventies'. Based on research and testing, I forecast launch campaign sales of 107250, just over £3 million revenue. The actual was 106780 – a fluke, but it was rare for any forecast to be out by more than 10 per cent.

Moreover, *Reader's Digest* devotes up to 15 per cent of its marketing budgets to testing. The benefits are more informed promotion and creative decisions. The payback from testing is tangible and measurable in higher profits. In one test series for a new product launch we discovered that by offering a premium with the product we could charge a higher price. This winning test offer doubled profits, increasing them by over £300000. The cost of the test was £6000 – a payback of 50:1. Gains of this scale are routine and testing is ingrained within the company's processes.

Reader's Digest develops an intimate knowledge of customer interests and motivations. This has an impact on the company's culture as well as its financial performance: management listens to customers, decision-making is informed and democratic, and the basis for decisions is long-term return. Costs are not cut to improve the bottom line short term, and investments in products, systems and marketing are evaluated on their long-term payback.

Knowledge about the customer is shared. Management systems ensure this through international information sharing and worldwide conferences. Testing in each country is prioritised, findings are shared and lessons are actioned around the world. As a result, a *Reader's Digest* manager is never short of proven promotional ideas and marketing is continuously innovative.

The company is unusual in that marketing drives its investment in computing. The company was an early IBM business systems' customer, but it is no pioneer of new technology. Its investments in IT are linked to results in the market-place. When marketing submits proposals for new technology and new customer information, it must support its case with an increased sales and profits forecast.

Reader's Digest captures all customer data legitimate to its business and uses this data to make better product and marketing decisions. My first task in the company as a statistician was to develop data analysis and modelling to improve the targeting of direct mail. I recruited and developed a team of analysts, responsible for the selection of over 50 million mail contacts each year. We were evaluated on the increased contribution to profits we achieved through targeting.

Reader's Digest is an excellent marketer because it learns about customers as individuals and creates products to meet their needs and interests – directly.

The strategy is relevant to every company, but the creative and promotional tactics are only appropriate for certain types of brand. *Reader's Digest* core brand values are convenience and quality. The magazine and condensed books summarise and package reading. Each special book is a comprehensive summary of its subject and each music collection a definitive record of the repertoire of an artist or musical era. The purchase decision is low risk because no self-image is involved: the products are cheap and used at home.

Inertia is the main barrier to purchase. To overcome this, *Reader's Digest* uses hard-hitting, incentive-led direct mail. Each direct mail package sizzles with competitions, prizes, games and gifts to involve the customer. Every package element is tested to prove its contribution to sales. I tested a new paragraph that, alone, increased sales by over 15 per cent, a new mail format that increased sales by over 25 per cent, and a new envelope *colour* that increased sales by over 40 per cent.

The products are excellent value and quality, and the customer service is of the highest standard. Yet the promotional techniques are mocked, despite their success – at the same time as they are much plagiarised. This does not help the company's image as many people equate junk mail with *Reader's Digest*. But as I will show, the tactics are right for low price, low involvement brands in any sector.

The Membership Model and the Development of Customer Relationships

Knowing the customer creates the opportunity to sell more to the customer, to turn a sale into a relationship, and a customer into a *member* of the company.

In the Membership Model, direct communications to members are more important than mass market advertising. Membership is a contractual relationship between company and customer, based on the provision of agreed services over a defined time-scale. The customer must renew the contract to continue to receive membership benefits, or suffer the opportunity cost of losing the benefits.

By developing a relationship with customers, two further benefits result. Members are retained longer than customers and buy a wider range of products and services. Membership generates two revenue streams: the fee or subscription and the sale of other products and services. The psychology of a membership relationship is powerful: members are more likely to use products and services and respond to invitations that are exclusive to them.

Data collected in the enrolment of new members can be used to segment them into behavioural types. The most important segmentation is on the value of the member to the company. The higher the value, the greater the benefits offered. By creating a relationship based on membership, companies can track the behaviour of their customers: this is a vital source of competitive advantage. Customers differ in value, and membership enables companies to make their most valuable customers their most *valued*.

Membership provides the emotional benefits of recognition and belonging. The more contacts with a member, the greater the perceived value of membership. The better the recognition, the greater the customer's association with the company.

Data is used to offer products and services relevant to members as individuals, to create new products based on the analysis of their needs and behaviour, to reward them regularly for their custom, and to enhance the customer service they receive.

American Express and the Membership Model

If *Reader's Digest* is the archetypal Direct Model business, American Express is one of the most sophisticated Membership Model companies.

American Express recruits members selectively. A major recruitment medium is targeted direct mail, and another is the take one leaflet displayed at locations that accept the Card for payment. Tight credit control of applicants maintains a high quality cardmember profile. When working with American Express, I found it significant that the company referred to its customers as *cardmembers*, while competitors refer to them as cardholders. The difference permeates all aspects of the company's thinking and operations.

My first contribution to American Express was to improve the targeting of new cardmember recruitment. Finding prospects interested in membership was straightforward. The challenge was to identify and motivate applicants who would be accepted. We targeted prospects who would use the Card regularly and would not default on payment. We targeted for quality, not quantity.

Locations that accept the card are screened with similar rigour. American Express refers to them as *service establishments*, unlike competitive credit card companies that refer to them as retailers. Again, the terminology reveals the closer relationship American Express seeks with all customers.

The relationship with the new cardmember starts with a telephone call from the customer to activate the Card. There are security reasons for this, but the call establishes American Express's responsiveness and quality of service, and the call makes the customer relationship active. The importance of active relationships, in which customers contact the company as well as the other way around, cannot be underestimated.

Thereafter, cardmembers are billed monthly and mailed regularly. Other than to collect outstanding payments, there are four types of contact.

Customer contact

(i) To improve renewals, to increase frequency of use, and to control credit where default becomes a risk.

(ii) To offer other products and services related to travel and leisure, to generate additional revenue.

(iii) To create exclusive privileges for selected groups of cardmembers, adding to the perceived value of membership.

(iv) To recruit new cardmembers by member-get-member, the most effective source.

Customer data is collected at every contact. Application forms capture the demographic and financial profile of cardmembers, and transactions made using the Card record the value, type, place and time of the spend.

Gold and Platinum Card membership are offered to members with specific qualifications, and business users are offered Corporate or Company Cards. Younger, high-spending cardmembers are offered a wider range of financial services. The cardmember base is analysed to create new propositions and benefits for specific segments.

For American Express, customer information is not only an asset that creates value, it is an integral aspect of its marketing, its service and its product. Cardmembers receive reports and records of their transactions, an essential feature of the service through which American Express helps business customers manage their travel-related budgets. Service establishments and business partners receive cardmember profiles and advice from American Express on how best to market to cardmembers.

To qualify for the American Express card, applicants provide sensitive personal and financial data. Cardmembers understand why American Express requires this data, and expect the company to reciprocate with services and information relevant to them as individuals. The exchange of information between company and customer is a vital aspect of relationship management.

In the US, a division of American Express is responsible for selecting and endorsing third party merchandise, and mailing offers to cardmembers. In the late 1980s, the frequency of mailing and range of offers attracted some criticism. Each offer may have been profitable in its own right, but the focus on immediate sales may have damaged some long-term relationships. American Express responded by announcing a change in strategy, in which communications would be more closely coordinated and cardmember agreement solicited for certain types of offer.

This illustrates the mutual rights and responsibilities in every relationship between company and customer. *Reader's Digest* and American Express are criticised for the frequency with which they mail customers, but in fact both companies are highly sensitive to customer perceptions. They value the long-term customer relationship more than a short-term profit opportunity. They solicit and analyse customer data to ensure that communications are relevant, and monitor customer attitudes continuously to ensure that the messages and offers are welcome and relevant. They mail frequently because it is profitable for them and appreciated by customers.

Data protection legislation enables customers to *opt out* of receiving direct mail. This *opt out* is negative, and I believe that companies should invite their customers to *opt in* to receive information and offers. When customers feel in control, they welcome communication, and *respond typically six times more often when they have invited the contact*. Customers welcome relationships and they want companies to keep in touch, as the *Teleculture 2000* research by the

Henley Centre confirms. Sixty per cent are more likely to buy again from a company that keeps in touch. According to Maritz Telebusiness, the equivalent figure in the US is 80 per cent.[4]

The Customer/Channel Management Model

When companies market through a channel, three relationships are important: between company and channel, between channel and customer, and between customer and company.

When there is no direct relationship between customer and company, the company's brand is at the mercy of the channel. Historically, a company simply pushed its product through the channel, and supported the channel by pulling customers into it through advertising (Figure 2.1).

If the company owns or has exclusive rights in the channel, its priority is to maximise sales. There is no relationship with the customer, so the company finds it difficult to influence the sale directly or even collect information that would influence future sales. In consequence, financial services customers are sold the wrong products by sales forces, and a surprising number of car buyers do not buy their next car from the same brand or dealer.

If the channel is independent, competitors vie for a share of its business. The channel can squeeze the brand's margins while protecting its own, and can favour private label pro-

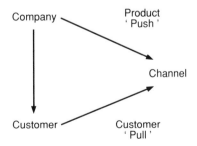

Figure 2.1 Company/customer/channel relationships: (i) Push/pull

ducts or competitive brands. In 1994, Amstrad withdrew its products from major retail chains and moved into direct sales, while Heinz initiated direct communications with customers in the face of overwhelming supermarket buying power. Both moves were prompted by loss of control over margins.

In contrast to the multiple chains, independent retailers are likely to be undercapitalised and their staff poorly trained. Poor merchandising of their stores and service to their customers can result in lost sales, and can damage customer perceptions of the brands.

The customer may be pulled to multiple and independent channels by the company's marketing, but conflict between the brand's values and the channel's service can disrupt the sale.

Virtually every company experiences problems in the management of channel relationships, whatever the ownership or remuneration arrangement. Some channels fail to meet the standards established by the company for quality of service. Some are reactive, and fail to exploit the opportunities offered by customers. Others are pro-active, but damage customer relationships by an aggressive push for sales to maximise their remuneration.

The Membership Model provides the best strategy for developing the company/channel/customer relationship. The best salespeople or outlets are identified and offered a new form of relationship: membership.

Membership provides rewards for performance and shared marketing support from a larger team. As in any membership relationship, company and channel have rights and responsibilities. Customers are allocated amongst members by geography, type of customer, size of customer, or by the products and services to be marketed. Marketing budgets are co-funded and customer information is shared. Remuneration can be based on long-term customer relationships rather than immediate sales.

In a membership relationship, marketing must ensure the training of qualified channel staff to improve performance in relationship management as well as in sales. Marketing communication programmes and systems can be provided

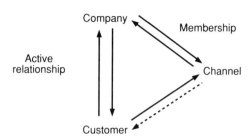

Figure 2.2 Company/customer/channel relationships: (ii) Membership

cost effectively by the company for use by the channel to communicate to customers and to collect information. A critical success factor is that this customer information is shared with the company rather than guarded jealously by the channel.

In the past, the only customers with whom companies talked directly were those with problems and complaints. The challenge now for companies that sell through remote channels is to identify all their customers directly, and to build relationships with them – often in partnership with their channels (Figure 2.2).

The Customer/Channel Management Model in Action: The Car Industry

The car industry grasped earlier than most that future profitability is more closely related to current customer satisfaction than to sales volumes. The league table of customer satisfaction, the Power Index (from the JD Power research company), has become an important motor industry barometer in the US. Customer satisfaction indices illustrate the change in priority from sales to customers, and are now ubiquitous in the industry.

A car is a high risk purchase because of the self-image involved in the choice of a brand. Customers search and evaluate before they buy. Prospective customers see the dealers and their sales people as order takers, not advisers. Customers search for information and make their purchase decisions *before* they see a sales person, so car manufacturers are heavy users of advertising to influence brand choice.

But less than 10 per cent of households buy a new car each year, and an interval of between one and seven years will elapse between purchases. A proportion of purchases is made by companies, but chosen by the employees who will drive the cars. The challenge is to identify and influence the small group of customers in the market at any one time, and this means tracking the customer and managing the relationship over time.

In most countries, car manufacturers are required to register new car buyers, so they have always known their private customers by name and address. They have used their customer lists to increase after-sales revenue and to make offers to existing drivers to increase repeat sales. Direct marketing has thus become an important sales tool: I have run programmes for a leading car manufacturer that were evaluated on the incremental sales generated each quarter by targeted direct mail to existing owners. But it is only more recently that car manufacturers have begun to understand that a relationship strategy, not a sales-led one, is vital to retain customers.

A customer relationship programme begins with pro-specting, as I will discuss in greater detail. The Ford Motor Company has been a pioneer in automotive direct marketing, and particularly in prospecting. Car manufacturers *prospect* for new buyers and *conquest* drivers of competitive marques to increase their market share. For the launch of the Sierra in the UK, for example, Ford identified 270 000 prospects, of whom about 200 000 were drivers of competitive marques.

Prospecting gathers data from drivers about their car ownership and purchase intentions. Data collection about cars illustrates a central principle of customer relationship management: that relationships are customer directed. The important data for cars consists of two dimensions:

(i) current and planned behaviour

(ii) customer needs and intentions.

Whereas most traditional direct marketing thinking emphasises the collection of historic, factual data – like transactions – the important relationship data is *need-directed* and *time-directed*.

Prospecting data in the car market

Traditional

— identity: name, address and telephone number

— purchase: current and previous car ownership in household

— contact: previous marketing, sales and service history

— profile: household composition, family demographics

Directional

— plans: timing of next purchase

— needs: type of next purchase and needs or use for a car

Different customers have different needs, and in the car market the different needs are for model variants like automatics, diesels and hatchbacks. By identifying needs, manufacturers can provide relevant information to help customers evaluate their models. Timing is important, and some customers are willing to let the manufacturer know when they next plan to buy a car. Alternatively, the manufacturer can predict the timing of the next purchase by analysis of current ownership and previous purchase history.

A particular role of data collection is to *qualify* prospects – to identify those of high value. Not all prospects who respond to Ford, for example, are in the market for a new Ford. There are brochure seekers and drivers who aspire to a new car but cannot afford one. Analysis of data about

. . . .

prospective customers allows Ford to rank prospects and to select the probable buyers.

Ford communicates regularly with qualified prospects. As they move towards their purchase window, Ford targets communications and offers to increase brand preference and purchase. The company communicates both as Ford itself and on behalf of dealers. Ford commmunications are designed to retain the driver, while the dealer communications aim to maintain service and parts revenue, and to motivate consideration of the dealer. Dealer support consists of a suite of marketing communications that can be bought by the dealer. Ford, like most car manufacturers, part funds and designs the programme, to exercise quality control.

Car manufacturer and dealer communications

Year one

— Welcome message from the dealer

— Post-delivery customer satisfaction survey from the manufacturer

— Service and parts invitation from the dealer

— Two/three added value messages, with information from the manufacturer

— First year ownership customer satisfaction survey from the manufacturer

---

In a relationship strategy, contact is maintained with the customer from one sale to the next, and the number of profitable contacts with the customer between sales is maximised. The objectives are to generate additional revenue through service and parts and to maximise share of repeat customer business.

In the fleet market, Ford faces the additional challenge that it does not know who chooses and drives its cars. Purchase decisions are typically made by user–choosers, employees who make their choice from a list approved by the employer. Until the early 1980s, employees had little choice over the cars they drove, and Ford was an automatic choice for fleet management. But Ford now faces a new environment, in which more employees exercise choice and the funding of the company car is one element of flexible remuneration.

To address this shift in customer decision-making, Ford adopted a relationship strategy in the company car market and implemented the strategy though the Talkback programme. Talkback involves prospecting and communication with company car drivers, including drivers of competitive marques. A distinctive characteristic of Talkback, as the name implies, is that most communications invite customer response. The programme was launched with the theme: 'You talk. We listen'. Participants are referred to as *members* of Talkback. They continue to receive the programme and enjoy its benefits if they continue to provide Ford with their feedback. Examples of Talkback feedback are customer surveys on motorway driving, safety and route planning. Talkback offers exclusive privileges to members and gathers extensive customer data, updated and enhanced with each survey.

Characteristics of the Ford Talkback Programme

— Identification and engagement of customers and prospects

— Communication relevant to customers

— Valuable information and offers

— Keeping in touch through continuous dialogue and data capture

— Messages timed in harmony with the customer's purchase cycle

— Close involvement of the dealer channel

Summary: The Critical Success Factors of Relationship Management

Ford, American Express and *Reader's Digest* are successful businesses which illustrate the evolution of relationship strategy by means of low involvement goods, financial services and high priced capital goods. The three companies represent best practice in their sectors.

Key characteristics summarised

Direct Model

— Maximisation of customer value, and investment in new customers based on customer value.

Membership Model

— Contract between company and customer, rewarding members with exclusive benefits and enhanced service.

Customer/Channel Management Model

— Development of direct relationships where customers were previously unknown, and management of customer relationships over time in partnership with channels.

Each of the three companies developed direct relationships with customers to sell more and to increase profitability. There are three elements of relationship strategy that are common to each company, and to the Direct, Membership and Customer/Channel Management models. Against each element of strategy, companies can test their commitment to recognising their best customers, developing relationships with them and maximising the value of their brands by maximising the value of their customers.

First element of strategy

— The focus on most valuable customers as assets representing current revenue and future potential; it pays to target valuable customers, to keep them with the company, and to increase the range of products they buy.

First test of strategic commitment to customers

— Do you know your 25 per cent most valuable customers, their current value to you, and your potential to increase their value?

Second element of strategy

— The development of a direct relationship with valuable customers; more influence can be exerted on customer choice, more appealing and relevant offers can be made, and customer revenue can be secured longer term.

Second test of strategic commitment to customers

— If asked, what more would your best customers say your company could do for them that your competitors could not, to help them in their business and domestic lives?

Third element of strategy

— The management of the customer interface; every contact is an opportunity to add value – more contacts create more value and the quality of contact depends on people.

Third test of strategic commitment to customers

— What do your customers gain from responding to, talking with and meeting people from your company, and what is special to them about dealing with your people and your company?

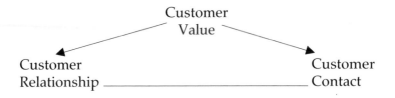

Figure 2.3   Elements of relationship management strategy

MARKETING STRATEGY FOR BRANDS AND CUSTOMERS 3

'One look, one voice'

Company-brand Strategy – People and Brands – The Definition of Relationship Strategy – Customer Relationships – Activating Customer Relationships I: Engagement – Activating Customer Relationships II: Involvement – Managing Customer Relationships – Customer Lifetime Value – Targeting Strategy – Translating Strategy into Action

---

Company-brand Strategy

In business, much of strategy's meaning and force has been lost through misuse. The *Oxford English Dictionary* defines strategy as: 'in circumstances of competition or conflict, as in the theory of games, decision theory, business administration, etc., a plan for successful action based on the rationality and interdependence of the moves of the opposing participants'.[1]

The 'participants' in marketing are the competition, the channels, the company's staff and customers. A marketing strategy must encompass relationships between customer and competition, customer and channel, and customer and staff (Figure 3.1).

Most companies share their customers with their com-

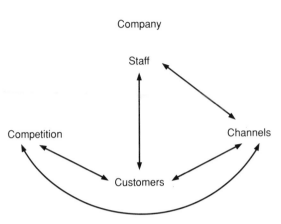

Figure 3.1 Relationships in marketing strategy

petition: the different brands in a market compete for a share of *customer repertoire*. How much the customer buys from the competition is an essential item of information. For example, two passengers may have identical flight histories with an airline, but one always flies with the airline while the other chooses it for one in five journeys. The two differ in their relationship and their potential value. One customer is loyal but low value, whilst the other is better treated as a high value prospect than as a customer. The marketing priority is to develop a relationship with this prospect and so to win a higher share of repertoire.

Most companies sell a number of products, under separate brands, to a wide range of customers, but do not relate the customer base of one brand to that of another. Traditional marketing practice separates brand advertising from corporate advertising. They are distinct in tone, message and target audience, with corporate advertising generally restricted to business and financial influencers.

In *Company Image and Reality*, David Bernstein comments on the paradox of brand and corporate advertising, using Bernstein's Law: 'Product advertising takes minor differences and maximises them. Corporate advertising takes major differences and minimises them.'[2]

In future, the trend will be to sell more brands to the same customer, rather than to different customers. The

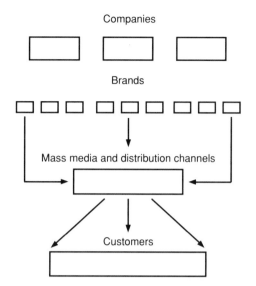

Figure 3.2 Companies, customers, competition and brands: historical

parallel trend will be to use specialist channels of distribution and specialist media to reach more tightly defined customer segments. Companies will maximise their share of a smaller number of customers, and the competitive value of the *company brand* will become a significant factor in marketing strategy (Figures 3.2 and 3.3). As *Brandweek* reports: 'As marketers from tissues to telecommunications seek consistency in their messages, one strategy gaining momentum is a "one-look one-voice" model to support a family of brands.'[3]

Companies will define their customer bases more tightly and sell a range of brands within a family to these customers. They will select specialist media and distribution channels to reach their tightly defined audiences, and build their private marketing databases to manage communication and distribution to customers. This is a model for the restructuring of giant companies like IBM and BT into separate business units or brand families.

In marketing, the major differences lie in companies and their people, not in products. Relationship strategy differentiates companies and I propose Pearson's Law:

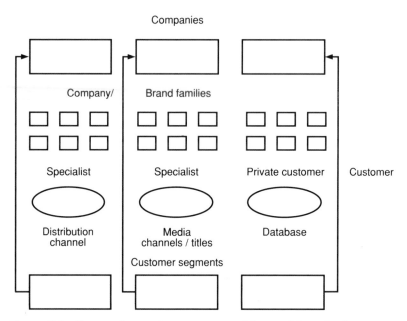

Figure 3.3 Companies, customers, competition and brands: future

'Customer relationship management takes what is special about a company and its people, and maximises it in every contact with customers.'

Relationships enhance marketing effectiveness. An offer from a recognised brand or company is more welcome than an unknown one. In my experience:

— If the company or brand name is known, sales increase by a factor of the order of three

— If the customer has an active relationship with the company or brand, sales increase by a factor of the order of six.

When markets were growing, the returns from launching new brands were often higher than from investment in existing brands or line extensions. Now, with intensifying competition and direct customer relationships, the payback is faster when new products are supported by the company brand or existing brand names. Compaq, a relatively new advertiser, recognises that a multiple brand strategy is dated: 'It's more cost-effective for us to put all our efforts behind the Compaq brand than to slice the budget in four or five different segments.'[4] This challenges traditional thinking which holds that line extensions dilute brand value; with a relationship perspective the opposite is true. By building customer relationships that embrace a wider range of products under the same brand, companies can reinforce their position with and value to the customer.

Long-established advertiser Lever Brothers has withdrawn Wisk, to concentrate on its core brands like Persil and Sunlight. It is shifting marketing processes away from individual brands to category management, reflecting the decision of multiple retailers to maximise the profitability of a category, not an individual brand.

There are five company-brand strategies.

Build the company brand, and use it to build customer relationships

Multiple pet owning households are responsible for a high proportion of spend in the pet food category. A strategic opportunity in this market is to win a higher share of repertoire in households owning several pets, by motivating them to buy as much cat and dog food as possible from the same company. But analysis of their brands reveals that different manufacturers have different likelihoods of taking advantage of the opportunity.

Pedigree, Mars' pet food market leader, is associated with one of its strong brands, Chum. So the company brand, Pedigree, cannot be used to add value to its other brands, including the other strong brand, Whiskas. Pedigree Whiskas does not make sense to the customer.

Quaker Oats owned Felix, the rising star of cat foods, but Quaker is associated with cereals, so the company brand could not be used to cross-sell other pet food brands to Felix users.

Dalgety's pet food unit, Spillers, was best placed to develop its company brand and to use the Spillers name to support all brands, including Felix when it acquired this brand from Quaker. The name Spillers is not closely associated with any individual brand, and it has a heritage of personal service appropriate to relationship management.

Launch a new brand designed to build stronger customer relationships

In financial services, many existing company brands are constrained by their heritage and cannot be used to breathe new life into customer relationships. New brands Firstdirect (Midland Bank) and DirectLine (Royal Bank of Scotland) are associated with access and responsiveness, values essential in direct banking and insurance. To convince customers that the holding companies, the banks, are accessible and customer oriented would require massive external and internal investment. A hundred years of customer experience cannot easily be reversed.

General Motors adopted a new brand strategy by launching Saturn, and by separating all aspects of operations and marketing from the company's established marques Cadillac, Chevrolet, Buick and Pontiac. With Saturn's success, GM now seeks to cross-fertilise its practices to other General Motors companies.

Add value to strong brands to develop customer relationships

Unilever brand Flora is manufactured by its business unit Van den Berg, and was one of the first to offer a free telephone careline to its customers. Flora press advertising invites customers to respond for information on healthy eating and to argue Flora's nutritional case against butter. The brand has an emotional appeal, developed through its distinctive television advertising, while a new press advertising campaign launched in 1994 adds the values of access and responsiveness to the brand.

Develop strong brands into company brands

Flora's packaging now features The Flora Food Company as the maker of the brand. The Van den Berg name is faceless and impersonal. Unilever is making Flora the company as well as the brand.

Develop a new umbrella for marketing different brands to the same customers

Kraft General Foods has created umbrellas for marketing programmes supporting brands targeted to consumer sectors – for example the newsletter 'What's Hot' targeted to families with young children. Similarly, Seagram has promoted its premium brands to the same customers under the umbrella 'President's Choice'.

Considerable competitive advantage can be gained from developing the company as a brand and from extending brands into families. All products from the company or the family can be marketed efficiently to the same customer base, as can short-lived brands linked to cinema, television or toy licensing. A relationship reduces the risks of failure in new product development; new concepts can be re-searched and tested, and new products launched to existing customers quickly.

A relationship strategy is a strategy for a company rather than for an individual brand.

People and Brands

The quality and personality of a company, as expressed by its staff, is a new dimension of marketing strategy. In discussing corporate advertising, David Bernstein says: 'I however believe that corporate advertising should treat a company as if it were a person. I'm stuck with this anthropomorphic view of companies. I can't help thinking of them as people.'[5]

The people behind a product or brand matter to the

customer. Research by the Henley Centre, *Teleculture 2000*, reports that customers' priority for service is a 'capable inside sales person'.[6] To build and sustain their brands, companies need to inject the commitment and personality of their people into their brand values.

Differentiation through people is stronger than any media advertising, explaining why fast-growing companies like Virgin and The Body Shop rarely advertise, yet have two of the most distinctive brands in the international market-place. Each has a distinctive personality, created by the founder and reaffirmed every time the customer contacts the company. Yet most companies invest in media advertising without backing up their promises with investment in the customer interface. The result is dissatisfaction and loss of sales, but these are rarely measured. Juliet Williams, of Strategic Management Resources, reports: 'up to 40 per cent of the potential return on your marketing spend is lost by the failure of your staff to live up to the promises you make to your customers. Brand images, perceptions and values are unwittingly undermined and eroded everyday at every point of contact along the customer interface.'[7]

Customer service telephone numbers – like Flora's – on product packaging and marketing literature add brand value by demonstrating *access* and *responsiveness*. In the future, I see these as universal brand values, just as reliability and quality have always been basic requirements for a brand to command any price premium. A free helpline or information service adds value in advertising – irrespective of the volume of response it generates – by guaranteeing the company's commitment to its customers.

When customers do respond, the company must match the promise made in advertising. Every staff member shares the responsibility, starting with those who interact directly with customers. Marketing strategy should give clear direction to plans and actions, and the direction must be understood not only by customer-facing staff but across the entire company. Relationship management *integrates* previously separate staff functions and activities.

The idea of integrated marketing is usually a campaign

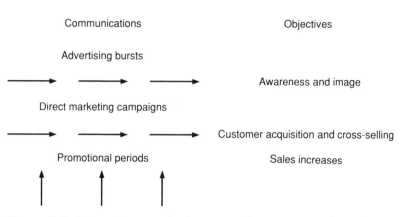

Figure 3.4 Integrating marketing around customer relationships: coordinated marketing

in which advertising, promotion and direct marketing all speak with the same voice and present the same image. This is a narrow view: it is more coordination than integration. The basis for the integration of marketing is the *customer relationship*, not the creative execution.

Response to advertising or redemption of a promotional offer is the start of a direct relationship. Marketing strategy should define the types of customer to be attracted by advertising and promotion, and the expectations to be created amongst those who respond. The strategy should encompass the short-term goal of the advertising and promotion – new customer acquisition, and the long-term goal – continuing customer relationships (Figures 3.4 and 3.5).

Coordinated marketing communications may 'look' the same, but advertising, direct marketing and promotion remain discrete activities with different objectives.

In a fully integrated model, the advertising message and promotional offer develop the customer relationship and increase the customer lifetime value using the appropriate media and all forms of customer contact, which combines advertising, promotion and relationship-building.

Integration does not stop within marketing but applies to the whole company, with every employee's contribution expressed as a contribution to the customer relationship.

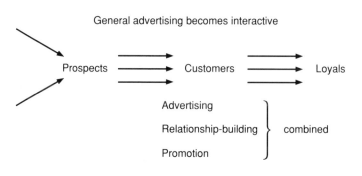

General advertising becomes interactive

Sales promotion becomes relationship-building

Figure 3.5 Integrating marketing around customer relationships: integrated marketing

Every employee can be empowered to invest in customer relationships. Recently in the US, for example, I came across hotel staff who are authorised to spend up to $500 to solve customer problems, because the value of a customer is many times that figure.

A relationship strategy integrates all company activities around the customer, not just communication. The strategy pulls together otherwise disjointed activities – advertising and customer service, trade sales and consumer promotion, sponsorship and direct marketing – whether or not these are within the remit of the marketing department.

At Ogilvy & Mather Direct, I led the development of customer-led programmes for Rank Xerox (UK). At our first meeting there were representatives from Management, Finance, Sales, Regional Sales, Service, Manufacturing, Advertising and Direct Marketing; we held separate meetings with Product Marketers responsible for product types. We found at least seven functions communicating separately to new customers during the six months after a sale, each with a different objective, style, contact name and number, and customer information base.

The solution was a programme called 'Customer Support'. A new external process managed customer contact and customer satisfaction and developed a dialogue to collect customer information. A new internal process shared customer information, solved customer problems and identified sales opportunities. We conceived and resourced a National Telephonics Unit to manage inbound customer contact and to increase the volume of outbound contact.

In another Rank Xerox marketing programme, we tested the effectiveness of direct mail, telephone, sales calls and service engineer visits in upgrading customers to a new generation of copier. The most effective contacts were by the service engineers. Customers trusted their advice about existing products, so they listened to what they had to say about new ones.

Relationship management builds brands by building relationships and trust between customers and company. Ultimately, people are the brand because people serve customers. And the brand is the summation of all customer experiences, of which advertising may be one of the weakest.

The Definition of Relationship Strategy

Relationship strategy has three elements:

(i) Build the brand by building customer relationships

(ii) Manage customer contact to enhance the total brand experience

(iii) Generate return on investment from customer lifetime value.

The development of strategy starts with analysis, in three phases: how customers use a brand and relate to the company that produces the brand; how the customer relationship can be best managed; and how much customers could be worth to the company.

The definition of a relationship strategy	
Analysis	Strategy
Customer relationships	Customer development
Customer contact	Customer management
Customer lifetime value	Customer targeting

Analysis of customer relationships

Research and testing evaluate the strengths and weaknesses of the customer relationship: how committed customers are to the brand, and how assured are the earnings they generate. Threats to customers from competitors are analysed and trends in customer behaviour are identified. The analysis of customer relationships drives *customer development strategy*. The objective is to increase *customer loyalty*, a frequently misused term. I define loyalty as 'the propensity of the customer to develop a closer relationship with the company, and therefore to buy more products and services'. My definition can be measured and linked directly both to brand value and financial performance.

Analysis of customer contact

Every customer contact is an opportunity to create value, and brand image is affected by a customer's total experience of a brand, not just by advertising. A vital analysis is an audit of all contacts with customers, to review effectiveness, potential for improvement, and opportunities to create more contacts. This is an audit that should include all sales and distribution channels, owned and independent, as well as all media. Analysis of contact drives *customer management* strategy. This sets out guidelines for all members of staff: when to contact customers, how to manage relationships, how to solicit feedback, how to identify opportunities, and how to collect information. Excellent staff performance is measured by results in the market-place – an area of company operations that should fall within marketing's remit.

Analysis of customer value

How much to invest in customer relationships depends on how much customers are worth. In future, companies will focus on the quality (i.e. profitability) rather than quantity

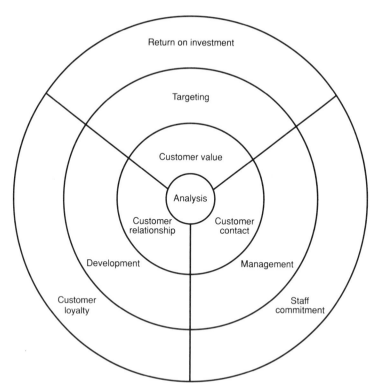

Figure 3.6 Relationship strategy wheel

of their customer base. Analysis of customer value drives *targeting* strategy, to determine which customers are currently most important, and which customers offer future potential. This analysis should involve business and financial as well as marketing management as the objective is to maximise return on investment. The targeting strategy will determine, for example, the allocation of budgets to media or direct relationships, to customer acquisition or retention, and to the sales force or direct channels (Figure 3.6).

Objectives	Return on investment	Customer loyalty	Staff commitment
Strategy	Customer targeting	Customer development	Customer management
Analysis	Value	Relationships	Contact

Customer Relationships

The *quality of relationship* between company and customer is a competitive advantage. The more closely the customer associates with the brand, the more likely the customer is to buy.

In traditional marketing theory, the analysis of relationships was based on a hierarchy of effects: awareness, knowledge, preference, purchase and repurchase. A customer becomes aware of a product, understands its features and benefits, develops a preference for it and purchases it. If use creates satisfaction, the customer repurchases it. But apart from purchase and use, the relationship is indirect and passive.

The *relationship* approach to marketing is based on the *activation* of customers. In an active relationship, the customer responds and becomes involved with the brand at times other than the sale. The effect of an active relationship on customer behaviour is strongest when the relationship is initiated by the customer. The customer wants control: to choose how, where and from whom to seek information about products and services. This desire to control the delivery of information and advertising underlies the growth in the use of the telephone and on-line media for

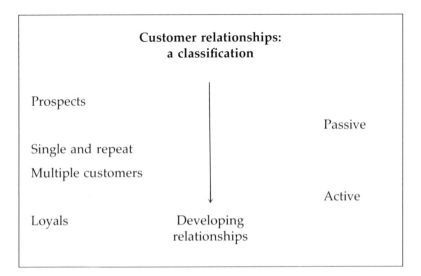

shopping and banking. The companies that succeed will offer customers more value and more control through active relationships.

I classify customers as prospects, single and repeat buyers (of one product or service), multiple customers (of more than one product or service) and loyals. The relationships with prospects, buyers and customers can be passive, but it is a characteristic of loyalty – to differentiate it from habit or absence of choice – that loyal customers have active relationships.

If prospects can be motivated to respond to a brand, for example to direct response advertising, they are more likely to buy. Direct response advertising is growing because it provides the opportunity to identify prospective customers, to provide them with information and offers, and thereby to motivate a higher proportion of them to select your brand.

Most relationships with customers are passive, even among frequent buyers. Customer interest in active relationships depends on the importance of a product category and the strength of their associations with brands in the category. Not all buyers of a brand will become active, the proportion will vary by category, but the challenge for every brand is to activate more customer relationships. I define three forms of active relationship that lead to loyalty.

Membership

When customers contract to receive products and services over time, the act of joining or subscribing is a positive decision. Membership must be renewed or the customer loses the benefits, and renewal of the commitment is also a positive decision.

Advocacy

When customers recommend the brand, they are effectively becoming its sales representatives. Word of mouth recommendation is a powerful force, and by inviting customers to become advocates, recommendation can become a powerful marketing weapon. Lexus in the US, for example, invites owners of its cars to become advocates when they attend special events at which they meet prospective buyers.

Association

The most active form of relationship is when customers volunteer to associate with the company and participate in its activities. Car manufacturer Saturn celebrated its fifth anniversary by inviting owners to travel to its Tennessee plant, at their own expense. A total of 44 000 made the journey – and revealed themselves as associates.

Associates will play an active role in company affairs. American Airlines invited its frequent flyers to lobby members of Congress to protest about the unfair terms on which British Airways gained entry to the US market.[8] Retail chain Neiman Marcus invites members of its 'InCircle' rewards programme to identify employees who provide excellent service.

Every company has customers willing to be associates, identifiable in correspondence and telephone calls. But few companies seek them out and make them active.

Activating Customer Relationships I: Engagement

Whereas advertising is concerned with a shift in customer beliefs, relationships are designed to change customer behaviour from P to C to L – from prospect to customer to loyal. The *quality or personality of the customer relationship* becomes the new fourth dimension to the brand, additional to its feature, benefits and values.

I call the move from P to C *engagement*, by which customers are motivated to respond and to identify themselves. Engagement makes a relationship between company and brand active.

The growth in direct marketing is usually attributed to the ability to target to customer or prospect databases. But I have always regarded the power of direct communications, and their ability to engage the customer, as at least as important. Two consumer brand examples illustrate the difference.

In 1985, Lever Brothers in the US targeted users of competitive soap brands with a mailing package inviting them to compare their brand with Lever's brand, Dove. A sample of Dove was enclosed, with a litmus test to demonstrate that Dove was neutral. Tracking research proved that the message had a powerful advertising effect and resulted in some brand switching. The communication was initiated by Lever, however, and demanded no active response from the customer.

The effect on customer behaviour is stronger if the customer is invited to respond and is engaged in the brand's message. In 1991, the Heinz Pet Foods brand Meaty Bone conducted research that proved it to be superior to its major competitor in blind testing. But Meaty Bone was not achieving trial among competitive brand users and its market share was static. The solution was advertising which invited dog owners to participate in a Taste Challenge. Respondents received a Taste Challenge Kit with samples of Meaty Bone and were encouraged to send back their feedback on a questionnaire.

Previous advertising had claimed Meaty Bone's superiority, but any claim is more credible when the advertising invites response and promises demonstration. Response to the Taste Challenge makes the relationship active, and because it is requested by the customer it is treated with greater attention. The questionnaire engages customers by inviting them to rate the brand's performance, motivating them to re-evaluate their existing brand choice.

This is a new challenge to advertisers, accustomed to creating advertising for passive viewers and readers; and to direct marketers, reliant on unsolicited direct mail. The trend in advertising and direct marketing will be from intrusion to invitation – from advertiser-initiated to *customer-directed* messages.

Activating Customer Relationships II: Involvement

I call the move from C to L, from customer to loyal, *involvement*. When customers become involved, the relationship between company and customer becomes a continuing dialogue. The Ford Talkback programme is a model of customer involvement, because it creates a continuing dialogue with company car drivers not previously known to Ford. When the driver receives the new car, the thrill of ownership and association with the brand may decline. By keeping drivers involved, Ford maintains its brand profile and adds value to the relationship.

A customer is fully involved if the relationship starts active and stays active. The importance of keeping the relationship active can be illustrated by customer magazines. Whereas many are bland, the best invite customers to write letters, ask questions, feedback their opinions and send in their stories for publication. For example, the children's magazines for the Disney and Nickelodeon cable TV channels in the US are based on the opinions and contributions of young viewers.

The best customer magazine programmes ask for commitment from the customer: information, proofs of purchase and even payment. Subscription to a publication (*Reader's Digest*), membership of an added value service (American Express) and participation in a regular dialogue (Ford Talkback) are methods of sustaining customer involvement.

I have never come across a company that did not have customers who wanted to be heard, and whose involvement would benefit the company. A model for customer involvement is the user group of a computer hardware or software company. Involving customers means listening to their opinions, solving their problems, and sharing the company's business with them. The British government has found the European concept of worker councils difficult to accommodate, although many leading UK companies accept their value. Similarly, every company should establish a customer council, a forum for involving a representative group of customer associates in the company's future.

Managing Customer Relationships

Traditionally, company processes are planned around transactions and staff are organised by function. When a relationship strategy is adopted, business processes and organisation are redesigned around customers.

Currently, marketing management is organised in a department where staff are responsible for each product and each form of communication: advertising, promotions, direct marketing and public relations. Relationships are often the responsibility of an individual, usually a sales person, who is often expected to perform the impossible: sell to the customer and nurture the relationship at the same time.

The worst feature of the traditional organisation is that customers are often a source of conflict: between marketing and sales, and between the company and the channel. The customer relationship is a battleground: contact with the customer is not coordinated, and ownership of customer data is jealously guarded.

To manage relationships, marketing needs to be organised by customer segment and implemented through a multi-disciplinary team. Customer teams comprise staff from disparate functions: sales, service, research, finance, distribution and manufacturing. A customer team allows for a mix of motivation, skills and expertise. Conflict can be resolved by organising teams by customer rather than function.

For the effective management of customer relationships by teams there are four critical success factors.

Access to customer information

Information enables staff to recognise the customer, manage contact and communicate results quickly to the team, reacting to problems and creating opportunities.

Shared goals

Performance standards are shared by all, with every team member able to make a contribution. As I will show, this becomes an opportunity to value the contribution of any member of staff, because the opportunities to increase customer value are always considerable.

Shared resources

Systems and technology can be shared and marketing communications conceived jointly and adapted to customer segments. A role remains for a guardian of the brand's values, but customer teams will want to customise both products and marketing for the customer segments for which they are responsible.

Decentralisation

Devolution of responsibility gives teams the confidence and authority to act on their own judgement. They are closest to customers and their decisions are the most informed. In the traditional organisation, management presents plans to customer-facing staff. But an organisation based on customer relationships learns continuously and shares understanding of customers, with staff presenting what customers are telling them to management. At Dell Computer in the US, customer service staff present to management every Friday morning.[9]

Financial reporting can be organised by team and customer segment, and all team members can be evaluated on their contribution to the increased value of their customers. This helps a forward-looking company invest in its staff, because it can measure the effectiveness of the investment by the value of its customers.

Customer Lifetime Value

Customer lifetime value (LTV) measures customer profitability over time. The value of a brand is the value of the customers who buy the brand, so customer lifetime value is the true basis for the valuation of brands. Increasing the value of a brand means increasing the lifetime value of its customers.

LTV is the net present value of the stream of contributions to profit that result from customer transactions and contacts with the company. Because it is cheaper to sell to an existing rather than to a new customer, profitability increases when many products are sold to the same customers rather than to different ones.

Most banks acquire customers through current, or cheque, accounts. These accounts are typically loss leaders, but the bank makes profits by selling other products and services with high margins (loans), fees (credit cards) or commissions (insurance). Most current account-only customers are unprofitable now, but some will be profitable in the future: these have high *potential* lifetime value because they will need other products and services in the future. These customers must be identified, relationships with them developed, and their future commitment secured before they will buy more products from the bank. Customers without this potential must be managed differently, perhaps by charging a fee to bring their relationship into profit.

A car manufacturer sells infrequently but there is a high margin on each sale. All sales generate similar revenues, but repeat sales to existing customers are considerably more cost-effective than first-time sales. Calculating the cost per sale encourages a car manufacturer to focus on repeat purchase from existing customers. From another perspective, the manufacturer has to invest in existing customers to prevent their defection.

Service and parts revenue is important to the dealer. Service and parts are also factors in winning repeat sales, because the dealer increases his rate of repeat purchase by offering privileged prices and excellent service to drivers. The economics of sales and service, and of manufacturer and dealer, are inextricably linked through the customer relationship.

For a pet food manufacturer, a single can or pack of a pet food brand may retail at 50p and deliver a margin of only 15p. But a pet owner with two dogs and two cats may spend over £1000 a year on pet foods, and contribute over £200 a year to pet food manufacturers' profits.

Through their different brands, manufacturers share the customer's purchase repertoire and their lifetime value. The difference between the current and *potential lifetime value* – if the company captured the complete customer repertoire – represents the scope for marketing to increase profitability. If the share of feeding regime in a multiple pet owning household held by one manufacturer is 25 per cent, this contributes £50 profit a year, but the potential is over £200. So the value of increased share can be up to £150 a year, if the manufacturer captures 100 per cent of the feeding regime.

The first step in calculating lifetime value is analysis of customers by their current behaviour, typically classifying them by frequency and value of purchase, and then seg-

---

Customer lifetime value analysis

Stage one

— Calculate current customer revenues
— Calculate current customer costs
— Calculate current customer profitability
— Determine policy for current customer lifetime value

Stage two

— Research potential customer revenues
— Project future customer costs
— Forecast customer potential lifetime value

Stage three

— Compare current and potential lifetime value to determine targeting strategy

menting them into behavioural groups with similar lifetime values. Costs are calculated for each behavioural group, on a marginal basis including manufacturing, distribution, service and support costs. Current customer profitability is the difference between revenue and cost.

Customer lifetime value is calculated from customer profitability using the interest rate and time horizon that reflect the company's investment policy. The more risk averse, the shorter the period, and the higher the rate.

The second step is to project potential value. One method is to model future behaviour from past behaviour, using transactional and other market data. Alternatively, research can predict potential by projecting future behaviour.

Three findings stand out in every analysis and research study I have conducted into customer lifetime value.

A surprisingly low number of customers contribute most of the profits

Even for mass market consumer brands and multiple retailers, 30 per cent of customers contribute 70 per cent of sales. These valuable customers cost less to manage because service is more efficient and problems are fewer than with the average. The result can be that these 30 per cent are responsible for all or more of the profits. Marketers can afford to spend more on cementing a relationship with these valuable customers because the opportunity cost of losing them is so high.

The highest spending segment is also the one with the highest potential

Although they are already profitable, the potential to increase the contribution of the most valuable customers is high. These are the customers who are very satisfied with the product and are loyal to the brand: they will buy more. Even among regular buyers of a brand, share of repertoire is often as low as a third, and these customers are most receptive to deepening the relationship. The customer segment with the highest potential is usually already the most valuable.

Marketing must be targeted – quality matters more than quantity

Since a small number of customers are responsible for a high proportion of profits, marketing must be targeted to avoid selling to unprofitable customers (Figure 3.7). Many companies have too many of the wrong customers, depressing their profitability, because they do not *target*. Marketing should be evaluated on quality and not just on quantity of customers and penetration of market.

Targeting Strategy

Targeting is the allocation of marketing investment among customer segments to maximise the increase in lifetime value.

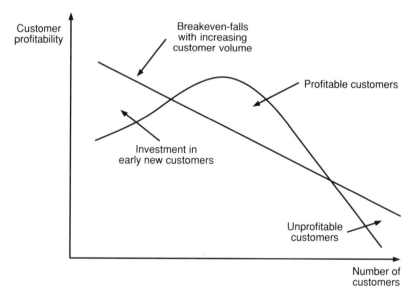

Figure 3.7 Customer profitability curve

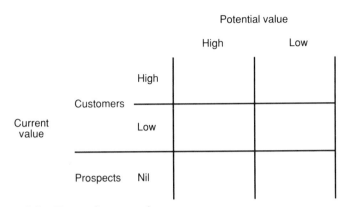

Figure 3.8 Targeting matrix

The simplest segmentation is customer and prospect. Customers can be segmented into high or low current lifetime value, and high or low potential lifetime value. Prospects have high or low potential value (Figure 3.8). *Marketing has three priorities: retain high value customers, develop high potential customers, and acquire high potential prospects.*

Not all customers or prospects are equally likely to respond. Additional to current value, the other dimension is responsiveness. Within each segment are customers and prospects with high potential value, who are receptive and whose custom can be developed cost-effectively. So targeting strategy has two dimensions:

(i)   The potential value of a prospect, or the increase in value of a customer

(ii) The propensity of a prospect to choose the brand (brand rate), or the propensity of the customer to buy more from the brand (loyalty rate).

I call the propensity of non-customers to choose the brand the *brand rate*, in itself a powerful measure of brand power. The propensity of an existing customer to buy more is the *loyalty rate*. Loyalty varies by customer and can be tested and predicted. A marketing science has evolved that uses sophisticated statistical and mathematical modelling of individual data to select customers and prospects most likely to respond to different marketing communications.

The Basis for Targeting Summary

Potential Increase in Customer Value
× Customer Responsiveness

Traditionally in advertising media strategy, the objective is to maximise coverage, subject to qualitative judgements about the appropriateness of different media. In relationship strategy, the targeting objective is incremental profitability from long-term customer relationships. Advertising is concerned with the number of impacts, rather than the quality of contact with the customer. An integrated relationship solution recognises the role of all contacts with customers, not just media.

Most traditional marketing planning ignores the power of direct and personal contact with customers. Options include direct media (mail and telephone), events and the many opportunities to contact customers face to face. There is a huge difference in impact between seeing a television commercial and meeting a member of the company's staff, or an existing customer who is an advocate. The greatest criticism that can be levelled at traditional marketing is that it focuses on media and neglects day-to-day contact between company and customer.

Lifetime value is *the* vital measure of marketing effectiveness. It is the basis for the evaluation of investment – in marketing or otherwise, and a new and better way of looking at the economics of a market and the financial performance of a company. The analysis of lifetime value redefines the finances of a company in terms of the customers it serves, rather than the products it makes.

Translating Strategy into Action

In *Competitive Advantage*, Michael Porter states: 'the failure of many firms' strategies stems from an inability to translate a broad competitive strategy into the specific action steps required to gain competitive advantage.'[10] Lifetime value analysis enables every company to take three action steps: identify customers whose change in behaviour will affect the bottom line, manage them better than the competition, and build relationships with them that last.

A relationship strategy defines the actions essential for a competitive advantage:

— The development of the customer relationship with the brand, and the use of communications to engage and involve customers in active relationships.

— The management of customers by internal teams.

— The retention of customers with high current lifetime value, and the targeting of customers with high potential lifetime value.

The strategy is driven by the potential to increase lifetime value – in my experience, the greatest untapped asset in every company.

CREATING VALUE FROM BRANDS AND CUSTOMERS 4

'Without an individual to take ownership,
nobody's accountable'

The Value of Brands and Customers – The Spiral of Prosperity – The New Economics of Marketing – Increasing Customer Value – The Dimensions of the Customer Relationship – Investing Externally in Customer Relationships – Investing Internally in Customer Relationships – Maximising Customer Profitability: Cross-selling – Planning the Investment in New Customers – Three Principles

The Value of Brands and Customers

There is no direct link between the value of a company and the effectiveness of its marketing. It is vital to create this link. If company value is the objective of marketing strategy, and the measure of marketing effectiveness, marketing can be treated as a strategic investment and can regain a critical role in company direction.

Currently, the valuation of a company is based on either:

— the value of its physical assets

— the net present value of its anticipated flow of future earnings, calculated on a multiple of current profits, the price/earnings ratio.

The valuation of brands is one way of linking marketing effectiveness to company value. The brand is, after all, the responsibility of marketing. To value a brand, analysts compare its earnings with those of unbranded equivalents in the sector, to give a figure for net brand-related profits; then a multiple based on brand strength is applied. Interbrand, the leading analyst, defines seven dimensions to brand strength: *leadership, stability, market, internationality, trend, support, and protection.*[1]

Some companies have put the value of brands on their balance sheets, for example food manufacturer Rank Hovis McDougall, and marketing services group WPP, which capitalised its JWT and O&M advertising brands. The practice is rare because accountants are prudent with intangible assets in an uncertain future. To value a brand, a complex set of influences and possibilities must be considered. Dramatic swings in brand valuation from year to year, and anomalies like the negative valuation of IBM, indicate that brand valuation methodology is not yet robust.

An alternative methodology is to value *customers* rather than brands. Customers are not used in current valuation methods, but it is logical to include them. All brand revenue flows from customer transactions and future brand revenue depends on future customer behaviour. The quality and reliability of brand revenue must depend on customer relationships – when we discuss the strength of a brand, we really mean the strength of the customer relationship with the brand. *Value lies in customers rather than brands.*

Marketing by a company and its competitors changes brand value, by changing customer relationships and behaviour. Channels and staff are also important factors in brand valuation. The effect of all marketing participants can be measured through their impact on customer behaviour and customer value. Relationships are complex and dynamic, but by keeping their finger on the pulse of customer/channel/competitive relationships, companies can monitor the health of their brands.

There is another reason to base valuation on customers rather than brands. Calculating the value of a *single* brand owned by a company ignores the customer relationship with the same owner's other brands. The potential value of a company is not necessarily the sum of the values of each of its brands; there are three possibilities:

(i)   If different brands compete directly for share of the same customers and the same value, the potential value of the company is less than the sum of the potential value of each its brands

(ii) If different brands target different customer segments, the potential value of the company is simply the sum of individual potential brand values

(iii) If different brands complement each other and meet adjacent customer needs, the potential value of the company may be higher than the sum of individual potential brand values.

In the following discussion, I refer to the brand as if it is synonymous with the company, but the arguments can be generalised to multibrand companies.

Customer lifetime value is the net present value of customer profitability. An element of the price commanded by the brand value, and thus the profitability generated by the brand, is the premium which customers are willing to pay for the perceived value of the brand. Customer profitability is the sum of this brand element and the manufacturing or generic element that could be realised by an unbranded alternative (Figure 4.1). The two elements correspond to Peter Drucker's view of the two purposes of business: marketing and innovation.

The brand element of lifetime value can be measured by analysing customer behaviour; it is directly affected by marketing, and it can be linked to financial performance. A brand can be strengthened by adding to brand value the new dimension of a direct customer relationship. Recruiting

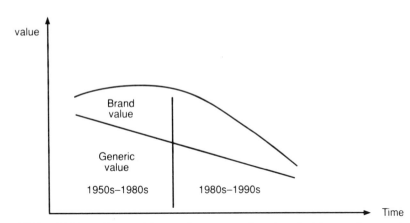

1950s–1980s: Competition reduces generic value, but innovation and marketing add brand value to increase total value

1980s–1990s: Competition and retail power exert continuing pressure on generic value, and now attack brand value

Figure 4.1 Customer lifetime value: brand and generic

customer as members, for example, can increase the brand's share of their repertoire, the probability of retaining their custom, the length of the relationship and thus the future earnings from the customers. Relationship-building increases the customer lifetime value that makes up brand value. Marketing effectiveness and brand value can be linked through customer lifetime value (Figure 4.2).

The Spiral of Prosperity

When I became music marketing manager at *Reader's Digest*, the division was loss-making. Our sales rates among existing customers were in decline and we were launching only four new products each year. We were selling fewer products to existing customers and not recruiting many new customers.

Our first action was to increase the rate of new product development, to be able to increase our mailing frequency to existing customers. A wider range of repertoire was

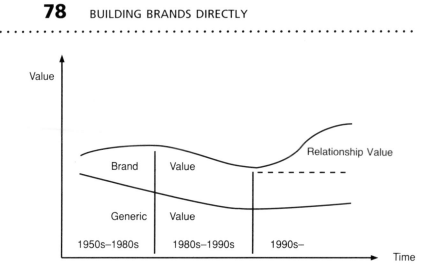

Figure 4.2 Customer lifetime value: relationship, brand and generic

mailed to customers, and the average frequency of mailing rose from five to eight times a year. Conventional wisdom suggested that the average response rates would fall with increasing frequency. In fact, they rose and I learned the value of increasing contact with customers.

We increased the personalisation of mailings, selected music more appropriate to individual customer tastes, and offered our best customers special discounts or gifts for repeat purchase. We solicited their interests and their opinions of planned new product development. So we recognised and rewarded our best customers and built closer relationships with them. Profits from customer marketing began to rise dramatically.

To grow the business, we needed to increase the size of the customer base. The most cost-effective way to do this short term was to prospect from magazine subscribers and book buyers who already had a relationship with the company. Using a simple questionnaire, we invited them to tell us their interests and offered responders music relevant to their tastes. This taught me the importance of the customer questionnaire or *census* – used to find out from customers which products they will buy and which marketing they will welcome.

We calculated how many new customers we needed to grow the customer base and the division's profitability, and how much we could afford to spend on each new customer, given our increasing returns from the existing customer base. Magazine subscribers and book buyers could not provide a sufficient flow of new customers, so we increased new customer acquisition by direct response advertising in the national press and on television. Our more frequent mailings to customers were delivering an increasing lifetime value, and our forecasts assured us that we could afford to invest in new customers – to accept a small loss in acquiring them. In practice, we acquired customers at a small profit from press advertising and purchased television airtime on a PI (per inquiry) basis, guaranteeing us a fixed cost per new name.

In the first two years of this strategy, with heavy investment in new product and new customers, we accepted a short-term decline in the product line's financial ratios. We were confident that our investment would pay back. More and better quality customers were acquired cost-effectively, and faster payback generated from existing customers. We returned the business to a sustainable high profit level in the third year.

The experience illustrates the four stages in the development of customer relationships:

(i) Prospecting

(ii) Acquisition

(iii) Cross-selling

(iv) Relationship-building.

I call the process of developing relationships through these stages the *Spiral of Prosperity*, and first sketched the concept in 1983 to summarise how marketing creates financial value (Figure 4.3).

Investment in new customers generates a new asset, and ongoing revenue stream. By cross-selling a wider range of products to customers, their profitability is increased. By building sustained relationships, customer lifetime value is maximised.

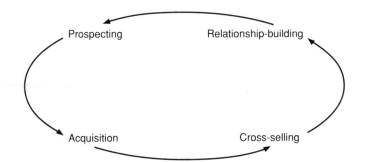

Figure 4.3 The spiral of prosperity

The Spiral of Prosperity highlights the crucial economics of marketing:

— LTV: Customer lifetime value

— CRC: Customer relationship cost

— AIM: Allowable investment maximum in a new customer.

The lifetime value (LTV) is achieved from developing customer relationships, and the cost of managing the relationship is the customer relationship cost (CRC). These two figures determine the allowable investment in new customers (AIM). Long-term profit results when lifetime value exceeds the investment cost in a new customer.

$$\text{Return on investment} = \frac{\text{LTV} - \text{CRC}}{\text{AIM}}$$

The profit generated from customer relationships can be reinvested in marketing, to acquire more new customers and develop more value from existing customers. By looking at a company and its finances in terms of customers, the value of marketing can be planned and its effectiveness measured.

Most marketing plans analyse the market, the competition and the brand in isolation from financial performance.

Using the Spiral of Prosperity:

— marketing investments can be determined for each type of activity: from advertising and promotion, to retention and loyalty

— marketing budgets can be set in the context of both short- and long-term effects on customer behaviour

— the payback from marketing investment can be calculated

— the payback from different marketing strategies and plans can be compared.

The New Economics of Marketing

Profits grow when lifetime value exceeds the cost of acquiring customers, and increasing lifetime value generates more profits that can fund more investment in marketing. This builds the customer base and further increases lifetime value. If the returns from marketing are re-invested in customers, the company is on an upward spiral.

If lifetime value is less than the cost of acquiring new customers, the company cannot grow profitably. Either fewer customers will be acquired or new customers will be unprofitable and overall profitability will decline. In either case, the company will enter a downward spiral.

Suppose that lifetime value is higher than the cost of recruiting a new customer, but the profit reinvested in marketing is only enough to maintain the size of the company base. The company will remain profitable, and by reducing the investment in new customers it is possible to increase short-term profits. But the company is not maximising profits.

Suppose that the company does not invest enough to maximise the potential of customers and thus their lifetime value. It cannot afford to acquire as many new customers as otherwise. Again it remains profitable but does not maximise profits.

In practice, I have never come across a company that

could not increase its customer lifetime value by investing more in its existing customers – and thereby afford future investments in new customers. In my experience, most companies do not calculate the financial value of their marketing. The profits from marketing are not reinvested: they are retained, distributed as dividends, or invested in other activities as part of the general surplus. Because the profits from marketing are not measured, the reinvestment of these profits in the next period's budget is rarely a subject of discussion.

Using the Spiral of Prosperity, marketing in a growing company can demonstrate the payback on investment, prove its financial case and become responsible for its funding. A static company, or one in decline, must determine the extent to which the problem is inadequate customer lifetime value or excessive new customer acquisition costs – or both. Only then can it determine the appropriate corrective action.

When it comes to allocating marketing budgets, most companies behave in a fashion opposite to the dictates of common sense and basic arithmetic. For example, most devote the largest proportion of a brand's budget to the initial launch, rather than to the development of the customer base over time. I believe this is a specific reason for the failure of so many new brands. Most companies, moreover, devote most of their marketing budgets to general media and promotions. The general media acquire some – but not many – new customers, and the promotions are redeemed by existing customers who would have bought anyway.

Marketing must focus on the critical changes in the customer relationship: from prospect to buyer, from single to repeat to multiple buyer, and from multiple buyer to loyal. These steps make the difference to the value of the brand.

A test of a company's commitment to profit maximisation lies in its allocation between existing and new customers of budgets, staff and resources. Most staff in marketing departments, and most marketing budgets, are devoted to the acquisition of new customers. Most sales forces devote disproportionate energy to new, not existing customers.

A subject for audit

% Budget, staff and resources devoted to increasing sales from existing customers

vs

% Budget, staff and resources devoted to acquiring new customers

---

A company that does not track new customer acquisition, or monitor existing customers through the stages of the relationship, cannot forecast its future size. A company that does not measure the lifetime value of existing customers, and the investment cost in new customers, cannot know whether it is maximising profit.

Most companies do not maximise profits because:

— they spend too much on new customers, not existing customers

— they do not spend enough in total on their customers, new and existing

To set the marketing budget, the starting point is not the advertising budget. The critical figure is existing customer lifetime value. The process starts with existing customers because:

(i) Investment in customer relationships is most likely to generate the highest returns; to determine how much to spend on new customers it is first necessary to determine the profitability of existing ones

(ii) Learning what motivates existing customers usually helps to define how best to acquire new customers.

In setting budgets, the critical evaluation is to determine the potential for *increasing* lifetime value, which determines the allowable investment in a new customer. With in-

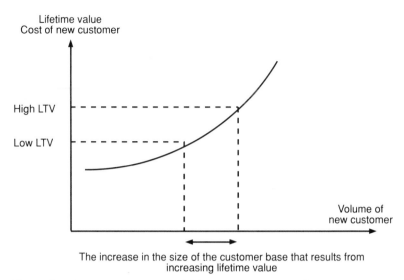

Figure 4.4 New customer acquisition investment profile

creasing volume, new customers are progressively more expensive to acquire. At some volume of new customers, the cost will equal the potential lifetime value, and this will be the maximum number of customers that can be acquired cost-effectively (Figure 4.4).

Increasing Customer Value

The process by which customer value and profits can be increased can be summarised in four stages.

For each stage, objectives can be established that link marketing results to financial performance. The objective of cross-selling to, and relationship-building with, *existing* customers is their future earnings (their lifetime value); multiplied by the probability of achieving the earnings (the customer loyalty rate). The objective of opening relationships with *new* customers is again their future earnings, multiplied by the probability that the customer can be acquired (the brand rate).

This provides the framework for justifying marketing investment. The process starts at the top, with existing

Increasing customer value		
Stage	Objective	Plan
1	Maximise potential customer lifetime value	Relationship-building
2	Maximise current customer profitability	Cross-selling
3	Maximise valuable customer base	Acquisition
4	Maximise future valuable customers	Prospecting

Relationship objectives		
Stage	Plan	Measure
1	Relationship-building	Loyalty rate: increases with customer involvement in relationship
		×
2	Cross-selling	Lifetime Value: increases with products and services used by customer
3	Acquisition	Potential Lifetime Value: increases with customer potential to buy more products and services
		×
4	Prospecting	Brand rate: increases with perception of brand values

customers and the development of closer relationships with them.

The Dimensions of the Customer Relationship

The concept of a relationship requires definition; I recognise five dimensions, summarised by the acronym CARES. I illustrate the dimensions of the customer relationship with reference to two successful US retailer programmes.

Building customer relationships:

CARES

Contact

Affinity

Rewards

Extra value

Service

Contact

The more frequent the customer contact, the more opportunities to sell to customers and the more secure the customer relationship. The effect of contact with customers is a function of frequency and impact, and can be tested and modelled.

US retailer Sears has evaluated the frequency of mailing to best customers, and reports that it takes six to eight communications a year before customers feel special. This is communication to the customer's home, and additional to the special recognition that best customers receive in-store. Sears has two programmes for best customers:

(i)   A Bonus Club, offering merchandise certificates on spends of $200 or more

(ii) A Best Customer programme to 4.8 million customers selected from 28 million active charge accounts, offering added value benefits like priority installation, repair services, special offers and events and free catalogues.

The impact of contact on customer behaviour varies by type of contact – options include mail, telephone, electronic media, events and representative visits. Different contacts have different costs, and different customers prefer different approaches. Customers polarise by their liking for mail and telephone contact: most distinctly prefer one or the other. Research can be used to probe customer responses to different approaches, and to measure the effectiveness of different forms of contact.

In 1984, US retailer Neiman Marcus launched its relationship-building programme, InCircle. Customers spending over $3000 a year are eligible, so the customer base is affluent. Neiman Marcus found that InCircle members welcomed a quarterly communication, and that with this frequency they preferred a short newsletter to a glossy magazine. Neiman Marcus reserves magazines for special occasions, like the 10th anniversary of InCircle in Autumn 1994.

In active relationships, contact is initiated by the customer as well as by the company. Neiman Marcus motivates contact with InCircle members by promotions like a Treasure Quest game in the 10th Anniversary magazine. The magazine announces 'buried treasure' in the stores and invites members to search for it. Customer participation is encouraged by offering new clues to members each week through calls to a special telephone number, 1-800-350-CLUE.

Regular events bring members together in the stores. In 1990, the 15 000 best customers were invited to special events launching the company's Christmas book. Special overseas tours and holidays are also organised, exclusively for members.

Affinity

Affinity means the tailoring of products and services to the specific needs of selected customer segments, or even the customisation of them for individuals.

Sears identifies five high value customer segments and creates affinity marketing programmes for each:

(i)   KidVantage for families with young children

(ii)   College Advantage for students

(iii)   Mature Outlook for the over 50s

(iv)   Craftsman Club for those interested in DIY

(v)   New Movers.

In developing affinity marketing programmes, a mass marketing company effectively transforms itself into many specialist companies. Sears KidVantage is a brand in its own right. The programme's benefits include warranties against wear and tear as well as rewards and discounts – 10 per cent for a $50 spend, 15 per cent for $100 or more. KidVantage marketing includes multimillion catalogue mailings to drive store traffic before the back to school season. Similarly, the Craftsman Club offers information, benefits and discounts on Craftsman-labelled DIY products in Sears.

For mass marketers, affinity marketing by customer segment is a strategic response to specialist or niche competition. The benefits of the company brand values and customer relationships are retained, but by customising features and benefits to specific audiences new value can be added.

Rewards

Rewards are tangible benefits, offered in exchange for continued custom and for frequent or high value purchase. A familiar form of reward is the point or collection scheme. Neiman Marcus InCircle members, for example, accumulate points for dollars spent, and at the end of the year receive a cash back voucher against future purchases. Special rewards, in the form of bonus points, are available at selected shopping times, at member-only events and for the purchase of selected merchandise.

Rewards are a form of promotion, but two relationship strategy features make them distinctive from traditional sales promotion:

(i) Rewards are offered selectively to individual customers based on their behaviour and interests

(ii) Rewards are dependent on continued custom.

The principle underlying both features is that rewards are not wasted on customers who would have bought anyway. They are targeted to increase customer lifetime value cost-effectively. Rewards are a form of differential pricing: they reward the customer for continued custom and motivate an increase in the level or range of purchase. They offer more value to the customer than straight price discounts, and because they are private and linked to continued customer there is no erosion of brand values through overt discounting. Tangible rewards should be distinctive to the brand and should be accompanied by extra value, as otherwise they can be emulated by competition.

Extra value

Extra value consists of privileges, services and offers exclusive to best customers. Each Sears affinity programme offers extra value relevant to the target audience. The over 50s save money by shopping during quiet store periods; students receive discounts on books, music and clothes; house movers receive a priority service at the time they need it.

Extra value can be provided through special arrangements with business partners, at no cost to the company. Neiman Marcus, for example, has business partners in airline travel, holidays, car rental and magazine publishing. Neiman Marcus involves InCircle members directly in creating extra value, as with a series of cookbooks sold to benefit charity, available to members only, with the recipes provided by members. To date, 200 000 cookbook sales have resulted in donations of over $600 000.

Service

Customer service adds access and responsiveness to the customer relationship, and provides help, information, problem-solving and complaint management on demand.

InCircle members reach dedicated customer service staff by calling the free number, 1-800-CIRCLE. Customer service's profile is raised by involving members: InCircle members receive four service stickers each year; when they experience superior service, they redeem a sticker in reward for points, naming the member of staff responsible.

Sears involves local store management in the delivery of its programme benefits. Sears senior marketing manager for customer marketing, Al Malony, says:

> We're using our local store managers within the stores and making them the heroes, the focal point, so that communications don't come from Sears, they come from an individual in a store where you shop. Without an individual to take ownership, nobody's accountable. But if its John Smith, the hardware department manager, in charge of the Craftsman Club, then John Smith has a better commitment to it and we get much better execution.[2]

The investment in internal customer service reflects the parallel investment in external customer relationships.

Investing Externally in Customer Relationships

The affordable investment in a customer relationship is based on a forecast of the potential to increase lifetime value. Rewards are the most direct form of investment in customers, and to achieve payback the cost of funding rewards must be more than recovered in the increase in customer profitability that results from additional sales.

In the accounting of customer rewards there are six factors: three positive and three negative:

Investment in customer rewards: short to medium term

A pro forma for the planning and evaluation
of customer rewards

Segment	Current Value	Potential Value		Effects
Customers	High	High	Reduction in margin	−
			Increase in sales	+
	Low	High	Increase in sales	+
	Low	Low	Reduction in margin	−
Prospects		High	Increase in sales	+
		Low	Increase in sales	−

In the short to medium term, the payback from investment depends on the difference between the margin for increased sales and the cost of funding the rewards. In the longer term, payback depends on the effectiveness of rewards in achieving a sustained change in customer behaviour: moving more customers and prospects into the high lifetime value categories.

··

Investment in customer rewards: long term

A pro forma for the changes in behaviour
achieved by customer rewards

Segment	Current Value	Potential Value		Effects
Customers	High	High	Increase in number	
			Reduction in margin	−
			Increase in sales	+
	Low	High	Decrease in number	
			Increase in sales	+
	Low	Low	Reduction in margin	−
Prospects		High	Increase in number	
			Increase in sales	+
		Low	Increase in sales	−

If they are to work, rewards must be motivating to
customers and offer value in return for the customer's
commitment. Less obviously, they must be relevant and
distinctive to the brand. Research can be used to evaluate
the relevance of rewards to the brand, as well as their
appeal to customers. I cannot emphasise enough the importance of:

— selecting rewards that are distinctive to the brand

— balancing tangible (hard) rewards with (soft) relationship benefits

— investing internally to communicate the brand personality through people and to deliver service excellence through operational efficiency.

The programme will not be distinctive to the brand, if
customers are not contacted regularly, rewards are not
customised for them as individuals, and extra value is not

one of the benefits they receive. It will be copied by competitors, margins will be eroded, and it will not change customer behaviour.

There are two opportunities to generate additional funds to defray the investment in customer relationships:

(i) Special privileges and offers may be funded in partnership with other companies or business partners; there is the potential to make the customer base a profit centre

(ii) Customers may be willing to pay for enhanced customer service and to enrol in a membership relationship; every brand should test the potential of paid membership.

Neiman Marcus combines both in a 'second tier' program, NM Plus, for customers who do not spend $3000 a year but are willing to pay a $50 membership fee – which they receive back immediately in the form of a complementary American Airlines $50 travel certificate

Once a relationship management programme is established, different thresholds can be set for entry qualifications and investment in customers. Analysis of customer behaviour can establish profitability thresholds, above which VIP programmes can be offered for higher spending customers, to strengthen their loyalty. The psychology is such that once customers achieve a higher status, they become unwilling to lose the greater privileges that accompany it.

Investing Internally in Customer Relationships

The analysis of return from investment in customer relationships applies as much to the two essential internal investments, in customer information and customer service.

Customer Information

A customer information system and customer data are fixed assets. The return from investment in these assets lies in the additional contribution to profit from more developed customer relationships, enhanced customer contact, and better targeted marketing. In the accounting of computer systems, the usual benefits are assumed to lie in increased operational efficiency, and in cost and labour-saving. With a relationship perspective, the returns from investment in information technology can be sought from increased revenues and profits.

Accounting for information technology

— Systems that allow enhanced management of customer relationships can be evaluated on the increase in the duration of the relationship and thus in customer lifetime values

— Systems that allow better targeting of offers to customer needs can be evaluated on the increase in customer profitability, and thus again on the increase in customer lifetime value.

Relationship management has the useful by-product of a framework for management to project and measure the value of investments in information technology.

Customer service

The goal of customer service is to meet and surpass customer expectations. Research and testing can be used to determine the investment in customer service, by measuring customer expectations and by evaluating the effect of improvements in service on customer behaviour. A watch on competition – benchmarking against competitive standards – is important, as competitive service can change customer expectations (Table 4.1).

Enhancing any of these aspects of service has a cost. Service performance across all of these factors affects customer behaviour. The change in the behaviour can be

Table 4.1 Components of internal customer management, as experienced by customers

Service aspect	Customer expectation	Competitive benchmark	Cost profile
Enquiry processing			
Quality of information			
Order despatch turnaround			
Quality of delivery			
Billing and payment methods			
Returns and exchanges			
Problems and complaint management			

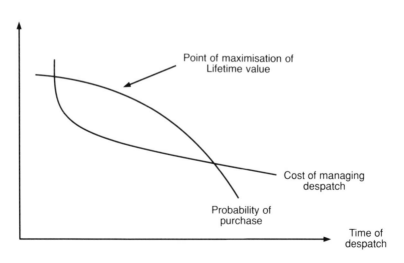

Speed of despatch of information in response to advertising enquiries

Figure 4.5 Customer service, relationship-building and lifetime value: an illustration

measured, and the opportunity cost of not providing the service can be determined and compared to the increased costs of providing it (Figure 4.5). Again, customer lifetime value is the basis for investment.

Maximising Customer Profitability: Cross-selling

Within a relationship strategy, customer profitability is increased by up-selling and cross-selling. Relationships have primacy, in that customers will not buy more products from brands with which they do not have relationships. So given relationships are developing, cross-selling is a necessary condition for maximising customer lifetime value. The objective is to sell as many products and services to customers as are relevant and acceptable to them.

These are the two critical success factors:

— to be efficient, cross-selling must be targeted

— to be effective, cross-selling must be welcome.

Targeting is driven by the analysis of customer data which identifies the products and services the customer needs and might buy. Data is critical because customer needs are individual. Analysis of a customer's behaviour and profile predicts if the customer is likely to buy further products and services. Detailed analysis reveals patterns or product purchase, helping to guide the sequence in which products are offered to customers. For each product and each customer, a probability of purchase can be measured and an ideal promotional sequence planned (Figure 4.6).

Analysis predicts opportunities to develop the customer relationship, or possible risks to the relationship if no corrective action is taken. The times at which sales may decline or customers may be lost completely to competition are critical and analysis can predict these watershed points in a customer relationship.

The best source of customer data for cross-selling is a *customer census* which can identify interest in or need for a product. A census is a regular survey of the customer base and an important aspect of every relationship management programme. The census allows customers to invite the sale by soliciting information on products or services. Cus-

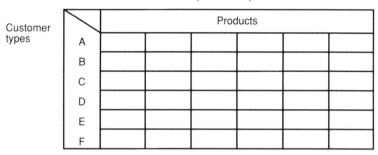

For every customer type the appeal of each product can be calculated, and the sequence with which products should be sold can be planned.

Figure 4.6 Customer/product array

tomers who opt in appreciate and welcome the marketing messages they receive.

Cross-selling need not be restricted to existing products. Any company has the potential to sell a wider product portfolio to existing customers. Research can be used to investigate the products and services that would be appreciated by the best customers. The company has the option of developing the highest ranking products or offering them to customers through business partners. There is a strategic choice between recruiting more customers, generally at rising cost, or broadening the product portfolio and cross-selling more to existing customers. In my experience, most companies concentrate on acquiring more customers and neglect opportunities to increase profits by selling more to their best customers. Many do not even determine the potential.

Reader's Digest and American Express are among the few companies to maximise opportunities. Managers in both companies bid to promote their product to customers and there are more bids than opportunities. Other managers are responsible for identifying new products and new business partners – and there are more new products than opportunities to sell them. Optimisation models allocate opportunities to products by customer segment, according to a plan that will maximise *company* profitability. The process is not driven by profitability alone. In both companies, management exercises judgement in shaping customer communication programmes, with house rules limiting the frequency of contact. Exploitation of the customer relationship could be damaging, even if analysis indicates that short-term profitability could be increased.

Planning the Investment in New Customers

The acquisition of new customers is driven by targeting strategy, and the focus is on high potential lifetime value customers. Targeting is no longer based on a vague definition of a general advertising audiences, defined by socio-economics or demographics. Targeting is based on value: on spend in the product category and on competitive brand relationships.

A useful basis for planning is to segment customers and prospects by quartile in terms of their lifetime value (Table 4.2). In many markets, for example, only the top lifetime value quartiles may be worth targeting. The relationship between lifetime value and acquisition cost is important as it determines the investment profile. The best customers are often the most expensive to acquire – they may currently be frequent users of competitive brands.

The cost of acquiring customers rises with increasing volume, and at some volume will be greater than the allowable investment maximum.

Prospecting is any activity that identifies potential customers by name and address and collects data about them.

Table 4.2 Planning investment in new customers

Market quartiles	Customer lifetime value	Customer acquisition costs
1		
2		
3		
4		

By analysing individual data, prospects can be qualified and their potential lifetime value predicted; unqualified prospects with low-potential value can be eliminated or allocated limited marketing investment. The strategy focuses on the best prospects, with lifetime value in the upper quartiles.

Customer prospecting and acquisition

Step 1 Determine allowable investment in new customers
  2 Determine the profile of upper quartile lifetime value customers
  3 Evaluate alternative media and contact with target customers
  4 Test alternative methods of engaging prospects
  5 Track quality of new customers acquired by each method and source

Prospecting is a priority for the whole company, not just the responsibility of the marketing department, as the range of prospecting opportunities reveals.

Name generation and data collection opportunities

direct response advertising
response promotion
sampling and field promotion
sales force and trade
data rental or purchase
in-pack or on-pack data collection
guarantee and warranty registration
customer service and helplines

The analysis of customer lifetime values will prompt most companies to review the targeting of their advertising. The result is likely to be a shift to more targeted media. The

more targeted the media, the greater the customer involvement and higher the impact of the advertising. The Henley
Centre *Media Futures* study, for example, reports that the
effectiveness of specialist magazines may be underestimated
by most advertisers.[3]

Investment in direct relationships was once cost-effective
for higher priced products only, but this is no longer so.
The cost per effective contact of direct media is rapidly
approaching that of general advertising media. Any consumer brand can use advertising response, promotional
redemption, and face-to-face sampling to target new customers; followed by mail and telephone to build relationships. The more data available about prospects, the better
the targeting, and the higher the affordable investment in
the customer contact. By analysing data about individual
prospects, sales can be maximised by selecting the right
message, at the right time, delivered with the right offer
through the right channel.

A model for every company's prospecting and acquisition
is *The Mill* – so called because it grinds prospects into
customers over time. The quality and cost-effectiveness of
different prospecting sources can be determined by a test
programme using The Mill (Figure 4.7).

Prospecting generates leads from a variety of sources,
including advertising, list rental and sales forces. Prospects
are analysed and segmented on the basis of their predicted
potential value as customers. A contact plan is designed for
each type of prospect, and the investment in the contact
plan and relationship is matched to the potential of the
customer. The plans use direct mail, telephone and sales
visits.

The results of The Mill are:

— immediate sales, captured on the customer database,
and eligible for cross-selling and relationship-building
programmes

— immediate rejections, excluded from future campaigns

— non-respondents: inclusion in future activity depends
on their potential; non-response reduces their potential

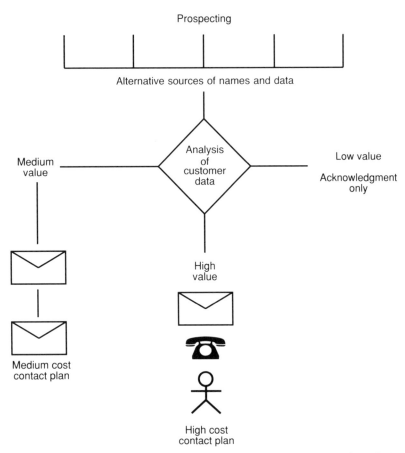

Figure 4.7 Illustration of name generation test design, and analysis for new customers of a consumer brand: The Mill

    value, and the probability that they will become customers

— respondents who indicate an interest, but do not buy. They are now better qualified, and are fed back into The Mill for further contact.

Three Principles

Three principles underlie the creation of value from brands and customers:

(i)   Focus on customers with two characteristics, both of which can be modelled: high potential lifetime value, and high propensity to increase their purchases

(ii)   Add the values of access and responsiveness to the brand, and build the customer relationship with the brand before trying to up-sell and cross-sell

(iii) Match the investment in external marketing to the customer with internal investment in customer information and service.

PART II: PLANNING

FROM IMAGE TO INTERACTIVE ADVERTISING 5

'Involve me and I'll understand'

> The Growth in Interactive Advertising – Image or Interactive Advertising – The Roles of Interactive Advertising – Image-led Advertising – Complementary Image and Response Advertising – Direct Prospecting Advertising – Direct Challenge Advertising – Double Duty Advertising – Support Advertising – Interactive Advertising Media Planning – Direct Response Television Planning – Managing Customer Response – The Relationship Dimension of Brands

The Growth in Interactive Advertising

Increasingly, advertisers invite customers to respond to press and television advertising. I define interactive advertising as communication that motivates customers to take a direct action towards an experience of, and relationship with, a brand.

Three factors underlie the trend to interactive advertising: brand development, product information and marketing effectiveness. Interactive advertising adds to brands the values of access and responsiveness, generic qualities

103

essential in the 1990s. It creates a channel by which manufacturers can communicate information to their customers.
At the same time, making advertising interactive makes it
more effective. Advertising should be measured not by
awareness or image but by brand rate: the propensity of
high lifetime value prospects to trial the brand. *By inviting
trial of the brand and experience of the customer service that
underlies the brand, interactivity maximises advertising's impact.
By generating the names of prospective buyers, interactivity
maximises advertising's sales effectiveness.*

Flora margarine advertising, headlined 'Fact or Fiction',
presents comparative figures on the saturated fat content of
Flora and butter. In the footnote to the advertisement is the
invitation: 'For more information, ring the Flora Careline
free on 0800 136959.' Prudential Assurance runs advertising
in which the headline is all invitation: 'Want a chat, quiet
word, tête-à-tête, natter, parley, an interface (interface?),
confab, gossip, chinwag, pow-pow, heart-to-heart, rabbit,
conversazione . . . ? Talk to Prudence. Phone 0800 000 000.'
Here response is not the primary objective, which is to add
value to the brand by developing the fourth dimension, the
customer relationship. Response is a secondary objective,
and the advertising also results in enquiries, information
requests and even complaints, all of which are valuable
customer contacts.

A further trend is for advertising to invite customers to
test or sample the product. As the Yankelovitch Partners'
1993 *Consumer Trends Monitor* reports: 'The idea of offering
concrete proof instead of vague guarantees is key to
marketing to today's consumers.'[1] Whatever the take-up
of the invitation, the confidence in the brand increases
the force of the advertising. In the US, brands are made
accessible by descriptive telephone numbers, like 1-800-
THE-CARD owned by American Express. Special numbers
and touch tone telephones make it easier to incorporate
customer service messages in television and radio advertising. The resistance to direct response in general and
customer service telephone numbers in particular, mainly
from advertising agencies, is luddite.

Many advertisers have found that adding response

improves even traditional measures of advertising like spontaneous awareness. In 1992, I invited a student to study this development for his business studies thesis. He found that even general advertising agencies expected a rapid growth in response advertising, and saw the advantages to their clients as 'a measurement tool and a means of maintaining and enhancing image advertising'.[2]

There is a narrow view of interactive advertising that should be resisted. For example, the UK advertising for Mazda that motivates the viewer to turn up the volume has been described as interactive. The execution is powerful because it prompts action, but the viewer is interacting with the medium and not the advertiser's message. More significant is US advertising for Coca-Cola's new soft drink brand OK, inviting viewers to phone in their first experiences of the brand. The advertising heightens involvement in trial of the brand and invites the customer to feedback their response. The viewer interacts with both brand and company. But this is still not truly interactive, in the sense intended by P&G's Artz. Callers to OK advertising received no reward or acknowledgement. In my definition, interactive advertising rewards customers, exchanges value with them, and uses the contact to develop an ongoing relationship.

Paul Ashby of the Interactive Marketing Group quotes an old Chinese proverb to demonstrate the principles of interactivity: 'Tell me and I'll forget. Show me and I may remember. Involve me and I'll understand.' IMG has created interactive television and print advertising around the world for major advertisers that include Procter & Gamble, Nestlé, Mars and Colgate-Palmolive. Its programmes have been tracked by major research companies that include AGB and Gallup. They report higher spontaneous awareness, prompted awareness, and purchase intention for customers exposed to the advertising. They report higher sales from responders to the advertising. But they also confirm significantly higher sales from customers exposed to the advertising who did *not* respond. Over a number of campaigns for packaged good advertisers in the Australian market, for example, brand awareness rose 13 per cent, advertising awareness 57 per cent, past four-week purchase 55 per cent and next four-week purchase 45 per cent among customers who were exposed to interactive advertising. In every case this was the result of a spend that was a fraction of usual general advertising budgets.

Ashby observes: 'Image advertising doesn't give the information needed to buy knowledge-driven products.' Moreover, he argues: 'Communication results from an interaction in which two parties expect to give and take . . . Audience members must be able to give feedback. Media practitioners must be sensitive to the information contained in the feedback. This give and take can result in real understanding or real feedback.'[3]

Image or Interactive Advertising

Direct response is the forerunner of modern interactive advertising techniques. The philosophies and methods of image advertising and direct response are contradictory. Image advertising is emotive, direct response is rational; image advertising works by changing beliefs, direct response by changing behaviour; image advertising is imaginative, direct response is factual; image advertising appeals to the emotions and senses, direct response to needs and desires – even to greed and ambition. The essential difference is that image advertising communicates ideas, whereas direct response traditionally communicates offers.

The gulf between image and response is vast. It is exacerbated by the division of responsibility within marketing departments into separate advertising and direct marketing functions, and by the appointment of different agencies to create the two types of advertising for the same brand.

John Caples was an advertising professional who studied direct response, and summarised what he called the scientific principles of advertising in *Tested Advertising Methods*. This book opens with the immortal line: 'The most important things to discover in the study of advertising are facts', and proceeds to chapter heads that include: 'The Most Important Part of an Advertisement' (the headline), 'Twenty-nine Formulas for Writing Headlines', 'Finding the Right Appeal', 'Twenty Ways to Increase Selling Power of Copy', and 'Thirty-two ways to Get More Inquiries from Your Advertising'.[4] There are two major international awards in direct marketing: the Echos and the Caples. While the former are based on marketing effectiveness, it is ironic that the awards named after John Caples are judged on creativity alone, and not on results.

As David Ogilvy writes in his foreword to Caples' book: 'The purpose of this book is to tell you how to write advertising that produces immediate sales for your product or service.' The difference between the two approaches results from their differing objectives and time horizons: direct response advertising is designed to achieve immediate results, image advertising to build a brand and market share over time. In contrast, a direct response campaign with the same creative execution almost always suffers falling response over time: the first advertisements attract the best prospects and the later advertisements pull fewer, lower value respondents.

When I was responsible for direct response advertising for music at *Reader's Digest*, even the most successful creative execution ran for only a few months before it began to wear out. Our solution was to rotate creative treatments: a new advertisement would raise response again while the first execution was rested. When the first advertisement ran again, response rose after an interval, although never to the level achieved in the original burst of advertising. In direct response, change in pace in creative and offer is vital.

Yet in image advertising the opposite is true: consistency in creative is important. The advertising is evaluated on recall and brand awareness, image and preference. As an advertising schedule progresses, the opportunities to see (OTS) increase, and so do the measures of recall and awareness. The advertising is reinforcing, building over time. Consistent creative in advertising usually runs for an extended period of time, often for years (Figures 5.1 and

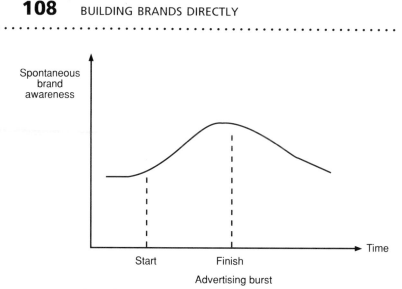

Spontaneous brand awareness is the preferable traditional measure of advertising effectiveness. The usual effect of advertising is an S-shaped curve

Figure 5.1 An advertising impact curve over time

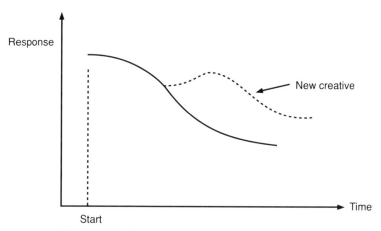

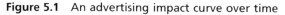

Response falls sharply after initial media insertions. New creative can raise the level of the curve but does not prevent long term decline in response

Figure 5.2 A direct response curve over time

5.2). Any advertiser that changes creative regularly is much criticised.

The challenge for advertisers is to create a synthesis between image and response advertising. This is *not* as simple as adding coupons and telephone numbers to image advertising. I was once consulted by an insurance company that had spent £2.5 million on television, and added a telephone number to the end frame of their commercial. Anticipating a sizeable response, they had printed 100 000 information packs but had less than 1000 enquiries. The telephone number – which was not memorable – was not on screen for long enough. No invitation to call was made in the voice over, and no benefit promised to customers as a reward for calling.

Traditional direct response tactics are inappropriate for advertising that builds brands. Advertising led by offer and reliant on a rational appeal does not differentiate. This is illustrated by the oldest direct response advertisers, the mail order catalogues. Most of their advertising leads on the gifts awarded with first purchase, and if one catalogue finds a new offer it is quickly matched by the competition. By competing on offers rather than on customer service or brand values, mail order advertisers fail to differentiate their individual brands, and fail to create a high perceived value for catalogue shopping in general. They should consider advertising strategies based on the added values of contact, affinity, reward, extra value and service rather than incentives.

The Roles of Interactive Advertising

In relationship strategy, the synthesis of image advertising and direct response is interactive advertising which is more salient, more involving and more effective.

Advertising historically divides into two broad schools: the creative and the propositional. The propositional school is associated with Rosser Reeves, who devised the Unique Selling Proposition (USP). The creative school is associated with Bill Bernbach, who is famous for Volkswagen Beetle advertising in the US: 'Think Small', 'It Makes Your House Look Big', 'Ugly is Only Skin Deep' and 'Lemon'. Bernbach famously rejected the emphasis on the USP. 'I am absolutely appalled by the suggestion, indeed the policy, of some agencies that once the selling proposition has been determined the job is done.'[5]

In practice, successful advertising learns from both schools. Researcher Millward Brown, for example, proposes three types of advertising:

(i) 'Immediate Challenge' confronts established perceptions with a significant new benefit or an appeal to a new audience

(ii) 'Interest-Status' renews the association with an existing aspect of the brand

(iii) 'Enhancement' reinforces the consumer's experience of the brand in use.[6]

Each of the three forms of advertising creates the opportunity to enhance the interaction with the customer:

— trial offers, product samples and demonstrations for immediate challenge

— new information, advice and help for interest-status

— rewards and extra value for enhancement.

An interaction with a customer is an opportunity to learn about the customer as an individual. The 'direct' communication that results from a customer response can be targeted or triggered to the customer as an individual, and increases the advertising effect by amplifying and developing the advertising message. The advertising invites the customer to participate in a continuing relationship.

I identify six interactive advertising strategies:

(i) Image-led

(ii) Complementary image and direct response

(iii)   Direct prospecting

(iv)   Direct challenge

(v)   Double duty

(vi)   Support advertising.

Image-led Advertising

All advertising need not call for a response. There are media, in particular outdoor, that do not lend themselves to response. And there may be better ways to prospect and interact with customers.

Cigarette manufacturers, despite severely constrained advertising opportunities, continue to invest heavily in brand image advertising. They have invested in other forms of prospecting to identify smokers: sampling in leisure sites, interviews with smokers at point-of-sale, collection of existing smoker data in-pack, and syndicated sources of cigarette brand usage data. The cigarette manufacturers have become among the most proficient of marketers in their focus on the identification and retention of their declining customer franchises.

Sometimes cigarette manufacturers like Imperial in the UK (with the Embassy catalogue) and Marlboro in the US (with the Marlboro Adventure Team) feature their customer reward schemes in advertising. The advertising supports the schemes, and increases the acquisition of new members through other sources like in-store promotions. Communicating the rewards associated with the brand adds more value to the brand image.

However I have frequently heard in research groups: 'If there was somewhere to write to, I might do something about it'; or: 'Why do they never give you their telephone number to contact them?' Customers appreciate the invitation to learn more, and a trend is for companies to complement their brand advertising with a customer information service.

There are precedents for this. Specialist magazines have

traditionally offered a Reader Reply Service, a convenient way for readers to respond at the same time to a number of advertisers. In the US, radio and television stations are experimenting with the same concept. CouponRadio, designed for commuters, is an experimental car radio system with a built-in smart card, enabling listeners to push a button to register their interest in advertising. Television network NBC has launched the NBC Viewer Service, a telephone response line shown during advertising breaks that enables viewers to call for information from commercials. NBC is testing NBC Preview, a viewing guide mailed to responders to advertising and the other promotions run by the network.

The growing demand of customers for information makes it imperative for advertisers to provide answers. Information is a competitive advantage and is becoming an essential aspect of brand value. Failure to communicate information can be expensive. Unilever's public relations disaster with the launch of Persil and Omo Power resulted from a failure to communicate the conditions under which the new formulation would provide superior performance. Procter & Gamble's aggressive criticism was hampered by a similar failure to communicate objectively the results of its own and other trials of the powder. As a *Financial Times* editorial concluded: 'Both Unilever and P&G have learned in recent months that they can no longer hide behind the carefully manipulated image of their brands; they have to explain themselves and their activities more effectively to consumers and the wider public.'[7]

As companies make themselves accessible to their customers they will need to orchestrate all their communications. Advertising, customer service and public relations will need to be integrated within a total relationship management process.

The growing use of the telephone and the increasing penetration of PCs in businesses and homes potentially puts customers on-line to advertisers. Electronic response options to advertising put control in the hands of the customer:

— automatic menu-driven telephone response handling allows responders to request information and register their own needs automatically

— fax-on-demand allows responders to reply by fax, and to request immediate fax transmission of the information they seek

— on-line information networks allow prospective customers to request their own information, and to browse information databases

— PC video systems linked by telephone allow responders to request information, watch demonstrations and talk live with a company representative.

Complementary Image and Response Advertising

Image and direct response advertising can be complementary. Image advertising creates awareness and draws attention to the rational appeal and call to action of response advertising. Response executions reinforce and complement the image advertising, picking up on the interest created and moving the prospect towards an enquiry or sale. The two forms of advertising should be coordinated, sharing personality, tone of voice and company-brand values.

Under the panoply of image advertising, response advertising can be customised:

— where the image advertising supports the company-brand, the response advertising can feature specific products and services

— where the image advertising addresses a wide audience, the response advertising can appeal to distinctive customer segments

— where the image advertising communicates a general message in general media, the response advertising can be adapted to the culture and style of targeted media.

Response advertising can be used for tactical offers and in reply to competitive advertising. As the new model year approaches, car manufacturers mix short direct response commercials into their television advertising schedules, inviting prospects to send for information on new models, offers and promotions. This is the most effective use of direct response television: not stand alone, but integrated within image advertising plans.

The Heinz Meaty Bone direct response campaign in the US referred to in Chapter 3 used a 50:50 mix of image and response executions. The image message centred on Meaty Bone's 2:1 preference in blind taste tests, supported in direct response commercials by the 'Taste Challenge', an illustration of Immediate Challenge advertising. Dog owners were invited to ring 1-800-SAY-DOGS to receive free samples and money-off coupons, and half of responders were competitive brand users. Meaty Bone achieved 70 per cent awareness of the 2:1 preference, and year-on-year sales increased 300 per cent.

Kaffee Hag, also in the US, illustrates how complementary image and direct advertising can amplify Interest-Status creative, and target an important audience segment. Against the backdrop of image press advertising, morning radio was used to reach the over-50s, and invite competition entry. Winners were announced at 4pm on the same day. The advertising offered a Kaffee Hag Friendship package, associating the brand with entertainment and community. The advertising generated response at a cost of only $3.50 per name, an acceptable investment in brand trial among a heavy consuming segment of the market.

Direct Prospecting Advertising

At the other extreme of the image-interactive continuum is a form of pure direct response that is not consistent with image advertising and does not even feature the brand. I call this direct prospecting.

Direct prospecting is the appropriate advertising execution where the objective is to identify competitive brand users. It is particularly effective for brands with a minority of the market, as the majority of the responders will be competitive brand users. The message in direct prospecting may be completely rational, or there may be elements of the brand's values disguised in the creative treatment. The creative itself, the offer, and the media selection determine the appeal of the message. If the company has brands in most sectors of the market, it will pay to appeal widely and to collect customer data useful to all brands. Direct prospecting can generate competitive user names for any of the brands in a company's portfolio, in particular for the smaller brands that could not afford their own activity.

Direct prospecting cannot be completely unbranded, as data protection legislation demands that the identity of the advertiser is revealed. But a holding company name can shield the real identity of the brand or brands. A company strategy for prospecting is more cost-effective than individual brand activities.

The follow-up to direct prospecting reveals the source of the advertising and offers trial of the brand or service. The mystery and challenge inherent in this strategy add to the interest and appeal. One of the most celebrated instances of 'mystery' direct prospecting was run by Philip Morris for its Merit cigarette brand. Smokers were invited to send for a free pack of a mystery cigarette and the sample packs were unbranded. The brand identity was revealed in a second mailing with a further free pack, offers and a questionnaire. In the UK, United Distillers has tested direct prospecting for an unnamed whisky brand. The follow-up reveals the brand as Bells, tells the brand story and heritage, and offers a discount voucher against purchase.

Direct Challenge Advertising

Most image advertising takes the form of enhancement, and is designed more to retain the custom of existing users rather to recruit new users to the brand. Existing users 'note' the advertising most highly, while non-users 'screen' the advertising, switching off their attention. Unless the advertising has news, interest or a challenge, it has little impact on competitive brand and non-users. Advertising is a relatively weak force in prospecting for new users.

If a brand is well known in its market, the majority of respondents to its advertising will be users of the brand. Interactive advertising can be used to issue a direct challenge to motivate their attention and interest of competitive brand users. The challenge can be overt, with the advertising identifying the competitive brand user in the headline. The advertising does not 'knock' the competitive brand: it simply makes an invitation and offer.

In the US, the RJ Reynolds brand Winston has run direct challenge press advertising, using dominant double page spreads in national magazines, with a bound-in insert between the two pages. On the left-hand page, Winston smokers were invited to enter a promotion offering rewards for continued purchase. The rewards were branded merchandise, designed to appeal to existing users who identified with the brand. On the right-hand page, in a direct appeal to smokers of the leading competitive brand, Marlboro, an incentive was offered for a combination of Winston and Marlboro pack tops. Response was by a coupon or the prepaid reply card included on the bind-in card. The premium brand end of the US cigarette market is fiercely competitive. Marlboro retaliates to Winston's challenge by using direct mail, containing a questionnaire and a sheaf of coupons to motivate brand switching.

Another illustration of the direct challenge is advertising by BMW in the US of a 'Comparison Drive'. Drivers are invited to test drive a BMW and competitive marques, including their existing models, through a specially designed course. The greater competitiveness of US markets in comparison to Europe is evidenced by the greater need for propositional and interactive advertising, working harder to build brand values and generate sales.

Double Duty Advertising

Image and response combined in a single execution is called 'double duty' advertising by Rapp and Collins.[8] Double duty advertising balances image building and response generation.

Dell Computer has been one of the fastest growing businesses in the world over the last decade. The company built its brand and market share using double duty advertising. For Dell's UK launch, the challenge was twofold: to build the brand and to generate immediate sales directly from advertising. In the early days, virtually all sales could be linked to advertising: today, the brand is so well established that a steady flow of leads is received irrespective of advertising. But at first, the advertising budget for each month was determined by the sales generated from advertising in the past month. This illustrates how marketing can fund its own investment.

The advertising creative was stylish and distinctive. Dominant formats were bought – a high investment in the early days, but larger spaces, special positions and bound-in inserts generate higher response in cluttered media. One of the most effective formats for Dell was the first double page spread plus gatefold in a computer magazine. A consistent creative style developed the brand. An abstract picture on the left was accompanied by headline, text and call to action on the right. But the creative execution also followed proven direct response tactics. The call to action was at bottom right, to where the layout led the eye. A large free telephone number was positioned above the coupon. Telephone response was preferable as it was an opportunity to learn more about customers, and to demonstrate the Dell brand personality 'in action'. Telephone pulls in more immediate prospects.

Dell France followed the same advertising strategy with equal success, but reported an occasion when the company moved away from established direct response practice. It suffered poor results when it hired an image advertising agency which did not understand direct response tactics.[9]

With fragmented media, marketing will be increasingly targeted in a smaller number of specialist media. Jack Daniels whiskey, Felix cat food and Häagen-Dazs ice cream are all brands that have been developed cost-effectively by concentrating advertising on a small number of press titles.

Double duty advertising makes advertising budgets go further. With developing market share Dell now advertises in the national press. Whereas in the specialist press Dell still buys dominant positions and expensive formats, in the nationals it uses smaller spaces and different messages. While other media communicate product innovation, the visual style in national press has moved away from images and the messages are service-led, each using a Dell customer service representative as a spokesperson for the brand.

In the US, Ryder Trucks' television advertising performs a double duty. A feature of all its commercials is a response invitation, with a booklet on moving home to appeal to families who are considering renting a truck. The offer generates leads and adds value by presenting Ryder as a company that helps people.

Some brands are inherently responsive, like Apple in the computer market, whereas others, like IBM, are not. If a brand continuously invites response, more customers in the market gain the experience of contact with the company. The invitation itself demonstrates a willingness to relate to the customer and has a positive effect on perception of the brand. Responsiveness is an aspect of the brand rate, the brand's power in the market-place. Responsiveness is self-reinforcing – calling for response, and excellent management of response, add to brand values with the result that the brand becomes even more responsive.

Support Advertising

Support advertising is the use of broadcast media to support other targeted media. The wide coverage of television is particularly valuable in directing customer attention to the other media and increasing their impact.

The classic support campaign is a short burst of television advertising run before, during and after a large direct mail campaign or door drop. Since the objective is to support print advertising, television typically shows the print vehicles on the screen. I helped plan the first use of television support by *Reader's Digest* in the UK. We found that it was important to concentrate the advertising within a short time-scale: no more than five days before and after the direct mail was delivered. We evaluated the balance between frequency and coverage, tested different schedules and weights in different television regions, and found that coverage mattered more than frequency. Television support increased direct mail response rates by 30–40 per cent.

The first support advertising featured the late Robert Dougall, formerly a BBC newscaster. In research, he was perceived as a credible presenter and, more importantly, a credible endorser of *Reader's Digest*. In testing, we attempted to move away from the endorsement formula but failed to find a more responsive approach. One of the *Reader's Digest's* most powerful direct mail copy lines, Three Stages, became the theme for the voice over of the television commercial – an illustration of the value of applying results in one media to others.

Interactive Advertising Media Planning

The objectives of interactive advertising differ from those of image advertising. Evaluation is on the numbers, cost and above all the quality of response. So planning is designed to minimise the customer acquisition cost and maximise the future lifetime value of responders. Response media planning is founded on a totally different premise from that of image advertising. Response advertisers spend their budgets more scientifically and frugally than image advertisers.

For direct response as opposed to image press advertising, smaller space sizes, specific positions and certain media are most effective. Response falls with smaller press size, but not proportionately. In any newspaper or magazine there are hot positions that are most effective for direct response. The best are pages on or opposite facing matter of considerable interest, and positions across which there is a high level of reader traffic. Right-hand pages generate a significantly higher response than left-hand pages. This information can be used in negotiating advertising costs with the publications. Insist on prime positions, and on right-hand pages. If left-hand pages are used, because of their low cost, it is worthwhile to produce a version of the advertising with the coupon in the left-hand corner.

Certain media are inherently more responsive than others. The weekend press, in particular the Sunday supplement magazines, are read during leisure time, and generate higher response, while monthlies generate a longer response 'tail' than weeklies. Each type of medium – national press, weekends, supplements, TV listings, monthlies – has its own response pattern. This can be used to project final results from early response, and therefore plan future advertising.

Direct response advertising involves the increased usage of a range of non-traditional media. Important direct response media are inserts in press, product despatches and door-to-door distribution.

In Alan Ayckbourn's play 'Henceforward', actor Ian McKellen walked onto the stage and, before speaking, raised an audience cheer by opening a magazine, from which a hundred inserts scattered. Around the same time, I placed an insert campaign for a client who, one morning, was not pleased to find Waterloo station strewn with his discarded advertising material. Yet his campaign beat its target – despite the wastage, and despite being seen by only one reader per copy, inserts demand more attention than space advertising and generate between three and ten times more response. This is not well understood and inserts are a neglected media. A particular advantage of inserts is the ability to use small runs in different media to test creative and media.

Bound-in inserts compensate for the disadvantage that only one reader of the publication may see the insert. But the extra cost of production and binding rarely pays for the increase in response. Tip-ons combine higher impact for the

Direct response indices by media format	
Off-the-page	1
Door drop	4
Loose insert	6
Bound-in insert	7
Tip-on card	7
Product despatches	8
Direct mail	30

first reader with the use of space advertising to address all other readers.

Door-to-door material can be delivered through the Royal Mail in the UK – it arrives with the post and usually achieves a higher response. Or with free newspapers, shared with other advertisers, or solus through other distribution companies. A solus drop can be targeted more accurately, by postcode, to selected demographic and lifestyle areas, and to defined retail catchment areas or sales territories.

Inserts in other company product despatches are another neglected medium. Distribution is out of your control, but with the right match of audiences product despatches can produce higher response rates than inserts. Many companies neglect their own product despatches for further advertising messages.

Direct Response Television Planning

Just as direct response press differs from image advertising in objectives, strategy and execution, so does television. Historically, most direct response television advertising is stand-alone and measured on immediate response and sales. The quality of television airtime available is vital, with response rates generally higher as a percentage of the audience at off-peak times. The direct response planner avoids most of the peak airtime for which image advertisers are bidding. Direct response television is particularly appropriate for cable and satellite television channels, where the entry costs are lower, the audiences are more targeted, and the opportunities to test are greater.

Testing can be used to determine the most cost-effective length of commercials and the scheduling of the spots. Some media owners encourage the testing of direct response by offering space or time on a per inquiry or PI basis, where the advertiser pays only a certain amount for each response achieved. As in press, there are hot spots in television schedules. Low involvement, off-peak programming is more cost-effective to buy and generates higher response rates. Response advertising in breaks surrounded by soaps, drama, news, quizzes and sports is likely to be the most expensive and the least responsive. Advertising during the day, and within lower interest programming receives the greatest attention because the audience is less involved in the programming. The first position in an advertising break generates higher responses than at the middle or end of a break.

Managing Customer Response

In my experience advertisers fail to match the promises they make in advertising with the quality by which they manage the customer's response. The effects of lack of attention to the back end are lost sales and customer disenchantment.

A television advertising campaign by Fidelity Investments in the US exploits the disenchantment with the information that financial companies send to their advertising responders. Fidelity has created a service, Fidelity Fundmatch, to match investors' needs to suitable investment vehicles. In the television advertising for Fundmatch, a couple is shown searching through competitive information that is confusing and unhelpful. In contrast, the Fidelity Fundmatch information pack is presented as practical and useful, consistent with Fidelity's brand values of access and responsiveness.

Prompt follow-up to advertising response is essential. I have found that the percentage of responses converted to sales can decline by 50 per cent if response is delayed by several weeks. The familiar but dated message, 'please allow up to 28 days for delivery', is not acceptable.

Customers respond to advertising for information, and the principles of effective response management are:

— to exceed the customer's expectation, by the speed of delivery, the quality of the content, and additional benefits unanticipated by the advertising: surprise and privilege are important

— to involve the customer in the information: using questionnaires and new forms of information delivery, including audiocassettes, video, computer disks and CD-ROMs

— to motivate immediate customer action and feedback, even if only to understand that the customer has no further interest

— to time follow-up in stages, especially where the purchase cycle is long

— to collect further customer data to understand the total potential of the customer.

It has always astonished me how some companies keep trying to sell before they have developed any form of relationship. A financial company created an information package for responders to advertising for a new Investment Bond. The offer was simply to invest in the bond, but I proposed several tests. A special discount, only announced in the information package, cost-effectively increased the conversion rate of enquirers to sales, illustrating the power of an unanticipated offer. The request for feedback, and in particular the request to the customer to advise their lack of interest, also increased sales, because it acted as a prompt for some customers to reconsider. Another test invited responders to indicate their interest in other types of savings and investment vehicles. As a result the sales of the bond went up even more and for each sale there were five enquiries for other products.

This illustrates two vital lessons. Do not let advertising responders go. And do not just sell – build relationships with them.

The Relationship Dimension of Brands

The role of advertising in the future will be to build all the dimensions of the brand: features, benefits, values and relationships. Just as any product must be built to a quality standard and perform reliably, so every brand must provide more information, be accessible to its customers at all times, and responsive to their needs and problems. Brand values are simply an aspect of advertising, and result from a total brand experience. Advertising must communicate and invite customers to experience the brand.

The objectives of advertising are twofold: short-term sales, and long-term brand image and customer relationships. Advertising planning must combine image and response executions in schedules that address both objectives and time-scales. Advertising, direct response and promotion must be integrated to maximise the number of effective contacts between company and customer. Marketing innovations like British Airways' 'World's Biggest Offer' combined elements of all three disciplines and achieved three results: a major advertising impact, far in excess of the media budgets for the campaign; a boost to sales in the immediate aftermath of the Gulf War; and a qualified database of customers and prospects for future relationship-building.

FROM SALES TO RELATIONSHIP-BUILDING PROMOTION 6

'An Extra Dynamic'

The Three Promotional Traps – Relationship-building Promotion: Promotion: Targeting – Relationship-building Adding Value – Relationship-building Promotion: Involvement – Promotions and Data Management – Promotion and Media Planning – Relationship-building Offers – Database-building Events: New Ways of Meeting Customers – The Sales Force, Trade and In-store Promotions – Integrating Promotion

The Three Promotional Traps

Sales promotion is defined by Petersen, in *Sales Promotion in Action*, as an activity consisting of 'a featured offer, of tangible advantages not inherent in a product or service, for the achievement of marketing objectives'.[1]

Expenditure on promotion includes both the direct costs of funding consumer offers and the indirect costs of funding retailer promotions and price discounts. The proportion of marketing budgets devoted to promotion has become an issue of some controversy. Expenditure on promotion is somehow held to be reprehensible, especially by advertising agencies concerned that promotion money would be better invested in building brands – witness the *cri de coeur* from

David Ogilvy, in *Ogilvy on Advertising*: 'In 1981, US manufacturers spent 60 per cent more on promotions than on
advertising, and distributed 1 024 000 000 000 coupons.
Bloody fools.'[2]

Most surveys agree that spend on promotion has increased
at the expense of advertising. In *Brand Marketing*, William
Weilbacher notes: 'By 1993 the proportion of total marketing
expenditures devoted to trade and consumer promotion
probably exceeds 70 per cent and may have reached 75 per
cent. The fraction of this that finds its way into retailer's
hands may account for three fifths of the total.'[3]

Analysis confirms that brand management should be
concerned about their returns from the investments made
in sales promotion. Andrew Ehrenburg in *Repeat Buying*[4]
reports most promotions as failing to achieve a long-term
increase in market share. In a US study, reported by Aaker
in *Managing Brand Equity*,[5] only 16 per cent of promotions
achieved a measurable long-term increase in sales. In *What's
in a Name*, John Philip Jones reports a Nielsen study that
promotions seem to increase the sales of growing brands,
decrease the sales of declining brands, and have no effect
on the sales of stable brands! He concludes: 'Consumer
promotions can be seen then as a sampling device, something extremely important for a new brand, an extra
dynamic to the short and medium term sales trend of an
established brand, speeding the success of growing ones,
but hastening the failure of those going down.'[6]

Companies use promotions because they increase sales
immediately. Often manufacturers have little discretion in
managing their promotional budgets: they are forced to
respond to competitive promotion, and forced to support
multiple retailers to stock and display their brands. As
Weilbacher says, manufacturers fund a high proportion of
retailer promotions as well as their own. Because it is perceived as a cost of doing business, the effectiveness of
promotion is not closely questioned – unlike advertising
and direct marketing. Promotion is much criticised but rarely
analysed.

Most sales promotion is 'general' in the sense that it is
untargeted: the usual media are press, door-to-door, in-

store and on-pack. Historically, promotional response has been the first source of customer data for many consumer brands, and the starting point for tests of customer communication and relationship-building. I have analysed many promotional data sets for leading brands and tested the behaviour of promotional responders. My observation from analysis, research and testing is that there are three traps inherent in most forms of general sales promotion:

(i)   most promotions are redeemed by the wrong customers

(ii) most promotions reduce perceived brand value

(iii) most promotions have no long-term effect on behaviour.

Analysis of sales promotion responders usually reveals a preponderance of existing users and inveterate promotional responders. In both cases, the promotional budget is largely wasted because there is no long-term increase in the brand's volume. Many promotions are redeemed by existing users who would have bought anyway – one study published in *Forbes* magazine in the mid 1980s claimed that the proportion was 92 per cent. Frequent promotional responders trade around all the brands in a category for the best offers, and switch out of brands when promotions close. Promotion, and in particular price promotion, damages perceptions of brand value. Promotion conditions the customer to expect offers and lower prices, and comes to dominate brand values. Customers won on price are soon lost on price.

Promotions involve customers, but only momentarily. After the excitement of the promotion and the experience of the brand customers are left to their own devices. Most continue their previous shopping patterns because the momentary effect of the promotion is not significant enough to change behaviour. There is a threshold above which customer behaviour will change, but most promotions do not rise above that threshold. The threshold must involve a significant positive experience of the brand and enough repeat purchase. It is important to know what experience of a brand will change customer behaviour. From their tracking of smoker behaviour cigarette manufacturers believe that five packs are the absolute minimum required to motivate a new smoker to switch. I believe that to rise above the customer's threshold the brand experience must deliver added values new to the customer. The best way to maximise the impact of promotion and motivate sustained change in customer behaviour is to stay with the customer: to build a relationship with the customer distinctive to the brand.

Whether promotions are good or bad is a sterile debate: promotions are necessary. They are effective because they increase sales measurably. A relationship strategy must address the challenge of designing promotions that build the brand by building the customer relationship in addition to their sales impact. The objective is to achieve a long-term payback starting with a short-term promotional effect. This requires a shift in perspective: promotions should be evaluated not just on increased sales but on the potential lifetime value of the customers who are responsible for the extra sales.

Promotional evaluation:
A pro forma

Current   Incremental sales

Analysis   Breakdown of sales under promotion into:
— sales from new customers, and profile of new customers

— sales from existing customers, and impact on existing customer margins

Research   Projection of:
— future sales from new customers: propensity to stay with the brand

— future behaviour of existing customers: any effect on perceived brand value

Future   New customers × lifetime value   +
Existing customers × future value   + or −

Net lifetime value effect

Relationship-building Promotion: Targeting

Targeting is the key: a promotion must reach only the customers whose behaviour it is designed to change. Markets can be segmented into non-users of any brands, the highly price conscious customer, repertoire users, competitive brand users and existing brand users. The promotion must avoid the customers who might redeem but whose long-term brand usage will not be affected. The promotion must target customers likely to redeem and who have high lifetime value.

If the objective of the promotion is to increase brand penetration, targeting should avoid existing users and the price conscious segment of the market. If the objective of the promotion is to retain existing users and increase their rate of sale, targeting should avoid non-users. Targeting requires investment in customer data. Many companies concerned about making an investment in customer databases should compare the costs with the huge amounts they waste in their promotions (Table 6.1). The cost of mistargeted promotions can be enormous yet rarely visible.

A multiple brand owner can coordinate promotions across all brands in the company's portfolio. Users of competitive

Table 6.1 Evaluating the targeting of offers and cost of wastage: a pro forma

Segment	Quantity	Redemption	Cost	Benefit
Users				
Competitives				
Repertoire				
Price conscious				
Non-users				

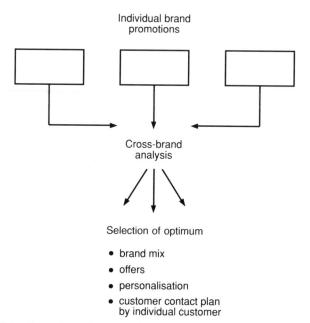

Figure 6.1 From brand promotions to company–customer relationships

brands can be analysed to determine the brand or brands that they are most likely to try to use on the basis of their current brand usage and promotional response history. Different brands can be targeted to each individual customer. Customers who respond to promotions for one brand can be targeted with relationship-building communications for another. The appropriate selection of brand or brands can be made using selective printing and mailing technology that translates customer data into personalised messages and offers (Figure 6.1).

Like many US manufacturers Quaker Oats has found that its traditional promotional vehicle, the newspaper 'free standing insert' (FSI), has declined in effectiveness. FSI redemption rates are falling and competitive promotions by other manufacturers are cancelling each other out. In 1991, Quaker launched a targeted direct mail promotion drive, offering coupons for seventeen of its brands to 18 million households. Quaker invited non-competing manufacturers to place inserts in the package, for a fee. CBS Television was a sponsor, perceiving the opportunity to attract Quaker's different audiences to relevant programming. Each mail package was individually targeted – using data drawn from a syndicated lifestyle database – by food category usage and demographics. The brands promoted and the coupon values in each mail package were selected by household composition (with especial reference to children and pets) and by usage of Quaker brands. The campaign achieved a significant impact. Research after mail delivery reported that 80 per cent of households either had redeemed or were planning to redeem.

But the programme was discontinued. Although the targeting was effective, my observation is that the promotion did not add value to the Quaker brand, nor did it build customer relationships with Quaker. The emphasis in the message was on coupons for individual brands rather than Quaker's company brand values. Most coupons were only for short-term redemption and no relationship was developed with promotional redeemers.

A targeted promotional campaign inevitably involves high redemption costs. Direct mail is so powerful that a high redemption rate on short-term coupons can be guaranteed: in my experience redemptions usually exceed 30 per cent and can be as high as 70 per cent. But short-term redemption has little effect on behaviour. Promotions can only achieve long-term effects when they:

— persuade new customers to try the brand and to stay with it over time

— motivate existing users to increase the share of the brand in their purchase repertoire

— add value to the brand through a continuing relationship.

Relationship-building Promotion: Adding Value

Coupons are popular promotional vehicles because they are a straightforward method of delivering an incentive to a customer, who gains instant gratification by redeeming them at point-of-sale. Couponing is the fastest way to increase sales, and a powerful tactical tool. But couponing is too frequently used where the strategic requirement is to build the brand by adding value and by rewarding the customer in ways other than price.

The usual development of price couponing is a collection scheme. Customers collect vouchers, labels or pack tops and redeem them for premiums, gifts or other forms of rewards. A relevant premium with close associations to the brand is always more effective than a price discount of similar cost to the manufacturer. While discounts reduce perceptions of value, premiums add value. Two factors drive the design of a collection scheme. The first is the customer threshold, described above: the collection levels can be designed to give the customers enough of an experience of the brand to move them over the threshold, to develop their appreciation, and to lock them into the brand. The second is to set an achievable level of collection. The entry level should be easy for a non-user to achieve. If the top level offers very attractive rewards it will 'pull through' regular users. But redeemers at the low level can be 'pulled through' by attractive rewards, and if they redeem early should immediately be offered a follow-up with a higher entry level. After they have 'qualified' themselves as willing to purchase the brand, their experience of the brand can be developed by rewarding a yet higher commitment (Figure 6.2).

Targeting is vital to manage promotional collection schemes cost-effectively. Rewards can be triggered, personalised to the customer as an individual, and selected to match the customer's potential lifetime value. In a points collection scheme, customers with the greatest potential value – users of key competitive brands – receive the highest number of free points. Prospects with the least potential value – buyers of cheap brands and own label – receive the lowest number of free points.

Another approach is to add value through business partners. A campaign in the US by Maxwell House coffee illustrates how promotions that add value can achieve more than short-term sales. This campaign, Sip'N Shop, ran on

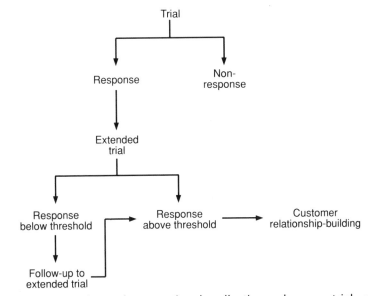

Figure 6.2 Design of promotional collection schemes: trial and extended trial

the Home Shopping Network (HSN) and on Maxwell House packaging, advertising and in-store promotion and offered a $15 voucher for a purchase from HSN. Redeemers and existing HSN subscribers received a $5 continuity club coupon for three proofs-of-purchase for Maxwell House. The campaign also used targeted direct mail to promote the offer to users of competitive brand Folgers. Sip'N Shop generated the largest number of new users ever for a promotion and Maxwell House became the leader in its category: the campaign was targeted, added value through the Home Shopping Network offer, and followed up redeemers to build repeat sales.

This was not the first use by Maxwell House of direct mail to motivate repeat purchase. In my days at Ogilvy & Mather Direct, the New York agency created a three-part mail programme to competitive users to add value to the brand, with the theme 'That's Entertaining'.

In another US extended trial, responders to promotions for the Mighty Dog pet food brand received ten time-sensitive personalised coupons. The coupons were sequentially dated, encouraging the consumer to purchase over time, and covered the full 'Mighty Dog' range, encouraging the consumer to use the brand throughout the pet's feeding regime. In addition to coupons, the consumer could collect proofs of purchase for gifts.

Acknowledging promotional respondents pays because it increases repeat sales. In the UK, Beecham Bovril Brands was conscious that it had delayed despatch of gifts to responders to promotions for its Ribena drink. It mailed an apology, using brand characters the 'Ribena berries' to add personality. Thirty-three per cent redeemed an extended repeat purchase offer, despite the delay in despatch of their gifts.

In my experience, it always pays to follow up promotional responders selectively, capitalising on the customer's appreciation of the brand and the promotional reward. The follow-up can double repeat purchase rates and brand switching.

Relationship-building Promotion: Involvement

The third promotion trap is reliance on hard rewards. Tracking many promotions we find that once the premium is gained or the price returns to normal, sales fall back to their pre-promotion level. But promotions should not have close dates and should not rely on hard rewards. As the customer experiences the brand a relationship can be developed that changes the reward from a hard, short-term incentive to soft long-term benefits linked to continuing purchase.

To recruit new customers and develop customer loyalty, US whiskey brand George Dickel created not a promotion but a society: the Tennessee Water Conservation Society. Customers are invited to become members of the society. The core communication to members is a newsletter, the society's 'Review'. The first issue of the 'Review' invited users of the brand to attend the Grand Opening of the society at the George Dickel distillery's home town. Registrations for membership were invited in-pack through the mail and at the 'Grand Opening'. Responders received a membership wallet card and formal Proclamation of Membership. Further editions of the 'Review' introduced members to the community and the people who lived and worked around the distillery, reinforcing the brand's values by describing the expertise and skill with which the whiskey is produced. Members of the society become brand advocates. They receive a Dickel 'Duel Kit' containing a sample bottle of Dickel and a leading competitor, to try with their friends.

The absence of a close date, and the emphasis on the soft benefits of membership rather than hard rewards, marks this as a relationship-building rather than a sales promotion.

Advocacy is the ultimate test of the strength of a relationship. Also in the drinks sector, Chivas Regal in New Zealand invited existing users to nominate their friends in a programme entitled 'Pay the Ultimate Compliment'. Fifty-seven per cent of users provided the names of friends to whom Chivas mailed a package under the banner 'True Friendship has its Rewards', offering an introductory discount with the compliments of the friend.

Promotions and Data Management

The quickest way to build a database is to use direct response and there are two variants of the direct response promotion: one and two stage. In a one-stage direct response promotion, the consumer redeems by sending proofs of purchase. In a two-stage promotion, the consumer sends for the entitlement to the reward which they redeem on receipt. When the promotion is redeemed through retailers, the customer details are returned to the manufacturer after a time lag.

I define the data required for promotional targeting in three categories: profile, behavioural and directional.

Profile data

Profile data is lifestyle and demographic. Both manufacturers and retailers have been seduced by the opportunities to profile their customers with greater insight, but have found that the differences between the users of different brands are small. The same types of people seem to prefer different brands. The differences between customers are attitudinal and behavioural, and seem unrelated to lifestyles or demographics.

Demographics, however, do influence the potential value of a customer: the younger the customers, the longer the time ahead for consumption, and the larger the household, the higher the spend in many product categories.

Behavioural data

Behavioural data identifies brand choice, the level of usage in the product category, and the customer's response to marketing. A warning: brand usage data from consumer response to promotions is usually biased. More customers claim to use the promoting brand than actually do, as they naturally believe that they will have a higher chance of winning a prize or receiving a better reward if they are seen to be existing customers. Since repertoire behaviour is the norm in many markets, a request for 'up to three brands in order of frequency used' solicits more useful data.

Brand usage data can be collected from promotional redemption, including coupons. When coupons are re-deemed through retailers, ask for customer information, and about a third of consumers will reply. The proportion can be increased by offering an additional reward to con-sumers who identify themselves on the coupon.

Directional data

The most important data to learn about customers from promotions is directional: their interest in offers, added values and continuing relationships. Data protection re-quires that customers are allowed to 'opt out'. *In planning and managing promotions manufacturers should also invite customers to 'opt in':* to indicate their interest in the alterna-

tive forms of promotion and relationship-building programme. This enables the manufacturer to identify the
segment of the market who will respond to added values
and to relationships, and the segment that should only
receive tactical offers and price promotions.

Competitions and prize draws are a regular feature of
sales promotion. Their role is often misunderstood: it is to
overcome consumer inertia, and to prospect. To create
interest and capture the consumer's attention, competitions
and draws dominate the promotion, and where they work
they add significantly to response and to sales. They generate responses from non-purchasers, prospects who may
have potential value. *Reader's Digest*, for example, treats a
prize draw 'no' as a good prospect, as the customer
has responded and created an opportunity to build a
relationship.

In increasing sales, competitions and prize draws are
most appropriate for intrinsically low involvement brands,
as is illustrated by their importance to *Reader's Digest*. For
higher involvement brands, the competitions and promotions need not, and in most cases should not, dominate
communication. They are ineffective in increasing sales and
they may distract attention from brand values. Their role
should be firmly assigned to the collection of data, and to
the low key reward to prospective customers for their time
and information.

In using competitions and draws to prospect, a balance
must be found between quality and quantity of response
(Table 6.2). This balance is affected by the prominence of
the incentive in communication, the perceived value of the
prizes and the relevance of the theme and the prizes to the
brand. Incentives too high in value and too prominent in
promotion will generate response from low value customers
and degrade the quality of the data collected.

Promotions and Media Planning

In planning media for promotions, the traditional approach
has been to maximise volume and coverage, and so less

Table 6.2 Testing the balance between quantity and quality: a pro forma

Response	Cost per response	Predicted lifetime value	Quality index
No incentive			
Premium incentive			
Prize draw incentive			

Promotional effectiveness should be based on:

$$\text{Quality index} = \frac{\text{Predicted LTV} - \text{Cost per response}}{\text{Cost per response}}$$

Table 6.3 Evaluation of new customer engagement: a pro forma

	Press	Inserts	Mail
Cost			
Volume			
% redemption			
Redeemers			
% new trialists			
Cost per new trial			

targeted media are favoured: in particular off-the-page coupons in press and door drops. More targeted media can be more cost-effective, even if a lower volume of coupons is distributed with a higher cost per contact.

Promotions that engage new users are an investment. Whether they pay back depends on potential lifetime value of the new customers acquired, and on the effectiveness with which the customer relationship is developed. The failure rate of new brands is high, and occurs not because new brands fail to win penetration but because repeat purchase rates are low. There is investment in the media but no investment in the relationship. Even if a brand secures a share of the market at launch, this is often the high water mark and thereafter it declines to a steady state. A launch really is a once-in-a-lifetime opportunity to establish the place of a brand in its market – and to win most of its customers.

SmithKline Beecham in the UK launched a new hot malted chocolate drink, Chox, to appeal to families with young children. A targeted door drop offered a free sachet (trial), a coupon (repeat purchase) and a consumer questionnaire (feedback). Analysis of the questionnaire confirmed high rate of use of the sample, appreciation of the product and intention to use the coupon. But coupon response was low because no budget was available for follow-up to positive questionnaire responders. The bulk of the marketing effort went into trial and not into repeat purchase.

Repeat purchase rates are critical to the economics of promotion (Table 6.4), as the earlier example illustrates.

Evaluation of long-term payback illustrates the fallacy of the cost per trial mentality. The most profitable plan has the highest cost per consumer contact and cost per trial. Promotions are a special case of customer acquisition, and lifetime value is the basis for calculating the affordable investment in promotions and the detailed promotional design, includ-

Table 6.4 Evaluation of new customer development: a pro forma

	Press	Inserts	Mail
Cost per trial			
Volume			
% conversion			
Regular users			
£ of regular users			
(2 year LTV)			
Total 2 year LTV			
Total cost			
Net gain			

ing the upper limit on the value of a premium or gifts in a collection scheme.

Lifetime value is the motivation for database-building initiatives by brands once regarded as mass market. For several years Pepsi-Cola in the US has run summer promotions, targeting diet cola drinkers. Redeemers receive a plastic card, entitling them to discounts from third party products and services. One summer, the theme was 'Gotta Have It!', which was endorsed by Cindy Crawford and offered discounts on a range of products and services. Another year, in 'Licensed to Chill', consumers rang an interactive telephone response service that captured their brand usage and profile, as well as their name and address. The motivation for these promotions is the lifetime value of the regular diet cola drinker – less than 10 per cent are responsible for over 75 per cent of consumption. The objective of the promotion is twofold: to motivate the target audience to try the brand, and to identify them on a database.

Relationship-building Offers

Promotions are generally discussed in the context of frequently purchased brands, but offers are equally important in the marketing of high price, infrequently purchased brands. The three principles of relationship-building promotion are relevant to offers.

(i) Targeting: making the most appealing offer to prospects most likely to buy

(ii) Added value: making offers which enhance experience of the brand, and making offers unanticipated by the customer

(iii) Relationship: following up initial offers with rewards for repeat purchase.

Free trial is the most appealing offer, and the higher the price the greater the power to motivate trial: car manufacturers offer test drives, as have computer manufacturers like Apple. Direct marketers have learned the power of approval offers, which increase response rates by a factor of six against cash with order. The customer is billed on receipt of product and is free to return it without commitment. Continuity marketers use free trial and free approval: a first book free offer for the *Reader's Digest* condensed book product line achieves response rates in the 30–40 per cent range, whereas when the first book is full price, although offered on approval, response is in the 8–12 per cent range.

The returns or rejectors of products offered on approval can be as high as 20–30 per cent. *Reader's Digest* can afford the high rejection rate because it is more than compensated for by the increase in response, and because the approval offer is targeted. The majority of customers are honest, and credit control can identify and screen most frequent rejectors or previous bad debtors. So targeting is again the key. The offer should be selected for the customer segment. Free trial is only cost effective if it is targeted. And a free trial offer should be followed by a continuing purchase offer.

A direct mail offer of a free sample for a malt whisky brand, for example, achieved a response rate of over 70 per cent. With their sample, customers received a voucher against purchase of the brand. The investment in the trial was worthwhile because the offer was made only to regular purchasers of other malt whisky brands. The investment in the trial pays back through the immediate offer of repeat purchase.

Making an unanticipated offer at the time of trial or demonstration is powerful. With trial of a computer or office system, for example, a software offer can be added. After a test drive of a car, an unanticipated special offer can be made at the discretion of the sales person.

Offers that add value to infrequently purchased brands work by enhancing the experience of the product in use, or by reducing the long-term cost to the customer. Opportunities are:

— add-on offers, like software with computer hardware

— support offers, like warranties on car purchase or maintenance contracts on equipment

— finance offers, like special loans, credit terms or even credit cards linked to the purchase, as pioneered by GM in the car market

— exclusive offers, through a membership relationship or club, and regular communication programmes

Database-building Events: New Ways of Meeting Customers

Sampling is one of the most powerful promotional techniques to gain trial and increase the penetration of a brand. Sampling can be combined with data collection to create a personalised follow-up to a product trial or demonstration, using the positive image and experience created by sampling to motivate repeat purchase. Data can be collected from customers 'in the field', at a variety of locations, whether or not the contact is used to sample the brand. There are the options of contacting the customer with the brand up-front, or of using a low level of branding to maximise contact with competitive brand customers. Field data collection can be effective where there is an opportunity to characterise the customer by sight, and in some cases to identify brand usage. Cigarette manufacturers request to see the current pack smoked. In pubs, representatives of drink manufacturers check the brand being consumed. This requires management and training of field staff to exercise consistency and quality control over data collection.

One approach to sampling, prospecting and database-building is to create an event. The most famous example of a database-building event is 'The World's Biggest Offer' by British Airways. With international travel in the doldrums after the Gulf War, British Airways created 'The World's Biggest Offer' to revitalise the market – and to build database. The campaign was launched by direct response advertising. Worldwide response was 5 million in ten days. BA learned the characteristics of entrants and their travel aspirations and gained a database for ongoing marketing.

Sometimes it is necessary to prospect to identify your own existing customers. The mobile telephone market is one in which the customer relationship has traditionally been held by a service provider. In the US, mobile telephone manufacturer Cellular One created a traffic-building event for their dealers to identify users, by offering a free 'tune-up'. The offer recognised concerns with phone quality, and it was important that users did not associate network problems with their telephone brand. The event identified users, and captured data, enabling the manufacturer to develop a relationship and to motivate upgrades. The event won the goodwill of dealers by generating traffic and revenues through their outlets.

In 1992, Apple Computer in the UK ran a similar event to target users of competitive brand PCs, and to motivate them to visit Apple dealers. Media inserts invited users of low performance machines to 'Recycle your PC' at an Apple Centre. Dealer merchandising and display material, including a 'recycling bin', was linked to the advertising. The Apple customer base was involved – Macintosh users were invited to place stickers on other PCs in their companies, saying 'I'd rather be a Macintosh'.

The Sales Force, Trade and In-store Promotions

Promotions can be used to motivate prospecting by sales forces and trade. There may be significant cultural barriers to overcome as ownership of names is jealously guarded. The generation of names needs to be incorporated within the remit and remuneration of the sales force, and incorporated within the relationship between the company and its channels.

An approach is to invite sales force, dealer and independent retailers to nominate their customers for inclusion within relationship marketing. They can retain control of the programme, and select the promotion and offers they wish to see made to their customers.

Promotions are more effective when they include rewards for sales and dealer personnel. Their cooperation is essential to maximise the effectiveness of in-store promotions in particular: front-line staff can draw customer attention to promotions and encourage their participation.

This is important in marketing to the independent trade, a sector neglected by many companies. Investment in relationships with the top performing and the most motivated outlets can be valuable, but it is as important to segment the trade as it is any customer base. My experience is that the potential of small business trade partners is related to attitude as well as to size of outlet. Many are informed businessmen who will respond to a promotional proposal, but there are cynical and apathetic members of every sector, and there are manipulators who will accept promotional support but do little to work with the brand owner to maximise joint sales.

As with the consumer market, trade marketing is most effective when 'customer-directed'. By inviting their participation the forward-thinking members of the sector can be identified and enrolled into cooperative programmes. The most effective support a manufacturer can offer lies in advice on merchandising to increase category sales, and special offers and added values for the retailer's customers.

As with any form of promotion, in-store runs the danger of attracting existing buyers. To address the need to target, new smarter in-store promotional systems are emerging. Catalina, for example, is a selective coupon distribution system at supermarket checkouts. The system reads transaction data, and selects coupons depending upon the contents of the individual consumer's shopping basket. Manufacturers can use the system to reward their existing users and to target competitive users. The retailer can use the system to promote own label lines. The coupons are issued for redemption on the next visit.

Other systems offer even more selective in-store support. In the US, the Vision Value Network system uses sophisticated hardware programmed by satellite for individual stores. Customers are issued with membership cards that record their shopping patterns not just on each visit but over time. When the customer swipes the card at the checkout, a selected promotional message is played on video, enabling the manufacturer to replay television advertising. The system enhances promotion as well as advertising, dispensing selective coupons. The Vision Value system can even print the equivalent of a mailing package with offers that the customer redeems by mailing directly back to the manufacturer. The customer receives electronic mail at point of sale.

Integrating Promotion

The conflict among advertising, direct marketing and promotion is unproductive, and a relationship strategy integrates the three different disciplines around the common objective of building brands by building customer value. Promotions in external media and in-store are the 'front end' of the customer relationship.

By developing direct relationships with their customers, companies will be able to redress the unequal balance of power between brands and retailers. The strategic opportunity is to regain control of customer relationships, and one consequence will be to reduce the reliance on short-term promotion in general, and on discounts to the trade in particular.

The effect on promotion will be to complement creativity with a greater degree of rigour in design and measurement. The evaluation of promotional investments can be put on a scientific basis.

FROM BRAND LOYALTY TO CUSTOMER LOYALTY 7

'Worth an investment'

The Principles of Customer Loyalty – Loyalty and Customer Targeting – Loyalty and Customer Relationships – Loyalty and Customer Management – Loyalty and Membership – Loyalty and Unanticipated Value – Loyalty and Low Involvement – Loyalty and Association – The Dimensions of Loyalty – Total Loyalty System

The Principles of Customer Loyalty

Customer loyalty is a concept central to many marketing plans, but defined by few. Many companies have embarked on 'customer loyalty' programmes without the understanding that loyalty is an *objective* rather than an activity – that loyalty results from investment in a total business system rather than just marketing communications. I define loyalty as the propensity of customers and staff to behave so as to maximise customer lifetime value.

Loyalty is the result of building the brand by building customer relationships.

Management consultants and marketing gurus have recently discovered the universal truth, known to direct

146

marketers for decades, that profitability is a function of how long customers stay and how much they spend. They report another finding well known to direct marketers: that it costs more to sell to a new as opposed to an existing customer. Their analysis of the recent performance of brands and marketing leads them to conclude a decline in brand loyalty.

My analysis is that there has not been a change in the character of brands but a shift in the forces that drive customer decision-making. My research into customer behaviour confirms that the values of leading brands are as much appreciated as ever, but are no longer compelling. Two factors, both a consequence of competition, have intruded on the cosy world of automatic brand choice:

(i) Competition has intensified and created greater choice, so customers demand more and better information to guide their decisions

(ii) Competition has educated customers to expect greater value, customer expectations have risen, and customers are both more demanding and less tolerant.

Customers are not inherently less loyal: they will remain with a brand, but the brand must work harder to earn and retain their loyalty.

Taking my definition one stage further, loyalty means the propensity of customers to behave *in the face of competition and choice* so as to maximise lifetime value. A loyal customer has a high propensity to choose the brand, *irrespective of competition*, because of the unique values associated with the brand and the customer's continuing relationship with the company that produces the brand.

I define six principles of loyalty:

(i) Loyalty is about customers, not brands: some customers may become loyal, but many can be so constrained by price or regulation that they will never exhibit loyalty; similarly, some customers can be loyal to companies in some product categories but not in others.

(ii)   Loyalty cannot be the result purely of lower prices, as customers conditioned to buy on price will switch to a new lower-priced competitor without compunction; but privileged prices for best customers only can be an important aspect of a relationship programme that develops loyalty.

(iii) Loyalty requires the positive involvement of the customer and not simply regular purchase: customer loyalty is more than customer satisfaction, although satisfaction can be a necessary condition for future loyalty.

(iv)   Loyalty develops over time and is a two-way exchange between company and customer – before customers become loyal to a company, the company must be loyal to its customers, recognising and rewarding their custom.

(v)   Loyalty is the total experience of the brand and is not just an objective of advertising or even of communication to customers; every aspect of a company's business is an aspect of loyalty.

(vi)   Loyalty is a result of the total relationship between company and customer, and the loyalty of the company staff is the major factor in developing the loyalty of its customers.

Loyalty and Customer Targeting

Loyalty is not to be confused with retention or cross-selling. Loyal customers stay longer and buy more. Retention, regular purchase and cross-selling, however, are the results of loyalty, not the cause.

When a brand is in decline, it can lose its best and oldest customers as quickly as its occasionals, and the loss is all the more devastating. When a brand is growing, the greatest contribution to increased sales can often come from existing rather than new customers, and as we have seen this is the most cost-effective way to build market share.

Loyalty is not as likely in some markets as in others: different degrees of loyalty exist in different product categories. The potential for loyalty depends upon the degree of customer *involvement* in the purchase decision. High involvement means high risk, that a wrong decision by the customer may result in dissatisfaction or loss. In high involvement markets, the risk may be significant and the decision-making complex: purchase may require a protracted search among alternatives. High price markets are naturally high involvement: examples are cars and other capital goods. Much business-to-business decision-making is high involvement: a multiple decision-making unit confers to define the needs, conduct the search among alternatives, evaluate the options, and make a mutually acceptable choice.

But many low price markets are high involvement. Examples are drinks, cigarettes, beauty products and pet foods. Purchase involves self-image, and a degree of risk if the product is not acceptable. High involvement purchases represent a significant degree of perceptual risk – to the consumer's self-interest, self-image or peer group status – as well as financial risk.

Examples of low involvement sectors are: white and brown goods, cleaning products like detergents, and general insurance. Many customers have a repertoire of brands. Repeat purchase is a function of habit rather than positive choice. Loyalty scarcely exists because involvement is low: the brand choice is simply not important.

Loyalty is also a characteristic of some customers and not others. In every category there will be customers to whom brand choice and the use of the product is more important than others. But if loyalty can realistically be an objective only for a segment of the market, this will be the segment responsible for most of the profitability in the market.

In Chapter 3, I predicted that companies will increasingly focus on a smaller number of customers, and in Chapter 4, I presented the importance of developing active relationships with high lifetime value customers. A relationship strategy should realistically aim only to develop the loyalty of a small segment of most valuable customers. A loyalty scheme for all customers is a contradiction in terms, and a failing of many 'customer loyalty' schemes is that they do not tightly define their customer segment.

The more involved the customer in the purchase decision, the more likely the customer to become loyal to a brand. In collecting data and learning about customers, the priority must be to understand which customers are already loyal and which might be prepared to give their loyalty to the brand. This is why the most important question to ask customers and the most important data to collect is:

— usage of and interest in the product category

— interest in involvement with the brand and participation in its activities.

Loyalty is an opportunity for only certain customers: not for the price conscious, not for frequent promotional responders, and not for infrequent buyers. Loyalty only matters to the heavy users of a product or service. Loyalty implies choice, and loyalty is the antithesis of behaviour where choice is made mainly on price.

Loyalty demands targeting. The strategic question is: on which segment will a company focus its efforts? The answer is to examine a company's strengths, and to design products, services and marketing that fit the company's strengths and match the needs of well-defined customer segments.

Loyalty can be based on lifestyle. In the US, the Cadillac company identified golf as the principal leisure interest of its customers. So General Motors made its credit card the official card of the USPGA golf tour, and Cadillac sponsors famous golfers Arnold Palmer and Lee Trevino on the Cadillac Senior PGA Tour Series. Cadillac targets advertising in golfing publications and sponsorship at golfing events, and has even endorsed a special golf cart bearing the name of one of its models. Cadillac's objective is to build loyalty among a customer segment defined by a lifestyle characteristic. If pursued, the strategy becomes self-reinforcing – Cadillac will sell more cars to golfers and reinforce the loyalty of its existing golfing drivers.

Loyalty can be based on demographics. All banks try to win customers when young, but the Clydesdale bank in

Scotland has differentiated its services with targeted marketing to families, based on a cartoon character 'Clyde'. The programme appeals to parents by helping to educate children in the handling of money and bank accounts.

Different credit card services are designed and priced to appeal to different sectors. There are cards with low interest rates, cards with fees but many benefits, cards with no fee but few frills, cards with charity links, cards related to car purchase, cards for frequent travellers, and cards linked to retail purchase. Similarly, different insurance companies are learning to target different customer segments, matching their different degrees of risk with differential pricing and service.

Loyalty is fostered by adding value closely related to the interests of the selected customer segment. Analysis of customer data can derive new product concepts with which customers have a close affinity. American Express, for example, analyses its membership data to identify new segments and new opportunities. *Direct Marketing* magazine described one initiative, 'The Style Report', as 'a women's magazine/catalog geared towards fashion-conscious female cardholders'. The report says that 'selective binding and ink-jet printing technology . . . will be able to target specific niches and send different copies to prospects and customers'.[1]

A company must select the customer segments that represent its future, and concentrate its energies on the customers in these segments with the potential for loyalty. The decision drives the re-engineering of manufacturing, operations and service around the needs of these customers.

Loyalty and Customer Relationships

Relationships are vital to loyalty because they enable the company to identify and *anticipate* customer needs before competition. A marketing priority is to build relationships with long-standing customers and regular buyers, not because they are necessarily loyal but because the cost of losing them to competition could be devastating. The longer the length of the relationship – all other things equal – the higher the repurchase rate. Loyalty can be fostered by recognising and rewarding long-standing customers: 'anniversary' rewards and 'long service' bonuses are opportunities that most companies neglect. A high retention rate is a requirement for profitability, but past retention rates are no guarantee of future loyalty.

Regular purchase of a brand is insufficient to ensure future loyalty. No matter how high the current earnings of a brand, a low level of loyalty from customers makes future earnings vulnerable, and the future of the business may be at risk to new competition and shifts in customer decision-making. This is precisely the threat faced by many long-established and apparently secure brands: past performance has become increasingly irrelevant as an indicator for future results. Past customer decision-making was often based on habit rather than positive choice. Around the world many near-monopolies and newly privatised industries face competition for the first time: any measure of past 'loyalty' has simply reflected an absence of choice.

Purchase of a range of products under the same brand, or a range of brands from a company's brand portfolio, is also an indicator of loyalty. Banks know that their retention rates on current accounts increase in direct relationship to the number of other accounts that customers open. Yet inertia is the major factor keeping customers with their banks, and multiple product holdings may only increase inertia: they do not mean that customers will want to buy even more products.

Loyalty may be more closely related to the recency than to the frequency of purchase. In direct marketing, the three most important variables in predicting repeat purchase are 'RFM': recency, frequency and money, in that order. Satisfaction with a recent purchase is an indicator of loyalty, but the experience is that satisfaction is only a necessary but not a sufficient condition for loyalty. US car manufacturers have focused on customer satisfaction since the early 1980s. The JD Power customer satisfaction indices are influential, were dominated throughout the decade by Japanese brands and predicted the rising Japanese market share. All US car manufacturers have now focused on customer satisfaction with product and sale. The result? The industry has raised satisfaction rates above 80 per cent – only to see average retention rates stuck around 40 per cent. The above average performers include brands already discussed here, in parti-cular Lexus and Saturn, with a strategy to develop customer relationships and not just satisfaction.

The evidence in most industries is that satisfaction pre-dicts future purchase only at the very top of the scale – only the 'very, very' satisfied have a high propensity to repeat buy. Satisfaction is backward looking, and measures the customer's evaluation of product performance and the company's management of the transaction. Loyalty is forward-looking and predicts the customer's response to a future marketing proposition.

Satisfaction surveys are now routine and are designed to measure performance, and to identify and solve problems. But if only the 'very, very' satisfied have a high propensity to repeat buy, the majority of responders to satisfaction surveys represent problems! I believe that satisfaction surveys should be complemented and enhanced by a regular customer census: a data collection exercise for all major purchases and transactions with customers:

— an invitation to the customer to describe their product usage, purchase plans, and individual preferences in the category: i.e. their current loyalty level

— an invitation to the customer to participate in a con-tinuing relationship programme.

Usually a minority of customers return customer satis-faction questionnaires. All customers should be contacted, by telephone or in person if necessary. A customer satisfac-tion survey is not another research study but the starting point in the development of a customer relationship. It pays to identify and 'loyalise' the lukewarm as well as the dis-satisfied: to fight for and earn the loyalty of as many custo-mers as possible.

Loyalty and Customer Management

Every contact between company and customer is an experience, and the effect of every positive experience is to increase loyalty. In marketing, advertising and customer service are usually considered as separate activities. They are in reality all aspects of building the brand by building customer relationships.

For a single, infrequently purchased product like a car, the usual measure of loyalty is the probability that the customer purchases your brand next time. But even in the car market the concept of loyalty is not as simple as it seems. Loyalty also encompasses the propensity of the customer to purchase an extended warranty, service the car at the recommended dealer, and buy the parts made by the manufacturer. When loyal customers use recommended dealers to service their cars, the performance of the dealer affects the customer's ownership of the product and experience of the brand.

Every customer contact and transaction influences loyalty. Advertising is only one of the many forces that influence loyalty, and indeed advertising may well be one of the weakest.

Car companies advertise heavily because they want the customer to choose the marque before entering the dealer showroom. Advertising invites customer enquiry but mostly as an afterthought. Car companies competently despatch information to enquirers but there is little about the process that reflects the brand's personality or adds value for the customer. The car companies do not match their investment in advertising with investment in the prospective customers who respond directly or who walk into dealer showrooms. They mistrust the ability of an independent dealer sales person to 'close the sale', so they are happy to put an offer into the hands of any prospects, again before they visit the showroom.

Because every customer contact is a part of the total brand experience, it pays to invest in the management of contact, to reflect the brand personality in customer contact, and to motivate company and channel staff to volunteer value that is unanticipated by the customer. Car companies can transform their competitiveness by matching their advertising with investment in customer contact and staff motivation.

Because each customer contact is an opportunity to increase loyalty, it pays to increase the frequency of contact. Previous transactions and customer contacts can effect loyalty by influencing the customer's perception of value. Car companies can further transform their effectiveness by more frequent contact with all customers.

The effects of past actions and contact decay fast, which is why recency is such an important marketing factor. Every company recognises that it must continually innovate its products and refresh its values to retain its customers. Otherwise customer relationships, like brands, wither and die. Every contact with the customer is an opportunity to revitalise and reinforce the brand proposition – and to sell more to the customer. Every contact is equally an opportunity to identify problems and prevent the loss of a vulnerable customer. Direct marketers in particular have learned the value of customer contact. No enquiry is answered, no order taken, no product despatched and no bill mailed without another offer, and without an invitation of customer feedback.

Customers welcome contact from companies with whom they do business. Research by the Direct Mail Information Service[2] demonstrates that 85 per cent of consumers agree that companies should mail their customers with relevant information. The same research shows that, despite general antipathy to unsolicited direct mail, over half of all consumers agree that companies should mail prospects with information they believe is relevant.

Increasing the frequency of customer contact increases retention rates and sales. In the US, the Customer Development Corporation (CDC) reports: 'Without a single mail contact, ABC Insurance had only a 43 per cent chance of holding onto a customer who had been with the company for a year or less. Retention jumped to 82 per cent among the same new customer group with four or more contacts during the year.'[3] CDC also reports that the type of communication matters less than the frequency. I have found that it is better to mail frequent 'hi-touch' cards and acknowledgements than to send customers a smaller number of more lavish mail packages.

Despite these findings, most companies simply do not keep in touch with their customers frequently enough. Some are inhibited by the fear that they will 'upset' their customers. Others are prevented by their failure to organise and manage the process. Yet I have never encountered a situation where customers would not welcome and respond positively to stimulating and relevant contact.

Loyalty and Membership

Loyalty requires a positive decision, a commitment by the customer to an active relationship. The decision to 'join' or become a member is the most obvious evidence of loyalty. But since the membership term is limited, and loyalty is open-ended, membership should be perceived not as an end in itself but as a stage in the process of building the customer's loyalty.

Car manufacturers have traditionally marketed extended warranties, but it is only with the advent of personal financing schemes and credit cards that they have begun to realise the marketing benefits of 'membership'. Financing helps win additional sales, and credit cards accrue points towards discounts on car purchase and so 'lock in' a proportion of customers before their next car purchase. But the strategic marketing role is to create a relationship, enabling the manufacturer to increase the frequency of contact, add value and 'loyalise' the customer.

Credit cards increase retention rates not just because customers accrue points towards rebates, but – more importantly – because the manufacturers use the card to develop customer relationship. Monthly statements and solus mail target messages to cardholders, and the database of cardholders and their transactions can be used to run local marketing efforts in cooperation with dealers and offer added values through business partners. These are all techniques pioneered by American Express which uses the contact opportunities with the customer to add value as I describe in Chapter 2. Personal financing and associated insurance, warranty and recovery benefits add value to the car purchase transaction for the customer, and make it a more profitable one for the company and its dealers. It also keeps the manufacturer in contact with the customer and by rolling over finance it increases the retention rate.

In any market the shift from a momentary to a continuing relationship offers new opportunities. In the UK most charities face a retention problem: a high proportion of donors give once only in response to an emergency or urgent appeal. The motive for support is immediacy and the relationship with the charity is once-off. Yet charities need a regular income to fund their work and a large supporter base as a channel through which to communicate their mission to society at large. To develop relationships that last many charities have developed 'continuity' products, where the supporter makes a regular contribution in return for feedback and involvement in a specific aspect of the charity's work. Examples are Action Aid's child sponsorship and Oxfam's 'Project Partners'. The donors who participate in these programmes are retained longer and a proportion continue to give in response to specific appeals.

Books are a market in which frequent buyers represent a high proportion of the value. The US retail chain Waldenbooks has redefined its relationship with its customers by creating a Preferred Reader programme. For an initial fee, members receive a regular newsletter and discounts on all purchases. Waldenbooks contracts with members to supply helpful information and books at privileged prices, and receives a fee in return. Members purchase more frequently than before, and by tracking their behaviour Waldenbooks has the opportunity to influence customer behaviour directly, and in particular to activate infrequent users.

Also in the US, Carnation Pet Foods has tested a direct delivery service 'fresh to your door', with their dog food brand, Perform. In test marketing the service achieved a 2.24 per cent response rate from media inserts and a 3.37 per cent response from direct mail. The costs per member were \$29.41 for inserts and \$31.25 for direct mail – well below the allowable maximum investment for a dog owning household. Carnation has combined both the membership and direct models in relationship management for a frequently purchased retail brand. Carnation has added to its brand values a new service. The payback results from new customers whose desire for the enhanced service influences brand choice, who will pay more for the service, and who become dependent on the manufacturer for supply.

Each of these case histories illustrates the shift from individual transactions to a continuing relationship – from product sales to a contract based on service. *The shift must be accompanied by added value.* The wider advantages to the company are significant: the ability to track customer behaviour means that customer relationships can be managed, and increased contact with customers means more opportunities to cross-sell. The result is to lock in the customer, increase the stream of earnings, and add the fourth relationship dimension to brand value.

Loyalty and Unanticipated Value

As the Institute of Direct Marketing observes, the two most important words in marketing are not 'new' and 'free', but 'thank you'. Marketing is an exchange of value and customers appreciate recognition. But they appreciate even more when recognition is accompanied by extra value, above all when it is not conditional on extra spend. The element of surprise is powerful: in the exchange of value between company and customer, it can pay the company to invest in rewards *unanticipated* by the customer, without guarantee of return.

United Airlines uses customer censuses to understand the interests of its members. These surveys achieve up to 50 per cent response and enable United to target precisely its extra value offers. United analyses flight patterns on its database and selects customers for special offers on selected routes that they use frequently. Hal Brierley of United's agency Brierley & Partners reports a European cruise offer to 8000 frequent flyers, selected on the basis of their interests from the 500 000 cruisers on United's 20 million database. The offer generated revenue of $250 000 for a spend of only $5000.[4]

A common failing of 'customer loyalty' programmes is that all the benefits are anticipated by customers. The result is boredom. If rewards simply match expectations, customers do not perceive added value. The company is doing nothing to earn their loyalty.

When rewards are unanticipated, they are all the more appreciated and motivating. There is a common misunderstanding that *Reader's Digest* is a 'club', which it is not. Yet the company achieves astonishingly high rates of repeat purchase and cross-selling. It markets a continuing stream of new products to its customer base, continually innovating creatively. Best customers receive new offers and new promotions every three weeks, each unanticipated and each offering more value.

From any company, the best customers should expect innovation in its marketing as well as in its products: better prices, better rewards and better service.

Loyalty and Low Involvement

Loyalty in low involvement markets is a contradiction. Loyalty can only be enhanced by developing the customer's involvement in the category and in the brand. General insurance is a typical low involvement category, and US insurance company USAA illustrates how to win customer involvement by offering more value. USAA focuses on military personnel, and builds customer involvement in its products by a non-profit USAA Foundation to promote understanding of personal financial management, a *USAA Guide to Services* to inform customers about the use of insurance, and a membership card with telephone numbers for USAA's advisory and information services.[5]

Customers have always had relationships with food brands, but most relationships were passive and so most brands were low involvement. A typical case is the children's soft drink brand Kool-Aid, which had suffered years of declining market share. Brand owner Kraft General Foods (KGF) launched the Wacky Warehouse programme to support Kool-Aid and rebuild children's involvement with the brand by linking it to television and toys. The programme is targeted to blue collar households with pre-teenage children: a high lifetime value segment. Members of the programme collect points from every Kool-Aid soft drinks package: the 'hard' rewards from the relationship. But points are collected for merchandise and redeemed at toy shops: 'soft' rewards and emotional involvement for the children. Enrolment in membership enables KGF to capture name, address and birthday: using the relationship to learn about customers. Using the database, mailings are sent separately to mothers and their children, including birthday mailings: triggering customer contact. The programme is supported with advertising, with television used to promote the fun and games in the programme: adding more value to membership.

The Wacky Warehouse is a long running programme that has changed the customer–brand relationship from low to high involvement, and is credited with increasing Kool-Aid's market share by twenty points.[6]

Loyalty and Association

In *A Recovery Strategy for Europe*, Yao-Su Hu writes: 'with Anglo-Saxon firms, shareholders come first, with customers and employees a distant second and third. With Japanese companies, employees come first, customers second and shareholders third . . .'.[7]

I argue that there is a class of customer who should be treated equally with shareholders and employees, and in Chapter 4 call this loyal customer an 'associate'. Associates have two defining characteristics: high lifetime value, and a desire to be involved in the brand and the company's activities. They want to 'belong' to the company – if only they were asked.

The new General Motors Saturn car division illustrates

both principle and value of association. To celebrate its fifth anniversary in June 1994 the company invited its 650 000 customers to a 'homecoming', a special celebration at its factory in Spring Hill, Tennessee. Saturn helped them make the journey from all over the US, offering assistance on hotel bookings and services along the way through its dealer netork. A total of 44 000 Saturn owners attended.

While its competitors continue to advertise their indistinguishable new model features, Saturn can advertise the appreciation shown by its customers. A three page advertisment in *USA Today*[8] illustrates Saturn customer loyalty: 'One of the many walls around our plant where Saturn owners gave us the most important award of all: their thanks.' The advertisement says that 10 743 owners contributed to these walls, and shows a sample of their testiomonials. The advertisement says nothing at all about the product! Saturn is a company not a product brand: its dealers are branded as Saturn and not by their local name, and the advertising strapline puts company before product: 'A Different Kind of Company. A Different Kind of Car.'

A characteristic of associates is that they seek out other customers with whom they share an interest in the brand. The Harley Davison owners club in the US has a membership of over 200 000 and is a major factor in Harley's dominance at the top end of the motorcycle market.

My experience is that most companies are surprisingly 'shy' of involving their customers. Yet there are numerous opportunities to develop a relationship with valuable customers as associates. Invite customers to participate in regular panels to assess new product development ideas – the secret of Reader's Digest NPD success. Ask them to seek out and reward excellent customer service – as Neiman Marcus does by providing customers with special awards to hand out to staff. Involve them in business policy – as American Airlines did by inviting members to write to Congress.

Customers are often described as 'stakeholders', to put them on a level with shareholders. Shareholders have a financial 'stake' in a company and are another segment in which loyalty can be developed. When I worked on the

Forte Gold Card, one of our simplest and most effective initiatives was to market the product to the company's shareholders. Shareholders can be invited to become a company's representatives or ambassadors. Oil company TOTAL has invited its shareholders to become 'eyewitnesses'. In advertising in the *Financial Times*, TOTAL invited shareholders to volunteer 'to travel on fact-finding missions, and be the eyes and the ears of all those interested in TOTAL'.[9]

Both shareholders and customers can be a company's 'eyes and ears'. Many will be willing to assist in keeping the company informed about outlets where the product is out of stock or the merchandising is poor. Invite them to special events, where they will meet other customers and recommend the company and the brand to prospects – as car company Lexus does in the US. Even ask for their direct help in sales and marketing.

Associates make excellent advocates – sales people in their own right – and the 'member-get-member' concept is a proven direct marketing technique. The wider relationship perspective is to exploit the value of active customer relationships in communicating to the market-place. The most powerful way of winning a new customer is not through general media or direct media, or even through face-to-face contact with staff, but through a person known to the customer who is an advocate of the brand. *'Word of mouth' is the great unrecognised marketing weapon, and a relationship network can develop word of mouth and propel the brand message around its market-place.* A customer who recommends once is likely to do so continually. American Express never exhausts the potential in its cardmember base to recruit new members, perhaps because the company recognises frequent recommenders and rewards them with special offers.

Brands can develop *relationship networks* (Figure 7.1) which encompass their shareholders and staff as well as their best customers.

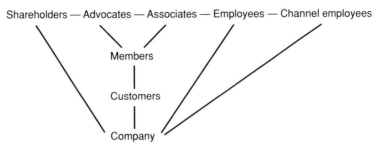

Figure 7.1 A relationship network

The Dimensions of Loyalty

Loyalty is complex and dynamic, and cannot be measured absolutely: it is a function of the competitive environment as well as a prediction of customer behaviour. A basic measure of loyalty is the customer's willingness to pay a premium price for the brand: premium pricing generates value and profits. But to measure customer rather than brand value I use three further wider dimensions of customer behaviour:

(i)   Repeat: propensity to repeat purchase the brand

(ii) Range: propensity to purchase the full range from the brand

(iii) Related: propensity to buy related services from the brand.

How do these apply to a leading brand like Sony which operates in a range of markets, many of which traditionally exhibit low levels of loyalty?

The first measure is propensity to repeat purchase. Sony's repeat purchase propensities will differ across the company's product lines: from low price consumables like cassettes and disks, to high price appliances like music systems and professional products. How likely is a buyer of one of these lines to continue to buy that product from Sony?

The second measure is the range of products that the customer is likely to buy. Loyalty research questions include: how likely is a music system buyer to buy Sony cassettes, a Sony Walkman, a Sony video machine, or Sony disks at work? Each of these is progressively further from the customer–brand relationship created by the initial transaction.

The third measure is the probability that the consumer will buy related products or services if offered under the brand umbrella. For a Sony, for example, this could mean software such as music, video or film products which are marketed under different brands or 'labels'. Can the Sony endorsement increase the share of recommended products? Does Sony's ownership of music label CBS influence the music purchase's of Sony hardware owners? Can Sony use its software to add value to its hardware product?

Companies often make acquisitions in related industries, and the announcement of the deal usually refers to the considerable potential for 'synergy'. There are only two possible benefits from synergy, and they lie either in more efficient manufacturing and operations or in more effective marketing to the same customers. Loyalty research can help companies determine how far their brand values influence customer choice, and whether they can realise the advantages of synergy by using the competitive advantage of customer relationships to increase their sales.

In designing customer loyalty research, all of the questions must be related to an actual or possible competitive environment. All of the customer's answers in research, like their behaviour in the market, depend on competitive marketing, and on competitive pricing and offers in particular. A measure of the strength of a brand is the 'resistance' of customers to competitive prices, features and benefits. Will a buyer of Sony tape continue to buy if competitors reduce their prices? Will a previous buyer of Sony buy again when a competitive product has new features? Loyalty measurement reveals the 'margin of error' available to a company in its pricing and product development. When loyalty is higher, the brand is less 'at risk' and its earnings are more secure.

Table 7.1 Customer loyalty measurement: a pro forma

	Weight	*Probability*	*Value*
Propensity to repeat purchase the brand			
Propensity to purchase the full range from the brand			
Propensity to buy related services from the brand			
Propensity to pay more than competitive prices			
Weighted total brand value			

For each dimension of loyalty there is a probability or a risk that can be measured by research. There is a potential increase in value or a cost associated with loss of the customer, or a decline in purchase frequency. A customer loyalty rate can be constructed that is a weighted average of these customer propensities. The weighting will be based on management assessment of the relative importance of the four factors (Table 7.1), and marketing's prediction of the risks associated with competitive action. The value of a brand or company can then be predicted as the product of loyalty rate and the potential lifetime values in the customer base.

$$\text{Customer value} = \text{Customer lifetime value} \times \text{Customer loyalty}$$

Customer loyalty results from two factors: active customer relationships and added value. The process of developing loyalty starts with the activation of customer relationships, and the objective is to develop an active relationship based on one or more of the three forms: membership, association and advocacy. In measuring customer loyalty it is important to determine how willing customers are to form a deeper relationship with company or brand.

Propensity to join – to commit to repeat or regular purchase

Propensity to advocate – to recommend other customers to buy the brand

Propensity to associate – to become involved in the brand and with the company

---

Figure 7.2 Measuring customer propensity to develop active relationships

Total Loyalty System

Despite an understanding of the financial payback from customer retention and despite investment in customer satisfaction, the car industry has generally failed to achieve growth in repeat purchase rates because it has failed to develop all dimensions of the customer relationship. Each of the major developments – in customer communication, financing, credit cards, roadside assistance and dealer training – has been piecemeal. Manufacturers still distance themselves from customers – even keeping their customer clubs at arms length, providing advice, very modest financial support, but no direct involvement. The car market illustrates the difference between loyalty as a set of marketing activities, and loyalty as a business objective.

A total loyalty system encompasses targeting, relationship-building and customer management, and can be illustrated for a car manufacturer (Figure 7.3).

Our car manufacturer has four models, but identifies three principal customer segments:

(i) Young adults, mainly in urban areas, driving the upper end of the smaller two models

(ii) Young families, driving the two mid-range models

1 Targeting

Identification of customer segments with loyalty potential and value potential

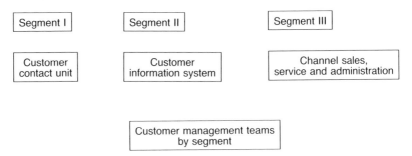

| Segment I | Segment II | Segment III |

2 Relationship-building

Adding value through relationships with each segment

	Segment I	Segment II	Segment III
Contact			
Affinity			
Rewards			
Extra value			
Service			

3 Management

Organisation of resources and motivation of staff to add value at each interface with customer, including channels

| Segment I | Segment II | Segment III |

| Customer contact unit | Customer information system | Channel sales, service and administration |

Customer management teams by segment

Figure 7.3 Total loyalty system

(iii) Older couples and single females driving the lower end of the smaller models.

The manufacturer audits customer interface – all points of customer contact – and invests in:

Table 7.2 In a total loyalty system, investments in processes and people match investments in communication to customers

Customer interface	Customer management	Added value volunteered
Customer enquiries	Managed by company staff, no longer outsourced to supplier	All enquiries receive unanticipated free gift and promise of special treatment by dealer; appointments are made with dealers at times appropriate to each segment
	Manufacturer and dealer customer information systems are linked on-line	
Dealer visits	Managed by staff trained to relate to customer segments	Customers have privacy to view cars and study information on video and CD-ROM without sales person
	Staff are recruited and trained for customer care to work in teams with sales force	Qualified customers are offered option of delivery of test car and/or information on them
	Adminstrative staff are trained to manage and distribute customer information	For selected segments morning or evening events are organised to add interest and overcome inhibitions
Post-purchase	Company staff have responsibility to check the satisfaction of all customers, visiting them where necessary	All customers are contacted, to check their satisfaction, and the contact is also used:
		to determine customer plans so that the company can add value to regular and holiday travel

Table 7.2 *Continued*

Customer interface	*Customer management*	*Added value volunteered*
		to determine customer preferences for information and contact by the company and dealer e.g. newsletter, calls, events
		to motivate customers to service their cars with the dealer
Regular customer contact	Company and dealer staff liaise to manage customer contact according to customer preferences	Customers are invited to participate in events and to recommend dealer and company's models to family and friends
	Customers are allocated employees of the company and the dealer as their account representatives	Customers are invited to join a membership association in cooperation with their local dealer
	The manufacturer integrates its own communications, at the same time as it co-funds and designs the 'shells' of dealer communications	Customers receive newsletters customised to their segments and their individual interests
	Dealers are rewarded for customer loyalty rates as well as sales	Customers have an annual 'check' of their satisfaction and future plans so that new and unanticipated offers can be offered

- — enhanced customer management systems and processes
- — staff training and motivation to volunteer added value to customers (see Table 7.2).

FROM MASS TO DATA-DRIVEN MARKETING 8

'Information is the only asset'

The Total Brand Experience – Integrated Media and Relationship Planning – Marketing to the Individual – Customer Contact Rules – Four Market Types – Markets with Complex Decision-making – Markets with Variety-seeking – Markets with Positive Choice – Habitual Purchase – Increasing Brand Value by Increasing Relationship Investment

The Total Brand Experience

The traditional model of the buying process consists of five stages: problem recognition, information search, evaluation of alternatives, purchase and post-purchase evaluation. Based on these stages, marketing theorists have developed a parallel model for marketing communications called the hierarchy of effects. Marketing planners explicitly or implicitly use the hierarchy of effects to assign appropriate roles to the different disciplines and media used in marketing.

> ### Traditional models of the buying process, hierarchy of effects and role of marketing communications
>
> | *The buying process* | *The hierarchy of effects* | *Communications* |
> | --- | --- | --- |
> | Problem recognition | Aware of brands | Advertising |
> | Information search | Knowledge of brand features and benefits | Advertising |
> | Evaluation of alternatives | Brand preference | Advertising |
> | Purchase decision | Brand choice | Promotion or direct marketing |
> | Post-purchase evaluation | Brand reinforcement | Customer service |

The Hierarchy of Effects model is a theory increasingly unrepresentative of real-life behaviour. Implicit in the model are the assumptions that customers are rational, make considered decisions and use information to choose amongst alternatives. In reality decision-making is emotional as well as rational. Many purchases are made on impulse, habit or simple convenience. Customers do not perceive that decisions are worth the investment in time and effort to search for information: their time is valuable, and anyway information is not readily available. In the traditional theory, beliefs drive behaviour: decisions are made in the sequence 'think, then do'. In the modern economy this is patently unrealistic. Most decisions are made in the sequence 'do, think, then do again'. Experience drives beliefs and behaviour.

To make a difference, marketing must change behaviour directly. Advertising has little effect because it limits its ambition to the creation of a favourable image for a brand. This can reassure existing customers but fail to motivate new users. Even the apologists for advertising emphasise its role in reinforcing behaviour and maintaining brands. They concede that if the objective is to change behaviour, advertising is a weak force.

Image advertising is in fact one of the weakest forces affecting customer behaviour, as some of the more thoughtful advertising agencies realise. Dan Wieden, of US agency Wieden and Kennedy, says: 'We have to relearn the relationship (between) brand and consumer. A brand is not a thing but a series of dynamic relationships. Brand is a verb, not a noun.'[1] Wieden and Kennedy is one of the small number of advertising agencies that understands the value of encouraging the customer to interact with the brand, but they only seem to see the contact as momentary. Direct marketing agencies use response advertising to generate customer contacts, but their motive is equally narrow: to build a database.

Neither advertising nor direct marketing agencies have grasped the importance of the interface with the customer as a force in building brands, and as the key to developing the total customer experience of the brand.

To build brands marketing must influence behaviour and experience directly. Brand experience is not limited to advertising or marketing communication but encompasses all forms of contact with the brand, including the channel that distributes it and the people who make up the company that manufactures it.

The idea of the total brand experience explains the success of leading brands that have been built without advertising. Modern examples are Virgin and The Body Shop. The owners of each of these companies are obsessive in differentiating themselves, and in creating powerful personalities. Every contact with the customer matters, because every contact is an opportunity to reaffirm the brand personality and develop the customer relationship.

Responsibility for a brand once belonged to the advertising agency. Now the strategy that guides advertising planning should drive:

— the recruitment and training of staff

— the management of customer response by telephone

— the quality of customer service

— the interface with the customer by sales forces and retail staff

— the presentation of the brand by the staff of independent distributors

— direct communication between customer and company.

Companies which understand the total brand experience see advertising, direct marketing, sales promotion, public relations and customer service all as aspects of the brand experience – and of similar importance to operations like manufacturing and distribution. Marketing *is* operational: it is as important to target, develop and manage customers as it is to manufacture and distribute products to them. *Marketing cannot be switched on and off. Without adequate marketing the link in the chain to the customer is broken.* The customisation of product, distribution and marketing to the individual customer can become a seamless and integrated process.

How customers relate to a brand depends upon their personalities and lifestyles. How customers perceive a brand depends upon their individual experiences of it, their use of the product and their relationships with the people in the company or channel that delivers the product to them. Every customer is different and the most effective marketing is closely related to the individual customer. Moreover, personal experience is significantly stronger than advertising imagery. A relationship network of associates and advocates can propel the brand into its market-place faster and more cost-effectively than any mass media. Every motivated member of staff and loyal customer can recommend and recruit many new customers, every day. Marketing can build brands from the bottom up rather than from the top down: individual by individual.

This new perspective suggests different roles for marketing communications. Perhaps advertising should be used to identify prospective customers and direct communications to develop their business as individuals. The new perspective suggests a new role for marketing. Marketers must think beyond communication and take responsibility for the motivation of staff and the management of the customer interface. Above all, they must invest in customer information and use that information to optimise marketing to the individual.

The shift from mass impersonal marketing to data-driven personal marketing is experiential and technological. Loyalty is created when the brand experience adds unanticipated value and exceeds customer expectations. Loyalty depends on recognition of individual customers at every potential point of contact with the brand, and also on technology: on the collection, analysis and distribution of customer information.

Integrated Media and Relationship Planning

Integrated marketing is the organisation of all customer contact to create business value from customer relationships. Integration applies not simply to creative but to media, sales, service and all channels of distribution. Broadcast and print media, the traditional focus of media planning, represent only one end of a spectrum that includes any contact between company and customer. Most media are planned on the basis of target audience coverage. Integrated plans build customer relationships and are designed to maximise engagement and involvement:

— by engagement I mean the power of communication to motivate a customer response: the brand rate

— by involvement I mean the impact of the communication on the customer's relationship with the brand and thus on propensity to choose the brand: the loyalty rate.

Media planning is usually based on cost-efficiency. A more useful objective is cost effectiveness. Different media and customer contacts differ in power as well as in cost:

quality matters more than the traditional objective of maximising quantities at the lowest cost.

Media and relationship planning: a checklist

Media	Network television
	Cable or satellite television
	Radio
	Newspapers
	Magazines
	Inserts
Relationship	Direct mail
	Catalogues
	Customer Publications
	Video/CD-ROM
	Telemarketing
	Remote personal contact
	Trade event contact
	Seminar contact
	In-store contact
	Personal sales contact

With each communication can be associated a cost per contact (very low for general media, very high for any form of personal contact), and an index of the power to engage and involve (also low for general media and high for personal contact). The mistake made by most companies is to neglect the power of personal contact – to invest most marketing money and effort in general media and not to match media expenditure with relationship investment.

By reducing media planning to a minimisation of the cost of cover, media buying has become a mixture of computer evaluation and hard bargaining over rates. The creative use of media has become neglected. As usual exceptions prove the rule. Mercury, Britain's second telecommunications company, buys bottom left and right positions in facing pages, commanding a double page spread and motivating higher readership. To launch its new Micra model, Nissan

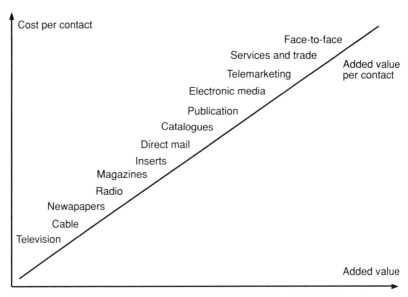

Figure 8.1 Media and relationship investment: customer segmentation planning

created a distinctive emblem of a cartoon car, and invited media to place the emblem in unusual positions, in particular on pages that rarely contain advertising.

In their quest to minimise cost of cover, media planners also neglect the power of different media positions and formats. Direct marketers measure response and therefore know the differences between a right- and a left-hand page, an early or late position, and a specialist magazine or national newspaper.

Media planning is usually a separate activity from distribution planning, sales force coverage or customer contact management by direct mail and telephone. An integrated media and relationship-building plan will assign a role to each form of communication (Figure 8.1).

Every media or direct customer contact can add value. Media advertising can communicate new information or offer extra value in the form of a special offer.

Similarly, with the management of the telephone enquiry that is a result of the advertising, the customer need is information. The usual routine is that the company exchanges the information the customer wants for the customer's name, address and other relevant data. Yet it is even more important than in advertising to add value, affirm the brand personality and exceed the customer's expectations. Even this simple enquiry management process can be enhanced. Excellent service by staff can increase the customer's perception of value and a distinctive personality can differentiate the company from its competition. The personality of the staff and scripting of the call can reflect the brand. The call can offer more to the customer, perhaps in an unanticipated offer or in privileged service. More value can be added and more information sought. For example, customers can be invited to say how, where, when and by whom they would prefer follow-up.

Companies that treat customer contact as routine are failing to differentiate themselves as brands, and failing to develop their customer relationships.

The more personal the contact, the greater the effect. Integrating media and customer contact has a multiplicative effect: for example, the Institute of Direct Marketing[2] reports the relative effects of different business-to-business media (Table 8.1).

Effective marketing planning integrates all media and all forms of relationship-building customer contact. The basis for planning is the individual customer. The roles of general advertising and promotion are not simply to reassure or reward existing customers – their roles become more precisely defined:

Table 8.1 Response to business-to-business contacts (percentages)

Direct mail	1
Telephone	2–10
Direct mail plus telephone	3–7
Telephone plus direct mail	5–15
Telephone plus mail plus telephone	10–20

— to increase trial among the high value prospects in the target audience

— to motivate infrequent or lapsed users to experience the brand anew.

They are the 'front end' of a process of building relationships with customers, in which each receives marketing messages relevant to them as individuals.

Marketing to the Individual

The management of marketing with a relationship strategy differs from traditional planning in one important respect. Advertising and promotions are typically conducted in 'campaigns' or 'bursts' and run over a period of months. Relationship management is a continuous process for marketing to individuals.

Many companies plan their advertising to coincide with seasonal peaks. The result is that every financial institution advertises mortgages and loans in the spring, every retailer concentrates on the run-up to Christmas, every car manufacturer promotes their best offers at the same times and every tour operator advertises in two bursts: after the summer and after Christmas. Impact is lost amidst the competitive noise at seasonal peaks, and marketing budgets cannot sustain advertising support outside the peaks. The concentration of advertising in the whole market is reflected in the 'softness' of the television airtime market at the beginning of the year and in the summer. Marketing is increasingly concentrated in short campaigns because few companies can afford a sustained media presence throughout the year.

Each campaign is managed and evaluated separately. Updating is necessary to maintain the topicality of the message and the competitiveness of pricing and offer. But updating creates the temptation to change the message more fundamentally: as is often said, companies and their agencies become bored with their advertising long before their customers. Updating campaigns places a considerable workload on the marketing department and creates a burden for customer-facing staff, who must continually be rebriefed on the latest marketing initiative. Because each campaign is 'new', staff may not be well informed and the company may not learn from the results in isolation. In most companies marketing is one of the least well-structured activities: it is not conceived as operational and as a continuing business process, and as a result has been slow to adopt and benefit from information technology.

As well as organising their marketing by campaign, most companies manage separately the communication of their message in different media. Different themes are used in advertising, promotion and direct marketing. This is an obvious inefficiency, measurable in lost sales: I have seen companies increase sales from 15 to 100 per cent by the simple expedient of running their advertising in harmony with their promotions or direct marketing. I have also tracked significant increases in advertising awareness when customers receive direct mail that reflects and develops the advertising theme. Customer communication can make the media advertising budget more efficient.

Many companies are improving the consistency and coordination of all messages, answering the call for at least one form of integration. But there is an even greater lost opportunity: customers are neglected and sales are lost in the absence of a process to manage customer relationships. Lost sales – or preferably – customer opportunities include:

(i) High value prospects who are unfortunate enough to be in the market outside the peak periods during which special offers are available

(ii) Enquirers who receive information but no special offer or trial privileges and whose subsequent behaviour is unknown

(iii) New customers whose dissatisfaction with their first purchase is not detected and who do not repeat buy

(iv) Regular customers who start to buy competitive products because they are not encouraged to buy more of your company's products

(v) Customers who are lost because no effort is made to retain them and to renew the relationship with the excitement with which it began.

The true meaning of integration is that all marketing – communication and distribution – is organised around the individual customer relationships. Relationship management is a continuous business process, developing the customer from prospect to customer to loyalist. The role of IT in marketing is to support this process by distributing information to everyone in contact with customers and in collecting information from every customer interface. As management consultant Tom Peters has said: 'information is the only asset most companies need to own'.[3]

The relationship-building process is managed by *customer tracks*, defining:

— the external media and promotions that generate names, and any source of prospects and customers

— the types, sequence and timing of internal contacts with customers, and the marketing messages they deliver

— the content and personalisation of each message to the individual customer

— the decision 'rules' that select customers to receive messages, based on individual customer behaviour and data

— the roles and responsibilities of members of the customer team

— the internal communication of customer information which drives the management of the customer relationship.

A customer track informs all staff in the company involved with customers, and integrates their contributions to the development of the customer relationship. As a process, a customer track is designed for efficiency and for quality: targeting the right message to the right customers is the key to efficiency, and adding value to the brand by distinctive contact with the customer is the driver of quality. The results of the track are continuously monitored and the key variables tested so that targeting and content are refined. The content of the messages within the track is updated over time but there is no need to reinvent the process for a new season or campaign (Tables 8.2 and 8.3).

Communication in a customer track is driven by customer behaviour and data. The database is an intelligence gathering system, with the information gleaned and the signals read used to prompt interaction with the customer and thus to generate incremental sales and profit. The process is *customer directed*, the most explicit form of customer direction being to allow the customer to select the marketing communications as well as the products they prefer. Customers can be invited to select the contact they prefer: mail, telephone or personal visits. And they can be invited to indicate the content they find useful and relevant.

A customer track should be designed as a *closed loop*. When the customer declines to participate the company should endeavour as far as possible to determine the reason. A lost sales opportunity or even a lost customer is a beginning as much as the end of a relationship. The customer may have decided to choose a competitive brand, to delay purchase or not to buy at all. By understanding the customer's behaviour and motivation the potential for a future sale and relationship can be determined.

The investment in the customer relationship and the design of the customer track are driven by the potential to increase customer lifetime value. Increasing the frequency of customer contact measurably increases sales, a fact well known to experienced direct marketers. Many marketers are strangely coy about keeping in touch with their customers, even though research proves that customers welcome contact, and results confirm that increasing contact increases sales. The Henley Centre reports in *Teleculture 2000*[4] that 60 per cent of customers are more likely to buy

Table 8.2 Customer contact tracks: structure

	Eligibility for customer track	
Customer contact plan	*Customer selection – decision rules*	*Contest and personalisation of individual messages*
Type, timing and sequence of messages to customers in the track	Rules to select customer to receive specific messages, based on status of relationship or probability of increasing customer value	Content of message by media – text and contents of mail package;
– initiated by company or – initiated by customers	– selected by criterion or model; or – triggered by event, signal or anniversary	– script guide for telemarketing; – briefing for staff at the customer interface Personalisation of offer, information and copy by individual customer
Creation and implementation of messages	Management and distribution of customer information	Management of customer contact, and evaluation of feedback
	Customer team responsible for customer segment and track	

again from a company that keeps in touch. A customer communication programme to frequent flyers increased an airline's share of their business from 11 to 27 per cent in one year.

Investing in the customer relationship pays, and the

Table 8.3 Customer contact tracks: an illustration

Home PC owners			
Plan	*Week*	*Decision rules*	*Content*
Welcome Package (mail) plus Customer census	1	All customers	Personalisation by – dealer channel of purchase – configuration of PC
Welcome Call (tel.) plus Customer census	3	All non-responders to welcome package	Personalisation by – dealer channel – configuration of PC
Software offer plus Software club offer	5	Selective offers according to census response	Personalisation and offer by – PC usage – software owned – children in family
Software club	7	Respondents to club offer	Registration data based on application form
Dealer mail	9	All census responders with dealer relationship confirmed	Customised offer by dealer in consistent presentation
Software newsletter	11	All customers	Club and non-club versions
Customer satisfaction check Mail or Telephone to mail non-responders	13	All customers, excluding complainants	Club and non-club versions Personalisation by – dealer channel – PC configuration – software usage/ ownership

payback is maximised by using customer data to drive customer contact *selectively*.

Customer Contact Rules

The decision rules for selection are based on analysis of customer data. Decision rules can be simple criteria, based on one or two customer characteristics like recency of order and type of product purchased. As the quality and complexity of customer databases grow, more sophisticated decision rules are required. Analysis of customer behaviour can be used to derive models that predict an individual customer's future behaviour (Figure 8.2).

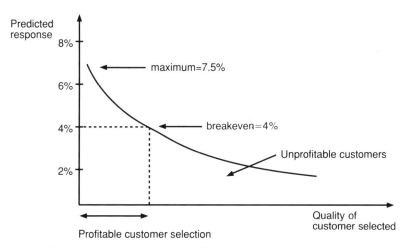

Figure 8.2   Customer models: an illustration

Models can be developed to predict any aspect of customer behaviour: their role is ultimately to drive marketing on the basis of the profitability of the *individual* customer. Models select customers to receive the appropriate contact, or exclude them if contact is likely to be unprofitable. Models allocate customers to high investment media like

Model to predict customer response
to a cross-selling offer for product A

Predicted response		*Variables*
=0.0155		
+0.0125	if last purchase is last 6 months ⎫	Time
0.0100	year ⎪	since
0.0005	two years ⎬	last
−0.0150	greater than three years ⎭	purchase
+0.0150	if three plus products held ⎫	No. of
	↓ ⎬	products
+0.0075	two ⎭	purchased
−0.0050	if customer is male	Gender
+0.0075	if customer is 25−35 ⎫	
+0.0125	35−45 ⎪	
+0.0050	45−55 ⎬	Age
−0.0075	55 plus ⎭	
+0.0150	if product X held ⎫	
−0.0075	Y held ⎭	Product

Maximum score/predicted response − 0.0750 or 7.5% for female, aged 35–45, with 3 plus products held including product X and last purchase within last 6 months

Decision rule might be:

Select all customers with score greater than 0.04 i.e. with probability of response greater than 4%

This would be appropriate if cost of promotion equals £1 but margin on Product A = £25; as

$$\text{Breakeven} = \frac{\text{Cost}}{\text{Margin}} = \frac{£1.00}{25.00} = 0.04$$

The model can be represented graphically as in Figure 8.2

Table 8.4 Customer models/customer actions

Model predictions	Customer actions
High probability of purchase	High investment contact cycle, e.g. multiple mail contact, offer of meetings, and telephone follow-up plus
Medium probability of purchase	Medium investment contact cycle, e.g. solus mail, offer of telephone discussion or face-to-face dialogue
High possibility of 'lost' customer, high value	High investment contact cycle, with high value 'offers' and 'rewards' to retain customers
High possibility of 'lost' customer, medium value	Medium investment contact cycle
Low possibility of purchase or High possibility of 'lost' customer, low value	No action

the sales force, or low investment media like direct mail. Models identify customers with high potential and trigger appropriate cross-selling messages, or they identify customers likely to be lost and trigger special actions to 'save' the relationship (Table 8.4).

Customer contact rules are based on judgement and experience as well as on analysis, but are modified by testing and further analysis. If a particular part of the contact cycle is unprofitable, the criteria are tightened to exclude poorer

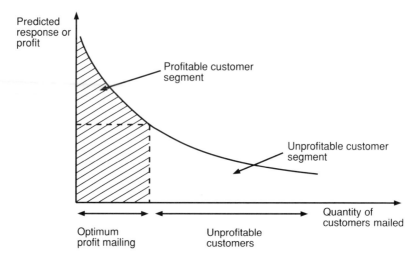

Figure 8.3   Modelling and increases in profitability

The shaded area under the graph represents profit, the unshaded area less. Any customer base or segment can be analysed to differentiate between

Profitable customers x% representing £y profit

Unprofitable customer $(100 - x)$% representing £z profit

Total profit $\pi = y - z$

Even an unprofitable customer base can be marketed successfully if the profitable segment x can be identified by data analysis.

customers. The effectiveness of selection rules and modelling depends on the quality of customer data, and the best source of data are customers themselves (Figure 8.3). As part of an active relationship and dialogue with customers, they should be asked to feedback their responses to past marketing and their preferences for future contact. An important aspect of the process is that contact with the customer is triggered by 'events', 'signals' or 'anniversaries'.

An *event* is any occurrence that creates an opportunity to contact or sell to the customer. The obvious customer event is a purchase, to which every company's response should at least be a 'thank you'. The contact rule selects purchasers to receive a 'thank you' card, and may allocate high value customers for contact by telephone by customer service representatives. The most valuable customers might be called by a manager or director in the company. Any customer contact with the company is a potential event, and so an opportunity to express the brand personality and build the customer relationship.

A *signal* is a change in the customer's status or behaviour that triggers a contact. A customer signal might be a change or decline in the customer's purchasing pattern. The company can respond by triggering an offer to restimulate purchase, and/or a query to identify the cause of the change in the customer's behaviour. Any new development in customer behaviour is a signal indicating a marketing problem or opportunity.

An *anniversary* occurs a defined period of time after an event (Figure 8.4). Examples of anniversaries are:

— a five-day anniversary: five days after despatch of information to enquirers a follow-up is triggered to understand the customer's response and 'close the loop'

— a three-month anniversary: three months after the sale a customer service call is made to check customer satisfaction and future intention to repeat buy

— a one-year anniversary: one year after a sale a customer census is sent to understand why customers have not yet repeat purchased and to offer them a specific reward for doing so

— a five-year anniversary: five years after their first purchase customers receive an unanticipated reward, and special acknowledgement and recognition of their status.

To implement a customer track a system is necessary to route customer data to the staff responsible for the

Current cheque accounts

Events	: balance enquiries at branch	— information about telebanking services
	: high cheque usage in branch	— offer of credit card and cash card for ATMs
	: request for information about mortgage	— assignment to home financing team and relationship-building messages
Signals	: low activity	— call from member of customer team, to invite change of main account
	: build-up of balances	— information on bank's savings products
	: early overdraft	— offer to discuss long-term financing needs
Anniversaries	: one month	— satisfaction call from member of customer team
	: six month	— invitation to meet member of customer team
	: one year	— thank you message, privileged offer on other products and appropriate gift

Figure 8.4 Customer events, signals and anniversaries: an illustration for a bank during a cheque account customer's first year

customer relationship. The internal communication of customer events, signals and anniversaries is a critical success factor for efficient marketing and effective customer service.

The more individual the contact with the customer, the more it is effective. A measure of the sophistication of any marketing is the degree to which messages are personalised for individual customers. Any aspect of content can be personalised: tone, language, products, and offers. Customers respond significantly better to personalised contact. Personalisation elevates a 'sales' offer to the status of added value and enhancement of service.

Marketing technology, linking customer databases to selective printing and binding, can support infinite variations. The US magazine *Farm Journal* is published in 8000 versions according to the size, crops, locations and interests of subscribers, and can personalise advertising messages for individual readers. Selective printing and inserting can tailor addressed copy and non-addressed contents of mailing packages.

Marketing driven by customer data is 'marketing with a memory' rather than by campaign.

Four Market Types

There is no single formula for planning the investment in customer relationships, but there are principles common to the major types of market. The most useful classification of markets is according to the method of customer decision-making, and there are two important dimensions to decision-making: involvement and price.

Involvement is the importance of the purchase decision to the consumer. High involvement means high risk. It means that the consumer will search for alternatives, and that the decision-making process is protracted. High involvement markets are typically high price; examples are cars and other capital goods. Much business-to-business decision-making is high involvement: a multiple decision-making unit confers to define the needs, search among alternatives, evaluate, and make a choice. But many low price markets are high involvement; examples are drinks, cigarettes, beauty products and pet foods.

Market types and decision-making	High involvement	Low involvement
High price	Type I Complex decision-making *Automotive* *Financial planning* *Cruises*	Type II Variety-seeking *White and brown goods* *Loans* *Holidays*
Low price	Type III Positive choice *Pet food* *Credit cards* *Hotels*	Type IV Habitual purchase *Detergents* *General and life insurance* *Train and bus*

Figure 8.5 Four market types

High involvement purchases represent a significant degree of perceptual risk – to the consumer's self-interest, self-image or peer group status. High price purchases represent a significant degree of financial risk – if the transaction turns out to be a mistake in any way. Price is a second measure of the importance of the purchase decision to the consumer.

There are four types of market and decision-making (Figure 8.5). *Complex decision-making* occurs in markets characterised by high involvement and high price. *Variety-seeking* is an appropriate description of behaviour where the category is high price but decision-making is low involvement. In lower price markets, *positive choice* is exercised by the consumer where involvement is high. *Habitual purchase* describes consumer decision-making when involvement with the category is lower. Examples of the decision-making types can be illustrated by product categories drawn from three business sectors: manufacturing, finance and travel.

There are different priorities for media and relationship investment in the different market types.

Markets with Complex Decision-making

In complex decision-making, purchase is relatively infrequent and customers move in and out of the market. Sales are typically 'one-offs'. The objective of the relationship strategy is to acquire new customers cost-effectively and build sustained relationships with existing customers to motivate repeat sales.

The value of relationships is demonstrable by the spiral of prosperity. The potential to increase marketing effectiveness by focusing on customer relationships (Figure 8.6) is based on:

— increasing the number of identified prospects as they move into the market

— increasing the brand rate: the propensity to prefer the brand

— increasing the conversion of prospects to purchasers

— increasing the customer lifetime value by cross-selling

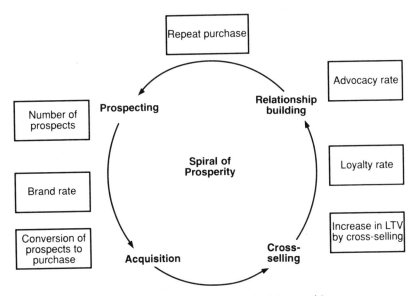

Figure 8.6 Relationship plan for complex decision-making

— increasing the loyalty rate: especially the propensity to repeat purchase

— increasing repeat purchase.

Japanese car manufacturers first penetrated the American market in volume on the heels of the twin oil shocks of the 1970s. In the 1980s, General Motors, Ford and Chrysler lost share, but confidently expected Americans to switch back to home models. Their second, and greater, shock was the high level of repeat purchase achieved by the Japanese – described in *The Reckoning* by David Halberstam, who uses the reversal of the balance of power in the car market between the 1940s and 1980s as a metaphor for the gulf between Anglo-Saxon and Japanese business cultures. Halberstam describes the breakdown in relationships between US car companies and their customers: 'What was truly worrying about Detroit's plight was that many previously steadfast customers now believed that there had been a breach of faith . . . many Americans now believed that the Japanese made better cars.'[5]

Toyota's luxury Lexus brand has a repeat purchase rate of nearly 80 per cent, compared to an industry average of under 40 per cent because Lexus invests in the process of relationship-building. Lexus makes the ultimate test of customer allegiance in inviting prospects to social functions at which they are paired with existing drivers. Lexus knows that the best salesman is a loyal customer.

Korean manufacturer Hyundai became the third largest importer of cars to the US behind Toyota and Nissan by focusing on customer satisfaction in the company's launch marketing strategy – before it had recruited its first customer. As *Marketing Communications* magazine reported: 'Hyundai's management team understood the importance of customer satisfaction as the key to referrals and repeat sales. For a fast start, it was important for positive word-of-mouth recommendation to supplement Hyundai's visible advertising campaign and strong distribution plans right from the beginning.'[6] Hyundai developed a customer satisfaction development programme and added value to the ownership of the marque through surveys, free membership of a club and a free customer hotline. The company sold more vehicles than any other importer in its first year in the US, illustrating the value of matching the investment in media with investment in customer relationships.

US car manufacturers have fought back and the Saturn company is a leading example of a successful relationship strategy, regularly topping the customer satisfaction rankings for example.

The car market is a powerful illustration of the value of investment in customer relationships in a marketing with complex decision-making (Table 8.5).

Markets with Variety-seeking

In variety-seeking, customer involvement with brands is low: brands are less established and brand values are less well defined. Product features dominate customer choice and pricing is a powerful factor. The objective of relationship strategy in Type II markets is to deepen customer involvement, engage the consumer more closely in the decision and build the brand by adding values through ongoing involvement. The challenge in Type II markets is to change customer behaviour to Type I, by finding added values within the company and the customer's relationship with the company, to motivate customer choice.

There is an opportunity in any variety-seeking market for the first major user to 'own' relationship management, which is what American Airlines achieved with AAdvantage – the first and still a leading frequent flyer programme.

The potential to increase marketing effectiveness by focusing on customer relationships is based on:

— increasing the customer lifetime value by cross-selling

— increasing the loyalty rate: especially the propensity to repeat purchase

— increasing the advocacy rate: prospects recommended by loyal customers

— increasing repeat purchase and lifetime value.

Table 8.5 Modelling the investment in customer relationship: a car manufacturer (margin per sale £500)

First cycle	Current strategy	Relationship strategy	Effects
No. of prospects	400K	500K	Interactive advertising
Relationship investment	£800K	£5m	Increasing contact
Media investment	£20m	£20m	No change in spend
Conversion to purchase	25%	30%	Each increased point in conversion rate is worth 5000 cars or £2.5 million

Summary		
No. of customers	100K	150K
Revenue	£50 million	£75 million
Mktg costs	£20.4 million	£25 million

Second cycle	Current strategy	Relationship strategy	Effects
No. of customers	100K	150K	
Relationship investment	£3m	£18m	Increase contact
Increase in profits/lifetime value	£6m	£13.5m	Increase in value less than investment in relationship
Repeat purchase rate	40%	45%	Each increased point in repeat purchase rate is worth 1500 cars or £750 000

Summary		
No. of customers	40K	67K
Revenue	£26 million	£49.25 million
Costs	£3 million	£13.5 million

Variety-seeking markets have been relatively slow to adopt relationship strategies: because of the lack of differentiating brand values. Brown and white goods have been particularly slow to adopt relationship marketing. An exception is General Electric in America. The GE Answer Centre is a customer service centre with a free telephone number featured in all GE advertising, product packaging and literature. The centre manages problems and complaints from customers and supplies help and information to trade distributors. The centre enhances customer satisfaction, but also generates incremental sales from solving problems and managing enquiries from customers and trade.

Sony has launched a customer club in America. The motive is clear. An affluent household will buy a range of hardware: televisions, radios, cassette players and music systems. The lifetime value potential is considerable. As the lines between television and computers blur, ownership of a relationship with consumers could allow Sony entry to the emerging markets for multimedia. The household will also buy software – potentially allowing Sony to cross-sell the titles of its subsidiary, CBS.

Type II markets are volatile. Because branding is weak, new product features can rapidly win a higher share. Relationship management provides a defence to competitive developments, or a platform for the brand to launch its new products into the market more dramatically.

Markets with Positive Choice

In positive choice brand values are powerful. To motivate a change in customer behaviour is difficult, often expensive. The value of a customer is higher the more frequent the purchase. Heavy users in the category have high lifetime values. The objective of relationship management is to retain the most valuable customers, and to target and switch users of competitive brands who have high lifetime value potential (Figure 8.7).

In lower price markets, the decision-making process is

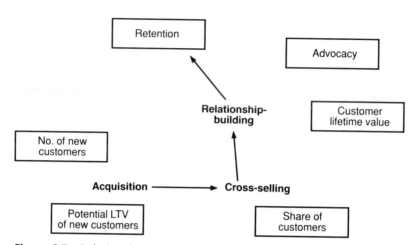

Figure 8.7 Relationship plan for positive choice

less a pyramid, as in the hierarchy of effects model, and more of a circle, a process of 'do-think-do'. Behaviour drives beliefs, rather than the other way around. A single purchase of the product carries little risk. Trial creates knowledge of the product. If the customer associates with the brand values, trial creates a liking for the product and preference for the brand. Consumption reinforces liking and preference.

In Type III markets, shifts in market share are gradual. Brands are strong and it is difficult to switch competitive brand users. Often it is more profitable to increase the value of existing brand users than to try to switch competitive brand users. In these markets, advertising works to maintain the status quo. Direct communications, significantly more powerful and targeted than general advertising, can win new share where advertising fails. One particular opportunity in many markets is to use customer engagement strategies to open relationships with new entrants to the market. Winning the first purchase can be the key to developing a relationship and retaining the customer's business long term. Marketing effectiveness is improved by focusing on:

— increasing the number of identified prospects as they move into the market

— increasing the brand rate: the propensity to prefer the brand

— increasing the quality of customers: the potential life-time value

— increasing the customer lifetime value by increasing the share of customer

— increasing the loyalty rate: especially the propensity to continue purchase

— increasing the advocacy rate: prospects recommended by loyal customers

— increasing retention.

A consumer sector in which relationship management has been rapidly adopted is pet foods. Brand values are distinctive. Customer lifetime value is high. One of the most successful users is the '9 Lives' brand. The 'representative' of the brand, Morris the cat, was once voted the best known personality in America, ahead of the then President Bush. Customer communications were centred on a magazine *The Morris Report*. The first issue of the magazine contained letters to Morris, merchandise offers, information and offers helpful to cat owners – as well as a Morris centrefold. It requested not only letters, but also features from aspiring writers. And it was offered on subscription – illustrating how a consumer brand can develop a relationship based on paid membership.

Lifetime value is high in pet foods. A manufacturer once asked me to justify data capturing 70 000 dog food promotional responders. I did a quick 'back of the envelope' calculation to estimate the annual expenditure of 70 000 owners on dog food. The total was over £5 million. The data capture cost of £10 000 was approved.

High lifetime value drives short- and long-term investment in customer relationships (Table 8.6).

Table 8.6 Modelling the investment in customer relationships: a petfood manufacturer

	Relationship		New
	Current Investment	Effect	customers and ROI
New Pet Owners 20% share of 2m new pet owners p.a., worth £50 each p.a. Current contribution £20 million	£20 each in 1m of the new owners. Cost £20 million	Increase in share to 40% among new owners contacted	Additional 200K customers worth £10 million p.a. for initial investment of £20 million
Competitive Users 2m competitive only users. Current contribution zero	£15 each in best 20% of 400K competitive users. Cost £6 million	Switching rate 5% each new user worth £100p.a. each	Additional 20K customers worth £2 million p.a. for initial investment of £6 million

Light Users 2m competitive and light users. Current contribution £50 million	£10 each in best 50% of light users. Cost £10 million	Switching rate 5% to heavy users and 5% to regular, worth £150 and £100 respectively	Additional 50K customers worth £5 million (£3.75 million incremental) and additional 50K customers worth £7.5 million (6.25 million incremental) – extra £14 million p.a. for initial investment of £10 million
Regular Users 1m regular users. Current contribution £100 million	£10 each in all regular. Cost £10 million	Switching rate 20% to heavy users worth £150 p.a.	Additional 200K customers worth £30 million (£10 million incremental) for initial investment of £10 million
Heavy Users 500K heavy users. Current contribution £75 million	£15 each in all heavy users. Cost £7.5 million	Increase in consumption worth £15 each by reduction in loss rate	Additional £7.5 million p.a. for initial investment of £7.5 million

Segment	Investment (£ million)	Payback (£ million p.a.)	Decision
New	20	10	Invest for L-T value
Competitive	6	2	Do not invest
Light	10	14	Invest
Regular	10	10	Invest for maintenance
Heavy	7.5	7.5	

Habitual Purchase

In habitual purchase, brands are not powerful. Repertoire purchase is the norm. Lifetime value is low other than among heavy users, and there are relatively few heavy users. The critical success factor is to deepen involvement, to change the passive nature of decision-making, and to encourage more heavy users.

Decision-making in Type IV markets is characterised by inertia. The decision does not involve any risk. The choice is not important. The process can be described as 'do-think-do'. A purchasing pattern emerges and becomes a habit. The habit is not difficult to break – which is why promotions are ubiquitous and (apparently) successful in these markets. But customers will move in and out of brands easily if the promotional offers are strong.

To describe the customer as promiscuous is inappropriate. The customer is simply not involved. The challenge is to shift customer behaviour to Type III, to motivate customer involvement, and an active relationship is an innovation. A customer rewards or frequent customer programme is the usual strategy in these markets, but competitive schemes can cancel each other out and reduce margins for the sector. The retail petrol sector is a glaring example. There must be real *interest* in information, real added value services and excellent customer care.

In Type IV markets, relationship marketing has the potential to engineer a permanent shift in the value of the whole sector, and marketing effectiveness can be increased by focusing on:

— increasing the quality of customers recruited: the potential lifetime value

— increasing the customer lifetime value by increasing the share of customer

— increasing the loyalty rate: especially the propensity to continue purchase

— increasing the advocacy rate: prospects recommended by loyal customers

— increasing retention.

The Kraft General Foods brand Crystal Light illustrates how customer relationships can be developed for a habitual purchase brand. In the early years of the programme, members received six newsletters each year. The direct communications added emotional values to the brand, complemented by rewards for regular purchase and offers on related services.

Insurance is a habitual purchase product. A relationship strategy for an insurance company selling through an independent channel is to build a closer involvement between the customer and the channel. *Direct Marketing* magazine reports the organisation of marketing support for agents used by the Allstate insurance company:

> To Allstate, relationship marketing is getting down to the heart of their distribution channel. The strategy recognises that one of the deepest human needs is to feel important . . . All communications with Allstate customers appear to come from their agents. Each event, 'moments of truth' in the company jargon, gives both company and the local field agent an opportunity to build loyalty.[7]

A newsletter keeps customers in touch with new products and services, and adds value by providing information and services related to insurance, with the content personalised to the insurance agent. Allstate builds the relationship between customer and agent, but maintains control over the quality of contact.

Insurance is a low involvement and undifferentiated product category with some of the greatest opportunities to build brands by developing individual customer relationships:

(i) Increasing the amount and quality of information to guide customers, and increasing the contact with the customer from company and/or channel – contact strategy

(ii) Tailoring insurance products and rates to customer segments – affinity strategy

(iii) Rewarding customers who have held the same policy for a number of years and further increasing their above-average renewal rate – rewards strategy

(iv) Offering extra cover and related car, household or health services – extra value strategy

(v) Improving claims service, quality of staff and systems and all-round customer support – customer service strategy

(vi) Creating an association or membership for customers to gain the benefits above.

Although insurance is one of the least differentiated categories, both product and marketing can be related to the individual customer. The challenge in this, one of the lowest involvement categories, is to match investment in customer information with investment in the staff who can develop customer relationships one-to-one.

Increasing Brand Value by Increasing Relationship Investment

In every market there is the potential to increase the value of the business and the brand by investing in customer relationships. The investment takes two forms:

(i) The experiential: the quality of personal contact in adding value to the customer, differentiate the brand and increase loyalty

(ii) The technological: the customer information and systems to distribute data and develop the whole organisation's understanding of and relationship with the customer as an individual.

The return on investment from customer relationships can be planned and measured. Companies have to date failed to match their media spends with investments in their customers, their staff and their information technology. There is no direct trade-off between these investments and media, but with the declining coverage and increasing cost of mass media will come the requirement for them to justify themselves on customer-based measures, in particular on new trial. This will change the characteristics of media advertising from general image to targeted and interactive messages.

PART III: SKILLS

CREATING INTERACTIVE ADVERTISING 9

'Pleasing customers'

Creating Advertising – The Development of Creativity – Direct Response Creativity – Creating Interactive Advertising – The Proposition and the Company Personality – The Call to Action – The Prompt to Thought – New Interactive Response Media – Short Form Television Advertising: DRTV – Long Form Television Advertising: Infomercials – Summary: The Creative Brief

Creating Advertising

Creativity resists analysis, and advertising creativity in particular defies attempts to define the factors that underlie success. Advertising is a commercial activity, so must result in sales, but the process by which advertising leads to sales is not well understood. The result is that for business management advertising is often a matter of faith – it is not uncommon to hear of managers who either 'believe' in advertising, or otherwise.

There are three contrasting views of how advertising works:

(i) From the neutral standpoint of an economist, advertising improves economic efficiency by communicating information to consumers, to help them maximise the value they gain from transactions

(ii) Critics argue that advertising manipulates consumers into the purchase of products they neither need nor want; a famous diatribe against advertising is to be found in Vance Packard's *The Hidden Persuaders* – the chapter titles summarise the content, and include: 'Marketing Eight Hidden Needs', 'The Built-in Sexual Overtone' and 'The Psycho-seduction of Children'[1]

(iii) The advertising industry itself sees its role as building brands by communicating them creatively and by associating them with prevailing ideas, fashions and culture – what Stephen Fox in *The Mirror Makers* calls: 'the favorite metaphor of the industry: advertising as a mirror that merely reflects society back on itself'.[2]

In the accepted definitions of advertising, customer beliefs drive behaviour, so to change behaviour advertising must change beliefs (Figure 9.1). The information communicated by advertising, and the method by which it is communicated, create the desired consumer *'take out'* – what the customer has learned from exposure to the advertising message.

Advertising planners analyse a product to find an attribute or set of attributes that *differentiates* it from its competition,

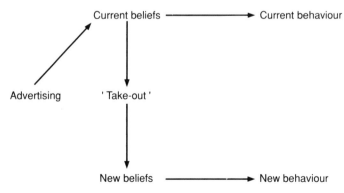

Figure 9.1 Beliefs drive behaviour

and they analyse customers to identify the needs which the product meets. Their objective is to define a *proposition*, an attribute that differentiates the product from others in the market-place *and* meets an important customer need. A strong proposition is one that can effect a significant change in customer beliefs: based on a motivating proposition, competitive strategy and advertising creativity develop the brand.

The competitive strategy summarises how the product will be differentiated from others in its market-place. The role of advertising creativity is to use imagination to express the proposition as an *idea*, which is a development rather than an obvious or literal expression of the proposition. A 'big' creative idea informs, interests, involves, challenges, entertains or even amuses customers. The idea and its communication summarise the proposition and create the brand. Alternatively, branding differentiates the product from its competition by adding the values contained within the big idea and its communication.

The big idea must be based on the attributes that make up the proposition. The ultimate crime in advertising, known as 'borrowed interest', is to use an idea that has nothing to do with a brand or its products, feature and values. The result can be powerful and original advertising, but it will not build a brand that customers value. A big idea is inextricably linked to the brand, which can be said to 'own' the idea.

Research is used throughout the process of creating advertising: to understand the customer's needs, derive the proposition, and test the power and relevance of the proposition. Most research is qualitative and does not provide quantitative forecasts of advertising effects.

The idea becomes an advertisement by the execution of the *technical skills* of the practitioners (Figure 9.2). Technical skills include copy, design and production. Copy attracts the customer's attention and delivers the required information. Design uses relevant visuals to highlight and support the message. The quality of typography in press and production of television are important to ensure that the intended message is forcefully communicated.

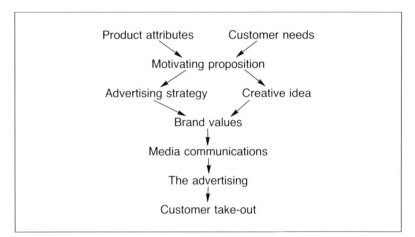

Figure 9.2 Creativity in action

In a number of respects, this advertising descriptive of branding is incomplete:

— The competitive strategy is led by company rather than product attributes; there are small differences between competing products, and successful strategies are founded on the unique competencies, assets and staff of companies – and the mission statements that guide their destinies

— The process that P&G uses to create a soap powder brand must differ at least in degree from the branding of a complex service like information technology and a multidisciplined company like IBM

— The emphasis on belief as the driver of behaviour is appropriate only for communication media that are passive, in particular television; the effect of other customer experience of product or company is ignored.

Creativity must develop to embrace all aspects of the total brand experience.

The Development of Creativity

In Chapter 5, I discussed the two schools of advertising, starting with the scientific. In *Reality in Advertising*, Rosser Reeves described how to research a product to derive a simple and powerful proposition, which he called the unique selling proposition or USP. Reeves claimed that 'for the first time we have an auditing approach to advertising'.[3] Reeves was known as the 'prince of the hard sell', and his Bates agency was legendary for taking a feature or benefit of a brand, making it the brand's dominating proposition and emphasising it remorselessly – hammering it into the customer's consciousness. Sometimes, the proposition was not particularly significant to consumers, and sometimes it was not even unique to the brand – but repetitive advertising made it important to the customer and bolted it strongly to the brand.

With Reeves, and before him Claude Hopkins, three ideas became associated with the 'scientific' school:

(i) 'Hard-sell', 'literal' advertising based on a single feature or benefit

(ii) Rigorous research into advertising development to determine the unique selling proposition

(iii) Equally rigorous measurement of advertising effectiveness.

In the 1960s came the 'creative revolution' led by Bill Bernbach of Doyle Dane Bernbach (DDB), who declared about Reeves and his acolytes: 'They forget that advertising is persuasion, and persuasion is not a science, but an art. Advertising is the art of persuasion.'[4] Advertising was not a matter of communicating a brand proposition. Bernbach's work emphasised the role of imagination and intuition in the leap which created powerful advertising ideas. The result was advertising with one or more of the three characteristics: it was stimulating, sometimes challenging and sometimes entertaining; it was intelligent; and it was honest. Honesty became a particular hallmark of DDB's work, as is revealed by the agency's long-running campaigns 'Think Small' for Volkswagen and 'We're No 2. We try harder.' for Avis.

In the 1970s, the fashion swung again towards the scientific school and the hard sell. As David Ogilvy said at the time: 'Today, thank god, we are back in business as salesmen instead of pretentious entertainers.'[5] The emphasis returned to the proposition, rechristened 'positioning' by Al Ries and Jack Trout. In updating the USP, Ries and Trout shifted the focus of analysis from the product to the customer: they saw advertising as 'the battle for your mind'.[6] But, as with the proposition, a combination of customer research and competitive analysis was used to derive a unique position in the market, which can only be defined in relation to competitive brands and the different 'positions' they occupy: Seven Up, for example, was the 'uncola'. The language of positioning is military: brands must conduct their marketing in an evershifting battlefield, as competitors continually seek the high ground, challenge each other's positions, or make indirect 'flanking' attacks.

The swings in advertising fashion have continued, and in the 1980s the emphasis returned to creativity. The most famous advertisement of the decade was Apple Computer's '1984', which cost $400 000 to produce and $500 000 to broadcast just once, during Super Bowl. In a scene reminiscent of George Orwell, a 'Big Brother' figure rants and raves to an auditorium of passive, grey 'proles'. A woman in athletic gear enters and hurls a sledgehammer into the screen, disintegrating 'Big Brother'. The announcement is: 'On January 24th, Apple Computer will introduce Macintosh. And you'll see why 1984 won't be like "1984"'. The advertisement established Apple as the revolutionary alternative to IBM, and communicated the mission of Apple's founders to make personal computing friendly and universally accessible. So powerful was the advertisement and its reverberations that some commentators believe its memory still – ten years on – hinders Apple, now in alliance with IBM but with a flat market share.

'1984' illustrates creativity at its best; the exceptional powering of a company's values into the market-place.

Much of the creativity of the 1980s is less well regarded and is held up as one of many signs of the transience and superficiality of the decade. JWT's Jeremy Bullmore sums up: 'It came to a point in the 1980s when some clients were telling their agencies that what they wanted was famous advertising – advertising that people would talk about. It was a vanity thing, and really quite preposterous.'[7] Bullmore is accusing agencies and many clients of mistaking originality for creativity, of relying too often on 'borrowed interest', and of neglecting their brands.

In the less extravagant and more austere 1990s, the balance has tilted again from the creative towards the scientific school. The increasing pressure on advertising budgets and the search for accountability are leading a trend towards advertising which is interactive and responsive. It is significant that on the page opposite Jeremy Bullmore's quote above is IBM advertising that invites direct response through the Internet.

Direct Response Creativity

The words of Claude Hopkins, a figure from the earliest days of advertising, best illustrate the scientific approach. Writing sixty years ago in *Scientific Advertising*, Hopkins concludes: 'The time has come when advertising has in some hands reached the status of a science. The causes and effects have been analysed until they are well understood. Advertising, once a gamble, has become, under able direction, one of the safest business ventures.'[8]

Hopkins was a direct response disciple. How can the views of Bernbach and Hopkins be resolved? Does the rule book of direct response preclude the imagination of advertising?

The essential characteristics of successful direct response are:

— a quickly explainable product proposition

— a motivating offer

— a powerful call-to-action.

Most response advertising is akin to scientific advertising in that it relies on a single offer as the proposition. The result is a literal as opposed to an imaginative expression of the proposition, emphasising a tangible offer rather than emotional values. The offer and call to action overshadow the brand and its values.

The creation of direct response advertising follows well-established rules. I learned the rules at *Reader's Digest*, where I oversaw a large increase in the Music Division's use of direct response press advertising. Although the company had a superb in-house copy and design department for direct mail, and a relationship with a large general advertising agency, *Reader's Digest* turned to a small agency, Trenear Harvey Bird & Watson (THB&W), to improve its direct response. In two split-run tests, against *Reader's Digest* own creative, THB&W doubled sales. For several years the agency and I tested creative themes, copy and layout, and a wide range of media, positions and sizes. The lessons we learned are typical of direct response.

Direct response advertising 'rules'

— Headlines are the most important feature of the advertisement

— The use and position of visuals affect response significantly: the best ads closely associate copy and visuals – the 'word-picture lock' – and when visuals intrude between headline and copy response falls

— Colour only pays for its extra production costs for certain products in certain media

— Serif typefaces are significantly more readable than sans serif

— Reversed out text and capitals are strong in short headlines but reduce readability otherwise

Further, testing reveals layouts that work better than others, copy themes that pull the highest response, and how to design the all-important call-to-action and coupon. We found many ways to increase sales from 5 to 25 per cent by superior technique. We created a formula for successful music collection advertising which we applied successfully to every product. Ten years on, the same formula is still used.

But the most important lesson we learned was how to increase our advertising effectiveness by a more imaginative expression of the *Reader's Digest* music proposition. In a split run test, the losing advertisement was headlined: 'The Swinging 60s: 112 Great Hits at 24p a track', the visual was a 'pack shot' and the copy emphasised value for money.

The winning advertisement, *doubling sales*, more imaginatively and emotionally invited readers to 'Bring Back the 60s'. The visual was a silhouette of a dancing couple wearing distinctive 1960s style fashion, and the copy emphasised the care with which *Reader's Digest* selects the music on behalf of customers. The advertisement appealed to the imagination of customers as well as to their desire to gain value through a great offer. Similar results were found in tests for other products: the most effective response advertising had a powerful emotional pull.

In direct response as in image advertising, the power of emotion in communicating the proposition is greater than the power of technique. The established 'rules' of direct response are increasingly irrelevant. One rule is that humour does not sell. Yet in the UK, National Savings commissions Gary Larson to create 'Far Side' cartoons to illustrate the benefits of its savings products. The cartoons differentiate the advertising visually and communicate the advantages of the high yield but secure investment products. In the US, the Quality Paperback Book Club uses Matt Groening cartoons to caricature the commitment selling of rival book clubs, and support the promise of its headline: 'With QPB, you get more than we do.'

Creating Interactive Advertising

The skill in interactive advertising lies in integrating direct response tactics with an imaginative and emotionally-based strategy to develop brand values. The critical success factors for interactive press advertising are:

— power: attracting attention with a strong headline, arresting visuals and layout leading to the call to action

— privilege: promising a reward for the customer's action or response to the advertisement

— personality: expressing the motivation of the company and its people

— personalisation: writing the headline in the language of a specific type of customer

— participation: engaging the customer in the message.

The Lands' End catalogue company has developed both a strong brand and a growing customer base with advertising consistent in look and tone of voice. All the advertising executions have five elements: strong headline and visual, the promise of reward from the product or from customer service, the commitment of the company to quality, the focus on a particular product interest or customer need, and the invitation to call or send for the free catalogue. The layout always directs the eye from top left to bottom right, helping readability. A series of Lands' End advertisements in *New Yorker* magazine illustrates some of the best combinations of brand building, direct response creativity.

'It takes 12 miles of cotton to make a Lands' End Pinpoint Oxford. And that's just the beginning' has a classic direct response layout, with product visual above headline, which leads into three columns of copy: headline below visual is a tactic that pulls more response than vice versa. The call to action is the offer of a free catalogue. Another product interest advertisement is headlined 'If our Attachés could talk, what stories they would tell.' This layout juxtaposes the headline and an unusual visual of an attaché case filled with concrete paving blocks. Again, three columns of copy, broken up by 'quotes' from Lands' End products lead towards the coupon and call-to-action in the right hand corner.

Two further Lands' End advertisements have a customer service theme: 'Like, who has time to shop anymore?' and 'Now, we're just two short days away.' The layouts are visual above headline, which juts into the one column of copy. As in all Lands' End advertising the sign-off 'Guaranteed. Period' appears immediately above the coupon, which is always at bottom right.

Most Lands' End advertising is black and white, but the advertisement for 'The Lands' End Turtleneck Dress' uses colour to highlight the product. In most media the extra cost of colour is not covered by the extra response. The headline 'What happened to the turtle? It turned into a swan.' is centred above a shot of a model wearing the dress, with the copy in two columns on either side of the advertisement.

Any advertiser will find a study of Lands' End advertising of interest, as the series illustrates how direct response has moved on since Caples. Small spaces, for example, are not necessarily appropriate, as in cluttered media a larger size may be needed to make more impact and to develop the brand.

Prudential Assurance's image advertising was well established by the time the company came to advertise the Prudence Bond. The image theme for many years has been 'I Want To . . .', and direct response advertising headline echoes and develops the theme with: 'Of course I want growth. I also want to be able to sleep at night.' Human interest is added by an inset customer photograph and a free booklet, 'An Introduction to Investment', is an incentive for response. The advertising personalises the image advertising to a specific product and target audience. The photograph identifies the specific audience, and the layout guides the eye towards the call to action. Using relationship-building creative skills, the copy invites the reader to speak to the Prudential, to listen to its advice and experience of investment before acting further.

In its direct response advertising, Mercury *one2one* echoes its image advertising directly, by showing a photograph of the personality who represents the company in television, press and posters above the coupon. Consistency in visual, typography and tone of voice from image to interactive advertising is essential. To relate image to response advertising, consider the image execution on page 3 of a newspaper followed by the response execution on page 5.

Persil illustrates the shift to advertising that is both interactive and responsive:

— image advertising becomes interactive and features the Persil Careline, promising: 'One of our specially trained advisors will be happy to help with any washing problems or questions you may have'

— direct response advertising offers a £2.50 cash back on new formulation Persil Power that is 'Easy To Use. Easy To Refill. Easy to Buy.'

The practice by which image advertising is created by advertising agencies and response advertising by direct marketing agencies is inefficient. The creators of advertising should take a view of the brand that encompasses customer relationships, and the creators of direct response should have an understanding of the brand and its values, and the company and its personality. It is desirable that they are the same people and can combine both skills.

The Proposition and the Company Personality

If the sole motivation for the customer to respond is rational then, as previously discussed, the advertising cannot be differentiating. Interactive advertising must offer emotional and intangible values as well as tangible rewards for response. One factor above all other makes a company different: its people and its customer service. *Every company has its own culture, value set and commitment to customers.* How the company expresses these through contact with customers is its most powerful source of differentiation and added value. The advertising proposition must encompass company personality as well as brand values. It is significant that in its Christmas 1994 UK catalogue Lands' End features both the very first British customer and the customer service representative who took her order – illustrating the community between people in the company and customers.

Even in the highly competitive computer industry, driven by faster speeds, bigger memories and lower prices, company personality and customer service are at least as significant as product performance. In an earlier advertising phase, Dell Computer featured its leadership in customer satisfaction scores. Dell now headlines its people, complementing product advertising with a campaign featuring customer service representatives: one execution is addressed: 'To all our nit-picky over-demanding ask-awkward question customers. Thank you, and keep up the good work.' The advertisement closes with a call to action, promising: 'Our suggestion box is more of a crate, and it's always open.' Direct seller Viglen uses the classic visual of a picture of customers above the headline: 'At Viglen, PC simply means "Pleasing Customers".' Both companies emphasise the advantages they enjoy from direct relationships with their customers, implicitly knocking competition that still sells through dealers.

In its UK advertising, Lands' End points out the misplaced apostrophe in the headline – '. . . every time we think about it, it reminds us that we're human' – as a way of emphasising its guarantee. The advertising's headline is: 'To err is human. To guarantee, divine.'

The Call to Action

An important aspect of an interactive advertisement is the call to action. There are at least ten distinct opportunities to call for a response in advertising:

(i)   Communicate information

(ii)   Generate sales leads

(iii)   Sample product

(iv)   Collect data

(v)   Recruit new customers

(vi)   Sell product directly

(vii)   Offer rewards

(viii)   Invite association

(ix)   Offer customer service

(x)   Solve problems.

The method by which response is invited, the reward for response, and data collected at response are all factors that affect brand image as well as response levels.

Method of response

It is desirable to offer customers alternative methods of response, and certainly a choice of mail or telephone. Some customers prefer post, and others telephone: with post the customer remains in control, while with telephone the customer can respond more quickly, so telephone enquirers are higher potential than those who use the post. The 'Response Research Survey' by the Direct Mail Information Service reveals that asking for a direct response enhances a company's image.[9] The more friendly and helpful the call to action, the greater the benefit to brand image. Reply paid postage and free telephone numbers enhance image as well as – in all my experience – increasing response cost-effectively.

Reward for response

The reward for response should offer value to the customer and differentiate the brand. Too much direct response advertising simply invites customers to send for product information.

Business-to-business advertising is among the least interesting in this respect – but advertising by the printer company Kyocera illustrates more imagination and more value. The advertising invites customers to send for a report: *The Shocking Truth About Office Printing Costs*, to substantiate Kyocera's claim to offer the lowest cost per page. The report is delivered on a disk, and includes software that allows customers to analyse their own printer ownership costs. Printing the report prompts customers to think about their costs even further.

Data collection at response

Response advertising of any kind is an opportunity to learn about customers. Car manufacturers ask prospects to tell them about the cars they drive and their plans to change. The value of the response is higher if the manufacturer also collects data on the customer's interest, for example: estate, diesel or automatic versions, and preferred method of financing the purchase. Similarly, a leading US book club includes a questionnaire in its response coupons to capture the interests of new members, who tick the types of fiction in which they are interested.

The Prompt to Thought

A response is an immediate change in behaviour in itself, but effective interactive advertising has an effect whether or not there is an immediate response. Interactive advertising intervenes directly in the decision-making process (Figure 9.3). The creative challenge is to *own the customer's decision-making process*.

The creative motives in inviting customers to interact with advertising are:

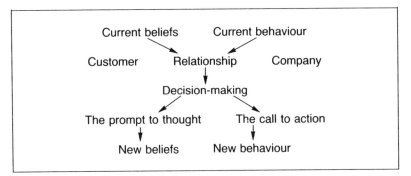

Figure 9.3 Interactive advertising: changing behaviour by intervening directly in decision making

— the prompt to thought: to intervene in the decision-making process and to prompt a change in current beliefs

— the call to action: to offer a reward for the customer's interest, to demonstrate access and responsiveness, and to affect customer behaviour directly.

Most image advertising is less effective than it might be because it concentrates on a long-term change in beliefs, to the exclusion of any immediate effect on behaviour. In every market advertising should aim for short term effects, to increase sales among customers currently in the market. The call to action is an invitation and reward for these customers. To change established beliefs takes time. The change in belief arises either from persuasion over time – the role of the prompt to thought – or as a result of behaviour – the customer's direct experience of the brand. The advertising's long-term effects work both through beliefs and behaviour.

So sometimes the prompt to thought and the call to action lead to an immediate response, but even where they do not the advertising can affect behaviour, especially in Type IV markets. I have already quoted the results of the Interactive Marketing Group's campaigns for habitual purchase of fast moving consumer goods brands, in which immediate sales increases were recorded for customers who were exposed to the advertising, but who did not respond. In these markets it is easy for customers to make immediate purchases on their next store visits, and these purchases are the equivalent of a direct response.

Direct response advertising is a subclass of interactive advertising and is of most value in markets with complex decision-making and variety-seeking, where the interval between purchases is extended, and where direct communications to customers before they enter their purchase windows can add value, raise brand preference and increase sales.

Computer manufacturer Unisys has run a high profile advertising campaign, inviting companies to evaluate their ability to 'customerise', with the whole advertisement consisting of a questionnaire. The questionnaire is a powerful prompt to thought: potential business customers of Unisys are motivated to consider how well their companies perform, and to reconsider their thinking on the role of information technology in that performance. The advertising is clearly designed to differentiate Unisys, by associating the Unisys brand with the business value of the customer interface – the theme of this book.

Car manufacturers intervene in the decision-making process and try to win brand preference before the customer enters a showroom. It will pay them to invest more in direct response because the resulting database is a private channel of communication to prospective buyers.

In markets with positive choice and habitual purchase, the other sources of name generation are more effective in producing direct response from high value customers. By featuring the Persil Careline, Unilever is making its advertising interactive and creating a channel of communication through which it can communicate:

— help to customers who have experienced problems with their washing

— advice to customers on the treatment of special garments and materials

— recommendations and added value offers on washing machines

— information on new product formulations, and the role of different Persil products for different clothes.

The use of a Careline could have averted many of the problems encountered by Unilever in the launch of the new Persil and Omo Power formulations.

Persil has also featured a promotional offer in advertising. This might have been communicated better by targeted promotion to light users of Persil and users of competitive brands.

The exceptions to the rule that direct response advertising is not for habitual purchase markets are 'Direct Challenge' and 'Direct Prospecting' advertising, where the objective is to generate the names of competitive users.

Advertisers are recognising that an important factor in television's decline is the medium's passivity. Interactive advertising is simply more powerful. Advertising once said to the consumer: 'Don't just sit there – watch and think!'. Interactive advertising says: 'Don't just sit there – do something, learn and tell us what you think'.

New Interactive Response Media

Most interactive advertising is a mix of image and direct response in print and broadcast media, with response by mail and telephone. With changing technology and economics, new media and response methods will emerge. I classify six overlapping forms of interactive response media: remote interaction, electronic response, on-demand information, on-site advertising, scanning and live interfaces.

The creative skills for the interactive advertising of the future will require the ability to hold the customer in a dialogue, and an understanding of all aspects of the human/computer interface.

Interactive response media

Remote interaction: Hand sets enable television viewers to send back signals through a cable, telephone or satellite link

Electronic response: PCs linked to on-line networks; also mobile telephones and portable PCs, making radio, for example, a more attractive medium

On-demand information: Touch tone telephones are a basic form of menu selection, but advertisers will increasingly set up on-line databases of information, products and services for customers to interrogate

On-site advertising: New electronic shopping kiosks are in test in retail outlets and in other sites with high levels of through traffic

Scanning: Personalised smart cards can download and upload data between company and customer; bar code readers are already used for research surveys, and could become a way of tracking customer transactions

Live interfaces: Live contact with advertisers and their staff though PC–video systems; the customer can not only see the advertiser's staff, but can be shown live information and products displays

---

Short Form Television Advertising: DRTV

Reader's Digest Music used direct response television advertising (DRTV) as well as press at a time when the independent television channels in the UK were experimenting with 'per inquiry' (PI) advertising. The commercials we created followed the received wisdom for direct response television.

Direct response television	
Length:	at least 60 seconds, and ideally 120 seconds
Introduction:	primes the viewer by establishing that this is a response commercial, and may introduce the offer
Message:	sequence is product, offer and call-to-action
Voice over:	must include offer and call-to-action
Call to action:	repeated several times, and ideally on screen for at least 20 seconds

American Express advertising in the US illustrates the difference between image and direct response. The company has always featured its free 1-800-THE CARD number at the end of its television advertising, only for a few seconds and without reference in the voice over or a call to action. The response is only a trickle of new card applications. But by creating 60 and 120 second direct response commercials, American Express has been able to generate over 200 000 new card applications annually.

Where television is used to engage customers for established brands, and for frequently purchased brands in particular, the received wisdom about the format of commercials may no longer be relevant. Short response commercials, sometimes as brief as ten seconds, can generate volume response if they use a memorable telephone number, are run frequently and are supported by image advertising. Ideally, short DRTV commercials are run within the same commercial breaks as the image executions.

In the US, leading advertisers have experimented with commercials that 'wrap' direct response messages around the image commercial. In the simplest form, an announcer opens the message by saying that he or she is about to show a commercial for an interesting brand, and encourage the audience to look out for an offer and to get ready to take down a telephone number. The short image film runs and the announcer makes the call to action. These hybrids are inelegant but illustrate the possibilities for shorter and more cost-effective DRTV.

Long Form Television Advertising: Infomercials

In the US, a new long form of television advertising has developed: the infomercial. The growth of this format results from the availability of low cost airtime on cable and satellite channels, but major advertisers are increasingly experimenting with infomercials because of the wider marketing opportunities.

The infomercial is a hybrid, information commercial. The infomercial advertising format is typically thirty minutes in length, and is driven by the advertiser's desire to communicate more information than is possible in a traditional fifteen to sixty minute length film. Infomercials have been used to market complex and high price products: direct response infomercial users, for example, have included Nordic Track, the makers of exercise equipment.

The infomercial is a powerful way of launching a new product: one of its most dramatic uses has been for innovative household products like electric juicers – harking back to the early days of DRTV when most of the advertised products were unusual appliances sold to housewives. A leading infomercial user has sold over 100 000 juicers direct and close to 1 million through retail. Experienced users of infomercials predict that from three to ten times as many sales are generated from retail sales as from direct response.

Car maker Saturn tested a half hour format 'Spring in Spring Hill', while Volvo used the extended time to provide testimony to drivers who owed their lives to the cars' safety engineering. Telephone companies have tested infomercials to communicate complex telephone equipment and the increasingly sophisticated range of optional services. Holiday company Club Med has used an infomercial to communicate the experience of its resorts, filming customer testimonials at the resorts. Even retailers have used infomercials to promote specific products – Sears, for example, has tested an infomercial for a high priced vacuum cleaner.

Infomercials have been used by major brands with a wide product portfolio or an interesting product story. Braun's infomercial 'What's New in the Kitchen' featured a range of its domestic products. Fragrance and cosmetics manufacturers have tested infomercials, using them as extended product demonstrations. SmithKline Beecham created 'The Good Night Show' for its over-the-counter sleep aids for insomniacs.

The American Medical Association created an infomercial, 'How to Quit', to advise smokers how to stop and to promote an anti-smoking kit available direct and in retail.

Infomercials thus have a range of marketing roles:

— communicate information

— educate consumers

— generate direct response

— achieve major impact

— penetrate new markets

— create a marketing event

— add brand value.

In creating long form advertising, the experience is that while media costs are a major factor, the production costs are less of a barrier. The incremental cost of a thirty minute film over a thirty second commercial can be small.

Long form advertising has wider applications. The BBC Select service was something of a pioneer in this respect, with plans to offer doctors and other special interest groups special programming, downloaded overnight to their video cassette recorders. With the growth in the number of channels and the fragmentation of the audience, long form will become more interesting. A major opportunity is to broadcast to employees who are distributed geographically, and to agents and dealers.

Summary: The Creative Brief

The creative brief for interactive advertising is a natural development of the brief for image advertising, encompassing the prompt to thought and call to action.

A way of summarising the change is that advertising must communicate the *'human face'* of the company. There should be a seamless transition from advertising through the management by the company of the customer's response, to the delivery of information to the customer and the opening of the relationship with a customer. Interactive advertising will not lack in imagination, as the battle to attract and to maintain the customer's interest will be fiercer than ever in the future. But by delivering more information and providing more service to customers, advertising will support decision-making that is more rational and more accountable.

The brief for interactive advertising should incorporate all potential contacts with the customer – a new challenge for advertising planning and creativity.

From image to interactive advertising

Content of the Brief:	Changes to make the advertising interactive
Product:	Encompasses company as well as product
Target audience:	Characterised by current behaviour and brand usage as well as demographics
Proposition:	Includes company and staff as well as product attributes
Prompt to thought:	Imaginative engagement of customers through one or more of: contact affinity reward extra value service
Call-to-action:	Invites response Rewards response Collects data
Media:	Includes all general media and relationship-building contacts: mail, telephone and face to face between customers and company staff, i.e. a complete customer track

CREATING INTERACTIVE MAIL 10

**'The only medium that can make a
personal approach'**

Attitudes to Direct Mail – The Junk Mail Syndrome – The
Qualities of Interactive Mail – Brand-building Mail – Relation-
ship-building Mail – Customer Publishing – Interactive
Electronic Mail – The Mail Future

Attitudes to Direct Mail

Writing forty years ago in *How to Sell Successfully by Direct
Mail*, John Cassels says: 'Direct mail is the only advertising
medium that can make a personal approach'.[1] Direct mail is
at the same time an old medium and the first of the new
interactive media. From direct to electronic mail is a technological, not a marketing leap. How customers receive and
use direct mail by post is relevant to the future of all personalised communication media.

The traditional direct mail format was developed to a fine
art by direct marketers, in particular by *Reader's Digest*. In
the Direct model the role of mail is to sell: to acquire new
customers and cross-sell to existing customers.

The traditional direct mail format

Envelope: Features prize draws and offers

Personalisation: Refers to area in which customer lives

Copy: Long copy, in letter and leaflet

Contents: Large number of individually designed items

Letter: Unpersonalised and up to four pages in length

Leaflet: Fold out, with product sell

Involvement: Games and gimmicks, e.g. 'scratch-offs', 'peel-offs'

Endorsement: Support to selling copy from company representative

Call to action: Often separate 'yes' and 'no' envelopes

Customer attitudes to direct mail have been conditioned by experience: they expect direct mail to sell, rather than offer help or advice; to promote an offer, rather than useful information; to advertise mail order catalogues, magazines, books and music, rather than leading brands. Experience of direct mail has created low customer expectations of the medium.

Direct mail volumes in Europe are low and vary enormously per head of household:[2] in 1991 the figures were 109 in Switzerland, 56 in Germany, 55 in France, 38 in the UK, and 23 in Spain. The closest comparable figure in the US, for households rather than heads of households, is 977!

The potential for direct mail in Europe is astonishing. Attitudes to direct mail are not conditioned, as is commonly feared, by over-mailing but by a lack of positive and enjoyable experience of the medium.

Research by the Direct Mail Information Service summarises attitudes to and usage of direct mail. The good news is that 89 per cent of UK consumers personally open all their mail and 68 per cent read the contents. Only 17 per cent say they would never respond or buy through the post, 85 per cent agree that companies should mail their customers, and 56 per cent agree that companies should mail to prospects information in which they are likely to be interested. At least 69 per cent agree that when direct mail is relevant and contains new information they feel more favourably about the company.

The bad news is that only 14 per cent agree that direct mail is informative, compared with 33 per cent for television and 43 per cent for press. Only 9 per cent agree that direct mail is honest, compared with 36 per cent for television and 30 per cent for press. Moreover, 40 per cent feel direct mail is intrusive, and only 9 per cent say that it helps people buy products of interest to them – the comparable figures for television and press are 46 and 33 per cent respectively.[3]

How are we to reconcile these figures with the overwhelming evidence that companies that mail their customers increase their retention and sales? Because the objective of most direct mail has been to achieve an immediate sale, the 'advertising' effect of direct mail has been neglected in favour of the 'promotional', and the personal relationship-building role forgotten in the desire to cut the cost per direct mail contact.

The Junk Mail Syndrome

Marketers new to direct mail need to understand the limitations of the traditional direct mail 'formula' and its inappropriateness for brand development and customer relationship-building. Whereas advertising uses imagination to communicate ideas, direct mail is literal. The format of direct mail offers the space to expand an advertising idea, but most creators of direct mail fall into the 'kitchen sink' trap. Most direct mail contains too many selling arguments, spread across different letters, leaflets and other inserts, and set out tortuously in long copy.

The creators of direct mail forget that marketing is an

exchange of values and information, that advertising is persuasion, and that customer motivations are a mix of the rational and the emotional. As a result, direct mail is patronising, leaves little to the imagination, and induces in most customers an overpowering sense of boredom.

Worst of all, most direct mail is impersonal – a damning indictment on the quality of a medium that is the only one, in Cassels' words, to enable a 'personal approach'. The impersonality of traditional direct mail is ironic in a medium which in theory is data-driven and one to one. In practice, most direct mail has been employed as another form of mass communication, direct mail successes have mostly been attributable to power rather than personalisation.

Finally, in this catalogue of uses and abuses, much direct mail plagiarises successful Direct Model techniques, but applies them to products and customer decision-making types for which they are inappropriate. I have seen the creative techniques used successfully to sell a £10 book applied to customer mail launching a £10 000 car. Unsurprisingly, research among car owners revealed that the result was to associate the manufacturer's brand with sales gimmicks rather than with distinctive added values.

Most direct mail has deserved the description 'junk' mail. In frequent group discussions I have watched customers recognise junk mail immediately by the signals that give it away, even before the envelope is opened:

— Mailsort postage insignia

— Cheap paper quality

— Errors in name and address

— No recognisable brand name

— Unanticipated and unsolicited.

I contrast junk mail with *interactive* and *relationship-building* mail.

The Qualities of Interactive Mail

Interactive mail is a communication that is selective and welcome, and that turns the recipient into a participant.

The marketing success of *Reader's Digest* lies primarily in the power of its direct mail to interact with customers and motivate their participation in the message: total *Reader's Digest* response rates exceed 40 per cent. *Reader's Digest* demonstrates the value of interactivity in general and non-order response in particular: the non-orderers who enter the prize draw but do not buy the product this time around have opened a relationship, even if it is tenuous, and are therefore good prospects for future products (Table 10.1).

It is instructive to examine the qualities of *Reader's Digest* mail – the envelope, letter copy and contents – to determine why it works, why it is so powerful, and how these qualities can be harnessed to build brands and customer relationships.

The envelope

Reader's Digest direct mail is undeniably *powerful*. Its impact starts with the envelope. Two tests illustrate the importance of envelopes:

(i)   Changing the colour of an envelope from white to yellow stock, with no other change in the package, increased

Table 10.1 Typical *Reader's Digest* response rates: acquisition of new magazine subscribers (percentages)

	Order response (%)	Non-order response (%)
Prospects	10	20
Customers	15	25

sales by 40 per cent: yellow is a 'live' colour and the package stood out in the mail

(ii) A new envelope originally tested for the US magazine was adapted for the UK, increasing sales by over 30 per cent; its important features were its buff paper (authenticity), official copy (credibility), prize draw preview (attention), promise of offers (anticipation), and a perforated tear off opening (convenience): versions of this envelope are still in use ten years later.

There is a common misconception that the objective of the envelope is to motivate opening, yet as research confirms, most envelopes are opened anyway. The misconception results in two forms of error: many financial institutions use 'private and confidential' for mass mailings, and many direct marketers who should know better believe that the envelope should carry no copy at all.

The objective of the envelope is that mail is opened with interest and *anticipation*. In years of testing I have never encountered a situation where special envelopes do not achieve superior results – if they are relevant to the customer and appropriate to the brand.

The letter

Reader's Digest letter copy illustrates the principles of selection and *privilege*. The recipient feels specially singled out for the message and the reward.

One example of privilege, and a significant breakthrough in response, was the 'Three Stages' copy, first tested in 1981 in one of my campaigns. The copy describes how the customer has successfully passed through the first two stages of the prize draw: the selection of the customer's name and the issue of the customer's personal prize draw numbers. All that is required is that third stage: the customer to return his or her numbers to enter the draw.

Over ten years later, 'Three Stages' is a mainstay of *Reader's Digest* direct mail copy – and of television support advertising scripts. Nothing exemplifies better the power of selection and privilege in copy: as the introductory copy in a recent *Reader's Digest* mail package says: 'many people eliminate themselves, by failing to return their numbers in time for the draw'.

Direct mail letters should say, in summary:

— why the customer has been selected

— what is the occasion, for example the event, signal or anniversary

— what is the purpose of the message

— how the customer should respond

— what reward and values the customer can gain for responding.

Unlike *Reader's Digest*, however, brands should offer real benefits associated with selection. And so a feature of effective copy is *personalisation*, used to substantiate the privileges offered. The most effective form of personalisation is to refer to previous purchase history, for example in 'thank you' mailings to recent buyers. Other examples of effective personalisation are new customer status ('welcome') and lapsed customer status ('we've missed you').

Contents

Reader's Digest success in the mail owes much to *participation*, and a typical direct mail package has several participation devices, usually peel-off labels or scratch-off mystery gift cards. The benefits of the promotion and the features of the offer are always presented in an interesting format, like a booklet of personalised tickets. *Reader's Digest* mail is not read passively: you have to do something with it. At *Reader's Digest*, we were also among the first to use questionnaires to learn more about customers, and questionnaires are another form of participation.

Interactive mail with these five qualities demands a

The five qualities of interactive mail

Power

Privilege

Personalisation

Participation

Personality

---

response – even if it is a 'no'. Every company needs to evaluate how to harness the power of mail to interact with its customers.

Brand-building Mail

My first experience of working with a consumer brand was with the Elida Gibbs division of Unilever. At Ogilvy & Mather Direct we developed a direct mail programme to promote a line extension for the Impulse body spray brand. The target audience was previous Impulse promotional responders and selected consumers in the brand's demographic heartland. The campaign illustrated the characteristics of brand-building direct mail.

The objective of an envelope is to 'prime' the target audience, and the Impulse outer envelope promised 'Something special for your skin', with an attractive illustration of a flower. Research confirmed the copy, and design created an accurate expectation of a message about cosmetics or fragrance. A one-page letter introduced the new product and a spokesperson for the brand. Brands short-cut communication, and direct mail for well-recognised brands, does not need extensive copy.

A PS in the letter invited Impulse users to write in with their news and stories – making the company and its staff accessible. Thousands replied, without incentive, revealing the interest in associating with the brand.

At the same time as direct mail, television presented the new product through a film about a journey on the Orient Express, and direct mail developed the story, written in the first person from the viewpoint of a customer. The product story was contained within a more interesting description of the journey. There were two calls to action:

(i) Personalised coupons for the customer to try the new product

(ii) A competition which invited the customer to nominate what was most important to her in beauty.

The competition was relevant to the Elida Gibbs brand portfolio, and responders to the competition received a thank you letter and – as reward – further coupons.

Research showed that over 90 per cent opened and read the package, over 80 per cent recalled the key aspects of the new product message, over 40 per cent claimed an intention to try the new product. The immediate result was that over 30 per cent of mailed customers entered the competition, and a brand relationship was developed with triallists, participants in the competition, and the many customers who wrote unsolicited letters.

Characteristics of interactive mail

Envelope:	recognition, privilege, and engagement
Letter:	opening copy that explains selection and privilege
Leaflet:	information new and helpful to the customer
Copy:	from a real person, a brand spokesperson
Reply:	simple and customer-friendly
Response:	invite every form of response

Relationship-building Mail

In the folklore of direct mail long copy sells. This is true to the extent that enough information must be conveyed to substantiate the brand proposition and to involve customers in brand values. But with time at a premium, and advertising intensity on the increase, customers welcome simplicity and clarity. With the decline in literacy, moreover, visual images will become more important. Brands have well-recognised attributes, and it is inappropriate and unnecessary to repeat these in every contact with brand users. Many are low price, and so the barriers to purchase are lower. And since the purchase may be made later in a retail outlet, it is inappropriate to emphasise a direct call to action.

The most important but most neglected aspect of direct mail is personalisation. The more closely a message is related to the individual reader, the higher the customer's appreciation and response. As many elements of mail communication as possible should be personalised, in particular the letter, the offer, the call to action and the contents. Powerful personalisation includes reference to:

— previous contact or purchase

— lack of previous contact or purchase

— time since first or last contact or purchase

— sales person or retailer with whom the customer has a relationship

— customer interests previously identified.

Traditional direct mail has a single-minded call to action: 'reply within 14 days' is the familiar instruction. But to build brands direct mail that is welcome will invite the customer's participation and *any* form of response. Even if the primary objective is to sell, any response should be encouraged because every contact with customers is an opportunity to build relationships.

'Negative' response should be encouraged:

— to allow customers to confirm and explain their lack of interest: they may after all be interested in future and it is valuable to identify this

— to determine customer interest in other related products and services, creating other sales opportunities

— to collect customer data

— to record changes in customer status and changes of address

— to allow customers to decline to receive future communications.

Interactive mail builds the customer relationship:

(i) by reinforcing and developing brand values

(ii) by reflecting the personality of the company and its staff

(iii) by inviting the customer's involvement and association with the brand, emphasising access and service

(iv) by motivating the customer to take a further step in the relationship, increasing loyalty and lifetime value.

This is quite a task for any single communication and a common fault in direct mail is to try to do too much. In the design of customer tracks different direct mail executions should be created for prospecting, acquisition, cross-selling and relationship-building.

Direct mail and prospecting: advertising plus response

The prospecting objective is to identify new high value customers and encourage them to volunteer information about themselves. The classic form of prospecting mail is simple: a letter, and a questionnaire and/or invitation for response.

Car manufacturers use prospecting to add the owners of

competitive marques to their databases. In its first work for Peugeot in 1988, my agency, DMB&B Direct, ran a prospecting programme to validate a database, mailing questionnaires that generated a response rate of over 20 per cent. The data was used to target specific sales activities, including the launch of a new estate model, for which we were able to identify 20 000 confirmed estate prospects from a database of over 500 000.

Several years later, a prospecting campaign helped to launch the new 106 model. A direct mail package to selected competitive car drivers invited them to guess which award-winning manufacturer was about to launch a new car which had style and quality, was a breakthrough in design, and offered irresistible driving pleasure. The identity of the manufacturer was only revealed in the shape of Peugeot's 'Lion' on the invitation form. The invitation was protected by delivery in a square 'box', standing out in the mail. The high response rate built a list of new prospects for dealers to invite to the launch events. This is an execution through the mail of Direct Prospecting.

Prospecting combines an advertising message in print with the involvement of ä uestionnaire. The importance of the advertising message is illustrated by a campaign for health insurer BUPA, the UK market leader. The target audience were households new to BUPA, but with demographic and lifestyle characteristics matched to BUPA's ideal high lifetime value new customer profile. The problem was that BUPA was the sector generic, and the company's superior products and services were not well appreciated. The challenge was to confront established beliefs about the company and several propositions were tested. In the test, the winning proposition increased the leads generated significantly, and in research even non-respondents reported that the mail changed their view of BUPA and their understanding of health insurance.

In business-to-business prospecting, the physical impact of the mail must be higher to compete for the decision-maker's attention. Software company Oracle prospected successfully for IT directors who were unwilling to respond to a straight sales call. The mailing was a metal can with a distinctive label carrying copy: 'All we can offer in exchange for your time is peanuts.' The can contained the promised peanuts and a questionnaire, and prompted interest from a significant number of IT directors in major companies.

Direct mail prospecting combines an interest-status or immediate challenge advertising message, with a questionnaire and call to action.

Many companies use mail to sell when they would be better advised to prospect first. Prospects often need more information before they are ready to buy, and need to learn about the company before they are ready to choose it as a brand.

Because direct mail is so powerful, the response rates in prospecting are high and in my experience can exceed 70 per cent.

Direct mail and acquisition: power and personality

Copy and visuals to create anticipation about the contents of direct mail before it is opened are vital. When communicating to non-users, or to prospects with whom there has been no previous relationship, it is generally more effective not to reveal the brand name on the envelope. This is especially true for low involvement brands in mature markets.

In the UK, for example, Pedigree Petfoods mails cat owners who use its Whiskas brand messages about Whiskas in clearly branded envelopes, but messages about its premium brand Sheba in envelopes that 'prime' the cat owner to expect something different, but do not reveal the brand name. These are small square envelopes, printed on quality parchment stock, used by Pedigree to invite users of other brands to sample Sheba. The envelope copy refers to an occasion – Sheba offers have been mailed on Valentine's day, at Christmas and on the cat's birthday.

When communicating a message about a brand to prospects with whom there has been a previous contact or relationship, the brand should be signalled on the envelope.

Land Rover invited qualified prospects to test drive their new model year vehicle by mailing a box containing a booklet, *The Joys of Motoring*. The copy on the envelope is: 'The Directors of Land Rover Great Britain request the pleasure of your company at a most refined occasion.' The invitation is confirmed on a card which is also a bookmark. The special booklet adds value to the relationship. Car manufacturers have experimented with high impact direct mail, with videos based on film of new models, and with interactive computer disks with new model details and specifications.

A feature of the use of direct mail to acquire new customers is that a mailing *series* may be necessary. A 1993 US Echo award-winning campaign to market SmartFood popcorn in the US used three mail contacts: two colourful postcards as 'advance' notification, followed by a box with a free sample and feedback questionnaire.

Direct mail and cross-selling: recognition and reward

Direct mail to cross-sell starts with an envelope that gains immediate recognition from the customer, and previews the reward.

American Express cardmember mail illustrates cross-selling. An example is the launch of a cardmember offer of a 'Far West Festival', in partnership with Euro Disney. The envelope is a distinctive, 'portrait' design, and buff in colour to differentiate it from regular cardmember communications. The copy reads: 'American Express invites you to participate in an exceptional event.'

When the challenge is to cross-sell a range of brands, a solution is to create a new 'umbrella' brand for the programme, like the Kraft General Foods mailing programme 'What's Hot' cross-selling brands for families with children, or Sears with its 'Mature Outlook' programme for older customers. Another US award-winning campaign for the Eckerd drug company consisted of a series of mailings with envelope headed: 'Especially for Eckerd Care60+ customers', 'Especially for Eckerd DiabetiCare customers', and 'Especially for Eckerd BabyCare customers'.

Previous purchase personalisation is particularly important and effective in cross-selling. One of the most successful mail campaigns on which I have ever worked was for the Royal Mint. To previous buyers of a special coin we mailed an offer of a second, with the copy line on the envelope: 'To buyers of the Welsh Variant Coin, be the first to acquire the Scottish variant.' We customised the envelope, and sales were over 70 per cent.

Direct mail and relationship-building: locking in the customer

At the other end of the Spiral of Prosperity, direct mail has an important role to play in the development of customer loyalty.

Role of direct mail in relationship-building

Thank You

Welcome

News

Keep in touch

Feedback

A 'thank you' message can increase repeat purchase rates without offers or incentives. An illustration of 'thank you' mail comes from the Wells Fargo bank in California. A small friendly envelope announces itself as 'just a note', and inside a card is personally signed by the manager of the bank branch – not by some anonymous head office functionary.

A *Reader's Digest* test of a 'thank you' card to all previous buyers of Music increased sales by almost 20 per cent. We included the card in our continuous stream of mailings to recent buyers, in which we matched the most relevant next offer for each customer.

British Airways Executive Club members receive regular mail. Consistent features are *Executive News*, which combines up-to-date information, new developments and special club member offers. In the summer of 1994, *Executive News* flagged the forthcoming relaunch of BA's European business class, Club Europe. A countdown to the relaunch date was begun with an advertisement reading: 'Ten, Nine, Eight, Seven, Six, and counting', which was also carried in the national press. Two weeks later, the countdown is completed on a specially designed envelope for the next Executive Club mailing, reading: 'Five, Four. Three, Two, One.' BA's customer communications are integrated as a programme, and combined with the airline's advertising.

BMW mails existing customers regularly. Major product developments are communicated by the manufacturer, while dealers are responsible for regular mailings about events, service and other relevant developments in areas like car security. A particularly customer-pleasing touch is an invitation to view new models at the dealership – even though customers may not be in the market for that model, or even ready to switch. The invitation, ahead of advertising, confirms that the customer is part of the BMW family.

An example of British Telecom customer communication is a summer offer to regular charge card holders. The envelope design highlights the audience for which it is intended, carries a summer theme and summarises the offer. A calendar for the summer adds some interest, drawing attention to the period of the offer.

BT has also used direct mail to restimulate a dormant or passive customer relationship. A mailing to non-users of its charge cards carried on the envelope the message: RSVP, and invited the charge card holder to say: Yes, Maybe, or Cancel.

Personalisation is a must in customer communication and greatly enhances the value added by mail. Here are a number of examples of how a supermarket, for example, could personalise its customer communications and build its customer loyalty.

Personalisation: illustration for a supermarket

By audience:

Welcome to our neighbourhood

We care about families – and we'll prove it

Remember our creche facilities . . .

By occasion:

Mondays are quiet, so we offer you . . .

Free coffee every Sunday morning . . .

By product:

Our new butcher is eager to meet you . . .

Try our new widget range – everyone wins a prize this week

We've changed since we last saw you . . .

Rapid delivery to our regular customers' homes . . .

By relationship:

You're busy – register to use our exclusive fast checkout lanes

For members of our valued customer programme . . .

Association

Bring a friend – both of you collect a voucher

Your invitation to our Christmas launch

Help us clean up the neighbourhood

Customers are more likely to buy from companies that 'keep in touch', and I am often asked the best frequency to write to customers. The only possible answer is as often as you have something interesting to say, beneficial to the customer and profitable for yourself.

After thank you, the next important words to a customer

are, in effect: 'How was it for you?' Direct mail is valuable in surveys of customer satisfaction and can be the start of data-driven cross-selling. Surveys or censuses should be repeated at regular intervals: to identify problems, to update the customer's status and substantiate the company's interest in the customer.

Customers are even more likely to buy more from companies that recognise them as individuals. I am also often asked what is the best way to keep customer data up to date. The answer is to ask customers to do it for you. Always invite an update on the customer's status and interest in your various products and services. Every contact is an opportunity to learn more, offer more and deepen the customer's association with the brand.

Customer Publishing

A particular form of mail is the magazine or newsletter. Despite the rapid development of specialised publications serving their industry sectors, more and more companies are developing their own publications. This is not 'vanity' publishing. It puts across the company's view without distortion or challenge by independent journalists. It intro-

---

Principles of customer publishing

Interest

Format

Information

Privilege

Personalisation

Contribution

People

---

duces products and offers in a 'non-selling' environment, and thus sells subtly. It keeps customers informed and makes them part of the company's community by inviting them to participate in the publication.

The successful customer publishing programme is one that develops customer loyalty rather than acting as a mouthpiece for company propaganda.

A basic interest in the idea of receiving the publication is essential. Before launching their 'Talk of the Trade' programme, Coca-Cola & Schweppes Beverages surveyed their independent trade customers to find out what form of contact was most welcome to them. A regular newsletter was a popular choice, from a list including visits by sales representatives and soft drink consultants, road shows, merchandising seminars and telephone calls.

Oxfam used to publish *Oxfam News*, a quarterly magazine. This was expensive and research confirmed that many supporters saw it as inappropriate. A lighter newsletter and a questionnaire invited supporters to nominate the information they would like to receive, and the frequency with which they would like to receive it.

Expensive magazine formats are often perceived by customers as unnecessarily lavish. More purposeful and economic newsletter formats convey a greater sense of current information, and can also be produced more cost-effectively. There is a significant opportunity to link the customer database to selective publishing technology, to customise the content to a segment, or even to individuals.

Apple Computer launched the newsletter *The Edge* to customers who had explicitly indicated an interest by response to surveys. *The Edge* illustrated several of the critical success factors in customer publishing:

— all issues were topical, related to imminent news and events, providing customers with genuine information from 'inside' the company

— customer contributions were solicited

— Apple personnel were introduced, to explain their roles and responsibilities

— each issue contained a special offer.

The best customer publications create a community between the staff of a company and its best customers in a new role as associates.

Full colour customer magazines of similar quality to full price publications can be effective where there are few alternative information sources available to customers. In the US, the 'Nine Lives' pet food brand used a magazine, *The Morris Report*, launched in 1987 with introductory copy that included: 'we want this to be your magazine'. The contents of the first issue illustrate the principles of customer publishing: 'news', 'letters', 'the Morris mart' (special offers), articles from contributors ('The History of Cats'), advice ('How to travel with your cat'), care ('The Art of Caring for the Elderly Cat'), book reviews, entertainment for adults ('Cat Folklore') and children ('The Baker's Cat's Kittens') – and customer stories. There is an invitation to customers to contribute, and special offers.

The Xerox *Best of Business* magazine illustrated customer publishing as an added value service. The magazine compiled and packaged the best current business writing for the convenience of senior management at Xerox customer and prospect sites. In the US, research revealed that the magazine had higher readership and interest than other business publications like *Forbes* and *Fortune*, illustrating how *Best of Business* built and added value to the customer's relationship with Xerox. The advertising effect was to associate Xerox with business strategy: to help Xerox enter decision-making in the board room.

Interactive Electronic Mail

Interactive mail services are not new, and in the computer and software industries have been available since the early 1980s. In the form of e-mail they have penetrated business office systems, supplanting paper-based memos and internal communications. Two forms of system have developed to offer interactive mail services to wider communities, and to create opportunities for electronic communication which could potentially supplant both media advertising and the postal system. The penetration of these systems is likely to be gradual and restricted to specific audiences, with the emphasis remaining in the business and academic world.

The first is a closed group with a service based on fees, like the US based on-line networks. While these services offer advertising, access to advertiser messages is made by users of their own volition. Advertisers can put their messages and their services on the system for a fee, and can flag their availability on the network, but they have no means of communicating directly to selected users. As yet there is limited ability to analyse the memberships of the on-line networks and select users likely to be interested in specific products and services. There is a paradox that the media cost of communicating on the networks is low, yet there is no apparent demand for advertising. This is the nightmare scenario for advertisers, who foresee a future where a potential high quality segment of their audiences is happy to pay a fee for information services on a network which will have no demand for advertising funding.

The other form of development is the Internet, an open system which has evolved as a free information exchange and dialogue – a natural development of the telephone. The early commercial use of the Internet has been unwelcome to users, who possess powerful sanctions against advertisers who in any way misuse the free access and unimpeded communication capabilities. The risk of 'flaming' – thousands of users retaliating against advertisers whom they perceive as misusing the network – should make any potential advertiser pause for thought. Unhappy network users can broadcast their disenchantment around the network, potentially destroying an advertiser's image and reputation immediately. 'The word on the Net' will be even more powerful than 'word of mouth'.

In the future, it is likely that on-line network users will be invited to register their interests in information. Users will programme their own 'agents', software tools that interrogate messages, search databases and select material and data of relevance to them. Advertisers will be able to reach customers when they create products, services or information relevant to the customer as an individual.

This is exactly how direct mail should operate: irrespective of data protection legislation, advertisers should invite customers to indicate their interests and to 'opt in'. The mail that results is welcome to users because they perceive it as being solicited by them.

The Mail Future

Mail will play an increasingly important role in future marketing communications and in customer tracks. For the sender mail is cost-effective, personal and highly responsive. For the recipient mail is relevant, informative and private. I predict rapid growth in the remainder of the 1990s both in direct mail through the postal system and in new electronic mail through closed user groups and open networks like the Internet.

Developments in data management and printing will permit mail to become more selective and personal. The emphasis will shift from mail campaigns to mail as an integrated component in the process of customer relationship-building.

Companies will also empower the staff in their customer teams to use mail to inform and keep in touch with customers. The fabled Joe Girard was for years the man who sold more cars than anyone else in the US. Girard was famous, long before computers, for building card index files about his customers and prospects, and using every event, holiday, and anniversary to mail them. Mail is a medium that can empower all customer-facing staff to make their own contributions to the customer relationship.

UNDER- STANDING 11 CUSTOMER BEHAVIOUR

'Advertising . . . one of the safest business ventures'

The Role of Testing – The Value of Testing – Test Designs – Customer Understanding and Qualitative Research – The Fusion of Data and Research – Customer Data – Customer Relationship Data – The Analysis of Customer Data – Customer Modelling – Summary: Building an Information Network

The Role of Testing

Marketing is generally held to be an uncertain investment. Even the editor of *Admap*, the magazine devoted to the research and quantification of advertising, confesses that advertising is inherently risky and asks: 'It is a truism that advertising, at least in the eyes of those who pay for it, seems chancier than virtually any other form of capital expenditure . . . will it work?'[1]

Contrast this with Claude Hopkins's view, expressed sixty years ago, of advertising as 'one of the safest business ventures'.[2] How far have we progressed since his time in predicting and measuring advertising effects?

Hopkins was working and writing during a time of simpler market structures, with mass distribution and multiple retailing in their infancy. Manufacturers employed agents to call on the small and independent retail outlets to whom they sold directly. There was no national advertising, only regional and local press. As the transfer of information across the country was slow, regional and local markets were isolated. Through their agents and sales forces, manufacturers gained direct feedback from the trade and from the trade's customers. Agents had personal relationships with retailers, who knew many of their customers as individuals. Information flowed back from customer to manufacturer.

Sales were measurable in each of the small areas managed by agents. Measurement enabled Hopkins and his peers to test different marketing in different areas and monitor the effect on sales. Trying different approaches in different areas enabled Hopkins to make the claim – outrageous today – that he had analysed and understood the causes and effects of advertising.

Advertising takes on the characteristics of a science when

The scientific advertising formula

(1) Analysis of customer behaviour to identify the main behavioural types

(2) Selection of customers by type

(3) Control of messages to different customer types

(4) Targeting of message by customer type

(5) Measurement of response of different customers to different messages

(6) Comparison of results to determine significant differences

(7) Prediction of the most effective advertising message and targeting

the message can be controlled – targeted – to selected customers, so that different messages can be tested and their effects measured and compared. The ability to test is a result of the ability to measure, and enables marketers to learn what works and what does not, and to optimise their marketing.

Mass marketing and multiple distribution have enabled manufacturers to reach large audiences at low cost. But by disrupting the flow of information back from the customer, manufacturers have surrendered control. In complex channels of distribution they are reliant on sales forces and agents for customer information and understanding, yet even with managed sales forces the flow of information is inefficient, and with independent agents or retailers it is non-existent. The greatest threat to manufacturers comes from retailers because they own the customer interface. As a result it is the retailer who ultimately controls everything shown and said to the customer, and it is the retailer who develops a greater understanding of the customer.

This knowledge is the source of market power. Multiple stores are test laboratories in which electronic point of sale systems provide retailers with instantaneous sales reports by category and brand. The information flow minimises stocking and optimises distribution, but the significant competitive advantage lies in the marketing arena: like Hopkins of old, retailers can measure the effects of product, merchandising, pricing and promotion, and determine the optimum mix by outlet. Some retailers can place new products in test stores and within hours evaluate the demand, incremental contribution and return on the investment in space.

Over the last sixty years, manufacturers have gradually surrendered the customer interface to retailers. Now, by developing direct relationships with customers, they can regain control of their marketing and collect the information that is essential for them to compete for the customer. A relationship strategy enables marketers to target and measure. They can test, learn what works and apply the lessons to improve their marketing effectiveness and profits.

Experiments can be designed to measure the effects of different marketing strategies in action, with different customer samples receiving different propositions. In a relationship strategy both communication to and response from the customer are individual and private. Testing can replicate exactly the 'live' marketing environment.

Testing reduces risk and uncertainty. The effects of marketing in general and advertising in particular can be tested, analysed and forecast with precision. Small investments in testing reduce the risks inherent in mainscale marketing programmes. In new product development, in particular, testing can represent the difference between success and failure.

The decisions taken as a result of testing are based on the response of customers. In a direct relationship customers exchange value and information, creating a feedback loop from customer to company. Every contact with the customer is an opportunity to collect information, and every response from the customer develops understanding – in particular different responses to different marketing stimuli. Making the right decisions becomes a matter of understanding and experience rather than of guesswork or opinion.

Testing makes decision-making more informed. At the same time, it develops marketers' intuition about their customers. By codifying and sharing their experience of customer response, marketers develop a fund of knowledge about customers that makes them more effective and becomes a valuable company asset.

Excellent marketers devote significant proportions of their budgets to testing, in some cases up to 15 per cent. It is their form of 'R&D', their investment in the future. Testing is an illustration of what the Japanese call *kaizen* – the commitment to continuous improvement. The excellent marketers test before committing to significant expenditure, and then 'reverse' test when they roll out their plans, to confirm the validity of their major decisions and gather information for the future. A successful test increases the return on marketing investment, so companies that do not test cannot be optimising their profits.

The Value of Testing

One of my early agency assignments was to test market a new product after a first test, conducted by another agency, had failed badly. Sharing a cautious view of the market with our client, we tested extensively: different target audiences, offers, calls to action and creative concepts. We staged the tests over several months to measure seasonality. The differences between the best and worst results for each marketing factor were significant and revealing.

Illustration of test results

(1)	the difference between the best and worst targeting	×6
(2)	the difference between the best and worst offer	×2.5
(3)	the difference between the best and worst timing	×2
(4)	the difference between the best and worst call-to-action	×1.5
(5)	the difference between the best and worst creative	×1.3

The results illustrate the importance of isolating marketing factors to measure their separate effects. Multiplying the differences, the best marketing plan was *fifty-eight times* more effective than the worst, certainly representing the difference between success and failure. The results also illustrate test priorities: targeting, offer, timing and call to action before creative. Creative is *not* unimportant, but creative effectiveness only makes a significant difference when the other marketing factors are optimised.

The value of testing lies in information and profit. At *Reader's Digest* all personnel have access to a worldwide library of test results, an asset that enables the company to launch new products with higher rates of success and faster

---

Variables to test in marketing

(1) Targeting: the target audiences and media

(2) Offer: the pricing, terms and incentives

(3) Timing: either the season, or the customer trigger

(4) Response: the method of customer engagement

(5) Creative: the copy and design

---

return on investment than could any competitor. As well as maximising profits, test information enables marketers to predict results, helping them to improve their company's operational planning, including production, distribution and cash flow.

A financial value can be assigned to testing, as an example illustrates.

Early in my career I designed the test marketing for a new book title, the most important to be launched by the company for some time. The proposed price point for the book was significantly greater than any comparable publication, and a test objective was to determine the resilience of the customer base to a higher priced product. Even so, the marketing manager held a view that the book could command an even higher price. He proposed that the test measured demand at three prices, and hoped to increased the perceived value of the book by offering it with a relevant premium. To meet his objectives I used a factorial design to measure the combined effects of price and premium. There were nine test samples: the three prices were each tested without a premium, and with two alternative premiums (Table 11.1).

The winning offer was *80 per cent more profitable* than the control, and only the factorial test design enabled us to identify it. Without any test, marketing judgement would have been to offer the book at the lowest price, and with a premium – a combination which would have achieved one of the least profitable results (index = 100). A conventional

Table 11.1 Illustration of factorial test design

Profit indices Control = 100	Low price	Medium price	High price
No premium	100	105	80
Medium-value premium	90	125	145
High-value premium	80	130	180

test of prices without a premium, or of different premiums at the lowest price, would have led to a launch offer of medium price without premium (index = 105). The test proved the marketing manager's hypothesis that the perceived value of the product/premium bundle was enough to command the significantly higher price.

Testing is an aid to, and not a replacement for, marketing judgement. Companies hungry to maximise their profits test, and keep testing. The *value of a test* is the additional profit resulting from the better marketing decision, less the cost of the test.

A decision to test can be treated as an investment and the return on the investment evaluated. How much to spend on testing is a function of risk involved: the costs of inaccurate targeting or suboptimal pricing are considerable, and so it is almost always desirable to test targeting and pricing. Statistical decision theory can be used to evaluate the investment in testing against the opportunity cost of less than optimal marketing decisions. Business and financial management can challenge their marketers to prove that they have assessed the risks and evaluated the costs of testing when they present their marketing budgets (Table 11.2).

Even companies with no requirement for direct mail as a strategic marketing medium should consider the use of mail

Table 11.2 The economics of testing: decision rules

	Predicted gain or loss	Probability
Before test:	Gain £750 000	0.5
	Loss £250 000	0.5

$$\text{Expected profitability} = 0.5 \times 750\,000 \\ - 0.5 \times 250\,000 \\ = £250\,000$$

After test:	Gain £600 000	0.9
	Loss £200 000	0.1

$$\text{Expected profitability} = 0.9 \times 600\,000 \\ - 0.1 \times 200\,000 \\ = £520\,000$$

The value of the test in increased certainty
or risk reduction is
£520 000 − £250 000 = £270 000

for testing, because it can be precisely controlled and its effects measured. The larger the sample size the more reliable the result, but the larger the sample the higher the cost (Table 11.3). A common failing in test design is the use of inadequate sample sizes, because to the statistical differences in results must be added the real-life variations which occur in the management of tests, any of which can increase the risk of making a wrong decision based on the results.

Testing involves two investments, in the cost of the test and in the loss of time required for the test and the analysis of the results. In my experience the very modest investment in testing will almost always pay back in higher profits. The major inhibition to testing is time: in many competitive marketing situations, the time required for testing may simply not be available. Even here, as I demonstrate below, there are testing methods which can be deployed quickly.

On occasion I have seen marketers afflicted by testing

Table 11.3 Illustration of test reliability and sample sizes: 95% confidence intervals (i.e. the actual result will be within the two bands 19 times out of 20)

Response rate =	5%	Lower band	Upper band
Sample size =	1 000	3.65%	6.35%
	2 500	3.86%	6.14%
	5 000	4.40%	5.60%
	20 000	4.70%	5.30%
	50 000	4.81%	5.19%
	200 000	4.90%	5.10%

Increasing sample sizes reduces risk more slowly

paralysis, unable to risk any decision without testing, and testing differences of no consequence: much 'creative' testing falls into this category. But in the vast majority of companies the problem is that they rarely test at all, take unacceptable risks with their marketing and often waste their budgets through imprecise targeting, ineffective offers and unappealing creative.

Test Designs

In the design of a test, the 'control' is the planned marketing mix, and the objective of the test is to beat the control. Some tests against a control – perhaps all – will fail, but even failures provide information.

The best test media are mail and telephone because they are the most controlled, as is the loose insert, a flexible and efficient method of testing media. Alternative test designs are:

— Wet tests: live direct mail, replicating real marketing: the customer is unaware of the test

— Dry tests: live direct mail, but testing products before committing to their production: customers who respond are offered a gift and an apology, but dry testing is now illegal

— Reservation tests: live direct mail: the customer is invited to 'reserve' a product for which production is planned, but the test objective is to determine the marketing plan and forecast volume before production is committed.

Other test methodologies overlap with quantitative research. Benefit testing, for example, uses mail and/or telephone questionnaires to measure customer response to alternative products, offers and premiums; or to invite customers to rank in order of appeal alternative added values and copy benefits.

I have always been astonished by how little research and testing is used to guide the selection of offers and the design of promotions. Research is often used to evaluate creative, yet offers and promotions can make a much greater difference.

A sample of the target audience can be invited, by a mailed questionnaire or a telephone interview, to rank a range of offers, gifts or premiums in appeal. The sample is also asked to consider how relevant to the brand is each of the offers. My experience is that test rankings predicts behaviour faithfully, another illustration of the value of involving customers in the direction of marketing.

A comprehensive testing plan using mail and telephone includes:

(i)   A questionnaire test, by mail with telephone follow-up, inviting customers to rank alternative propositions and concepts

(ii)   A further questionnaire test, with the winning proposition and by mail with telephone follow-up, inviting customers to rank features and benefits in order of their appeal

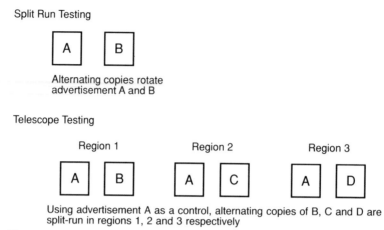

Figure 11.1 Media testing

(iii) A 'live' marketing test by mail of prices, offers and communication formats, copy and design: also used to forecast response from the mainscale marketing launch.

Testing can also be conducted in press and on television. Newspapers can 'split run' their circulations, with consecutive papers receiving different advertising copy. Regional tests can be conducted in many national press media, and on television, with control regions established as the benchmarks against which sales trends in the test region are measured (Figure 11.1).

A comprehensive test design for a brand manufacturer, developing a prospect database and direct relationships with customers for the first time, combines all of these elements (Figure 11.2).

Testing does not stop with a successful launch. The proportion of the marketing budget devoted to testing is a benchmark of a company's customer orientation and forward thinking.

Name generation

Area 1		*Area 2*	
Concurrent TV		*No concurrent TV*	
Direct response	Promotion collection	Promotion sampling	Lifestyle data
Inserts	Offers	Offers	Source
Press	Media	Location	Selections

Evaluation on cost per qualified prospect

Segmentation into brand users and prospects, and into high
and low potential

Tests

Offer tests	Response tests	Timing tests	Creative tests

Evaluation on new customer acquisition cost, and projected
customer lifetime value and return on marketing investment

Figure 11.2 Brand test schematic

Customer Understanding and Qualitative Research

Testing is invaluable because it measures how many customers respond to differing marketing stimuli, but testing alone cannot tell why customers respond or which customers respond. The 'why' is answered by qualitative research, and the 'which' by customer analysis.

Research is appropriate at all stages of development of a relationship strategy, but essential to two aspects of strategy in particular:

(i) Engagement: overcoming inertia and inhibitions and motivating customers to participate in direct relationships with the companies that market their brands

(ii) Involvement: planning and delivering the added values that change customer behaviour and increase loyalty to their brands.

In addressing these objectives, the role of research is to make customer communications welcome and helpful, as leading UK qualitative researcher Michael Herbert observes:

> Qualitative research can raise response rates, and lower the alienation of non-responders by making communications more relevant and helpful to the customer. Qualitative research can get you closer to the customer in two ways. It can help you relate your specific message to the customer's beliefs and needs. And it can help you understand how the message itself is received and how it might help the customer in his or her decision-making.[3]

A research plan for relationship management asks the customer to consider:

— contact: how would I like to hear from this brand, and what information would be helpful to me?

— affinity: what could this brand do to help people like me?

— rewards: what would I expect to receive as one of this brand's best customers?

— extra value: what other benefits and services would be helpful to me when I buy and use this brand?

— service: what can this brand do to improve its service to me?

Throughout, research evaluates customer perceptions of the personality of the brand and customer expectations of the people who represent the brand. A 'laddering' technique can be used to explore how customers will develop closer relationships with companies (Figure 11.3).

In the development of direct relationships, the delivery of the message is as important a subject for research as the content. A caveat: in direct mail, qualitative research cannot predict what will work. Customers do not admit to the

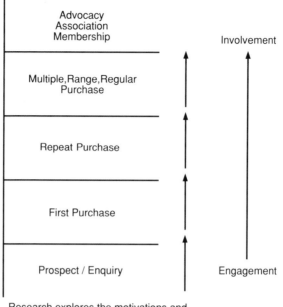

Figure 11.3 Laddering

desire to win money or buy cheaply, so they minimise the effects of prize draws and discounts on their behaviour.

Direct mail research should explore production values, envelope signals, flow of the message from the envelope through the package, letter copy, visual appeal – and, overall:

— comprehension of the salient elements of the message

— the power of the message in prompting thought

— the effectiveness of the call to action.

Research into direct mail reveals general truths: clarity and honesty are paramount; quality and visual differentiation are vital but neglected; humour and 'cleverness' are dangerous; content must contain new information; and offers must be meaningful. The message must start with current customer perceptions and it is effective to create different messages, even different envelopes, for different target audiences.

Issues to explore in direct mail research

Envelopes

— initial signals they communicate to the recipient

— perceptions created when the company or brand is revealed

— appropriate size

— appropriate colour(s)

— level of design, if any

— addressing: window or 'closed face' – labels are to be avoided

— type of postage and the postage insignia.

Letter

— length of the letter

— strength of opening paragraph

— communication and comprehension of the copy

— tone of voice

— language and vocabulary

— signatory.

Leaflet

— visual appeal

— effectiveness of product or service description

— comprehension and take-out of features and benefits.

Reply invitation

— ease of use

— perception of value offered

— expectations created of delivery or general customer service.

General

— signposting of package

— perceived company and brand values

— customer intent to 'engage' or become 'involved'.

Qualitative research is invaluable in guiding language, tone and presentation. For modest investment and with skilled interpretation, research measurably increases customer response and sales. A comprehensive programme for the development of relationship strategy includes research and testing in complementary roles.

Research and testing plan

(1) Initial quantitative research (telephone or mail question- naire) to estimate the size of the market, and the elements of the customer decision-making process

(2) Initial qualitative research (group or depth interviews) to probe customer motivations, the competitive frame, and the potential for added value through relationships

(3) Further qualitative research (group or depth interviews), with relationship-building concepts as stimulus, to test customer response to different propositions, and to evaluate their perceived relevance to the brand

(4) Quantitative research (mail questionnaires and/or telephone interviews) of the most promising proposi- tions, incentives, and copy

(5) Testing of marketing communication of developed con- cepts (direct mail and other direct media)

(6) Testing of data sources, and modelling of customer potential for targeting (direct mail and other direct media)

(7) Tracking on non-response, and effects on awareness, image and intention-to-buy (telephone and direct mail)

With a background in direct marketing, I believe quantitative research and testing are vital to maximise profit, yet are badly neglected. I do not dismiss qualitative research. Early in my career at *Reader's Digest* we discovered from focus groups that our customers related to the description of the music of the great composers as 'classics' rather than 'classical'. By changing the tone of voice, language and the mood of the design we transformed our classical music sales.

Yet traditional marketing places too much reliance on qualitative research, which is not predictive. I agree with Kevin Clancy and Robert Shulman, authors of *The Marketing Revolution*, that: 'Focus group research has value from the perspective of giving insight into the language that consumers use, but it has no value when it comes to helping companies making multi-million dollar decisions.'[4]

By comparison with qualitative methods, quantitative research and live testing are predictive, and demonstrably increase profitability.

The Fusion of Data and Research

In the definition of the Market Research Society: 'Market research is the means used by those who provide goods and services to keep themselves in touch with the needs and wants of those who buy and use those goods and services.' A code of conduct ensures that the information collected in research is not used for selling. The practice of selling under false pretences, encouraging customers to lower their guard under the guise of research, is known by the unattractive term of *sugging*, and is expressly banned by the code.

In relationship strategy, data collection is transparent and conducted with the willing participation of the customer, who volunteers information in the expectation of a reward for expressing his or her needs and interests. The data collected is not valid as descriptive research, as respondents are self-selected and not representative of the market. Direct feedback from customer to company is prescriptive and an invaluable source of information: revealing problems and identifying opportunities.

Relationship data is collected only from customers who welcome a deeper relationship with the brand, while market research data is representative of all customers in a market – including those who have no interest in or value to the brand.

Strategy development involves the fusion of market and relationship data:

— initial research gathers data from a representative sample of the market

— analysis of the research sample reveals important customer beliefs and behaviour

— further analysis develops customer segmentation current and potential lifetime value, and drives targeting strategy

— in the market-place, data about important beliefs and behaviour is collected to determine the current and potential value of customers, and to assign them to the appropriate customer segment.

Customer Data

The growth in relationship management has fostered new sources of customer information. The richest sources of customer data lie in the consumer market, where they can be characterised as postal, geodemographic, lifestyle and commercial.

Data associated with the *postal* system is essential for the control of names and addresses (Figure 11.4). Intelligent name and address software processes names and addresses, corrects obvious errors, completes missing elements, and identifies and merges duplicates. Quality control is important: incorrect addressing and duplicate mail damage brand image. Name and address software is generally based on the Postal Address File (PAF), maintained and published

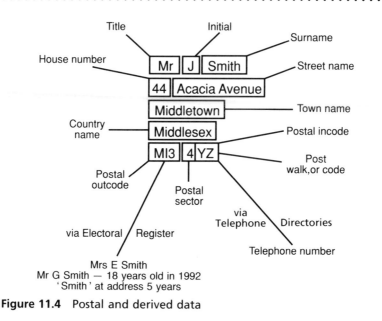

Figure 11.4 Postal and derived data

electronically by the Royal Mail. In the UK the Electoral Register, although not commercially available in all regions, identifies all adults at a household every October. Telephone lists can be matched to name and address lists to add telephone numbers.

In the UK, the Royal Mail has introduced barcodes, unique to addresses or delivery points, to automate the processing and delivery of mail. Barcodes help the coding of customer transactions, the control of customer identity and the tracking of customer behaviour on the database.

Geodemographic information systems (GIS) use the national census, combined with other data sets linked to postal geography, to profile and map small areas. GIS applications include site location, sales force coverage planning, media planning and local business potential analysis. When linked to name and address databases like the Electoral Register, geodemographic systems provide some targeting capabilities, but they are weaker than data sets that contain the specific characteristics and behaviour of households and individuals. Geodemographic data sets contain either:

— geodemographic codes, like Acorn or Mosaic, summarising the type of area

— specific geodemographic variables, like the penetration of teenagers, cars or professional workers in an area; by analysing their own customers against specific variables companies can build their own tailored versions of Acorn or Mosaic.

Syndicated data collection, built by mass market consumer questionnaires, is an opportunity to collect individual demographic and lifestyle data in volume and with shared costs. Brand marketers have the option of sponsoring questions about their product category on an exclusive basis. If no competitor has taken up that option, data can be rented, at lower cost but without exclusivity.

The major variables on syndicated databases are:

(i)	demographics:	age, occupation, income, and size, type and ownership of home
(ii)	lifestyles:	car ownership, travel patterns, credit card usage, and hobbies and interests
(iii)	category/brand usage:	use of products in a category and brand repertoires.

In the UK, the major syndicated databases are managed by National Demographics, Computerised Marketing Technologies (both subsidiaries of Polk in the US) and International Data & Communications. The sponsorship of syndicated data collection does not provide total market coverage and is biased towards households who respond to questionnaires. There is no interaction between the brand and the customer, so communication is unsolicited and response is lower than to other prospect sources.

The most powerful profiling systems integrate all the above data sources, and overlay the external data on internal data about a customer's identity, purchases and marketing contact history:

— identity: name, address, household composition
                 and telephone number

— purchases: recency, frequency, value, payment his-
                 tories and types of purchase

— contacts: recency, type, offers made, response
                 received.

Business data is analogous in structure, with the additional complexity of multiple decision-making units (dmu)
and corporate structures:

— multiple dmu: names, titles, responsibilities,
                          locations of all members of the
                          dmu – with telephone, fax and
                          e-mail contacts

— corporate structure: holding company and subsidi-
                          aries' names, addresses and tele-
                          phone numbers.

The equivalent of demographics, lifestyles and category/
brand usage are business profile, purchase behaviour and
category/supplier usage

— business profile: industry, revenue, work-
                             force size and composition

— purchase behaviour: purchasing process, tender-
                             ing, criteria, attitudes

— category/supplier usage: regular suppliers and pro-
                             ducts generally purchased.

Customer Relationship Data

In direct marketing, the received wisdom is that the important customer data is: recency, frequency and monetary
value of purchase (RFM). In a relationship strategy for
branded goods, this data is necessary *but not sufficient*.

For frequently purchased low price brands, the relationship objective is to win a higher share of the individual customer's repertoire. For infrequently purchased high price brands, the relationship objective is to motivate preference for and repeat purchase of the brand. Customers are people, and people matter more than data. The most important data is concerned with the brand and the customer relationship. Customer have always had relationships with a brand, and in learning more about customers, the important data to capture is association with the brand and willingness to respond directly to the brand's marketing. Data that describes the customer relationship is either *derived* or *directional*.

Derived data is, as the description suggests, based on analysis of the core data captured about customers. The analysis predicts the customer's value and behaviour. Derived data includes:

(i) A segmentation code, signifying the customer's potential

(ii) A product indicator, indicating its relevance to the customer
or
a profitability score for the customer and product

(iii) A timing for the likelihood of next customer purchase.

For banks I have built models to derive the timing of a mortgage customer's next house move, the next account that the customer is likely to open, and the expected return from a mailing to the customer. This derived data establishes triggers for personalised communication to customers.

Directional data is volunteered by the customer, and reveals:

(i) the customer's full brand repertoire

(ii) the customer's needs, interests and intentions.

Directional data is even more powerful than derived data: it is more direct to ask mortgage customers to indicate the

Table 11.4 The importance of data

Low	Secondary	Primary	Dominant
Geographic	Size	Brand repertoire	Source
Demographic	Income	Frequency	Interest
Lifestyle	Spend in category	Pattern	Participation

source of their current mortgage and their moving plans than to predict the event. The data is collected by questionnaires that can be included within every customer communication and dialogue, and updated by a regular census. The enquiry to the customer is a natural aspect of the relationship-building process (Table 11.4).

Most companies that have built customer databases have

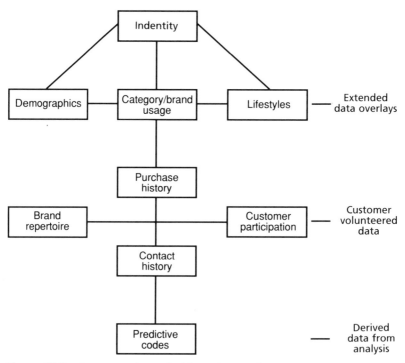

Figure 11.5 Consumer household: customer data structure

invested in the wrong data: external demographics and past purchases rather than the customer's current behaviour and interest in participation. Historical data is of value only where it helps make predictions about future behaviour. A relationship strategy builds a database as it markets, and asks customers to volunteer information and direct the marketing they receive as individuals (Figures 11.5 and 11.6).

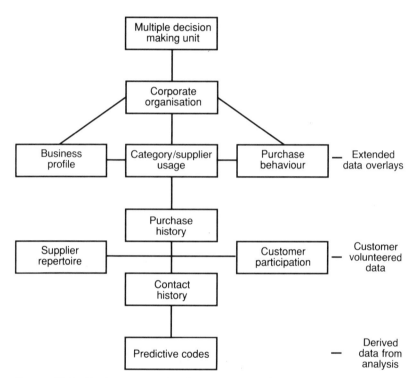

Figure 11.6 Business organisation: customer data structure

The Analysis of Customer Data

The analysis of customer data is typically organised in two phases.

In the first phase, all readily available data is analysed: this phase is usually dominated by response and transaction data, with the overlay of demographics and lifestyles. The analysis provides a profile of the current customer base, and a summary of its current behaviour and profitability, but is unlikely to identify the potential or the future behaviour of customers. In particular, this is because the data may not include competitive customer behaviour.

In the second phase, the data input to analysis is enhanced by the collection of directional data from customers and/or the derivation of data about customer potential and behaviour. The analysis provides a profile of current and potential lifetime value, and the development of a segmentation scheme to target marketing investment.

There are two kinds of data analysis technique:

(i) Descriptive analysis, for example cluster analysis which classifies customers into groups on the basis of similarities in their characteristics and behaviour.

(ii) Prescriptive analysis, for example multiple regression analysis which predicts the customer's propensity to respond to a marketing proposition or the customer's future lifetime value.

Comparison of data analysis techniques	
Descriptive	*Prescriptive*
qualitative	quantitative
meaningful labels	numbers
versatile	one-use
segments	special groups
over time	at one time

Just as I believe quantitative research is neglected in favour of qualitative, so I observe that marketers neglect prescriptive in favour of descriptive analysis. Quantitative research and testing has value as the basis for analysis

Tests of customer segments (% response/£1000 value)

		High value	Low value	Cost per contact
Tests of marketing investment	High cost	15% £9000	9% £3000	£6
	Low cost	5% (£1500)	4.5% £250	£2
	Lifetime value income for respondents	£100	£50	

Analysis of response

High value	Best	80%	17.75%	£1750
	Worst	20%	4%	(£2000)
Low value	Best	50%	7%	£1500
	Worst	50%	2%	(£1000)

Figure 11.7 Quantitative testing and prescriptive analysis: illustration of test design

of customer response to model behaviour and optimise targeting – further increasing profitability. It is the combination of testing and analysis that makes a relationship strategy 'one of the safest business ventures' (Figure 11.7).

The example above illustrates the power of customising the offer by customer segment:

— the power of prescriptive analysis in increasing profitability, by excluding unprofitable customers

— the increase in profit from matching marketing investment to the potential to increase lifetime value; the use of the high cost contact plan only for high value customers significantly improves profits.

The test design evaluates the effects of different levels of marketing investment on two customer segments, with high and low potential to increase lifetime value; the tests of marketing investment are a high cost promotion like a multiple contact plan with telephone vs. a low cost like a single mail contact

The profitability of the offer is $£ = LTV \times P - C$

where

— LTV is projected increase in lifetime value
— P is the response rate
— C is the promotion cost

The optimum contacts plans are then:

— high cost for high value customers: projection £9 per customer
— low cost for low value customers: projection £0.25 per customer

Analysis of response enables targeting within the two segments to achieve a further improvement in profitability and return on marketing investment:

— target: best 80% high value customers
            response 17.75% and projection £11.75 per customer
   exclude: remaining 20% high value customers
            response 4% and projection a loss of £2 per customer
— target: best 50% low value customers
            response 7% and projection £1.50 per customer
   exclude: remaining 50% low value customers
            response 2% and projection a loss of £1 per customer

Cluster analysis is useful in an early stage of development and helps describe the different types of customer. The analysis, however, should be linked to lifetime values and future behaviour, as a typical cluster analysis for a credit card illustrates (Figure 11.8).

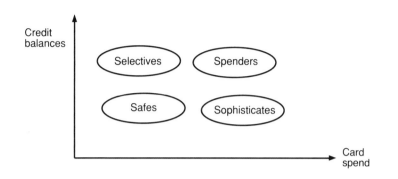

Spenders:	high spend/high credit balances young families
Sophisticates:	high spend/low credit balances older families, and higher income individuals
Selectives:	irregular spend/moderate credit balances older families, and lower income individuals
Safes:	low spend/low credit balances older families

Figure 11.8 Cluster analysis: four credit card clusters (characterised by behaviour, profiled by demographics)

Prescriptive analysis techniques predict customer behaviour and customer value, and are directly applicable to marketing planning. The data analysed includes the results of marketing as well as data about customers, and this 'dependent' data can include response and value. The starting point is exploratory data analysis to explore the relationships in the data, and in particular the customer characteristics that are correlated with response and value. The simplest technique is known as CHAID, and is an interactive process which breaks the analysis sample down into ever-smaller segments based on response or value.

Multiple regression analysis, discussed in Chapter 4,

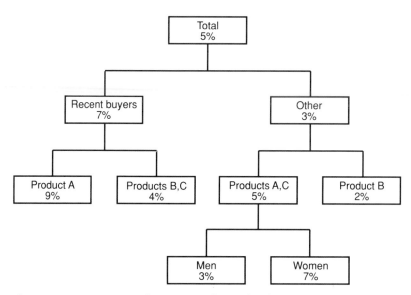

Figure 11.9 CHAID: exploratory analysis of a direct mail test

is the most popular of the techniques used to predict customer behaviour and value. The analysis of response or value derives a regression 'formula' or 'model' which 'scores' an individual customer to predict their response rate and profitability. The final result is a 'gains chart', relating the number of customers to predicted scores.

The gains chart is a decision-making tool: by setting a cut-off point for regression scores marketing can select customers for appropriate contact plans.

Variations on the basic regression technique include bayesian and logistic regression. Increased computing power has led to the development of data analysis algorithms that search through possible solutions for the best possible fit to the actual data. These algorithms, known as neural networks, can be trained to seek an ever closer fit to actual customer behaviour.

The analysis of data to target marketing is critical. It avoids wastage, by selecting the appropriate offers and behaviour for each type of customer. By comparing the likelihood of response and the potential customer value, different offers can be targeted to different customer types.

Customer Modelling

Analysis of the customers of a credit card illustrates the methodology in practice. At the time of analysis, the credit card was barely profitable, despite volume recruitment of new cardholders. For a credit card the customer behaviour which drives revenue is the size of spend and credit balance: the credit card company generates income from commission on spend and interest on credit balances. On the other side of the customer profitability equation, the cost of a credit card customer is made up of billing, administration and service elements.

I found that only 15 per cent of the credit card customers were profitable – and that these customers were responsible for over 120 per cent of the profits. The remaining 85 per cent of customers were unprofitable as their card usage was infrequent, or they always paid off their outstanding balances.

I profiled the customer base, segmented by level of spend and use of credit. Heavier spenders and higher credit takers had some common characteristics: they owned fewer credit cards in total (competitive behaviour in the product category) and were typically borrowers rather than savers (stronger relationships with the company). In contrast, non-users of the card were older and single, and lived in different geographic areas. The analysis reveals two important principles:

(i) Customer behaviour is more important than customer profile

(ii) Source of customer is an important aspect of behaviour.

The credit card recruited new customers through a variety of sources, and it was immediately apparent that source was an important factor: most of the profitable customers came from certain types of source.

The next step in analysis is to relate the customer base to the total market. This defines a framework for planning new customer acquisition.

Second phase analysis and research were conducted to predict potential customer value. The major factors in the potential value model were the household income and demographics of cardholders. To model potential value means measuring sales not yet made, or sales made with the competition. A database is no help here, as it records only current and not potential transactions.

For the credit card, we conducted two studies. First, we analysed the best customers, and built a targeting model to predict which of the non-users and the low spenders were most likely to use the credit card, and therefore most likely to increase their spend. We knew the competitive cards held (the data is captured on the application form), and the type and number of competitive cards held was an important factor in the model. Second, we mailed a research questionnaire, to identify the customers intending to use the card and their motivations for changing the credit card they preferred to use.

The targeting model and the research drove a marketing programme to activate selected non-users and low spenders.

Summary of credit card analysis

Analysis of customer behaviour by all variables to determine drivers of profitability

Segmentation of customer base into major behaviour types

Analysis of current and competitive customer segment profiles and values, relative to market sizes

Enhancement of customer data by research and questionnaires

Analysis of potential customer behaviour and values

Building targeting models, possibly for each segment, to predict potential value

Use of models to select customers within segments for appropriate contact to shift customer in low profit segments into high profit ones

---

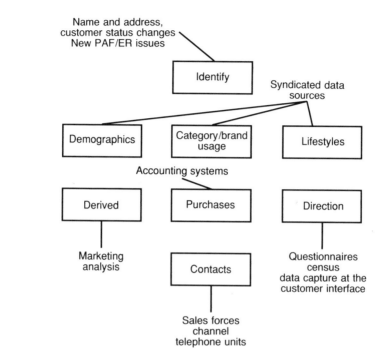

Figure 11.10 The information network

Summary: Building an Information Network

In Chapter 7, I introduced the concept of a relationship network, through which shareholders, employees and customer associates drive a brand message in the market-place and develop relationships with other customers. The internal counterpart of the relationship network is the information network (Figure 11.10), through which information flows back from the market-place to the company.

CONTROLLING MARKETING INVESTMENTS 12

'An annual audit and autopsy'

The Dynamics of Financial Decisions – Expenditure Planning – Marketing as an Investment – Investment in Customer Systems and Information – Calculating Customer Lifetime Value – Calculating Customer Relationship Costs – Modelling Marketing Investment – The Measurement of Marketing – The Primacy of Marketing in Business Strategy

---

The Dynamics of Financial Decisions

Finance and marketing are not natural partners. Financial management prefers to invest in assets of known value, but marketing objectives like brand image are intangible. Financial management dislikes risk and discounts forecasts which carry a significant level of uncertainty, but marketing is inherently speculative. Financial management deals in numbers, but marketing is not rigorously measured.

Financial management intuitively understands the importance of marketing, but is rarely presented with information to quantify the effects of marketing and justify the investments in brands.

In company accounts, marketing is treated as current expenditure. Some marketing activities like promotion

284

demonstrably affect current period sales – but many do not. Advertising in particular may have little effect on immediate sales, but no one disputes its contribution to longer term measures like market share and brand image. Although it is clear that the effects of marketing carry forward, there is no formal methodology for the allocation of marketing costs over time. Even the small number of companies that value brands on their balance sheets do not formally allocate their marketing expenditure to the capital value of brands.

As a result, marketing does not feature in capital budgets, and cannot compete effectively for capital allocation with investment in 'real' assets such as new factory equipment or computer systems. The treatment of marketing as current rather than capital expenditure has serious consequences for the funding of marketing.

Capital expenditure is planned in depth, usually well in advance of inclusion in budgets. The projected returns are scrutinised and purchase decisions subjected to careful analysis of the alternatives. Fixed costs are committed step by step, enabling management to examine and judge each item. Every individual capital expenditure item has to be authorised, often at the highest level.

As current rather than capital expenditure, marketing is not usually subject to the same control. There are rarely formal limits to expenditure at different management levels. Expenditure plans are presented and approved in summary. The component parts of the marketing budget and the particular activities proposed are rarely interrogated by management. The effects of past marketing decisions are not closely analysed, and the incremental sales effects of planned marketing expenditures are not forecast. The merits of alternative ways of allocating the marketing budget are hardly ever debated within a senior management forum.

Marketing is generally treated as an overall 'lump sum' expenditure line: management questions total marketing spend and its effectiveness, but is rarely involved in analysis of the process by which marketing delivers results. Because marketing is not structural, is rarely measured, and is often a relatively small percentage of costs, it receives limited attention from finance. Marketing is therefore at a severe disadvantage in bidding for funding against other forms of expenditure and in resisting budget reductions.

If marketing is to compete for management support and funding, it needs finance as an enthusiastic ally rather than a sceptical neutral within the management team. It needs to involve financial management in planning, budgeting and evaluation, so that investments in marketing are treated on a par with other uses of company resources. But every specialisation develops its own language, and finance is no exception. Marketing needs to learn the language of finance and work within the decision-making framework expected by financial management.

Above all, marketing needs to sell itself to finance as a capital investment, inviting more control and accountability at the same time as it receives more cash.

A simple model summarises the dynamics of financial decision-making. The model is illustrated first for a manufacturing company, which divides its costs into fixed and variable elements.

A manufacturing company P&L		
	Sales Income	100
Variable (or direct) costs	Materials	50
	Labour	20
	Distribution	10
Gross margin		20
Fixed costs	Overhead	8
	Marketing	2
		10
Profit before tax		10

In their accounts, manufacturing companies treat marketing costs as an element of fixed costs, and it is immediately apparent why they are not a priority for financial management. The greatest scope for the improvement of profitability in manufacturing lies in the management of variable direct costs.

A service-led company has a different cost profile.

A service company P&L		
	Sales Income	100
Variable (or direct) costs	Sales costs	<u>20</u>
Gross Margin		80
Fixed costs	Premises	10
	Systems	10
	Staff	40
	Marketing	<u>10</u>
		70
Profit before tax		10

In a service company, fixed costs are higher and are dominated by staff and employment. In service companies the expenditure on computer systems is becoming an increasingly significant element of the fixed costs of running the business. Marketing is a greater cost than in the manufacturing sector, but remains the only significant expenditure line that does not require a long-term commitment.

Marketing is therefore the easiest cost to cut: the largest item in most traditional marketing budgets is for advertising media, and most media are paid for short term even if they are planned long term. The marketing budget is vulnerable and in many companies suffers regular review and cutback during the financial year. The process has become so routine that many marketing departments operate on the assumption that the budget available to them will be reduced throughout the year. They therefore have a stronger incentive to spend the budget quickly than to spend it wisely, which has the perverse effect of creating irrational and sometimes profligate use of scarce funds.

Expenditure Planning

To evaluate proposed expenditure plans, finance starts with an expected income forecast. This is the product of sales by their likelihood. The exercise of proper financial control demands prudence, and the sales forecasts provided by marketing are discounted according to their likelihood. The better the information and more relevant the experience on which sales forecasts are based, the greater the reliance placed by finance on forecasts, and the higher the expected income used by finance in planning expenditure.

Expected sales income = Forecast revenue × Probability

The justification for capital expenditure is straightforward in the case of a fixed asset like a new machine tool for the manufacturing company. A projection is made of the year-on-year expenditure and sales effects of the investment (Table 12.1). Cash is spent up-front, in return for an incremental revenue stream. It is probable that a new machine results in reductions in running and maintenance costs, and so the investment also increases the gross margin. Most new machinery is labour saving and so enables a reduction in the manufacturing workforce and fixed overhead, as well as in variable operational costs.

Capital expenditure does not directly reduce current period profits because in the profit and loss account the investment is depreciated over time (Table 12.2). A principle of accounting is to match costs with income and so the investment cost is spread into the future.

Capital investments are evaluated in one of three different ways:

(i) Payback period: the point at which cash flow on the project becomes positive, i.e. how quickly does the company get its money back; this method is used for shorter term investments.

(ii) Rate of return: the discounted value of the cash flow generated by the project; this method is used for longer term investments, and to compare different investments against alternative uses of cash, including investment in financial markets.

(iii) Return on capital: the discounted value of the profits generated by the investment.

Table 12.1 Cash flow forecast for manufacturing

	Year				
	One	Two	Three	Four	Five
Sales income	100	110	115	120	125
Variable materials	50	52	53	54	55
Labour	20	19	19	18	18
Distribution	10	11	11	12	12
Gross margin	20	28	32	36	40
Cash expenditure					
Overhead	8	8	9	9	10
Marketing	2	2	2	2	2
Capital	20	—	—	—	—
	30	10	11	11	12
Net cash effect	(10)	18	21	25	28
Previous cash flow	10	10	10	10	10
Net (or marginal) cash impact of investment	(20)	8	11	15	18

The investment results in increased sales, reduced materials and distribution costs as percentages of sales, and reduced absolute labour costs. It pays back in just over two years and doubles the gross margin in five years.

Table 12.2   Profit and loss account for manufacturing

	Year				
	One	*Two*	*Three*	*Four*	*Five*
Sales income	100	110	115	120	125
Variable materials	50	52	53	54	55
Labour	20	19	19	18	18
Distribution	10	11	11	12	12
Gross margin	20	28	32	36	40
Fixed costs overhead	8	8	9	9	10
Marketing	2	2	2	2	2
Depreciation	4	4	4	4	4
	14	14	15	15	16
Profit before tax	6	14	17	21	24

Because of the size of the investment (20% of sales) profits reduce in year one, but increase thereafter rising to 240% above the previous level after five years.

Many companies establish a hurdle rate as the minimum rate of return they will accept from any investments. Corporate treasurers are responsible for maximising return on corporate funds, and the search for higher returns has led many to invest in new financial products like derivatives. These forms of investment have become more attractive precisely because they are more measurable and, apparently, more certain than investment in a company's marketing. But major companies including Procter & Gamble have been burned by their experiences with arcane financial instruments, and an issue for society in general and shareholders in particular is that investment in the company, its employees and customers might yield better long-term growth in shareholder value.

This is the environment in which marketing must present its case for investment.

Marketing as an Investment

Marketing has a responsibility to provide the sales forecast. In forecasting sales marketing can improve its case for funding in two ways.

Marketing can improve the precision of its sales forecasts by supporting the forecast with more information. The more certain the contribution to sales that marketing can promise, the larger the marketing budget – and the less likely it is to be reviewed and cut.

Marketing can also demonstrate the sales leverage of marketing expenditure: the direct effects of marketing on customer behaviour. To make this meaningful to business and financial management, marketing must demonstrate how customer behaviour translates into cash generation both short and long term.

If marketing has a communication problem with finance, it may face an even more serious lack of understanding in the ultimate arbiter of financial decisions, the chief executive. In their book, *The Marketing Revolution: A Radical Manifesto for Dominating the Marketplace*, Kevin Clancy and Robert Shulman argue that most chief executives do not understand marketing and that they would achieve greater performance in the market-place if they did. They recommend detailed analysis and reporting of the last year's marketing performance: a 'marketing audit' to compare expenses against results and a 'marketing autopsy' to report which marketing investments had been successful, and which had not.[1]

The information which forms the basis for a marketing forecast is of two kinds: experience and judgement. In making their forecasts marketers must be prepared to quantify their experience and to stand or fall by their track record. More weight will be attached to marketing forecasts if the quality of past forecasting as well as past marketing is proven. Even where results have deviated significantly from forecast, marketing should be in a position to explain the factors that caused the deviation, and to demonstrate that the lessons have been incorporated within the new forecasts. Marketing needs to develop a process which monitors actual against forecast, and isolates the causes of the differences. It needs to understand not only the effects of competition, price and other changes in the market-place – but also the effects of its own decisions.

Marketing forecasts will be perceived as more reliable if supported by facts, and in particular by tests. Here is one of the most compelling reasons for an increased level of testing: to prove the case for investment. Increased measurement and testing will lead to the assignment of higher probabilities to marketing forecasts, and to higher marketing budgets. More accurate forecasts win the confidence of business and financial management. The rule is: to forecast accurately, forecast more often.

A new approach to marketing planning is needed. The traditional approach in most companies is to plan marketing and budget for marketing expenditure as a fixed annual sum. Although the amount is not committed and may be changed through the year, it is agreed in principle. The process involves the usual negotiating games. Marketing bids high, knowing that it will only receive a proportion of the total. Marketing spends its budget early in the year, to avoid the third and fourth quarter cuts.

The new approach is to plan and forecast marketing on a rolling basis, on an incremental and regular basis throughout the financial year. At each stage current results are compared with previous forecasts and accompanied by analysis that explains the differences. Forward forecasts are continually adjusted to incorporate trends and build in the findings of ongoing testing and research. Marketing responds more quickly to customer behaviour, and marketing budgets adjust to incorporate market dynamics and company priorities. The process integrates marketing with regular financial reporting and involves finance closely in marketing evaluation and decision-making.

In discussing this shift in culture, I have encountered a concern in some companies that finance would exert control without understanding. I believe that the opposite will be the case. If finance wishes to control marketing, it is because it does not understand the causes and effects. Indeed it would not be an overstatement to say that in many companies finance fears marketing – or at least the risk that marketing expenditures represent. The objective should be that finance is as convinced about marketing as was Hopkins in the 1930s that advertising is one of the 'safest business ventures'.[2]

If marketing is to be credible as a quasi-capital expenditure item, it is essential that marketing demonstrates the effect it has on sales and profits *over time*, to demonstrate the effect of expenditure now on future customer behaviour, and to show the future cost of not investing in customers. The methodology of customer lifetime value provides the basis for the evaluation of marketing as an investment. In the simplest form of this evaluation, marketing expenditure results in the acquisition of an increased number of new customers and in an increase in sales to existing customers.

As I have described in Chapter 4, the effectiveness with which new customers can be acquired is a function of the perceived values of the brand in the market-place. The effectiveness with which sales can be increased among existing customers depends upon the level of loyalty within the customer base. The degree of certainty in the marketing forecast can, by analogy with the investment in a fixed asset, be represented as equations.

Expected income from sales to new customers =
Brand rate × New customer lifetime value

Expected income from increased sales to existing customers =
Customer loyalty rate × Customer lifetime value potential

A model of the business can be constructed in terms of customers, with income and variable costs re-evaluated in terms of customer lifetime value, customer management costs and the acquisition cost of a new customer. The cash effects of marketing investment can then be analysed in the same format and using the same language as for fixed assets.

Marketing as an investment: customer economics

The marketing budget of '2' is devoted 50% to investment in new customers and 50% to relationship-building with existing customers. Analysis of customer economics and behaviour reveals:

Customer Economics

	Year				
	One	Two	Three	Four	Five
Acquisition	(1.0)				
Net lifetime value	–	2.0	2.0	2.0	2.0
Relationship-building	(1.0)				
Increase in lifetime value	1.0	1.5	1.5	1.5	1.5

The effect of increasing marketing investment to 5 in year one, allocated 2 (1 additional) to acquisition and 3 (2 additional) to relationship-building is:

Marketing as an investment: customer cash flow model

	Year				
	One	Two	Three	Four	Five
Sales income	103	109	115	121	172
Variable costs	81	82	83	84	85
Gross margin	22	27	32	37	42
Cash expenditure overhead	8	8	9	9	10
Marketing	5	5	5	5	5
	13	13	14	14	15
Net cash effect	9	14	18	23	27
Previous cash flow	10	10	10	10	10
Net (or marginal) cash impact of investment	(1)	4	8	13	17

The effect is cash positive soon after year one because the payback from relationship-building with existing customers quickly outweighs the investment in new customer acquisition. Financial management could depreciate the extra marketing investment in customers over four years (4 × 0.75) and thereby eliminate even the year one impact on profits thus:

Marketing as an investment: P&L model

	Year				
	One	Two	Three	Four	Five
Sales income	103	109	115	121	172
Variable costs	81	82	83	84	85
Gross margin	22	27	32	37	42
Costs					
overhead	8	8	9	9	10
Relationship-building	1.5	2.0	2.5	3	3
Acquisition – depreciated	1.25	1.5	1.75	2	2
	10.75	11.5	13.25	14	15
Net cash effect	10	14	18	23	27
Previous cash flow	10	10	10	10	10
Net (or marginal) P&L effect of investment	1.25	5.5	8.75	13	17

The evaluation can be considerably more sophisticated if the model includes:

— the increasing cost of acquiring customers as the volume of customers rises

— multiple customer segments each with different lifetime values and management costs, and the effects of marketing expenditure on switching between segments

— the effects on overheads in general, and labour costs in particular, of different marketing expenditure

— the effect of investment in existing customers on the allowable acquisition cost of new customers.

Investment in Customer Systems and Information

For a service company, the investment in the hardware and software for a new computer system can be evaluated as capital expenditure. Systems decisions are, however, usually made on the basis of competitive advantage: without the system the company may not be able to match competitive prices, service and distribution. The decision rests simply on whether a company wants and can afford to play in a higher league.

The benefits of the new system lie in increased sales from new product features and more competitive pricing, and in cost-savings from reduction in administrative and management staff. The system is treated as a fixed asset, although the accounting treatment of hardware and software is generally stricter than for plant and machinery because of the rapid rate of obsolescence in technology.

Accounting for investment in computer systems is notoriously problematic. The subject is dealt with in depth by Paul Strassman in *The Business Value of Computers*, who begins this 500 plus page book with the humbling sentence: 'There is no relationship between expenses for computers and business profitability.'[3] Strassman's overriding conclusion is to focus on management productivity as the key to achieving return on investment simply because management are the principal users of computers. He shows in particular that as IT spending on sales and marketing increases, the proportion of the budget spend on sales and marketing overhead decreases. In most studies this is a consequence of operation efficiency in general and labour-saving in particular.

Computers entered business to automate finance and operations, and the primary motive for computerisation has been to improve productivity, in other words to reduce costs. More recently, IT has become an important competitive weapon in the interface with customers and has made major inroads in sales and marketing. Airline reservation systems are the most dramatic examples of operational 'super systems' that have transformed business efficiency. At the same time as reservations systems have increased the sales of tickets they have enhanced the customer interface. IT allows the airline to recognise and reward its best customers at the point of sale and at all points of contact from check-in to arrival at the passenger's final destination.

Most system developments in service industries increase productivity by reducing the number of employees, although new skills will be necessary to manage the increased sophistication of the new system. The number of staff required will reduce although at the same time the qualifications and training of the staff will increase. As backroom clerical tasks are automated, companies have the opportunity to reduce their fixed employment costs, or to redeploy staff in customer-facing roles where they can contribute directly by increasing customer lifetime value. Telemarketing will be one of the fastest sources of new employment in the developed economies over the next decade, as companies invest in customer contact centres and in customer service representatives.

Calculating Customer Lifetime Value

With the perspective of relationship management, customers are assets. Customers transact with the organisation and purchase products and services. The outcome is a flow of revenue from customer relationships. Customer value is the difference between the revenue from customer transactions and the costs of managing customer relationships. The net present value of these income and cost flows is the *customer lifetime value*.

To acquire customers requires investment. Payback may be immediate, but is more likely to be realised over a period of years. Using customer lifetime value, the budgets for marketing can be planned on the basis of projected returns. The effect on customer behaviour can be measured and the contribution to profits can be calculated.

In forecasting it is the potential customer lifetime value that matters. On the revenue side, this means analysing past behaviour and future opportunities. Past behaviour is analysed by research, and by analysis of past transactions. The objective is to determine the total potential of customers, including what they buy from competition, and what they might buy in future from the company.

The objective is to identify the 'ideal' customer from whom the company generates the maximum lifetime value. More than one type of ideal customer may exist and it is important to determine the profile of each type.

There are two approaches to the projection of customer lifetime value, looking backwards or forwards.

Backward analysis of lifetime value is based on analysis of customer characteristics and transactions. Certain customers' characteristics may influence customer lifetime value significantly. Examples are the number of children in the household, the value of the property if owned and the size of business by revenue or number of staff. A profiling exercise of characteristics and value enables the development of a model that predicts customer lifetime value.

To project customer lifetime value forward, a prototyping method can be used. The prototypes are the different types of customer relationship, and the analysis prototypes the behaviour of different types of customers as the basis for forecasting their contribution to profits, the costs of managing relationships with them, and thus their lifetime value.

In both forms of evaluation, modelling and forecasting, lifetime value will be projected for different types of customer. Lifetime value is individual. The segmentation will be specific to company and its brand portfolio, but a basis for planning is to segment on the range of brands and the potential value, by quartile and by types of relationship.

Customer lifetime value matrix

Quartiles	New	Relationship A	B	C
I				
II				
III				
IV				

The calculation of lifetime value can be illustrated for a bank, car manufacturer and pet food manufacturer.

For the bank the analysis of customers is based on the type and number of accounts, and the customer's use of the accounts, i.e. transactional data. The bank can analyse its profitable customers and look back at their sources and early accounts. Or it can research its customer base to understand their competitive behaviour and their future value, and to prototype ideal customer relationships. The drivers of customer lifetime value for a bank are identifiable as:

— age

— financial assets

— expenditure

— net income.

Many banks around the world have invested in new young customers, but been dissatisfied by the returns. Their retention of new customers has been disappointing and they have been unable to generate long-term lifetime value. Home ownership is a better customer lifestage around which to focus marketing investment. Potential long-term lifetime value peaks for home owners because of the high margin of the mortgage product, the opportunity to cross-sell to the mortgage customer, and the relationship

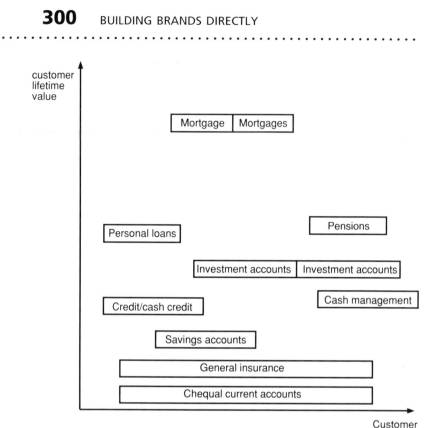

Figure 12.1 Potential, future customer lifetime value for a bank

created by the mortgage that gives the bank the opportunity to market fee-earning services (Figure 12.1).

For the car manufacturer the analysis is also based on transactional data: the model of car owned, number of previous purchases, and time since purchase. Lifetime value of purchasers is enhanced if finance and service revenues result. Repeat purchase is related to any factors that develop a sustained relationship between the customer and dealer and/or brand manufacturer – which is why the growth in personal leasing offers manufacturers a major remarketing opportunity. The major predictors of potential lifetime value are then:

— relationship with dealer and/or brand manufacturer

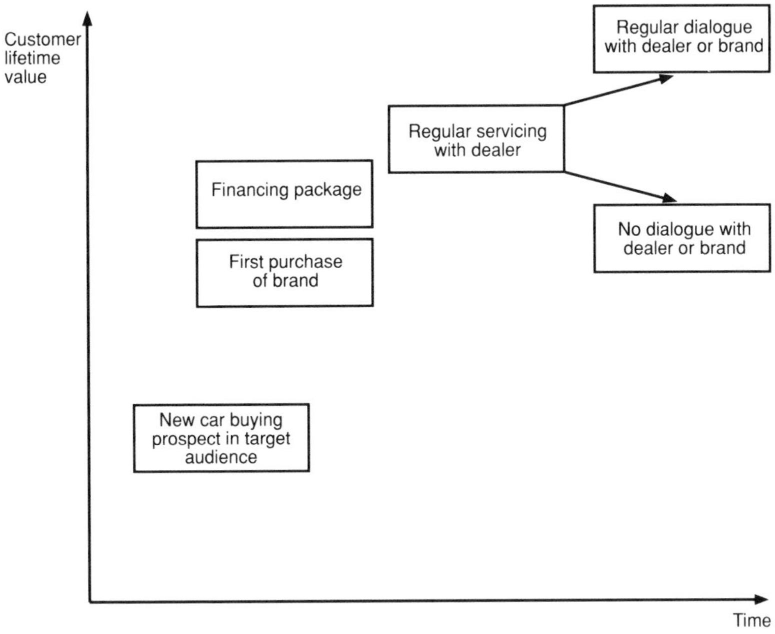

Figure 12.2 Potential, future customer lifetime value for a car manufacturer

— past purchase history, especially if previously with the brand

— number of cars in household

— age and family size.

The calculation of lifetime value is at its most straightforward here, although account should be taken of multiple car ownership to calculate lifetime value for households rather than for individuals (Figure 12.2).

In the business market, lifetime value can be determined by researching companies or by modelling their size and business profile to predict their fleet size and composition.

For the petfood manufacturer the analysis is based on brands used and volumes of purchase, and since the transactions are made in retail outlets, the base data must be collected directly from customers by survey. The petfood manufacturer can capture competitive brand usage in the survey and predict the customer's total usage in the category. The key variables that predict potential lifetime value are:

— number of pets in the household

— ages of pet owners

— ages of pets

— size of dogs

— household income

— pet feeding behaviour – a proportion of the market prepares its own foods.

Calculating Customer Relationship Costs

To determine the cost side of the lifetime value equation it is important to determine what lifetime value does *not* include. This leads to an important change in the accounting of marketing because it is important to differentiate between marketing and operating costs.

The calculation of lifetime value includes all cost elements inseparable from delivering the product and service to the customer, and from managing the customer relationship. To determine customer management costs activity-based techniques are necessary. These differ from traditional budgeting techniques in two ways:

(i)   costs are allocated to customers as well as to products

(ii)   costs are summed for processes, customer tracks, rather than by function.

An activity consists of the staff involved and the resources they use to manage the customer relationship. As a structured business process, a customer track links a set of activities together to increase the value of a customer. The cost of an activity is a function of the volume of customers involved at each stage in the customer track, and the company's investment in customer contact, itself a function of the quality of personnel and their training, the systems and the materials used in the process.

Any customer can then be characterised in terms of the activities in which he or she is involved and their costs, and a cost determined that is unique to the customer or, in large volume businesses, unique to the customer type.

Activity-based costing divides fixed costs in a different way from conventional costing systems, separating the costs related to customers from the costs related to overhead. This enables a company to separate three forms of cost:

(i) customer relationship costs fundamental to managing and developing the customer relationship

(ii) supporting costs necessary to maintain the infrastructure in which the company and its staff operates

(iii) all other non-essential costs.

By identifying non-essential costs companies can identify their source and organise to eliminate them. By separating the marginal cost of a customer from infrastructure accounting companies can identify the true contribution. Activity-based costing and the evaluation of marginal customer costs will typically highlight that the true lifetime value of a new customer is higher than might otherwise have been estimated using conventional accounting.

The process will also reveal significant cost differences between different types of customer. Some findings include:

(i) Membership companies which have realised how quickly lifetime value increases with length of membership, because retention and service costs are so much less for experienced customers

(ii) Financial service companies which have learned a similar lesson, and shifted their emphasis from the acquisition of high cost youth accounts to lower cost and higher potential value mature customers

(iii) Insurance companies that have measured that the differences in customer claims and service costs vary more by customer demographics and profession than by geography.

Many costs traditionally counted as marketing costs can be reclassified as operating costs. The implication that the costs of customer contact, affinity, rewards, extra value and customer service should not be included in marketing costs. Companies should consider accounting for these as operating costs rather than as current marketing expenses, because they have become the costs of being in business rather than discretionary current expenditure.

In the case of an airline frequent flyer program, for example, the marketing operating costs comprise:

— contact: regular mailings and newsletters to frequent flyers as well as special programmes to create contact between airline management and staff and best customers

— affinity: special offers and promotions to selected customers (e.g. foreign nationals, unaccompanied children, handicapped) designed to increase their usage of and loyalty to the airline

— rewards: the funding of free miles, upgrades and third party benefits, offers and promotions – some of which could be revenue earning and thereby reduce the cost of the programme

— extra value: the costs of enhancements to service and other additional benefits offered to the best customers

— customer service: the costs of enhanced customer service at all points of contact with the customer.

Impact on financial budgets: customer and operating costs – a service company P&L		
	Sales income	100
Variable (or direct) costs	Sales costs	10
	Customer relationship costs	5
	Gross margin	85
Fixed costs	Premises	10
	Systems	15
	Staff	35
	Marketing	10
		70
Profit before tax		15

Profit is increased by using customer relationship strategy to leverage sales effectiveness and raise the productivity of personnel

Marketing costs which are not operating costs can be considered either as current customer maintenance or as investments in the customer relationship. Current customer maintenance is the proportion of advertising that is designed to maintain company awareness and image, or sales promotions that are designed to defend the current customer base against competitive activity.

By evaluating the payback profile of expenditure that definitely represents investment in the future, marketing can propose that these costs are capitalised and allocated according to the pattern in which they generate return on investment. All marketing costs would then be allocated to one of the three areas: current customer maintenance, customer management or operating costs, and customer relationship-building investment. The basic unit of accounting can be changed from product to customer. In this new model, customer segments and the customer teams responsible for them become profit centres.

Modelling Marketing Investment

To plan marketing requires decisions to be made about the targeting of investment in customers, and the nature of that investment. Targeting is to customer segments and types, and the focus of investment should be against both opportunity and risk. Targeting should be directed to customer segments where the opportunity to increase customer lifetime value *profitably* is the greatest. Targeting should also be directed to customer segments where future customer lifetime value is most vulnerable to competitive threats or to changes in the market environment, and where this future flow of value can be sustained *profitably*. The key word in both paragraphs is, of course, profitably.

The model described here is a method of comparing:

— the levels of investment in the customer relationship likely to change behaviour

— the levels of increase in profit likely to result from the change in behaviour.

In both cases the investment should be calculated quantitatively to deliver a return on investment subject to the projected change in customer behaviour, and designed qualitatively to change customer behaviour short and long term, to deliver a competitive edge.

Marketing effectiveness and investment can be analysed using a cost-benefit model as illustrated in Figure 12.3. The model is practical, and helps put numbers, even when they are estimates or judgements, to forecasts. It helps to quantify judgement, not to replace it. It is an aid to decision-making, a means of setting budgets and targets, and a tool to check the sensitivities and risks involved in alternative marketing plans.

The model is based on two principal factors. The first is

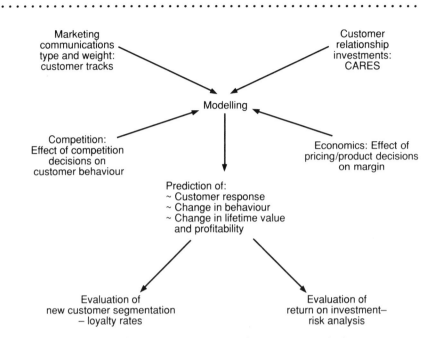

Figure 12.3 Evaluating marketing effectiveness and the return on investment model

an understanding of the market, its segmentation and behaviour by segment. The second is an understanding of the likely impact of alternative strategies and activities by segment. The model will guide the evaluation of which strategies and activities are likely to yield the greatest returns. It will also help the allocation of effort and investment by customer segment.

The role of the model begins with planning, of:

— relationships between costs, and customer behaviour

— projection of target response rates, conversion

— linking costs to customer values

— recommendation of size and allocation of budgets.

The model can be used to test the assumptions underlying plans and thus the robustness of alternative plans:

— design of testing to measure sensitive variables

— evaluation of customer service investments or rewards

— evaluation of tests against targets

— input of test findings to market forecasts.

The model can also evaluate the downside risks involved, for example to determine the need for insurance or to prepare contingency plans. The model can be shared between marketing and finance to develop their common understanding of the results of marketing investment, and to ensure that proposals for marketing are based on sound financial criteria, that the opportunity costs of not funding marketing are well appreciated, and that the evaluation of marketing effectiveness is rigorously analysed.

The core output from the model is the evaluation of the return on investment from loyalty programmes. This will include the effect of the change in sales on margins, and of the change in loyalty on projected customer lifetime value.

As well as changes to existing customer behaviour, a customer relationship strategy can also be projected to reduce customer losses and increase customer acquisition. The model can factor in these effects.

The model can also be used to reveal scenarios where investments in customer relationships do not pay back.

The Measurement of Marketing

A rigorous measurement system is necessary to evaluate the full effects of relationship strategy, and is a critical aspect of planning customer tracks. The direct measures of success are customer response to, participation in and sales made through relationship activities.

The incremental sales generated are the only visible measures.

The quality of response and or sale is a critical factor. Promotions which generate promiscuous buyers achieve little long-term benefit. Some activity will generate new customers of more value than others. And some response and sales would have occurred without any marketing – with no incremental gain.

Customer research: proforma

Category

— level and type of product usage in the product category
— spontaneous brand awareness
— spontaneous advertising and direct communications or contact awareness and experience

Brand

— rating of brand values on a range of dimensions
— brand repertoire and experience in the category
— relationships, e.g. membership with brands in the category

Marketing

— participation in marketing activity and response to offers
— appreciation and impact of marketing

Customer

— brand loyalty measures
— customer response to possible market changes or competitive actions
— customer intentions

Future

— customer ranking of alternative marketing propositions
— customer willingness to enter a membership relationship
— customer willingness to become an associate
— customer willingness to become an advocate

Sales are the tip of the iceberg. The 'advertising' effect of relationship investment cannot be ignored. Customers within relationship marketing tracks can be researched, to evaluate the 'advertising' measures which reflect the longer term impact – awareness, image and preference. Additional research can track the loyalty rate and relate these measures to lifetime value.

Brand management is much criticised for its short-term orientation. But the problem lies with the measures by which brand management is judged, typically the change in market share from period to period. Alternative measures should focus on total brand value based on a forward projection of customer lifetime value, measurable by loyalty rate and brand rate tracking. Brand management will be encouraged to invest in customer relationships because it will be measured on the propensity of the customer to repeat buy. Small differences in marketing effectiveness, and in particular in predicted customer retention rates, can result in dramatic swings in profitability, in customer lifetime value and thus in total brand value. If the company capitalises the database then brand management will also be encouraged to invest to build the database, and to shift customers to higher value customer segments.

Research is part of any measurement system for the evaluation of direct marketing. The effect of direct market-

---

Quantitative effects of relationship programme

£ cost per prospect
% conversion to new customer
£ cost per new customer acquisition
% conversion to multi-buyer from cross-selling
% return on investment from cross-selling
% return on investment from relationship-building
£ lifetime value per customer
£ total cost per customer
% return on investment from relationship

ing is not only response. Nor is it immediate sales. There is an effect on non-respondents. And there is an effect on longer term behaviour. A measurement system will include the quantitative effects shown at the foot of the opposite page.

A measurement system will also include these qualitative effects (see below).

Qualitative measurement of direct marketing

Participants vs Control

Spontaneous awareness
Brand imagery dimensions
Preference ranking of competitive
 brands
Intention to buy/repeat buy
Loyalty rate

The Primacy of Marketing in Business Strategy

If marketing is to regain its proper position in business strategy and in the company boardroom, then it must become recognised by financial management as an investment. This requires a cultural shift. Marketing must invest in information to support and justify its activities and to learn from success and failures. It must share this information with financial management without inhibition, and make finance its partner. Above all marketing must establish:

— the direct communication of customer behaviour and value from the market-place to the company management

— the direct contribution that staff can make to customer behaviour and thus to customer value

— the direct effect of customer lifetime value on brand and company value as perceived by management and shareholders.

PART IV: APPLICATIONS

BUILDING 13 CONSUMER BRANDS DIRECTLY

'Keeping the brand relationship alive and well'

> The Forces Shaping Consumer Brand Marketing – Consumer Brand Relationship Strategy – A New Agenda for Consumer Brand Marketing

The Forces Shaping Consumer Brand Marketing

The pressures from intensifying competition and demanding customers are the greatest for consumer brands. Their marketing options are limited by the increased cost and fragmentation of media, and by the growth in retail power which has robbed them of most of their ability to compete at the point of sale. Brands have as much to fear as retailers from the potential of home shopping. If brands have little control of their display on supermarket shelves, they have even less opportunity to differentiate themselves on the telephone or on-line through PC and television screens. There are no longer significant differences in quality among brands themselves, and between brands and their private label equivalents. So customers are no longer willing to pay the significant price premium which generated the brand manufacturer's profits.

Every consumer market faces the threat of commoditisation: of undifferentiated products competing only on price.

To maintain their momentum in the 1980s, manufacturers relied principally on line extensions, and research, development and marketing investment was ploughed into them. Although at first many extensions created incremental share for the brand, by the low growth 1990s most manufacturers found that the line extensions simply cannibalised their total share. The fragmentation of messages and budgets in the market-place became confusing, and a marketing budget sliced into ever smaller amounts was dissipated amidst the competitive clutter.

In contrast to the developments and acquisitions of the last two decades, many brand manufacturers were forced by competition and declining earnings to downsize. In 1993, Sara Lee cut $250 million from its costs and announced a plan to reduce its workforce by 8300.[1] Quaker Oats also announced cuts in overheads and staff.

One of the key areas for personnel cuts has been the direct sales force, superseded by lower cost alternatives to distribute to the retailers whom manufacturers have always considered as their customers. The alternatives include independent distributors like Cash & Carries in the UK, merchandising staff out-sourced from third parties, and telesales to take orders direct. Often it is not clear that the new channel to the retailer fulfils the original role of the sales force in providing a personal contact to the retailer and a channel through which the company can monitor the retailer's response to its products and marketing. The excising of direct sales forces represents another retreat by brand marketers from the customer interface.

Confronted with the need to focus their energies and budgets, even the primacy of brand management is under review. The retailers through whom manufacturers must sell focus on maximising the profit from the various product categories that occupy their shelves. To mirror the retailer's focus, manufacturers are reorganising their marketing departments around brand families and even around product categories rather than individual brands and their line extensions. Some, like Elida Gibbs in the UK, have even abolished the title of marketing director to locate decision-making closer to product categories and their retail customers. Closer relationships with retailers are essential for brands to regain some control over their marketing, as one US observer writes: 'The tactical price-based relationships of the present, in which marketers essentially pay for the right to be on the shelf, is precisely the wrong approach . . . To achieve proprietary consumer access the marketer must change the retail environment into a brand environment.'[2]

The efficiency of consumer brand marketing expenditure is a subject of concern in boardrooms. Media inflation and fragmentation have reduced advertising efficiency, and the shift to trade promotion has been dictated to manufacturers by retailers. In their willingness to experiment with every new in-store and promotional vehicle, manufacturers are simply expressing their need for new media and new channels to change customer behaviour. Manufacturers can choose from options that include:

In-store

— interactive kiosks

— coupon issue at checkout

— video advertising on trolleys

— point-of-sale – requiring expensive promotional support

— in-store radio

— advertising in retailer publications

— sampling teams.

Out-of-store

— syndicated sampling

— syndicated databases

— joint promotions to retailer databases

— new local media

— coupon books syndicated and distributed by national and local media.

A strategy is required for manufacturers to make sense of the communication options and guide the allocation of the marketing budget among so many competing opportunities.

At the same time as their traditional communication channels are in decline, retailers face customers demanding more sophisticated communication and information. Customers no longer take manufacturer promises for granted: they want information to convince them that products are environmentally sound and nutritionally pure. They welcome help and advice in choosing products that reconcile four important concerns:

 (i) Family: products must be good for their families, in particular for children

 (ii) Responsibility: products must represent good value for money

(iii) Environment: products must not damage the environment

(iv) Convenience: products must make the shopper's life easier: in particular when it comes to running the home and preparing food.

Consumer brands must reassure the shopper on all four counts, and at the same time must often appeal to other members of the household who are the ultimate consumers of the brand: children are playing an important role in the marketing of many product categories, and research confirms that they are more susceptible to advertising and to fashions in brands.

Consumer brand marketing was once the simplest of affairs: research the market, find a new need or niche, develop the product, book sufficient television airtime, negotiate the distribution with retailers desperate for new products to increase their sales – and go. Manufacturers now confront fragmented markets, demanding customers, dynamic behaviour; and retailers whose shelves can no longer accommodate new products and customers who may buy new products but whose total spend will no longer increase.

Above all manufacturers must make sense of complexity. The new environment demands a new strategy.

Consumer Brand Relationship Strategy

For frequently purchased consumer brands, the idea of the total brand experience is central to the new relationship strategy. The customer's relationship with the brand is not restricted to advertising, and encompasses purchase in-store and consumption in-home. Advertising cannot be separated from purchase and consumption: as Professor Giep Franzen, quoted by Larry Light, the chairman for the US Coalition for Brand Equity, says: 'the constant interaction between brand and use and advertising helps to reinforce attitudes leading to universal brand loyalty.' Light urges consumer brand manufacturers to learn from American Airlines, Philip Morris, American Express and book retailer Waldenbooks in developing loyalty programmes and in 'keeping the brand relationship alive and well'.[3]

Consumer brand manufacturers have fought shy of relationship strategy and individual marketing because they did not believe it could be economic for low price brands and because of the poor image of 'junk' mail. But basing the strategy on the customer lifetime value to the company as whole transforms brand manufacturer thinking. An investment in many selected individual customer relationships is no different from an investment in media advertising: it achieves short- and long-term returns.

The falling costs of setting up a customer service capability, communicating directly with customers and managing customer data make these sound investments, when compared to the potential lifetime value of the ideal customer, regularly purchasing all of a company's brands. These investments have the simultaneous effect of reducing the hidden costs of promotional wastage: sales promotion expenditures can be absorbed within the relationship management budget, their effectiveness enhanced and their accountability ensured.

Consumer brand manufacturers can make these investments in three steps.

Step one: customer service

A free customer service line can be cost-justified on the basis of the value of solving customer complaints and retaining complainants: the economics are straightforward (Table 13.1).

A customer service resource has wider benefits:

— for interactive advertising: the distribution of new information to customers

— for relationship-building promotion: the management of premium and reward redemption

— for public relations: a crisis line to communicate the company's viewpoint to customers – retailers and the ultimate consumer.

Step two: customer communication

With changing media economics, direct mail communication to customer becomes a viable complement or alternative to media advertising and promotions. Direct mail can be targeted, and even for the largest of brands relatively small numbers of households represent:

(i)   the brand's current loyal base of heavy consumers whom it is vital to retain

Table 13.1 Evaluating the return on investment from customer service: pro forma

	Before customer service	*After customer service*
No. of problems		
No. of complaints		
Cost of complaint management		
Retention rates		
Customers: Very satisfied Quite satisfied Not very satisfied Very unsatisfied		
Incremental customers retained		
Customer lifetime value		
Return from complaint management		
Net return from investment		

(ii) the light users of the brand among whom significant volume increases are most likely to be achieved cost-effectively

(iii) the heaviest competitive brand users in whom it is worthwhile to invest to attempt a change in their behaviour and introduce a new brand into their repertoire

(iv) the new entrants into the market, in particular the formation of new households.

Direct mail to selected individual consumer brand users is proven as a combination of powerful advertising and promotion.

Step three: customer relationships

A relationship strategy involves a dialogue, with communications from customer to company as well as from company to customer. The usual context for a dialogue is one or more of:

— regular, exclusive offers for which customers apply

— a customer publication like a newsletter, to which customers contribute

— a collection scheme, in which customers redeem points for rewards

— a membership or club, formalising customer eligibility for exclusive benefits.

A dialogue enables brand manufacturers to go beyond what Larry Light calls brand marketing's 'Fable No 1: Marketing's job ends with the sale'[4] and take responsibility for enhancement of the total brand experience and management of the total customer relationship.

Brand marketer's can also use the membership model to develop their relationships with retailers. Retailers and manufacturers can compete or cooperate over the customer interface, and not surprisingly many manufacturers seek cooperation. Speaking at the 1994 EDMA Forum in Brussels, Mary Petersen of Quaker Oats stressed the value of co-operative marketing and described how her company seeks participation in retailers' frequent shopper programmes: 'Retailers have very active databases – and if they haven't, they will get them. We have consumer insight.'[5]

Manufacturers should seek to integrate their trade and consumer activities more closely, and to involve independent retailers as well as the multiples. They should develop relationships with the independents based on personal contact and added value service, helping retailers maximise their profits through:

— economic packaging and pack sizes

— guaranteed distribution

— advice and support for merchandising

— tailored promotional offers by retailer type and size

— local marketing support campaigns to drive volume.

To manage their relationships with independents manufacturers should invest in systems and personnel as they do for the ultimate customer.

In many respects the tobacco sector has become bellwether for consumer brand marketing. Although it is an observation that some may find reprehensible, cigarette manufacturers are setting standards of excellence in consumer brand marketing. They confront:

— a rapidly declining market

— high taxes forcing steady price rises

— legislative restrictions on advertising media and messages

— tight data protection rules.

The response of cigarette marketers to these threats illustrates the power of relationship strategy for consumer brands.

A New Agenda for Consumer Brand Marketing

Philip Morris is the largest tobacco manufacturer in the US and as *Brandweek* describes: 'Even with the problems, it's a clinic in brand marketing.' The Philip Morris response to the declining share of its flagship Marlboro brand has been described in outline in Chapter 1. By the summer of 1994 Marlboro's share had risen back to a record 28.5 per cent of the US market. This success was not purely attributable to the price cut, and Philip Morris brand strategies increasingly included relationship management programmes.

Philip Morris has focused on brand families after a series of line extensions like Marlboro Medium, B&H Special Kings and Merit Ultra achieved little gains in overall share. Marketing now downplays the line extensions and seeks to create a total brand imagery to support all products in a family.

At the same time, value added database management programmes play a growing role within brand families. For several years Marlboro users have been rewarded by participation in the Marlboro Adventure Team, and this was updated in 1994 as the new Marlboro Country Store. The value added by these programmes is summarised by Marlboro's agency, Leo Burnett: 'The Adventure Team brought the West into the 90s context. Country Store is much more the Cowboy focus. It's authentic.'[6] These programmes have made Marlboro the fifth largest user of direct mail in the US. Direct mail does not simply reward smokers: in the form of newsletters and bulletins it communicates Philip Morris's point of view about the legal issues concerning smoking and government activity.

In its focus on brand families and customer involvement, Philip Morris illustrates the key steps in an agenda to build consumer brands directly.

Brand families

The payback from developing customer relationships across a brand family is illustrated by Weight Watchers in the US with 250 products in seventy-eight different categories. Before 1992 Weight Watcher products were managed by separate category management teams in the organisation of owner Heinz. The decision was taken to integrate all products within a brand family under a single management team, and to develop a database management programme, 'Winners', linked to the membership of the autonomous Weight Watchers clubs. The objectives of the programme included the increase of club attendance rates and of Weight

Watcher foods brand volume. Customer club attendance and brand purchase were both rewarded by points which could be redeemed for premiums. The penetration and rate of sale of different Weight Watcher food categories were managed and developed by a series of mailings with incentives varied by the customer's individual brand usage:

— high value coupons where the objectives were penetration and cross-selling

— bonus points for repeat purchase where the objective was retention[7].

In communications to the customer base of a brand family, selective insertion of product information, combined with personalisation of copy and offers to individual customers, enables the brand manufacturer to maximise the penetration of all the brand's products and the total share of the customer base 'owned' by the brand.

Measurement and accountability

Weight Watchers 'Winners' illustrates the ability of a relationship management programme to be tracked in the finest detail. By comparing customers in the programme to a control sample of customers not in the programme and by adjusting for trends and differences between areas, the effects and payback of 'Winners' could be determined. For its entry to the 1992 'Brammy' sales promotion awards, the effects of the programme were reported as:

— a customer participation rate of 45 per cent

— a 66 per cent increase in brand volume over three months

— a payback in ninety days, agreed jointly by marketing, research and finance

— a 45.5 per cent after-tax internal rate of return.

Whatever a brand manufacturer's commitment to relationship management, the capture of individual customer data can be used to create control samples and test streams that will provide more effective tracking of customer behaviour and marketing effectiveness than current research measures.

Making advertising interactive

The potential for interactive advertising by consumer brands has already been discussed. With the deregulation of European television and the growth in cable and satellite channels, direct response television (DRTV) is likely to be a new media option. Short-form DRTV can be used to sample brands and motivate customer trial at the same time as it contributes to the building of brand values. The demand for programming will create opportunities for long-form infomercials. Every brand manufacturer should consider testing the role of both forms within their brand strategies.

Avoiding the promotional traps

The shift from short-term, untargeted couponing to promotions integrated within and targeted by a relationship strategy is illustrated by a case history from the petfoods market. The Iams brand delivered three offers within one direct mail package:

(i) a free sample to create familiarity with the brand and encourage trial

(ii) coupons to motivate repeat purchase

(iii) rebates for prolonged usage of the brand.

The campaign achieved a 3.6 per cent response, $1.4 million incremental sales and new brand users at a cost of only $24.23 each.

Promotions integrated within a relationship strategy:

— bounce back to respondents to advertising and promotions to maximise brand usage and customer share

— contain product messages and offers designed to increase brand penetration and usage cost-effectively

— add relationship values to the brand and build customer involvement as well as incentivising purchase.

Develop a club or membership

The development of a club to support and build a consumer brand is illustrated by the Philip Morris Raffles brand, marketed in the UK by Rothmans. The Raffles Club was launched with a collection scheme which offers members exclusive premiums and offers in exchange for points. The Raffles brand proposition is based on style, and the target audience have lifestyles based around their homes: there is a high propensity to shop from home and a high level of interest in games and competitions. The presentation of the club and the selection of gifts support the stylish image, but the club does not simply rely on tangible rewards. The differentiation of the Raffles Club from competitive collection schemes reinforces the differentiation of the Raffles brand from competitive brands. Membership is managed by a friendly and personable customer service team, and personalised mail adds value to the brand by regular communications that include:

— vouchers to increase participation

— defence against competitors' price cuts

— games, quizzes and competitions to raise involvement

— third party offers to increase perceived value

— a club newsletter to develop association with the brand.

The Raffles Club represents a significant investment in the customer relationship. To manage the investment and develop the relationship, 'entry' to the club is managed through a customer track that takes promotional responders through an extended trial of the brand before they become eligible for membership. The club has contributed to a significant increase in smoker loyalty to Raffles: members are less likely to be repertoire purchasers and less likely to switch when competitors promote or discount.

Marketing 'sensitive' categories

A relationship strategy is highly appropriate for brands in 'sensitive' product categories where customers welcome privacy. Peaudouce in France distributed 4 million samples by mail of its feminine protection brand Nana, achieving up to 5 per cent response to coupons offered with the package and a competition to generate customer data. A relationship strategy can also improve recommendation by medical influencers: also in France, Sanofi-Winthrop sent five mailings in sequence to 30 000 doctors under the banner 'Les France du Cholesterol' to inform them of its anti-cholesterol drug, and averaged a 10 per cent response to each: collecting data and distributing samples.[8] In Germany, I presented a relationship strategy for P&G's brand Attens, designed to help adult incontinents, which included the establishment of a customer advice service and communications to the medical profession.

Investment in a relationship strategy targeted to influencers can drive a brand's share by developing its relationship network. In the US petfood market, Carnation supported its Chew-eez brand with a programme of bi-monthly mail containing educational information and samples for vets, achieving a 68 per cent recommendation rate.

Adding value to families with children

P&G has been a major user of direct mail to distribute its Pampers brand, although the most celebrated use of a database to distribute baby nappies was by competitor Kimberly

Clark in the early 1980s with a programme 'The Beginning Years' that began before birth and continued for the first eighteen months of a baby's life. The Kool-Aid 'Wacky Warehouse' programme described earlier illustrates how value can be added through a relationship strategy to mothers and their children, the ultimate consumers. Kid's Clubs are a growing feature of consumer brand marketing: the Burger King Kid's Club is reputed to have members in one in ten US households and the club newsletter is one of the highest circulation children's publications.

In a 'first', Breyers Ice Cream launched a joint credit card with the Marine Midland Bank and a charity, the Children's Miracle Network. Breyers contributes $2 for each successful card application, and a percentage of the spend on the card is donated to the charity.[9]

Cooperative brand and retailer marketing

Another cigarette manufacturer, RJ Reynolds, has focused on the development of cooperative marketing programmes with retailers. It has programmes with 200 retailers and its support includes the management of a membership club for smokers who are customers of its retail partners.

Most trade promotion funding supports the display and often inefficient in-store promotion of a manufacturer's brands. Manufacturers can redeploy their trade budgets into activities that offer more value to retailers and their customers:

— selective and automated couponing in-store

— targeted offers to retailers' frequent shopper databases

— enhanced in-store display and demonstration

— local marketing by the brand to increase its share and the retailer's.

To compete with the specialist beauty stores, giant Wal-Mart has developed the concept of an in-store 'Beauty boutique', said to have been supported by P&G. There are many opportunities for manufacturers to go into retail stores and work with retail staff to enhance the quality of the shopping experience for customers and the rate of sale of its brands for its retail customers.

Building relationships with independents

The independent sector has been squeezed by multiple retailers but remains of considerable importance. It remains a sector in which brand manufacturers can exert considerable influence over the point of sale, and in many categories its share may increase as new buying points are needed to meet new customer demands. The independent sector typically perceives itself as neglected by manufacturers and lacks the capital base to invest in marketing, but in my experience it is enthusiastic about support which:

(i)   increases their sales without significant investment on their part

(ii) does not simply shift stock from the manufacturer to their shelves.

Retailers will increase their stock if they know that it will turn rapidly, so manufacturers must match any offer to drive distribution into the retailers with the support to drive customer demand that will move the stock off the retailer's shelves. Support can be provided in-store in the form of merchandising and point of sale, but independents particularly welcome offers that help them to provide more value for their customers and help them increase their margins. Manufacturers can also offer retailers participation in local marketing support, perhaps as customised up-weighting of nationally planned activity.

In France, Les Brasseries Heineken has made a longer term commitment to independent distributors with Le Cercle Pelforth. The initial motive was to compete with aggressive marketing competitor Kronenbourg's 1664 brand.

But the strategy was long term oriented, launching Le Cercle as a club to 25 000 outlets, at the same time as it moved nearly 100 000 additional cases of the beer. Most significantly, 28 per cent of outlets registered for Le Cercle Pelforth.[10]

Direct distribution

In an economy with increasingly complex distribution and fragmented markets, many consumer brands could build relationships with, and distribute directly to, high value customer segments. There is particular potential for:

— baby products, including foods

— pet foods

— drinks

— cosmetics.

The direct model is appropriate for any consumer brand which is bulky or difficult to carry, is bought frequently or is sensitive. The combination of the direct and membership models can provide an added value service to customers:

(i) Delivery according to a cycle designed to meet the needs of the individual customer

(ii) Instantaneous capability for the customer to add to regular orders

(iii) Privileged pricing

(iv) Added value in the form of information, extra value and enhanced customer service.

BUILDING FINANCIAL BRANDS DIRECTLY 14

'A lifetime of service'

> The Forces Shaping Financial Marketing – A Financial Relationship Strategy – A New Agenda for Financial Marketing

The Forces Shaping Financial Marketing

Financial products are the ultimate in services. The basic banking product is simply the transmission of money between seller and buyer in a marketing transaction. Banks and other retail financial institutions – building societies in the UK, savings and loans in the US – generate a margin on the transmission of money by lending long term at a higher rate of interest than they pay on short-term deposits. Similarly, life assurance and general insurance companies generate a margin between the price individuals are willing to pay to insure against risks, and the value of claims they make. The delivery of financial services involves huge administrative complexity. Billions of transactions are recorded, processed and reported – a task that before computerisation required armies of clerical staff, few of whom ever met customers.

As the funds deposited with financial institutions grew, customers sought higher returns. Financial institutions became the major investors in company equities, managing large portfolios on behalf of millions of small investors. Competition created a new market for complex financial products, with elements of life assurance, savings and equity investment. The skills and knowledge of the designers of the products and the managers of the funds determine the return on investment achieved.

People have become the driver of competitive advantage in financial services. A merchant banker confided to me that investment analysis had become so complex that it was compared to 'rocket science', literally so in his case as the products underlying his bank's success had been designed by a pair of mathematicians recruited from NASA.

Other than historical funds, a financial services company has only two assets: customers and staff. Yet most institutions have the wrong people in the wrong jobs and at the wrong locations to face the challenges of the new competition and the new customer. By the late 1980s, to deal with a bank required an inconvenient visit to a branch open for a limited time. Most customers became treated as strangers as they were unlikely to use their original branch.

Competition had forced down the margins from borrowing and lending, and banks were forced to adopt a commercial rather than a personal view of customer relationships. Lending decisions were made centrally rather than by local management, and banks began to promote promising staff and remove them from their local communities.

As customers began to demand higher levels of service, banks and other financial companies were ill-equipped to respond. Their goal of earning higher margins from fee and commission-earning products was constrained by their lack of trained staff and supporting systems: they failed to appreciate that to sell an increasing range of products required them first to build their brands by developing their customer relationships.

Four companies which have given priority to customer relationships illustrate how to address the forces shaping financial services markets: three are British: Firstdirect,

DirectLine, and the Cheltenham & Gloucester (C&G) – and the fourth is US-based Fidelity Investments.

The Firstdirect brand values are access and responsiveness. Advertising demonstrates commitment to customer service, supported by testimonials. The promised customer service completes a total brand experience with a personality reflective of the company's staff. Firstdirect is a twenty-four hour, seven day telephone banking service with well-trained, young, friendly staff who are supported by systems that allow them to recognise customers as individuals and help them manage their accounts more easily than do traditional banks.

Firstdirect recruits current account customers dissatisfied with their existing banking services: over 40 per cent of new Firstdirect customers are recommendations from friends and family. The objective of the bank is to build relationships with customers that will enable it to sell them a wider range of higher margin products. The economics are based on the maximisation of lifetime value, and the company is interested only in high potential customers: Firstdirect rejects 40 per cent of applications.

DirectLine advertising positions the company as the champion of the customer against the overpriced insurance cover offered by other less accessible and responsive financial institutions. DirectLine has captured a growing share of the motor insurance market by automating the quotation and processing of policies, and dealing directly with customers.

DirectLine's low prices are based on two factors. By eliminating broker commission and simplifying administration, DirectLine has been able to slash premiums. By focusing on low risk customers, DirectLine has been able to avoid the cross-subsidisation of higher risk customers, and offers privileged pricing to the company's selected target audience. By offering telephone access and rapid responsiveness to claims, DirectLine has achieved high levels of customer satisfaction and retention. The company's objective is to build relationships with customers that will enable it to sell a wider range of higher margin products, and in 1995 it will offer loans and mortgages. Founder Peter Wood is also establishing a new brand and differentiated service, Privilege, that will target higher risk motorists.

Both Firstdirect and DirectLine are engaged in a two-stage 'steal' of customers from their established competition. First build a relationship, then sell the profitable products that achieve lifetime value.

In contrast, the C&G offers savings and investment products with the highest rate of interest on postal savings and investment accounts. There is no added value here, and C&G makes no bones about its strategy: the society's strapline is: 'We're here to make you richer.' But C&G is able to offer the highest interest rates because it is the society with the lowest cost–income ratio of the majors, and has – relative to assets – the lowest investment in the bricks and mortar of branches.

Fidelity serves a more sophisticated investor than the C&G and the majority of its business comes direct from customers. Although Fidelity first established a presence in the UK market with distinctive product-led advertising, the company's competitive advantage is based on the quality of its service and its people. A shift in advertising strategy in 1994 expresses product performance through people values, and the skill and experience of the Fidelity fund manager. Fidelity customer service representatives are mostly graduates, and are supported by systems that deliver to their desktops up-to-date product and investment information while they are on the line to customers.

The core brand values of Fidelity combine excellence in product and people: investment expertise delivered through helpful and informed customer service. Fidelity expects the customer to make his or her own decisions. I described earlier the US direct response television advertising for Fidelity Fundmatch, dramatising customer confusion with the hard sell communications of Fidelity's competitors. Responders to Fidelity advertising receive information that guides customers through the alternative investment options, and helps them make up their own minds and choose the solution appropriate to them as individuals.

This tone pervades all Fidelity communications and service: investment is an intensely personal decision, it is for the customer to decide, and Fidelity's role is to provide knowledge and expertise as well as competitive products.

The four companies illustrate the forces shaping financial marketing:

(i)   Personal service, available whenever and wherever the customer needs it

(ii)   Competitive pricing, based on operational excellence

(iii)   Differential pricing, not based on averages but on the costs of servicing individual customers

(iv)   Information and education, enabling customers to make their own decisions about increasingly complex products.

A Financial Relationship Strategy

Most of the higher margin products that financial companies want to sell to build customer lifetime value are of interest to a minority of the population. They consist broadly of lending products like mortgages and personal loans, or high rate savings and long-term investment vehicles. Both types of product are only relevant to customers at a certain lifestage. Once they buy a product, even a smaller minority of customers remain in the market and actively manage their financial portfolios. Most relationships with customers are passive.

Although financial companies sell principally to existing customers and their products appeal to a narrow minority, general advertising is justified on the grounds that it builds the brand. Yet there is little evidence that branding has achieved any significant differentiation in finance. Most gains are the result of distribution trends, in particular towards 'bancassurance', the sale of life products through retail branches rather than sales forces.

Direct mail is used to promote specific products but is not well regarded by customers. Because financial companies have built databases of transactional rather than directional data, their mail is poorly targeted. And because there is a belief that most financial products are sold rather than bought, their messages are dominated by offer, incentive and price. Financial direct mail has contributed little to brand differentiation; as one commentator puts it: 'Many offices spend a great deal of money on direct marketing activity which you would think would be carefully designed and written in order to feed off, and indeed feed into, the brand communication. Not a bit of it. Everyone is saying and showing the same things, using the same language.'[1] My own research reveals that at best financial mail is regarded as low interest – at worst it demonstrably damages brand values.

The first priority for a financial relationship strategy is to target customers at the time in which they are in the market for financial products. The strategy must be to collect directional data about customers' needs and intentions, and use this data to time and trigger messages appropriate to them as individuals. Existing customers should receive special offers and privileged pricing as a reward for their custom – a differential pricing strategy to customers increases profitability as well as response rates. Although the message should feature a reward, the communication must put the customer in control: adding value to the relationship by providing helpful information and guidance on the options available to the customer.

Most customers have a passive relationship with their bank, building society and insurance company: their continued custom is matter of habit. Collecting data about customers is an opportunity to add value and activate the relationship. The company should focus attention on the 'handraisers' who represent high potential lifetime value. Even for the clearing banks only a minority of customers offer potential, and affinity marketing programmes should be developed to maximise the relevance of products and services for selected customer segments. As Mike Patterson of USAA Investment Management Company advises: 'take the 20 per cent of your customers that generate 80 per cent of your revenues – and get intimate. If you do it well, you'll find you've entered into a marriage made in heaven. But you'll also have to get serious about your database.'[2]

Financial services marketers have failed to achieve the cross-selling rates they originally set themselves after deregulation in the mid 1980s. They have failed because they did not first develop their customer relationships and their customer involvement. Most did not offer any meaningful privileges or substantive rewards for buying more products from the same company. Encumbered by clerical work-forces and antiquated systems, most were unable to make themselves accessible and responsive to customers. Their challenge now is to focus on a manageable number of high potential customers, and develop distinctive relationships with these customers that add value.

Financial companies have largely been marketed on a product basis, but the relationship perspective is to identify the mix of products appropriate to the individual customer. Prospects for multiple products can be managed through customer tracks that include relationship-building as well as product communications. Product communications can be data-driven: targeted, timed and triggered by events, signals and anniversaries.

Financial companies must rethink the content of their communications and the design of their products and services. The mass of the population was inhibited by money management, but the new customer demands control of the financial as well as the other aspects of their lives. Financial companies must develop the knowledge of their customers, help them overcome their insecurity and partner them in making their money work to achieve their aspirations.

At the same time, a financial company can develop its brand personality and customer relationship by inviting customers to participate in a wider range of activities. Opportunities to create customer association with financial brands include: surveys, financial education programmes, customer magazines, extra value offers, charities and local community projects.

To deliver on the service promise investment in people is vital. Firstdirect gives new staff six weeks training, three weeks of which is spent with a trained representative on live calls. For customers for whom face-to-face relationships are important, financial companies must rethink their staff policies and their organisational structures. A study reported in *Director* magazine reveals that the movement of branch staff is one of the constant complaints that customers hold against banks, in contrast with Germany where turnover of staff is significantly lower.[3] In a presentation to the spring 1993 Direct Marketing Conference, Frederick Reichfeld of Bain & Co reported a study that branch profitability rises with the length of tenure of branch management.[4] Financial companies need to establish a customer management strategy and customer team structure, empowering local staff to implement their own marketing programmes and make more of their own decisions.

A New Agenda for Financial Marketing

Financial brands must demonstrate access and response, communicated with a personality distinctive to the company and its people. Innovative and competitive products are not enough – in finance most innovations can quickly be matched by competition. Products only exist to meet customer needs: to buy and protect homes and cars, achieve financial security and enjoy a higher quality of life. Money is a means to these ends, and financial companies can add value:

— by helping customers through important transactions that can involve anxiety and stress

— by helping customers realise their aspirations.

Successful relationship-building means eliminating the customer's fear of the unknown, simplifying the complexity of transactions and helping customers make better use of their money to achieve their ambitions.

Building brand value

Financial brands must encompass a number of generic values:

— clarity

— information

— flexibility

— helpfulness

— problem-solving

— personal service

— advice

— reputation.

Building a brand means building a total experience. The mission of the company and the personality of its people are the factors that will make a financial brand distinctive and motivating to customers. The brand promise must be reaffirmed in the way in which customer needs are met and customer relationships are managed. Prudential has invested heavily in the advertising theme 'I want to be', and research confirms that: 'Its brands values are understanding people's aspirations, integrity and fair dealing.'[5] But Prudential must demonstrate these values in every contact with customers.

Like any of the major financial companies, Prudential will also need to segment its broad customer base, and develop affinity relationship management programmes with their own personalities and brands within the Prudential brand family. This is easier, and is the survival strategy for a smaller player. Clerical Medical is a medium-sized company that has focused on professionals and achieved high awareness from a modest advertising budget. But Clerical Medical must enhance its products and combine them in innovative ways to deliver on its brand promise.

Developing the brand into a relationship

USAA is one of the leading financial institutions in the US and achieves among the highest customer retention rates. A major aspect of USAA's relationship strategy is to develop the brand into an added value relationship by packaging a number of products together and overlaying additional customer services:

(i) Movers Advantage offers help and savings with relocation, travel and telephone in a combination with a home loan and insurance package

(ii) Auto Pricing offers help with current car price lists and model options, and USAA will even negotiate with a dealer on behalf of a member in combination with a finance package.

USAA's objective is that 'there is only one place to buy a car . . . only one way to move, that's the USAA way'.[6]

UK financial companies have developed similar added value concepts. Mortgage customers are high value and the mortgage transaction is a trigger for other financial needs. The TSB has created a series of videos to guide customers through home purchase and finance, and savings and investment options. The Leeds Permanent building society has developed a 'Home Arranger' service to help customers through all aspects of the home purchase process. The Home Arranger service develops a one-to-one relationship between the customer and the Home Arranger, a member of staff located in the customer's local branch.

Every financial company can re-engineer a product forwards and backwards to develop a transaction into a relationship: home extensions and holidays (after cars the two major reasons for loans), and wills, births, marriages and deaths all create new customer needs which the company can meet.

Developing satisfaction and loyalty

For a sector with low levels of customer satisfaction, the development of service must be a priority. Research into lost bank accounts shows that only a minority switch because of price: the major reasons are either major problems or a series of small errors in the management of the account or the handling of the customer relationship. Interactive communication with customers – more surveys of customer opinion and censuses of customer needs – perform two functions: they demonstrate that the company is interested in its customers and committed to helping them, and they identify customers with serious problems and allow the company an opportunity to solve the problem and save the customer. An important investment for most financial companies is in a 'customer save' programme to identify and retain high risk/high value customers.

To develop meaningful loyalty financial companies must activate their customer relationships. In particular they must shift from 'hard sell' financial junk mail to interactive communications:

— delivered in information-led formats, like newsletters, videos, interactive disks and on-line services

— offering new guidance and advice

— adding entertainment value

— soliciting customer feedback at all stages.

Putting the customer in control

The increasing sophistication of customers has changed their relationship with financial institutions from parent-to-child to adult-to-adult. The conventional wisdom that products are sold and not bought is out of date. Financial companies must communicate to customers both their full range of services and the information and advice that will equip customers to understand and use the products.

I have found that one of the most appreciated communications to customers is a 'menu' of services which describes in context the financial products available and illustrates their value by customer case histories. The 'menu card' concept can be usefully developed into a 'financial catalogue', a guide to rather than a mere listing of financial products. As in any sector, customers enjoy and benefit most from human interest stories and the experiences of their peers. Financial services become real to customers when their role in improving quality of life is illustrated.

Financial companies can add value by customising information like:

(i) A regular report of their major transactions and how they have used their accounts

(ii) A regular update on their eligibility for lending products, and privileged pricing on savings and investment products.

Product promotions succeed only when they arrive during the narrow window in time when a customer is in the market. Personalised, menu-driven communication builds customer awareness of the products, and can be used to prompt customer response data to drive triggered communications.

Creating customer access

Putting the customer in control means giving the customer direct access to services and information. The rapid acceptance of ATMs in the 1980s demonstrates customer demand for more convenient access: two ATM transactions are now made for every cheque transaction in a bank. For up-to-date account and product information, personal service by telephone is not a customer priority and is too expensive for companies to provide to a mass market. New solutions will include:

— Automated telephone services, using touch tone and other intelligent devices that allow the customer to obtain information and execute simple transactions; BSV Bank in Germany has introduced an interactive communications system called 'Telekonto' linked to its operation in Luxembourg

— On-line visual links through television or PC to information and a live customer representative; Centraal Beheer in Holland has a system it calls the 'Visual Telephone' which can communicate to over 70 per cent of Dutch households using the Astra satellite.

The principle is simply to give customers access to the information they need wherever they are and whatever the time.

Managing local marketing

The centralisation of decision-making and marketing in financial services may have improved operational efficiency, but has distanced companies from their customers. It is arguable that locally made lending decisions were superior to those made under central control, even with sophisticated risk analysis tools. Technology can make these tools available to local customer representatives. If branches are to become financial retailers in the true sense of the term, their staff must be empowered to manage customer relationships and supported with marketing tailored to their customer base.

The trend to bancassurance and the conditions imposed by legislation are reducing the ranks of self-employed financial sales forces and independent agents. Companies that wish to maintain these channels of distribution need to develop tailored marketing support systems. Typical local marketing programme options include cross-sell, traffic-building referrals, customised offers and local community support activities. These programmes can be centrally managed by locally planned and implemented. Local staff select from a menu: the customers they wish to target, the information and product offers they wish to make to these customers, and their choice of copy and personalisation. A central marketing team manages the selection, printing and mailing of the communications. By combining the requests of many branches, economies of scales are realised in the production and management of the campaigns. Local content and personality increases the effectiveness of the campaigns and builds local relationships consistent with the national brand personality (Figure 14.1).

Bankers and insurance agents were once props of their local communities. Where companies have a heavy concentration of branches and so a major presence in the

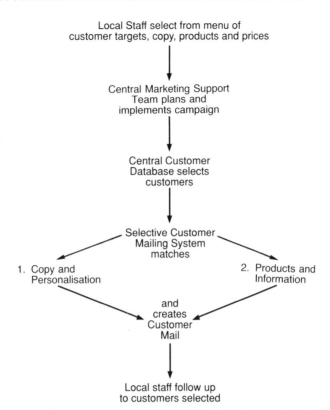

Figure 14.1 Local marketing system for branches, sales forces and agents

community, they should empower their staff to develop community-based initiatives and involve customers in these initiatives.

Developing customer management

An integrated strategy for customer management encompasses four major types of media and customer contact opportunity:

(i) Brand-led advertising, direct marketing and promotion communicate general themes and messages over time, in

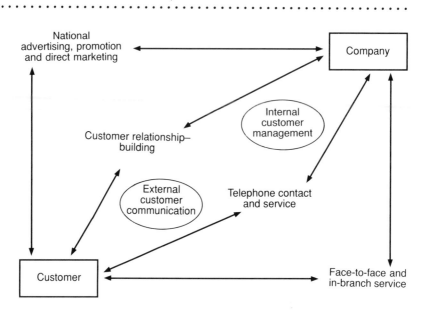

Figure 14.2 Customer management

Table 14.1 Customer management: illustration – mortgages

Brand-led communication	Relationship track	Telephone contact	Personal contact
Advertising of new mortgage rates and personal service	Update of regular communication to existing mortgage holders	Special scripts to all mortgage enquirers	
Targeted direct mail to future movers and holders of competitive mortgage accounts	Triggering of special offers to previous respondents in a home owner programme	Special cross-sell scripts to selected callers and transactors on other products	
In-branch promotion to motivate dialogue with branch staff	Internal communication of best prospects to telephone teams and branch staff	Special scripts for customer service and public relations	

particular new product information, and new pricing, terms and conditions

(ii) Customer relationship-building messages are delivered through customer tracks

(iii) Customers can access the company by telephone to make enquiries and manage transactions: during customer-initiated calls relationship-building messages can be prompted, and company-initiated calls can enhance relationship-building tracks

(iv) The same customer data available to marketing is available to customer-facing staff in branches, to manage transactions and prompt relationship-building.

Marketing planning assigns to each of these four layers of communication an appropriate role and set of messages (Figure 14.2 and Table 14.1).

Design customer tracks

Financial products are pure information and financial services demands data-driven marketing. The elements of a system to drive customer tracks in financial services are:

— Enhancement of transaction data with customer response data, using censuses and surveys to prospect among customers and identify the events, signals and anniversaries that create selling opportunities

— Design of an expert system that analyses customer data and selects the appropriate offer, method of contact and timing: the system selects products, pricing, and sequence and predicts profitability and response rates

— Communication of customer selections to customer service representatives at local sites and in telephone contact centres, and to automated customer mail centres

— Customer teams are briefed to contribute to the contact, and informed of the products likely to be of interest to customers if they initiate the contact

— Mail is customised, using standard stationery with in-fill of messages appropriate to the individual customer and referring to the customer's usual company contact; specific offers and pricing are in-filled, and general information relevant to all customers is automatically inserted.

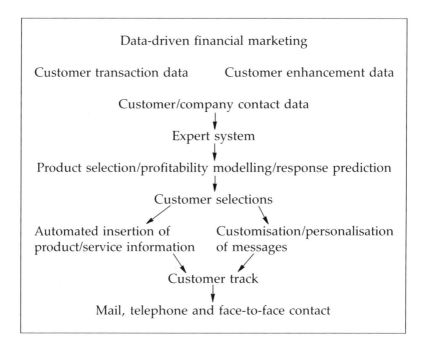

Data-driven financial marketing

Customer transaction data   Customer enhancement data

Customer/company contact data

Expert system

Product selection/profitability modelling/response prediction

Customer selections

Automated insertion of   Customisation/personalisation
product/service information   of messages

Customer track

Mail, telephone and face-to-face contact

Increasingly, financial services providers will focus on well-defined customer segments, and their marketing will be targeted within selected customer tracks. Firstdirect and Fidelity illustrate companies with a proposition designed for a specific customer belief and behaviour. By contrast, USAA sells to an audience defined by demographics and occupation, and seeks to maximise its share of the customer's financial portfolio: USAA's strapline is 'A lifetime

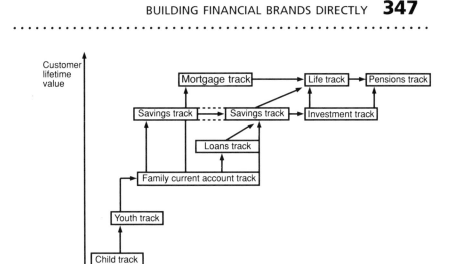

Figure 14.3 Lifecycle marketing and customer tracks

of service to you and your family'. Customer tracks can themselves be integrated to meet customer needs throughout their financial lifecycles: marketing from 'cradle to grave' (Figure 14.3).

BUILDING BUSINESS BRANDS DIRECTLY 15

'Who's talking to your customers if
you're not?'

The Forces Shaping Business-to-Business Marketing –
Business-to-Business Relationship Strategy – A New Agenda
for Business Marketers – Enhancing Contact by Telephone

The Forces Shaping Business-to-Business Marketing

The changing organisation of business and the rapid advance of technology have increased the complexity of
business-to-business decision-making. Many business
marketers could once identify the relatively small number
of decision-makers in their target audiences. As business
hierarchies become flatter and technical specialists grow in
influence, the buying points in customer organisations have
increased in number and the varying influences on the
buying decision have become more difficult to identify. The
balance of power in the traditional model of the multiple
decision making unit (dmu) has shifted, away from management, to specialists and users who are also choosers
(Figure 15.1).

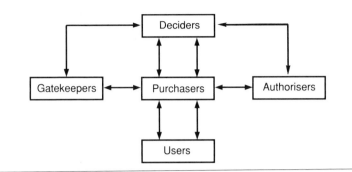

Deciders	Senior management, motivated by the impact of the purchase on the company's competitiveness and image.
Authorisers	Financial management, concerned with capital budgeting, the financing of the purchase and the stability of the supplier.
Gatekeepers	Technical specialists, concerned with the specification of the solution and its fit with the company's strategy.
Purchasers	Operational managers, concerned with the supplier's ability to deliver a solution that is efficient and effective.
Users	Managers and staff, concerned with the ability of their solution to enhance their working lives.

Figure 15.1 Multiple decision-making unit

The growth in the number of self-employed and professionals who work from home has increased the size and the importance of the 'SoHo' market: small offices and home offices. One of the consequences of fragmentation is that business-to-business marketing is becoming more like business-to-consumer marketing. External influences on a company's decision-making are increasingly important, and word-of-mouth, reputation and awareness of a supplier play a greater role. Above all, brand image and values are increasingly important in business-to-business decision-making.

The fragmentation of decision-making has been accompanied by a proliferation in specialist and trade media. The costs of producing and distributing magazines has fallen sharply, and in every industry there has been an increase in the number of titles and advertising pages available. Competition for business advertising is fierce. Many business magazines serve well-defined target audiences and satisfy the needs of these audiences for industry news and information. In the US, the industrial magazine *New Equipment Digest* advertises itself as 'The hardest working magazine in America', challenges advertisers to consider: 'Who's taking to your customers if you're not?', and offers a guide to high yield advertising as means of influencing advertisers to include the magazine in their media schedules.

The business marketer has an enormous range of sales opportunities and marketing media to evaluate: from advertising to direct mail to trade shows and seminars. The priority is to cut through complexity to talk to the right buyer. Among important relationship trends are the building of customer databases and the publication of customer magazines as private channels of communication between manufacturers and their customers.

A change of supplier can involve a significant dislocation of a customer's operations. The costs of switching suppliers are large, customers are loath to change, and to win new customers is difficult and expensive. At the same time, any company complacent about its own customer base is living dangerously. Rapid technological change and product obsolescence mean that buyers are constantly aware of and tempted by new solutions. Suppliers must keep in close contact with their customers to monitor their changing requirements. But the fragmentation of buying decisions and the increase in the number of technical influencers makes it harder for any supplier to build relationships with more contact points within the customer and retain control of a customer's entire purchases within a category.

There are more buying decisions to cover, yet sales forces are more difficult to recruit and retain, and more expensive to train and support. Sales persons must match the increased sophistication of buyers, and require greater general business knowledge and technical understanding to negotiate and sell more complex products and services. Companies are increasingly concerned with the control they exercise over the presentations made by sales people and the relationships they build with customers. To exert more control they invest in portable technology to enhance sales force communication and in technical and support staff to enhance customer communication. These investments further increase the costs of calling on customers and managing relationships face to face.

Companies who distribute through a dealer or agent network have different concerns: the quality of the sale and the value added by the distributor. The inability to control the point of sale and the customer interface is perceived as a limiting factor, and the quality of the staff in independent outlets and the professionalism of their marketing are potentially damaging to manufacturers' brand values. Independents owe no particular allegiance to any manufacturer, sell competitive products and have incomplete geographic coverage. These factors frustrate manufacturers from maximising their revenues and developing the penetration of new products and services.

Concerned with the cost of sales forces and quality of independent distribution, business marketers seek new routes to market. They are forced to participate in the new retail formats: as in the consumer market business-to-business category killers like Staples (office supplies), PC World (computer hardware) and CompUSA (computer software) have emerged to satisfy the growing range of products and the proliferation of buying points. But as in the consumer market, distribution through multiple retailers squeezes manufacturers' margins and divorces them from their customers.

In contrast, the Direct model offers access to the total market, control of pricing and the opportunity to develop quality customer relationships.

Business-to-Business Relationship Strategy

The increasing complexity of business markets demands increased marketing sophistication and greater invest-ment in research and analysis. To target their marketing companies must be able to identify the location and timing of buying decisions within a market and understand the decision-making processes within the companies that make up the market. A research and analysis plan identifies:

— the number and size of buying decisions, the proportion of decisions in which the company was a candidate and the reasons for success and failure

— the decision-makers within the buying company, their information sources and motivations, and their roles and relative importance in the buying decision

— the timing and cycle of decision-making and the cus-tomer's planning and budgeting process.

These analyses drive the targeting strategy, and under-standing of customer information sources and decision-making drives the planning of message and media within the strategy (Figure 15.2).

I have developed three generic business-to-business communication strategies to address the different members of the multiple dmu:

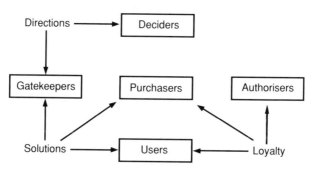

Figure 15.2 Multiple decision-making unit: message strategies

(i) *Directions* Communication to Deciders and Gatekeepers, who may not be directly involved in the process, but with whom it is important to develop a dialogue; senior company management must foster relationships with their peers in customer organisations, and special communication tracks that include information bulletins, conferences and seminars can be developed for technical specialists.

(ii) *Solutions* Communications to purchasers and influential users should emphasise the effectiveness of solutions and the future direction of the supplier's products; they should also emphasise the supplier's commitment to total service.

(iii) *Loyalty* Communications to users should involve them in the effective use of the solution and build an association with them so that they become advocates of the supplier; it is particularly important to identify and solve problems and concerns with the solution. Communications should also address authorisers and exchange value for repeat purchase.

The value of a customer governs investment in the customer, the contact plan and the design of customer tracks to develop relationships. The conventional segmentation of a business market is by key and major accounts, industry sectors like finance and government, and small business. Business decision-makers are allocated direct sales or remote customer representatives. The relationship strategy is to focus on the potential of a customer and the probability of winning a higher share of the customer's business.

The company's representation to the customer consists of a multidisciplinary team rather than an individual sales person or account manager. In the customer team are at least three types of personnel: sales, technical support and customer support (Figure 15.3). Technical and support personnel are accessible by telephone, and teams may also be backed by information analysts responsible for database management, the updating of customer information and monitoring of industry trends.

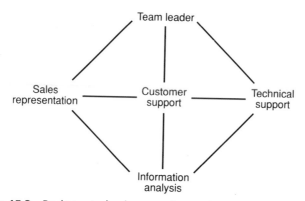

Figure 15.3 Business-to-business customer team: structure

Most companies neglect the updating of customer information: one study reported that in one year 61 per cent of decision-maker details had changed, and 27 per cent of decision-makers had moved to other customers.[1] An essential for relationship management is to track customers, and decision-maker moves can create new opportunities. The information function also scans for industry and customer news, and should seek to identify the events and signals that reveal customer needs and sales opportunities.

The team concept enhances the quality of relationship between company and customer. The customer relationship is no longer owned by an individual member of staff, protecting the company from loss of that individual to a competitor. The management and development of a customer relationship is a task beyond any individual, and the team with complementary skills, personality types and motivations can add value to all the dimensions of my CARES model:

— *Enhanced Contact*   The customer has more contact with technical and customer support as well as sales, and all members of the team can send the customer information of interest and relevance; the different members of the team match and develop a dialogue with the different members of the customer's decision-making unit, from senior management to technical specialists

— *Enhanced Affinity* The team develops and shares specialist knowledge of the customer's industry and business, and can tailor the company's products and services more closely to the customer's needs

— *Enhanced Rewards* Increased knowledge of the customer and the decentralisation of responsibility to the customer team allows members of the team to compete in tenders and to tailor pricing to the customer; a particular responsibility of the team is customer accounting and profitability measurement, and – if measured on lifetime values – the team can make more informed decisions about preferential customer pricing across all products and services and maximise their share of the customer's business

— *Extra Value* Better customer knowledge allows the team to compete for customer business by offering extra value relevant to all members of the customer's decision-making unit; customer profiles and cultures vary and marketing is more powerful when it is customer-directed

— *Enhanced Customer Service* The increased resources in the customer team allow the company to deliver superior service.

Customer teams create an organisational structure in which all contact with customers can be integrated, reaffirm the brand personality and add value to the customer relationship. A team is simply an effective method of managing the customer relationship, and a productive organisational response to increasingly diverse customer needs. In particular the reorganisation of sales, service and marketing into customer teams eliminates the damaging 'turf' wars between sales and marketing and between head offices and regional sales.

The new generic brand values of access and responsiveness are particularly important in business-to-business markets. A customer contact centre is an essential organisational resource, and information systems should support the internal communication of customer data from the centre to teams. Information systems should respond to customer events, signals and anniversaries, alert all representatives in the team and trigger appropriate action with the customer.

A New Agenda for Business Marketers

In business markets a significant element of a company brand is defined by its relationship with customers, and customer information is a critical competitive advantage. The choice of a supplier is important not only because the supplier's products benefit the customer, but because they ultimately enhance the customer's service to *its* customers. An intimate knowledge of the customer's business is valuable precisely because it helps suppliers get closer to an understanding of how their products and services can add value to end-users. Business brands must encompass access, responsiveness, service and a distinctive element which represents the benefit to the customer's end-users.

Adding access and responsiveness to brand value

In *Managing Brand Equity* David Aaker describes the fate of the software company MicroPro, manufacturer of the first successful word processing package WordStar. In analysing WordStar's dramatic loss of market share to WordPerfect, Aaker says: 'WordStar lost position in large part because it turned its back on its installed base.'[2] WordStar neglected the needs of existing customers by launching new products incompatible with existing software, and failing to provide information and service to customers. Meanwhile, relative newcomer WordPerfect supported its customers through change with an unlimited access, free telephone support service.

The software market illustrates the cost to the customer of switching and the importance of managing the customer through change, both to retain and develop existing customers and to win new customers. Business marketers can use new technology to enhance their accessibility and responsiveness. Information can be supplied through fax on demand services, automatic call distribution systems can switch customer callers directly through to their own customer representatives and teams, and electronic mail links can be created between teams and their customers.

Embedding partnership values within business brands

Companies seek long-term business partners rather than single solution suppliers. Two essential values for business brands are:

(i) *Investment* Business marketers must demonstrate their commitment to invest, to learn and to meet the specific needs of their customers

(ii) *Development* Business marketers must demonstrate their investment in the future: the proof that they have products and services to meet the future needs of their customers.

Partnership is a generic value that can be demonstrated by the direct involvement of customers in product development.

Combine customer service with relationship management

Dell Computer is the best example of customer service as a source of competitive advantage and brand value. For Dell, moreover, service is inseparable from relationship-building and sales.

Many companies use the telephone to manage customer enquiries, but these operations – especially when they are outsourced – do little more than despatch brochures. Other companies establish customer service operations, but separate them from enquiry management sales and distribution functions. The result is that customers may need to deal with a number of contacts within the company, each of whom works in isolation of the others. If customer information cannot be distributed to and shared among the different functions, the results are gross inefficiency for the company and frustration and confusion for the customer.

Business marketers most reorganise sales, service and marketing into teams, and allow important customers direct access to these teams. At the same time, they should support customer teams by updating and distributing customer information.

Maximising customer value

The opportunity to increase customer profitability by increasing share of the customer is significant in business as in any market. A relationship with a customer enables the business marketer to identify other buying points within the same customer site, at other customer sites and even in the international divisions of the customer. To maximise customer value requires:

— the continuing research and update of buying points and decision-makers

— the continuing communication to and feedback from customers.

As well as establishing responsive customer contact centres, business marketers should develop proactive customer communication programmes to maximise customer awareness of their total range and to increase cross-selling to their existing customers. I designed a sales force and lead generation programme for Rank Xerox that generated an 18 per cent response rate, but two-thirds of respondents were interested in products and services other than that featured in the mail: revealing the huge potential for increased contact with customers.

Business decision-makers receive a considerable volume of mail, so it is vital that mail engages and involves them, and reflects the brand personality in distinctively presented messages. Mail that calls for a response achieves the highest awareness. The power of interactive mail to gain attention and build relationships is illustrated by a mail programme to board-level decision-makers in major industrial customers of Midlands Electricity. The strategy was to use case histories to demonstrate the value of Midlands Electricity consultancy and services, and the executions were audio-cassettes which featured recorded interviews with customers. The first package featured a photograph of and introduction to the Midlands Electricity's designated representative, and the cassette recordings were given personality and continuity by using a fictional detective as the narrator.

Direct mail in business markets is most effective when it expresses both the values of a company and the personalities of its staff. Business products and services like electricity processes may be highly technical, but ultimately it is the people in the supplier on whom customers depend. The cassette series was a platform for subsequent tactical offers, and the distinctive personality of the Midlands Electricity team was maintained: an invitation to a seminar about industrial drying processes was mailed in a leaflet packaged in a water bag containing cartoon fish. Senior decision-makers applauded the entertainment value and the seminars were a success.

Enhancing Contact by Telephone

Mail contact can be supported and enhanced by telephone. The customer contact track should include regular telephone contact between customers and members of the customer team on a 'keep in touch', even when there are no specific sales messages. The combination of mail and telephone is powerful: mail communicates information that a customer can assimilate in a non-selling environment, while telephone follow-up can capitalise on the interest created. I have known a mail programme generate only a 1.8 per cent response rate, which rose to over 9 per cent when mail recipients were contacted shortly after by telephone. A factor of 6:1 for telephone over mail is typical.

Driven by the growth in telephone as a marketing communication medium and the scarcity of telephone skills, there is an increasing trend towards the outsourcing of telephone services and the management of telephone contact on a cost per contact basis. Both trends are dangerous because of the power of telephone as part of the total customer experience of the brand. Companies should invest in the training of telephone personnel in their contact centres and in representatives in their customer teams. The effectiveness of telephone contact should be measured not on the number of calls per hour but on the value added to customers and on the customer's propensity to buy: in other words, on customer loyalty.

Mail and telephone contact are particularly important in an area neglected by most business marketers: maximising the conversion of prospects into sales. Most companies fail to follow up leads if they do not show an immediate interest in purchase, yet US research has revealed that 56 per cent of respondents were still in the market six months after enquiry, and 33 per cent had retained the company's literature and had still budgeted to buy the product.[3]

Building an association of customers

Customer publications are a private medium through which companies can talk to their customers, and are most effective when the strategy is to use the magazine to articulate the voice of the customer – not just to deliver what I once heard a research attendee describe as 'company propaganda'.

In designing business-to-business customer magazines I have learned two lessons. The first is to make much of the material about the staff in the company, and to balance company and product information with contributions from customers: their own stories, information and questions.

As the editor of any consumer magazine knows, people

like to read about people. Many business marketers run small user groups, but their proprietary magazines could become the linchpins of wider customer associations.

The second lesson is to invest in the content of the publication rather than the quality of the production. Because business decision-makers are time-pressured and bombarded by information sources, most magazines have a short life-span – if they are read at all. Full colour magazines may not be cost-effective on a regular basis, and should be reserved for special occasions. Simpler production using desktop publishing technology can allow shorter lead times and more topical content.

Customer publishing programmes can be targeted to different levels in the decision-making unit. Xerox in the US and Rank Xerox in Europe created the magazine *Best of Business* to communicate to senior decision-makers that the company was positioned in the information technology as well as the office product market. Federal Express launched its magazine *Via FedEx* in November 1991 to target 350 000 secretaries, the ultimate users of courier services. Federal Express recognised them as neglected by other publications but as key influencers in the choice of despatch services. The content of the magazine is designed to help secretaries use delivery services, but also to add value to their working lives: as *Via FedEx* editor Joan McPeak says: 'we knew what an eager audience this was . . . We want to help educate office professionals . . . give them something to help them improve in their jobs'.[4] Federal Express also targets magazines to other decision-maker roles: a quarterly to senior executives, and a semiannual covering economic and business issues to decision-makers in the Far East.

The role of customer magazines should be to build the brand and customer relationships. The magazine content should be selected to offer extra value and information consistent with desired brand values. The editorial thrust should motivate customer response and participation in the magazine.

Customer magazines are notoriously difficult to justify and many have been cut when budgets are tight. The impact of magazines can be evaluated by their role in generating customer leads and incremental sales. Every issue should be tracked by a telephone sample to measure use and readership of the publication, and impact of the content on intention to buy and loyalty.

As an alternative to customer magazines, business marketers can offer key decision-makers complementary subscriptions to other publishers' magazines. Digital Equipment Corporation offered a free subscription to *International Business Week* to board directors of the top UK companies and delivered the magazine to home addresses. Every quarter Digital inserted supplements on developments in information technology and Digital's role in these developments.

Cutting through the advertising clutter – 1

The importance of specialist magazines as advertising media has been discussed in earlier chapters. *Marketing Director International* reports research that confirms the effectiveness of business magazines in gaining the attention of readers:

— three-quarters of readers read more than half the content of an issue

— more than three-quarters of readers read every issue and often go back to them several times[5].

Many conventional advertising formats like double-page spreads are less effective than in newspapers because advertising not positioned opposite receives little reader attention in a thick 'book'. To maximise the effectiveness of magazines, business marketers should evaluate higher impact formats:

— multiple pages in succession opposite editorial

— gatefolds at front and rear of magazine

— bound in and loose inserts

— special multi-page advertising supplements.

And they should use these formats for prospecting as well as for advertising.

Cutting through the advertising clutter – 2

To maximise the impact of magazines, business-to-business marketers can use advertising to generate qualified prospects, and follow up with mail and telephone contact to build relationships. Advertisers can achieve step changes in their advertising and lead generation by switching from space advertising to inserts and mail. In a presentation to the Montreux Direct Marketing Symposium, Irene Allanson, formerly of Ogilvy & Mather Direct and now of Direxions in Brussels, describes inserts for Data General that generated 11 per cent response and a direct mail programme for Oce copiers that raised spontaneous awareness from 20 to 42 per cent with two mailings, and to close to total awareness with five mailings.[6] I have developed a programme for Digital to develop their share of the Workstation market that turned the advertising theme into a multidimensional mail programme, and used a questionnaire as insert and in mail to lead generate and build a private database for regular contact.

Integrating Sales and Marketing

The role of technology in automating lead generation and sales force contact is now widespread. Customer information is communicated electronically to remote sales forces, and the results of sales force contact captured on from local and portable PCs are automatically uploaded overnight to the company's customer database. But information technology can be used to control (the company's objective) as well as enhance (the company's sales force's objective) all contacts between its representatives and customers:

(i) *Automatic Proposal Generation* Software is available to automate proposal writing and the description and costing of services in complex tender documents

(ii) *Multimedia Presentations* Presentations can be prepared centrally and downloaded to sales force systems fully customised for individual customers; presentations can be left with customers on floppy disk for use by more decision-makers

(iii) *Remote Presentations* PC video and video conferencing systems can involve more members of a company team and more customer decision-makers in a direct dialogue

(iv) *Customised Product Configurations* Customer service representatives can configure products and services on-line for customers, and directly place tailored orders with manufacturing once the customer's specifications are met

(v) *Automated Distribution* Any member of the customer team can track the progress of a customer's order through manufacturing and delivery.

Managing customers internationally

Customer service can be provided from any location. The US marketing community has seized with alacrity upon the opportunities offered by the recent international trade agreements. US marketers are used to dealing with diverse and geographically distant markets: one direct marketing magazine's response to the North American Free Trade Agreement was that it 'will be like adding another million zip codes to the US marketing universe'.[7] The same source offered this prediction:

> American Direct Marketers will be able to centralise marketing and management activities and use regional warehouses in Europe and other territories. The globalisation of American catalogues will be a fact in the new century. Conventional retailing will survive, but more consumers will turn to non-store shopping, so it should be an exciting era for interactive marketing, cable shopping and catalogs.

Cataloguers can manage relationships and distribute product through international call centres, which offer savings in development costs and benefits in shared knowledge. International toll-free numbers route calls from any country and high volume call centres receive significant discounts from telecoms suppliers. Customers in different markets and in different sectors have different expectations about language, but multilingual staff can be employed.

Telecom Ireland advertises its call centre services as a gateway to the EU market of 340 million consumers. One major company to locate its call centre in Ireland is Kao Infosystems, the world's leading manufacturer of 3.5 inch diskettes which has call-centres in Ireland and California. Sun Express Europe, the direct marketing subsidiary of Sun Microsystems, selected the Netherlands as the location for its telephone centre supporting its cross-border sales force. The location of a Customer Contact Centre can reduce telecommunication costs, minimise staff costs, benefit from government incentives, and harness local skills in the selected site.

Launching a direct channel

The effect of all the forces shaping business markets will be to lead companies to build their brands and customer franchises by direct distribution of their products to customers. Direct now accounts for over 15 per cent of the US PC market, driven by leaders like Dell and Gateway 2000. By combining competitive product quality with high service values both companies have built their businesses as brands in their own right. Other independents like MicroWarehouse and PCs Compleat are cataloguers who sell branded PCs, peripherals and accessories on price, and see themselves as channels rather than brands. As PCs Compleat says: 'We view ourselves as a Good Housekeeping seal-of-approval kind of company. Having our own brand would be kind of a taint on us.'[8]

The established manufacturers confront direct sellers who have built their brand values on access and responsiveness while in the recent past they themselves have focused on product or customer rather service: while Dell has been advertising the commitment of its people, IBM has continued to advertise its product. While Dell has built awareness of its support and accessibility, Apple has remained restricted by its established dealer and retail sales channels.

Manufacturers with established sales and distribution systems face a twin challenge:

(i)   To revitalise their brands to include the values of access and responsiveness, commit to support customers wherever the product is purchased, and offer a direct relationship to every customer so that they can deliver on this promise; in practice this will mean that they will have to leapfrog the direct sellers and the cataloguers in the quality of service they offer

(ii) To offer direct access as an additional purchase channel without alienating existing channels of distribution unduly; in practice this will mean that they must increase their support for existing channels at the same time as they introduce the new direct channel.

A distinctive business brand must combine a competitive product offering with a total commitment to guarantee the customer's own effectiveness: partnership is the value that best expresses this commitment to customers and can best build a direct channel. To deal directly the customer the customer requires a guarantee. The promise of partnership is the guarantee of a company's commitment to direct customers.

BUILDING RETAIL BRANDS DIRECTLY 16

'Bound to attract customers'

The Forces Shaping Retail Marketing – Relationship Management for Retailers – A New Agenda for Retailers – Summary: The Retail Experience

The Forces Shaping Retail Marketing

Shopping is no longer an essential household chore but a popular leisure pastime. The shopping experience has been enhanced by giant superstores, and by shopping malls that offer hundreds of stores under the same roof in combination with restaurants and entertainment: a complete family 'day out'. The extension of opening times to twelve-hour days and seven-day weeks makes the experience available to everyone. Clustered together in retail centres, parks, precincts and malls, departments stores and specialists offer an ever widening range of goods from around the world.

In retailing the conventional wisdom used to be that the critical success factor was location. Retailers used the science of geodemographics and techniques like gravity modelling

367

to analyse local markets and forecast the business potential of alternative sites. But precise location no longer matters and geodemographics is increasingly irrelevant. The leading multiples, superstores and malls create their own centres of gravity, attracting customers by car, bus and train wherever they are located.

The growth in the power of multiple retailers has been a relentless trends for decades, and has been accompanied by the development of retail names as brands in their own right. The leading food and department store chains like Wal-Mart and Nordstrom in the US, and Sainsbury's and Marks & Spencer in the UK, have grown by rapid geographic expansion in their own countries. Wal-Mart is forecasting sales of $100bn in 1995, which would make a retailer one of the ten largest companies in the world. Led by Sainsbury's the multiples' share of UK food sales has risen from under 50 to over 80 per cent in the last twenty years. Specialists like Benetton of Italy, IKEA of Sweden and The Body Shop of the UK are international, and the US fast food chains like McDonald's and Pizza Hut are everywhere. The same products are increasingly available from the same names on every continent.

Retailers have benefited from sustained growth in the disposable income of their customers, and the most successful have harnessed growth by combining operational efficiency and quality goods at competitive prices with a distinctive in-store customer proposition. Nordstrom, originally from Seattle, is the fastest growing US department store chain and comparison of Nordstrom with its longer established competitors like Saks 5th Avenue and Macy's are instructive: in most US cities they are within walking distance. In Nordstrom, the store layout is better organised and goods are better displayed.

But the most noticeable difference lies in the better presentation, training and motivation of the Nordstrom sales personnel: while Nordstrom's people seem genuinely committed to helping their customers, the staff in the other stores seem by comparison to be there to ring up the tills. At Nordstrom quality of people matters as much as quality of product. Every successful retail brand encompasses the

ιopping experience and the quality of the people
ʳve the customer.

the early 1990s may come to be recognised as the
ʳater mark of the rising tide of retail power. The limit
ɪil ambition is geographic saturation. There is a fear
ɪe US is 'over-malled', that the available shopping
exceeds the customer's demand for product. Harris
ɔn of Deloitte & Touche calls the constant building of
ɜites the 'Field of Dreams' mentality: retailers believe
'if we build new stores they will come'.[1] Fears of
ation by UK supermarkets have depressed share prices
ʲorced Sainsbury's, Tesco and Safeway to cut back on
new store building plans. The multiple retailers may
ɔnd to saturation in their home markets by international
nsion, but their track records overseas are not promis-
the *Financial Times* reports well-publicised failures that
ɪde France's Printemps in Japan and even the UK's
ks & Spencer in Canada.[2]

he threat of saturation is accompanied by new competi-
ɪ from the low cost category killers. Specialist competition
ʲating away at the market share and forcing down the
ʲes and gross margins of the multiples. The category
er is one of only two retail formats showing real growth
the US. The other is, in the words of *The Economist*, 'more
ɡhtening for retailers than for consumers':[3] interactive
ɪme shopping. Currently, home shopping is a small pro-
ɔrtion of retail sales, even in the US mail order represents
ɪly $70 billion out of a $2.1 trillion industry, or 7 per cent
ʲ all non-food sales. But the potential for remote access to
ɪ-line databases and remote browsing of electronic stores
ɪ enormous. The technology exists, although no one
ɪnows how customers will want to use it. Trials by Time-
Warner in Orlando and BT in Colchester were the first tests to
measure how customers would use interactive media and
ɜhopping.

An alternative to shopping at retail sites already exists in
traditional mail order, now referred to by the more fashion-
ɪble description of home shopping. Even food and grocery
ɜtores must fear home shopping if the example of Holly, a
'Phone-In Supermarket', is anything to go by: 'Consumers

choose products from a catalogue – updated with flye
listing weekly specials – phone in orders, and groceries a
delivered on the same day.'[4]

The potential of an on-line future using telephone c
interactive media does call into question retailers' inves
ments in ever more sites and ever larger stores, and make
it imperative that retailers explore a new agenda.

The forces shaping retail marketing

Geographic saturation

Category killer competition

Interactive home shopping

Relationship Management for Retailers

Competition forces retailers to think about their customers
as individuals, analyse their share of customers and calculate
their customer lifetime values.

The results are more targeted marketing and a greater
focus on the relatively small number of high value customers
on which even the most mass of multiple retailers depends.
As the *New York Times* reported: 'Knowing more about the
customer can lead to greater customer retention for supermarkets . . . It is estimated that a typical supermarket loses
40 per cent of its customers each year and gains about 40
per cent.'[5]

To identify customers as individuals, retailers have built
databases using in-store data collection and applications for
store cards. To retain these customers, retailers have
launched frequent shopper programmes in which customer
spend accrues for rewards and special benefits. The database
is also used as a private medium for interactive communication to make special offers, drive store traffic and add
value outside the in-store relationship.

Analysis of retail brands reveals the importance of personal relationships as well as product and pricing. Customer information can develop the customer relationship by enhancing the total customer shopping experience. Frequent shopper and VIP programmes enable staff to recognise their best customers and deliver a privileged service.

'Soft' membership rewards include priority service, gift wrapping, enhanced guarantees and sales prenotifications. 'Hard' benefits include privileged rewards and extra value offers as well as straight discounts.

By swiping membership cards customers can use in-store technology to receive selective rewards based on their purchasing patterns: targeted mail delivered into the customer's hands at point of sale. This is more efficient and more effective, as the *Times* also reports: 'It is estimated that these electronic coupons also generate four to five times the response rate of free-standing insert coupons.'

The quality of management of the customer is becoming an increasingly important source of competitive advantage. The investment in external marketing to customers should be matched by the education and training of staff to enhance customer service. Local store management can be empowered to maximise the value of each customer visit and to manage localised marketing programmes to customers and prospects in their catchment areas. Analysis of customer behaviour can guide *store merchandising* to match the profile and purchasing habits of local markets, and even the needs of shoppers at different times of the day. To confront the challenge of interactive home shopping, retailers can set up their own tests: finding new ways to distribute their products through direct selling in home or home shopping catalogues. Retailers can test electronic versions of their stores on the on-line information services.

A relationship strategy for retailers is to build the brand and the value of the customer by enhancing the total shopping experience in the store, adding value outside the store, and testing new methods of communicating and distributing to customers.

A New Agenda for Retailers

In evaluating a shift from mass marketing to relationship management retailers must think about their customers as individuals. Starting with an understanding of the value of their customers, this new perspective will confront them with the realities of their business and set a new agenda for their marketing.

The value of a customer

Calculating customer lifetime value gives retailers a new perspective on their markets. Pizza Hut has determined that its best customers are worth over $2500 over their lifetimes. The company considers its customers as assets and customer information as the source of competitive advantage. It views every local market in terms of the profile and number of individual households. If Pizza Hut has 30 per cent of a market of size 10 000 households, the strategy is to target the highest spending 10 per cent within the competition's customer base: the objective is to identify and switch only 700 households because these are crucial to sales and profits in the area.

Because the company appreciates that customers are not created equally, the Pizza Hut strategy is to tailor value added benefits to different customer types. The database of past transactions enables it to recognise customer preferences and tastes, and to select offers likely to appeal to customers as individuals. Because it knows that the way to build its business and its brand is area and by area and customer by customer, Pizza Hut in the US is assigning marketing responsibilities to personnel within its local stores.

The concentration of customer spend

When retailers analyse their customers as individuals they always find that a surprisingly small number is responsible for a high proportion of sales. This is true even for sup-posedly mass market multiple retailers: at US department store chains Bloomingdales and Saks, the best 10 per cent of customers are responsible for over 40 per cent of sales, and the best 25 per cent for 70 per cent of sales. There is the apocryphal story of the president of an audio chain in the US who was so alarmed to learn that nearly half of his sales came from only 10 per cent of his customers that he installed a red telephone in his own office and each of his managers', and invited the best customers to call regularly with any problems. The most valuable customers are vital for any retailer and must be identified and retained.

The value of a customer and the concentration of spend by customers force retailers to view their marketing priorities with a new perspective. To maximise the value of a custo-mer a retailer should seek to maximise shopping frequency and the size of the individual's shopping basket. This re-quires information about the customer as an individual. Retailers can use the opportunity of a customer visit to capture information as well as sell.

The capture of customer information

Every visit is an opportunity not just to sell but to identify and learn about the customer as an individual. Data capture questionnaires can be displayed in the store, handed out by staff and enclosed with the merchandise purchased by customers. The best way to build a retail database is by a card marketing programme. The original motive for store cards was to manage customer credit and gain the increased margin from a credit transaction.

Card applications create a database that can be used to manage and develop the customer relationship. Trans-actions made by the card, ideally scannable, record trans-actions and update the customer behaviour. Card marketing is a powerful retail weapon whether the card is a member-ship card, a frequent shopper card or a fully fledged credit card. Using the techniques pioneered by American Express, card transactions and cardmember communications become opportunities to develop the customer relationship.

Customer information to increase in-store sales

The real power of customer cards is not only to record customer transactions, but to enhance the customer's shopping experience. When the customer is in the store the card can be read and the customer information analysed to create selective, added value offers. The electronic device that reads the card can be hooked on to a local PC or networked to the retailer's central customer information system. The reading device can be positioned at the entry to the store, at a key point of sale position in the store or at the checkout. When they swipe their cards, customers receive special offers which can be redeemed immediately.

Electronic kiosks at the entry to the store generate electronic coupons. Some systems issue personalised paper coupons, while others scrap paper and automatically discount the shopper's bill at the checkout on purchase of participating manufacturers' brands. The Ukrops supermarket chain in Virginia, one of the first to develop a customer loyalty program, uses a Citicorp system with two PCs for in-store data processing that dispenses with paper coupons.

Checkout systems like Catalina issue selective coupons on the basis of the shopping transaction, usually for redemption on the next visit. More sophisticated technology, like the Vision Value Network, combines a card reader, a video screen and a selective printing system. Transmitting to its Vision Value terminals via satellite, Advanced Promotion Technologies delivers to shoppers in the checkout lanes of participating retailers a series of five- to seven-second long televised promotions that are financed by manufacturers or the retailer.

By swiping their cards and pressing selective buttons, shoppers can receive instant print out of coupons, and information such as recipes, promotional messages and offers. The system can even print mail packages with offers that invite redemption by direct response to brand manufacturers. A year-long test of the Vision Value Network has confirmed the potential of technology and customer information to add value to the shopping experience, change customer behaviour, and increase retailer sales and brand share:

— average number of shopping trips increased 15 per cent

— Vision Value member spending increase 18 per cent

— average order value increased 3 per cent

— the 20 per cent of 'secondary' shoppers reduced to only 2 per cent

— average sales from participating brands increased 8 per cent.

A Swedish supermarket placed an interactive terminal at the front of the store. By swiping their frequent buyer card once per week, customers received coupons, special offers, free coffee and cake on their birthdays. The system also prints a report of customer spend by department.

Promoting Store Traffic magazine estimates that 40 per cent of cards are used each week, 5000 of 7000 families in the store town hold the card, and cardholders spend 95 per cent more than non-cardholders.[6] In the US, ActMedia achieved redemption rates of 27 per cent from its in-store Instant Coupon Machine, nine times higher than coupons delivered by free standing insert.[7]

The benefit of in-store customer interaction is not simply the increase usage of coupons and offers. By analysing customer data the offer is targeted, avoiding the promotional traps: offers can be targeted only to non-users; the 'surprise' factor of an immediate, unanticipated offer adds value rather than damaging the brand; and rewards can be offered by individual customer for repeat purchase.

Communication outside the store

Retailers use marketing communications in the form of advertising to build their brands, and promotions to drive their store traffic. The concept of individual customer communication outside stores, however, is alien to retailers. They are concerned by the incremental costs, and unconvinced by the necessity to add a new form of dialogue when most customers are exposed to the store's message on the occasion of each visit.

Yet communication outside the store can add value cost-effectively. Successful Montreal supermarket chain Provigo has sponsored *Le Magazine Provigo*, distributed to 2.2 million homes which represent over 80 per cent of the homes in Quebec province. The magazine has increased readership of Provigo's promotional flyers, with research confirming that with the magazine 75 per cent of customers consult and use flyers in their purchasing decisions. Provigo's director of marketing says: 'We can cut TV, we can cut radio, but there's no way we can cut flyers.'[8] *Le Magazine Provigo* is now a monthly, part-funded by brand manufacturer advertising.

Provigo originally built its database by questionnaires. A multimedia campaign won a US Direct Marketing Association Award, producing 136 000 active members from a spend of $3 million for Provigo's 'Club Orange', which provided exclusive offers and a personalised newsletter.[9] At a cost of less than $25 per recruit this is a modest investment in a regular supermarket shopper.

Frequency of communication depends on the market and the retailer category. Neiman Marcus mails members of its InCircle scheme quarterly. Members of the Ukrops Valued Customer programme receive a monthly 'Valued Customer News' plus a list of the month's special offer items. The newsletter features added value through a column by an expert in nutrition, and includes surveys to feedback customer opinion and attitudes.

A database creates the opportunity for selective customer messages to increase traffic and the size of the shopping basket. Direct mail is a powerful tool to generate new buyers and reactivate lapsed customers. Supermarket chain A&P launched a new store in Atlanta with a direct mail campaign that achieved a 12 per cent visit rate and recruited over 10 000 new customers. Retailer and author Murray Raphel reports a local supermarket store that defended its customer base against the opening of a new national chain with a mailing with two coupons each week for the four succeeding weeks: one coupon for a free item, one for a discount. Redemption ranged from 15 to 20 per cent.

John Goodman of Helzberg Diamonds in the US has pioneered the use of databased direct mail in the jewellery retail trade. Customer data is captured using guarantees, service and insurance policies. Direct mail programmes include seasonal offers at Christmas, Valentine's Day and Mother's Day and individually triggered Thank You, Birthday and Anniversary offers.

Direct mail is a flexible weapon for special discounts and sales, launching new ranges, building traffic on special events, and clearing previously unsold stock.

Motivating the staff to volunteer value

The quality of in-store service is a key factor in differentiating the retailer and in winning a higher share of a customer's spend. Gary Ostrager reports a survey that asked whether shoppers would ask for the same salesperson on their next purchase visit: 'the yes responders were more likely to give the store an 8, 9 or 10 rating. Conversely, shoppers unhappy with their salesperson gave the store very low performance marks on overall service and performance.'[10] A frequent shopper programme can increase sales simply because it is accompanied by a drive to motivate staff to recognise their best customers and offer them superior service.

By identifying and recognising their best customers retailers should seek to foster the community relationship between them and their staff. The training and development of staff can be accompanied by a delegation of marketing responsibilities to the management of local stores, who are closer to their markets and customers. A system to manage local marketing programmes can be developed that allows the local manager to select the targeting and offers for his own store:

— The central marketing team manages and quality controls the customer data, and prepares 'shell' marketing programmes for local store managers to in-fill their own messages and offers

— The local manager calls on the central team to create a programme, specifying the customer selections, messages and the offers.

Adding value and building relationships in-store

In a feature on 'The Future of Shopping', *The Economist* warns that whatever the future: 'Retailers will re-learn an old lesson: consumers prefer shops that do not treat them like cattle.'[11] A common thread running through all retailer applications is the identification of customers as individuals and the development of a relationship that offers customers more value and reward for continuing sales.

A newer lesson that retailers are learning is that 'customer loyalty' schemes that offer only tangible rewards without adding value and without enhancing the shopping experience have no lasting effect. Indeed, by associating the brand with discounts or irrelevant offers, the scheme may damage customer perceptions of the brand and reduce the brand value. The scheme must build the brand by building the total store experience.

IKEA developed IKEA Family as much to motivate retailers, all of whom are franchisees, to enhance customer service and the store experience as to reward customers. The IKEA Family Card is a membership programme with four objectives:

(i) to increase store traffic from IKEA Family members

(ii) to increase the sales of members on each visit

(iii) to increase empathy for IKEA as a home furnishing store

(iv) to offer a local marketing vehicle for the local management.

IKEA recommends to its franchisees six mailings per annum, including welcome and birthday mailings. Mailings achieve average response rates of 25–30 per cent. The pro-gramme is supported by internal marketing to educate staff to manage the programme locally, and to follow-up custo-mers who respond to the programme.

A machine at the entry to the store swipes the card and issues a special offer to the customer on every visit. Items in the store have special family prices, and special merchandise has been developed for a substore, the IKEA Family shop, which sells products out of the home furnishing range and helps to make IKEA Family a profit centre. IKEA monitors the additional visits, sales and profits generated by the programme. The value of membership is increased by Family evenings and sales events, and in Sweden IKEA Family has 600 000 members who receive discounts from petrol stations.

IKEA Family illustrates a relationship programme con-sistent with the development of the core brand values and the quality of customer management by store management and personnel.

The direct model for retailers

In the US, most retailers have developed their own catalo-gues and many leading cataloguers have opened their own retail stores. The motivation for a retail catalogue can be to build store traffic and the value of store sales, to generate home shopping business, or a mixture of both. UK retailer The Body Shop has a catalogue that it sells in-store in the UK but uses to generate home shopping sales in the US. In the UK, the company is testing Body Shop Direct, which is the in-home selling of Body Shop products by appointed representatives outside towns in which Body Shop has a presence.

In testing a catalogue, a retailer must be sure of distin-guishing between:

— incremental sales to new customers

— incremental sales from existing customers.

Some retailers like the book stores in the US combine frequent shopper programmes with home shopping. Members of the scheme can also order books directly.

Retailers can enhance the range of goods they offer in-store through CD-ROMs in electronic shopping kiosks. US shoe retailer Florsheims has tested kiosks that allow shoppers to view a wider range of shoes, complete with a sales presentation. Grocery retailer Cub Foods has tested an interactive kiosk that combines the issue of coupons with other travel and information services. In the UK Argos and Woolworth have both tested kiosks: Woolworth's features a comprehensive catalogue of music and film: 12 000 CDs, 9000 cassettes and 4000 videos. In Europe, Zanussi has placed kiosks in electrical stores to demonstrate its products and highlight their benefits over competition.

Interactive home shopping

Interactive media are natural developments for any telephone-based service. In France, the mail order catalogue industry takes a third of its orders through the Minitel videotex system, but the customer has previously used the printed catalogue to reach a buying decision. Similarly, the move by pizza delivery services to on-line ordering is a natural development of telephone ordering, and car companies are testing on-line 'showrooms' to allow prospects to view models, and check features and prices.

There are early and significant developments of complete 'virtual' stores on on-line networks. The most promising technology for on-line shopping is the PC-Video system in which the customer talks to an on-screen sales representative, who simultaneously presents a product or service demonstration. The customer can access the company through his or her own PC at home or at the office, or through special kiosks in public locations and shopping malls.

Summary: The Retail Experience

Because the retail experience has become a popular leisure activity, it is vulnerable to new competition for customers' entertainment. The potential threat of home shopping will only become a reality for retailers that fail to entertain and involve their customers. Significantly, in the first UK advertising specifically designed to counter own label colas, Coca-Cola attacked the idea of supermarket shopping by presenting a family experiencing a visit to a 'grey' and soulless monolith.

In the US, retail analysts are reporting that the average shopping trip is down in duration and concluding that customers are losing interest. To stop them retreating into their homes, retailers must fight for their custom and enhance their in-store experience. Interactive systems are effective simply because they offer unanticipated rewards for the shopper in-store.

People power is more important than technology, and customers seek information and entertainment as the reward for the time they invest in visiting stores. Retailers can offer involving product demonstrations, and games and amusements as well as special prizes and rewards. Technology enables retailers to interact with customers in all of their stores from one central location – using celebrities, for example – to demonstrate products, but they must not lose sight of the reality that if price, convenience and choice are the only reasons for customers to use their store, then their businesses will be superseded by home shopping, which will eventually beat retailing on all of these benefits.

It is the quality and value added by the total experience in-store that will determine the loyalty of the retail shopper.

PART V: ACTION PLANS

ACTION PLAN ONE
Developing a Marketing Organisation

'It is people who offer the personal one-to-one service we all want'

Summary

If companies are to realise the value of their customers, changes in organisational structure are essential. The trend in US and British business, unsympathetically referred to as 'delayering', is towards leaner and flatter organisations. In their rush to cut costs, however, many companies have neglected the potential of their people. And in their attack on middle management in particular, many companies have neglected the role of this level in communicating across the company and in orchestrating the efforts of different functions.

Companies must organise around their customers. Marketing must take the lead in developing company resources and customer focus. In an article, 'Marketing – A

Mid-Life Crisis', Professor Malcolm McDonald urges: 'With marketing largely an attitude of mind vested solely in the department bearing the same name, the critical issue is how to introduce and sustain customer focus across a company.'[1]

Marketing should develop its remit to give internal communication to staff equal weight with external communication to customers. This is an action plan for a reorganisation of the marketing function, the integration of marketing with other business functions, and the development of customer focus throughout a company.

1. Change the marketing organisation

1.1   Change the marketing organisation from product-based to customer-focused.

1.2   Break down the functional disciplines of advertising, direct marketing, sales promotion and public relations and develop communication skills across all the four disciplines.

1.3   Breakdown current and potential customers into key behavioural segments on the basis of first, their characteristics and behaviour, and second, their value to the company.

1.4   Decentralise decision-making and responsibility to customer teams based on customer segments.

1.5   Assign to the customer team responsible for a behavioural segment responsibility for product design and distribution as well as marketing communication.

1.6   Assign to customer teams responsible for best customers priority in resource allocation to enable them to provide higher levels of service.

2. Integrate marketing within the organisation

2.1   Integrate marketing communication – the traditional role of the marketing department – with customer service, and with sales and channel management, to form multifunctional customer teams.

2.1 Build close working relationships between customer teams and product development, research and manufacturing.

2.3 Develop marketing planning and budgeting jointly with finance, and design rolling evaluation and forecasting systems for reporting to senior management.

2.4 Invest in the collection and dissemination of market, competitive and customer information to the teams.

3. Develop staff skills

3.1 Define the skills sets required by staff to ensure a competitive advantage and brand differentiation, and develop training programmes to develop the necessary skills.

3.2 Focus training on five skill sets:

(i) Teamworking
(ii) Understanding of IT, and basic computing
(iii) Project management
(iv) Quantitative analysis and qualitative evaluation
(v) Business and financial appreciation

3.3 Establish and share best practice across customer teams – especially across different countries in a multinational company – by Customer Manuals and Quality Circles, motivating staff to revise and update best practice on the basis of innovation and experience.

3.4 Establish the equivalent of an internal college, and recognise staff training and educational achievements in remuneration and career development.

4. Design customer information systems

4.1 Define sources of customer, market and competitive information, and assign responsibilities for its collection and dissemination.

4.2 Design a customer information system (CIS) to store and manage the information.

4.3 Design access to the CIS and the systems and procedures to obtain feedback from customers to the CIS from all parts of the organisation.

4.4 Design the processes by which customer understanding and learning are shared throughout the organisation, including:

— Feedback from customer-facing personnel to all other staff, including management
— Formalised reporting of experience, especially research and testing
— Regular meetings among teams to report achievements, assign priorities and progress a shared customer development agenda.

5. Develop customer contact centres

5.1 Develop the personnel and technology to manage all forms of customer contact.

5.2 Designate roles and responsibilities for the organisation to manage and communicate the results of all forms of customer contact.

5.3 Ensure the inclusion of staff contact details on all customer communications so that customers learn to know and recognise appropriate staff and contact points.

5.4 Define customer management by need and allocate to appropriate staff, specifying different treatment of:

— Enquiries
— Complaints
— Technical issues
— Best customer contacts.

5.5 Determine quality of service standards for all staff at any customer interface.

5.6 Set objectives for all customer contact through the design of Customer Tracks.

6. Develop automated customer communication

6.1 Design Customer Tracks to develop relationships with customers in high potential lifetime value segments.

6.2 Link company systems to automate the process of creating, implementing, customising and modifying customer communications:

— Customer planning system
— Customer information system
— Product information system
— Picture library system
— Electronic publishing system
— Automated addressing, enclosing and mailing systems
— Telemarketing systems.

7. Design measurement and feedback systems

7.1 Design research and tracking to measure customer sales, profitability, loyalty and predicted lifetime values.

7.2 Support customer measurement with objective feedback from customers and staff through anonymous surveys, for example 'mystery shopping'.

7.3 Share reporting of results among all participants in customer teams throughout the organisation.

7.4 Link marketing results to financial performance, establishing brand rates and customer loyalty rates as key performance indicators.

8. Redesign evaluation and remuneration systems

8.1 Base staff evaluation, within customer teams, on customer loyalty and predicted customer lifetime values.

8.2 Develop rewards and career progression not simply to progress up a hierarchy but based on the individual's contribution to customer lifetime values.

9. Manage channel relationships

9.1 Redefine channel relationships based on membership, and define rights and responsibilities of membership.

9.2 Develop channel-specific and local marketing support systems:

— Enabling local, field personnel to select their own marketing programmes

— Managing the delivery of the programmes centrally to ensure quality and efficiency.

10. Share the total brand experience with all customers and staff

10.1 Create an association of customers, including opportunities for staff to meet and hear from customers.

10.2 Translate brand and relationship values into meaningful actions for all personnel.

Footnote

Ray Jutkins, a leading speaker on international direct marketing says: ' . . . it is people who offer the personal one-to-one service we all want. Sure, machines make much of what we call service better. But so far, robots and voice mail and other technical things cannot do what people still do best.'[2]

ACTION PLAN TWO
Developing a Customer Information System

'Information is a company's only asset'

Summary

There are three types of software in a customer information system. A *relational database management system* (RDBMS) stores and organises data efficiently. A *user interface* provides staff with access to the data. *Applications* software enables staff to carry out various tasks using data.

Customer information system

Applications

User Interface

RDBMS

Database

. . . .

A customer information system should be integrated within a general companywide IT strategy and database design. Customer data and marketing applications can be linked to those of other key functions, including planning, customer service, sales, personnel, finance and order processing. Applications range from the strategic through management to the operational. In a companywide solution, data is shared, but the user interface and application can be specific to a customer team or an individual staff member.

Customer marketing software

Planning   Marketing   Service   Sales Personnel   Finance   Order

Applications

| User | User | | User | User | | |
| interface | interface | | interface | interface | | |

RDBMS

Dbase   Dbase   Dbase   Dbase   Dbase   Dbase   Dbase

Within a companywide database strategy, marketing has access to all data relevant to its customers. And all functions and staff involved with customers can access and use customer data collected by marketing. Customer data is *integrated* with other data, and is *distributed* to all users throughout the company.

1. Planning the scope of the system

1.1   To plan the scope of a customer information system requires:

— Evaluating the desired applications of all users
— Determining the costs and benefits
— Forecasting the data sources and volumes

— Determining the usage and performance of the system
— Selecting the appropriate hardware and software solution
— Planning the build of the system
— Delivering the system with user training and documentation.

2. Define relationship management applications

2.1 The major relationship management applications are customer analysis, external campaign management and internal customer management.

2.2 The applications comprise the *functionality* of the system. Within the system functionality, each major application can be divided into a number of discrete subapplications for design and programming, including:

— Customer marketing planning
— Customer track management
— Campaign management
— Financial planning
— Customer service
— Sales management
— Channel management
— Personnel management
— Order processing
— Billing, payment processing and credit management.

2.3 Reporting from the system should be designed as a specific application, and users equipped with the capability to create their own customised reports.

3. Plan the external view of the system

Design an *external* view of the system, summarising the interfaces that gather customer information, and the transformation of data into information.

Customer information system: external view

Customer information sources

| Customer profitability models | Customer potential scores | Customer status reports | Sales territory profiles | Trade/ retail profiles |

Applications

User interfaces

Geodemographics & lifestyles   Postal & telephone

Database(s)

Update

Customer questionnaires   Staff inc. sales data collection

| Information brokers | Retailers & distributors | Customer orders & data | Prospecting data |

| Disk/modem | EPOS | Sales | On-line | Telephone | Mail |

---

4. Structure the build of the system

4.1 Structure the system build by merging of data from disparate sources, to identify customers uniquely, eliminate duplicate contact and understand the total relationship with the customer over all brands marketed by the company.

4.2 Design quality checks on individual records and variables to ensure data integrity.

5.   Build the internal view of the system

5.1   From an internal perspective, the database provides access to customer data to staff in all departments.

Customer information system: internal view

Management   Planning   Finance
              Marketing   Research
Sales   Service
              Customer Information
       Retail   Production   Trade

---

6.   Link customer access technology to the system

6.1   Link all external sources of data to the customer information system:

— Advertising response management by telephone and mail data entry
— Promotion response management by telephone, mail data entry and coupon data capture
— Sales management and contact systems
— In-store customer data capture through point-of-sale terminals and kiosks
— Remote customer ordering, by telephone or interactive on-line system
— Customer enquiry, complaint and service calls.

6.2   Link customer contact technology to the information system.

— Automated call distribution
— Call sequencing
— Voice messages
— Interactive voice recognition

— Fax-on-demand
— Electronic mail
— Electronic data interchange.

7. Link system to customer track and campaign management

7.1 Link the customer information system to project management software to automate the management of:

— Customer tracks
— Specific campaigns and communications within customer tracks.

7.2 Link the project management software and information system to:

— Laser printing
— Production
— Enclosing
— Publishing
— Selective binding

plus:

— Telephone and sales contact, by print lead sheets or electronic communication.

8. Recruit/assign a database manager for the system

8.1 The Database Manager (DBM) is responsible for system administration, data integrity, applications development.
8.2 The DBM's role is to ensure that the system meets user needs.
8.3 The DBM communicates with business and IT man-

agement to develop goals, plans, budgets and policies for the system.

8.4 The DBM establishes standards and guidelines for operation of the system.

8.5 The DBM establishes and maintains a Data Dictionary defining the source and meaning of all information in the system.

A warning

The timing of development and investment must be managed with reference to the benefits. At an early stage in the adoption of a relationship strategy, development costs should be minimised. With successful experience, a roll-out will require more applications to be developed. Once the full scope of the required system is determined, the full set of applications can be developed in-house.

There are typically two barriers to development of customer information systems.

Some companies have invested in CIS without allocating the budgets to collect data or use the names. There is cost, but little return. Some companies have not invested at all in CIS. As a result they have not controlled major relationship management programmes with quality. There are returns but major problems and poor customer service. The lesson is that system development and marketing spend must be closely coordinated.

To manage investment, there are three phases through which a company can move in its development of a customer database:

(i) In the first stage, a company can subcontract the capture, processing and management of customer and marketing data; there is no capital investment and the company can move faster up the learning curve by working with outside experts

(ii) In the second stage, the company will begin to build its own developments in-house; initially these systems may be stand-alone, and other systems will continue to be outsourced

(iii) In the third and final phase, all systems can be integrated internally.

ACTION PLAN THREE
Opening a Direct Channel

'Putting the customer in control'

Summary

Opening a direct channel of distribution has two overriding advantages related to sales and service. Without significant investment in infrastructure, the direct channel generates incremental sales, usually from new customers, but potentially from existing customers as well. Direct can be complementary not competitive to retail. But the second advantage is that a direct channel enables a company to regain control over the customer interface, and over all the decisions about product, pricing and promotion that it may have surrendered to retailers.

1. Define direct objectives and brand values

1.1 The selection of objectives for a direct channel is made from amongst the alternatives:

— Incremental sales from new customers whom existing channels could not reach
— Incremental sales from new types of customers or whom the existing channels were not relevant

— Incremental sales from existing customers of products which the existing channels could not support
— Incremental sales from existing customers from the use of direct communications as a private channel and the development of direct relationships.

1.2 The direct channel must develop its own brand and/or enhance the existing brand by offering added values:

— *Contact*: in particular recognition
— *Affinity*: customising product, offer and service to the needs of segments and individuals
— *Reward*: preferential pricing, offers or terms for multiple or regular purchase
— *Extra value*: additional services directly or through third parties
— *Service*: superior service to existing channels and competitors.

1.3 The brand personality must be reflected in all communications, in particular:

— *The virtual store*: the cover of the catalogue or – perhaps in future – the customer interface to electronic media
— *The virtual sales person*: the expertise, presentation and dialogue of telephone staff.

2. Select the delivery system

2.1 Evaluate the potential of the traditional delivery system, mail order, through:

— *Print media*: mail order could be appropriate for any media, for example, in the US Kraft General Foods markets premium coffee brand Gevalia Kaffee through direct response press advertising and direct mail
— *continuity programmes*: customers can order auto-

matic and regular shipments of their Gevalia coffee selections.

2.2   Evaluate the potential for direct response television:

— Short form commercials that sell product directly
— Long form infomercials that sell product ranges, direct brands or catalogue shopping concepts.

2.3   Negotiate distribution through a shopping channel intermediary:

— Special promotions with existing catalogue merchandisers
— New channels, in particular QVC, on BSkyB in the UK, which offers segmented programming with each hour its own merchandise theme, and adds value through presentation: 'one-third the principles of direct marketing, one-third the principles of theater and one-third the principles of retailing . . . putting the customer in control.'[1]

2.4   Test new electronic media:

— CD-ROMs, for search and demonstration of product information, potentially linked to on-line services for direct ordering
— Internet services, like the Internet Shopping Network in California, with the opportunity to customise the shopping experience for the individual subscriber and to capture data on browsers: 'we have a tremendous amount of information because as people click the mouse, we record everything they do'[2]
— Electronic kiosks in retail outlets, shopping malls or other locations with high traffic flows.

3.   Develop motivating creative and promotion

3.1   To recruit new customers, communication must overcome the different forms of risk from shopping direct:

— *Financial*: the despatch of money to an unknown company
— *Performance*: uncertainty about product quality and suitability
— *Social*: latent perception, historically based, that home shopping is either downmarket or anti-social.

3.2 Communication must present the advantages of shopping direct as well as the intrinsic product value:

— accessibility
— availability of more information, in a non-selling context
— time for consideration of options
— time saving in ordering
— wider choice
— convenience of home delivery.

3.3 Communication must address and overcome the perceived disadvantages of buying direct:

— Customer cannot touch product – but new on-line services enable the customer to see product

— Waiting time to delivery
— Accuracy of order
— Uncertainty about return if product fails to provide satisfaction
— Rental of names and addresses to third parties.

4. Manage economics of direct channel

4.1 Marketing for the direct channel must be designed to maximise customer lifetime value and not just sales.

4.2 Merchandising policy must ensure there is an adequate product and service range to deliver target lifetime value and thus establish the allowable investment in a new customer.

4.3 Testing must measure the cost of acquiring a new customer for comparison with the allowable investment

5. Manage the customer relationship

5.1 A customer welcome programme should be designed to motivate new customers to repeat buy quickly: single buyers should not be counted as customers until they buy again.

5.2 A customer save programme should be designed to minimise the loss of regular buyers, using questionnaires to determine the reasons for any decline in custom.

5.3 A customer development programme should be designed to interrogate customer interests and develop new products and services to increase lifetime value.

5.4 A customer membership scheme should be evaluated to retain customers, by offering added value in exchange for increased frequency and higher retention rates.

5.5 A customer association should be considered to involve best customers with the company, its products and its marketing.

5.6 A customer advocacy – or member-get-member – programme should be a regular feature of the customer dialogue

6. Manage the database

6.1 The database should be monitored by key variables recency, frequency, monetary value and types of products that either have been ordered or in which interest is expressed.

6.2 Customer models should be developed to predict:

— The products a customer is likely to order
— The timing and value of next order
— The probability of losing customer.

6.3 The database should be segmented by value, and the investment in promotion weight and frequency should be varied by potential customer value.

6.4 Customer segments and individual customers should receive individual treatment and personalised communications.

6.5 Regular customer censuses should be used to validate and update database information.

6.6 The database should be analysed and customer behaviour monitored to discover new opportunities, for example for niche promotions or catalogues to segments of the base.

7. Design catalogue to reflect brand personality

7.1 Establish appropriate investment in the catalogue in relation to brand, to target audience and to allowable investment in customers: a catalogue operation should cost no more than one-sixth the equivalent of a new retail store.

7.2 Consider different covers for new and existing customers:

— For existing customers new products or enhancements in services are important for change of pace

— For new customers the cover should present the brand personality and promise.

7.3 Develop copy theme and style that are both emotional and factual: romance the product and sell the features and benefits.

7.4 Maximise the sales value of the 'hot spots' in the catalogue: inside front cover, centre pages, inside back cover, next to order form, within reply envelopes.

7.5 Develop a theme or promotion that builds traffic through the catalogue, encouraging customers to study all pages.

7.6 Decide whether to compartmentalise products: in business this is the right strategy: in consumer markets it seems to have no effect on sales.

7.7 Present the human face of the Direct channel, the personnel that provide information, take orders, handle problems, choose products and despatch products.

7.8 Make ordering as easy as possible.

Footnote

The decision to establish a direct channel represents a company commitment to meet customer needs anytime, anywhere and anyhow. Many companies make the mistake of not appreciating the implications – and they fail to establish the new infrastructure and change the organisation's mentality to deal directly with customers. Compaq Computer, which was once wholly committed to selling through independent dealers now says: 'The key decision was to shift this company from being a product-centric to becoming a customer-centric company . . . we sell computers wherever the customer wants to buy them. If they want to buy them in gas stations, that is where we will sell them.'[3]

ACTION PLAN FOUR
Building a Relationship/ Loyalty System

'A business resolution'

Summary

Customer loyalty is the ultimate driver of business profitability, but loyalty is only given where it is earned. Loyalty accompanies change in strategy and process. Companies must change from mass marketing to a focus on the customer as an individual, and to earn the loyalty of customers must offer them demonstrably superior value. Customers will give their loyalty in exchange for more value. Companies must change from hierarchical organisations divided by function to teams based on customers and designed to manage process.

The added values that earn customer loyalty, moreover, cannot consist exclusively of tangible incentives unrelated to product or service. To differentiate their products and justify their premium pricing, companies must build on and revitalise their brand values by adding a relationship dimension. Through closer relationships with customers, companies can express their brand personalities through their people, and involve customers more closely in their products and marketing. To build these relationships the

403

company must simultaneously earn the loyalty of its staff, and motivate them to volunteer added values to customers.

In a report on new flexible manufacturing organisation, *The Economist* comments: 'After 80 years of me-too mass production, consumers are once again demanding infinite variety.'[1] To earn their loyalty, marketing must be designed around customers as individuals and offer the same 'infinite variety'. Companies must not mistake loyalty marketing as another mass activity – and the 'reward' system in the 'loyalty' agenda below is thus just one element of a total relationship strategy.

1. Customer analysis, research and audit

1.1 Analyse customer behaviour and segment the market by customer lifetime value, identifying the segments with highest current and potential value and the customer behaviour that drives value.

1.2 Research customer perceptions of brands, company and its channels, identifying the greater needs of current customers that might be fulfilled by the company and the triggers that might motivate new customers to become involved with the company and its brands.

1.3 Audit current customer contact, evaluate the effect of current contact between company or channel and customer, and determine how current customer contact might be enhanced and how added value can be offered through new opportunities to recognise and interact with customers.

2. Customer development

2.1 Plan the development of customer relationships and the differentiation of the company and its brands through:

— Contacting customers more frequently
— Customising the proposition to affinity segments
— Rewarding increased purchase

    — Offering extra value through added products and
       services
    — Supporting the relationship with superior cus-
       tomer service.

2.2 Determine how to involve existing customers in a
    closer relationship, evaluating:

    — Membership
    — Association
    — Advocacy.

2.3 Determine how to engage new customers to open a
    relationship, through a mix of:

    — Prospecting
    — Acquisition.

3. Customer management

3.1 Design customer tracks to manage contact with cus-
    tomers in each behavioural segment, integrating:

    — Advertising and promotional response
    — Direct mail
    — Telephone
    — Sales
    — Service
    — Channel contact.

3.2 Reorganise the marketing function in customer-focused
    teams, encompassing all marketing communication
    disciplines, together with customer service and sales.
3.3 Design the business processes and information flows
    to manage and report customer tracks.

4. Customer targeting

4.1 Compare potential to current lifetime values to deter-
    mine priority customer segments for investment.
4.2 Build models to predict customer behaviour and value,
    and determine customer-focused investment strategy.

4.3   Work with finance to develop a customer-based return on investment model of the company, its brands and their markets; set return on investment targets and profiles.

4.4   Develop a planning and evaluation system to track the short- and long-term effects of marketing on the basis of lifetime value and loyalty measures.

5.   Marketing integration

5.1   Determine the role of advertising to increase the brand rate and the potential of interactivity to increase impact and build database.

5.2   Determine the role of promotion to increase customer lifetime value and the potential of direct response to identify high lifetime value customers and prospects.

5.3   Determine the role of public relations to communicate information about the company and its brands to the marketplace.

5.4   Determine the role of customer service, its development to encompass all forms of contact from customers and its payback in lifetime value.

5.5   Determine the integration of sales within customer tracks, how they can offer customers added value, and their role in creating an information flow from customer to company.

5.7   Determine how channels can be motivated to volunteer added value to customers, and how marketing support can be tailored to their needs and markets but managed by the company.

6.   Customer relationships

6.1   Develop a plan for the change in customer relationships from purchase- to relationship-based, and from transactional to membership.

6.2   Develop a plan for customer association, and for the involvement of best customers in company affairs, events and strategy.

6.3 Develop a Relationship Network, and maximise the power of advocacy throughout the market-place.

7. Customer rewards

7.1 Research the tangible rewards and preferential pricing that motivates customers to change their behaviour and pays back in increased lifetime value.

7.2 Select rewards within a strategy that includes increased contact, customisation to affinity groups, extra value, and enhanced customer service.

7.3 Develop the process that targets rewards only to customers with potential for increased lifetime value, and links rewards to sustained increases in revenue from these customer segments.

8. Customer information

8.1 Build a customer information system to support the relationship strategy, with emphasis on relationship data: derived and directional.

8.2 Plan the capture of customer data and feedback through an Information Network across the company and its market-place.

8.3 Develop the management of customer tracks by automated data selections from the customer information system.

8.4 Design the information flow that communicates customer events, signals and anniversaries to customer teams and customer-facing staff.

9. Staff development

9.1 Evaluate skills requirements and develop a programme of training, and both staff and team development.

9.2 Establish processes to learn from customer feedback within teams, and to share customer learning across teams.

9.3 Develop and maintain Best Practice and Customer Value manuals.

9.4 Build customer-based measures into staff and team rewards and remuneration structures.

10. Total brand experience

10.1 Enhance brand value strategy with relationship values associated with the uniqueness of a company and the personality of its staff.

10.2 Translate brand relationship values into meaningful and actionable guidance to all staff in customer teams.

10.3 Communicate the value of a brand as the value of the company's customer relationships to all the company's constituencies: shareholder, staff and customers as associates.

References

1 A time for change

1. P. Kotler, *Marketing Management*, 6th edn, Prentice-Hall, Englewood Cliffs, NJ, 1988.
2. A. Nove, *The Soviet Economic System*, George Allen & Unwin, London, 1977.
3. P. Drucker, *The Practice of Management*, Harper & Brothers, New York, 1954.
4. *Marketing at the Crossroads*, Coopers & Lybrand, London, 1993.
5. P. Kennedy, *Preparing for the Twenty First Century*, HarperCollins, London, 1993.
6. M. Albert, *Capitalism against Capitalism*, Whurr Publications, London, 1994.
7. C. Baker (ed.), 'The Volkswagen Golf 1984–1990', *Advertising Works 7*, NTC Publications, Henley, Oxfordshire.
8. A. Ourusoff, 'What's Hot', *Financial World*, August 1994, New York.
9. 'Don't Get Left on the Shelf', *The Economist*, 2 July 1994, London.
10. J. Kochner, Presentation to Spring Direct Marketing Association Conference, New Orleans, 1993.
11. Quoted in M. Thompson-Noel, 'Of Fish 'Eads, Baked Beans and Cola', *Financial Times*, 31 October 1994, London.
12. P. Kotler, *Marketing Management*.
13. *The C-Box Project*, Final report to the Newspaper Publishers Association, Collect Research, London, 1992.
14. *Planning for Social Change 1993/94*, Henley Centre, London, 1994.
15. S. Yahn, 'Advertising's Grave New World', *Advertising Age*, 16 May 1994, Chicago.
16. *Direct Marketing*, Hoke Communications, Garden City, New York.
17. T. Levitt, *The Marketing Imagination*, Free Press, New York, 1983.

2 Successful business models

1. S. Kiener, 'Megatrends 2000 – Challenges for Mail Order Businesses', presentation to the Direct Marketing Association Conference, San Francisco, 1994.

409

2. C. Hopkins, *Scientific Advertising*, Bell Publishing, New York, 1923.
3. A. Perruzza, 'The Customer Service Response/Retention Model', presentation to the Direct Marketing Association Conference, San Francisco, 1994.
4. *Teleculture 2000*, Henley Centre, London, 1994.

3 Marketing strategy for brands and customers

1. *Compact Edition of the Oxford English Dictionary*, Clarendon Press, Oxford, 1987.
2. D. Bernstein, *Company Image and Reality*.
3. K. Benezra, 'Mixed Messages', *Brandweek*, 25 July 1994.
4. G. C. Bisone, Compaq Computer, quoted in K. Benezra, 'Mixed Messages', *Brandweek*, 25 July 1994.
5. D. Bernstein, 'Company Image and Reality', 1986.
6. *Teleculture 2000*, Henley Centre, London, 1994.
7. J. Williams, *Strategic Management Resources*, 1994.
8. M. Gunn, 'The Advantage Programme', presentation to the Spring 1993 Direct Marketing Association Conference, 1993, New Orleans.
9. J. Kochner, 'Dell Computer', presentation to the Spring 1993 Direct Marketing Association Conference, 1993, New Orleans.
10. M. Porter, 'Competitive Advantage', in *Creating and Sustaining Superior Performance*, Free Press, New York, 1985.

4 Creating value from brands and customers

1. A. Ourusoff, 'What's Hot', *Financial World*, August 1994.
2. G. Gattuso, 'Relationship Retailing: A Two-Way Street', *Direct Marketing*, Hoke Communications, Garden City, NJ, February 1994.
3. *Media Futures 1993*, Henley Centre, London, 1993.

5 From image to interactive advertising

1. P. Weisz, quoted in 'Only a Matter of Trust', *Brandweek*, 25 July 1994.
2. L. Smith, 'Direct Response Advertising', unpublished, 1992.
3. P. Ashby, 'The Future of Advertising is Interactive Marketing Communication', Interactive Marketing Group, London, 1994.

4. J. Caples, *Tested Advertising Methods*, Prentice-Hall, Englewood Cliffs, NJ, 1974.
5. S. Fox, quoted in *The Mirror Makers*, Vintage Books, New York, 1985.
6. 'How Advertising Affects the Sales of Packaged Goods', Millward Brown, 1993.
7. 'Soap and Chips', *Financial Times*, 21 December 1994, London.
8. S. Rapp and T. Collins, *Maximarketing*, McGraw-Hill, New York, 1986.
9. Aude de Tuin and Prisca Michel, quoted in *En Direct*, Dunod, Paris, 1993.

6   From sales to relationship-building promotion

1. C. Petersen, *Sales Promotion in Action*, Associated Business Press, London, 1979.
2. D. Ogilvy, *Ogilvy on Advertising*, Pan, London, 1983.
3. William Weilbacher, *Brand Marketing*, NTC Business Books, Lincolnwood, Ill., 1993.
4. A. Ehrenburg, *Repeat Buying*, Oxford University Press, 1988.
5. D. Aaker, *Managing Brand Equity*, Free Press, New York, 1991.
6. J. P. Jones, *What's in a Name*, Gower, Aldershot, 1986.

7   From brand loyalty to customer loyalty

1. 'AmEx Developing Catalog Around Database', *Direct Marketing*, June 1993, Garden City, NJ.
2. Customer Survey, Direct Mail Information Service, London, 1992.
3. 'Customer Loyalty – Worth an Investment', Advertisement in *Target Marketing*, March 1994.
4. H. Brierley, 'The Art of Relationship Management', presentation to the Direct Marketing Association Conference, San Francisco, 1994.
5. M. Patterson, 'Relationship Marketing: Get Serious', *Dateline: DMA*, New York, April 1994.
6. L. Di Bella, 'Not Just for the Litttle Guys', *Direct Marketing*, May, 1991; L. Egol, 'Wacky Warehouse Builds Kool-Aid's Market Share', *Direct*, January 1990.
7. H. Cowie and J. Pinder (eds), *A Recovery Strategy for Europe*, Federal Trust, London, 1993.

8. *USA Today*, 12 October 1994.
9. 'TOTAL shareholders. Now is your opportunity to become an eyewitness', *Financial Times*, 4 November 1994, London.

8 From mass to data-driven marketing

1. 'American ad chief issues "end of era" warning', *Campaign*, 29 July 1994.
2. The Institute of Direct Marketing, Teddington.
3. *The Economist*, 17 February 1990, London.
4. *Teleculture 2000*, Henley Centre, London, 1994.
5. D. Halberstam, *The Reckoning*, Bloomsbury, London, 1986.
6. 'Hyundai taps into a "hidden sales force"', *Marketing Communications*, October 1988.
7. *Direct Marketing*, Hoke Communications, Garden City, New York.

9 Creating interactive advertising

1. V. Packard, *The Hidden Persuaders*, Penguin Books, Harmondsworth, 1981.
2. S. Fox, *The Mirror Makers: A History of American Advertising and its Creators*, Vintage Books, New York, 1985.
3. R. Reeves, *Reality in Advertising*, Knopf, New York, 1960.
4. Quoted in S. Fox, *The Mirror Makers*.
5. Ibid.
6. A. Ries and J. Trout, *Positioning: The Battle for Your Mind*, Warner Books, New York, 1981.
7. M. Thompson-Noel, 'An Explanation for Advertising', *Financial Times*, 12 December 1994, London.
8. C. Hopkins, *Scientific Advertising*, Bell Publishing, New York, 1923.
9. 'Response Research Survey', Direct Mail Information Service, London, 1992.

10 Creating interactive mail

1. J. W. W. Cassels, *How to Sell Successfully by Direct Mail*, Business Publications, London, 1954.
2. *Direct Marketing in Europe: An Examination of the Statistics*, European Direct Marketing Association/NTC Research, Brussels, 1993.

3. *Direct Mail Monitor*, The Direct Mail Information Service, London, 1994.

11 Understanding customer behaviour

1. *Admap*, May 1994.
2. C. Hopkins, *Scientific Advertising*, Bell Publishing, New York, 1923.
3. Michael Herbert Associates.
4. K. Clancy and R. Shulman, *The Marketing Revolution: A Radical Manifesto for Dominating the Marketplace*, Harper Business, New York, 1992.

12 Controlling marketing investments

1. K. Clancy and R. Shulman, *The Marketing Revolution*, Harper Business, New York, 1992.
2. C. Hopkins, *Scientific Advertising*, Bell Publishing, New York, 1923.
3. P. Strassman, *The Business Value of Computers*, Information Economics Press, Connecticut, 1990.

13 Building consumer brands directly

1. J. McManus, 'Moving the Needle When the Needle Don't Want to', *Brandweek*, 13 June 1994.
2. H. Hastings, 'At Retail Level, Brands Must Entertain, Involve, Inform', *Advertising Age*, 1994.
3. Quoted in L. Light, 'Brand Marketing Fables Lead to Loyalty Declines', *Advertising Age*, 10 January 1994.
4. Ibid.
5. Quoted in M. Petersen, *Direct Marketing International*, June 1994, EDMA Forum, Brussels.
6. F. Warner, 'Philip Morris Defends its Turf as Anti-Smoking Forces Grow', *Brandweek*, 18 July 1994.
7. 'Best Promotion Brammy, Food & Beverage', *Marketing*, April 1993.
8. 'Nana dans les bôites aux lettres' and 'Les France du Cholesterol', *Direct*, no. 33, Paris.
9. L. Frenette, 'Breyers Scoops Affinity Cards', *Direct*, 20 July 1989, Paris.
10. 'Pelforth en brune et blonde', *Direct*, no. 33, Paris.

14 Building financial brands directly

1. L. Camp, 'Marketing Focus', *Marketing*, 20 January 1994, London.
2. M. Patterson, 'Relationship Marketing: Get Serious', presentation to the DMA Conference, Toronto, October 1993.
3. M. Bose, 'Learning How Not to Lose Friends', *Director*, August 1991.
4. F. Reichfeld, 'Customer Loyalty', presentation to the Spring DMA Conference, New Orleans, 1993.
5. L. Camp, 'Marketing Focus'.
6. M. Patterson, 'Relationship Marketing: Get Serious'.

15 Building business brands directly

1. J. M. Coe, 'The Decay Rate of Business Databases – A Surprise', *DM News*, 14 February 1994.
2. D. Aaker, *Managing Brand Equity*, Free Press, New York, 1991.
3. S. Kapp, 'Prospects Stay Interested Six Months', *Business Marketing*, March 1990, Chicago.
4. T. Eisenhart, 'On-Target Delivery', *Business Marketing*, April 1994, Chicago.
5. I. Locks, P. Dear, P. Cutts, 'The Secret Success of Magazines', *Marketing Director International*, 1994.
6. I. Allanson, 'Building Awareness and Image Using Direct Marketing Methods', Montreux Symposium.
7. *Direct Marketing News*, 20 December 1993.
8. Quoted in *Brandweek*, 6 June 1994.

16 Building retail brands directly

1. H. Gordon, 'Managing Database Marketing Technologies for Success', presentation to the Spring 1993 DMA Conference, New Orleans.
2. N. Buckley, 'Retailers' Global Shopping Spree', *Financial Times*, 12 October 1994, London.
3. 'The Future of Shopping', *The Economist*, 20 October 1994, London.
4. C. Sandys, 'Holly Fills Market Niche', *Canadian Direct Marketing News*, 1 March 1991.

5. N. Kleinfield, 'Targeting the Grocery Shopper', *New York Times*, 26 May 1991, New York.
6. 'Program Greens in Sweden', *Promoting Store Traffic*, Hoke Communications, 1 June 1992.
7. L. Petersen, 'ActMedia Rolls Out Coupons', *Adweek*, 11 February 1991.
8. A. Cranin, 'Bound to Attract Customers', *Advertising Age*, 11 February 1994, Chicago.
9. 'Club Orange', Direct Marketing Association Echo Entry, 1 October 1990.
10. G. Ostrager, 'How Retailers Can Use their Customer Databases', *DM News*, 4 July 1994.
11. 'The Future of Shopping', *The Economist*, London, 1994.

Action plan one

1. M. McDonald, 'Marketing – A Mid-life Crisis', *Marketing Business*, May 1994.
2. R. Jutkins, 'Why the Hi-tech Profits of Doom Have Got it Wrong', *Direct Marketing International*, June 1994.

Action plan three

1. Target Marketing, March 1994.
2. J. Emerson, 'CommerceNet Linkup Helps Internet', *DM News*, May 1994.
3. 'Compaq, But It's Perfectly Formed', *Financial Times*, 25 July 1994, London.

Action plan four

1. 'The Celling out of America', *The Economist*, 17 December 1994, London.

Index

417

Operational Risk Control with Basel II

Operational Risk Control with Basel II

Basic principles and capital requirements

Dimitris N. Chorafas

ELSEVIER
BUTTERWORTH
HEINEMANN

AMSTERDAM   BOSTON   HEIDELBERG   LONDON   NEW YORK   OXFORD
PARIS   SAN DIEGO   SAN FRANCISCO   SINGAPORE   SYDNEY   TOKYO

Elsevier Butterworth-Heinemann
Linacre House, Jordan Hill, Oxford OX2 8DP
200 Wheeler Road, Burlington MA 01803

First published 2004

British Library Cataloguing in Publication Data
A catalogue record for this book is available from the British Library

Library of Congress Cataloguing in Publication Data
A catalogue record for this book is available from the Library of Congress

ISBN 0 7506 5909 2

For information on all Butterworth-Heinemann publications
visit our website at www.bh.com

Composition by Genesis Typesetting Limited, Rochester, Kent
Printed and bound in Great Britain

Contents

Foreword

Understanding risks in the modern economy

It is with great pleasure that I write this Foreword to the book by Dimitris Chorafas on 'Operational Risk Control' as he set out to tackle an almost impossible problem: How to deal with the many risks that financial services firms, and insurance companies in particular, face in the operational risk dimension. As Chorafas rightly explains in Chapter 1, the prevailing definition of operational risk comes from the Basel Committee on Banking Supervision. In their consultative document Operational Risk – Supporting Document to the New Basel Capital Accord of January 2001, the Basel Committee on Banking Supervision writes on page 2 that operational risk is '*the risk of direct or indirect loss resulting from inadequate or failed internal processes, people and systems or from external events*' and adds the footnote '*This definition includes legal risk*'. One could make a case that such a broad definition is not particularly helpful. As a reaction, many other definitions of operational risk have been proposed, only to come back to the above one. In practice, more often than not, operational risk seems to comprise all those risks that are not dealt with by any other specific control mechanism in a company. This makes it especially awkward to deal with the issue, as there is a tendency to push anything and everything into the category of operational risk whenever any of the other – more traditional and therefore with a clearer framework – risk areas do not appear to apply or fit the situation.

In addition, there is another problem as operational risk does not have its own special champions. Chorafas underlines this by writing in this book that '*everybody is accountable for operational risk control*'. Insurance risks like technical provisions are for the actuaries, financial planning and reporting risks like asset-liability matching are for accountants, information technology risks like computer failures are for the IT experts etc. So who are the operational risks for? Chorafas deals with this issue in a direct or indirect way in many parts of his book. He establishes that they are for human resources specialists as they deal with the people as a source of risk. They are for lawyers as they concern legal issues. They are for economists as they deal with economic events. And so on. However, the main question remains: Who takes ownership in a direct and focused way as the core of his profession? The only real operational risk experts are often the senior management of a company with enough broad overview and understanding of, but at the same time also responsibility for, a company's exposure, conduct and performance. Unfortunately, they are by training actuaries, accountants, economists, lawyers, engineers etc. who have accepted a shift and an enlargement of their activities to become (more or less) operational risk experts.

The International Association for the Study of Insurance Economics, or by its short name 'The Geneva Association' was established in 1973 for the purpose of promoting economic research in the sector of risk and insurance. It is a unique world organization formed by a maximum of eighty chief executive officers from most important insurance companies in the world. Its main goal is to research the growing importance of worldwide insurance activities in all sectors of the economy. It tries to identify fundamental trends and strategic issues where insurance plays a substantial role or which influence the insurance sector. In parallel, The Geneva Association develops and encourages various initiatives concerning the evolution – in economic and cultural terms – of risk management and the notion of uncertainty in the modern economy. The Geneva Association also acts as a forum for its members, providing a worldwide unique platform for the top insurance CEOs. It organizes the framework for its members to exchange ideas and discuss key strategic issues. The Geneva Association serves as a catalyst for progress in this unprecedented period of fundamental change in the insurance industry. It seeks to clarify the key role that insurance plays in the further development of the modern economy. The issue of operational risk has featured prominently in many of the past conferences and seminars of the organization.

As recently as in its February 2003 conference, the Amsterdam Circle of Chief Economists, an international network of the key insurance economists and strategists founded and managed by The Geneva Association, has dealt with the intricacies of operational risk. The group came to some sobering conclusions. Probably the key one being the view that risks from internal operations are fairly well understood today. However, risks from the business and economic environment and other external sources are much less understood.

Operational risk has a lot to do with the concepts that are at the basis of insurance. The modern world, as an integrated production system for economic and social goods and services, is no longer viable without properly functioning insurance solutions. Our actions depend on so many other actors and what they do, that questions of how to join these processes together with tolerable risk exposure have become a central preoccupation of society. Thus, today the insurance industry does not play the role of a standard widget-maker that simply produces a good or service and leaves it up to the market to decide whether to accept it or not. In a globalizing environment where risks are pushed increasingly onto the individual, insurance becomes an essential prerequisite for a modern service economy. Whether with regard to risks associated with the life or the non-life industry, it seems that we all need more and better insurance solutions to manage our existence. We also need, as Chorafas writes, a much better understanding about the operational risk that accompanies our actions and processes.

The economic and financial performance and reliability of humanity has increased greatly. At the same time, our perception of risks and vulnerabilities – partly as a consequence of a higher level of knowledge – has increased to the point of producing feelings of insecurity. This is not only a psychological attitude, but is linked to the fact that every system needs to be controlled, guaranteed and financially protected against failure. This is the context in which insurance and risk management can improve their image and underline the fact that they operate at the very core of our modern society and economy. This effort needs to be accompanied by an adequate understanding of the theoretical basis of insurance and risk management issues. It is in this light that I am so supportive of the work by Dimitris Chorafas.

It is a paradox that humankind's obsession with certainty and predictability, supposedly created by a better, more scientific understanding of the world, has led to the insight that we are facing more and more risks every day. As a blind person gradually learning to see, the additional information has not led to the elimination of all risks as was formerly thought but, on the contrary, to a more pronounced understanding of what the vulnerabilities are and where they lie. The blind walking by an abyss are blissfully ignorant of the danger they are in. The ignorance does not eliminate the risk objectively but removes it on a subjective basis – at least as long as nobody falls down the precipice. Is the world of the blind a better place? Definitely not. We can in some instances try to avoid risky situations, but life without risk is unimaginable. We thus have to learn to live with risks and dangers to our lives and the social and economic fabric that we put in place. The solution cannot be to close our eyes but, on the contrary, to open them wide and deal with any challenges in an informed and proactive way. Operational risk issues are a special case in point. Those risks exist in a very real way, but the risk perception is not always there, and if it is, then often the right management tools do not exist or are not applied. I hope that this book can make a difference in this way.

However, despite great efforts, let us not forget a fundamental truth. The advancements in theoretical and practical understanding have led to the application of calculations that convert a fuzzy understanding of risks into a more or less exact scientific discipline. The key problem here is not the 'more or less' but rather the notion of an exact scientific discipline. As Heisenberg demonstrated, there are limits to the exactness of science. This is not the outcome of our limited understanding about the world and its inner mechanisms but rather an inherent part of what constitutes life in itself: the notion of only transitory balances and equilibria that give way to dynamic adjustment processes. We have learned reasonably well to coexist with this uncertainty. Nevertheless, even the best understanding of operational and other risks will not prevent us from suffering important accidents, catastrophes and other misfortunes.

As I wrote in the editorial 'Towards the New Insurance World' for the *Geneva Papers on Risk and Insurance – Issues and Practice*, vol. 27, no.1, of January 2002 (Blackwell Publishers, London), '*Insurance is the science of the improbable and the art of the impossible*'. I am delighted to see that Chorafas has decided to include these reflections in Chapter 10 of his book. Insurance is the ultimate expression of, and test for, risk understanding and management. It is the science of the improbable as risk coverage is usually given for improbable events. Understanding the frequency and severity of a potential claim is a necessary precondition for sound insurance business. More information and better understanding, more efficient tools and instruments will improve this part of the business. However, insurance is also the art of the impossible. We are, from time to time, confronted with events that we would have qualified ex ante as impossible, unrealistic or that we were simply unaware of. This dimension of risk management has also to be applied to operational risk control – perhaps even more to this particular risk category, as it comprises so many different sources of risks.

As any good risk manager knows: If a risk can be sold in the marketplace at reasonable conditions, then risk management is either already efficient or can be made so. Many operational risks, however, are difficult to place as Chorafas explains in Chapter 11. This is not only true for the fairly new categories of operational risks, but especially for internal operational risks that are closely linked to the established processes of an entity. Those internal operational risks often violate some of the necessary preconditions for obtaining insurance – the absence of moral hazard, adverse selection, asymmetric information etc. This is an important reason for paying special attention to them. While for many risks there is a ready choice to transfer them to another party or otherwise outsource them, internal operational risk is often so closely linked to the very fabric of a company that selling it is very difficult and costly. And if it is sold, then there are carefully worded clauses that protect the buyer from undue exploitation by the seller of these risks. It will be especially interesting to see how the insurance industry and its potential clients will cope with this type of risk in the future. Some interesting solutions will doubtlessly emerge while other aspects of the business will remain uninsurable and the management of those risks will firmly rest with the companies.

Dimitris Chorafas' book is worth reading for anyone who has an interest in understanding operation risks and their management and control. It provides very useful insights in some of the key issues facing modern companies, their risk managers and the insurance and reinsurance industry.

Patrick M. Liedtke
Secretary General and Managing Director
of The Geneva Association
www.genevaassociation.org

Preface

Knowledge wears out if we don't use it. This book is about knowledge connected to operational risk control, and what we know that can be implemented to help financial institutions and other organizations overcome their operational risk problems. The text is written for managers and professionals, because managers are responsible for a company's success or failure, as well as for the control of the risks that confront it.

The book addresses practitioners in business and industry: commercial banks, securities houses, service companies, merchandising firms, manufacturing companies, and consulting firms. Members of the board, chief executive officers, chief operating officers, financial directors, back office managers, members of audit committees, auditors (internal and external), lawyers (corporate and partners of law firms), financial analysts, operations managers, information technology officers, and, evidently, operational risk managers and their staff, will all find some of the answers they seek in these pages.

Because the past is not behind us but within us, like rings in a tree, the past is part of the knowledge we have in operational risk identification and control. Therefore, the text brings to the reader's attention both basic principles and practical examples through case studies. Both should also be of interest to regulators, and certified public accountants. The same is true about forward-looking models presented in this book, like high frequency/low impact and low frequency/high impact of risk events.

A special audience is that of insurance. As a major case study, five chapters present technical risk and operational risk in the insurance industry. Technical risk is taken by insurers in their daily business through the contracts they underwrite for their clients, whose operational risk is quite often the technical risk of the insurer. An example is insurance on malpractice, which amounts to an insurer's significant exposure to somebody else's operational risk.

Organization of the text

The text divides into four parts. Part 1 explains how and why operational risk is present in every enterprise, at any time, in any place. Chapter 1 presents ways and means for management to be in charge. It explains what constitutes operational risk events; why operational risks are embedded in all transactions, and at all organizational levels; which strategies help most in bringing operational risk under control; and how control activities can be turned into a senior management tool.

Chapter 2 addresses the issues of classification, identification, and monitoring of operational risk. It starts by following the directives of the Basel Committee, then it capitalizes on past experience from auditing and internal control. A practical implementation example is presented in Chapter 3, with legal risk. The definition of legal risk is followed by examples on operational risk management with contractual risk, crossborder legal risk, and legal risks taken with securitized products.

The theme of Chapter 4 is management risk in all its manifestations. A practical example is taken with the power crisis in the United States. Other case studies included in this chapter are at the junction of operational risk and credit risk, since the former can morph into the latter. Chapter 5 brings to the reader's attention technology risk, and what this means for the financial institution. The subjects range from operational risks associated to trading, payments, and settlements, to operational risks resulting from system unreliability as well as from outsourcing and insourcing.

Capital requirements for operational risk, and their modeling, are the subject of Part 2. Chapter 6 explains how the allocation of operational risk capital can be effectively done by means of the methodology advanced by Basel II, provided the institution and its senior management are willing and able to undergo a cultural change. The chapter also brings to the reader's attention the difference between economic capital and regulatory capital.

Chapter 7 analyzes the first four of the five methods of capital allocation for operational risk, by the Basel Committee on Banking Supervision: the basic indicator approach, standard approach, internal measurement approach, and loss distribution approach. It also explains why the latter two, which are advanced measurement approaches, require leadership in databasing and datamining – which are themselves among the operational risks faced by the institution.

The subject matter of Chapters 8 and 9 is how to establish a scoreboard approach. To provide the proper conceptual base for its development, Chapter 8 addresses itself to high frequency/low impact (HF/LI) events, as well as low frequency/high impact (LF/HI) events. Having defined the concept and the method, it explains what is needed for system design for operational risk control. Through practical applications of Six Sigma, the text explains what can be done.

Chapter 9 focuses on market discipline to be assisted through the scoreboard approach. The level of difficulty in implementation goes from relatively simple templates to sophisticated practices. The text also includes, in connection to operational risk control, extreme value theory and genetic algorithms, and also the method followed by a common op risk project undertaken by 12 major financial institutions.

The focal point of Part 3 is operational risk in the insurance industry. Chapter 10 defines the science of insurance and the notion of technical risk. Risk factors are identified, the role of actuaries is brought into perspective, technical provisions are discussed and, with them, the role played by profitability models. Attention is evidently paid to reinsurance.

The use of insurance policies to mitigate risk is analyzed in Chapter 11. The cost of equity is compared to the cost of debt and the cost of insurance. Alternative risk transfer (ART) is a central theme, while op risk securitization is associated to possible moral hazard. Chapter 12 examines the role of rating agencies in insurance, and insurance-linked cases. It explains how insurance companies are rated, presents a case study with marine insurance underwriting, and elaborates on why and how insurers should do their homework.

Chapter 13 focuses on tort and its relation to operational risk. It presents the thesis of proponents of and contrarians to tort reform; explains what can be learned from the Y2K crisis; and it brings into the picture different outsized compensation for operational risk claims like asbestos. It also explains why tort and management risk correlate. The challenge of terrorism is the subject of Chapter 14, starting with business disruption. While the events of 11 September 2001 are in the background as an extreme event, many other examples are taken to lead the reader into rethinking insurability. Part 3 concludes with the case of governments as insurers of last resort.

The theme of Part 4 is the importance of cost-consciousness in operational risk control. The message it brings to the reader is that costs matter, and that costs and op risk management correlate in many ways. As Chapter 15 documents, deficient cost control is the result of management risk. Emphasis is therefore placed on the need to be a low-cost producer, with practical examples taken from the financial industry, particularly from companies that have been able to keep their overhead at rock bottom.

Chapter 16 brings to the reader's attention that, apart the cost of doing business, there is also the cost of staying in business. Operational risk interacts with both of them. The text examines whether mergers are a good way to cut costs, explains what's behind being an innovator of financial services, discusses how to sustain a transnational advantage in an era of globalization, and concludes with ways and means for capitalizing on the evolving role of financial institutions in the economy.

*   *   *

This integrative approach to operational risk management has been necessary because, until quite recently in banking and finance, operational risk has taken a back seat to credit risk and market risk. This is no longer true. Prompted by the new capital adequacy framework (Basel II), by the Basel Committee on Banking Supervision, and its rules, financial institutions are busy rethinking and revamping their operational risk control. This text is a contribution to their efforts.

I am indebted to a long list of knowledgeable people, and of organizations, for their contribution to the research that made this book feasible. Also to several senior executives and experts for constructive criticism during the preparation of the manuscript. The complete list of the senior executives and organizations who participated in this research is shown in the Acknowledgements.

Let me take this opportunity to thank Mike Cash for suggesting this project, Jennifer Wilkinson for seeing it all the way to publication, and Deena Burgess and Elaine Leek for the editorial work. To Eva-Maria Binder goes the credit for compiling the research results, typing the text, and preparing the artwork and index.

Dimitris N. Chorafas
June 2003

Acknowledgements

The following organizations, through their senior executives and system specialists, participated in the research projects that led to the contents of this book and its documentation.

(Countries are listed in alphabetical order)

Austria

National Bank of Austria
Dr Martin Ohms
Finance Market Analysis Department
3, Otto Wagner Platz
Postfach 61
A-1011 Vienna

Association of Austrian Banks and Bankers
Dr Fritz Diwork
Secretary General
11, Boersengasse
1013 Vienna

Die Erste (First Austrian Bank)
Franz Reif
Head, Group Risk Controlling
8, Neutorgasse
A-1010 Vienna

Bank Austria
Dr Peter Fischer
Senior General Manager, Treasury Division

Peter Gabriel
Deputy General Manager, Trading
2, Am Hof
1010 Vienna

Creditanstalt
Dr Wolfgang Lichtl
Market Risk Management

Julius Tandler
Platz 3
A-1090 Vienna

Wiener Betriebs- and Baugesellschaft mbH
Dr Josef Fritz
General Manager
1, Anschützstrasse
1153 Vienna

France

Banque de France
Pierre Jaillet
Director, Monetary Studies and Statistics

Yvan Oronnal
Manager, Monetary Analyses and Statistics

G. Tournemire, Analyst, Monetary Studies
39, rue Croix des Petits Champs
75001 Paris

Secretariat Général de la Commission Bancaire – Banque de France
Didier Peny
Director, Control of Big Banks and International Banks
73, rue de Richelieu
75002 Paris

F. Visnowsky
Manager of International Affairs
Supervisory Policy and Research
   Division

Benjamin Sahel
Market Risk Control
115, Rue Réaumur
75049 Paris Cedex 01

**Ministry of Finance and the Economy,
   Conseil National de la Comptabilité**
Alain Le Bars
Director International Relations and
   Cooperation
6, rue Louise Weiss

Germany

Deutsche Bundesbank
Hans-Dietrich Peters
Director

Hans Werner Voth
Director

Dr Frank Heid
Banking and Financial Supervision
   Department
Wilhelm-Epstein Strasse 14
60431 Frankfurt am Main

Federal Banking Supervisory Office
Hans-Joachim Dohr
Director Dept. I

Jochen Kayser
Risk Model Examination

Ludger Hanenberg
Internal Controls
71–101 Gardeschützenweg
12203 Berlin

European Central Bank
Mauro Grande
Director
29 Kaiserstrasse
29th Floor
60216 Frankfurt am Main

Deutsches Aktieninstitut
Dr Rüdiger Von Rosen
President
Biebergasse 6 bis 10
60313 Frankfurt-am-Main

Commerzbank
Peter Bürger
Senior Vice President, Strategy and
   Controlling

Markus Rumpel
Senior Vice President, Credit Risk
   Management
Kaiserplatz
60261 Frankfurt am Main

Deutsche Bank
Professor Manfred Timmermann
Head of Controlling

Hans Voit
Head of Process Management,
   Controlling Department
12, Taunusanlage
60325 Frankfurt

Dresdner Bank
Dr Marita Balk
Investment Bank, Risk Control

Dr Hermann Haaf
Mathematical Models for Risk
   Control

Claas Carsten Kohl
Financial Engineer
1, Jürgen Ponto Platz
60301 Frankfurt

Volkswagen Foundation
Katja Ebeling
Office of the General Secretary
35 Kastanienallee
30519 Hanover

Herbert Quandt Foundation
Dr Kai Schellhorn
Member of the Board
Hanauer Strasse 46
D-80788 Munich

GMD First – Research Institute for
   Computer Architecture, Software
   Technology and Graphics
Prof.Dr Ing. Wolfgang K. Giloi
General Manager
5, Rudower Chaussee
D-1199 Berlin
75703 Paris Cedex 13

Hungary

**Hungarian Banking and Capital
   Market Supervision**
Dr Janos Kun
Head, Department of Regulation and
   Analyses

Dr Erika Vörös
Senior Economist, Department of
   Regulation and Analyses

Dr Géza Nyriry
Head, Section of Information Audit
Csalogany u. 9–11
H-1027 Budapest

Hungarian Academy of Sciences
Prof. Dr Tibor Vamos
Chairman, Computer and Automation
   Research Institute
Nador U. 7
1051 Budapest

Iceland

The National Bank of Iceland Ltd
Gunnar T. Andersen
Managing Director
International Banking & Treasury
Laugavegur 77
155 Reykjavik

Italy

Banca d'Italia
Eugene Gaiotti
Research Department, Monetary and
   Financial Division

Ing. Dario Focarelli
Research Department
91, via Nazionale
00184 Rome

Istituto Bancario San Paolo di Torino
Dr Paolo Chiulenti
Director of Budgeting
Roberto Costa
Director of Private Banking

Pino Ravelli
Director Bergamo Region
27, via G. Camozzi
24121 Bergamo

Luxembourg

Banque Générale de Luxembourg
Prof. Dr Yves Wagner
Director of Asset and Risk
   Management

Hans Jörg Paris, International Risk
   Manager
27, avenue Monterey
L-2951 Luxembourg

Clearstream
André Lussi
President and CEO
3–5 Place Winston Churchill
L-2964 Luxembourg

Poland

Securities and Exchange Commission
Beata Stelmach
Secretary of the Commission
1, Pl Powstancow Warszawy
00–950 Warsaw

Sweden

**The Royal Swedish Academy of
   Sciences**
Dr Solgerd Björn-Rasmussen
Head Information Department

Dr Olof Tanberg
Foreign Secretary
10405 Stockholm

Skandinaviska Enskilda Banken
Bernt Gyllenswärd
Head of Group Audit
Box 16067
10322 Stockholm

Irdem AB
Gian Medri
Former Director of Research at
   Nordbanken
19, Flintlasvagen
S–19154 Sollentuna

Switzerland

Swiss National Bank
Dr Werner Hermann
Head of International Monetary
   Relations

Dr Christian Walter
Representative to the Basel Committee

Prof. Urs Birchler
Director, Advisor on Systemic Stability

Robert Fluri
Assistant Director, Statistics Section
15 Börsenstrasse
8022 Zurich

Federal Banking Commission
Dr Susanne Brandemberger
Risk Management

Renate Lischer
Representative to Risk Management
   Subgroup, Basel Committee
Marktgasse 37
3001 Bern

Bank for International Settlements
Steven Senior
Basel Committee Secretariat

Hirotaka Hideskima
Basel Committee Secretariat

Claude Sivy
Head of Internal Audit

Herbie Poenisch
Senior Economist, Monetary and
   Economic Department

Ingo Fender
Committee on the Global Financial
   System
2, Centralplatz
4002 Basel

Crédit Suisse
Christian A. Walter
Vice President, Risk Management
8 Paradeplatz
8070 Zurich

Ahmad Abu El-Ata
Managing Director, Head of IT Office

Dr Burkhard P. Varnholt
Managing Director, Global Research
12/14 Bahnhofstrasse
CH-8070 Zurich

Bank Leu AG
Dr Urs Morgenthaler
Member of Management
Director of Risk Control
32, Bahnhofstrasse
Zurich

**Bank J. Vontobel and Vontobel
   Holding**
Heinz Frauchiger
Chief, Internal Audit Department
Tödistrasse 23
CH-8022 Zurich

Union Bank of Switzerland
Dr Heinrich Steinmann
Member of the Executive Board
   (Retired)
Claridenstrasse
8021 Zurich

UBS Financial Services Group
Dr Per-Göran Persson
Executive Director, Group Strategic
   Analysis

George Pastrana
Executive, Economic Capital
  Allocation
Stockerstrasse 64
8098 Zurich

University of Fribourg
Prof.Dr Jürgen Kohlas

Prof.Dr Andreas Meier
Department of Informatics
2, rue Faucigny
CH-1700 Fribourg

Swiss Re
Dr Thomas Hess
Head of Economic Research &
  Consulting
Mythenquai 50/60
P.O.Box
CH-8022 Zürich

United Kingdom

Bank of England
Richard Britton
Director, Complex Groups Division,
  CGD Policy Department

Ian M. Michael
Senior Manager, Financial Industry
  and Regulation Division
Threadneedle Street
London EC2R 8AH

Financial Services Authority (FSA)
Lieselotte Burgdorf-Cook
International Relations
7th Floor
25 The North Colonnade
Canary Wharf
London E14 5HS

British Bankers Association
Paul Chisnall
Assistant Director
Pinners Hall
105–108 Old Broad Street
London EC2N 1EX

Accounting Standards Board
A.V.C. Cook
Technical Director

Sandra Thompson
Project Director
Holborn Hall
100 Gray's Inn Road
London WC1X 8AL

Barclays Bank Plc
Brandon Davies
Treasurer, Global Corporate Banking

Tim Thompson
Head of Economic Capital

Julian Knight
Manager, Group Risk Analysis and
  Policy

Alan Brown
Director, Group Risk
54 Lombard Street
London EC3P 3AH

Abbey National Treasury Services plc
John Hasson
Director of Information Technology &
  Treasury Operations
Abbey National House
2 Triton Square
Regent's Place
London NW1 3AN

Citigroup
Dr David Lawrence
European Head of Risk
  Methodologies and Analytics
33 Canada Square
Canary Wharf
London E14 5LB

Rabobank Nederland
Eugen Buck
Managing Director
Senior Project Manager Economic
  Capital
Thames Court
One Queenhithe
London EC4V 3RL

ABN–AMRO Investment Bank N.V.
David Woods
Chief Operations Officer, Global
   Equity Directorate

Annette C. Austin
Head of Operational Risk
   Management Wholesale Client
250 Bishopsgate
London EC2M 4AA

Bankgesellschaft Berlin
Stephen F. Myers
Head of Market Risk
1 Crown Court
Cheapside, London

Standard & Poor's
David T. Beers
Managing Director, Sovereign &
   International Public Finance Ratings

Barbara Ridpath
Managing Director, Chief Credit
   Officer, Europe
Broadgate West
9 Appold Street
London EC2A 2AP

Moody's Investor Services
Moody's Risk Management Services
Samuel S. Theodore
Managing Director, European Banks

Alastair Graham
Senior Vice President, Director of
   Global Training

Lars Hunsche
Project Manager, KMV

Lynn Valkenaar
Project Manager, KMV

David Frohriep
Communications Manager, Europe
2, Minster Court
Mincing Lane
London EC3R 7XB

Fitch Ratings
Charles Prescott
Group Managing Director

David Andrews
Managing Director, Financial
   Institutions

Travor Pitman
Managing Director, Corporations

Richard Fox
Director, International Public Finance
Eldon House
2, Eldon Street
London EC2M 7UA

A.M. Best Europe
Jose SanchezCrespo
General Manager
1 Minster Court
Mincing Lane
London EC3R 7AA

Merrill Lynch International
Bart Dowling
Director, Global Asset Allocation

Elena Dimova
Vice President, Equity Sales

Erik Banks
Managing Director of Risk
   Management
Merrill Lynch Financial Center
2 King Edward Street
London EC1A 1HQ

The Auditing Practices Board
Jonathan E.C. Grant
Technical Director

Steve Leonard
Internal Controls Project Manager
P.O.Box 433
Moorgate Place
London EC2P 2BJ

International Accounting Standards Committee
Ms Liesel Knorr
Technical Director
166 Fleet Street
London EC4A 2DY

MeesPierson ICS
Arjan P. Verkerk
Director, Market Risk
Camomile Court
23 Camomile Street
London EC3A 7PP

Trema UK Ltd
Dr Vincent Kilcoyne
Business Architecture
75 Cannon Street
London EC2N 5BN

Charles Schwab
Dan Hattrup
International Investment Specialist
Crosby Court
38 Bishopsgate
London EC2N 4AJ

Charity Commission
Susan Polak

Mike McKillop

J. Chauhan
13–15 Bouverie Street
London ECAY 8DP

The Wellcome Trust
Clare Matterson
Member of the Executive Board and
    Head of Policy
210 Euston Road
London NW1 2BE

Association of Charitable Foundations
Nigel Siederer
Chief Executive
2, Plough Yard
Shoreditch High Street
London EC2A 3LP

IBM United Kingdom
Derek Duerden
Technical Strategy, EMEA Banking
    Finance & Securities Business
76 Upper Ground
London SE1 9PZ

City University Business School
Professor Elias Dinenis
Head, Department of Investment
Risk Management & Insurance

Prof.Dr John Hagnioannides
Department of Finance
Frobisher Crescent
Barbican Centre
London EC2Y 8BH

TT International
Timothy A. Tacchi
Co-Chief Executive Officer

Henry Bedford
Co-Chief Executive Officer

Robin A.E. Hunt
Martin House
5 Martin Lane
London EC4R 0DP

Alternative Investment Management Association (AIMA)
Emma Mugridge
Director
10 Stanhope Gate
Mayfair
London W1K 1AL

Ernst & Young
Pierre-Yves Maurois
Senior Manager, Risk Management
    and Regulatory Services
Rolls House
7 Rolls Buildings
Fetter Lane
London E4A 1NH

Brit Syndicates Limited at Lloyd's
Peter Chrismas
Hull Underwriter

Anthony Forsyth
Marine Underwriter
Marine, Aviation, Transport & Space
    Division
Box 035
Lloyd's
1 Lime Sreet
London EC3M 7DQ

United States

Federal Reserve System, Board of Governors
David L. Robinson
Deputy Director, Chief Federal
    Reserve Examiner

Alan H. Osterholm, CIA, CISA
Manager, Financial Examinations
    Section

Paul W. Bettge
Assistant Director, Division of Reserve
    Bank Operations

Gregory E. Eller
Supervisory Financial Analyst,
    Banking

Gregory L. Evans
Manager, Financial Accounting

Martha Stallard
Financial Accounting, Reserve Bank
    Operations
20th and Constitution, NW
Washington, DC 20551

Federal Reserve Bank of Boston
William McDonough
Executive Vice President

James T. Nolan
Assistant Vice President
P.O. Box 2076
600 Atlantic Avenue
Boston, MA

Federal Reserve Bank of San Francisco
Nigel R. Ogilvie, CFA
Supervising Financial Analyst
Emerging Issues
101 Market Street
San Francisco, CA

Seattle Branch, Federal Reserve Bank of San Francisco
Jimmy F. Kamada
Assistant Vice President

Gale P. Ansell
Assistant Vice President, Business
    Development
1015, 2nd Avenue
Seattle, WA 98122–3567

Office of the Comptroller of the Currency (OCC)
Bill Morris
National Bank Examiner/Policy
    Analyst,
Core Policy Development Division

Gene Green
Deputy Chief Accountant
Office of the Chief Accountant
250 E Street, SW
7th Floor
Washington, DC

Federal Deposit Insurance Corporation (FDIC)
Curtis Wong
Capital Markets, Examination Support

Tanya Smith
Examination Specialist, International
    Branch

Doris L. Marsh
Examination Specialist, Policy Branch
550 17th Street, NW
Washington, DC

Office of Thrift Supervision (OTS)
Timothy J. Stier
Chief Accountant
1700 G Street Northwest
Washington, DC, 20552

Securities and Exchange Commission, Washington, DC
Robert Uhl
Professional Accounting Fellow

Pascal Desroches
Professional Accounting Fellow

John W. Albert
Associate Chief Accountant

Scott Bayless
Associate Chief Accountant
Office of the Chief Accountant
Securities and Exchange Commission
450 Fifth Street, NW
Washington, DC, 20549

Securities and Exchange Commission, New York
Robert A. Sollazzo
Associate Regional Director
7 World Trade Center
12th Floor
New York, NY 10048

Securities and Exchange Commission, Boston
Edward A. Ryan, Jr
Assistant District Administrator
(Regulations)
Boston District Office
73 Tremont Street, 6th Floor
Boston, MA 02108–3912

Microsoft
Dr Gordon Bell
Senior Researcher
Bay Area Research Center of
Microsoft Research
455, Market Street
Suite 1690
San Francisco, CA 94105

American Bankers Association
Dr James Chessen
Chief Economist

Mr Douglas Johnson
Senior Policy Analyst
1120 Connecticut Ave NW
Washington, DC 20036

International Monetary Fund
Alain Coune
Assistant Director, Office of Internal
Audit and Inspection
700 19th Street NW
Washington DC, 20431

Financial Accounting Standards Board
Halsey G. Bullen
Project Manager

Jeannot Blanchet
Project Manager

Teri L. List
Practice Fellow
401 Merritt
Norwalk, CN 06856

Henry Kaufman & Company
Dr Henry Kaufman
660 Madison Avenue
New York, NY 10021

Soros Fund Management
George Soros
Chairman
888 Seventh Avenue, Suite 3300
New York, NY 10106

Carnegie Corporation of New York
Armanda Famiglietti
Associate Corporate Secretary,
Director of Grants Management
437 Madison Avenue
New York, NY 10022

Alfred P. Sloan Foundation
Stewart F. Campbell
Financial Vice President and Secretary
630 Fifth Avenue, Suite 2550
New York, NY 10111

Rockefeller Brothers Fund
Benjamin R. Shute, Jr
Secretary
437 Madison Avenue
New York, NY 10022–7001

The Foundation Center
79 Fifth Avenue
New York, NY 10003–4230

Citibank
Daniel Schutzer
Vice President, Director of Advanced
  Technology
909 Third Avenue
New York, NY 10022

Swiss Re
David S. Laster, PhD
Senior Economist
55 East 52nd Street
New York, NY 10055

Prudential Securities
Bella Loykhter
Senior Vice President, Information
  Technology

Kenneth Musco
First Vice President and Director,
Management Internal Control

Neil S. Lerner
Vice President, Management Internal
  Control
1 New York Plaza
New York, NY

Merrill Lynch
John J. Fosina
Director, Planning and Analysis

Paul J. Fitzsimmons
Senior Vice President, District Trust
  Manager

David E. Radcliffe
Senior Vice President, National
  Manager Philanthropic Consulting
Corporate and Institutional Client
  Group
World Financial Center, North Tower
New York, NY 10281–1316

Permal Asset Management
Isaac R. Souede
President and CEO
900 Third Avenue
New York, NY 10022
(telephone interview)

HSBC Republic
Susan G. Pearce
Senior Vice President

Philip A. Salazar
Executive Director
452 Fifth Avenue, Tower 6
New York, NY 10018

**International Swaps and Derivatives
  Association (ISDA)**
Susan Hinko
Director of Policy
600 Fifth Avenue, 27th Floor,
  Rockefeller Center
New York, NY 10020–2302

Standard & Poor's
Clifford Griep
Managing Director
25 Broadway
New York, NY 10004–1064

Mary Peloqyun-Dodd
Director, Public Finance Ratings
55 Water Street
New York, NY 10041–0003

Moody's Investor Services
Lea Carty
Director, Corporates
99 Church Street
New York, NY 10022

State Street Bank and Trust
James J. Darr
Executive Vice President, US Financial
  Assets Services
225 Franklin Street
Boston, MA 02105–1992

MBIA Insurance Corporation
John B. Caouette
Vice Chairman
113 King Street
Armonk, NY 10504

**Global Association of Risk
  Professionals (GARP)**
Lev Borodovski
Executive Director, GARP, and
  Director of Risk Management,
  Credit Suisse First Boston (CSFB),
  New York

Yong Li
Director of Education, GARP, and
Vice President, Lehman Brothers, New
  York

Dr Frank Leiber
Research Director, and
Assistant Director of Computational
  Finance,
Cornell University, Theory Center,
  New York

Roy Nawal
Director of Risk Forums, GARP
980 Broadway, Suite 242
Thornwood, NY

Group of Thirty
John Walsh
Director
1990 M Street, NW
Suite 450
Washington, DC, 20036

Broadcom Corporation
Dr Henry Samueli
Co-Chairman of the Board, Chief
  Technical Officer
16215 Alton Parkway
P.O.Box 57013
Irvine, CA 92619–7013

Edward Jones
Ann Ficken
Director, Internal Audit
201 Progress Parkway
Maryland Heights, MO 63043–3042

**Teachers Insurance and Annuity
  Association/College Retirement
  Equities Fund (TIAA/CREF)**
John W. Sullivan
Senior Institutional Trust Consultant

Charles S. Dvorkin
Vice President and Chief Technology
  Officer

Harry D. Perrin
Assistant Vice President, Information
  Technology

Patty Steinbach
Investment Advisor

Tim Prosser
Lawyer
730 Third Avenue
New York, NY 10017–3206

Sterling Foundation Management
Dr Roger D. Silk
Principal
14622 Ventura Blvd
Suite 745
Sherman Oaks, CA 91403

Grenzebach Glier & Associates, Inc.
John J. Glier
President and Chief Executive Officer
55 West Wacker Drive
Suite 1500
Chicago, IL 60601

Massachusetts Institute of Technology
Ms Peggy Carney
Administrator, Graduate Office

Michael Coen, PhD Candidate
ARPA Intelligent Environment Project
Department of Electrical Engineering
and Computer Science
Building 38, Room 444
50 Vassar Street
Cambridge, MA, 02139

**Henry Samueli School of Engineering
and Applied Science, University of
California, Los Angeles**
Dean A.R. Frank Wazzan
School of Engineering and Applied
  Science

Prof. Stephen E. Jacobson
Dean of Student Affairs

Dr Les Lackman
Mechanical and Aerospace
  Engineering Department

Prof. Richard Muntz
Chair, Computer Science Department

Prof. Dr Leonard Kleinrock
Telecommunications and Networks

Prof. Chih-Ming Ho, PhD
Ben Rich-Lockheed Martin Professor
Mechancial and Aerospace
  Engineering Department

Dr Gang Chen
Mechancial and Aerospace
  Engineering Department

Prof. Harold G. Monbouquette, PhD
Chemical Engineering Department

Prof. Jack W. Judy
Electrical Engineering Department

Abeer Alwan
Bioengineering

Prof. Greg Pottie
Electrical Engineering Department

Prof. Lieven Vanderberghe
Electrical Engineering Department

**Anderson Graduate School of
Management, University of
California, Los Angeles**
Prof. John Mamer
Former Dean

Prof. Bruce Miller

**Roundtable Discussion on Engineering
and Management Curriculum
(October 2, 2000)**
Dr Henry Borenstein, Honeywell

Dr F. Issacci, Honeywell

Dr Ray Haynes, TRW

Dr Richard Croxall, TRW

Dr Steven Bouley, Boeing

Dr Derek Cheung, Rockwell
Westwood Village
Los Angeles, CA 90024

University of Maryland
Prof. Howard Frank
Dean, The Robert H. Smith School of
  Business

Prof. Lemma W. Senbert
Chair, Finance Department

Prof. Haluk Unal
Associate Professor of Finance
Van Munching Hall
College Park, Maryland 20742–5

Part 1

Operational risk is present at any time in every enterprise

1 Management control of operational risk

1.1 Introduction

The prevailing definition of operational risk (op risk) comes from the Basel Committee on Banking Supervision. It states that 'Operational Risk is the risk of loss from inadequate internal processes or failed internal control. These processes may regard people, tools, methods, procedures, or systems.' Operational risk also stems from external events that are not always under the control of *our* organization. Internal and external op risk factors are defined in section 1.2.

The concept of operational risk control is new, but the facts themselves – at least a good deal of them – have existed for some time. Many of the newer operational risks are the aftermath of the expanding business horizon, as well as of the fact that the company of the twenty-first century is transforming itself into an entity that is:

- Rich in professionals, and
- Thin in managers.

Therefore, operational risk control must take full account of the likelihood the evolving organizational structure will resemble an orchestra with 300 professionals and one conductor, as Peter Drucker suggests. An orchestra does not have sub-conductors, in the way industrial and financial organizations are presently built. It has a first violin, a top professional who distinguishes himself by being a virtuoso – and who himself is part of the operational risk landscape.

As the events of 2001–2002, including CEO malfeasance, have shown, one of the problems in modern business and industry is that companies have too many virtuosi poorly controlled by the board. Chapter 4 will explain that management risk is an inseparable part of operational risk. Often, too often to my mind, the bottleneck is at the top.

To account for operational risks that go beyond fraud and other well-known cases, many financial institutions have their own definition, which largely complements that of Basel and reflects what I just stated. For instance, Crédit Suisse defines operational risk as the: 'Potential adverse impact *improper* or *inadequate business conduct* will have on operations.' Banks class operational risk as the second most important category of exposure after credit risk. To face op risk challenges, they allocate part of their economic capital. This issue is discussed in Part 2.

John Hasson, of Abbey National Bank, aptly said that there exists no unique model on how to map operational risk into neatly organized categories. Nevertheless, a growing number of credit institutions tend to distinguish between five major operational risk classes: Organizational, policies and processes, technological, human-engineered, and due to counterparties or generally external factors. Banks that have studied the origins of op risk appreciate that:

- It is causal
- It is event-oriented, and
- Its aftermath is loss and damage.

Key indicators for operational risk include: outstanding risk claims; number of errors, by channel; frequency of other incidents; impact of each class of incidents in economic terms; legal issues connected to op risk; level and sophistication of staff training; staff turnover; and the way in which jobs are organized and supported – including information technology (IT) supports. Operational risk often results in reputational damage, over and above the costs associated with standalone events and op risks characterized by a certain synergy with one another.

Last but not least, to face the challenges associated to operational risk, banks must set aside adequate capital reserves. Following the third quantitative impact study (QIS3) of Basel II, changes have been made to the treatment of capital requirements for operational risk. The most significant is that of prompting banks to model or otherwise assess their operational risk requirements using one of the advanced approaches.

- Loss distribution (see Chapter 7), which is practically bottom-up, and
- Scoreboard (see Chapter 9), which is a top-down method.

With both advanced operational risk measurement approaches, initiative and guidance is the responsibility not only of regulators but also, and most particularly, of the institution's own top management. The board, CEO, and all executives must appreciate that operational risk represents a significant threat to the company's statutory objectives. There is no way to deny that this should be a senior management concern.

1.2   The presence of operational risk in an organization

Operational risks are present whether the business is regulated or deregulated; centralized or decentralized; proceduralized or free rein; old technology or high technology; local, nationally based, or international; characterized by simple products or by complex products; trading through a single channel or multiple channels. In banking, operational risk tends to partly overlap with market risk and credit risk, as Figure 1.1 demonstrates.

In a way similar to what we do with credit risk and market risk, operational risk should be examined from a strategic perspective. A strategic evaluation does not mean we have to be perfect. We only have to be better than our competitors. In credit risk terms, comparisons are made through grades assigned by independent rating agencies (see Chapter 13). But as Annette Austin, of ABN–Amro, suggested, such agencies do not provide rating in connection to operational risk. If and when they do so, independent rating agencies must take into account several factors, including:

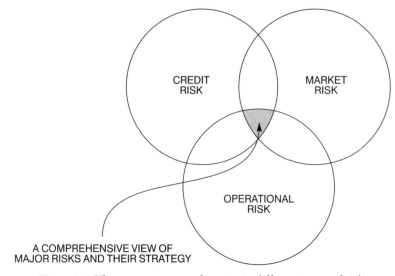

CREDIT
RISK

MARKET
RISK

OPERATIONAL
RISK

A COMPREHENSIVE VIEW OF
MAJOR RISKS AND THEIR STRATEGY

Figure 1.1 There are common elements in different types of risk.
Therefore, these risks partly overlap

- Quality of management
- Soundness of IT support, and
- Other issues that add up to op risk.

This will be tantamount to using an extra dimension than the one so far existing for evaluating credit risk. The exact nature of this dimension will depend on the industry we are in and the nature of the business we do. Operational risk tends to increase with sophisticated financial instruments characterized by many unknowns. And, as business characteristics vary, op risks tend to change. Therefore, to a large measure, each financial institution has its own profile of op risks.

Management risk, said one of the global banks, is our No. 1 operational risk. It represents one out six or seven op risk cases. Next in importance is *event risk*, including internal and external fraud. The third most critical op risk is technology risk, including:

- System reliability
- Analysis/programming, and
- Model risk.

The executive I was talking to made reference to value at risk (VAR), saying that 'VAR has clean parameters. But how do you value somebody's incompetence?' Banks tend to rely on models for transaction control and end up in a loop. A challenge is that we don't have enough data to model information technology risk.

This reference has another side. One of the problems with operational risk is that no two institutions look at it in the same way, or classify it in the same manner. This is equally true of constituent parts of op risk, as it is of remedies. Matters are made worse because internal control is often wanting, or simply not in place. It is therefore senior management's responsibility to:

■ Identify, monitor and measure operational risk, and
■ Put in place an internal control system that assures rapid and accurate feedback.

As my research has documented, a salient problem in operational risk control is that the staff are untrained and lack focus, and/or there is a lack of clear directives. Staff training should include the understanding of what drives people to obey or break the rules put in place to keep operational risk under lock and key. It should also deal with the four reasons reinforcing operational risk:

■ People don't know *what* is targeted
■ They don't understand *how* to control op risk
■ They don't *want* to do it in a rigorous way, in order not to touch other people's sensitivities, and
■ They don't *like* to be controlled in what they are doing.

Both focusing and prioritizing are most important. Headway will not be made by attacking all operating risks at once, but rather by selecting the top operational risk issues as salient problems, and bringing senior management's attention to them. The way to bet is that in the majority of companies the top three op risk issues are:

■ Legal risk (see Chapter 3)
■ Management risk (see Chapter 4), and
■ Information technology risk (see Chapter 5).

If anything is going really wrong in one of these areas, the whole financial institution can fall into hard times. This feeds in to the general understanding that, in every field of endeavor, one of the signs of good management is the ability to identify and deal with the salient factors. As my research documents, in the realm of day-to-day operations there are a good dozen operational risks which can be grouped in the three classes, as shown in Figure 1.2. Here is a description of each.

1 Management inadequacy at all levels, starting with the board and CEO.
2 Quality and skills of professionals and employees.
3 Organizational issues, including separation between front desk and back office activities.
4 Execution risk, including the handling of transactions, debits/credits and confirmations.
5 Fiduciary and trust activities, throughout supported channels.
6 Legal risk under all jurisdictions the bank operates, and compliance with regulations.
7 Documentation (a hybrid between other types of operational risk and legal risk).
8 Payments and settlements, including services provided by clearing agents, custody agents, and major counterparties.

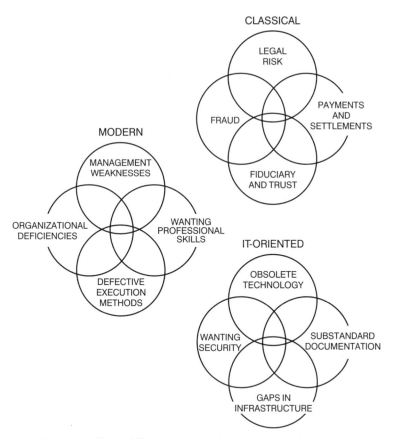

Figure 1.2 Three different groups of operational risk present in practically every organization

9 Information technology risks – software, computer platforms, databases and networks.
10 Security and fraud, including rogue traders (internal op risk), and external op risk sources.
11 Infrastructural services, for example, power and telecommunications.
12 Present and future operational risk associated with innovation and globalization.

This more extensive list contrasts to the event-type classification of operational risk by the Basel Committee on Banking Supervision. The latter includes seven op risks: internal fraud; external fraud; employment practices and safety; business practices, clients, products, damage to physical assets; business disruption, system failures; and execution, delivery, process management. We will talk more about these classes in Chapter 2 as well as in Chapters 6 and 7 in conjunction to capital requirements for operational risk.

No matter how we compose the list of specific op risks that we define and aim to control for our company, we must distinguish between core risks and non-core risks

– because this is fundamental in identifying salient problems and setting priorities. *Core risks* are those that an entity is in business to take, for instance:

■ Loans are core risks for credit institutions.

Non-core risks are those the firm has no clearly perceived comparative advantage in bearing, yet it is taking them. An example is:

■ Speculation through derivatives, as contrasted to true hedging.

This is an example from credit risk and market risk domain, but similar criteria also exist in connection to operational risk. It is the responsibility of the board and the CEO to make a formal determination of what the core risks are, how they should be faced, and how much capital should be reserved for them. My experience tells me that capital reserved for non-core risks may exceed that for core risks – and this helps in rethinking business strategy.

Core risks should evidently attract more attention in terms of perception, study, and evaluation than non-core risks. Core op risks are likely to involve; people, procedures, and systems at the same time. When I say *people*, I mean not only the persons *per se*, but also corporate culture, training, experience, transparency, willingness to cooperate and to perform. *Procedures* involve internal control, accountability, risk appetite, and leverage. The *systems* are networks, databases, knowledge artefacts, and real-time solutions (see Chapter 5).

1.3   The management of operational risk events

A good way to look at operational risk events is as the result of ill-defined, inadequate, and failed internal processes – or external impacts overwhelming internal defences. To control these happenings we must analyze the causes and effects of incidents which are either at the origin or lead to op risk. As we will see in Chapter 2, proper analysis followed by op risk identification and classification helps in:

■ Identifying
■ Monitoring, and
■ Interpreting operational risk data.

At its basic level, operational risk management is a comprehensive practice comparable to the management of credit risk or market risk. Aptly, the Basel Committee insists that the board should approve the implementation of a firm-wide framework to explicitly control op risk. An operational risk framework must include appropriate definitions that:

■ Clearly articulate what constitutes op risk in each bank, and
■ Reflect the bank's appetite and tolerance for operational risk.

Basel also presses the point that banks should make sufficient public disclosure to allow market participants to assess their chosen approach to op risk management. Sunshine is always the best disinfectant. It is also a good way to gain public confidence. Market discipline matters; it is Pillar 3 of the New Capital Adequacy framework (Basel II).

Operational risk control will be that much more effective when the board establishes the proper risk management policies, when we have available a sound methodology, and when our tools are dependable. Also, when the solutions we adopt are characterized by accuracy of execution and timeliness of execution. This requires rich operational risk databases and their on-line, interactive mining.

Typically, operational risk is magnified by globalization, because of crossing of jurisdictional boundaries with different laws, rules and compliance requirements (see Chapter 3). Globalization has many advantages, but it also amplifies business competitions, accelerates customer demands, sees to it that organizational responsibilities are no more clearly defined, and sometimes leads to breakdowns in planning and control. Also protracted changes in management, through musical chairs, increase the assumed operational risk.

As the Introduction brought to the reader's attention, the management of operational risk cannot do away with the fact that *management* itself may be part of the problem rather than of the solution. In the late 1990s, a study by the Bank of England – which involved 22 failed financial institutions – found that in 19 of these cases poor management was the top reason leading to bankruptcy. Box 1.1 shows the frequency of the identified reasons for failure.

Box 1.1   Bank of England study on why companies fail based on 22 bankrupt institutions (some failures were due to two or more reasons)

Six top reasons in order of frequency:

1 Mismanagement
2 Poor assets
3 Faulty structure
4 Liquidity
5 Dealing losses
6 Secrecy and fraud

Total management-oriented events:

No. 1 + No. 2 + No. 3 = 39 cases

Total financially oriented events:

No. 4 + No. 5 + No. 6 = 18 cases

Hence:

Mismanagement reasons 39/57 = 68.4% of all cases
Financial reasons 18/57 = 31.6% of all cases

It is not surprising that management-oriented reasons exceed those of a financial background by a ratio of 2:1. The board, the CEO, the executive committee are the parties that decide on the management of assets and liabilities, and on assumed risks. If the bank or the insurance company finds itself with poor assets, it is management's fault, not an accidental financial mischance. A similar statement applies with operational risks being taken, like cutting corners:

■ On legal issues, and
■ In terms of compliance.

Not only many operational risks find their origin in management decisions, but also several among them are interconnected. This is shown in Figure 1.3 using four operational risks as an example. Notice that *management intent* can be found in the background of all four, expressed by means of:

■ Fundamental principles
■ Decisions being taken, and
■ Rules and bylaws.

Principles, decisions, and rules are governing the strategy, policies, and procedures of an institution. Therefore, management decisions, and the reasons behind them, must be analysed for consistency. Fundamental principles are more important than rules, because people engineer their way around rules. However, rules can be audited; which

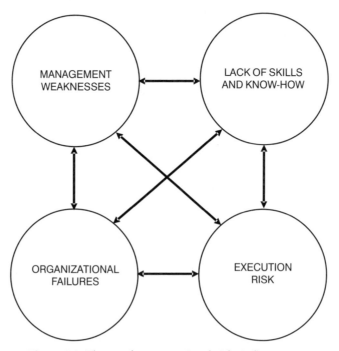

Figure 1.3 The top four operational risks influence one
another in a significant way

is not possible with fundamental principles (more on auditing and internal control in Chapter 2).

One of the basic principles to be observed in connection to the control of operational risk is materiality. As an accounting principle, *materiality* means relative importance – a concept critical to all procedures. In operational risk control, materiality is a challenge because of difficulties in weighting losses from op risks against the costs of their control within and across:

■ Product lines, and
■ Business units.

The correlation between operational risk type and loss experience might differ significantly depending on products, processes, and entities. Still, because of scarcity of operational risk data many banks collaborate with one another in establishing an op risk database. At the same time, however, several banks have adopted a two-tier strategy:

■ Short- to medium-term solutions with an interim, coarse-grain methodology, and
■ Longer-term solutions at greater granularity, using op risk indicators with predictive models (see Chapters 8 and 9).

Tier-1 banks have also established a policy of post-mortems, which helps to appreciate whether operational risks have been properly tracked – and at which cost – including op risk distributions before and after modeling; the shifting of distributions to lower frequencies or lower impact; and the savings *vs* cost analysis which can tell whether we apply the right level of control for each operational risk.

Say that we decide to go after operational risks in a back office environment. Then among our priorities should be to match confirmations, check undocumented trades, minimize litigation costs, eliminate handling errors, protect from reputational risk. Auditing IT applications and projects is an integral part of this effort:

■ What's their track record?
■ How late are they?
■ How secure are transactions over networks?
■ How much does [a given service] expose our organization to operational risk?
■ What's the cost and benefit of the controls we apply?

In conclusion, while everybody agrees that operational rules must be managed, their steady and focused control has a price. It does not come free of cost. We must therefore optimize, and this means deciding between absorbing some losses, or establishing tighter control over operational risk events (see Chapter 8 on high and low op risk impact).

1.4 Supervisory response to operational risk

Supervisory response to operational risk is expressed through increased monitoring, the requirement that companies take remedial action, and provision of additional capital to face op risk aftermath. The Basel Committee has advanced some standard models estimating capital needs for op risk. These are discussed in Chapter 7. But Basel also promotes more sophisticated approaches, such as loss distribution and the scoreboard.

By all evidence, capital requirements for operational risk will be subject to frequent redefinition. This is the more likely as credit risks and market risks may be morphing into operational risks. For instance, the management of collateral was associated to credit risk. Now it becomes part of operational risk. This redefinition is sure to impact on Pillar 1: Capital Adequacy, as seen from the regulators' capital requirements viewpoint.

Experts participating in my research pointed out that as the operational risk landscape becomes better understood and more clearly defined, questions will also be posed on the impact of op risk on Pillar 2: Prudential Supervision. By all evidence, this will include the growing importance of three underlying principles:

■ The bank's own responsibility
■ Supervisory evaluation, and
■ Supervisory intervention.

To answer prudent supervision requirements in an able manner, old business lines, for instance the branch office network and loans, need to be rethought in operational risk terms. Beyond this, new implementations, like e-banking, require a structured operational risk analysis, as well as a factual cost and risk versus benefit study.

As these references are documenting, the rightsizing of operational risk exposure poses several challenges. Resources allocation that supports and sustains market discipline – which is Pillar 3 – is one of them. Another example is a realistic evaluation of the challenge of avoiding business disruption. In conjunction to the challenge of terrorism, Chapter 14 elaborates on the challenge of business disruption and needed countermeasures.

Here is the concept in a nutshell. Because in the first years of the twenty-first century terrorism has become a real threat, supervisors are increasingly concerned about the aftermath of operational risk connected to business disruption. Management should not lose sight of the fact that because of globalization and high technology, financial markets work around the clock.

■ Major business disruptions can become killer risks.
■ Just-in-time supply chains can be put on hold.

This is one of the cases where credit risk, market risk, and operational risk correlate. As business confidence gets a beating, financial flows can dry up. Intangible assets, too, can be at risk, because killer events provoke herd-like:

■ Runs on liquidity
■ Flights from damaged assets, and
■ A high degree of volatility.

Therefore, a critical evaluation of operational risks requires stress scenarios and drills, as well as a broader perception of possible consequences. To properly evaluate business disruption we must attach great importance to *system* performance, not just to standalone products and services. An important pattern is the transition from high frequency/low impact (HF/LI) to low frequency/high impact (LF/HI) events (see Chapter 8).

Supervisors are also paying growing attention to catastrophic, or killer operational risks. These should be given priority. Relatively large size killer events existed before 11 September 2001 (9/11). Some of them have been financial; others are operational. But as we will see in Part Three, 9/11 has changed the supervisors' and the financial industry's perception of business interruption. Questions pertaining to this issue are:

- How does a company survive when some of its key personnel have been killed?
- How can a firm operate when its computers, networks, and databases are destroyed?
- Which back-up should be in place in case the main premises are put out of commission?

Some aspects of business interruption might be insured, but because this is a new major operational risk it will be difficult to satisfy the insurer that everything abides by the contract – or, for that matter the regulator. Regulators appreciate that critical assets like top management could be rapidly shattered, and recovery may not be easy. Yet, confidence in management drives:

- Future investments
- Product innovation, and
- Customer trust.

This is an issue where the interests of regulators and of the regulated entities support one-another. Innovation, imagination, and flexibility are not only vital to business survival; they are as well a cornerstone to our ability to face operational risk challenges. 'One does not plan and then try to make the circumstances fit those plans,' said General George Patton. 'One tries to make plans fit the circumstances. I think the difference between success and failure in high command depends on the ability, or lack of it, to do just that.'

For his part, Sam Walton, one of the most successful businessmen of the post-World War II years, described in the following manner the way his mind worked: '*If* I decide that I am wrong, I am ready to move to something else.' The operational risk manager's mind should react in a similar way. When the current op risk control method has not been able to deliver as promised, *then* the manager should change the method and the tools.

As a way of bringing together what has been discussed in this section, Figure 1.4 outlines 13 vital steps in operational risk management. They integrate the input received in my research and, between them, they constitute a better, more adaptable method than the one used by each individual organization.

The pattern in Figure 1.4 is a feedback mechanism. Operational risk results and assessment – both short-term and longer-term – must be fed back to senior management. They should also be fed into a database for future datamining. Agents (knowledge artefacts)[1] must steadily examine the evolving op risk statistics as well as the key indications. Stress tests should be done:

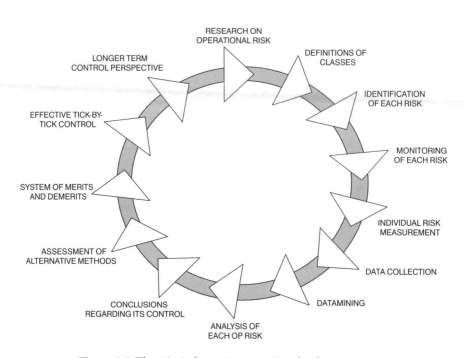

Figure 1.4 The 13 vital steps in operational risk management

- By changing the parameters of topmost op risks, and
- By altering the control structure, and/or nature of controls.

As we will see in connection to advanced methods for operational risk control (Chapter 8), experimental design can help in analysis of variance when more than one factor changes. The existence of a *control group* permits the better appreciation of the impact of new tools or methods. It also makes op risk reports to senior management and the supervisors more factual and better documented.

1.5   A strategy for bringing operational risk under control

The key elements affecting operational risk will be better identified and controlled if we are able to assure early involvement by senior management. As we will see in Chapter 2, the proper operational risk identification is a senior management job, even if technologists and mathematicians are doing the legwork. The analysts should be responsible for examining op risk behavior and studying correlation between different operational risk types – but the final decision is management's responsibility.

In a nutshell, the strategy for operational risk control is described in Figure 1.5. Prerequisite to reaching the goal is the appropriate layout of analytical processes which permit getting to the core of the matter. Setting limits, controlling limits, and

ANALYTICAL PROCESSES

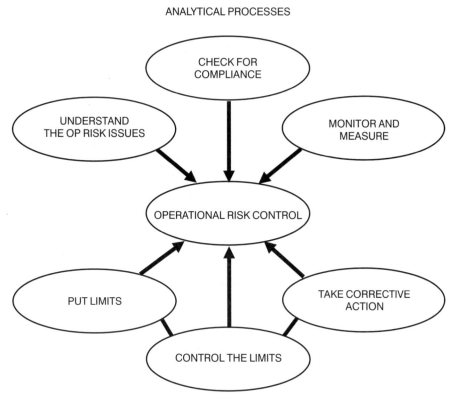

CONTROL ACTIVITIES

Figure 1.5 The able handling of operational risk needs both analytics and rigorous control

taking corrective action are the means for establishing a valid system of checks and balances. For every entity:

- The definition of operational risk is strategic.
- The analysis is part of the tactical approach to op risk control.

Analytical activities start with understanding the op risk issues proper to *our* enterprise, checking to make sure these represent the core of compliance, then following up with monitoring and measuring. To plan for risk assessment, the analysts should learn from control weaknesses that have been identified in the past, establishing the overall risk profile at two levels of reference:

- Restructuring of current operational risk control concepts and procedures, and
- Designing and implementing a new, more effective op risk management system that works in real-time.

This effort will be more successful if the risk control process becomes an integral part of overall business management, with outputs from op risk assessment incorporated in the design of *our* products and processing channels, existing or under development. As cannot be repeated too often, the early engagement of senior management assures that operational risks are considered as an integral part of the overall command and control system of the enterprise.

A company-wide approach able to cover operational risks where they exist, will evidently require different project teams working in parallel to one another. The downside of such a holistic approach is that operational risks may be identified and handled in heterogeneous ways in the different business units of the organization. Also, that the company may fail in establishing appropriate links between different classes of exposure.

The answer is co-ordination by senior management, keeping in perspective the fact that different business units may have a unique exposure profile and control framework, as well as heterogeneous exogenous factors. These differences can be effectively handled through operational risk classification and identification, as is explained in Chapter 2. The strategic prerequisite to this approach is that an enterprise-wide op risk control program is examined under all possible angles. Among crucial queries are:

- How clear are the objectives of *our* program?
- What is the overall level of certainty and uncertainty?
- How much experience do *we* have with this type of program?
- What is the potential to be released from staff upgrades?
- What is the degree of impact upon the customer base?
- How much change to existing IT solutions will be necessary?
- What is the degree of the legal and regulatory implications if we fail to take control of *our* op risks?

A strategic view of operational risk control will pay considerable attention not only to organizational issues but also to all *our* products and processes, the quality and accuracy of internal control, the calibration of the risk management system, as well as risk mitigation policies. It will also steadily evaluate the continued effectiveness of op risk controls, addressing issues that are both internal and external to *our* enterprise. For instance,

- Contractual terms with business partners, and
- Legal challenges, including creative accounting and creative marketing.

Reputational risk resulting from failure to control operational risk(s) should always be at the top of the list of priorities. Barings was not the only institution brought to its knees because of op risks, lax internal controls, wanting organization, and conflicts of interest. Another example is the British & Commonwealth (B&C) merchant bank, which in its day grew very fast under the aegis of its leader. One day, the auditor of the B&C discovered that in one of its subsidiaries, Atlantic Leasing, there was a hole of £800 million ($1.2 billion). Atlantic Leasing was in the rental business. The mainframes it rented depreciated very fast, but the company kept these mainframes in its books at full value. This beefed up the assets, but at the same time it opened a gaping hole in management control, due to *creative accounting*. One of the frequent op risk scenarios is that:

- Fair value is often discarded in an effort to make the assets look attractive, and
- Senior management is happy enough with the good-looking fake figures, and therefore it does not take corrective action.

Generally, creative accounting is not considered to be fraud, yet this is precisely the case. The aftermath is disastrous both to the company which practices creative accounting and to its business partners. Many firms who had delivered goods and services to Atlantic Leasing got burned. One of them, a service bureau, was owed £600 000 ($900 000). After the liquidation proceedings, it got 3 pence to the pound.

Because with operational risk all stakeholders are at the frontline, regulators have every interest in looking into the op risk control practices of the entities they supervise. Mid-October 2001, the Financial Services Authority was criticized in a report by Ronnie Baird, its own head of internal audit, for failing to spot key problems at mutual life insurer Equitable Life, in January 1999. The report said that the FSA should 'have recognized sooner a significant weakness in Equitable's solvency position.'

- Basically, this has been credit risk, but record-keeping, the analytics, and transparency are operational risks.
- Also an aspect of operational risk has been the fact that not all drawdown policy holders of Equitable Life were experienced investors.

The misrepresentation of product characteristics is a con game, and therefore an operational risk. Many clients of the mutual life outfit were mis-sold drawdowns without understanding the risks involved. At Equitable Life, the management set aside £200 million ($300 million) to pay investors who were taken for a ride.

Sir Howard Davies, chairman of FSA, has had his salary cut by his board for failures in the way the authority he heads handled the collapse of Equitable Life. The internal audit report also criticized the FSA for failing to appreciate fully the danger that Equitable could lose the costly legal battle over its treatment of guaranteed annuity rate policies. In July 2000, the loss of the House of Lords appeal left Equitable with a bill of £1.5 billion ($2.25 billion), plunging it into financial crisis.

The careful reader would take note that in spite of its precarious financial condition, Equitable Life was allowed to continue operating, even if it failed to meet regulatory solvency requirements set by the Financial Services Authority. By mid-November 2002 the Equitable warned that the financial uncertainties it faced could involve painful actions – like the announced cut of 30% on with-profit annuities affecting the pensions of 50 000 policyholders.

Bringing assets and liabilities back into line is sure to involve major policy value reductions and bonus cuts. By November 2002, the value of Equitable had dropped to about £14.5 billion from £18.6 billion at the end of 2001. Equitable Life also revealed that its fund for future appropriations (a measure of how much capital it has in excess of its liabilities) fell to $382 million from £1.1 billion at the end of December 2001.

While these are credit risks to Equitable's policyholders, for many of the latter the ordeal started with an operational risk: *creative marketing*. Because it rests on false premises, creative marketing is just as deadly as creative accounting, and it should be sanctioned by top management. Six Sigma is a powerful tool in the control of this operational risk. Chapter 8 explains why.

The examples I have just given underline some of the less known aspects of operational risk. Solutions must be polyvalent: strengthening management, training all personnel, studying emerging best practices, developing and using advanced measurement methods, as well as instituting sophisticated controls. Among other approaches we will follow in this book are doing risk mitigation through insurance, developing contingency plans, providing consistency in operational risk management, and considering operational risk along global business lines.

1.6 Operational risk must be managed at all organizational levels

Operational risk is present both at headquarters and at *all* business units, even if some of these units are more exposed to op risk than others. Creative accounting is (usually) a headquarters practice. Creative marketing often happens at the fringes, near the customer base. Therefore, the identification, classification, monitoring, measurement, and management of all operational risk types must be done at all organizational levels establishing:

- Dependencies, causes, enablers of op risks.
- Possible threats and control failures.
- Countermeasures and their effectiveness.
- Responsibilities for action plans to bend the curve of op risk growth.

After the basic homework is done in operational risk classification, identification, setting of limits, and analysis of cost-effectiveness of countermeasures, a company-wide system of traffic lights will help. The guidelines should be set at headquarters, but each business unit must be part of the picture in deciding on op risk priorities, because it is its responsibility to identify and manage operational risks.

Figure 1.6 shows an organizational structure which abides by the principles outlined in the preceding paragraphs. Senior management is accountable for global operational risk identification and control. It is assisted by a headquarters unit that establishes op risk control plans, elaborates the standards, and supervises local operations and functions. Headquarters should provide:

- Norms
- Analytics
- Guidance, and
- A system of merits and demerits.

Quantification and qualification of company-wide operational risk is a headquarters activity. But as the British Bankers Association was to say, you cannot quantify

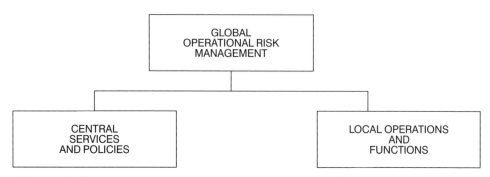

Figure 1.6 The organization and monitoring of operational risk controls must be done at two levels

everything connected to op risk. Much will have to be done on a qualification basis, and this increases the need for proper identification and classification of operational risks, discussed in Chapter 2.

The qualification of operational risk is specific case-by-case. This means there is no consistency bank-to-bank. But we should not be adverse in trading, up to a point, consistency for relevance. Relevance is very important in all three pillars of the New Capital Adequacy Framework.

- With Pillar 1, operational risk has a cost
- With Pillar 2, the regulator will be on our back, and
- With Pillar 3, op risk can lead to reputational damage.

While we can adopt an operational risk control methodology from another bank, or other entity selling such services, and get an idea about pitfalls based on other banks' experiences, we should not use the same solutions another bank uses down to every detail. Copycats have no place in the control of operational risk. The advice embedded in the following eight items helps in providing a unique approach and competitive advantages associated to it:

- Have a sound methodology for operational risk control.
- Emphasize management risk and ways to avoid it.
- Pay significant attention to legal risk (see Chapter 3).
- Understand how and why information technology is a major operational risk (see Chapter 5).
- Distinguish between high frequency/low impact and low frequency/high impact events (see Chapter 8).
- Provide analytical approaches to op risk control, to help with scoreboard developments (see Chapter 9).
- Use plenty of case studies from banking and insurance to demonstrate the attention operational risks deserve (see Chapters 10 to 14).
- Integrate cost control into the operational risk perspective (see Chapters 15 and 16).

Some of the case studies the reader will find in Part Three and Part Four demonstrate how other companies have compounded their operational risk problems by adding to their troubles through moves that are both unwise and ill-studied. Not only do creative accounting and creative marketing render a very bad service, but so also do other moves that might provide temporary relief but turn into longer-term liabilities.

For instance, triangular agreements are poison to operational risk control. My favoured case study in this regard is what happened with Sainbury and its IT. That Sainsbury had to improve the look of its balance sheet and that's why it went into the pains of leveraging its IT, was only a hypothesis when this deal was done. It became a certainty when on 7 April 7 2002, it was announced that Sainsbury intended to underline its recovery with a trading statement showing that it is gaining market share from rivals such as Tesco and Safeway, after having chosen a strategy of concentrating on its 'core activities'. Part and parcel of this strategy was getting rid of:

■ The company's real estate, converted from ownership to leasing, and
■ The company's information technology, outsourced wholesale to a consulting firm.

In my book, both real estate and IT, and most particularly IT, are core business of a merchandiser. Advantages to the balance sheet by getting rid of them are illusionary, and surely temporary. The aftermath of assuming operational risks by denying reality will come back and bite the outsourcer, while on the insourcer's side operational risk has plenty of opportunity to get out of hand.

In fact, despite Sainsbury's improved sales figures, some analysts were still unconvinced by its recovery strategy. Philip Dorgan, a long-time critic of the stock, has pointed out that, while Sainsbury has been good at generating extra sales, it has still to prove it can grow profits as quickly. Ian Macdougall, food analyst with Williams de Broe, said he was not wholly persuaded by Sainsbury's recovery; neither was he quite sure what the formula is, as in his opinion the company was coming off a very low base and it is hard to sustain momentum. For my part, I would consider the op risk associated with losing control over IT as being the merchandiser's soft underbelly.

Loss of control over operational risk can have serious spillover, as the *Exxon Valdez* case documents. The 1989 *Exxon Valdez* disaster has been a major operational risk. Exxon's tanker ran aground in Prince William Sound, causing the largest oil spill in history (at that time). The damage to Exxon included not only the financial cost of the environmental clean-up and the legal risk connected to civil and administrative liability, but also the potential impact of oil loss on the company's existing oil hedges.

■ Without the physical oil itself, any hedge suddenly became a source of risk.
■ With this, the effect of the *Valdez* accident went beyond legal risk and immediate financial risk, into risk associated to hedging.

What all of the foregoing examples have in common is the understanding that operational risk has the potential for loss due to top management decisions based on wrong bets (which is part of management risk), eventually resulting in operational deficiencies characterizing control processes or systems. By contrast, well-managed companies attempt to mitigate operational risk by:

- Maintaining a comprehensive internal control, and
- Employing experienced, well-trained dedicated personnel.

This is the right direction in operational risk control, but while necessary, by itself it is not sufficient. For each functional area deemed to be potentially of medium to high risk, senior management should perform a rigorous risk self-assessment. Its goals must be to evaluate the appropriateness of internal controls policies and systems; perform operational risk tests by type and business line, and provide emergency procedures as well as recovery plans.

1.7 Turning operational risk control into a senior management tool

Today, practically nobody has in place a system that can make operational risk control a senior management tool. Most companies just try to hedge op risk for the reserve bank, or other supervisory authorities. This is tantamount to being at the side of the problem, not at the heart of it. Failure to focus is one of the basic reasons why we will have to redo everything in operational risk control by the middle of this decade.

By being the most classical of all op risks, fraud can serve as an example of what I just said. The reality is that few companies think about fraud until they have suffered its consequences. Most institutions believe prevention is a good idea, but they never invest in it the time, money, and effort which is necessary – or use imagination and ingenuity.

When senior management makes a frontal attack against fraud, it puts fraudulent persons on their guard. By contrast, a better policy would be to emulate the successful island-to-island hopping strategy of General Douglas MacArthur, during World War II in the Pacific. MacArthur always moved against the strategic flank of the Japanese army, rather than fighting for every foot of land occupied by its tenacious and fanatical soldiers.

An island-by-island offensive against fraud will account for the fact that fraud is both an internal and external problem. Fraud experts point out that most financial fraud, even when organized by outside individuals, requires some cooperation from inside the company. Surveys suggest that more than 50 percent of all frauds are perpetrated by people within the company.

- Internal fraud is fed by a non-transparent culture, where people are not trained in its prevention and are not encouraged to find out what compliance is all about.
- Because many fraud prevention methods are superficial and substandard, in many cases detection is by accident, rather than as a result of regular controls.

The irony is that the increased use of information technology inside organizations has provided more opportunities for fraudsters to steal from companies. Fraud prevention can be encouraged by creating an environment where people feel comfortable speaking up when they feel something is not right. That's the flank of fraudulent people. Datamining aimed to uncover fraud patterns can also be instrumental in fraud prevention.

As Dr Brandon Davies, of Barclays Bank, aptly suggested, credit institutions have a wealth of data on fraud and other classical operational risks which they do not truly exploit. Yet we have today the technology, including knowledge artefacts, which permits accurate and effective datamining, leading to proactive solutions to fraud detection.

We can capture a lot of operational risk by using information available in the back office, Davies suggests. Such information accumulates over the years, but it is rarely exploited in an operational risk oriented manner. Brandon's very significant experience leads him to the concept that a good way to improve operational risk control is to:

■ Co-involve senior management in clarifying responsibilities for operational risk
■ Understand back office performance within the organization, and
■ Obtain a commitment on operational risk awareness, monitoring, measurement and control.

A good question is how a system along these lines of reference can be staffed. Some organizations have one person dedicated to operational risk per business line, responsible for giving advice and getting feedback. They use skilled people to review current practices and identify weak links in operational risk; and they require that a new product approval committee looks into a new product's operational risk.

Beyond this, I would suggest developing and implementing radar charts that map every manager's performance in terms of operational risk control. Figure 1.7 presents an example. Its focal point is a one-year evolution in op risk control, but the crucial variable being measured might also be a different one.

Well-managed companies also hold an annual operational risk forum, organized by the corporate operational risk office. This leaves open the possibility of critical evaluations and post-mortems – both being part of proactive approaches. Critical evaluations are necessary, for example, because while technology provides valid means for control of operational risk – if we use them the proper way – it also creates new ground in which op risks can grow.

For instance, the vulnerability of corporate computers to external hackers and viruses has opened new opportunities for fraud that were unavailable at an earlier time. The good news is that knowledge engineering used in conjunction with real-time systems has increased the capability of investigators to work out what happened and where it took place. In this regard, an excellent example of the use of knowledge engineering for operational risk control is in the domain of *fiduciary risk*, which has the potential for financial or reputational loss through the breaching of fiduciary duties, including:

■ Individual and corporate trust
■ Investment management custody, and
■ Cash and securities processing.

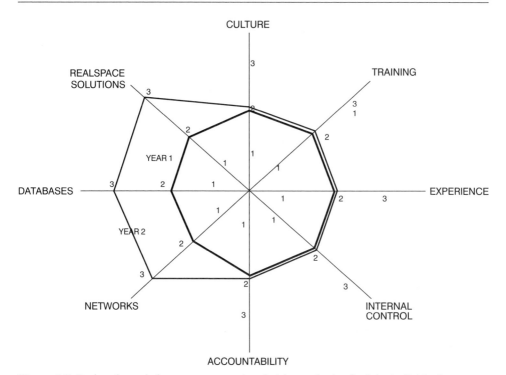

Figure 1.7 Radar charts help to map operational risks to the level of the individual manager and professional (3 is the highest grade)

Companies attempt to mitigate fiduciary risk by establishing procedures to ensure that obligations to clients are discharged in compliance with legal and regulatory requirements. In this connection, guidance and control should be provided through the board's fiduciary risk committee, but the nuts and bolts for operational risk control will be the knowledge artefacts working on-line on the bank's network.

Both the strategic and the tactical approaches are crucial. Senior management co-involvement is most critical because the extent of operational risk exposure being taken may go unnoticed and unchecked until it reaches a level that represents an unacceptable threat to the company's operations. On the other hand, to be effective the operational risk control framework that is established must be based on a whole range of methods of analysis, because:

■ There are many different types of operational risks, which can be both internal and external, and
■ They often go unnoticed until top management gives the message that *everybody is accountable* for operational risk control.

This brings our discussion back to this section's heading. Making op risk control a management tool means both personal accountability and the ability to challenge the obvious. Neither is self-evident, and their absence is a distortion built into today's system. One of the results of such distortions, for example, is that commissions are seen as extra compensation resulting from taking operational risk at the bank's expense. The failure of NatWest Markets because of options mispricing provides the evidence.

Challenging the obvious has prerequisites. The first in line is the board's and CEO's co-involvement. The next in importance is analytics: for example, finding peaks in the distribution of op risk, like those due to monthly and quarterly reconciliation. Hypotheses have to be made and they have to be tested. For instance, a hypothesis is that of assuming that in a back office and middle office environment small errors happen every day, but not all have the same impact. We must divide errors between:

- Minors, or those which are almost acceptable, and
- Majors, which have to be thoroughly controlled through a system of merits and demerits.

Critical to turning operational risk control into a senior management tool is our ability in developing and using early indicators. There should be a flashing light for all op risks to guide the hand not only of middle managers but also the CEO and the board. Audits must get into the act and audit tracking can be enhanced through clearly defined early indicators. This subject is treated in Chapter 2.

Let me close this chapter with a reference to contingency planning in connection to operational risk control. Operational risk control policy, according to the Financial Services Authority (FSA), is guidance on high level rules. The FSA's stated aim is to highlight issues for consideration, not be prescriptive. Policy developments cover:

- Legal requirements
- Management of people, including accountability
- Caliber of staff
- Availability of staff, including what to do *if* there is unavailability
- Management of processes and systems, including IT
- External changes, including effect on business continuity
- Outsourcing of services (see Chapter 5), and
- Insurance coverage (see Chapters 10 and 14).

As the reader will appreciate, an important consideration underpinning all eight points is preparedness for unavailability of vital services, which can disrupt even the best laid business continuity plan. This consideration focuses both on the company's own personnel and on dependability of supply chains and of outsourcers, which impacts upon business continuity.[2]

In regard to outsourcing, FSA advises setting minimum targets for business partner performance, as well as making appropriate contingency arrangements – given that contingency planning is an integral part of an operational risk control policy. FSA also underlines that operational risk disasters and their aftermath are most definitely senior management's concern.

Disaster containment represents a major challenge both in the longer-term and in day-to-day management responsibilities, because while disaster planning is longer term the availability of disaster recovery means and methods must be instantaneous. The longer-term policy should reflect the fact that:

- All firms are exposed to operational risk, and
- The breadth of operational risk impact can be wide.

To be effective any disaster recovery policy needs to assure that communications channels are always open, recovery and damage control goals are explicitly stated, and disaster recovery training is an integral part of every manager's responsibilities. All this comes over and above obtaining full support by senior management.

'Ultimately what are we looking for?' asks Lisa Wild of FSA.[3] She answers her own query by saying that FSA's goals in this domain target senior management buy-in; place emphasis on sound planning and control practices, not just minimum compliance; and require firm understanding of operational risks and of the way to control them. Also, FSA guidance calls for properly documented executive processes. All this together makes a sound operational risk management culture.

Notes

1 D.N. Chorafas, *Agent Technology Handbook*, McGraw-Hill, New York, 1998.
2 D.N. Chorafas, *Outsourcing, Insourcing and IT for Enterprise Management*, Macmillan/Palgrave, London, 2003.
3 As outlined in the lecture by Lisa Wild to the 'Basel II Masterclass' organized by IIR, London, 27/28 March 2003.

2 Classification, identification and monitoring of operational risk

2.1 Introduction

The many types of operational risks we have seen in Chapter 1 cannot be successfully controlled until they are properly recognized and identified. Only then can they be monitored and measured, with measurements datamined in real-time. (Manual approaches to database searches are too slow, too costly, and ineffectual in terms of required timely control action.) Therefore, prior to being able to exercise control over operational risks we must do our homework in their identification and classification.

Tier-1 banks appreciate the reasons for an *unambiguous* identification of operational risks. Experts, however, also point out that many op risks just don't sign up as such, because they are booked under other titles. For instance, Chapter 1 noted that collateral is usually considered to be credit risk, because that is how it has been handled until recently. But this is changing:

- In the coming years, there will be a huge transfer of issues from credit risk and market risk to operational risk.
- This transition will make data collection more difficult, unless we have in place a classification and identification system that assists in monitoring.

An operational risk classification and identification solution can in no way operate independently of the goals we set for op risk control. The latter include the monitoring, data collection and data analysis strategy we decide to follow. Data collection must be detailed and, to keep costs low, it should be largely piggy-backed on other systems, like:

- Accounting, and
- Financial information.

The right policy would aggregate and consolidate data collection solutions across business lines, mapping business lines to regulators' definitions, and our own aims. It will also create an appropriate verification process for management reporting and disclosure. Incident reporting on op risks must make sure that:

- The message is clear
- It leads to corrective action, and
- It leaves a historical trace for further analysis.

This is consistent with the fact that, as we gain experience and enrich our database, operational risk studies should target a significant detail. We are not yet there. Prior to reaching the necessary level of detail, we must assure that op risk studies address salient problems, a process assisted through classification and identification.

Regarding data collection *per se*, operational risk data must be captured at the source. This is not current practice, therefore, according to some estimates 30% of op risk entries are wrong. Wrong classification is co-responsible for errors in the operational risk database.

The polyvalence of operational risks, and its aftermath, must evidently be taken into account. I do not subscribe to the view of some experts that: 'You have to have a single operational risk scoring framework.' This is nonsense. There are so many types of op risks that we *cannot* have a single risk scoring frame of reference. (More on this in Chapters 8 and 9.)

But we can increase op risk sensitivity across the board. This is done by establishing correlation between risk indicators and actual loss experience. Risk sensitivity is upheld by sound measurements, a loss-gathering infrastructure, models, systems and procedures for their use, the ability to do stress testing, and periodic reviews of methodology and tools. All this must be done in a way that is consistent with directives by regulators.

2.2 Basel Committee directives in understanding operational risk

There is no way of avoiding operational risk in a service economy, but there are sound strategies for damage control. A fundamental understanding of both the type and quantity of operational risk taken by credit institutions, brokerage firms, insurance companies, and other entities is essential, as business and industry face up to increasingly demanding operational-type challenges. Because most financial institutions are ill prepared for operational risk control, the Basel Committee on Banking Supervision has provided the flexibility of different approaches.

- From the so-called 'basic' (which is too elementary),
- To the so-called 'standard' expressed in a matrix of seven risks and eight banking channels (see section 2.2 and Chapter 7), and
- To three advanced methods, the most sophisticated being known as the 'scoreboard' (see Chapters 8 and 9).

Financial institutions which have the know-how and skill to develop scoreboard solutions go well beyond the classical view of operational risk mainly related to fraud, payments, and settlements. This is precisely the approach this book takes. Bringing into perspective many different operational risks underlines the need for a methodology. The methodology I am suggesting is:

- To start with a classification, which helps to identify op risks
- To employ a battery of tests in tracking them
- To use several advanced tools in analysing them, and
- To develop methods which are open, flexible, and expendable to bring them under control.

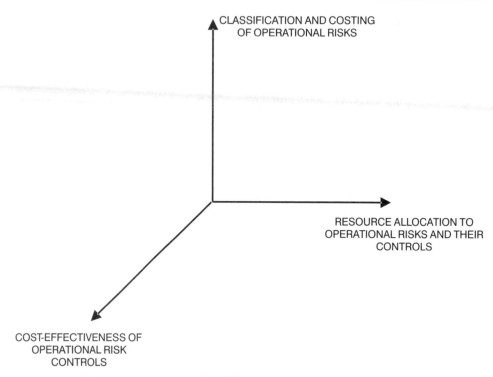

CLASSIFICATION AND COSTING
OF OPERATIONAL RISKS

RESOURCE ALLOCATION TO
OPERATIONAL RISKS AND THEIR
CONTROLS

COST-EFFECTIVENESS OF
OPERATIONAL RISK
CONTROLS

Figure 2.1 An advanced modeling framework for operational risk

The overall concept behind this approach is expressed in a nutshell in Figure 2.1. Notice that op risk control is three-dimensional; it is ineffectual in only one dimension because solutions are not linear. Costs matter (see Part 4). Resource allocation and cost-effectiveness must always be accounted for. Internal control is at the vertex. Credit institutions that are admired for their caution and their ability to control exposure:

■ Have in place a rigorous system of *internal control*, and
■ Their management is characterized by a deep sense of *personal accountability*.

The Basel Committee has defined an appropriate operational risk management environment in the following terms. Operational risk strategy must reflect the institution's tolerance for risk; the board should be responsible for approving the basic structure of managing op risk; and senior management must have the responsibility for developing op risk:

■ Policies
■ Processes, and
■ Procedures.

Aptly, the Basel Committee on Banking Supervision underlines the fact that internal control must enable senior management to monitor the effectiveness of all op risk checks and balances – while failure to address present operational risks increases the likelihood that new op risks go:

- Unrecognized, and
- Uncontrolled.

There are plenty of new sources of operational risk, as the reader will recall from Chapter 1. Some of them come from the fact that more and more financial institutions engage in risk mitigation techniques, which produce new sources of op risk. Credit derivatives[1] and asset securitization are examples of instruments designed to mitigate credit risk, but they bring along a share of operational risks because:

- The pool may be heterogeneous, and
- The rating of the tranche may be misquoted.

Credit derivatives, asset securitization, and other financial instruments which became popular in the 1990s are largely technology-enabled activities. The astute reader is already aware of the fact that while technological innovations must be steadily incorporated into op risk management, technology also engenders its own operational risks. One of them is that the viability of integrated IT systems is put under stress by:

- Mergers
- Spin-offs, and
- Consolidations.

Basel does not say so, but all three of these points increase operational risk. Among newer banking activities, growth in Internet commerce brings up other op risks with many aspects not yet well understood. Examples are:

- The rebirth of external fraud, and
- A greater than ever challenge to system security.

Matters are not helped by the fact that, sometimes, in search of profits banks seem eager to assume an inordinate amount of operational risk even if this leads to reputational risk. This is the case with what is now called 'guessing game derivatives' commercialized as investments. These essentially amount to a big bank casino and, in a regulatory sense, they should require a gambling license – over and above the necessary risk management procedures which are not in place.

In early October 2002 Deutsche Bank and Goldman Sachs began offering investors this casino-type gambling. The banks are giving their clients a chance to profit by guessing through call options the level of American non-farm payrolls.[2] Other guessing games focus on the manufacturing index, and figures for retail sales. All this is heralded as another great hedge. It is not. No more are those instruments targeting:

- Financial market risk such as falling share prices
- Guessing the likelihood of borrower default, or
- Betting on changes in $/euro, $/yen and other exchange rates.

Apart from being nonsense in the investment sense, these involve an inordinate amount of legal risk (see Chapter 3). Clients are very likely to sue in court because very few gimmicks really work. For instance, attempts by banks to offer derivatives on property prices and on inflation have failed.

The operational risk embedded into pseudo-novel, untested, and largely misunderstood instruments is so much more pronounced because most of these gambles are masquerading as hedges. Yet, guessing the level of non-farm payrolls, for instance, has greater similitude to horse racing than to investing. As a business it is not serious, and it should not be promoted by banks to trap egg-headed investors.

There is a huge amount of reputational risk and operational risk embedded into this sort of silly business, beyond operational risk associated with more classical activities, like clearing, payments, and settlements where technology (and its risk) also plays a key role. For example, the provision of payments services includes:

■ Clearing of trades
■ Payments proper, and
■ Delivery of assets (settlements).

In every one of these aspects, payment services require the same type of skills banks use in lending: fraud prevention, credit analysis, and ability to retrieve funds improperly sent. Besides this, payment services are expensive; they are the largest cost component in securities trading. Their operational risks, which include security breaches, add significantly to the cost of transactions, and pose the challenge of payments efficiency – hence of technology.

2.3   Classification of operational risks and the Basel Committee

Operational risk presents a complex picture, and the Basel Committee has given guidelines for its identification. Basel is suggesting that *op risk identification* is critical to the development of control solutions and *risk indicators* are a 'must'. Risk indicators are statistics and metrics (often financial) that provide insight into the op risk's impact. Furthermore, Basel says, identification should include determination of which risks are controllable. Senior management must estimate procedures necessary for measuring, monitoring, and controlling op risk, including:

■ The event's probability (high frequency, low frequency), and
■ The event's potential size of loss (high impact, low impact).

Overall, this approach is sound and, by all likelihood, it will constitute the mainstream methodology for handling operational risk. Where I have reservations is the level of detail to be followed by financial institutions for the clarification and identification of operational risk both:

■ In terms of the bank's product lines, or channels, and
■ In connection to the number of operational risk categories as well as their component parts.

As we will see more extensively in Chapter 7, the Basel Committee has advanced five alternative approaches for the calculation of capital reserves connected to operational risk: basic, standard, and three advanced measurement approaches (AMA); Basel's standard approach uses a matrix of:

- Eight business lines, and
- Seven operational risks.

As shown in Figure 2.2, this matrix is not adequate for sophisticated banks. AMA permits more degrees of freedom, but though credit institutions choosing the advanced measurement methods are given nearly free rein to develop their own identification and classification system, there should be a downwards compatibility with the standard method. This is provided by the Chorafas system, presented in section 2.5.

Operating Risk / Business Line	Internal Fraud	External Fraud	Employment and Workplace Safety	Clients, Products, Business Practices	Damage to Physical Assets	Business Disruption, System Failures	Execution, Delivery, Process Management
Corporate Finance							
Trading and Sales							
Retail Banking							
Commercial Banking							
Payments and Settlements							
Custody and Agency Services		.					
Asset Management							
Retail Brokerage							

Figure 2.2 Matrix of standard business lines and standard operating risks

Behind this statement lies the fact that a consistent classification and identification of op risk helps in the definition of regulatory capital in a manner permitting cross-industry comparisons. The bottom line is that compatibility is measured in *money units*, but money becomes the common denominator in operational risk control if, at a chosen level of comparison, the classification/identification system used by different banks is homogeneous enough to provide a solid reference base.

Another fundamental reason for downwards compatibility is statistics. As I never tire repeating, my fifty long years of hands-on experience with computers and models documents that in simulation of real life situations, which is what we aim to do with operational risk control,

- 80% of the problem data, and
- Only 20% of the challenge is algorithms and heuristics.

Chapter 1 has made reference to cooperative efforts among major banks – which otherwise are competitors – aimed to establish, by working together, a richer operational risk database than each could do on its own. Today, operational risk data are in short supply, though some exceptions do exist here and there.

■ Cooperative databases will not succeed, unless classification and identification of op risks are homogeneous.
■ At the same time, credit institutions should have the freedom to choose their own methodology rather than having to live with a straitjacket.

The parallel code system presented later in the chapter reconciles the otherwise contradictory statements made by the above two points. It also allows us to bring into the solution a significant amount of detail, which goes beyond the taxonomical approach. This is done through 'further definiens', whose use is explained in the next section.

A detailed matrix of operational risks corresponding to product lines, products, and processes should not start with money but with *functions* and *events*. Structural aspects are unavoidable, like the distinction made between 'retail banking', and 'other commercial banking', in Figure 2.2, but as sections 2.4 and 2.5 emphasize,

■ The classification must be generic, and
■ It should go all the way to the most elementary op risks.

This is indeed a challenging job requiring lots of homework and skill. Using money as a common denominator would superficially simplify the work to be done, but in the longer term it will be counterproductive. Therefore, it should not happen at the outset of a classification and identification study because it will bias the results.

Finally, as we will see in Chapter 7, a pivotal point of Basel in computing capital requirements for operational risk is *gross income*. However, a big question in connection to using *gross income* as proxy concerns the recognized but not yet realized gains and losses. As the computational system is refined, these will have to be included in gross income because at their origin are derivative financial instruments, which involve legal and other op risks.

Other critical problems to be considered, in an op risk solution, are errors in measurements, consistency in reporting, cost-effectiveness of op risk control, and changes in criteria for effective computation of capital for operational risks. (More on these issues later).

2.4   A classification and identification system for operational risks

Nobody will dispute the need for identification in human society. We all have a name and ID card. Many of us who travel internationally have a passport with our name, certain vital life details, and a photo. But this concept of identification article-by-article and entity-by-entity has not yet taken hold in the physical world of commodities; neither has it been considered, until recently, a requirement in the logical world of accounts and financial (virtual) goods.

This policy of doing without a system of rigorous identification is currently being challenged. Internet commerce, online supply chain requirements, and advances in technology available at low cost have made the change mandatory. We are starting to appreciate that we live in a physical and logical world with, correspondingly, real and virtual objects that need to be uniquely identified.

■ This is necessary to face the challenge of connecting the physical world to the virtual (data) world, and
■ The implementation of reliable ID solutions brings to the foreground the concept of classification, which is prerequisite to automatic identification.

Financial goods are part of the supply chain. Experts believe that the next wave of changes in the supply chain will see to it that our concepts of handling inanimate objects will evolve as radically as with Henry Ford's assembly line at the beginning of the twentieth century. There are good reasons for this change.

The revolution currently under way in financial services, as well as in merchandising and distribution, parallels that of the assembly line in terms of depth. At its roots is a unique identification (ID) code for each individual item: it will be embedded in products, printed on packaging, used for storage, transmitted over short and long distances, provide information to a reader, as well as receive and store information.[2]

At the basic level, in the post-PC era low cost intelligent devices with resident agents and telecom gateway will receive and read signals, translate their code, pass information to a computer directly or through the Internet, and generally do something with the received data stream. Knowledge-based systems will permit multiple platforms and software modules to talk to each other, sharing data streams and commands, while other software modules execute accounting and logistics operations without human intervention.

The system solutions of the future that I am describing will resolve some of the current problems in the origin of operational risks, but they will also create other op risks which must be approached in a proactive way. There is no free lunch.

It may help a better appreciation of the point made here if we keep in mind that the notions underpinning a supply chain did not change until the industrial revolution altered the means of transportation, making possible large transfers over long distances at an affordable price. This was a nineteenth-century development. Then, in the twentieth century, came the assembly line, which resulted in a big step forward in production chores. Twentieth-century type industrialization, however, did not change the linkages to the other key nodes of the supply chain; for those major developments we had to await the advent of the Internet. The effects of this delay can be summed up in the following two points:

■ Information about current status, therefore visibility, did not greatly improve in the first 50 years of computer usage.
■ With new financial products, which are more flexible and more risky than grandfather banking, reduced visibility resulted in lack of reliable information about accounts and financial statements.

This second deficiency resulted in latency in the feedback from the users of information to its producers. The financial scams of 2001 and 2002, plus the regulators' emphasis on the causes of operational risk and their control, changed this perspective.

- Correct identification is now becoming a fundamental operational requirement,
- But unique, reliable identification of goods, accounts, and other wares is not possible without a rigorous classification system.

Precisely for the reasons explained in the preceding paragraphs, the classification of operational risks is a prerequisite to their identification. The problem is that classification is difficult in general terms because organizational differences between banks blur business lines and adversely affect classification codes that aim to be universal.

The previous section has shown that with the standard approach to capital allocation for operational risk, the Basel Committee promotes eight business lines. The British Bankers Association has 14 business lines in its database, because that is how British banks work. Fourteen is more detailed than eight, but this does not mean that the 14 such business lines fit the business of every British bank, let alone foreign banks. For the same reason, it is virtually impossible for all regulators to have the same classification code.

There is a way out of the straits created by pursuing the dual goals of compatibility and flexibility. This is a parallel code system whose taxonomical part is universally homogeneous – at least at the top two levels – while the lower end of the classification *and* the identification code are specific to the entity which has to solve a classification/

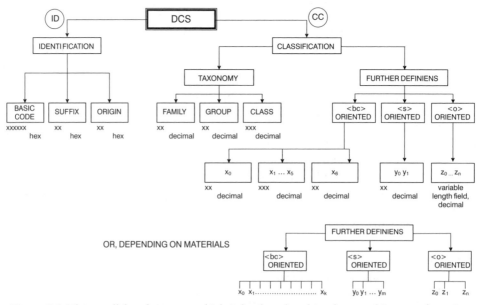

Figure 2.3 The parallel code system which I developed and implemented in manufacturing companies and financial institutions

identification problem. This is as true of operational risk as it is true of credit risk and market risk.

Figure 2.3 shows the parallel code system I have developed, and which has been implemented by manufacturing companies and financial institutions. In one of its implementations it has helped in reducing operational risk in the expediting of wares to business partners. Improvements have been significant by an order of magnitude.

2.5 The Chorafas parallel code system as an organizational infrastructure

Let's look first at *classification* since, as explained in the sections above, it should precede the identification of objects. The best way to classify a population of objects is taxonomical. In the parallel code system, the higher level of classification is done through a 10×10 matrix (each column and each row identified by 0 to 9).

- A 10×10 matrix has 100 pigeonholes – well beyond the eight or 14 business lines – identifying families.
- Not all pigeonholes need to be filled, and each bank can select from the filled those appropriate to its operations.

The family is the highest taxonomical level of the parallel code system. Each family can be exploded to greater detail, again using a 10×10 matrix. This matrix, second in a taxonomical sense, helps to classify the groups of financial products belonging to the same family. Type of product or service *and* process serving are the characteristics bundling together group classification. Note that there exist 100 groups per family.

- Between family and group there are 10 000 pigeonholes, a high multiple of what is needed for unique product identification.
- Below that level, essentially corresponding to each group, is the 10×10 matrix of each class of operational risk. This greater taxonomical detail provides 100 op risk pigeonholes as classes.

Taxonomical classification is not only a practical issue for operational reasons, but also a state of mind. As in the case of manufacturing and merchandising, successful approaches to operational risk management in the banking industry have to be based not only on a clear distinction between products and their associated credit risk, market risk, and operational risk, but also on an unambiguous distinction. Among the different categories of op risk,

- The *families*, *groups*, and *classes* are organized in the taxonomical way.
- Families and groups address the whole range of products and services; classes focus on operational risk per group.

Figure 2.3 also brings to the reader's attention that operational risk classification can go beyond the class level, therefore outside the taxonomical approach. This is done through *further definiens*, which, as their name implies, define the op risk in each class to further detail.

■ Each credit institution can use its own further definiens, which may not be compatible to those of the other institutions.
■ The common ground is provided by the operational risk class. (Note that some further definiens are <bc> oriented, others are <s> oriented. More on this later.)

The need for a taxonomical approach to the classification of operational risks is not appreciated in all quarters, yet it is the cornerstone of their control. As the preceding paragraphs brought to the reader's attention, to properly identify all the operational risks we are faced with, we must first classify them in a taxonomical way. This is the role played by families, groups, and classes.[3]

Families, groups, and classes represent among themselves 100×100×100 pigeon-holes. Contrasted to this one million classification possibilities, the standard approach identifies eight product lines and seven op risks, which is too summary and many banks say it is also arbitrary. Remember also that the British Bankers Association follows 14 product lines. However, several banks:

■ Have 15, 20 or more channels, and
■ Their classes of op risks are 12 or more.

This is why I have insisted on the fact that a proper classification methodology should start with products and processes pertinent to all banks, going down to the detail that is specific to *our* bank; and that it should also account for databased historical risk information, because if the history of op risk is taken out all there is left is guesswork.

Notice the flexibility of the method underpinning the parallel code system. The classification methodology, as we have seen, allows us to go beyond taxonomy into further definiens. The latter makes possible a one-to-one correspondence between classification and identification, whenever the taxonomy is not detailed enough.

A possible critique of this system is that some operational risks, for instance internal fraud, may be present in more than one taxonomical group. This, however, is not a problem but an opportunity. It is always wise to associate operational risk to the product-and-process, because it enables it to be tracked more effectively. Then, homogeneous op risks can be grouped together in the parallel code system – for instance, by using the suffix.

The best classification is one that has the maximum number of business lines, products, and services integrated towards a global classification system at the top, but one that can also be exploded in terms of detail and of specific identification requirements. Detail is crucial for unambiguous identification.

The parallel identification code has three components:

■ A *basic code*, <bc>, written in hexadecimal (radix 16), which corresponds one-to-one with classification, and is supported through a parity check.
■ A *suffix*, <s>, which allows linkages outside the classification – for instance operational risk across taxonomical boundaries.

■ An *origin*, <o>, which makes possible identification outside the classification and which may, for example, identify the branch.

For any practical purpose the identification number corresponds one-to-one to the classification number, but their characteristics are different and so is their use. A valid classification system will also account for migration from credit risk and market risk to the operational risk category. There is plenty of work to be done within the perspective examined in this section.

In conclusion, lack of proper logical classification of operational risk results in difficulty (or impossibility) in understanding it and measuring it. Ideally, a classification must see to it that defined operational risks are mutually exclusive and comprehensively exhaustive. This is not easy, because many op risks are cross-functional and usually overlapping – but it can be done. The more polished the work we do, the better it will observe the rules outlined in the previous three sections (2.2, 2.3, 2.4). Compromises in classification and identification usually lead to trouble and therefore they should be avoided.

2.6   Quantitative and qualitative approaches to operational risk identification

When asked about best practices in identifying and measuring operational risk, many companies responded that while they aim at identifying, monitoring, and controlling operational risk, clear-cut norms are still missing, and op risk measurement frameworks are still at a developmental stage. Some credit institutions have added that best practices will necessarily involve both quantitative and qualitative approaches. Not everything can be quantified. Indeed, the Basel Committee suggests a list of crucial qualitative elements of effective op risk control:

■ Senior management involvement
■ A good management information system (MIS)
■ Strong internal controls
■ Personnel training, and
■ Contingency planning.

These are valid for all financial entities, of any size and scope. Qualitative analysis is just as important as quantitative analysis and, on many occasions, the one assists the other, as demonstrated by the following paragraphs.

Quantitative approaches to operational risks are discussed extensively in Chapters 7, 8, and 9, along with toolboxes for analysis. Therefore, I will not elaborate on them in this section, but would like to make three points that provide perspective when we talk of quantification, analytics, and the evaluation of the results being obtained.

The first is a reminder of the point made earlier: that all types of analytical treatment of quantification are 80% a data problem and only 20% a mathematical problem. In other words, *if* we have no data *then* we have no chance of doing quantitative analysis even if we have available the best toolbox. As Chapter 1 has explained,

- To understand the pattern of op risk we must datamine the information elements we have in operational risk classes.

But, as stated above:

- We will never have the op risk data we need unless we apply a rigorous methodology for classification and identification – *plus* op risk monitoring and recording.

The second critical point regards the sophistication of the toolbox that can be used to address analytical and modeling requirements for operational risk control. Our tools should include: hypothesis testing, experimental design, analysis of variance, autocorrelation,[4] regression, least-squares, extreme value theory, non-linear programming, and confidence intervals.

Just as important is to perform symbolic logic operations, fuzzy engineering, Bayesian logic, genetic algorithms[5] for time- and frequency-domain analysis, spectral analyses, and filtering. It is also important to visualize processes and analyze images. As this list suggests, operational risk problems cannot be successfully attacked in the quantification domain through simple business statistics – which essentially means worn-out tools.

The third point concerns using the past as a predictor and estimating the model risk involved in this approach. It is quite wrong to suggest we can tell what will happen tomorrow by what happened yesterday. But to say it is not possible to benefit from an analysis of past events, or from a peer comparison within a group, is to imply everything is totally random and is not subject to research.

To close the gap between these two statements we must use the concept of confidence intervals with practically everything we estimate. The *mean value*, x, of a variable which we study represents very little in terms of information if we don't know the *variance*, which is the second moment of a distribution. The use of the standard deviation (s, square root of the variance, v) allows to understand the distribution's pattern and to identify a level of significance. Using statistics from the Bundesbank, Figure 2.4 gives an example at the 95% level. The 95% level of confidence is equal to $x \pm 1.96s$ (mean plus or minus 1.95 standard deviations) in a two-tailed distribution.

Readers familiar with the use of confidence intervals, fuzzy engineering, and genetic algorithms will appreciate that all three are an interface between quantitative and qualitative methods. They help to quantify an abstract notion, like the 95% level of significance, or to quantify belief functions. Fuzzy engineering converts into pattern concepts like:

- More or less
- Higher (or lower) than . . ., and so on.

Let's now turn our attention to the qualitative drivers for operational risk control. These are many. Large-scale, they include the operational risk management framework we adopt, as well as the classification of op risks along homogeneous lines

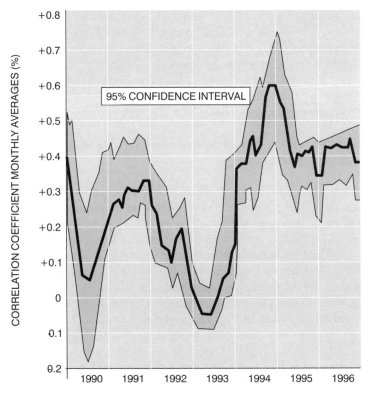

Figure 2.4 Spillover of yield volatility from the American debt securities market to the German market (*Source:* German Bundesbank)

(see sections 2.4 and 2.5); small-scale, they focus on causation clauses in operational procedures, application of extra control over large transactions, tracking fraud attempts during holiday periods, and similar instances which cannot always be successfully quantified, but which are present nonetheless.

Other qualitative factors in operational risk control are greater consistency in risk measurement, management transparency, communication of findings, explanation of op risk impact on the organization, definitions of expected and unexpected losses, and adequacy of capital provisions – which could be quantified through confidence intervals, in line with the model in Figure 2.4.

The focus on awareness and op risks training and self-assessment are yet more examples of qualification factors. Among qualitative drivers with a punch are incentives (merits) and disincentives (demerits). The same is true of independence of operational risk management and control functions, as well as of ways and means for mitigation of operational risk.

Among organizational issues that have to do much more with management beliefs and culture than with analytics, is the balance between centralized and decentralized functions in regard to operational risk control. For instance, the Deutsche Bank has a centralized group of 12 people, and decentralized small groups which look after op risks in all its operations. Other banks depend solely on centralized op risk control.

A crucial question is how to identify and measure qualitative factors in operational risk. My answer is the use of the Delphi method,[6] which I have found to be the best approach in operational risk identification, and in the definition of valid control solutions. Delphi is based on systematic pooling of expert opinion. The rules are:

- Select a sample of knowledgeable and independent-minded people.
- Create the proper conditions under which they can perform, then let them rate an issue.
- Use considerable caution in deriving from their opinion *both* diversity in thinking and a convergent position.

Delphi is typically conducted by means of a focused questionnaire given to the experts. The object of this approach may be strictly qualitative, such as identifying operational risks; or it may be somewhat more quantitative, such as asking for their educated guesses on the frequency of a given op risk, or on its impact. The use of fuzzy engineering and the Delphi method have many things in common.

In conclusion, operational risk has both qualitative and quantitative components. The latter are not served through too detailed algorithmic expressions, complex and obscure equations, or an inordinate amount of theory. What is needed for an able solution is sensitivity to qualitative factors, and this is what Delphi provides.

2.7 A framework for monitoring operational risk

A study done by Kodak in the early 1980s gave evidence that six consecutive years of mismanagement can bring a great company to its knees. In 2001 and 2002 we had plenty of examples of companies fitting this pattern (see also Chapter 4, on management risk). The most frequent reason behind this failure has been senior management itself – which is an operational risk.

Following the identification of operational risks, management must decide how to control the exposure associated to op risk. While at least in selected areas, risk transfer might be done through insurance, in the majority of cases operational risk must be controlled through a methodology fitting our bank's business perspective – and leading to immediate corrective action.

- *If* the problem is at the top, which means the CEO, then the board must take action and change the management.
- *If* the problem is legal risk (see Chapter 3), then the board and the CEO should work together with the legal counsel to solve it or mitigate it.
- *If* technology is the weak spot in the chain, then the CEO and the other members of the executive committee must come forward forcefully to change IT direction, and maybe the chief technology officer (CTO) as well.

These are senior management actions and they have to do with forceful decisions, not necessarily with money. Nevertheless, capital charges for operational risks are also necessary (see Part 2), and are currently demanded by regulators. In the longer run, qualitative criteria, organizational solutions, quantitative tools, interactive databases, *and* capital should work in unison. Money alone does not represent an effective substitute for adequate management.

Another 'must' is open communications lines and feedback. In this connection, the best answer is rigorous internal control and corrective action with senior management taking the lead. Senior management is the only authority able to control operational risk in the longer term.

The board and CEO will be much better positioned to act in the direction of operational risk control *if* the institution has in place a framework that assists in taking action. Based on a project along the principles outlined in Chapter 1 and in this chapter, Figure 2.5 presents such a framework for the evaluation of global operational risk.

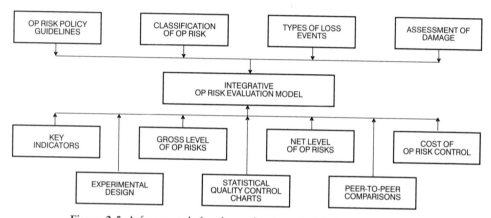

Figure 2.5 A framework for the evaluation of global operational risk

What this figure misses is the detail. This is intentional, because detail is specific by bank in the sense that it is always expressed within an operational environment. It can never be given in an abstract sense; it should also reflect the finite elements of a bank's product channels and processes, in conjunction to the operational risk classes on which we have chosen to concentrate.

For example, these may be the seven classes proposed by the Basel Committee: internal fraud; external fraud; employment and workplace safety; clients, products, and business practices; damage to physical assets; business disruption; systems failures; execution, delivery, and process management. (They have been presented in Figure 2.2.) Or, we may break down these classes into further detail. As an example, at least 14 different operational risks are included in just one class – system failures: networks, databases, central processors, servers, workstations, the software associated to each of these groups, analysis and programming staff, operators, help centers, and IT management.

The previous section brought to the reader's attention that the advanced measurement method entails that the classification of op risks may be quite different from that outlined by Basel's standard method. For instance, one financial institution chose to emphasize operational risks associated to:

- Business continuity planning
- Business concentration
- Litigation
- Legislative changes
- Compliance
- Development and use of models
- Insider trading
- Taxation.

In connection with operational risk, major activities in which a financial institution, and any other organization, finds itself engaged should be examined both in a holistic form and in detail. An example is outsourcing, which some banks have begun to practice widely on the wrong assumption that in this way they delegate part of their responsibilities. This is tantamount to underestimating operational risks. A Basel Committee document of July 2002 on sound practices for op risk supervision has brought attention to outsourcing risks by stating that 'Growing use of outsourcing arrangements . . . can mitigate risk, but can also present significant other risks to banks.'[7] Therefore, Basel advises that institutions should:

- 'Establish sound policies for managing the risks associated with outsourcing,
- 'Understand that outsourcing should be based on rigorous legal agreements, with clear allocation of responsibilities, and
- 'Appreciate that the use of third parties does not diminish the responsibilities of the board and senior management.'

A study I conducted subsequently to this document identified some two dozen issues raised by IT outsourcing which are operational risks. These include: quality of human skills, proven capability for advanced solutions, technology infrastructure, 'factory processing' in one location, system reliability, availability, and data integrity.

Among other operational risks (in the same list) are lack of homogeneity of platforms, lack of homogeneity of basic software, lack of sophistication of applications software, age of applications software, and maintenance of applications software. Also, security (physical and logical), effective handholding, cost-effectiveness of contracts, outsourcer bankruptcy risk, fall-back, backup, and optout.

Critical operational risk factors are, as well, relationships created in other jurisdictions, auditing of outsourcer(s), contagion of op risks among related business lines, and business-partnership-wide internal control. These are examples of the detail that is needed to fill the pigeonholes of the classification framework which we looked at above, and therefore provide a reference structure that can keep operational risk under control.

2.8 The art of operational risk modeling

As of March 2003, nearly four years after the first consultative paper on Basel II and in the aftermath of QIS3, one of the major developments is that both regulators and commercial bankers are inclined towards the two poles of the proposed system. Namely, the simpler and more advanced alternatives, rather than half-way solutions.

This means a marked preference for loss distribution. Of some twenty international banks participating in a 2003 meeting in London, the large majority had chosen the loss distribution approach. Two had gone for the scoreboard, where a key challenge is that of correlations. There were no takers for IMA. Whether loss distribution or scoreboard solutions are preferred, models and modeling are in the front line.

If a major problem with the scoreboard has been that of correlations, what about the challenges presented by the loss distribution approach? The answer is that a loss distribution solution has to be data-rich, in order to permit the bank to compute its own correlations. Besides, these correlations have to be tested and they must be reasonable.

Therefore, the downside is lack of op risk loss data as well as the challenge of developing and recognizing empirical correlations in operational risk losses across application areas, which reflect the pattern of individual op risk estimates. The Basel Committee permits the institution to do so, provided the institution can demonstrate to a high degree of confidence that:

- Its system for measuring correlations is sound
- Modeled processes are implemented with integrity, and
- Solutions take into account the uncertainty surrounding any correlation estimate.

Another basic requirement is that the system for analysis, calculation, and testing can work in periods of stress. To provide such guarantees the bank must validate its correlation assumptions through analytics. Moreover, risk measures for different operational risk estimates must be added for calculating regulatory minimum capital requirements.

It is appropriate to note that challenges regarding correlation are present with all operational risk control approaches by Basel II, except the basic indicator (see Chapter 7). For this reason some experts suggest that, in the absence of op risk databases, many banks may choose the basic approach to avoid the correlations requirements that start with the standard approach and progress with the three advanced methods.

There are also other queries relevant to implementation of operational risk solutions which involve modeling approaches and the models themselves. One of the major ones is that of partial use of each op risk control methodology, and of the measurement method associated to it. For instance, what about a bank's ability to use different approaches in:

- Different countries, and/or
- Different subsidiaries.

The first paragraphs in this section spoke about the choice of loss distribution and scoreboard, but the AMA methodologies are not necessarily applicable to small entities. The way to bet is that a loss distribution or scoreboard approach for the big bank cannot be used in one of its small subsidiaries – while, at the same time, the basic and standard approaches are not an option for large banks.

Another, closely related, problem connected to operational risk tracking and control is that of databases (see also Chapters 5 and 8). Today several banks are actively working to solve the database bottleneck – whether through a consortium or by themselves. Many develop an operational risk data collection and analysis methodology targeting the loss distribution approach – in appreciation of the fact the latter absorbs op risk data like a sponge.

A good example of solving this challenge is the ORX consortium, a project set up by a dozen major banks that have combined forces and information elements on operational risks (more on this later). But Barclays Bank, which also adopted the loss distribution approach, chose a lone wolf strategy. The way senior management looks at it,

- The bank can gain more value out of eigen scenarios
- While it is quite difficult to add value by combining forces with other institutions.

Still another interesting issue connected to development and implementation of operational risk models, one which is always present whether a consortium or a lone wolf strategy is chosen, is the question whether operational risk databases should be centralized or distributed. There is no unique answer to this query, which, to a very significant extent, relates to technology risk (Chapter 5).

2.9 The role of internal control and auditing in operational risk management

As underlined in a research paper by the International Organization of Securities Commissions (IOSCO), verification procedures relating to controls should be a function of both internal and external oversight. Based on the experience of its members, IOSCO advises that there should be four levels of defense:

- Internal day-to-day management
- Internal auditing
- External auditing, and
- Action by the supervisors.[8]

All four levels of reference must have tools and procedures to report logical and physical inadequacies, misbehavior, security breaches, and system breakdowns. Like bank supervisors, the securities commissions, which are members of IOSCO, underline that while these events may take place way down in the organization, the final responsibility and accountability for them rests with senior management.

Both the securities commissions and the bank supervisors aptly maintain that capital charges for operational risks – while they are necessary – don't represent an effective substitute for adequate management. Rigorous internal control is the answer, because the only authority within an organization to control operational risk is senior management.

Internal control is a process that evolves over time.[9] As more functions are being added, new and old internal controls coexist. Typically, the elder type of internal control has been used to address abuse, fraud, and errors. But during the past 10 years, new targets have been added to this short list:

- Compliance
- Breaking of credit limits
- Dynamic haircuts
- Market risk exposure
- Breaking of trading limits
- Changes in organizational behavior
- A long roster of operational risks.

One of the questions I have researched in depth during the past few years is the difference between internal control and risk management.[10] Is risk management part of internal control or is it the other way around? The two do overlap even if, more specifically, risk management uses mainly quantitative tools, namely:

- Statistics, and
- Models.

By contrast, in internal control top criteria are qualitative:

- Accountability, and
- Due diligence.

But while they differ in some respects, at the same time risk management and internal control have many things in common both between themselves and in connection to accounting and auditing, as shown in Figure 2.6. According to the Basel Committee, the scope of internal audit is broad and includes major areas:[11]

- Internal control processes
- Adherence to legal and regulatory requirements
- Risk management policies and procedures
- Financial information systems
- Testing of transactions, systems, and procedures
- Testing of compliance to regulatory requirements
- Special investigations.

Nearly all banks consider the auditing of accounting records within the scope of internal audit. Regrettably, this is not true of the banks' financial statements – as it should be the case. The result is an inordinate amount of operational risk, as the 2001–2002 cases of CEO malfeasance have demonstrated.

The reference to internal auditing must be qualified. Contrary to internal control, which is a process, auditing is a function. Audit reports are a good basis for validating operational risk events. But there should be no amalgamation between:

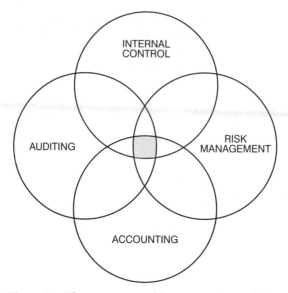

Figure 2.6 The areas covered by accounting, auditing,
risk management, and internal control overlap, but
each also has its own sphere of interest

- Auditing, and
- Operational risk management.

Auditing is a function of inspection largely based on sampling. Validation through auditing is done in a rigorous but intermittent manner, which must carefully review external and internal loss data. The control of operational risk is steady and, as we have already seen, it should use quantitative and qualitative drivers such as:

- Event categories
- Frequency of operational risk events
- Evidence on loss data
- Compliance to regulatory rules.

Auditing should evaluate the ability of the bank's current culture, as well as of its organization and structure, to manage and control operation risk. It should prompt group-wide op risk control, supported by technology. Both auditing and op risk control must be done in a cost-conscious way, and they should be effective.

When it comes to evaluating the role auditing can play in operational risk control, it is appropriate to keep in mind that, in most banks, internal audit is not a sizeable activity. It represents, on average, 1% of the workforce. Yet, its scope has considerably expanded to include:

- Financial audit

Assessing the reliability of accounting, information system support, and financial statements.

■ Compliance audit

Evaluating the quality and appropriateness of internal control in regard to compliance to laws, regulations, and internal policies.

■ Operational audit

Focusing on organizational structures, its solutions, methods, procedures, and transactions.

■ Management audit

Targeting the quality of management, its approach to risk, and the control of exposure – in accordance to the bank's objectives.

Some banks are outsourcing their internal audit. The Basel Committee on Banking Supervision says that regardless of whether internal audit is done in-house or is outsourced, the board, CEO, and senior management remain ultimately responsible. They are accountable for assuring that the systems of internal control and internal audit:

■ Are adequate, and
■ Operate effectively.[12]

The Basel Committee also underlines that internal audit is a core function of all banks. An institution might outsource the auditing work but it can never outsource the auditing responsibility. Neither can it outsource its responsibility for operational risk control. All these issues form a pattern of management responsibility and accountability. Therefore, they affect in an important way the classification, identification, monitoring, and control of operational risk.

Notes

1 D.N. Chorafas, *Credit Derivatives and the Management of Risk*, New York Institute of Finance, New York, 2000.
2 D.N. Chorafas, *Integrating ERP, CRM, Supply Chain Management and Smart Materials*, Auerbach, New York, 2001.
3 For practical implementation examples, see Chorafas, *Integrating ERP, CRM, Supply Chain Management and Smart Materials*.
4 D.N. Chorafas, *How to Understand and Use Mathematics for Derivatives, Volume 2 – Advanced Modelling Methods*, Euromoney Books, London, 1995.
5 D.N. Chorafas, *Rocket Scientists in Banking*, Lafferty Publications, London and Dublin, 1995.
6 D.N. Chorafas, *Modelling the Survival of Financial and Industrial Enterprises. Advantages, Challenges, and Problems with the Internal Rating-Based (IRB) Method*, Macmillan/Palgrave, London, 2002.

  7 Basel Committee on Banking Supervision, *Sound Practices for the Management and Supervision of Operational Risk*, BIS, Basel, July 2002.
  8 Report by the Technical Committee of IOSCO, *Risk Management and Central Guidance for Securities Firms and Their Supervisor*, IOSCO, Montreal, 1998.
  9 D.N. Chorafas, *Reliable Financial Reporting and Internal Control: A Global Implementation Guide*, John Wiley, New York, 2000.
 10 D.N. Chorafas, *Implementing and Auditing the Internal Control System*, Macmillan, London, 2001.
 11 Basel Committee on Banking Supervision, *Internal Audit in Banks and the Supervisors Relationship to Auditors*, BIS, Basel.
 12 Basel Committee, *Internal Audit in Banks and the Supervisors Relationship to Auditors*, BIS, Basel.

3 Legal risk

3.1 Introduction

The origins of legal risk are infinite, and each case has its own characteristics. What most of them have in common is that, in their source, operational risks are connected either to current mistakes or errors of the past. As we will see in this chapter, legal risks get amplified because of deregulation and globalization, which have somehow reduced visibility as well as the counterparty's obligation to perform.

Put in basic terms, legal risk is an operational risk that comes above the better known, and therefore appreciated, credit risk and market risk. Yet, in spite of its importance, the impact of legal risk has received scant attention in international financial dealings. Experts say that, if tested in court, many of the current transnational agreements will not stand.

- This will have disastrous effects on business confidence, and
- It may even disrupt global trade, because confidence is at the heart of the financial system.

Globalization brought into perspective the inconsistency prevailing in laws and regulations among different countries. By doing so, it amplified the aftermath of mistakes made in the present and in the past. These may concern the choice of a counterparty or of a business partner; entering a new market without due diligence in learning its laws and its culture; being caught between two different and incompatible systems of laws and regulations; paying scanty attention to compliance; and plain errors of judgement.

An integral part of legal risk is technical glitches, including the 'not invented here' and 'would not happen to me' sort of thinking. An example is lack of advance scrutiny on the counterparty's obligation to perform, which may not be enforceable because of differences in the letter of the law and the:

- Breakdown of the law enforcement industry (judiciary and police)
- Crony capitalism and the impact of occult interests
- Political greed and corruption, and
- Exploitation of different loopholes existing in the letter of the law.

Globalization, deregulation, and the move toward litigation as a way to settle differences, as well as the turn to the judicial system into a sort of regulatory agency, as shown in the case of the US Department of Justice against Microsoft, have amplified the legal risk landscape. Because global markets have so many unknowns and unpredictable events, litigation has become a way of thinking.

For many instances, therefore, legal risk is now the means for solving fairly significant difference in legislation and regulation prevailing in different countries where a financial institution and its counterparties operate. What many people and companies fail to appreciate is that legal risk often amplifies other risks. The principle with litigation is that unless you are getting into it with thorough knowledge of the law *and* your eyes wide open, it is not the right process for you.

The goal this chapter has set itself is to demonstrate how in the modern, global economy legal risk has taken on a totally different dimension than the one characterizing it in the past. Also to convince that both persons and companies should think very carefully about this operational risk, because a great deal of the success or failure of any enterprise depends on the solution to be provided through court decisions.

3.2   Back to basics: the definition of tort

In modern business, companies have numerous lawsuits filed against them, asserting various reasons. Often, these include class actions and stockholder derivative actions. The results of complex legal proceedings are difficult to predict. Moreover, many of the complaints being filed do not specify the amount of damages that plaintiffs seek, making it nearly impossible to estimate in advance the possible range of damages that might be incurred should these lawsuits be resolved against the company.

Apart from the fact that lawsuits distract management from its main objectives, the uncertainties to which the previous paragraph made reference are a major unknown in regard to a firm's continuing well-being. An unfavourable outcome or settlement of one or more lawsuits could have a material adverse effect on its:

- Financial position
- Liquidity, or
- Results of operations.

Even if the outstanding lawsuits are not resolved against the company, the uncertainty and expense associated with unresolved legal cases could seriously harm its business, including its reputation. An unwritten law of business is that when something goes wrong, the aftermath seems twice as bad as might be the real case.

Theoretically, uncertainty should not exist in connection to legal risk because since the time of Hammurabi in 1700 BC laws have been codified and written down, and a main theme in any litigation is to know exactly what one wants to defend or to achieve. This allows us to prepare our arguments and elaborate on our legal strengths and weaknesses, as well as to keep an eye on the give and take certain to follow in any negotiations.

Along this line, it is wise to know the bare minimum we can accept and the maximum we are hoping for. Once we have studied what the law says, and have these levels of reference, we are well on our way towards facing legal risk – or, that's what the theory says. In practice, matters are more complex. First and foremost, we must put ourselves on the other side of the table and:

- Study what drives our opponent(s) in a legal case
- Evaluate whether our opponent has political or occult means to influence the judiciary, and
- Estimate how much we hope to get, or how little we are willing to accept, in a negotiated settlement.

The way to bet is that such a settlement will have regard to assets and liabilities, therefore possessions. A *possession* is single and exclusive. Two different parties, not being joint owners, cannot have at the same time possession of the same thing. Therefore, if one of the parties loses the court case, there is going to be transfer of assets.

Critical in connection to litigation is the role of *motive*. There are several torts with a motive in which liability may be an integral part. The word *tort* stands for any private or civil wrong, by act or omission, for which a civil suit can be brought. This definition is all-inclusive, except breach of contract. An example of tort is asbestos litigation (see Chapter 12).

Experts believe that multibillion dollar cases in the twenty-first century will have tort in their background, rather than breach of contractual clauses. Though in the general case the laws, jurisprudence, and ways to define legal risk are quite different from one country to the next, such differences are much greater with tort than breach of contract, including procedural issues characterizing each jurisdiction. The US and UK provide an example:

- In the US, legal risk frequently involves class actions; judgment is done by jury; there is unlimited liability; and there exists a high environmental liability as well.
- By contrast, in the UK there are no class actions; the judge (not a jury) decides on compensation; and there is liability cap. Also environmental liability is much lower than in the US.

As mentioned in the preceding paragraphs, the background to tort is motive; which signifies the reason for the conduct. It may be an evil motive, or tort may be done wilfully without cause or excuse. Motive often refers to *intention*, a term that describes the basic reason for conduct and its desired consequences. Motive influences the actor, but:

- If conduct is unlawful, a good motive will not exonerate the defendant, and
- If conduct is lawful apart from motive, a bad motive will not make the defendant liable.

There are, however, several exceptions to this second point. The first point, too, has exceptions; defenses like necessity being an example. Fundamentally, it is the act, not the motive for the act, which is judged. If the act, apart from motive, gives rise to damage or injury, the motive will not relieve the actor of liability.

An example of unlawful conduct is the false statement. A *false statement* is one with knowledge of its falsity, or recklessness. Doing something recklessly means knowing the statement is false and being consciously indifferent about it. This is much more than gross negligence. It is intention, with the actor bearing the consequences of his act.

Another example is deceit. *Deceit* originally had a narrow meaning of swindling a court in some way, and it has been one of the forms of abusing legal procedure. The concept of deceit, however, has expanded over time. Still another example is *defamation*. Lawyers say that no domain of litigation is more fertile than defamation. Nor has any branch of legal practice been more perplexed with minute distinctions.

When two or more people combine for inflicting unlawful injury upon another person and cause damage to that person, they commit the tort of *conspiracy*. Originally the law regarding conspiracy had a narrow meaning: that of combination to abuse legal procedure. Its meaning however has expanded, bifurcating into civil and criminal conspiracy. Both have legal consequences:

- In principle, damage to a plaintiff is an essential part of tort.
- Combination of different people's actions leads to tortuous conspiracy.

Persons are said to be joint actors in tort when their shares as actors are done in common design. In this case, they share joint responsibility. On the other hand, mere similarity of design on behalf of independent agents is not enough. To involve joint responsibility, the action must be concerted to a common end.

There may be actions by a single party, or several in unison, which involves negligence. This, too, can have a legal aftermath. *Negligence* is the omission to do something that is part of one's duties. This is often linked to a reasonable person's behavior, which is an abstract concept but has real impact when associated to a person's behavior in the execution of his or her duties.

3.3   Responsibilities resulting from legal risk

In business, unlawful acts bring up the issue of liability resulting from the master–servant (or employee) relationship, as well as from other relationships which are not of a contractual nature. Historically, the master is liable for any tort the servant commits in the course of his or her employment; though the servant himself is also liable. This idea of vicarious responsibility is common, founded on a good deal of ancient law, starting with the law of Hammurabi.

Laws, however, are not cast in stone. Over the centuries the concept of complete liability for the wrongs of servants changed to that of liability only where there has been command or consent on the part of the master to the servant's wrong. In the Middle Ages the master's liability was considerably narrowed to the point that he was no longer liable unless he *particularly* commanded the very act done – with one exception.

The exception has been the case that the master is liable if an implied command could be inferred from the general authority he had given to the servant. Eventually, with merchandising this exception took on significant importance, and was at the root of the eighteenth and nineteenth century extension of the master's responsibility.

Trade has been responsible for this evolution in legal risk because trade became too complex to allow the original direct command concept, which suited the old simple relation of master and servant. The expansion of liability covered persons such as agents, who were not accustomed to take their orders from a medieval master. Late in the nineteenth century the implied command concept theory was displaced by the scope of *employment* which is now the rule.

The question however remains: *Who is the servant?* As far as vicarious liability is concerned, a servant is one whose work is under the direct control of another person. In this sense, the servant is distinguished from an *independent contractor*, who undertakes to produce a given result, but in the actual execution of the work is not under the order or direct control of the person for whom the work is done.

Contrary to a servant, an independent contractor may use his or her own discretion in things not specified beforehand. At the same time, however, an employer is not liable for the torts of his independent contractor. The employer will be liable, if he gives the contractor authority to do some careless act, which falls under the definition of tort given in section 3.2. Theoretically, this would seem to characterize the relationship between:

- An outsourcer, and
- An insourcer.

The outsourcer may be a bank which, for instance, delegates the execution of its information technology chores to a third party. The latter is the insourcer, who functions in a way similar to what has been said, in the preceding paragraphs, about the independent contractor.

Practically, in the case of a financial institution, this delegation of responsibility does not hold. The central banks and regulatory agencies of the Group of Ten (G-10) countries have made it clear that full responsibility for execution of outsourced IT remains with the board, CEO, and senior management of the outsourcing bank. The insourcer, too, is responsible – but the top management of the outsourcer is in the frontline of personal accountability.

Another example where the coming years may hold surprises in terms of responsibilities for legal risk is that of expert opinion. In 2001–2002 we had plenty of cases of equity analysts who misinformed investors. Merrill Lynch, for instance, paid a $100 million penalty for this reason. An interesting case for the future is *legal risk* connected to *rating agencies*. Such risk exists at two levels:

- The process of credit rating, and
- The issue being rated.

In the case of the issue, rating is a function of the bond's structure, issuer, bankruptcy law, covenants, and country. In some countries security due to covenants is worthless in a bankruptcy court. For example, in France the judge can override covenants and put all lenders, secured and unsecured, at same level. In other countries, the court may be corrupt.

Transactions made in good faith where *ex ante* legal opinion is overruled are not unheard of. Examples are those of the Hammersmith judgment in the UK, and of a power utility in Washington State in the US. My research on legal responsibility derived from documented formal opinions that credit rating agencies have to look very carefully at:[1]

- Legal risk connected to their rating, and
- What both investors and regulators can and cannot do with such opinion.

In the United States the freedom to express one's opinion is protected by the First Amendment. But the case of such opinion being taken as a basis for investments and capital reserves, as specified by Basel II, has not yet been tested in court. Experts participating in my research underlined that this issue is particularly important in structured finance.

The same experts made the point that legal risk is greater in countries where there exists a tendency to sue. Rating agencies, for instance, must be very careful in the US. There has already been a critique about the rating of Enron debt, in the sense that nobody reacted in a way that would inform the bondholders ahead of time. So far this case has not led to court action.

Nevertheless, evidence provided during research interview and meetings suggests that following Enron there is more focus on legal risk at the rating agencies side. For instance, more stringent procedures are now followed by their credit policy group, which confirms the ratings and oversees all matters from legal and other viewpoints. The crucial question is how to act as a rating agency, given the likelihood of tort.

Some rating agencies commented that the aforementioned type of legal risk cannot be deadly, because in court it is necessary to prove negligence. Apart of that, rating agencies rely on the company's financial statements. This, however, is an argument Andersen brought up – and it did not stick. The reliability of financial statements is part of accounting risk, which incorporates the likelihood of fraud.

- *If* there is no fraud,
- *Then* there is management risk (see Chapter 4).

Another component of legal risk is documentation risk, largely a human resources and technology problem. Compliance falls in the same category (see section 3.8). In establishing the nature of tort, and the extent of liability associated to tort, it is important to evaluate in a pragmatic way the master–servant connection, and what we might expect from our opponent(s) in terms of unfavorable surprises. This permits us to gauge the outcome. Only in the light of what we can conclude from this analysis about our legal position in relation to the motive(s) of our potential opponent(s) can we establish a valid strategy for defense.

The strategy of our opponent(s) and his (their) history of deception, as well as the economic and political environment within which litigation takes place, usually weigh greatly on the outcome. Legal risk has to be judged by taking full account of the legal and economic environment characterizing business operations, as well as the evolution of jurisprudence over time.

3.4   Contractual aspects of legal risk

An examination of contractual aspects of legal risk is important because, fundamentally, the business of a credit institution can be analysed as a series of contracts. In all likelihood, operational risk will be embedded into each one of them. The probability of future legal risk is highly influenced by:

- The clauses in the contract with the counterparty, and
- The credit risk and market risk assumed by each party.

New laws may bring up new contractual risks. The Gramm–Leach–Bliley Act of 1999, which repealed the Depression-era prohibition against combining commercial and investment banking, could be used against a credit institution. The law requires diversified financial companies to be not only *well-capitalized* but also *well-managed*. On 18 July 2002, federal regulators limited the activities of Pittsburgh-based PNC Financial Services on those grounds.

In principle, institutions most at risk of scrutiny are those involved in complicated financial deals, such as special purpose vehicles (SPVs), and events like pre-pays, which have been a curious financial instrument used by major credit institutions. JP Morgan Chase and Citigroup found themselves in trouble with the pre-pays they had arranged for Enron out of Jersey Island, an offshore.

Contractual risk and tort correlate; by so doing they drive other risks. But contractual risk has hues. Typically, contracts with correspondent banks are *hard*. By contrast, retail banking contracts established with customers tend to be *soft*. For instance, repayment of a mortgage is one of the ambiguities in a contract.

Other things being equal, clauses in hard contractual agreements are more likely to lead to legal proceedings, claims, and litigation arising in the ordinary course of business. Theoretically, these are pure legal challenges. Practically, they are as much financial as they are legal, because they are not determinable in advance and the ultimate costs to resolve them can have a material adverse effect on the company's:

- Consolidated financial position
- Results of operations, and
- Projected cash flows.

Plaintiffs, for example, may allege that defendants have made false and misleading statements, purporting to assert claims for violations of securities laws. As a result, they will in all likelihood seek compensatory damages and other relief. The company may believe such claims are without merit and defend its actions vigorously. It may also ask for an injunction.

An *injunction* is an order of the court, or judgment, restraining the commission or continuance of some wrongful act, or the continuance of some wrongful omission. An injunction is given by discretion of the court, but it cannot be demanded as a matter of right. There are several ways of classifying injunctions, one of them being into:

- Interlocutory, and
- Perpetual.

An *interlocutory* injunction is issued provisionally until the case can be heard upon its merits, or until further order. The court does not profess to anticipate the determination of the dispute, but merely indicates that there is a substantial question to be tried. Eventually, if the plaintiff proves that at all events he is entitled to relief, the Court will make the injunction *perpetual*. In the opposite case, it will dissolve the injunction.

There may also be *derivative suits*. For instance, Cisco's 2001/2002 annual statement makes the reference that beginning on 23 April 2001 a number of purported shareholder derivative lawsuits were filed in the Superior Court of California, County of Santa Clara, and in the Superior Court of California, County of San Mateo. The statement adds that there is a procedure in place for the Northern District of California, and those federal court actions have been consolidated. The complaints in the various derivative actions include claims for:

- Breach of fiduciary duty
- Mismanagement
- Unjust enrichment, and
- Waste of corporate assets.

These court actions are based on essentially the same allegations as the class actions. They seek compensatory and other damage, disgorgement, and other relief. Some legal actions against entities focus on *compliance risk*. This, too, is an operational risk. It refers to the possibility that a company will be found guilty of wrongful acts, by:

- A court
- Arbitration panel, or
- Regulatory authority.

Having failed to comply with an applicable legal or regulatory requirement exposes an entity to lawsuits, or arbitration claims. These may be levied by clients, employees, or other third parties. The company may be brought to court in the different jurisdictions in which it conducts business (see section 3.5 on the complexity of transborder legal cases).

Some legal risk may be the consequence of management's lack of attention to rules and regulations. New laws or rules, and changes in application of those currently applicable, could affect our company's manner or type of operations. Violations of enforceable statutory and regulatory requirements could subject *our* company and its directors, officers, and other employees to:

- Disciplinary proceedings, or
- Civil or criminal liability.

Also tax considerations increasingly determine the legal liability of a firm. Sometimes companies get into trouble through a process they call 'tax optimization', which they consider to be different from tax evasion. Often, however, tax optimization involves cutting corners and/or it frequently requires a rapid adaptation of policies to changing legal conditions.

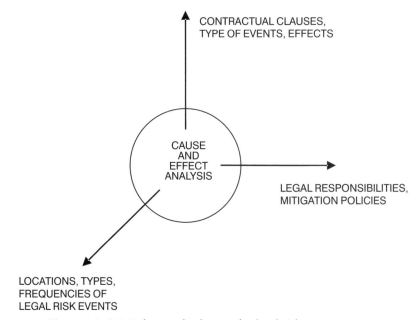

CONTRACTUAL CLAUSES,
TYPE OF EVENTS, EFFECTS

CAUSE
AND
EFFECT
ANALYSIS

LEGAL RESPONSIBILITIES,
MITIGATION POLICIES

LOCATIONS, TYPES,
FREQUENCIES OF
LEGAL RISK EVENTS

Figure 3.1 A 3-D frame of reference for legal risk management

Senior management should always keep in mind that in the present day markets are characterized by litigation more than ever before. Being able to fence-off legal risk is synonymous to being able to survive the increasingly severe competitive struggle. Figure 3.1 presents in a nutshell a three-dimensional frame of reference for legal risk management, which includes cause and effect analysis as its pivot point.

Cause and effect should be studied proactively in terms of legal and financial aftermath, not just post-mortem. Proactive solutions provide visibility, while post-mortems teach a lesson. In its long legal troubles in the early 1990s, Prudential Securities let it be known that, during the reign of George Ball as its CEO, the company made many unwise commitments mainly connected to new and untested products.

■ Customers to whom these products were sold brought the company to court.
■ This untangled the legal maze behind a court action which took nearly 8 years, at an estimated cost to Prudential Securities of $1.4 billion.

This is a risk the company assumed for very meager rewards. The board and top management should always keep in mind that litigation can be costly, time-consuming, and disruptive to normal business operations. The costs of defending lawsuits, particularly class actions and stockholder derivative actions, could be quite significant and may not be covered by insurance policies (see Part 3). Often, the defense of these lawsuits results in continued diversion of senior management's time and attention, away from business operations.

3.5 Crossborder legal risk and bankruptcy laws

Here is an example of cost of transborder legal risk. In the early 1990s, two banks, one operating in London the other in New York, were ordered by one of their clients to transfer $5 million from one institution to another. This was done by cable, and there was fraud. The case went to court. In the end, it cost $6 million in legal fees, and there was no solution to the legal issue behind the court action.

This case illustrates what makes crossborder legal conflict so complex. Legal risk, and other operational risks, are augmented by the fact that in a globalized economy credit institutions and other companies often engage in crossborder transactions that are:

■ Initiated in one jurisdiction
■ Recorded in a different jurisdiction, and
■ Managed in yet another jurisdiction.

Differences in legislation and regulation have always existed. However, the globalization of business has magnified the differences that prevail between countries. At the same time, legal risk problems get more complex because with rapid innovation in financial instruments there is no jurisprudence which may offer guidance regarding:

■ The way courts may react, or
■ How the law enforcement industry may operate.

Globalization has increased legal risk in more ways than one. A recent example is the ongoing discussion on changing national and international laws to set up a legal process for restructuring sovereign debt. The plan being advanced calls for consolidating the bankrupt country's loans and bonds, and instituting a committee of creditors which would bargain with the government to rollover debts.

Parallel to that, IMF and the debtor nation are expected to work out a long-term rescue program that could put the country on a sound footing, permitting creditors to be repaid even with rescheduling and reductions to interest rate and/or capital, which amounts to haircuts. Solutions are not forthcoming because they involve considerable political and social implications, let alone the technical minefield of laws and regulations themselves.

Some experts suggest that the hurdles to setting up such a global legal system are so many, that for any practical purpose it is not feasible. To start with, any solution worth its salt has to put aside the country's sovereignty, and put on hold all of its bankruptcy laws. Short of this radical approach, there will always be ways (including legal means) to bypass or outright block such a 'solution' even after it has been agreed upon.

Beyond that, all existing loans and bonds, world-wide, would have to be rewritten, and new financial paper with different provisions would need to be issued. This is a legal risk of magnitude and, even if it were for this reason alone, such a 'solution' will not pass. Changing contractual rules midstream and retroactively is illegal in most countries, and as Dr Ben Gurion used to say, two things that are wrong don't make one that is right.

Furthermore, not only the IMF itself would have to amend its bylaws, but also its member countries would need to change their statutes. The added hurdle is that of establishing a supranational juridical institution and giving it legal authority to mediate disputes. This, the experts say, would be a legal and political nightmare – though it might well turn into a lawyers' paradise.

In fact, as far as legal risk in global markets is concerned, the single biggest mess in international laws is in the domain of bankruptcy. Country-by-country, the bankruptcy laws may not be terribly different from one another, but they leave gaping holes characterized by operational risk. Companies with experience in transborder court issues suggest that such complex decisions tend to conflict with one-another.

The Basel Committee on Banking Supervision can recommend and approve capital requirements, but it cannot change the bankruptcy law, and other laws, of the different jurisdictions. This has led many bankers and other businesspeople to suggest that today bankruptcy laws are the Achilles' heel of globalization. Here are some examples.

■ In the UK, insolvency starts at *noon*.

This means that morning deals are covered.

■ Napoleonic laws prevailing in continental Europe specify *zero hour* insolvency.

This means last midnight. The morning deals are not covered. By all likelihood, it will take ages for insolvency laws to change and to become homogeneous both because of embedded interests in the current system, country by country, and for other much more practical reasons.

Legal differences in a globalized business environment are so many that they cannot be solved on the run. A sound system has to be built involving not only laws, regulations, counterparties and their management – but also the best legal skills available. An integral part of this effort will necessarily be information system support, feedbacks, and post-mortems. A pattern is shown in Figure 3.2.

In my book, a curious thing in the current environment is that the likelihood of a transborder court fight is rarely considered by investors, yet this constitutes a major operational exposure. Because of transborder legal risk, investors should think twice before lending to borrowers who can get into a global legal mess. This is true both with bonds and with loans. The basic question a bank should ask itself is:

■ Can I seize the borrower's assets?

The answer to the question: 'Can I seize the borrower's assets' is not that simple, and it brings into perspective the legal risk associated with the total entity *vs* single entity concept. In case of bankruptcy, Swiss law considers the assets of the New York branch of a Swiss bank as part of the mass of its assets. But US law says the opposite: the New York branch is a separate entity.

■ Hence, two different jurisdictions will make different judgments on the same bankruptcy case.

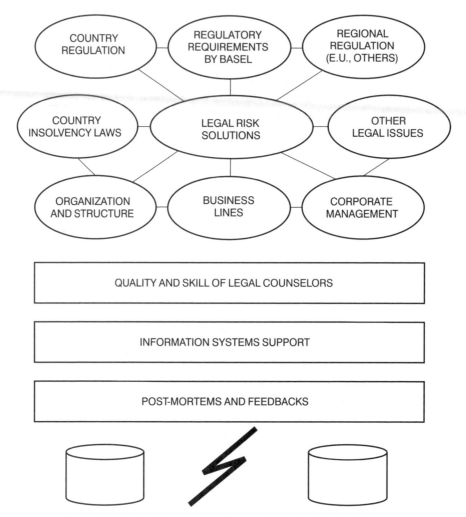

Figure 3.2 Basic elements of a framework for legal risk solutions

■ With the separate entity approach, assets and liabilities will be sorted out at local or national level.

Global business operations can hold many surprises, one of them being senior claims associated to insolvency. The 2001 annual report by UBS makes the following references in regard to its US operations: 'So long as UBS maintains one or more federal branches, the office of the controller of the currency (OCC) has the authority to take possession of the company's US operations. This federal power may pre-empt the state insolvency regimes that would otherwise be applicable to the bank's state licensed offices.'

The UBS annual report goes on to say that *if* the Office of the Controller of the Currency exercised its authority over the entity's banking offices pursuant to federal law, in the event of a UBS insolvency *then* all of UBS's US assets would be applied.

- First they will be used to satisfy creditors of its US banking offices as a group.
- Then they will be made available for application pursuant to any Swiss insolvency proceeding.

The last thing one needs in bankruptcy of a global company, or an international banking crisis, is courts fighting one another. Regulators can get together and, if the worst comes to the worst, they can agree much faster among themselves than judges do. The regulators' more rapid action, however, is necessary but not sufficient. Hence the wisdom of playing devil's advocate in all matters involving transborder legal risk.

With globalization, special attention has to be paid to the differences existing between insolvency laws. Insolvency laws in G-10 countries are by no means the same. In the UK, two parties, one of whom fails, can net their exposure; and only the resulting difference is brought to court. This is the English *set-off* law. By contrast, in continental Europe not only the set-off does not apply, but also each country has different legislation on the underlying issues.

3.6 Legal risk may be an impediment to a solution to a banking crisis

In case of bankruptcy, any solution requires legal certainty as to the owner of the claim(s) to future cash flows. This is achievable within a given jurisdiction, though some uncertainties may persist. By contrast, it is not really attainable without a global insolvency regime. Legal certainty does not exist if there is doubt as to the jurisdiction in which assets are located, a risk magnified by the fact that:

- Banks seek cross-border funds outsourcing.
- Competitive pressure drives transborder aggregation of institutions.
- More countries play host to foreign banks, which become economically important.
- Disclosure regimes differ markedly between countries.
- The location of the bank's assets is often uncertain.
- Banking failures are to a large measure unpredictable.

All these reasons contribute to legal risk and, vice versa, legal risk impacts upon them. The reasons the previous paragraphs have outlined also see to it that claims fail to materialize as expected. One of the interesting consequences of legal risk is that not all depositors have equal rights.

Because the complexity of legal issues and a legal fight among different jurisdictions might lead to systemic risk, according to J.M. Williamson, former Deputy Chief Executive of the Association for Payment Clearing Services (APACS) in London, to understand what it takes to establish a sound risk management process, a financial institution should look back at least 10 years and emulate the changes coming in terms of:

- New developments in financial instruments
- Risks, costs and profitability associated to them, and
- Legal and structural questions which impact upon the control of other risks.

Preparing for legal risk becomes more complex owing to the fact that our society is an information economy, with virtual assets. In contrast to real assets there is neither licensing in trading nor copyright in financial products. In modern finance, non-banking organizations come into banking and take away the business – while new financial products are likely to involve complex legal issues in a crossborder sense.

- A great deal of progress with payment systems depends on *sharing information* across borders.
- A salient problem is that of *uniform legislation* that will permit effective crossborder, multi-currency netting and settlement done in real-time.

Cross-country legal policies and procedures are necessary to strengthen the underlying transactional framework, in order to enhance financial responsibility. A redefinition of financial responsibility is inseparable from risk management, as any market can undergo times of stress. At the end of 1992 in the United Kingdom the real estate market collapsed for a second time in a few years and left many people who had taken mortgage loans with negative equity. The same thing can happen with the financial markets in trading crossborder off-balance sheet instruments.

Regulators are particularly worried about *systemic risk*. Today, reliable means for measuring the probability of systemic risk do not really exist. The central banks are nervous because they have no control over one of the main triggers of systemic risk – *sovereign risk*. Systemic risk can have several origins that test the financial system.

- What if two or three of the big money center banks fail at the same time?
- What if it is not possible to estimate the huge liabilities that will be created, because exposure figures steadily change?
- What if there is a snowball effect which engulfs other big banks, and from there the global market?

Ironically, one of the constraints in global risk management is technology (see Chapter 5). Very few banks have in place the technological infrastructure which would help their top management to properly estimate global exposure in a real-time sense. Legal constraints and technology constraints are both operational risks.

The lag in technology because of old concepts that are not commensurate to current risks is so much more surprising given the amount of money spent on IT. There is no doubt that practically all banks are nervous about risk and exposure both to on-balance sheet and to off-balance instruments. And there is no surprise in the fact that one major British bank has assigned a senior executive to deal with *systemic risk*.

- One of the reasons why financial institutions have been particularly alerted to this issue is that the regulatory authorities are demanding action.
- But in all likelihood, the real background factor is their own business sense. At long last they appreciate that the risks they have taken may no more be controllable.

Today, some big banks have a derivatives exposure which runs into trillions in notional principal amounts. At JP Morgan Chase, it is said to stand at $26 trillion; at Deutsche Bank, at $13 trillion; Citigroup and Bank of America have each nearly $12 trillion. While not all of notional principal is toxic waste, even demodulated to bring it down to the level of credit equivalence, this huge exposure is explosive stuff,[2] particularly if the bank faces class actions by shareholders.

Experts suggest that in the case of big banks overexposed to derivative instruments, to a high multiple of their equity, shareholder action is absolutely warranted (see also section 3.7). Avoiding legal risk because of inordinate exposure is a balancing act. It could be performed with some success *if*, and only *if*, rigorous standards of risk control are set by the board.

Legislation regarding limits to exposure and financial responsibility has to be clear and unambiguous, with well-delineated lines of personal accountability. As explained, legal risk can be amplified by management risk and IT risk. This is one of the areas of concern to central bankers. Take the international payments system as an example.

- Many banks now want real-time bilateral netting, with a further view toward multilateral solutions.
- But multilateral netting is very difficult because of differences in *laws*, legal systems, and *supervisory rules*.

Currently, most of what takes place in payments and settlements is improvised. Assisted by technology, human ingenuity brings things a notch further, but the necessary global legal infrastructure is simply not there. Until this happens, there is every reason to worry about the extent of legal risk and the uncertainties of litigation. Both damage the operating franchise of global business.

3.7 Huge credit losses, securitized corporates, and legal risk

Let's face it, the beginning of the twenty-first century has seen a rapid rise in exposure across the board: credit risk, market risk, and operational risk. On 17 September 2002, JP Morgan Chase warned that its third quarter operating profits would be well below those of the second quarter, because losses on corporate lending could more than quadruple, to $1.4 billion.

Not long ago, in the 1980s and early 1990s, there was a time when the securitization of loans allowed banks to discharge some of the credit risk in their portfolio, but by all indications this way of transferring exposure has by now been overdone. On 9 October 2002, Moody's Investors Service cut JP Morgan Chase's long-term debt rating to A1. With $713 billion in assets, the credit institution had:

- $278 billion in credit derivations
- Versus $207 billion in loans – which is, after all, a commercial bank's main line of business.

Evidence that shareholders do not appreciate these statistics is provided by the sharp and steady drop in the price of JP Morgan Chase's equity. But credit institutions that assume huge derivatives exposure are also opening their flanks to legal risk, particularly so when their loans business, too, is in trouble. *Loans* in default in US banking skyrocketed from $0.9 billion in 1997 to $19.6 billion in 2002.

Many of the JP Morgan Chase loans were made to now-struggling or failed telecom companies like WorldCom, in a bid to win investment banking business. This is an example of where synergy is producing more risks than one is bargaining for. These and other similar bad loans by commercial banks are part of the huge wave of debt turned sour which is flooding the financial system in the US, Europe, and Asia.

As dramatized in Figure 3.3, as of 1 January 2002 there has been a record $200 billion worth of corporate *bonds and loans* distressed or in default. Worrisome is the

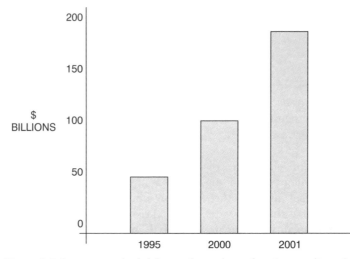

Figure 3.3 In one year bad debts and poorly performing syndicated loans nearly doubled. (*Source:* Statistics by Federal Reserve and Bond Market Association)

fact that this figure doubled in just one year (2001). Because the losses continue to mount, the biggest firms are facing not only an unprecedented credit risk but also legal risk. This comes in the form of a threat of legal action from investors who see themselves as the victims of a:

- Massive deception, and
- Colossal financial drain.

Experts say that the issues described by both these points are a result of securitized corporate loans and other alternative investments sold to individuals and institutional investors, in the 2000–2002 timeframe, by big banks – without appropriate wording about embedded risks. All sorts of investors have found themselves overexposed with loans made to highly leveraged telecoms and other unstable firms.

Central bankers, bondholders, and shareholders are nervous. But while the regulators are unlikely to go to court against the mismanagers of corporate wealth, the investors might. No JP Morgan Chase shareholder can be thrilled by the fact that the bank wrote off $3.3 billion in bad loans in the nine months through 30 June 2002.

To guesstimate the amount of legal risk which comes at the heel of huge loans losses and big derivative contracts turned sour, one needs to guess how vulnerable the big banks' enormous portfolio would be to, say, a sharp rise in interest rates (interest rate risk), or a fall in the dollar (foreign exchange risk). The way to bet about assumed derivatives risk is to demodulate this notional principle, or face value, by 6 in a worst-case scenario.[3] This will mean a black hole of $4.33 trillion – or 43% of the gross domestic product of the United States – in just one big bank: JP Morgan Chase.

How did we reach that point? 'The whole financial system has become corrupt,' says Dr Felix G. Rohatyn, formerly of Lazard Brothers and, also formerly, US Ambassador to France.[4] Big banks sold off major chunks of their corporate loans to:

■ Smaller banks
■ Insurance companies
■ Mutual funds, and
■ Other investors.

Many did so in a booming syndication market of more than $2 trillion. Then they moved on to repackaging consumer loans into securities, from mortgages to credit-card receivables, and sold them to institutions in what's now a $7 trillion securitization business, roughly divided (at the end of 2002) as follows:

■ $3.9 trillion in mortgage-backed securities
■ $1.4 trillion in corporates and
■ $1.7 trillion in other securitized loans.

Figure 3.4 shows this acceleration in securitization of loans – good and bad. By selling off the content of their loans portfolio, banks have been able to lend to yet more borrowers as they have generated a cash flow that enabled them to reuse their capital time and again. Critics now say that this facilitated:

■ Getting rid of loans the banks knew were about to turn sour, and
■ Making lending decisions based on investment banking projects, rather than on their own credit judgments.

There are several downsides to this process and each can lead to legal risk. The wholesale offloading of credit risk made the banking system both less stable and an agent of greater volatility. Critics add that the more business loans and corporate loans credit institutions securitized, the more conflicts of interest they faced regarding their decisions and the products they bring to the market.

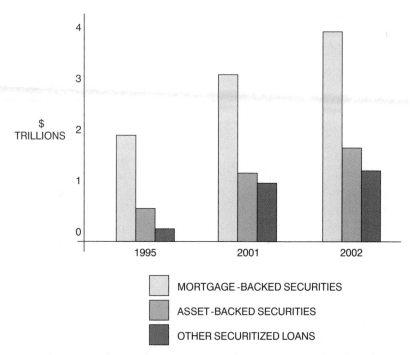

Figure 3.4 The rapid rise in securitized corporates matches that of
mortgage-backed securities

'This is the first time that the banking system has ever pre-distributed losses,' says
Martin Mayer, a guest scholar at the Brookings Institution. 'Banks are playing the
interest-rate market, and it is starting to explode,' suggests David A. Hendler, an
analyst with CreditSights.[5] Other experts have been expressing very similar
opinions.

Investors are angry about these happenings and, as is to be expected, some of the
majors are taking legal action. Pension funds and insurance companies are striking
back. CalPERs has joined with several other pensions funds to sue JP Morgan Chase
and Citigroup, the underwriters of WorldCom's last bond issue, an $11 billion deal,
for alleged lack of due diligence.

Experts say that banks who have entered into the corporates securitization channel
may have to pay up to $5 billion to settle over 300 class actions. Though the majority
of these court cases involve everything from hyping lousy IPOs to favoring their best
banking clients, securitized products that got sour are also in this legal risk picture.
On top of that, there are 25 class actions pending against equity research analysts,
employed by different firms who gave their clients a biased investment advice.

3.8   Compliance risk: a case study with the Year 2000 problem

Compliance is an operational risk with plenty of legal risk characteristics. The case
study in this section comes from the late 1990s. It focuses on compliance regarding

actions defined by the regulators in connection to the Year 2000 (Y2K) problem. Starting with the fundamentals, the Bank of England has defined Y2K compliance in a rigorous way:

- 'To be Y2K compliant you must be able to work any date in the 21st century.'

This definition blew out semi-measures taken by some firms and their consultants to face Y2K, like windowing (using 50 years of 1999 and 50 years of 2000) and other half-baked solutions. It also put into question the statement by everybody who claimed in the abstract: 'We are Y2K compliant.' Among the critical questions to be provided with factual answers have been:

- Is Y2K compliance a factual and documented statement?
- Even *if* the adopted IT solution is today valid, for how long may this be true?

This discussion on compliance will become more meaningful if we briefly examine how the Year 2000 problem came around. Computers started being used in other than military applications in 1954, with the first Univac I delivered that year to General Electric. But punched card equipment still dominated the landscape for another 15 years or so, and punch cards (at least the IBM version) only have 80 columns.

There is not much information one can write in 80 columns. Therefore, better be thrifty. In the 1950s and 1960s, the data processors thought there was no reason to spoil 4 columns to write the year; 2 would do. For instance 1955 could be written as 55. This works well if the application is contained in the twentieth century, but it creates lots of problems with dates in the twenty-first. For instance 55 could be interpreted by the machines as 1955, 2055, or the 55th year of any other century. Hence, the Y2K problem, to which there has been no precedent – but there was plenty of legal risk.

Lawyers did not fail to see the golden opportunity Y2K presented for their services. Until the US Congress acted to put limits to litigation in this specific case of tort, doing so just in time, litigation because of Year 2000 problems was thought to put the torrent of asbestos (see Chapter 12) and tobacco legal cases to shame. Experts said the first moves in a *decades-long* Y2K litigation would be lawsuits against technology companies. They were right.

Getting themselves ready to reap unspoken fees, lawyers attended seminars on how to *bring* and *defend* Y2K cases. Many people suggested that there would be more lawyer-driven cases, than customer-driven ones. Andrew Grove, of Intel, predicted that the US would be tied down in a sea of litigation because of the aftermath of the Year 2000 problem.

It did not happen that way because the law changed. Yet the prediction that technology companies would be in the front line came true. The first Y2K legal case has been by Atlas International, a New York computer vendor. against Software Business Technologies (SBT). The reason was that SBT asked for fees instead of providing a free patch to its software. Macola, a Chicago accounting software vendor, and Symantec were also sued by their clients.

The next domain in Y2K litigation was breach-of-contract suits against corporate officers of publicly quoted companies. The third wave of litigation was expected to involve insurance firms, as defendants sought to force their insurers to cover:

- Legal fees, and
- Damages.

Experts suggested at the time of this third wave that Year 2000 litigation would, in all likelihood, last more than 10 years. Had the US law not changed, and had regulators taken it easy instead of pushing hard the issue of compliance to Y2K fixes, this prediction would have materialized.

The size of the Y2K problem was tremendous. Each big company had 20 million to 30 million programming instructions in its applications software library, which had to be reviewed and all Y2K bugs corrected. Correctly, rather than having to face mammoth maintenance cost while still being left with old, patched-up software, the best managed companies took this opportunity to revamp and renew their applications programming library.

This has been the positive side of Y2K compliance. Yet legal costs of the Y2K bug still run high. The programmers' and computers' cost of Y2K finally stood at the $300 billion to $600 billion range, depending on how the costs are counted; legal costs and settlements in connection to Y2K litigation meant more money spent on this problem. In the US alone, 375 large law firms were active in Y2K litigation mainly involving software products that were materially defective in a Year 2000 sense, and the vendor failed to disclose it.

Before the US law changed, some 200 disputes have been decided out of court with each settlement involving between $1 million and $10 million – even if none of the plaintiffs had so far suffered actual Y2K-related losses. There has as well been an alarm connected to Year 2000 litigation in the insurance industry. The Independent Insurance Agents of America estimated that it could reach $65 billion.[6]

It did not happen that way, but insurers did not know it at the time and, therefore, insurance companies moved quickly to prevent suits by revising their policies, to exclude Y2K claims. The ground for this revision of insurance policies has been that Y2K perils were not known to exist when the policies were written. As a result, premiums were not collected for such coverage and the coverage itself did not exist.

Certified public accounts, too, build up legal defenses. In the UK, the Institute of Chartered Accountants warned that auditors may qualify accounts if there is no adequate record of preparations to adapt computers for Year 2000. While small, privately held companies did not see this as a threat, they were bound to face problems with loan approvals without an:

- Unqualified audit, and
- A Y2K compliance plan.

Had Standard & Poor's, Moody's Investors Service, and the other independent rating agencies taken account of the Year 2000 problem in companies rating? 'We have attempted to factor it in,' said Clifford Griep of S&P in a meeting we held in New York, 'but this is difficult for an outside observer, beyond questioning management.' In Griep's opinion,

- The Y2K is an opaque risk,
- Therefore, S&P encouraged disclosure.

To get as much information on Y2K as it could, S&P sent out a questionnaire. An interesting finding has been that in lots of cases management did not even know where the company stood in Y2K compliance. Few boards were aware of the fact that Y2K problems could hit every firm, including their own. The more far-sighted people suggested that the Year 2000 problem was a good opportunity to:

■ Make companies more transparent, and
■ Exercise a pro-active supervision by regulators.

Being pro-active has been a 'must' because no one was really out of Y2K danger. The regulators got active in promoting Year 2000 compliance because they appreciated that contagion could spread from systems exposed to the millennium bug, to those that had been streamlined. Even organizations who thought they have made the necessary technical adjustments could be vulnerable to disruptions if their business partners, clients, and suppliers failed to take care of Y2K compliance. As time went on, clauses were added to supplier contracts requiring them to be Y2K compliant. This is another reason why the Y2K problem offers a good precedent to several of the legal risk challenges facing companies in the twenty-first century.

Notes

1 The role of rating agencies is discussed in Chapter 13.
2 D.N. Chorafas, *Managing Credit Risk, Volume 2 – The Lessons of VAR Failures and Imprudent Exposure*, Euromoney, London, 2000.
3 D.N. Chorafas, *Stress Testing. Risk Management Strategies for Extreme Events*, Euromoney, London, 2003.
4 *BusinessWeek*, 7 October 2002.
5 *BusinessWeek*, 7 October 2002.
6 *Herald Tribune*, 4 May 1998.

4 Management risk

4.1 Introduction

In the aftermath of the big bankruptcies of 2001–2002, particularly in the United States, experts said that poor management is the most important operational risk. The Bank of England had already pointed that out through a 1997 study that proved that mismanagement was accountable for 19 out of 22 bank failures (see Table 1.1). Other studies have pointed in the same direction, presenting regulators with a salient problem regarding the financial institutions under their control.

'*Management risk*', said the senior executive of one of the global banks I met in London in the course of this research, 'is the No. 1 operational risk. It represents one out of six or seven op risk cases. Next in importance is *event risk*, including internal and external fraud.' Hence, management risk is more of a salient problem than fraud – the classical operational risk.

How poorly are companies really managed? Between the bear market and prosecution of CEOs for creative accounting and other manipulations, investors badly want to know what is their corporate governance exposure. Another interesting question is how it happened that all of a sudden management risk came up to the No. 1 spot in competition to legal risk (Chapter 3) and technology risk (Chapter 5).

The Financial Accounting Standards Board (FASB) says it is looking to refashion its financial statement reporting standards so that companies would not be able to find as many loopholes in financial reporting as they do now.[1] But FASB's regulatory overhaul will take years. In the meantime operational risks relating to management's actions and inactions will persist, and with them:

- The risk of tort, and
- The bending of business ethics.

Here are a couple of examples, with more to follow in the body of this chapter. In the second week of June 2002 Sam Waksal, who until a few weeks earlier was chief executive of ImClone Systems, was arrested on charges of insider dealing. His biotech company was already under regulators' scrutiny for misleading shareholders by withholding sensitive information. Waksal has been formally charged for wrongdoing.

Insider trading is not the only flaw. One of the best examples on how inside management positions are in a win–win situation, is what has followed the bankruptcy of Kmart. As it has been reported in the press, if the company's new chairman James Adamson brings Kmart out of Chapter 11 before 31 July 2003, he will get a pay package of about $8 million, subject to bankruptcy-court approval.

Whether through extravagant bonuses or options, excessive pay levels are also a management risk.

Neither is the $8 million a bankrupt company would have to pay its chairman the only blood-letting. Charles B. Conaway, Kmart's president, will also be richly rewarded. According to a clause on Kmart's performance, and to some other contractual clauses, he could get $16 million over 18 months. All this at a time when:

- Kmart struggles for its survival, and
- Even if it makes it out of bankruptcy it would not automatically become an enterprise able to afford such fat pay packages.[2]

Mismanagement is what brought Kmart into bankruptcy in the first place, and members of its board of directors suffered the consequences of their actions and inactions. The board's troubles include multiple investigations of company accounting, a $501 million profit restatement, and a federal grand jury probe into pay practices. Fat rewards are incompatible with the fact the board has been passive as the company's performance deteriorated before a bankruptcy filing in January 2002. And while Kmart was heading for the rocks the board approved $28 million in retention loans to 25 top executives.

Sweden's Ericsson is another informative case. In 2001 and 2002 it posted $5 billion in losses, and in October 2002 its formerly highly flying shares were selling at under a dollar – as a penny stock. Because new client orders plunged 49%, the company had to lay off 40 000 of its 110 000 workers, but the company was not forthcoming with cancellation of executive bonuses because of poor performance.

In Sweden, Ericsson's president Kurt Hellström is said to be the most hated man in the country. He is regularly vilified in the press. In 2001 one paper made its front page into a mock 'Wanted' poster.[3] Another consequence of mismanagement is that Ericsson's woes, and those of its suppliers, have shaved nearly half of 1 percent off Swedish gross domestic product (GDP).

4.2 Management risk in the power crisis in the United States

It is not always appreciated that the mismanagement of big private companies, who are employers, clients, and suppliers of a certain size, can hit the national economy like a rock. This is particularly true if these companies belong to a country's more sensitive sectors. The power crisis of 2000 and 2001 in California, and more generally in the US Pacific region, provides a vivid example of operational risk associated to corporate management.

Theoretically, the 2000–2001 power crisis in the United States was spiked by high natural gas prices. Practically, the primary reason was structural defects in the power industry which could mean the end of cheap electricity, which during World War II and the post-war years made the Pacific Northwest the center of the US aluminum industry.

Half a century ago, when I was a student at the University of California, energy companies pushed hard to increase power consumption – and the public was happy

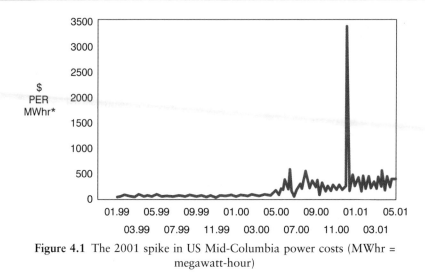

Figure 4.1 The 2001 spike in US Mid-Columbia power costs (MWhr = megawatt-hour)

to oblige. But times have changed. In 2001, the Bonneville Power Administration, a federal agency that supplies about half of the region's power, has requested its utility customers to implement *load reductions* with a view to:

- Cut down demand, and
- Stabilize wholesale power rates, which spiked as shown in Figure 4.1.

The result of this new policy has been that aluminum capacity, totalling 1.43 million metric tons of annual output, which roughly represents 8% of Western world capacity, has been significantly reduced in the US Pacific Northwest. To appreciate this reference, and its effect of energy shortages, it is necessary to recall that the production of aluminum is a very energy-intensive process requiring:

- Bauxite to be refined into alumina,
- Then turned into aluminum through smelting.

Figure 4.2 gives a birds-eye view of production costs, with power at the No. 2 spot. Low cost smelting can only be attained through the availability of low cost and plentiful electricity. This is why many smelters are now found in developing countries where electricity and labor costs are very low. The US Pacific Northwest was an exception, and the reason for this exception was its cheap power.

What happened in 2001 is a livid example of operational risk and its aftermath. In addition to the structural defects that were experienced in California, acute seasonal variations have added to the already serious power problem. Water levels in the region's dams are so low that the Bonneville Power Administration was forced to declare an emergency in order to move water out of storage that would have otherwise been saved for juvenile salmon migration.

The next major structural factor in the US power crisis has been the Pacific region's seemingly ravenous demand for electricity. The resulting crisis put the end of clean

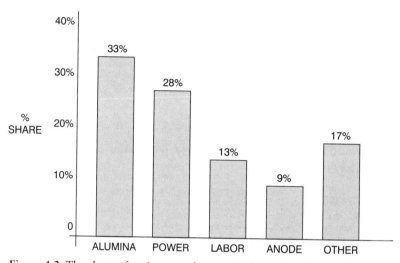

Figure 4.2 The share of major cost chapters in the production of aluminum

power in California squarely on the table, and with it the changing nature of the energy business, in which deregulation has played an important role.

Experts, however, add that while all these factors did play a major role, the lion's share of the energy crisis belongs in the realm of speculation. In November 2002, the State of California accused the energy traders of manipulating the market to cause the energy crisis. Heightened scrutiny led some of the traders to admit to wrongdoing, and lawsuits followed. In the aftermath:

■ Some energy trading firms watched their share prices plunge below $1.
■ By mid-2002, six months after Enron's default, several energy traders put their once highly profitable business up for sale.

California's major power production companies went bankrupt (see section 4.3), but also, nation-wide, other energy companies were confronted by credit woes, in spite of the hefty increase in the price of their produce. In real life, this difference between what might have been a cash flow and earnings glut and the companies' precarious financial situation is made by mismanagement.

By mid-October 2002, the *Wall Street Journal* said that 'The U.S. electric power industry is in its worst credit crunch since the Great Depression,'[4] and it may get worse as electric-energy firms will have to roll over about $50 billion in short-term debt. Standard & Poor's suggested that the debt load contracted in anticipation of growth in a deregulated market and led to half the electric power industry being downgraded to a triple B credit rating.

■ In the first nine months of 2002, there were 135 credit downgrades of utility holding companies, leaving one-third of the major firms on the watch lists.
■ Of the 320 companies followed by Standard & Poor's, 11% were rated at junk bond levels (double B or worse).

Apart from the giant California electric utilities, which filed for bankruptcy protection, Allegheny Electric defaulted on its credit agreements and TXU Corp said a credit downgrade of one of its European units may trigger an early bond repayment. At the equity side, Standard & Poor's Electric Utilities Index fell to its lowest level since the early 1990s. Both bondholders and shareholders paid for the energy companies' mismanagement.

4.3   The changing nature of energy business calls for high grade management skill

The changing nature of the energy business has meant that spot-market price speculation has replaced long-term contracts. This process, it should be noted, is not limited to the energy market. Similar trends are under way among other commodity producers, some of them having preceded the energy market, and all of them falling in an area which shares common ground between credit risk, market risk, and operational risk. Here is an example:

- At present, a single contract for West Texas Crude trades 15 times before it expires.
- This means that for every new barrel of oil pumped onto the market, 15 new *paper barrels* of oil are traded.
- It also provides plenty of opportunity for operational risk problems, including management risk and legal risk.

Both are reflected in prices. California's State Attorney General has sued electricity producers for allegedly overcharging consumers during the state's power crisis.[5] The Federal Energy Regulatory Commission has been slower to act, but California has put legal risk associated to energy manipulation on the table.

The leverage provided by derivative financial instruments has been amplified by organizational acrobatics. An example of operational risks is the transfer of electricity generating capacity out of regulated utilities, which both weakens the ability of state regulators to stop prices from spiking (a market risk), and paves the way for a rapid consolidation of mighty but highly geared power firms (a cross between credit risk and op risk). Enron provides an example – albeit a very bad one.

Looking at these changes, it is useful to recall the comments of former Enron president Jeffrey Skilling to *BusinessWeek*, in an interview published on 12 February 2001. Asked who should own the power plants, Skilling replied: 'Financial institutions, insurance companies, and pensions funds ... [But] they don't like to operate things. They don't like to take the risk on commodity prices. We ought to do that stuff and then sell them the underlying asset with kind of an annuity return.'

The fate of Enron, which filed for bankruptcy on 3 December 2001, is well known. Less known is the fact that the policy Skilling described led to the spike in energy prices – but also to the demise of Enron itself, which I view as an operational risk because it involved so much of management risk. Subsequently, the spike in prices put California's two largest utilities, Pacific Gas & Electric (PG&E) and Southern California's Edison (SCE), under financial stress and led to their bankruptcy.

Both PG&E and SCE were charged sky-high prices for the electricity they bought from the energy traders. Poor management lost control of the situation and they defaulted. Neither company could pass the higher energy costs for purchased electricity on to the customer. They accumulated approximately $12 billion in debts to purchase the higher-priced electricity, on top of another $7 billion of debt they already had in their books. At the end, they could not:

- Pay the debt, and
- Face their other obligations.

This is an operational risk which morphed into credit risk. PG&E and SCE owed substantial sums of money to Bank of America, Wells Fargo, and JP Morgan Chase, as well as to at least two dozen other banks, including Deutsche Bank in Germany and Crédit Agricole in France. Their lenders also included insurance companies, pension funds, and the Treasuries of California counties.

To face this crisis, the State of California created its own operational risk. It took $400 million from the Los Angeles Water District's Treasury, and used it to buy electricity and sell it, at lower prices, to the PG&E and Southern California utilities.[6] What this meant is that the Los Angeles Water District has been subsidising the speculators, so that the utilities could find a way out of the higher and higher costs of energy.

The decision to use water money to feed the speculators was flawed; it temporarily eased the energy crisis, but it did not avert the bankruptcies, as the numbers show. California's total costs for electric power, which were about $7 billion a year until 1999, soared to $27 billion in 2000. According to some reports, they reached nearly $70 billion in 2001. About two-thirds of California's state budget, which till then had America's largest surplus reserve fund, disappeared in the first quarter of 2001. As the state's giant energy companies fell, the smaller, in-state power-generating firms went out of business or took their power off the market.

Economist Steve Cochrane reminded the readers of the *San Francisco Chronicle* that 'everything we produce or consume requires power', and he predicted that the price tag for goods produced in California, and consumed all over the country, will rise 2% to 4%.[7] This was a conservative estimate. The Bureau of Labor Statistics said that the consumer price index for the Bay Area of Northern California had already risen 6.5% from February 2000 to February 2001.

California's citizens and its struggling utilities must be envious of their counterparts in New England. Several times during the past few years New England utilities have stood on the brink of blackouts like those that plagued California. Each time, however, the New England region was saved because:

- It had adopted aggressive energy conservation programs to cut electricity demand, and
- These policies saw to it that the power consumption curve bent somewhat and power outages were averted.

This is a good example of how operational risk can be kept in control through proper policies, provided these are established in time, are observed by everybody, and are shielded from the influence of covert interests and pressure groups. As the New England experience suggests, easing energy woes is not just about increasing supply, it is also about reducing demand through proactive policies which see to it that consumption tapers off, at least until supply catches up with increased challenges.

4.4   An operational risk which morphs into major credit risk

The mismatch of energy supply and demand in the US Pacific Coast region had major consequences that went well beyond the original operational risk. The effects built up over time, with the result that the volatility of equities of US power utilities increased by 220% between 1993 and 2000. The volatility of the Standard & Poor's electric utility stocks reached 22% in 2000 while in 1993 it was 10%.

Related to this has been the change in volatility of cash flows of electric power companies. NERA, a New York-based economic consulting firm, owned by insurance brokerage Marsh & McLennan, analyzed the utilities using *cash flow at risk* (CFAR). For each company, it assembled a group of similarly situated firms. If one member of this group had recently suffered a big cash flow shortfall, this was taken as a sign that the same thing could happen to others. It did. Four key measures had been chosen to help in determining how a company is grouped:

- Market capitalization
- Company profitability
- Stock price volatility, and
- Riskiness of the product line.

At the basic level, this approach makes sense. One shortcoming, however, has been that NERA lumped all the big electric utilities into the same riskiness group, but companies don't have to be in the same industry to be lumped together. Also, like value at risk (VAR), CFAR is based on historical data; it cannot forecast the impact of changes in business. Therefore, it could not have foreseen something like the California power shortages and price spikes.

This is a good lesson in model risk (see also Chapter 5) because sustained price spikes were at the origin of PG&E's and SEC's downfall. Where NERA can help is that the emphasis on cash flow can give warning signs to banks before they throw good money after bad in loans to firms under stress.

Which were the banks that did not interpret a fall in cash flow as a signal of coming trouble? In 2000, Bank of America led a group of credit institutions that extended a $850 million credit line to PG&E. This became part of $3 billion in delinquent credits Bank of America had to write off in 2001, as in April 2001 Pacific Gas & Electric filed under Chapter 11.

JP Morgan Chase had been the leader of a $1 billion credit to Southern California Edison. TIAA-CREF, too, had $336 million worth of bonds issued by the two California power utilities. The Prudential Utility Fund, America's largest utility sector fund, managed $4.5 billion in utility stocks. Big chunks of it have been at risk, in a cascade of power company defaults.

Investment funds that held stocks and bonds issued by the utilities lost their money. The manager of the $1.6 billion Franklin Utilities funds noted that 'the reverberations would be widespread, in the near term'. There were about 40 mutual funds specializing in utility stocks for decades considered to be the safest possible investment. Their total exposure was some $30 billion at risk in the case of a torrent of defaults.

Municipal districts, too, were exposed. The Orange County and Riverside County in California, the first already hit some years earlier because of the collateralized mortgage obligations (CMOs) fiasco, held $40 million in utility notes and commercial paper each. The income from those investments typically finances public schools, public transportation, as well as other essential infrastructure. In the aftermath of the losses budgets had to be cut.

In financial terms, California's operational risk reached international dimensions. In January 2001, Barclays Bank issued a statement that it need not make provision against its exposure to the default by PG&E, but refused to reveal what was its total exposure. Straight afterwards, ABN–Amro bank said that it was not at risk from the California crisis. At Wall Street, however, analysts noted that ABN–Amro was part of a syndicate that had a $4.2 billion agreement with PG&E.

While some of the details connected to red ink have been slow to emerge, it was reported that Japanese, German, and South Korean banks also had substantial exposure in the US utility sector. Experts suggested that because utilities are generally considered to be sound investments, it is not surprising that the problems of two well-known energy companies in California spiralled world-wide.

Neither were investors in energy utilities and banks that lent to near-bankrupt firms the only parties hit by losses. Bond insurers and guarantors were paying out claims on defaulted California utility debt. In January 2001, the Ambac Financial Group reported that its municipal bond division made interest payment on a bond for a California utility that was on the brink of bankruptcy, when it defaulted on payment. In total, Ambac had $75 million in exposure to SCE, and $73 million to PG&E.

Also, MBIA said that it expected claims of about $660 000 because of missed interest payments by Southern California Edison. Moody's reported that MBIA had a total of $445 million of exposure to Edison debt, and $590 million to PG&E debt. Financial Security Assurance, part of the Belgian-French bank group Dexia, also had millions of exposure to SCE and to PG&E. Bermuda-based ACE had about $138 million in aggregate exposure to both utilities, representing 15% of its capital base.

The size of the largely unexpected bankruptcies was of such dimensions that the thought that even California's two largest public power utilities might default on billions of dollars of short-term debt threw shareholders, bondholders, and lenders into a panic. Belatedly it was realized that a decade of poor management had brought the formerly mighty energy utilities to the abyss.

Speculation mounted on how the final bill would look. Experts said that default by the two California energy companies would set off at least $20 billion in cross-defaults on the utilities' other debts, and possibly the loss of electrical power in the state. This projection was based on the fact Southern California Edison and Pacific Gas & Electric had suddenly built up a horrendous short-term debt, borrowing from banks to pay wholesale electricity prices two orders of magnitude above what they were a year or so earlier. They were paying these hyperinflated rates to:

- Enron
- Reliant Energy
- Dynergy, and
- Duke Power.

These four companies had bought up California's power-generating plants under the deregulation act passed by Congress in 1996. Enron was still a going concern in early 2001, and in an arrogant way it was leading the pack of speculators blackmailing utilities in many parts of the US for power and natural gas. At the time, Enron's shareholders, bondholders, and lenders had no inkling of what was in store for them a few months down the line.

In an effort to stave off the crisis which hit California as a result of management risk, Gray Davis, the governor, held emergency meetings on 28–29 December 2000 with president Bill Clinton, Treasury Secretary Lawrence Summers, and Federal Reserve Chairman Alan Greenspan. Bloomberg News service quoted a Chase Manhattan economist warning that with US banks shutting off lending, 'a credit issue can pose the potential to become a systemic threat'.

Bloomberg drew an analogy between the Federal Reserve's emergency bailout in September 1998 of Long Term Capital Management (LTCM), aimed to save the stock market and derivatives market, and the looming default of California's utilities in 2001. LTCM's failure was the result of another major management risk.[8] The Fed of New York was more successful in its 1988 salvage operation than the US government in keeping the utilities above water.

As one misfortune never comes alone, the financial crisis of the California power utilities triggered a natural gas crisis as well: By late 2000 pipeline companies, including Enron, refused further sales of natural gas unless Southern California Edison and PG&E paid cash in advance for the deliveries. They also threatened to cut off electricity sales on the ground that the utilities would not be able to pay for them.

Then, on 4 January 2001, California's State Public Utility Commission raised the electric rates for customers of Southern California Edison by 9%, but as the subsequent bankruptcy of PG&E has shown this did the utilities no good. Instead, the utilities' stocks fell sharply, and Moody's Investors Service warned of further downgrade in their credit rating. The irony is that after the lambs were eaten, the wolf, Enron, died as well.

4.5 The derivatives losses of EDS: a different management risk

In the week of 16 September 2002, the equity of Electronic Data Systems (EDS), the computer services insourcer, fell more than 52% on its warning that earnings would be sharply lower than expected. Following that surprise profit warning by EDS' management, Merrill Lynch touched off a new rout after saying it believed the second largest IT insourcing company in the world was facing a major loss from its use of derivatives. Gambling and losing with derivatives:

- Hit hard the insourcer's bottom line, and
- Made it more difficult for the firm to fund large insourcing deals, because of their up-front capital costs.

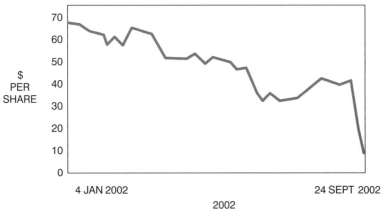

Figure 4.3 The 2002 crash of EDS' equity

On 24 September 2002 the shares of Electronic Data Systems plunged for a second time in less than a week. Investors were concerned about the company's huge loss on its derivatives trades – definitely a non-core business – that could wipe out its 2002 cash flow. The market's fears knocked a further 29% off the company's battered stock price, with shares closing down $4.84 at $11.68. Figure 4.3 dramatizes the downfall.

Speculative losses are always a sign of management risk, and customers took notice. After EDS shares began their free fall, in mid-September 2002, Procter & Gamble delayed awarding EDS an expected $8 billion outsourcing contract. The message the market got out of this piece of news was that:

- *If* Procter & Gamble, considered to be a well-managed company, kept its distance,
- *Then* this could be related to worries about the survivability of EDS, and the operational risks assumed by its clients.

Incidentally, this has not been the first time EDS faced management risk. When Ross Perrot quit General Motors' board, the company he left behind became more or less a mismanaged outfit. The automobile manufacturer was not versatile in selling computer-related services. Eventually, GM decided that it had better spin off EDS.

With the spin-off, management risk seems to have increased. In 1999 Richard H. Brown became the CEO of EDS, and the new chief executive focused his attention on outsourcing deals that provide steady revenue growth over their multiyear lifespan. This means emphasis on large, longer-term insourcing agreements which, however, have very significant start-up costs. These costs involve:

- Buying the client's data center
- Hiring its employees, and
- Carrying on a swarm of financial and technical responsibilities connected to insourcing.[9]

These deals were supposed to give EDS rich cash flows and 'guaranteed' profitability. In reality, however, they had a negative impact on both cash flow and profitability – at least in the shorter term. As if this was not enough, it subsequently came out that management misguided itself (and others) because EDS used a method known as *percentage-of-completion*.

- With it, costs and payoffs are estimated over the life of the deal,
- Then, as work is completed the customer is billed on a monthly or quarterly basis.

This approach is not uncommon with large projects, but it constitutes an operational risk because it inflates costs by bringing them upfront in a medium-to-longer term timeframe. It also makes miscalculations very costly. When EDS, or any other company, overestimates a contract's profitability, it has to:

- Take a charge to cover the loss, and
- Retroactively apply a lower, revised profit margin.

Besides that, the percent-of-completion method leaves ample room for wishful thinking and for errors, which add a great deal to the company's liabilities. The reader should keep in mind that, unlike banks but like certified public accountants, consulting companies and insourcers do not have a treasury able to withstand major financial shocks.

Severe shocks that put a company in peril can arise for several reasons. One of them lies half-way between operational risk and counterparty risk. In July 2002, EDS had to swallow $101 million losses from its huge contract with WorldCom when the latter went bankrupt. It also had to write off $69 million from its insourcing deal with also bankrupt US Airways.

These, and others, have been operational risks related to the type of business EDS had decided to pursue – and they were beyond the domain that could be described as *expected losses*. If indeed they were expected, then EDS should not have entered into longer-term insourcing contracts with companies who were on the brink of the abyss.

Management risk at EDS did not end there. The steep decline in the company's equity since the mid-September 2002 profit warning exposed its derivatives' extra-curricular activities. Like some other big technology companies, EDS used derivatives to try to reduce the cost of issuing shares under its employee stock options plans.

Steve McClellan, an analyst at Merrill Lynch, said EDS had settled derivative obligations related to 3.7 million shares on Friday 20 September 2002, at a cash cost of $225 million. Rod Bourgeois, an analyst at Sanford Bernstein, added the high-profile nature of EDS' profit warning could attract the attention of the Securities and Exchange Commission.

Other analysts were just as cutting in their comments. In different terms, EDS fell prey to its own greed using options for hedging the growing (if irrational) wave of executive options. The exact details pertaining to this particular foray into shareholders' equity are not precisely known, but participants at my London seminar on outsourcing and insourcing volunteered, as an example, the case of executive options-and-derivatives at Storebrand, the well-known Norwegian insurance company.

To cover the stock options it gave to its executives, Storebrand bought options from an investment bank. However, because the management of the insurer found that these hedging options were too expensive, it asked for better conditions and the investment bank offered to reduce the price, *if* no compensation were provided in case the insurance company's stock price dropped by 'x' percent. It did, and the same had happened to EDS.

In Storebrand's case, as long as the insurance company's price increased, there were no problems and no complaints. But then the market did not oblige; the stock price went down by more than 'x' percent. This saw to it there was no more option coverage. As a result, the insurance company lost money and the executive options ended by diluting shareholder equity in a big way. Quite likely something similar has happened to EDS, and to many other companies whose management has become some sort of sorcerer's apprentice.

■ The hedge provided by option coverage is often seen by management as a sort of compensation for the executive options because, when exercised, the options would be booked at market price.
■ In a bear market, however, such plans are chicken-brained. There are made by mismanagers who think it is possible to have your cake and eat it too.

With this sort of background in terms of management risk, financial analysts were puzzled about another questionable decision by EDS, namely to enter the market of *treasury outsourcing*. Some analysts asked why a company that could not manage its own treasury should want to manage the treasury of others – let alone the fact that companies which are outsourcing their treasury are simply looking for trouble.

Investors have also been questioning the generous 2001 $55 million pay package of EDS CEO Richard H. Brown, over and above the costly bet on EDS's stock options. Management risk was further brought under the spotlight when the company said third-quarter profits would fall as much as 84% short of estimates, to $58 million, due to slowing client spending and write-offs from problem contracts. Investors were not pleased by the fact senior management gratified itself with millions when:

■ Revenues, which were already revised downward to a 4–6% growth rate, were expected to decline by another 5%, and
■ The outlook for the fourth quarter of 2002 was dismal as well, with no clear signs of short-to-medium-term recovery in 2003 and beyond.

In conclusion, management risk and the options gamble left EDS $225 million poorer. Investors were angry not only for the losses but also because all this was done in secrecy. EDS said it did not disclose the deals because they were made in the 'normal course of business'. But the news set off fears that, as management risk mounted, EDS could face a cash crunch and have difficulty competing for capital-intensive contracts.

4.6 Management risk at Tyco International

Based in Bermuda with headquarters in Exeter, New Hampshire, at its high-water mark Tyco International had 240 000 employees and its products ranged from security systems and safety devices to financials and syringes. In the late 1990s the conglomerate was attracting the market's attention in a big way. Its investors considered it to be a sort of multi-identity holding company. But, in February 2002,

■ Fears about its opaque accounting had branded Tyco 'the next Enron', and
■ As investors fled, the market vaporized more than $160 billion in Tyco's capitalization.

Many lessons can be learned from the demise of Tyco. One of them is that investor indulgence does not help. When the shares of Tyco International were still rising in 1998, some of the main shareholders proposed that the company's board should be restructured to make a majority of its members independent. This resolution was defeated, partly because Fidelity Investment voted against it.

More independent directors might not have saved Tyco, but analysts did not fail to note that Fidelity's vote consistently supported the position of Tyco's management. The fact is that investors tend to abdicate their role as company owners:

■ When share prices soar, many institutional investors vote with management.
■ Then, when things go wrong, some institutional investors admit that, as equity owners (on behalf of individual savers), they should have done more to curb corporate excesses.

Because they had shied away from their responsibilities, institutional investors had only themselves to blame when management risk hit home in a big way. The market gave no reprieve; it saw to it that Tyco's $12 billion-plus in commercial paper and other debt obligations coming due through June 2002 came into the danger zone. CIT, Tyco's financial arm, said that an $8 billion bank line it tapped and another $4 billion to $5 billion more in securitization facilities, was covered for five months or so. The market had its doubts.

■ CIT was America's largest independent commercial-finance outfit, before Tyco bought it.
■ Suddenly, it was faced by enormous capital needs and it had trouble responding to them.

Even *if* CIT's problems were not present, Tyco's CEO, L. Dennis Kozlowski, had to deal with a mountain of debt left over from the $63 billion acquisition spree he went through between 1995 and 2001. After Enron went to the dogs, analysts and investors became aware that, by December 2001, Tyco's industrial companies had debts of $28.3 billion. This was more than 40% up from just $20 billion in March of that same year.

■ When this news became public, as 2001 came to an end, Tyco's stock slid in a matter of a few days to about $23 from $53.
■ When Standard & Poor's cut Tyco's credit rating by three notches in one shot, it effectively shut the company out of the commercial paper market.

Left without clout in a capital market suspicious of its financial condition, Tyco had to draw on its $8 billion backup bank lines of credit. Some analysts suggested that if dozens of companies were forced to follow, banks might soon face a liquidity crisis of their own. Others pointed out that management risk is somehow often able to lie dormant, until it explodes in a spectacular way.

Tyco is a good example of how some companies keep massaging their numbers, and take pains to avoid regulatory disclosure. Eventually, the market retaliates. The moment came when Tyco International was hit the hardest among S&P 500 companies: its stock plunged 51% in the first five weeks of 2002, and the slide gathered speed after the company said it had spent $8 billion since 1999 on acquisitions it had not fully disclosed to shareholders. Figure 4.4 shows the equity's impressive ups and downs.

Yet even after Tyco's equity had crashed, some analysts kept on recommending it to investors as a double *strong buy*. On 25 April 2002, a comment from Merrill Lynch, signed Phua Young, CFA, first vice president, and Farukh Z. Farooqui, vice president, stated in big letters:

■ 'Stock is a good value, Strong Buy'
■ 'Long Term, Strong Buy'

The more detailed comment was: 'Liquidity looks to be adequate. Near term, the change in strategy could require some time for investors to digest. However, even

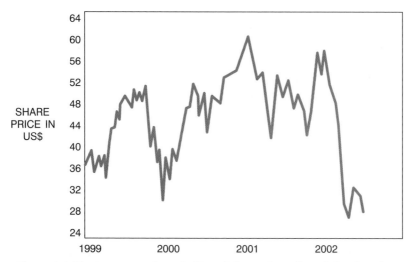

Figure 4.4 Playing yo-yo: the volatility of the equity reflected the changing fortunes of Tyco International

more importantly, the company's financial position appears to be good.' To say this is utterly misleading is to state the obvious. Some analysts render investors a negative service – which is an operational risk.

What those two analysts essentially advised investors was that Tyco is a *good value* stock for patient people. To their belief, the shares were attractive value because: 'As Tyco delivers results, and improves transparency, the shares and the P/E have healthy upside potential.' According to the two analysts' opinion, potential catalysts included:

- A higher level of confidence in management to execute (!)
- More in line results with strong cash flow (!)
- Discounting of the economic recovery
- Overcoming the transparency issue.

Listen to that 'higher level of confidence in management' four months after the leveraged empire began to unravel. Trying to pull itself up from its shoestrings in January 2002, a demoralized Tyco was making plans to split itself into four different companies. The market did not take it kindly, and Kozlowksi retracted.

In early February 2002 Tyco cancelled the planned initial public offering of CIT, its financial arm, cutting, at the same time, the company's full-year earnings estimate. Things had not improved a single notch when in late April 2002 Merrill Lynch recommended the stock as a strong buy.

By early May 2002, after Tyco International had abandoned plans to split itself into four companies, and after it unveiled a $1.9 billion loss in the second quarter, management said the firm would cut 7100 jobs and close 24 factories, mainly in telecoms and electrical equipment, due to weak trading conditions. At the same time, Tyco announced it would continue with an initial public offering of CIT, which it valued at $6.5 billion.

At Wall Street the experts doubted Tyco could raise that much money from the sale of CIT. Even if it did, it would still face a hefty loss. Tyco had bought CIT for almost $10 billion in cash and stock in 2001 – less than a year earlier. Management risk in this case stood at about 50% of CIT's value. More precisely, at 54%, as CIT was finally sold for $4.6 billion. That's one way to put a price tag on management risk.

The prospect of somehow getting some badly needed cash from somewhere was enough to temporarily put a lid on the tanking of Tyco's stock price. It also, up to a point, smoothed the gyrations of its bonds. However, drawing down the parent company's and CIT's bank lines contributed to more rumours. Tyco was caught in a spiral.

- A plan that it was thought would boost the share price by 50% backfired and actually cut it in half.
- As its financial condition turned from bad to worse, Tyco took one big write-off after another.

In October 2002 the write-off was some $2.5 billion for its disastrous foray into the undersea cable-telecom market. This came on top of a $6.7 billion write-down it took in early 2002 on the sale of Tyco's CIT for a mere $4.6 billion. Averting a liquidity crisis was not easy. While the sale of CIT helped boost Tyco's cash level to about $7 billion, nearly half of its short-term debt, which by then stood at $13 billion, was coming due by the end of 2002.

- As previous estimates of cash flow continued to be downsized, it looked like Tyco could come up way too short of what it needed.
- And there was still an awful lot of uncertainty, because lower margins and higher tax rates cut its earnings.

Companies that have gone through similar pains know that fire sales are no good way to raise cash, though they are evidence of bad management. Being squeezed for cash to the point of oblivion, Tyco had no chance to get more than a fraction of the premium paid by Kozlowski to buy companies during the bull market. Deeply discounted sales also forced further write-downs in the bloated $27 billion of goodwill Tyco still carried on its balance sheet. This, too, was a miscalculation and therefore an operational risk.

4.7 The CEO should be an example of virtue, not of malfeasance

Socrates defined virtue as knowledge that cannot be taught. If so, there are no teachers of virtue though there are virtuous people. Judging from the long list of prosecution counts which piled up in 2002 against Tyco's former CEO for alleged accounting fraud and tax evasion, Dennis Kozlowski was no virtuous person. He simply represented another example of management risk which became part of the problem of corporate America.

One of the things Kozlowski has in common with Kenneth Lay, Enron's former CEO, is that he turned an obscure company into a high-powered conglomerate. Tyco originally was a New England electronics maker. Enron used to be a gas pipeline. Another common characteristic is that both companies were a blip in industrial history: They started low, leveraged themselves, rose fast, and then plummeted to ground.

The executive life of Kozlowski, while chief of Tyco International, was characterized by spectacular spending during the boom times of the stockmarket and of the firm. Ironically, however, it was alleged tax evasion in New York which first landed him in legal trouble.

The original charges brought against Kozlowski alleged that he evaded sales tax on works of art, aggravated by grand larceny, corruption, falsification of records, and securities fraud. If convicted, he could face decades behind bars. Also charged are Mark Schwartz, former chief financial officer, and Mark Belnick, former corporate counsel of Tyco.

As time went on, more charges accumulated. By June 2002, Dennis Kozlowski faced new challenges because of alleged tampering with evidence, as law enforcement officials pursued their investigation. He was arraigned in New York State Supreme Court on charges that alleged he removed a shipping document from files kept at Tyco's offices at Boca Raton, Florida, before the file was delivered to the office of Robert Morgenthau, Manhattan District Attorney.

Other top brass at Tyco also came under spotlight, after the charges against Kozlowski sparked a broader investigation of Tyco's affairs, including whether there was a possible misuse of company funds to buy homes for senior executives. Tyco's new management filed lawsuits against Mark Belnick alleging that he received inappropriate payments.

The strategy of Tyco's new management was that of suing to recover allegedly looted funds and other assets, including a $17 million Fifth Avenue apartment, a $7 million Park Avenue apartment, another $5 million home, and the $30 million compound in Boca Raton, Florida. Smaller items allegedly bought with company money included a $17,000 sponge bag.

The Securities and Exchange Commission has also been examining whether the conglomerate's financial statements properly reported the dealings of its senior executives. Kozlowski was been accused by the SEC of running his company like a 'private bank', handing out hundreds of millions in unauthorized loans, and lavishing exorbitant gifts on himself and his lieutenants. At Wall Street, many analysts said that:

- Tyco's former CEO will be remembered as being at the top of a great corporate malfeasance by the company's own management, and
- Tyco itself will go down in business history books as a company that was not run on management principles, as companies are supposed to be.

Even as Tyco International ballooned to a $36 billion giant with 240 000 employees, Dennis Kozlowski allowed only a relative handful of trusted lieutenants to work with him at Tyco's headquarters, keeping out any prying eyes. This is precisely the environment where management risk multiplies. In September 2002, Tyco's new management said Kozlowksi arranged the payment of $96 million in bonuses to 51 employees so that they would pay off:

- Loans from the company, and
- Tax liability resulting from the forgiveness of those loans.

There were strings attached to this outrageous gift. All 51 beneficiaries were asked to sign an agreement that they would forfeit the money if they told anyone other than their lawyers and accountants about it. Kozlowski also concluded a secret agreement with Mark Belnick, which tied Belnick's remuneration to Kozlowksi's, thereby giving the corporate lawyer an undisclosed incentive to aid and facilitate the CEO's improper diversion of company funds.[11]

Operational risk at Tyco did not end there. As it was eventually revealed, not one or two but many of Tyco's supposedly independent directors had direct financial dealings with the company and the board altogether lacked vigilance. For instance, one director, Joshua M. Berman, was receiving $360 000 annually for 'legal services', according to SEC filings. That is small fry compared with the $20 million fee Kozlowksi paid to 'lead director' Frank E. Walsh, Jr for his services in helping to arrange Tyco's disastrous 2001 acquisition of commercial finance company CIT.[12]

But greed tends to retreat when the money-grabbing becomes public. Tyco's board finally forced Dennis Kozlowski to resign as chairman and chief executive, shortly before he was charged with tax evasion and related offences by New York authorities in connection with his purchase of valuable Impressionist paintings. Many more secrets became known by way of Kozlowski's indictment on tax evasion charges, and the events which followed it. The equity's rout gave Wall Street's short-sellers their day of glory.

4.8   Conflicts of interest: from IPOs to disappearing technology firms

Nobody would really question that the low business ethics of the late 1990s led to the débâcles of 2000–2002. Enron, Tyco International, ImClone Systems, Kmart, Adelphia Communications, Global Crossing, WorldCom are but a few examples of what has been going on behind the backs of unsuspecting investors who were being taken to the cleaners. The background to all this is lust and greed – but also conflict of interest, which is an operational risk.

In the mid-1990s to 2001 timeframe a major conflict of interest among investment banks was connected to initial public offerings (IPOs) and the unwarranted hanging of *strong buy* signs on their analyses and stock ratings (see section 4.6). Brokers were using their investment analysts to promote investment banking business. In early 2002, Crédit Suisse First Boston (CSFB) paid $100 million to settle charges that it gave certain hedge funds IPO shares in exchange for inflated commissions on other stock trades. CSFB also faced possible criminal charges on other IPO-related abuses.

In May 2002, Merrill Lynch also paid $100 million to settle charges by New York State Attorney General Eliot Spitzer that it traded favorable ratings on Internet stocks to bolster its investment banking activities. Eliot Spitzer, who called such actions a shocking betrayal of trust by one of Wall Street's most trusted names, has also been investigating Citigroup's Salomon Smith Barney for both IPO abuses and tainted research.

The National Association of Securities Dealers (NASD), too, has been investigating Salomon Smith Barney, charging it with issuing materially misleading reports on the telecommunications company Winstar. Salomon agreed to pay a trivial $5 million fine as Winstar, the company it promoted, collapsed. 'What occurred in this case was a serious breach of trust between Salomon and its investors,' said Mary Schapiro, NASD's head of regulatory policy.[13] Indeed there has been a serious breach of trust, but who is to right the balances?

Initial public offering was not the only game in town that defrauded investors. Some of the brokers recommended to their clients as *buys* companies that simply faded away from the radar screen – in the same mysterious manner they had come alive a few years earlier. Toronto- and Hong Kong-based Semi-Tech Group went public in 1993, and collapsed in 1999, wiping out the nest egg of thousands of investors, and leaving behind a huge trail of debt. The crash of its equity is dramatized in Figure 5.

A holding company, the Semi-Tech Group specialized in the rescue of fallen angels: well-known but tarnished brand names such as America's Singer Sewing Machine, and Japan's Sansui Electric, a manufacturer of consumer electronics. Theoretically at least, Semi-Tech employed 100 000 workers in a global setting said to include120 countries (!). Also theoretically, it racked up almost $5 billion in sales. By the mid-1990s, the

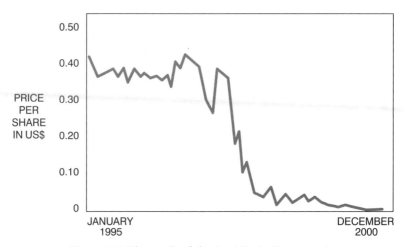

Figure 4.5 The crash of the Semi-Tech Group equity

'Group' boasted listings in stock markets around the world, including New York, Tokyo, Frankfurt, Hong Kong, and Bombay.

Post mortem, even critics admit that James Ting, Semi-Tech's founder, was successful at rebuilding companies that were not in great shape when he acquired them. But what has happened subsequently to these companies and to the equity they represented is anybody's guess.

Some people say Ting took the money and ran. Others are of the opinion he overplayed his hand leading to a chain of failures. No matter what the basic reason might have been, Ting's global web of businesses unravelled, culminating in the largest corporate collapse in Hong Kong history. AKAI Holdings, Ting's main Hong Kong subsidiary, fell apart after recording a $1.75 billion loss in 1999. By early 2000, most of the companies controlled by his holding:

■ Had stopped doing business
■ Slid into bankruptcy, or
■ Were absorbed by other firms at bargain basement prices.

Whatever happened, investors lost big sums. The crash left lenders and bondholders with unpaid debts estimated at $2 billion. In Hong Kong alone, HSBC tried to recover some $200 million, potentially its largest loan loss in more than 135 years of operating in the former British colony. On the surface, this is credit risk, but as a careful examination reveals, at the bottom line it has many operational risk characteristics – and above all management risk.

Notes

1 *BusinessWeek*, 4 November 2002.
2 *BusinessWeek*, 11 March 2002.

3 *BusinessWeek*, November 2002.
4 *Wall Street Journal*, 15 October 2002.
5 *BusinessWeek*, 16 December 2002
6 *EIR*, 6 April 2001.
7 *San Francisco Chronicle*, 26 March 2001.
8 D.N. Chorafas, *Managing Risk in the New Economy*, New York Institute of Finance, New York, 2001.
9 D.N. Chorafas, *Outsourcing, Insourcing and IT for Enterprise Management*, Macmillan/Palgrave, London, 2003.
10 *Financial Times*, 25 September 2002.
11 *Financial Times*, 25 September 2002.
12 *BusinessWeek*, 30 September 2002.
13 *EIR*, 4 October 2002.

5 Information technology risk

5.1 Introduction

A sophisticated information technology (IT) system can be instrumental in controlling some types of operational risk. At the same time, however, IT creates new operational risks, all the way from bookkeeping and payments to systems reliability and model risk. Low technology makes matters worse. This chapter explains why, and it suggests ways to bend the curve of IT-related operational risks.

For starters, information technology is pervasive. In the G-10 countries and many others, it can be found in any activity undertaken by modern enterprises. All automated processes are exposed to technology risk. Therefore, to study the operational risks associated to IT, we must first identify and make an inventory of what we have in:

- Computer applications
- Databased information
- Basic software endowment(s)
- Physical network(s), and so on.

This concerns not only software and hardware but also the processes running on the computers.

This being done, we must focus on risks such as:

- Threats to information
- Vulnerability in architecture
- Vulnerability in applications
- Vulnerability in security.

Not everything is quantifiable. As José Sanchez-Crespo, of A.M. Best, suggested to me: 'You cannot quantify all information technology risks. Some of them are more qualitative than quantitative.' System reliability is quantitative (see section 5.6); analysis and programming have both quantitative and qualitative aspects – and the same is true of model risk.

Some models are complex. But even if they are simple, how can we value somebody's incompetence in using the model? This question is vital because banks tend to rely on models for transaction control and can end up in a loop of uncontrollable actions.

One of the problems is that we do not have enough data to model IT risk. *If* we wish to get results in controlling exposure connected to IT, *then* the search for technology-related operational risk must be specific. An example is the role of computers, communications, and sophisticated software in risk management, and the deliverables which we get.

The good news is that knowledge and experience can be instrumental in controlling information technology risk – from overall system perspective all the way to implementation details. What did we learn from 45 years of computer applications, databases, and communications experience in banking? The A,B,C can be phrased in these terms:

- A   The able usage of information systems is a matter of *culture* – not of machines.
- B   We get little from our investment unless we have *clear goals*, and effectively use technology to reach them.
- C   Without challenging the 'obvious', results will be minimal while op risks will run high.

This emphasizes the importance of getting out of old structures that limit our ability to obtain results, and cost too much for the service they provide. The computer as we have known it for nearly five decades is dead. The new master of the technological domain is *system solutions*, which require both insight and foresight. We must use our experience in a productive and pragmatic way. The know-how we acquire should be applied to the job, it should not be left as a theory.

5.2   Technology risk defined

In an advanced industrial society, a company's operations are highly dependent on the integrity of its technology systems. Its success depends, in great part, on its ability to mine increasingly rich databases and make timely decisions in anticipation of client demands and industry changes. A company needs rich databases to be in control of risks assumed in the environment in which it operates.

A company's business is negatively impacted if it experiences system interruptions, errors or downtime; and also if it falls behind its competitors in the information technology which it uses – and the way in which it is using it. Therefore, every company must be committed to an ongoing process of upgrading, enhancing, and testing its technology, to effectively meet:

- Sophisticated client requirements
- Market and regulatory changes, and
- Evolving internal needs for information and knowledge management.

Technology risk includes the failure to respond to these prerequisites, as well as many other issues such as: human error; internal fraud through software manipulation; external fraud by intruders; obsolescence in applications and machines; reliability issues, mismanagement; and the effect of natural disasters. Technology risk is manageable, but it takes a significant amount of *will* and *skill* to do it.

Of all the operational risks connected to IT, which were briefly outlined in the preceding paragraphs, mismanagement may well be the most deadly. Not only in the general case is information technology seriously mismanaged, but there is also a trend to outsourcing, often improperly considered as relegation of senior management's responsibility for IT to a third party.[1]

Over the years, available computer power has tremendously increased; this however cannot be said of the sophistication of applications and of systems solutions. Figure 5.1 emphasizes this bifurcation between spending money on information technology and getting tangible benefits out of it. The difference is made by management, both at corporate level and of IT operations themselves.

- Companies benefit from advanced, highly competitive computer applications.
- The laggards pay the costs, but get meager results because they mainly think of the past, not of the future.

Today, continuing to program in Cobol is not just an operational risk, it is a criminal offence. What is surprising is that by 'tradition' rather than by choice, the majority of companies continue being criminal offenders.

A similar statement is valid about the continuing use of mainframes, which cost an inordinate amount of money for the trivial computer power they deliver. Client-servers, disk farms, and supercomputers are the answer. In the early 1990s supercomputer performance has been typically characterized by millions of floating-point operations per second (megaflops). Today, there are more than 50 super-computers on the Top 500 list delivering peak performance over a trillion floating-point operations per second (teraflops). This capacity has enabled their users to:

- Generate complex simulations, and
- Operate on high resolution grids.

High technology permits *visualization* (turning numbers into graphs and images), *visibilization* and *visistraction* (see section 5.4). These are powerful tools but few companies know how to use them. Any institution, or any other firm, which fails to

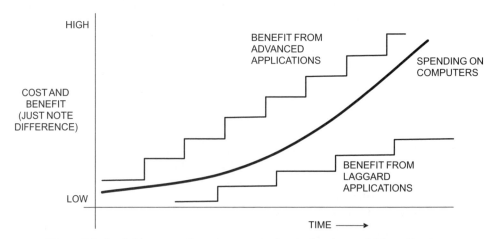

Figure 5.1 Available computing power and advanced *vs* laggard IT applications

capitalize on the best that technology can offer purposely exposes itself to operational risk.

Figure 5.1 and the preceding paragraphs drew attention to the fact that while practically all companies spend large amounts of money on computers, communications, and software only the leaders really benefit from their investments. Spending big sums of money on technology without the corresponding return of investment (ROI) is an IT-related operational risk. Take the financial industry as an example.

As an enabling technology, electronic banking significantly increases the complexity of business operations, which is being further intensified by the ongoing process of concentration in the banking industry. But while mergers are frequently seen as a means for cost savings, ROI is rarely a clear goal when approving IT expenditures (more on this later).

I classify routine in information technology operations, the so-called legacy systems, as a major IT-related operational risk. It is one of the important reasons why banks do not get their money's worth out of IT investments. There is also, however, plenty of other IT-related operational risk. The evidence collected in my research in 2002 among leading financial institutions indicates that banks consider IT as their second (or, sometimes, third) most important and most consistent operational risk. In the majority of cases, the approaches they take to control it are heterogeneous, lacking both:

- A common ground, and
- An enterprise-wide system view.

One of the major flaws is the continuing use of legacy applications as their basic frame of reference. This not only limits the implementation perspective but it also keeps the bank in a backwater. An example based on 12 crucial applications within one financial institution is shown in Table 5.1. It distinguishes between:

	Currently is	Should be
Currency risk	Partially RT	RS
Global market risk	Batch	RS
Interest rate risk	Partially RT	RS
Exchange rate risk	Partially RT	RS
Credit risk	Batch	RT
Investment risk	Batch	RT
Event risk	No IT support	RT
Position risk	Batch	RS
Sales conditions risk	Limits Only	RS
Funds transfer risk	No IT support	RT
Settlement risk	Batch	RS
Transaction processing risk	No IT support	RT

RT, real-time; RS, realspace.

Table 5.1 The missing technology for controlling risk at most financial institutions

- *Batch*, which was a solution of the 1950s, and today is an obscenity.
- *Real-time* with data capture at point of origin and instantaneous on-line information delivery at point of destination.
- *Realspace*, which is real-time on a global setting, collapsing operations which may be in five continents into real-time interactive reporting.

It can be easily seen that the information technology solution followed by this institution is substandard. It is way behind state of the art, and it is full of operational risks related to the use of obsolete concepts. Event risk, funds transfer risk, and transaction processing risk are not even supported by IT. Global market risk, credit risk, investment risk, position risk, and settlement risk are handled overnight in batch. By the time senior management gets the information, the bank may well have gone under.

Yet, this financial institution – like so many others among its competitors – spends an inordinate amount of money on IT. A big chunk of its technology risk is that its top management, and its IT specialists, fail to appreciate there is a world of difference between legacy approaches and new, competitive solutions which are able to respond to twenty-first century requirements. In terms of sophistication, the pattern shown in Figure 5.2 differs by an order of magnitude.

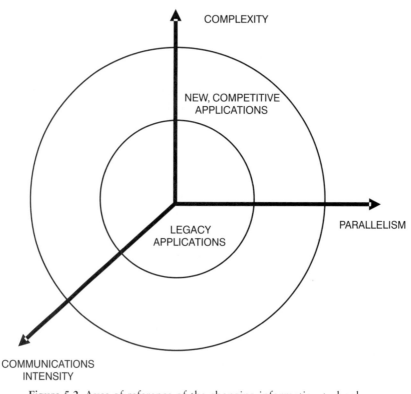

Figure 5.2 Axes of reference of the changing information technology environment and its systems perspective

At the top of the list of operational risks which I have found in connection to IT solutions, I distinguish:

- Risk of falling behind in IT
- Project management risk
- Quality and sophistication of software risk
- Risk of slow applications development
- Vendor failure risk, and
- Risk related to third party outsourcing.

Vendors can fail, but few companies have paid enough attention to protecting themselves against this eventuality. The usual approach is to put all of one's eggs in the same basket, quite often that of the bigger vendors. This is a very limited vision and it is wrong because big vendors, too, can fail. Look at Digital Equipment Corp. (We will return to this issue.)

5.3 The growing role of IT and its risks

In today's global markets, enterprises succeed or fail based on the speed with which they can respond to changing market conditions. Properly chosen and correctly used, information technology is a vital ingredient of rapid response. The fast development of sophisticated software is the cornerstone to competitiveness; therefore business solutions need to be put in place faster than ever before. Contrary to rules prevailing during the Palaeolithic age of computing (1960s and 1970s):

- In many cases it is no longer practical to build new business applications from the ground up.
- Nor is it always viable to deploy a package solution, as packages do not keep up with new, specific company needs.

Where business competitiveness is at stake, the answer is rapid prototyping and a fast track to implementation. Assembling a business application from software components is like using ready-made parts to build a car or house. The fast track offers a competitive solution to the dual problem of:

- Speed of response, and
- Flexibility in adaptation and upkeep.

At the same time, however, IT costs must be contained. Rapid software development is a good way to do so, because a huge component in the IT budget is personnel costs. Another vital ingredient in cost control is the avoidance of duplication of effort in regard to data capture, through a policy of one entry, many uses.

In classical 'electronic data processing' (EDP), the same information element is entered up to seven times. The average number of re-entries used to be 3.5. Now the average is 2.8. This is still too high, let alone the error in transcription which comes into the IT system through multiple entries made in incompatible formats and addressing heterogeneous files – usually corresponding to discrete islands of application.

No wonder that data entry costs and subsequent clearance of embedded errors have been consuming 20–25% of the IT budget in many companies. The best policy is one entry, many uses, but its implementation demands a deal of organization and self-discipline. Both are lacking from the majority of IT operations in the banking industry, with the result that operational risks are ballooning.

Another crucial policy in restructuring information technology operations, one that will have significant impact on operational risk control, is the emphasis that should be placed on system analysis for advanced applications. To appreciate that statement it is wise to underline the fact that, contrary to what is generally believed, the *main* objective of computing is not reduction in paperwork and clerical operations, but:

- Foresight
- Insight
- Analysis, and
- Design.

It is *not* the automation of classical data processing chores or of numerical calculations. High-technology data-handling should eliminate the low technology of the past. As Figure 5.3 suggests, there is a great need to increase the depth and breadth of analysis. This is perfectly achievable, but it requires appropriate board decisions and CEO guidance. The change from an environment characterized by the top half of Figure 5.3 to that in the bottom half will not come on its own.

Still another needed policy in information technology restructuring, indeed in changing the whole culture of IT, is the emphasis to be placed on return on investment (to which reference was made in section 5.2). Bankers Trust (BT) and the Mellon Bank, among others, have been examples of institutions that had a firm 22% rule on information technology ROI.

As a goal, high return on investment is reachable, but the decision to achieve it must be made by the board and the CEO – and it should be steadily controlled. Apart from the ROI side of the equation, which is very important, there is no better way to let loose IT-related operational risks than poor cost control.

- Large budgets have the nasty habit of breeding op risk.
- Tight budgets convey a sense of discipline, therefore they make everybody attentive.

IT expenses must be focused. Take risk management as an example. At Bankers Trust, information technology absorbed about 25% of the non-interest budget: $600 million per year out of $2.5 billion. Ten percent of all IT expenses went for risk management. If the restructuring of the bank's computers and communications systems to support risk control was included, the figure would be much higher.

Out of the IT risk management budget at Bankers Trust have come beautiful applications such as the risk adjusted return on capital (RAROC) and the Magellan corporate memory facility (CMF). But money alone was far from being the whole

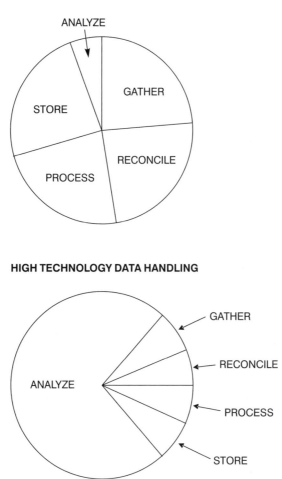

LOW TECHNOLOGY DATA HANDLING

HIGH TECHNOLOGY DATA HANDLING

Figure 5.3 The need to increase the depth and
breadth of analysis without increasing costs is served
by high technology

story in the BT solutions. Global risk management required effectively integrated systems and procedures implemented at:

- Front desk
- Middle office
- Back office, and
- Enterprise-wide.

Within this enterprise-wide perspective, a system must be put in place for operational risk identification and for timely reporting on operational risk events. Several banks included in my research expressed the opinion that operational risks

	Business unit		
	Internal control	Op risk exposure	IT service
Product X	Excellent	High	Very good
Product Y	Poor	Average	Average
Product Z	Excellent	Average	Not material

Table 5.2 Example of a macroscopic reporting structure for operational risk adopted by Barclays Bank

must be integrated into a homogeneous reporting format. A business unit by business unit reporting scheme by Barclays Bank, which is more qualitative than quantitative, is shown in Table 5.2.

A king-size operational risk associated to IT is the maintenance of obsolete applications software. Practically all financial institutions have in their library applications which are 20–30 years old. These have to be maintained:

- The maintenance of applications programs is labor-intensive and it is a highly ineffective job.
- Many banks are using up to 75% of their programming resources to maintain old programs, which is absurd.

Because the maintenance job is greatly mismanaged by the same IT people who should know better, I classify it near the top of IT-related operational risk. I know banks that use young IT graduates to maintain applications programs that were written before they were born.

5.4 Advanced IT solutions and smart environments

Several hypotheses have been advanced about what the business world will be like with smart environment technology, but none can be proved until the smart environment comes of age. A similar statement is valid about guessing what the 'killer' information technology applications will be. One has to build them and try them out. The same is true about the operational risks associated with new and old system solutions.

But the very fact that hypotheses (tentative statements) are made about the future is a good sign. Historically, information technology departments did not work that way. They did not make hypotheses, let alone validate them; neither did they pay attention to killer applications. What they have been mostly interested in is a shot-by-shot writing (not even program design) with plenty of heterogeneity in the system.

Enterprise management software helps to break that vicious cycle of short-termism. The first step in developing an information technology system able to support managers and professionals in an able manner, through interactive computational

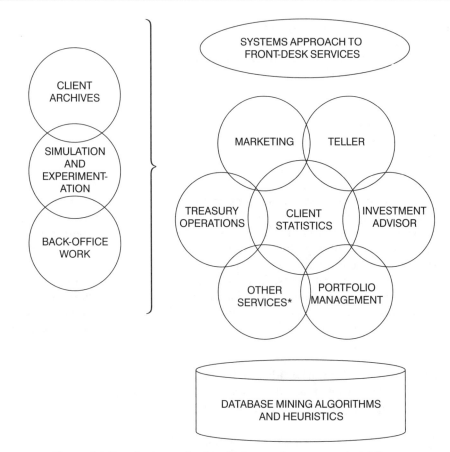

Figure 5.4 Developing and using the interactive computational finance architecture. (*Derivatives, currency exchange, legal advice, tax advice, ancillary services)

finance, is the development of the appropriate architecture. Figure 5.4 provides an example based on a project I carried out in the financial industry.

An enterprise architecture should have vision, be flexible, provide for system integration, employ prototyping, and use the latest technology.[2] The latter includes *agents* (knowledge artefacts)[3] and sophisticated decision support solutions. To enable *our* bank to be ahead of the curve, the architecture that we choose must definitely allow for adaptation to changing:

■ Market conditions
■ Customer requirements
■ Products and services, and
■ Corporate objectives.

The enterprise architecture should contribute to the control of other operational risks (see section 5.7), rather than adding to them. Because technology moves fast, customer needs change, and new operational risks come to the fore; therefore the technological infrastructure should be up for frequent review. The same is true about managing the distribution and configuration of software across the network. For this reason, IT departments should always keep a balance between:

- Innovation
- Speed of execution
- Reliability, and
- Overall control.

Sometimes the goals are conflicting. For instance, decentralizing IT responsibilities contributes to cost awareness and network performance, but makes it more difficult to enforce configuration standards and maintain control. By contrast, placing all application files in a few central locations gives IT better central control, but also leads to reduced flexibility and network reliability, which may end in user dissatisfaction with information services being provided.

System performance, reliability, cost and user-perceived quality of service are challenges which, to a significant extent, date back to the 1960s, even if they are still with us. What is new is the emphasis now placed on IT-oriented operational risk. The persistence of old problems and adding of new challenges in the IT landscape has three unwanted effects:

- It diverts attention from new, advanced applications.
- It invariably leads to end-user dissatisfaction with IT services.
- It contributes in a significant way in increasing information technology costs.

As we saw earlier in this chapter (section 5.2), cost/benefit optimization is a 'must' because the way to bet is that network-attached devices have a high cost of ownership. Some companies have estimated the cost to be $10 000 per desktop per year – a figure that mainly covers on-line support and maintenance, not installation or actually buying the unit. Neither is the tracking of IT-related operational risks included in this figure.

With such high cost, the returns obtained per workstation in terms of personal productivity, and decision support, deserve particular attention. Short of high returns in terms of deliverables, ROI will be dismal. Only advanced applications, including interactive datamining, graphics presentation, and agent-supported services, can provide high enough benefits to justify the cost.

Effective on-line searches and reporting solutions for managers and professionals have prerequisites. They require the use of filters so that specifics are reported in a way that is answering *each* end-user's requirements in a *personalized* manner. Computer response must be action-oriented. Based on an ongoing application in the financial industry, Figure 5.5 gives an example of visualization services (turning numbers into graphs and images) available through interactive computational finance.

Advanced applications are sensitive to reliability and uptime (see the next section). Reliability criteria and cost-effectiveness meditate against centralized solutions. A most vexing problem with centralization of network resources is the potential for

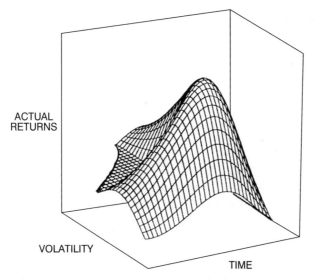

ACTUAL
RETURNS

VOLATILITY

TIME

Figure 5.5 A 3-D (color) presentation both permits more variables and better describes changing market situations

bottlenecks and downtime. Local area networks like IBM's Token Ring and 10MB Ethernet do not deliver acceptable response time when 100 or more clients simultaneously work on-line. Therefore, they are leading to IT operational risks.

Inability to support 99.99% reliability and deliver an acceptable low level response time is a recurrent operational risk, so much so that it looks permanent to the end-user. Besides significantly improving performance on these two fronts, high reliability and low response time, users demand a mechanism for easy development and distribution of applications programs, as well as a prototyping language which speaks *their* jargon.

The availability of flexible and comprehensible graphical users interfaces, and the existence of visual programming languages some of which are job-specific, helps in answering such requests. The more sophisticated end-users, however, go beyond simple visualization through graphics. They want to have available on-line:

- Market data *filtering*, parametrically set to their specific needs
- *Visibilization* facilities, permitting them to perceive and appreciate in real-time the very small and the very large
- *Visistraction* capabilities, which enable the comprehension of phenomena without direct physical interpretation as well as concepts.

All three points describe advanced applications. The nature of what is 'advanced' and what is not evidently changes with time. In the mid-to-late 1980s and early 1990s advanced IT applications were expert systems.[4] Today they are not, in the sense that banks, manufacturing, and merchandising companies that don't use expert systems as a matter of course are living in medieval times in terms of information technology.

Being in an IT backwater is a major operational risk, but few boards and CEOs are aware of this fact. The problem is that plenty of people in senior management are still computer-illiterate, though this is changing with the new generation of executives taking over. Because it keeps the company behind the curve of competition, computer illiteracy is an operational risk.

Both the IT applications and the infrastructure must be ahead of the curve. To serve its users in an able manner, the infrastructure itself should be smart, able to check if it is missing components and automatically reinstall those out of action. Also, it should be providing an automatic method of correcting software problems after they occur, and facilitate the installation of new software or changes to the configuration (as the system evolves) without interruptions, reloads, and restarts.

All these are prerequisites to advanced applications, because no IT implementation can be even remotely considered 'advanced' if what has just been outlined in a systems sense does not perform to the highest standard. Killer applications will themselves be killed by the substandard centralized infrastructure which characterizes so many IT operations, and operational risks will abound unless they are properly identified, classified, monitored, and corrected, as outlined in Chapter 2.

5.5   Business continuity and IT-related operational risk

Given a modern entity's dependency on technology, a major operational risk is that of hardware, software, and telecommunications breakdown. A prolonged timeout can be catastrophic. Protection from unexpected events as well as back-up and recovery are 'musts'. Policies and standards related to avoiding, mitigating, and recovering from unexpected and sudden loss of computing and communication resources must be established by every institution in a factual and documented manner.

The tragic events of 11 September 2001 have demonstrated the importance of assuring *business continuity* when major adversity hits. The better managed companies see to it that executives, at any time, in any place, are each responsible for preparing and upkeeping business continuity plans for their unit, as well as for following up on such plans. The goal is typically to:

- Minimize business disruption
- Evaluate in advance likely financial loss
- Protect the firm from regulatory and legal exposure, and
- Maintain a public image of world-class service provider, able to operate under most adverse conditions.

Business continuity has been discussed earlier in this book from an entrepreneurial viewpoint. This section adds to it IT-related concerns. For business continuity purposes every credit institution must assume that even under a worst-case scenario it will:

- Maintain official and corporate customer records
- Create, transmit, and process financial transactions
- Provide direct electronic service to customers, and
- Sustain compliance with regulatory and legal reporting.

Regardless of IT platform, for operational continuity reasons critical applications routines and data must be restored to the point-of-failure, within the recovery time specified by the criticality of the application. It is wise to always remember that IT is the cornerstone in maintaining business continuity. Standards concerning IT outsourcing, for example, must be configured to continue providing support under disaster conditions.

Fast recovery procedures should see to it that real-time connectivity is maintained at all times, to each business unit and desk. This requires detailed contingency planning. Furthermore, business continuity plans must be continually re-evaluated, and re-tested annually. Such exercises should include structured walkthroughs:

- Evaluating the business continuity plan and updating according to changing business conditions, and
- Testing expected results and examining deliverables through post-mortem, including audits.

Different levels of criticality must be established in connection to information technology and the operational risks connected to it (see also the discussion on HF/LI and LF/HI events in Chapter 8). Applications with real-time recovery from a disaster must be properly identified. This identification is vital, as such applications should be running within five minutes or less of a catastrophic event.

Other applications than those in the top priority class may be one notch less critical. For instance, they should be up and running within 2 hours; still others within 12 hours, or 24 hours. This type of identification and classification of the aftermath of IT-related operational risk should be determined by the company's exposure to each event, customer service prerequisites, and tangible monetary criteria.

As a matter of principle, business continuity solutions should be cost-effective. Usually, though not always, it is easier to assure business continuity in a structured information environment, than in an unstructured one. Figure 5.6 illustrates this further.

- A structured information environment is served through algorithms and long-established procedures.

Accounting is a prime example; relatively simple transactions are another. For business continuity purposes, accounting database(s) should be duplicated, but with all of them updated on-line. Simple transactions can be more easily reconstructed than complex transactions characterized by a multitude of database accesses.

It is evident that assuring business continuity in an unstructured or semi-structured operations environment costs more than doing so in a structured one. Typically, within a structured information environment operational risks will tend to be high frequency but relatively low impact (HF/LI). (More on this in Chapter 8.) The opposite is true of operational risk in an unstructured information environment.

- Information technology used in unstructured environments is heuristic by nature, and the reporting requirements are realspace (see section 5.2).

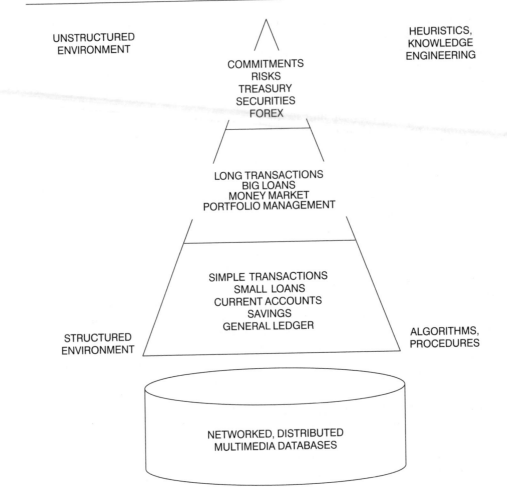

UNSTRUCTURED
ENVIRONMENT

HEURISTICS,
KNOWLEDGE
ENGINEERING

COMMITMENTS
RISKS
TREASURY
SECURITIES
FOREX

LONG TRANSACTIONS
BIG LOANS
MONEY MARKET
PORTFOLIO MANAGEMENT

SIMPLE TRANSACTIONS
SMALL LOANS
CURRENT ACCOUNTS
SAVINGS
GENERAL LEDGER

STRUCTURED
ENVIRONMENT

ALGORITHMS,
PROCEDURES

NETWORKED, DISTRIBUTED
MULTIMEDIA DATABASES

Figure 5.6 Information technology environments range from structured to
unstructured, depending on the applications they support

■ The transactions are complex, and the likelihood is that operational risks will be
high impact.

The examples presented in the preceding paragraphs document that the control of
IT-related operational risk is key to business continuity and represents a critical
management challenge. Companies must strive to handle in an able manner their
service delivery infrastructure and operational risks, as well as those originating at
their business partners. Key points of an op risk control plan include:

■ Unifying the weakest links in the technological base.
■ Rethinking customer service to upgrade quality and dependability.
■ Monitoring the entire network of operations for unwanted events.
■ Integrating service assurance to assist in isolating operational risk cases.

Upgrading service quality and IT dependability enhances business continuity and makes it feasible to support more revenue streams. Tier-1 companies have been eager to create a self-healing infrastructure, able to automate corrective action and avoid costly duplication of monitoring work. Knowledge artefacts (agents) can be designed and implemented to enable such a self-healing approach.

Able solutions, however, have prerequisites. One is identification, classification, and standardization of IT-related operational risks (see Chapter 2). Another prerequisite is the clear definition of quantitative and qualitative metrics connected to quality assurance. This makes feasible:

- Evaluating service quality easily, and
- Making documented changes to existing service agreements.

Making efficient provision for operational risk control decreases the time involved in activating new customer services, while it also permits the faster deployment of novel features and innovative products. Because forward-looking provisioning decreases the manpower necessary to run the system, it ultimately cuts down operational costs. Other benefits include:

- Reducing human errors, and
- Improving efficiency by providing an accurate view of the causes of operational risk.

Operational risk incidents have to be databased and datamined after having been identified and classified. Statistical evaluations will eventually permit their division into high frequency and low frequency. Costing of their aftermath, which also must be databased, will enable classification of their impact into high or low.

In conclusion, the op risk control solution to be adopted has to react to a situation that already may be causing operational risk problems to the company and its customers. The technology to be used must respond well in meeting customer needs associated with ongoing services. The move to a concept of self-healing infrastructure, which automatically takes corrective action and improves the cost-effectiveness of an operational risk control solution, requires a significant amount of skill.

5.6 System reliability should always be a major objective

Reliability is not an ability. It is the probability that a given component, subsystem, or system will perform without failure over a pre-established time period, within a defined operational environment, and under other conditions which characterize the operations this component, subsystem, or system is expected to perform. System reliability – or, more precisely, the lack of it – is a major operational risk.

Many people confuse the reliability of a given system component with that of the system as a whole. This is wrong. Other things being equal, the more complex the system the faster its reliability decreases. Figure 5.7 gives a bird's-eye view of the

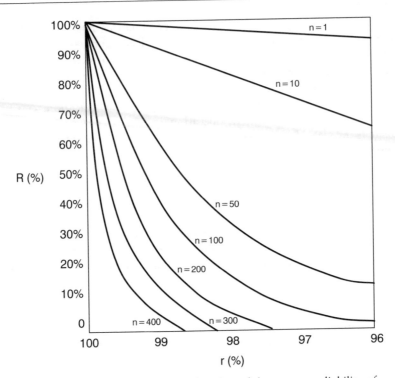

Figure 5.7 System reliability as a function of the average reliability of the components and of the number of components

relationship between system reliability, R, and component reliability, r. The algorithm connecting the two is:

$$R = e^{-t/\bar{T}} \qquad [1]$$

where:
e = the radix of Neperian logarithm
t = the pre-established operational period
$\bar{T}$ = Mean time between failures (MTBF)

MTBF is basic metrics in engineering. Another key measurement is mean time to repair (MTTR). With information systems we are also interested in other metrics:

- MTBSI, which stands for mean time between systems interrupts.
- MTOSI, which means mean time of system interrupt.

Reliability may also be defined as the extent to which a system or component performs its specified functions without any failures visible to the user (see also reliability applications feasible in connection to ship insurance, in Chapter 13). In this broader sense, instead of the reliability equation [1] many computer centers prefer to use the following calculation:

$$R = \frac{\text{System usage time}}{\text{Sum of interruptions}}$$

The total system facilities viewed as an integral source of a given technological capability can be categorized according to the responsibility of the provider of IT services, and according to the job done by the end-user of those facilities. Hardware, software, communications, and operational reasons will all have an impact on systems availability.

Availability is the probability that a system is running at any point during scheduled time. It is calculated as follows:

$$\text{Percentage availability} = 100 \times \frac{\text{System usage time (uptime)}}{\text{Scheduled time}}$$

where Uptime = Scheduled time − system downtime

Availability and reliability relate to the system running at any point during scheduled time, and must be examined and ensured within a life cycle perspective. As such, they also define the extent to which the system (all components of hardware, software, and documentation provided by the supplier) may be depended upon to provide complete, correct results when required, given any combination of inputs.

'Any combination of inputs' includes the certainty that the system will be up and running, able to evaluate these inputs and handle them in realspace. Some inputs, however, may be invalid, not because of system reliability reasons but because the prerequisite organizational study was deficient. Complete and correct results require error detection, correction (or rejection), and publication. In different terms:

- An IT system may be up and running,
- But its deliverables are characterized by 'garbage-in, garbage-out'.

This, too, is an IT-related operational risk. System reliability should not be confused with system dependability, which is primarily guaranteed through minute organizational work. Taking system dependability out of the operational risk list, calls for timely and accurate work centered on input-processing-output. By contrast, reliability rests on design characteristics incorporated at drafting stage.

Reliability, availability, and business continuity correlate. Operational risk must be examined from the viewpoint of all possible consequences to an entity, should it suffer a disaster that does not allow it to function properly. Notice that total system failure or a wider disruption can be caused by a number of reasons, including power outages – not only computer hardware and software failures.

An example along this line of reference is the train accident in Baltimore, Maryland, which derailed Internet traffic. This accident took place inside a rail tunnel in the week of 16 July 2001, and it did more than snarl city traffic or spread toxic fumes. It also highlighted the vulnerability of the growing web of Internet connections. The accident severed or melted fibre-optic cables running through the tunnel, affecting electronic commerce, Internet sites, and e-mail along the length of the US East Coast, including Washington, Philadelphia and New York. For more than two days, dramatic slowdowns occurred for many on the East Coast who sought access to the Web. As Internet traffic was re-routed to other cables, computer users encountered sluggish responses in cities as far away as Atlanta. However, companies which had enhanced system reliability through alternate links, were relatively unaffected by the accident.

Experts say that because fiber-optic lines often run along heavily travelled rights-of-way, they are vulnerable to such accidents. Another fiber-optic outage in Oregon, during that same week of 2001, was due to a construction crew digging a trench for a sewer pipe. Workers inadvertently slashed a fiber-optic cable with the result that at least 50 000 subscribers lost phone services.

Some months earlier, in November 2000, millions of Internet users in Australia were affected after Telstra, the country's biggest Internet service provider, was crippled. The hypothesis has been that a fishing boat or small earthquake might have damaged a cable that handled more than 60% of Telstra's Internet traffic. The cable lay beneath about 100 feet of water off Singapore.

Also, in March of 2000, Northwest Airlines was hamstrung for three hours when a construction crew cut a fiber-optic cable near its headquarters in Eagan, Minnesota. The accident crippled Northwest's communications with airports around the United States and the carrier found itself obliged to cancel 120 flights, while delaying hundreds of others.

These examples should be viewed within the pattern described in 2000 in a report from the US General Accounting Office (GAO).[5] The evidence provided in this report focused attention on several factors responsible for delays and outages, mainly regarding:

- Electronic trading systems used in the equity markets, and
- On-line brokerage models where traders employ high-speed Internet links to intermediaries.

Because of this, GAO's general conclusions are relevant to a number of information environment activities, including foreign exchange and fixed income markets. Most of the intermediaries contacted in connection to the GAO study noted that outages did not result principally from the incapacity of their computers to handle large transaction volumes, but rather from upgrades to:

- Expand capacity, and
- Improve supported capabilities.

The most common reasons for system outages involve problems with vendor-supplied trading system software. This is a good example of lack of coordination in outsourcing (see also section 5.8). Most companies operating on-line rely on vendor support for major parts of order processing. When these third-party systems experience problems, outages hit more than one firm.

5.7 Trading, payments, settlements, and operational risks associated to IT

Most success in tracking and control of IT-based operational risks comes by focusing on functional categories which have different characteristics and availability requirements. In other terms, an IT-related operational risk control program is more effective if it is specialized, with queries addressed within the context of the functional class under scrutiny. For instance:

- What is the cause of trading delays?
- Which are the operational risks associated to them?

According to the study by the US General Accounting Office, to which reference was made in section 5.6, trading delays in the environment that was investigated were primarily caused by heavy Internet traffic, particularly during periods of high market volatility. The GAO analysts found that several problems were attributed to Internet service providers.

Other reasons for delays and failures included hardware problems, procedural switches from manual to automated order processing, different reasons for system stress, problems regarding overnight updating of databases, and breakdowns in telecom equipment. The silver lining was that despite their frequency and (sometimes) length, outages and delays did not seem to have had *systemic* consequences. The apparent reasons for this are that:

- In most cases there was no coincident big market news to the outages
- These outages have not been too prolonged, so traders were able to delay trades, and
- Other ways to trade were still available, like elder electronic systems and telephones.

GAO noted, however, that when outages and delays were present trade activity was generally lower than on normal trading days. Also, some institutional and retail investors were reluctant to trade without the availability of centrally determined prices. This particularly happens outside regular trading hours when liquidity is low.

It is only reasonable that in order to minimize the chance of trading halts occurring, system providers and users should not only identify the pertinent operational risks but also be most careful in providing for contingency measures and backup procedures. These should be incorporated in every system designed for trading, payments, and settlements. The resulting reliability must be carefully measured. In a comprehensive sense, the provision of payments services includes:

- Clearing of trades
- Payment proper, and
- Delivery of assets (settlement).

Each of these functions carries potentially one or more operational risks. Interbank payment services require the same type of skills credit institutions use in lending:

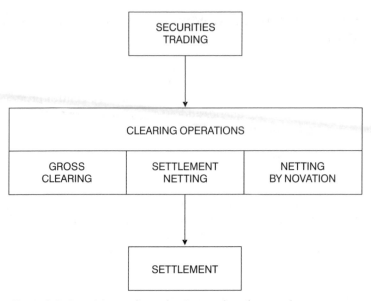

Figure 5.8 Securities trading, clearing, and settlement share common functions

- Fraud prevention
- Credit analysis, and
- Ability to retrieve funds improperly sent.

Payment services are expensive; indeed, they are the largest cost component in securities trading. Also, their operational risks may involve security breaches, which add significantly to the cost of transactions. Another challenge is payments efficiency, which can be improved through organization, technology, and op risk control.

Trading and settlement are closely related, as shown in Figure 5.8, by the European Central Bank (ECB). In this figure, *settlement netting* describes the case where net obligations are computed without impact on contractual obligations. *Netting by novation* describes the netting process which also includes the replacement of original contracts.[6] Settlement netting can be provided not only by central counterparties but also through securities settlement systems, which offer:

- Custody services
- Delivery versus payment, and
- Final delivery of securities from seller to buyer.

The last two points are payments and settlements advances enabled by technology which, however, also engender operational risks. On-line cash payment and settlement services is another challenge. Clearing houses and payment networks are exposed to legal risk and IT risk which should be looked at very carefully.

ECB operates a payments and settlements system, known as Target, which is a welcome addition to the technology of the European Union. Prior to it, the study which I undertook as consultant to major financial institutions in continental Europe showed that, to a considerable extent, operating risk was the most underestimated risk in the existing payment system made up of heterogeneous components that were not properly tested for built-in reliability. Yet, banking payment systems:

- Are linked on-line to the clearer, and
- They are interdependent in terms of existing operational risks.

A single systems failure, whatever the cause, can spread into other aggregates and it may have a domino effect. Therefore, the able handling of the consequences of security issues, reliability, and outages must be built into national and international settlement systems and procedures. Payment and settlement systems must continue to function regardless of the stress put upon them, even if at reduced capacity.

A modern economy requires on-line settlements, and in recent years progress has been made in the area of wholesale payment systems through the widening introduction of real-time gross settlement. Commercial banks, investment banks, other financial institutions, and the regulators appreciate that continuous linked settlements (CLS) are key to assuring that the clearing and settlement of foreign exchange transactions in the major currencies helps in keeping Herstatt risk under control.

5.8 Operational risk that may result from IT outsourcing and insourcing

Outsourcing is the delegation to another party – the *insourcer* – of the authority for the provision of services. The insourcer is a third party, and there are different types of outsourcer–insourcer relations, which are not the subject of this book.[7] Outsourcing is done under a contract that incorporates service level agreements (SLA; more on this later) including:

- Functionality
- Cost
- Quality, and
- Timeliness of deliverables.

The insourcer accepts the rendering of specific services, under the above four conditions (see in Chapter 4 the case study on EDS, which is one of the major IT insourcers). Companies outsourcing their information technology, or other services, must understand that risks and responsibilities cannot be delegated by the outsourcer to the insourcer. The board and CEO are always responsible for what they have outsourced. Every insourcer is faced with:

- The challenge of getting it right, and
- The cost of getting it wrong.

Taken together, these two points suggest that there are risks associated with outsourcing and insourcing. Outsourcing is not necessarily the best policy for every entity. The golden rule is: never outsource (or insource) what you don't understand. Moving away from this principle is synonymous with assuming a horde of operational risks.

Next to understanding what is involved in an outsourcing/insourcing business partnership comes the challenge of working out the clauses of the *service level agreement* (SLA). This is a 2-way contract which defines deliverables and their functionality, timing, quality, cost, and legal procedures governing the outsourcing/insourcing contract. Legal clauses should focus on:

■ The dependability of outsourced services
■ Operational risk associated to these services
■ The outsourcer's right to inspect facilities and staff of the insourcer
■ Resolution of eventual conflicts of interest between the two parties, and
■ Contract termination and exit from the agreement.

An SLA is part of a *collaborative level agreement* (CLA). Some companies consider the SLA and CLA as being synonymous. This is not a crucial distinction. What is important is that the clauses on SLA and CLA are thoroughly studied and all present or potential operational risks flushed out. Op risk must be properly identified and controlled *before* the contract is signed.

The question whether outsourcing is a good policy cannot be answered in a factual and documented manner in a general sense. Every case must be studied on its own merits. The principle however is that core functions should not be outsourced. Companies give different reasons for outsourcing services. Some of them are smoke and mirrors, others do make sense. The most frequently heard reasons are:

■ Reduce costs (35%)
■ Focus on core business (30%)
■ Improve functional performance or quality (16%)
■ Improve time to market (10%)
■ Foster innovation (3%)
■ Reduce non-productive assets on balance sheet (2%)
■ Conserve capital (1%).

The reader will appreciate that not all these reasons make sense. Costs are not *necessarily* reduced through outsourcing. The excuse of 'focus on core business' is that of the unable who has been asked by the unwilling to do the unnecessary; and so on. This does not exclude however that there may be some good reasons for outsourcing. Only a case-by-case thorough analysis can tell.

Another reasons for outsourcing which I was given in my research is a fast-rising one. It is also plainly ridiculous: that of using outsourcing to cut the head count. This is an excuse that proves that people and companies will do many irrational things, even if the background goal is rational. Here is an example from an investment bank which:

■ Outsourced its IT to downsize its employment.
■ Did so by transferring to the insourcer its own IT personnel.
■ But this personnel continued to work on the bank's premises.

The services provided by its former personnel were billed by the insourcer to the bank at a higher rate, with the result that the overall expense instead of being downsized went up. This was not seen to be important. What was important was that the company could report that it had reduced its workforce, because the board had decided that the head count haircut had to be near to the scalp.

In the above discussion on research findings, singularly absent as a reason for outsourcing is: to serve the company's strategic plan and its objectives. Yet, this should have been the No. 1 in the list – albeit a difficult one to meet. Well-managed companies should:

■ Tie the outsourcing strategy to their business strategy
■ Have a policy of knowing exceedingly well what they outsource, and
■ Analyse the operational and other risks associated to outsourcing.

Regulators have not been particularly happy with the practice of IT outsourcing, because while it may diminish some operational risks, it brings other op risks into the picture. Here are three guidelines by the Federal Deposit Insurance Corporation (FDIC) on choosing a software/service bureau outsourcer for banks.

■ Information technology is core business in banking.

Otherwise the Federal Reserve, FDIC, Office of the Controller of the Currency (OCC), and Officer of Thrift Supervision (OTS) would not have examined 350 software/service bureau providers in the United States in connection to Y2K (see Chapter 3).

■ Failure in outsourcing can be as fatal to a financial institution as failure of its own IT resources.

For this reason, in the US, the regulators rounded up, and phased out of banking, a weak service bureau with plenty of operational risks. In fact, many experts suggest that because IT outsourcing expands, the action of regulators needs to extend beyond banking to the insourcers, for all mission critical systems.

■ The board, CEO, and senior management have personal accountability for all outsourced service.

Outsourcing is no relegation of responsibility. Banking and information technology are indivisible. As Walter Wriston, the former chairman of Citibank used to say: 'Banking is information in motion', and 'information about money is as important as money itself.' Technology is a financial institution's infrastructure, and no bank can function with defective IT whether this is provided in-house or it is outsourced.

Notes

1 D.N. Chorafas, *Outsourcing, Insourcing and IT for Enterprise Management*, Macmillan/Palgrave, London, 2003.

2 D.N. Chorafas, *Enterprise Architecture and New Generation Information Systems*, St Lucie Press/CRC, Boca Raton, FL, 2002.
3 D.N. Chorafas, *Agent Technology Handbook*, McGraw-Hill, New York, 1998.
4 D.N. Chorafas and Heinrich Steinmann, *Expert Systems in Banking*, Macmillan, London, 1991.
5 General Accounting Office (GAO), Washington DC. Information published in 2000.
6 *ECB Monthly Bulletin*, August 2001.
7 D.N. Chorafas, *Outsourcing, Insourcing and IT for Enterprise Management*.

Part 2

Capital requirements for operational risk and Basel II solutions

6 Allocation of capital to operational risk according to Basel II

6.1 Introduction

The new capital adequacy framework (Basel II) requires capital reserves for operational risk. These can be computed through different methods advanced by the Basel Committee on Banking Supervision, which are presented in this and the following three chapters. Capital requirements for operational risk add to the other capital requirements computable by the credit institution in connection to credit risk and market risk exposures.

Algorithms alone are only part of the computational challenge. As the reader will recall from Part 1, a bigger hurdle is op risk data – and above all management policy and methodology. To assure better results, bankers should appreciate the sense of regulatory capital, that of economic capital, and the differences that exist between the two.

The objective of the present chapter is to convey this message. Basel I of 1988 was a capital accord that focused on credit risk in an age of globalization. Its great merit is that it provided a level ground for the global banking industry, followed in 1996 by the market risk amendment.[1] Basel II is a much broader accord, having three pillars.

- Pillar 1 is capital requirements.

One of the options the Basel Committee offers to banks is the standard method of Basel I. The better alternative is an internal ratings-based (IRB) method which would eventually become widespread and could lead to self-discipline in the capital reserves ratio.[2]

- Pillar 2 is regulatory validation and supervision.

Through Basel II, the role of supervisory authorities is strengthened. The real question is: In validating a particular capital allocation model do regulators let bank management off the hook in terms of errors in capital reserves? It is too early to respond to this question.

- Pillar 3 is market discipline.

The keyword is transparency, which is key to proper functioning of free economy markets. But there are also questions to which only time, and practice, can respond.

For instance: Is closer alignment of regulatory capital with economic capital good public policy (see section 6.2).

Because it represents loss resulting from inadequate or failed internal processes (including people and systems), and from external events, operational risk is present in all three of the pillars. Capital requirements for operational risk are on a firmer basis for those internal and external events that are quantifiable and amenable to computation of risk charges. Others are only qualifiable, and in this case the role of economic capital, which goes beyond regulatory capital, becomes supreme.

Account should also be taken of extreme value events. On 1 November 2002, the equity of one of the main British insurers dropped nearly 10% because of a rumor that it had a large liability in an asbestos case (see Chapter 12). With extreme events and qualifiable operational risks, a key role can be played by Pillar 2 and, most particularly, Pillar 3.

The best way to start this chapter is by going back to the fundamentals. Regulatory capital and economic capital have become keywords in banking; but while the notion of regulatory capital is fairly clear, that of economic capital is still in flux. What else does economic capital represent except guiding management's hand not to spread the company's resources too thin?

6.2   Regulatory capital *vs* economic capital

There is no problem in defining *regulatory capital*. The current 8% capital reserve for commercial banks, stipulated by the 1988 Capital Accord by the Basel Committee, is the best example. Banks adopting the IRB method will no longer follow the 8% rule. Regulatory capital will be computed through models, and it may end up being less or more than 8%. But the regulators have set no rules for *economic capital*. Defining it is the object of this section, leaving aside the rather foggy notion of entrepreneurial capital. Our focus will be the *total economic equity*, shown in a nutshell in Figure 6.1. It includes:

- Regulatory capital
- On-balance sheet assets and liabilities, and
- Off-balance sheet assets and liabilities.

Eliminating the notion of entrepreneurial capital has been a deliberate choice. In the late 1990s, economic capital and entrepreneurial capital were coexisting, but they were not clearly defined. Often, what one bank told me constituted economic capital the next bank would say: 'This is entrepreneurial capital' – and vice versa. Hence the decision to concentrate on economic capital and regulatory capital. Within this perspective, three concepts dominate the comparison of the one to the other:

- Regulatory capital is the *minimum* amount needed to have a license. It corresponds to *expected* risks.
- Economic capital is the amount necessary to be in and stay in business. For instance, providing a cushion at the 99% level of significance.
- Additional capital, beyond economic, is also necessary for extreme events and in order to gain market confidence.

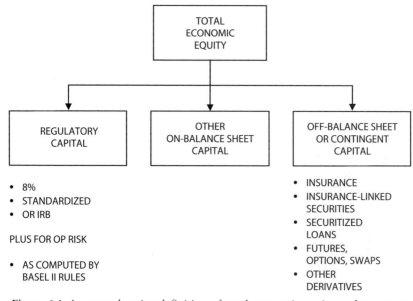

Figure 6.1 A comprehensive definition of total economic equity under current conditions

Economic capital, and that beyond the economic capital notion, essentially correspond to unexpected risks (more on this in section 6.3). Since 1988 regulatory capital is composed of two parts, the so-called *tier 1* (T1) and *tier 2* (T2). To appreciate the difference between T1 and T2 the reader must understand the philosophy behind them, and the criteria used to distinguish between them. These criteria are three:

■ Performance

Share capital is permanent; subordinated debt is not. Share capital is tier 1.

■ Possibility to stop payment

Dividends can be stopped; short of bankruptcy, interest to bonds and loans cannot.

■ Possibility of write-offs

We can write down equity without being sued in court. But we cannot write down debt without a court decision – or filing for protection from creditors under Chapter 11, or some other law protecting from creditors.

Tier 1 and tier 2 capital have been defined in connection to the 1988 Capital Accord. They have been, to a large extent, a compromise between the central bankers of G-10. It may not be appreciated as such, but a major challenge with tier 1 and tier 2 capital is pricing the bank's assets. The solution that *our* bank chooses must be within directives set by regulators. There are two alternatives:

- Marking-to-market, and
- Book value, the accruals method.

Using both approaches indiscriminately can lead to trouble. The results of the two methods, however, can be compared for benchmarking. *If* capitalisation is, say, $30 billion, and book value stands at $50 billion, *then* the regulators will ask for an explanation of the reasons for the difference.

There is an exception to the statement made in the preceding paragraph, and it has to do with the valuation of derivative financial instruments in the bank's trading book. While the majority of derivatives tend to be short- to medium-term, some are long-term. Interest rate swaps may go up to 30 years, which is not rational, but that's life.

Some regulators permit valuation of derivative instruments kept to maturity through accruals, while those for trading purposes are marked to market. The difference is made by *management intent*. This is, for instance, specified by the Statement of Financial Accounting Standards (SFAS) 133, in US banking. Let me repeat this statement. Provided the executive board clearly defines its intent to the regulators,

- *If* derivatives assets are for trading, *then* mark to market
- *If* for long-term holdings, *then* use accruals method.

Recently the notion of *tier 3* (T3) capital has come up. It derives from trading profits and other chapters, and it may be part of the additional capital we will be talking about. While the notion of T3 capital may seem appealing, it is appropriate to account for the fact that with derivative instruments what at this moment is trading profits, in a few hours' time may turn into trading losses.

So much for regulatory capital for the commercial banks. Regulators of other financial industries do not necessarily use the same criteria in defining capital requirements. According to José Sanchez-Crespo of A.M. Best, the insurance companies' independent rating agency, regulatory capital for an insurance firm is:

- The minimum solvency margin, and
- What an insurer needs to get a license and operate.

By contrast, economic capital is all the capital available to face the insurance company's liabilities. It includes shareholder funds, discounting of reserves to their economic value, and all the capital that can be utilized to pay policy holders. The latter incorporates part of the debt when the length of borrowing is 20 years – and it is known as 'hybrid' capital. (More on insurance companies in Part 3).

6.3   Economic capital and levels of confidence

What was presented in the previous section represents a good enough expression of notions underpinning regulatory capital. The question, however, remains: How are reserve banks looking at economic capital? 'Ideally, the level of economic capital should be the same as the level of own funds,' said a senior executive of the Austrian National Bank. Own funds consist of:

- Paid-up capital (share capital)
- Disclosed reserves (open reserves)
- Funds for general banking risks (provisions with reserve character)
- Hidden reserves (where the law allows them)
- Supplementary capital
- Subordinated capital
- Revaluation reserves, and
- Short-term subordinated capital.

Accepting this statement as a valid frame of reference, which it is, a challenge is the computation of the *holding period of return*. This is a management requirement, not a regulatory issue. No exact method is set for calculation of this holding period but experts think a daily profit and loss (P&L) statement computed in parallel to the daily value at risk (VAR) can be instrumental in providing the necessary metrics.

Clearly enough, the computation of daily P&L poses challenges; requiring both a first class management information system (MIS) able to provide in real-time such detail, and state of the art technology (see Chapter 5). These are prerequisites. Few banks have this capability at the present time. Those who do, call it a *virtual P&L* and *virtual balance sheet*. Both require intraday:

- Evaluation of assets and liabilities
- Identification of risks and their weights, and
- Effective resource allocation on an enterprise-wide basis.

Well-managed banks know how to meet these challenges. They also appreciate that once they do so, they are well on their way to classifying their capital requirements according to risk levels. Figure 6.2 provides a snapshot. It can be seen that regulatory

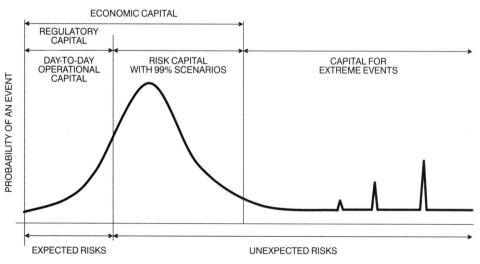

Figure 6.2 Classification of a bank's capital requirements according to risk

capital covers expected risks associated with day-to-day operations, while economic capital includes regulatory capital and capital associated to unexpected risks – up to a point. That point is the 99% level of confidence.

This means that 1% of events that might happen in the future are not necessarily covered by economic capital, the way most financial institutions define their economic capital reserves. In fact in one of the research meetings I had, the statement was made that:

- *If* an insurance company holds capital at the 99.97% level of confidence,
- *Then* this will correspond to about an AA rating in solvency terms (more on this issue in Part Three).

Wise management should not feel comfortable with a limited definition of economic capital, or one that is monolithic, because history shows that financial might can quickly turn to ashes. In 1989, at the apogee of the Japanese banks' brief rise in the world's financial capitalization, they had an impressive $400 billion in unrealized profits. Then this turned into a $1.2 trillion torrent of red ink – which is very serious because:

- Japanese banks were never strongly capitalized, and
- Their special reserves have been non-existent.

Not everybody appreciates the importance of special reserves, and in some countries they are illegal. Yet, they can be life-savers. On 15 November 2002, after injecting another $1 billion in Winterthur, Crédit Suisse seems to have exhausted its special reserves. This completely changed its risk profile.

The best and simplest way to look at economic capital is as a performance measure which can satisfy unexpected risks within the broader perspective described in this section – doing so by level of confidence. Beyond this, it should be noted that there are three different viewpoints to account for in the calculation of economic capital:

- Shareholders' perspective

The best way to look at it is through a virtual balance sheet and virtual P&L. This way, capital is calibrated against market prices; book value is too historical and market capitalization is volatile.

- Bondholders' perspective

Experts think that the best approach in this connection is the one focusing on intrinsic value, which is just as important as capital reserves. Account should also be taken of liquidity, liabilities, and assets.

- Regulators' perspective

Here the keyword is risk-weighted assets and liabilities, and their impact on regulatory capital. Regulatory capital and risk capital at least at the 99% level of confidence effectively contributes to financial stability; financial stability improves if banks hold capital and reserves beyond the 99% level of significance.

Thanks to the 1996 market risk amendment and the use of VAR, banking culture now widely embraces the 99% level. But what about going beyond 99%? This will be an important exercise in the coming years; a consequence of Basel II. To understand how it can be done, we should return to the notion of the balance sheet.

- Table 6.1 shows a typical balance sheet for a commercial bank.
- Table 6.2 presents a restructured balance sheet, along the lines suggested by Dr Werner Hermann.

The classical balance sheet, established by Luca Paciolo in 1495,[3] does not have levels of confidence. Even economic capital at the 99% level of confidence leaves 1% of all

Assets		Liabilities	
Cash and cash equivalents	0.8%	Inter-bank borrowing (deposits)	10.1%
Inter-bank lending	12.4	Customer deposits	60.4%
Securities	8.5	Debt securities	10.9
Loans and advances to customers			
Gross loan amounts	69.0	Other liabilities	4.6
Loan loss reserves	(0.8)		
Loans net of reserves	68.2		
Prepayments and accrued income	1.9	Accruals and deferred income	2.8
Tangible and intangible fixed assets	3.4	Loss reserves (provisions) for liabilities and charges	1.2
Other assets, including goodwill	4.8	Subordinated debt	4.5
		Total shareholder equity	5.5
Total assets	100	Total liabilities	100

Source: Basel Committee, 'Risk management practices and regulatory capital. A cross-sectoral comparison', November 2001

Table 6.1 Typical balance sheet for a commercial bank

Assets		Liabilities	
Current, medium, and long term at fair value	100%	Current and medium term	50%
		Capital at 90%	20%
		Capital at 90–99%	10%
		Capital at 99–99.9%	5%
		Capital at >99.9–100%	15%
			100%

Table 6.2 A restructured balance sheet by Dr Werner Hermann, of the Swiss National Bank

cases outside its limits. Usually this 99% of all cases does not include outliers and spikes, but the 1% does.

Extreme events may upset even the most carefully contracted balance sheet and cause default. Therefore, solutions are necessary that go beyond the 99% level. These must be proactive, and they should be designed to enhance the bank's financial staying power. This is precisely the advantage of Dr Hermann's proposal.

Let's recapitulate the message conveyed by this section. Because it is based on expected risks, the day-to-day operational capital shown in Figure 6.2 may be taken as a proxy of regulatory capital. Beyond this comes the tranche of economic capital which augments regulatory capital providing a cushion of comfort at the 99% level of confidence.

To face potential liabilities at the 99.9% level of confidence and beyond, we must restructure the liabilities side of the balance sheet. Not only should regulatory capital and economic capital not be confused with one another, but our bank must also bring into its assets and liabilities a concept of level of confidence that covers the probability of 99.9%, and even goes beyond that level.

6.4   A bird's-eye view of models for operational risk reserves

Prior to the new capital adequacy framework, money was set aside for operational risk largely on an ad hoc basis. Practically every credit institution used to have its own method, and to a large measure it still does so until Basel II takes hold in January 2006.

Well-managed banks, however, did not take lightly capital needs for operational risk. Many class it as the second most important category of exposure, after credit risk. Research by supervisors, based on data from credit institutions, suggests that the ratio of credit risk to operational risk in the banking industry is roughly 4:1. This being the case, the supervisors originally demanded (in the first draft of Basel II) a capital reserve for operational risk at the level of 20% of credit risk.

That's what the Basel Committee said as a first instance in June/July 1999, with the early draft of the new capital adequacy framework. Commercial banks reacted negatively to this 20% ratio because they found it to be too high, and in September 2001 it was reduced to 12% – still on a consultative basis.

This is an average, and no doubt both commercial bankers and supervisors appreciate that, in real life, averages do not mean much; they are only of indicative value. Every credit institution should do its own research to establish the relative weights most appropriate to its operational risk in the business environment(s) to which it addresses itself. Furthermore, it should be using its technology to continue upkeeping and fine tuning such weights.

Once again, the best approach is back to basics. Well-managed banks must provide for planning and control over the allocation of their financial resources. Figure 6.3 suggests a basic approach to compound risk management. While the three main channels in this figure are loans, investments, and derivatives,

- Operational risk is omnipresent and
- It is an integral part of each of them.

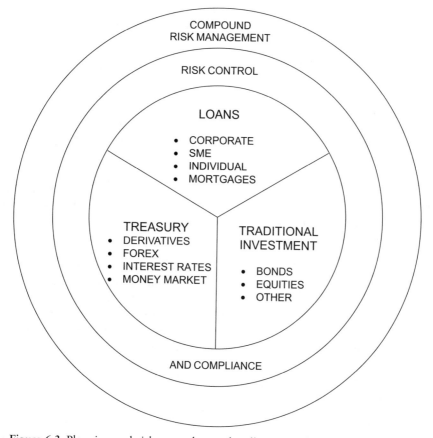

Figure 6.3 Planning and risk control over the allocation of financial institutions' resources

As we will see in Chapter 7, the Basel Committee proposes five different models for computation of op risk capital. Those of them that are more advanced are, however, not cast in stone. Speaking from past experience, as computational models for operational risks evolve, the way to bet is that both the criteria being used and the models will evolve – and will be neither purely quantitative nor purely qualitative.

The new capital adequacy framework advises that in countries subject to sizeable changes in economic conditions and banking practices, supervisors should consider imposing higher capital requirements to take account of operational risk, and most particularly legal risk. Fair enough, but it is also wise to account for the fact that factors relevant to operational risk change over time in practically all countries. Factors that today make themselves felt at a strategic level are:

- Business policies
- Management culture
- Type of products
- Market characteristics

- Diversification
- Size of equity and assets
- Level of technology, and
- Risk management systems.

With only a couple of exceptions, these are largely qualitative factors relating to people and their judgment. Change in people's attitude is key to operational risk control, but it is not easy to develop operational risk consciousness in an organization. Some people say, 'We don't have op risks.' The challenge is how to get people to:

- Identify their operational risk(s)
- Write them down
- Tally their frequency, and
- Evaluate their impact.

Some people know about the existence of op risks, but have not properly identified them. To do so, they must think of the unthinkable, project on extreme events, challenge current conditions, and evaluate operational aftermath.

As far as the computation of capital requirements is concerned, much of the challenge lies in the fact that management mechanisms, particularly methods of defining and quantifying operational risk, are still embryonic or, at best, at an early stage of development. No 'best approach' to operational risk has emerged so far but, as we will see in this and the other chapters of Part 2, the Basel Committee on Banking Supervision is working on different alternatives.

Some of these alternatives are based on a simple algorithm, others are more sophisticated; the latter are still at early stages of their development. Following consultation with the banking industry, Basel has specified five methods of measuring operational risks. In the following chapters we will scrutinize each of these methods. Here is a bird's-eye view:

- Basic indicator
- Standardized approach
- Internal measurement
- Loss distribution, and
- Scoreboard.

The last three methods are collectively known as the *advanced measurement approaches* (AMA). From the very simple basic indicator to the scoreboard which is the more sophisticated of AMA's, these five methods represent a range of possibilities for allocating operational risk capital. From simple to complex, these methods are characterized by increasing risk sensitivity and sophistication in computational solutions.

The reader should nevertheless appreciate that even the most sophisticated and accurate approach to the calculation of operational risk capital has the shortcoming that the established requirements change over time. There is no way out of the need for steady review and adjustment.

In my research, I asked many companies how they update their operational risk control requirements in a way that is cost-effective. The best answer I got is Citigroup's adjustment factor for economic capital allocation. The way Dr David Lawrence, Citigroup's European Head of Risk Methodologies and Analytics, phrased it, because the frequency of review is a compromise between precision and cost his company chose quarterly adjustment through the formula:

$$EC_1 = C_0 \sqrt{\frac{R_1}{R_0}}$$

where:

EC_1 = this quarter
EC_0 = last quarter
R_1 = revenue in channel k this quarter
R_0 = revenue in channel k last quarter

The method is easy to implement, uses existing data, and gives results that are reasonable. Revenue is taken by channel, not bank-wide. The square root rule was adopted because relation between economic capital and revenue is nonlinear. Studies have shown revenue by channel to be a better metric of gross income.

The quantitative square root rule is supplemented by qualitative adjustments that lead to scaling based on auditing results. This starts with the concept of business issues (BI) and major business issues (MBI), each MBI weighting three times a BI. The next important factor is *aging*, past the date the op risk should have been fixed. Then comes the auditing score and risk level (low, medium, high) leading to a quality weight which can range from 1 to 15. (The risk level affects the frequency of auditing.)

Dr David Lawrence kindly explained Citigroup's qualitative weights used in conjunction to the quantitative square root rule. These qualitative adjustments rest on the results of auditing which, after looking into operational risks, classifies them into:

- Business issues (BI), and
- Major business issues (MBI), weighting 3 × BI.

Another factor is *aging*, past the due date the operational risk should have been fixed. The algorithm is:

BI or MBI × Aging = Preliminary Issues Score (PIS)

Across the entire corporation, there could be hundreds of outstanding business issues. The peak is immediately following a large merger, but Citigroup's industrial engineers quickly redress the op risk pattern. An ogive curve like the one shown in Figure 6.4 converts PIS to an audit issues score (AIS).

AIS × Risk level = Quality adjustment factor (QAF)

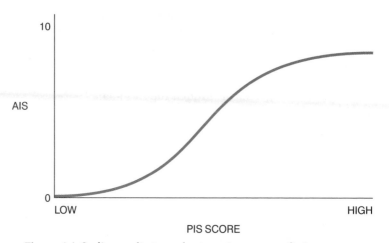

Figure 6.4 Scaling preliminary business issues to audit issues score

Three different risk levels – low, medium, and high – define frequency of operational risk audit. The computed values taken by QAF vary from 1 to 15, and they impact on economic capital allocation for operational risk. Altogether, Citigroup's qualitative and quantitative effort for operational risk valuation is a first class solution.

6.5   The choice among methods for operational risk modeling

Theoretically, but only theoretically, the more sophisticated modeling of operational risk is accompanied by a corresponding reduction in capital charges. The practice will most likely show otherwise. What is important to note, however, is that the existence of alternatives gives banks the freedom to move to more advanced risk management techniques. Supervisors should encourage them in doing so as well as guiding them in appreciating that they need both a policy and a model, to manage operational risk through time. Banks have to:

■ Create the database
■ Calibrate their model(s), and
■ Benchmark and stress-test the model(s).

For its part, senior management must understand the different levels of operational risk, and their change over time. The key to successful modeling, whether for operational risk or any other reason, is the existence of rich databases. This has led to consortiums of big banks pooling their data resources.

For instance, *ORX* is a consortium of a dozen banks, run by a joint steering committee. ABN-Amro is one of them. Among other credit institutions are: JP Morgan Chase, Deutsche Bank, BNP Paribas, and Canadian Imperial Bank of Commerce. (See Chapter 9 for a description of the ORX project.)

The first goal of the ORX Consortium is data pooling for creation of a wholesale banking operational risk database. Also part of the effort is the identification of key risk indicators. The other goal is mutual handholding in:

- Getting operational risk consciousness, and
- Developing op risk control expertise.

This is the point that was made in section 6.3 on economic capital. At ORX, particular attention is paid to organizational risk. We have spoken of management risk and organizational risk in Part 1, emphasizing the fact that they are at the top of the op risk pyramid of a modern financial institution.

Simple models like the basic indicator approach and the standard approach don't account for legal risk, management risk, and IT risk (see respectively Chapters 3, 4, and 5). But AMA solutions should do so. (The ORX consortium is using the loss distribution approach. An internal control matrix is described in Chapter 9 (see section 9.6, Figure 9.7).

A rapid identification of what each of the five Basel methods entails for operational risk control will help the reader to better appreciate the criteria that should enter into the choice.

The *basic indicator* is intended for small, unsophisticated banks; it practically does not involve measurement of risk. Capital charge is determined using an indicator such as gross income, according to the provisional definition of:

- Gross income = net interest income + net non-interest income

Net non-interest income includes fees and commissions receivable, less fees and commissions payable, the net result on financial operations and some other elements. This definition excludes extraordinary or irregular items. Income is to be stated before deduction of operational losses.

The shortcoming of the basic indicator method is that it involves just a generalized, not-that-reliable estimate of operational risk. It is only reasonable that bank supervisors expect medium size to larger banks, and surely the internationally active credit institutions, to use a more precise methodology. An upgrade is the *standardized approach*, which, however, does not account for the fact big financial entities have not only a significant but also a polyvalent operational risk.

With the standardized method, operational risk is measured using an indicator that reflects the volume of the bank's activities with each business line. For instance, retail banking, other commercial banking, trading, payments, and settlements. As has already been briefly discussed in Chapter 2, eight business channels and seven classes of operational risk have been identified by the Basel Committee (for greater detail see Chapter 7).

With this method, the operational risk is weighted by a capital factor specified by the supervisors. Remember, however, that this approach, too, represents only a rough measurement of risk, since it is not based on any *loss data* specific to the institution. Therefore, the Basel Committee would like to see banks advance from the standardized approach to the *internal measurements* method, which provides greater accuracy.

The prevailing opinion is that the incentive to opt for this upgrade is lower capital charges. This *might* be true if all goes well, but it is not a foregone conclusion. Neither should a sharp reduction in capital charges be a primary objective. This will expose the credit institution to unexpected risks, as discussed above in connection to economic capital (section 6.3).

- Downsizing capital charges should never be senior management's goal.
- Rather, the aim must be *right-sizing* and that's where models can help.

Experience will tell which way the chips fall in terms of operational risk modeling and its deliverables. Banks are given, by Basel, the option of applying the internal measurement approach only to some lines of business to begin with. Such partial use can lead to a more generalized application of sophisticated approaches.

Bankers with whom I discussed the internal measurement approach like the concept because it takes account of a credit institutions' individual experience of loss data connected to operational risk. The latter is measured by business lines and types of loss such as:

- Write-offs
- Legal costs, and
- Other charges.

A more complex version of this method is that a distinction is made not only by line of business but also by exact type of operational loss in each business line. Management determines the scale of expected operational exposure, by each type of loss and business line, on the basis of internal loss data, supplemented, when necessary, by external loss data. The latter is the objective of consortia like ORX.

With both versions of the internal measurement method, overall capital requirements are calculated by multiplying these expected losses by a capital factor specified by supervisors. This approach can be made more accurate by means of a fourth method currently under discussion, known as *loss distribution* – which is the second of the advanced measurement approaches.

Under loss distribution, banks may determine capital needs associated to their operational risk using their internal models. These will in all likelihood include risk mitigation techniques, such as insurance against some types of operational risk (see Part 3). The supervisory assessment of this possibility is currently being studied – including qualitative standards that have to be met to use the advanced approaches under discussion.

While the supervisors are open to more sophisticated solutions, commercial bankers find themselves constrained by the lack of both accurate and complete operational risk data. Throughout this section, the reader's attention has been brought to the fact that database deficiencies can well prove to be a stumbling block. This is particularly true of the most advanced of the AMA methods: the *scoreboard*.

To help the reader, a number of analytical methods and tools that can serve scoreboard solutions are described in Chapter 8 and 9. These are time-tested tools, and they have given, in other applications, first class results. It is wise to remember, however, that – as cannot be repeated too often – in all analytical solutions 80% of the challenge is with data, and only 20% lies with heuristics and algorithms.

6.6   Capital standards and operational risk control costs

Several national bankers associations have supported, and continue to support, the Basel Committee's efforts to align more closely capital standards with actual risk. They do so by promoting the opportunity for banks to use internal risk-oriented models to assess the adequacy of their capital reserves. An example is the internal ratings-based (IRB) approach, as well as the recognition of credit risk mitigation in setting the level of capital support.

The regulators suggest alternatives and they can provide guidance in implementing them, up to a point. But it is up to the commercial banks and investment banks to properly define the capital necessary for each major class of risk, within their own business environment, and establish valid ways to control it. Management control costs money. It is therefore necessary to optimize cost *and* the benefit under perspective.

As my research documents, many banks are still searching for an estimate of how much the *operational risk control* project is going to cost them. There are organizational and management costs that need to be budgeted over and above the necessary capital reserves. Early estimates by banks which have undertaken serious projects for the control of operational risk, indicate that costs connected to:

- The op risk study, and
- The system to be put in place

will be fairly significant. An estimate by the Bank of Ireland is that the cost will be at Y2K level (see Chapter 3). Other banks, too, have come to similar conclusions, citing the fact that because they are still in the learning phase of operational risk control, the project will be expensive. This is part of the cost of staying in business, as Chapter 16 documents.

Some credit institutions think of cutting corners in operational risk control studies, but others aptly suggest that in the longer run this will be counterproductive. Skipping the discovery and experimental phase, for example, will prove to be very costly later on. Rigorous operational risk control studies are justified because of:

- Technology and innovation
- Globalization and deregulation
- Intensifying competition
- Increased customer demands
- High profile op risk failures, and
- Steady regulatory pressures.

Both cost and benefit have to be demonstrated to justify a budget for op risk control. Money must never be thrown at the problem. The board and CEO should require clear evidence on cost/benefit, even if some expenditures might be considered mandatory within the realm of Basel II. Critical questions are:

- Where to focus first
- How much to spend, and
- What the company gets for its money.

None of the answers to these queries is evident a priori.[4] Will the operational risk controls, to be established, reduce the probability and financial impact of operational risks? In short: 'What's the value?' A valid answer requires documentation, which should include:

- The frequency and impact before the controls
- The frequency and impact after the controls, and
- The change in loss distribution over a period of time.

I would strongly advise using this method with all three advanced measurement approaches, briefly discussed in the previous section. Cost/benefit measurements should blend with the analytics (see Chapters 7–9). The most important factor, which may make or break the whole effort, is top management commitment to the control of operational risk.

Several commercial banks commented that operational risk should not be handled only from the viewpoint of capital adequacy connected to Pillar 1, but should include the monitoring and supervisory approach proper to Pillar 2. I would think that also Pillar 3, market discipline, is crucial. In fact, all three pillars should be reflected in operational risk control.

The problem with putting all hopes of control on one pillar is that no two banks have the same recognition of operational risk, which continues expanding to new areas. Figure 6.5 dramatizes this ongoing business expansion by means of overlaying areas that include a significant amount of operational risk.

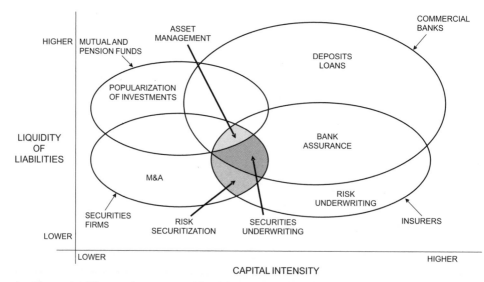

Figure 6.5 The overlapping worlds of financial institutions. (Modified from Swiss Re, Sigma, No. 7/2001)

- A very important organizational effort is needed to be in charge of this situation.
- Capital is important, but there should be no overemphasis on capital as a substitute to sound management and rigorous supervision.

Some commercial banks are concerned about the lack of detail on the variety of operational risk components. They criticize the fact that setting capital requirements for different op risk at approximately 12% of capital, is arbitrary and not consistent with their own estimates of operational risk exposure (which they say are much lower, but provide no statistics to prove it).

I am not impressed by these arguments. My own research has documented that most banks, indeed the majority, have only a faint idea of operational risk factors and of the exposure these entail. Capital for operational risk is not a matter that can be settled through horse trading.

At the risk of being repetitive, let me draw attention once more to the data problem, which further complicates the challenges I have just explained. Most banks have not captured the data necessary to evaluate operational risk, even theoretically. Attempts at capturing operational exposure through statistics reflecting historical market risk and credit risk losses – one of the options I heard about – are infantile, apart from resulting in double counting between operational risk, credit risk, and market risk.

It is not true that business diversity assists in reducing operational risk. If anything, it increases it. This is the background against which should be seen the effort at operational risk control. With this in mind, we should take another look at *regulatory capital* and *economic capital*, discussed in sections 6.2 and 6.3 above, as well as the means through which capital can be allocated to operational risk in a way that effectively supports the bank's objectives.

6.7 Allocating regulatory capital and economic capital to operational risk

Though our goal may well be one of the advanced measurement approaches, as a dry run it makes sense to start by checking what the regulatory charge capital may be for every business line and every risk factor defined by the standard method (see Chapter 7). This will be a good training for the people in the operational risk control project, and it will also provide a frame of reference. From there we can progress toward a detailed analysis concerning every product and service, and every op risk we choose to consider.

A dry run helps to define the more detailed method we will be using. It will also permit a first estimate of how much money we may have to put into the control of operational risk. Another benefit is that it teaches the analysts to be objective, not subjective, fencing reactions such as:

- 'This operational risk event will never happen to our organization.'
- 'Traditionally we did not have to pay attention to this type of op risk.'
- 'The probability of losses is a small fraction of what it takes to control this operational risk.'

The crucial issue in a dry run is that what we do is reasonable in respect of the method we are adopting, like hypotheses on the frequency and impact of operational risks, and economic capital allocation to each risk type. In fact, the dry run will be so much more successful if we take things that we know about operation risk, and try to cast them in a format fitting the problem we face.

When this preliminary phase of work has been accomplished, we will be faced with the problem of capital allocation. Money acts as a common denominator. But which money? The 12% advised by the Basel Committee? The gross income by major product line? Or, something else?

Some experts say start with book equity. That is not the right approach. Book equity is not a good measure, because book value rarely, if ever, corresponds to market value – or to economic capital in the broader sense discussed in previous sections. Also, book equity tends to have a weak correlation to operational risks, which may be the reason Basel did not adopt it.

Another problem is that book equity is most often a virtual notion, often with little reference to real assets that can back up operational risk reserves. Several banks working on AMA now consider economic capital as a better framework for calculating operational risk reserves than regulatory capital and the 12% of capital adequacy rule associated to it. The downside is that:

- Some operational risks are not easily correlated to economic capital, and
- As we have seen, economic capital has no unique industry standard, since a good deal depends on the level of confidence – if not its outright definition.

Deutsche Bank, for example, relates economic capital to return on equity (ROE) calculations for management accounting purposes. Other credit institutions still follow their own definition of entrepreneurial capital, which I advised at the beginning of this chapter that it is better to put at rest.

As a start, I would advise following either of two solutions. The one is to adopt the gross income level of reference, but by product line and eventually by single product. The other, is to take economic capital at the 99% level of confidence, also at product line and product detail.

If with this or a similar approach capital allocation for operational risk reasons is established, *then* the dry run will provide an initial capital allocation matrix. Its goal should be to enable project managers to evaluate advantages and limitations of the method, project on its accuracy, and evaluate its effect on operational risk control. Senior management should answer the following questions:

- Should the operation risk project choose a single methodology or different ones by type of op risk?
- How should we be pricing internally the operational risk control services?
- Should the audit committee and the auditors be involved in evaluation of results?

No bank, to my knowledge, has given 'best answers' to these questions, which might be looked upon as a de facto standard. And there is always the challenge of where exactly to start. There is also the age-old, but still ongoing, discussion about top-down and bottom-up approaches to identification of operational risk and capital allocation.

It is unwise to enter into top-down and bottom-up arguments because in the last analysis the background principle is the same: Whether top-down or bottom-up, the study should have as a goal to highlight operational risk, heighten awareness of it in the organization, and provide the funds to face op risk events. Just for the record, a top-down approach typically starts with:

- Corporate strategy
- Critical risk factors, and
- Enterprise-wide value-based analysis.

By contrast, bottom-up concentrates on:

- Data collection
- Modeling, and
- The choice of a capital allocation method.

The two will eventually map into one another. Therefore neither approach (whichever might be chosen) should be done independently of business operations, try to deliver everything at once, or lead to an unbalanced assessment of risks. Also neither approach should bet on quick gains, or give the impression of being a one-off effort.

In conclusion, the upside of a co-ordinated approach to capital allocation which is based on some critical choices for operational risk control and its funding, helps to highlight the bank's own op risk requirements with some accuracy. The method I have been suggesting in this section has already been used as an internal measure of credit risk exposure and it had the advantage that it led to annual benchmarking with peers. The following case study presents an example.

6.8 Capital at risk with operational type losses: a case study

Bank ABC has been an early starter in studying capital allocation for operational risk reasons. Along the line of the start-up framework discussed in the previous section, it computed capital allocation for five business lines and the seven types of risks defined by the Basel Committee on Banking Supervision. The chosen method was actuarial loss models constructed for each business line and for each operational risk event.

The first impulse was that of implementing game theory. This was chosen for two reasons. Game theory was considered to provide a faster, if not outright better, solution than extreme value theory. And, at the same time, it was thought that game theory would waive the need, for at least a decade, of a rich operational risk database – which simply was not on hand.

The deliverables of game theory, however, were disappointing, and this called for a change in strategy. Separate frequency and severity modeling was done using Monte Carlo simulation. Then, capital at risk was defined as a function of the loss distribution in each business line/event type junction, weighted on tail scenarios.

- Capital at risk was adjusted for diversification and correlation effects.
- Business line and bank-wide capital was determined through aggregation of cell results, junction-after-junction in an op risk capital matrix.

Superficially, it may look *as if* this is a totally different approach than the one suggested in the previous section. In reality this was not the case, because (as a start) the standard method was chosen – reduced to five product lines, but augmented in terms of sophistication regarding the tools being used. This is the very sense of the dry run to which reference was made.

As experience accumulated, within a reasonably short timeframe, high frequency and low frequency operational risk events were identified, quantified, and profiled. A compromise was sought between the ideal solution where an op risk model will use available information elements that contain specific types of characteristics, or can lead to them, and the practical fact that:

- The operational risks content of the database was wanting,
- While a great deal of available information, including opinions research, was qualitative.

Alternative scenarios to capital requirements were considered, such as getting insurance coverage for some of the operational risks. Senior management asked the question: 'Is buying insurance a good way to avoid too high capital reserves?' Theoretically, the answer looks as if it is 'yes'. Practically, however, the analysts found a number of limitations to this approach. Not the least were:

- The case of unforeseen events not covered by insurance policies, and
- Extreme events that insurers would not like to cover (at any premium).

One of the challenges faced by the analysts involved in this project has been the fact that what happened 'last year' may have very little to do with what happens 'this year' or 'next year'. As the project progressed, this challenge was magnified by the fact that:

- Some operational risk losses are rare indeed, and
- When they exist, dependable data is unavailable or sparse.

An integral part of the solution to this challenge was the assessment of forward-looking changes in the management of operational risk exposure. This was engineered through the definition of early indicators and the use of what was called 'non-loss data' such as the quality of a bank's internal control environment. An attempt to employ near-misses failed.

The Delphi method was employed to integrate expert judgment into a system of ranking operational risks.[5] A battery of tests was developed amounting to a multi-attribute decision model designed to accommodate qualitative information and to provide quantifiable results. By breaking decisions down into manageable parts, the methodology that was chosen facilitated the application of expert judgment not only to isolate key factors that determine relative risk rankings, but also:

- To measure operational risk likelihood, and
- To provide expert opinion on the most probable impact (mean value, range).

The results obtained through the Delphi method were used directly or as inputs to further analysis. This can be one of the most imaginative scoreboard approaches; others will be discussed in Chapters 8 and 9. To help along the aforementioned line of research and of reasoning, operational risks have been classified a priori into five types of impact:

- Catastrophic
- Severe
- Average
- Low impact
- Negligible.

Both catastrophic and severe are high impact. The difference between these two classes is that catastrophic disrupt business continuity. Three classes of frequency were chosen, the classifications being:

- High frequency
- Medium frequency (typical)
- Low frequency.

Expert opinion was used to evaluate impact and likely frequency. Senior management asked the project team to provide an evolutionary approach open to adjustments, as operational risk data is collected and deeper experience with losses associated to different business lines and op risk events grows. A richer database allows assumptions that have been made about frequency and impact:

- To be validated or rejected, and
- To be objectively updated as time goes on.

A rough statistic based on this project indicated that about 75% of operational risks being encountered are of the negligible/low impact/average type; while the balance comprises higher impact events (severe, catastrophic). Senior management decided that a unified rating system would be applied throughout the institution, after the pilot study moved into daily implementation in a couple of chosen channels.

This and similar projects provide insight which helps in understanding the evolution of operational risk control systems and practices. One of the lessons learned through the aforementioned experience is that policies and measures to control operation risk must account for the fact that:

- It is lurking in all operations, and
- A normalized frame of reference helps in developing enterprise-wide solutions.

Experts should be called into the act of projecting operational risks, so that it becomes possible to plan in advance, accounting for the aftermath of exposure to each operational risk under consideration. Policies must be in place to assure that each error, failure, and delay becomes:

■ Visible and
■ Measurable.

Visibility increases with real-time data capture, and evaluation standards becoming an integral part of the operational risk framework. Norms should exist for every type of operational risk faced by *our* organization, and they must be regularly updated. Tools should be in place to permit self-assessment. There is no such thing as a one-shot 'best solution'. If the operational risks being targeted persist, this should constitute a ground for deselecting an originally chosen method.

6.9   Operational risk control at the Erste Bank

The Erste, Austria's second largest credit institution, has 10.7 million customers in five countries and about €121 billion in assets. Senior management has chosen the loss distribution approach to operational risk control, under the assumption there will be incentives in terms of capital relief, and the Advanced IRB method for credit risk. Other product lines will start with Foundation IRB, with the goal to transit to A-IRB.

Because of the 1997 merger between the Erste and Austria's savings banks treasury institution (GiroCredit), which brought together two different systems, a large part of the data collection effort, including op risk identification, had to be done manually. This data collection project went back to 1999. Subsequently, it benefited from the fact that since 2001 op risk data collection has been decentralized on Excel spreadsheets.

Main sources of manual work have been the audit reports, security reports, and customer complaints. Business lines, event types, and operational risk processes have been defined and specified for all day-to-day tasks. This approach permitted value-added solutions. Control has been maintained by comprehensive features and a range of monitoring and reporting tools.

The Erste Bank study found lots of high frequency/low impact (HF/LI) events (see Chapter 8). Interviews with experts helped to identify LF/HI events, with scenarios based on significant losses. Particular attention was paid to op risk losses, which go directly into the profit and loss statement. The following points identify the major findings of this study, presented by Franz Reif, Head of Group Risk Controlling, Erste Bank, at the 2003 Basel Masterclass:

■ The quantification of risk requires frequency and severity to be modeled separately
■ Frequency is best modeled by a Poisson distribution
■ The severity distribution is lognormal, and
■ The integration of frequency and severity distributions is effectively done by Monte Carlo simulation.

FREQUENCY DISTRIBUTION WITH MEAN 10

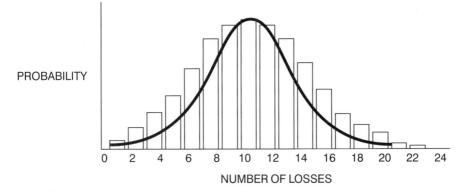

LOG NORMAL SEVERITY DISTRIBUTION

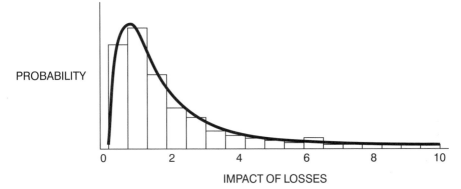

Figure 6.6 Quantification of operational risk at the Erste Bank. The Erste says that quantification of operational risk requires frequency and severity to be modeled separately

A snapshot of the two distributions is shown in Figure 6.6. The Erste Bank paid significant attention to tail events for which have been used internal data and scenarios elaborated between headquarters and the business units. Distributions obtained from public databases as well as from operational risk data consortia of other banks have also been of assistance.

With the aim of fulfilling high quality criteria, a risk assessment method has been developed in collaboration between the operational risk control project and the bank's risk management organization, as well as the security department, and auditing. Senior management expects that, with practice, the chosen approach to operational risk assessment and control will turn into risk self-assessment; and that it will also change the bank's culture in regard to risk management.

Notes

1 D.N. Chorafas, *The 1996 Market Risk Amendment. Understanding the Marking-to-Model and Value-at-Risk*, McGraw-Hill, Burr Ridge, IL, 1998.
2 D.N. Chorafas, *Modelling the Survival of Financial and Industrial Enterprises. Advantages, Challenges, and Problems with the Internal Rating-Based (IRB) Method*, Palgrave/Macmillan, London, 2002.
3 D.N. Chorafas, *Financial Models and Simulation*, Macmillan, London, 1995.
4 D.N. Chorafas, *Managing Operational Risk. Risk Reduction Strategies for Investment Banks and Commercial Banks*, Euromoney, London, 2001.
5 D.N. Chorafas, *Modelling the Survival of Financial and Industrial Enterprises. Advantages, Challenges, and Problems with the Internal Rating-Based (IRB) Method*, Palgrave/Macmillan, London, 2002.

7 Five models by the Basel Committee for computation of operational risk

7.1 Introduction

The five models advanced by the Basel Committee on Banking Supervision for computation of operational risk charges are shown in Figure 7.1 on a double scale: expected amount of capital allocation, and complexity. Top to bottom, they range from the simplest, basic indicator approach, to the more sophisticated scoreboard. In fact, there will be a family of scoreboard approaches, not just one of them. Practically every financial institution will develop its own, though these will undoubtedly have common elements outlined in Chapters 8 and 9.

The alternatives shown in Figure 7.1 are still under study, but financial institutions should not wait for the ultimate in operational risk control. The operational risk control solutions we are after, particularly the more complex, will be based on models. Several will be novel. Today nobody has the 'best' solution. As the reader is aware from Chapter 1, everybody is learning about operational risk and how to control it.

Companies should not be afraid to develop experimental approaches for operational risk control, even if they are imperfect. As pointed out in the preceding chapters, in 10 years from now nobody would have the same solution as they developed today. Mathematical models evolve over time. Opinions, hypotheses, algorithms, and heuristic solutions for operational risk control are and will most

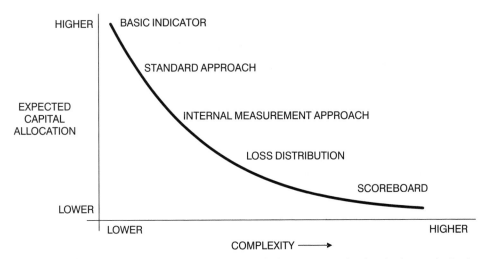

Figure 7.1 Capital allocation will likely vary with the operational risk calculation method being used

likely be different from one entity to the next, though we may have a consensus on:

- The kind of data that is necessary
- Its analytical treatment, and
- What constitutes acceptable cost for op risk control.

Chapter 6 has raised the cost/benefit question: At what point is the cost of operational risk immaterial relative to the cost of managing it under the dual perspective of high frequency events with low impact, and low frequency events with high impact? (See also Chapter 8.)

In a way not unlike the control of credit risk and market risk, providing solutions to operational risk problems is a learning curve. Therefore, companies that are serious about operational risk control do not try to address all types of operational risks at the outset. This is a prescription for failure. Chapter 6 has made reference to this fact. Solutions must be:

- Focused
- Pragmatic
- At the right strength level
- Implementable and manageable
- Scalable and changeable
- Cost-effective.

Valid solutions take account of different perspectives and definitions of operational risk. The way we manage operational risk is affected by the manner in which we view it, the board's and CEO's determination to come to grips with op risk, the skills and tools at the regulators' disposal, and our resolve to put op risk under lock and key. This is, in the last analysis, the reason why Basel II wants banks to put aside capital for operational risk control.

7.2   The effort to measure operational risk and the basic indicator approach

The point that operational risk control is everybody's responsibility – and most particularly every manager's – has been made on several occasions. The methodology shown in Chapter 2 in regard to operational risk classification and identification has in its background the need to develop an op risk control culture. Part of the discipline for operational risk control is gathering and databasing information through a rigorous data collection process.

- Tracking operational risk data by business line
- Monitoring loss events and gathering loss information, and
- Allocating op risk losses between properly identified risk classes.

These are basic prerequisites for the successful implementation of all of the five models advanced by Basel for operational risk control. The possible exception is that of basic indicator approach *if*, and only if, the bank plans to stay with it rather than graduating to more accurate – therefore more complex – and data-hungry solutions.

In the whole range of modeling possibilities, from the standard approach to the scoreboard, it is important to keep in mind that an operational risk is better managed when it is mapped to a risk indicator and has a cause-and-effect relationship.

■ With losses resulting from this op risk related to its appearance, and
■ With a control system being put in place able to follow op risk events and non-events step-by-step.

A basic prerequisite to an effective operational risk control is to understand the inherent frequency of operational risk events, as well as the likelihood of failure of prevention measures. By 'non-events' is meant op risk appearances that, according to cause and effect, should be there but fail to show up. The effective use of reporting practices to swamp operational risk, and the ability to minimize data collection costs, are two other prerequisites.

With the possible exception of the basic approach, no matter which of the Basel Committee methods we choose, our strategy should be to comprehend the operational risks we are confronted with, identify them, monitor them, transform them, and eventually accept minimal low impact op risks. This acceptance should be pragmatic. The British Bankers Association says: 'We don't believe you can measure operational risk in anything similar to the way we measure credit risk and market risk.'

At the same time, however, the British Bankers Association points out that there are some operational risks where tolerance must be zero. At its basic level, a credit institution's tolerance of operational risk has to do with:

■ Amount of losses in a worst case scenario
■ Frequency of appearance, and its underlying causes, and
■ Brand name risk and Pillar 3 of Basel, that is market discipline.

Again, no matter which of the Basel Committee models we choose, organizational and procedural changes, which help in controlling operational risk, cannot and should not be avoided. An example is so-called 'sunset clauses' for job descriptions. Because operational risk is, to a large extent, human risk, there must be clauses that, for instance, specify:

■ 'Approval to handle transactions is valid from time t_1 to t_2 *(say, one year)*', or
■ 'If a person does not do any of the authorized operations in time t, the authorization ends.'

Life-long learning about operational risk control is another basic requirement. There is always a learning curve. From time to time traders do a rare type of transaction, but in between the rules and regulations may have changed. Compliance will suffer if they are not updated on new rules. Also when the bank's internal policy changes without updating of skills, traders, loans officers, and other professionals will still execute in the old way, which leads to operational risk.

Sunset clauses on job description and the steady updating of skills aimed at swamping operational risk is a different way of saying that op risk events and their likelihood should also be examined from an applied psychology viewpoint. Applied psychology looks at operational risk from a triple perspective:

- Antecedents
- Behavior
- Consequences.

The most powerful classes of antecedents are those describing expectations and linking to results as well as to specific consequences. The human factors embedded in operational risk bring into perspective the wisdom of having in place a system of merits and demerits, which roughly corresponds to the proverbial carrot and stick.

This is not only true of complex approaches to operational risk control; even the standard approach requires that attention be paid to human factors. But, as I have already mentioned, the basic indicator approach (BIA) is so elementary that it might be exempt from the human factors requirements. Its capital charge is one lump sum, too coarse to allow reflections on individual performance in keeping operational risk under lock and key.

Banks using the basic indicator approach solution must hold capital for operational risk reasons equal to a fixed percentage denoted by α (not to be confused with α, the level of confidence in an operating characteristics curve). The algorithm is:

$$K_{BIA} = \alpha \bullet EI$$

where:

K_{BIA} = Capital charge under BIA
EI = Exposure indicator for the whole institution, provisionally based on gross income
α = Constant (fixed percentage) set by Basel

In September 2001, the formula became:

$$\alpha = \frac{0.12 \bullet MRC}{GI}$$

where:

MRC = Minimum regulatory capital (e.g. 8% of the bank's risk-weighted assets)
GI   = Gross income

Gross income is averaged over a 3-year period, α. Following QIS3, Basel set the fixed percentage $\alpha = 15\%$.

What exactly is represented by *gross income* is discussed in section 7.3. Notice that *if* GI is taken by each of eight business lines, and *if* we distinguish between seven different types of operational risk, *then* we transit from the basic indicator approach to the standard approach by Basel. This 8×7 operational risk matrix introduces enough detail to bring human factors requirements into perspective.

7.3   Capital charges under the Basel Committee's standard approach

One basic element the basic indicator approach (BIA) and the standard approach (SA) have in common is that they use gross income as a proxy of operational risk exposure. There the similitude ends, because contrary to BIA, which looks indiscriminately at the whole institution's gross income as indicator of op risk – and, therefore, as a basis for capital charge – as we will see in this section, SA differentiates between classes of operational risk exposure.

This makes Basel's standard approach a more detailed method for calculating capital requirements connected to operational risk, and positions it at the root of a family of modeling solutions whose gradual evolution in complexity is shown in Figure 7.2. Precisely for this reason, in Chapter 6 I have suggested that a dry run for capital allocation for operational risk can benefit by using the standard approach as a first step towards more detailed modeling. The Basel definition of gross income is:

Gross Income = Net Interest Income + Net Non-Interest Income

and

Net Non-Interest Income = fees + commissions
 – (fees and commissions payable)
 + net result of financial operations[1]
 + other income

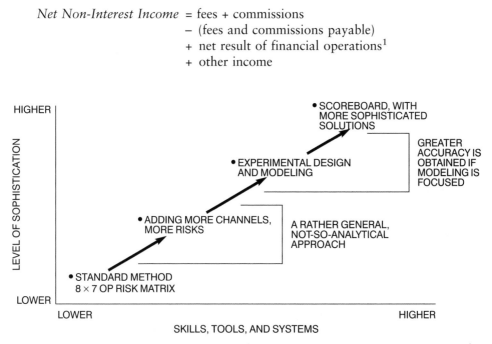

Figure 7.2 There is a progression in levels of sophistication, accuracy, and complexity of solutions

In the 'other income' component of net non-interest income should not include extraordinary or irregular items. This means that the measure of 'other income' should reflect income before deduction of operational losses.

With the standard approach, gross income is divided among eight pre-determined business lines. A β_i multiplier is applied to the income from each one of them (more on this later). The capital charge is the sum of these eight product line products. Note, however, that the Basel Committee is still considering the levels of β_i, and the same is true of α in connection to BIA.

Why should 'gross income' be taken as a basis for operational risk charges? This is a question often asked by bankers and the answer has been partially discussed in Chapter 6. An evident problem with gross income is that the more money an entity makes the more it is taxed in terms of op risk capital reserves – even if its business does not have a high level of operational risk.

But other methods, too, have their downside. One banker I spoke to suggested that an easy answer to the query 'Why should gross income be taken as a proxy?' is 'Why not?' He immediately added, however, that a more managerial response would be 'Which are our alternatives?' In the following, I have classified the operational risk indicators discussed by Basel:

Criteria based on financial statement figures

■ Gross income
■ Number of employees
■ Total compensation
■ Book value of assets
■ Market value of assets
■ Deposits
■ Number of client accounts
■ Number of accounts and their average balance.

Criteria reflecting actual value of transaction

■ Number of transactions
■ Value of transactions
■ Mean value and standard deviation of transactions, within a quarter
■ Idem, but in connection to annual value of transactions.

As the reader will appreciate, none of these alternatives is perfect. But an advanced method approach (see section 7.4) might select and use more than one of them. This is with the proviso that the regulators approve such a solution, and the bank choosing it is consistent in its application.

Let's now look more carefully into the operational risk capital charge under the standard approach. As shown in Figure 7.3, the financial institution's business activities are divided into eight major product lines, each having associated to it a constant β_i. (The reader will recall that we briefly looked into this matrix in Chapter 2, with another reference made to it in Chapter 6.) With SA, gross income must be calculated by major product line, each being characterized by its own β_i.

TYPE OF BANK	8i / 7j	BETA FACTORS	INTERNAL FRAUD	EXTERNAL FRAUD	EMPLOYMENT PRACTICES AND SAFETY	BUSINESS PRACTICES, CLIENTS, PRODUCTS	DAMAGE TO PHYSICAL ASSETS	BUSINESS DISRUPTION, SYSTEM FAILURES	EXECUTION DELIVERY, PROCESS MGMT
INVESTMENT	CORPORATE AND GOVERNMENT FINANCE, MERCHANT BANKING	β_1							
INVESTMENT	TRADING AND SALES	β_2							
COMMERCIAL	RETAIL	β_3							
COMMERCIAL	OTHER COMMERCIAL	β_4							
COMMERCIAL	PAYMENTS AND SETTLEMENTS	β_5							
COMMERCIAL	CUSTODY, AGENCY SERVICES	β_6							
OTHER	ASSET MANAGEMENT	β_7							
OTHER	RETAIL BROKERAGE	β_8							

Figure 7.3 i,j, business line/event type classification

Investment banking
β_1 Corporate, government, merchant banking
β_2 Trading and sales

Commercial banking
β_3 Retail
β_4 Other commercial banking activities
β_5 Payments and settlements
β_6 Custody, agency services

Other business lines
β_7 Asset management
β_8 Retail brokerage

Figure 7.3 also outlines the seven operational risks, j, retained by the Basel's standard approach. The first algorithm is the constant representing a fixed percentage set by Basel, relating required level of capital to level of gross income. The formula was:

$$\beta_{i,j} = \frac{0.12 \bullet MRC_i \bullet ORS_{ij}}{GI_{i,j}}$$

where:

MRC = minimum regulatory capital
ORS = operating risk share

GI   = gross income
I   = 1...8, business line defined by standard approach
j   = 1...7, type of op risk defined by standard approach

Capital charge is computed by summation of regulatory charges across major product lines through the algorithm:

$$K_{SA} = \sum_{i=1}^{n} \beta_i \bullet EI_i$$

where:

K_{SA} = capital charge under standard approach
EI_i = exposure indicator for each business line

Based on Basel Committee statistics, Table 7.1 presents the weighted average of β_i factors for the eight business lines in SA.[2] Notice that in corporate finance the standard deviation is greater than the mean, while in custody and agency services they are nearly equal. Because of this, with a one-tailed distribution a 99% level of confidence will be 347% greater than the mean – which of course leaves much to be desired.

With gross income (GI) taken as exposure indicator, the algorithm of the standard approach becomes:

$$K_{SA} = \sum_{i=1}^{n} \beta_i \times GI_i$$

Each business line must have its own multiplier βi. As of QIS3, Basel set β in the range 12–18%:

Business line	Multiplier
Corporate finance	18%
Trading and sales	18%
Retail banking	12%
Commercial banking	15%
Payment and settlement	18%
Agency services	15%
Retail brokerage	12%
Asset management	12%

To effectively handle operational risk through the standard approach a bank must be well versed in database management:

■ Identifying exposures to operational risks,
■ Assessing potential impact of risk on solvency, and
■ Implementing a system of interactive management reporting.

	Median	Mean	Maximum	Weighted average	Standard deviation	Weighted average of typical β by business line
Corporate finance	0.131	0.236	0.905	0.120	0.249	2
Trading and sales	0.171	0.241	0.775	0.202	0.183	8
Retail banking	0.125	0.127	0.342	0.110	0.127	1
Other commercial banking	0.132	0.169	0.507	0.152	0.116	3
Payments and settlements	0.208	0.203	0.447	0.185	0.128	7
Custody and agency services	0.174	0.232	0.901	0.183	0.218	6
Asset management	0.113	0.149	0.283	0.161	0.073	5
Retail brokerage	0.133	0.185	0.659	0.152	0.167	3

Table 7.1 Standardized approach with eight business lines. Experimental estimate of regulatory capital

7.4   The effort to develop advanced measurement approaches

With the exception of cause and effect relating to well-known operational risks, in cases already established beyond doubt, analytical studies are not only the better way to operational risk control, they are the *only* way. This section explains how and why analytical approaches help to uncover the reasons for and behavior of operational risks that can hit a company at any time with largely unexpected consequences, and it concludes with one of the advanced methods by Basel II.

In Basel Committee terms the more advanced studies associated with operation risk control and asset allocation come under the heading of Advanced Measurement Approaches (AMA). To my mind, they differ from the standard approach in the sense that they are analytical solutions. It is, therefore, necessary to explain the concept of system analysis and how it can be used in a practical sense, the way it is done by tier-1 credit institutions. As a term, *system analysis* is composed of two words.

- *System* means an assembly of constituent parts united by interdependence in functioning. The word system is also used to denote a universe.
- *Analysis* is a mental act of investigation and query. Analytical queries help to challenge the 'obvious', which may be beliefs, pre-established notions, or prejudices.

Prejudices, Albert Einstein said, are those notions that parked themselves in the human brain before the age of 6. Analysis in the sense of investigation usually, though not always, takes the road of dividing a whole, or system, into its constituent parts and looks at their roots. The next mission is to investigate each of these parts both on its standalone merits and demerits, and as an integral, functioning part of the whole system under study.

Put simply, system analysis makes the difference between what we 'need to know' and what we 'want to know'. Therefore, an analytical investigation truly helps *only* if management and the professionals know what they need, or what they are after. This contrasts to a standard solution, like SA, because the eight main product lines and seven operational risks which it uses have already been defined by Basel, while analysis, including cause and effect investigation, may be done within each of these business lines and op risk classes.

System analysis lies in the background of all three advanced measurement approaches: the internal measurement approach (IMA), loss distribution (LD), and scoreboard. The investigation promoted by system analysis makes the difference between the operational risk guidelines characterizing the standard approach (which is fixed) and the freedom to:

- Choose a different solution, and
- Bring greater detail to the business line.

To some extent, going towards richer analytics is a one-way street, because once the bank obtains supervisory approval for one of the advanced approaches, it cannot regress backwards. To a greater or lesser extent it has to follow along a line of greater sophistication, and rightly so since this is the sense of moving forward. The analytical approach is part of system thinking, which implies the following:

- Stop using humans as number grinding machines.
- Develop and implement mathematical models.
- Apply mathematical tests of significance.
- Steadily evolve the system concept in a feed-forward sense.

In a significant number of cases, the feed-forward element is introduced for prognostication reasons, and it is a basic element of system thinking that aims at framing the present as a function of the future – not of the past. Inference is the keyword in this connection.

AMA also features other prerequisites. A critical one relates to the database and requires that data should go back at least 5 years (see section 7.7 below). A bank must have high technology able to capture, filter, and report operational risk information. It is also necessary to integrate external operational risk loss data to test the model and strengthen model usage.

The Basel Committee says that over a period of time regulators will review and adjust the AMA method chosen by credit institutions. Basel also brings attention to the fact that effective usage of AMA poses challenges of openness, transparency, flexibility, readiness to change, and an action-oriented strategy. This is valid both:

- Within the organization choosing AMA, and
- In the banking industry as a whole.

Financial institutions developing AMA solutions must be expert in business case analysis as well as keen to choose an advanced operational risk measurement and monitoring methodology, best fitting their operations. The actual choice of an exact approach depends on many factors, some of which are internal while others are external (see Chapter 9 on Pillar 3 and market discipline).

Among the three AMA solutions advanced by the Basel Committee, the internal measurement approach (IMA) is the simpler and more structured. In essence, it is an intermediate step between the standard approach and more sophisticated methods. With IMA capital charge is computed by the algorithm:

$$K_{ij} = \gamma_{ij} \, EL_{ij} = \gamma_{ij} \bullet (EI_{ij} \bullet, PE_{ij} \bullet, LGE_{ij})$$

where:

EL_{ij} = expected loss in business line i because of op factor j
EI_{ij} = exposure indicator, ij, based on gross income ij
PE_{ij} = probability of event (that an operational risk j occurs)
LGE_{ij} = average loss given an op risk event
γ_{ij} = a multiplier translating the estimate of expected loss, EL_{ij}, into a capital charge, per i business line and j type of op risk event

The Basel Committee suggests that the γ_{ij}, for each business line and operational risk event type combination will be specified by banks, probably through consortia. γ_{ij} will be subject to acceptance by supervisors, with the overall charge calculated as the sum of capital charges for individual business lines/op risk event type matrix entries.[3]

The reader will remember that the standard approach outlines eight business lines and seven operational risk event types. An analytical internal operational risk measurement model should do better than that. It might take, for instance, twenty or more business channels and a dozen or more op risk event types. This shows that IMA is not a standard approach under a different name, but one that has built-in greater flexibility and can be adapted to the business lines and operational risks faced by a specific bank.

There are, however, shortcomings associated to the internal measurement approach, which mean that IMA is not so popular among commercial bankers and regulators. It needs a multiplier to move from expected losses to unexpected losses. The γ must be produced by business line, but doing so by event type becomes very complex. Most big banks have chosen the loss distribution approach; a few adopted the scoreboard solution.

7.5 Capital allocation with loss distribution approach

It is self-evident that a more advanced solution to measurement and monitoring of operational risk than IMA has to be based on sound internal loss reporting practices. This brings into the picture the need for data capturing, databasing, and datamining requirements discussed on several occasions in the preceding chapters. Accuracy in operational risk loss data is not obtained overnight. Historical information must extend beyond 5 years, and it should be validated and reliable.

The conditions I have outlined here are crucial whether we talk of a bank's own operational risk data, or of a database created as a consequence of a collaborative effort, like the ORX consortium, which was discussed in Chapter 6. With AMA, reliable operational risk data are necessary all the way:

- From the development of algorithms and heuristics,
- To calculations made through real-life op risk information, and
- Process control, helped by scenario analysis, simulation, and stress testing.[4]

Another integral part of the AMA approach, which is valid to all operational risks, is to have in place an action-oriented methodology that will allow operational risks to be brought under control. The analytical approach may be a powerful tool, but even the most sophisticated toolbox will be of little service if timely corrective action is not being taken to right the balances.

Take Basel's *loss distribution* (LD) approach as an example. What is aimed at here, the Basel Committee suggests, is that banks generate estimates of operational risk capital, based on historical measures of losses. Implicit to this statement is the fact that banks will do their utmost to bend the curve of targeted operational risks and cut their losses – hence they will exercise corrective action.

Here we are faced with two sets of loss data, and hopefully with two distributions: ex ante and post mortem to operational risk control. Hopefully, the post mortem mean and standard deviation will be smaller than the statistics of ex ante. However, judging quality performance in a dependable manner requires accurate and detailed operational risk information over a number of years:

- By channel, and
- By identified op risk.

Reporting standards, too, should be revised and upgraded. As Part 1 has underlined, reporting should be fully interactive, observe realspace requirements, and make extensive use of confidence intervals. The results we are obtaining from system analysis and operational risk tracking will vary quite significantly depending on the level of confidence we use. Figure 7.4 dramatizes this reference by showing:

- The mean value of a normal distribution and a skew distribution.
- The 95% and 99% confidence intervals corresponding to the skew distribution (more on this in Chapter 8).

A basic principle in system analysis is that action-oriented results must be presented in a way people understand the meaning and are comfortable working with them. This means that reporting solutions will have to be studied, negotiated, and implemented case by case, worked out with senior management and the professionals who will use the data to bend the curve of operational risk.

The 99% level of confidence should be observed throughout the institution, and it should be reported interactively. Operational risk information must be datamined on-line. Besides real-time operational risk data capture, databasing, datamining, and interactive reporting, attention must be paid to the algorithms that will be used. This

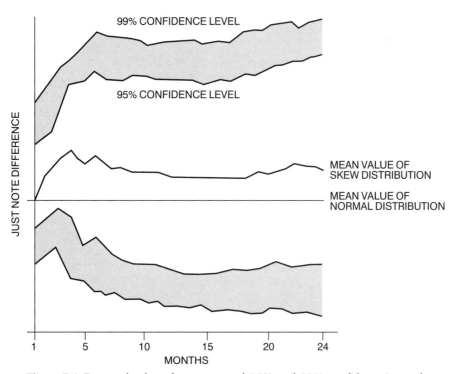

Figure 7.4 Expected value of exposure and 95% and 99% confidence intervals

is an important part of the choice to develop and implement advanced measurement solutions.

The good news is that the effort to develop AMA solutions faces challenges that have already confronted other sectors of the economy. Loss distributions have been investigated by the insurance industry in its work to price risks. A valid statistical loss distribution approach is, to a significant extent, an adaptation of the actuarial process:

■ Frequency and severity are modelled independently, and
■ The distribution of total losses is computed as a combination of the two.

Some experts have been suggesting that a confidence level of 99% is not enough. 'Three 9s' or 99.9% is better. I agree with this statement. Banks that choose the 99.9% level of significance should however appreciate that they have to put aside a greater amount of op risk capital reserves. Set against this, however, they obtain much greater assurance that they are well financed to withstand extreme events.

Let me add that, as of this moment, there is no industry standard for loss distribution, just as there is no industry standard for the scoreboard. Some people say LD is a bottom-up approach, while the scoreboard (see Chapters 8 and 9) is a top-down attempt to capture the loss profile. To my mind, that is nonsense.

■ Both loss distribution and the scoreboard try to be forward operational risk calculations, and
■ Both must have a rich quantitative basis, which implies a sound initial estimation, historical data, and post mortem data.

Also, both the loss distribution approach and the different scoreboard methods require steady vigilance through real-life tests, to determine a capital charge based on loss data, or some other chosen variable(s), and to allocate such capital charge to the business lines.

In 2002, the Basel Committee conducted an operational loss data collection exercise which can be valuable to the loss distribution methodology. This study gained information on 47 000 events involving operational hazards like fraud, system failure, and settlement errors. Data came from 89 credit institutions in several countries.

Because of the information it has provided, this Basel study on operational risk data is a milestone. The lack of loss information has hindered progress in developing advanced measurement approaches for assessing operational risk under Basel II. Evidence advanced by this exercise shows that loss data exhibits considerable clustering around certain:

■ Business lines, and
■ Event types.

For example, there is significant clustering in retail banking which tends to experience many frequent but small operational risk events. There are also business line/event type combinations with few to no op risks being reported. However, it is unclear whether low reporting frequency in these areas reflects:

- A short data collection window
- Gaps experienced in data collection, or
- Low probability of events types occurring for certain business lines.

Moreover, low frequency by no means indicates low risk, because operational risk events in this class tend to have high impact. Low frequency/high impact (LF/HI) events (see Chapter 8) are characteristic of exposure by banks and other financial companies to *long tail* risks. Stress testing can help to unearth valuable information about outliers and extreme events.[5]

A question discussed during the research meeting is where such calculations should be done. There is no one correct answer to this question. Some companies have decided that op risk capital calculations should be performed at group level, followed by allocation to business lines. Others follow the opposite road.

Whichever organizational approach may be chosen, implementation of loss distribution, like that of scoreboard solutions, requires design objectives. One of them is economy: attaining required performance at an acceptable cost. Another is performance, expressed in throughput, timeliness, and accuracy. Still another is implementability. The computational approach of the loss distribution may be based on a matrix of op risk cells:

$$X_{ij}$$

This matrix addresses two-by-two the axes in the three-dimensional frame of reference shown in Figure 7.5. The operational risk events being recorded and analyzed will be characterized by a distribution. Tentative statements concerning different types of distributions may be made: normal, lognormal, Poisson, skew, leptokyrtotic, chi-square, and so on. These hypotheses will have to be tested.

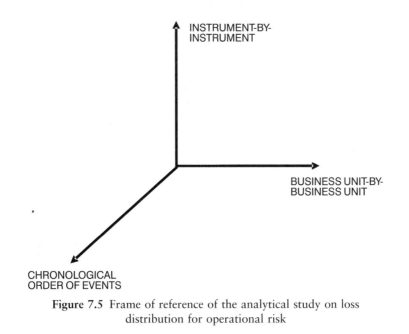

Figure 7.5 Frame of reference of the analytical study on loss distribution for operational risk

Sometimes compromises are necessary because, in the general case, one of the design criteria is availability of skills, data, and financial resources to do the required job. While money would not buy a solution, lack of money may inhibit developing one. Finally, due attention has to be paid to expandability. Credit institutions deal with almost steady change in their volume of transactions, nature of business, and losses from operational risks associated to both of them. A flexible model is the best approach, and senior management must look after this issue of flexibility.

7.6 Databasing and datamining information on operational risk

Typically, the underlying database for operational risks will consist of internal and external op risk loss data for all events being traded – including high frequency and low frequency, as well as high impact and low impact operational risks. The reader is by now aware of the fact that there are many prerequisites in developing an operational risk database. Examples include:

- Determining the loss data to be databased in practical business terms
- Tracking the drift from low impact to high impact events
- Costing the monitoring and measuring of operational risk losses
- Performing peer-to-peer studies on op risks, and
- Capitalizing from data swapping between financial institutions facing the same or very similar op risks.

Data swapping is particularly useful with loss information produced as a by-product, which may be of value to other firms in a bank's value chain. There is really no reason why credit institutions should not collaborate in operational risk control, and data swapping is a way of doing so – provided op risk identification, data formats, and files are homogeneous.

Operational risk databases have to be rationally designed, with both operational risk classification/identification (see Chapter 2) and interactive access and reporting in mind. Banks do not really have a choice of doing otherwise. The building of a first class operational risk event database has become mandatory, as the Basel Committee expects banks to:

- Include operational risk in their *loss event* records, and
- Have clear policies regarding the measurement of exposure by business line and op risk type.

One of the challenges that have to be faced is that of data uncertainty. Data uncertainty arises from incomplete data streams and from measurement errors, particularly in key variables of the model. It may also arise from faulty filtering. When a measurement error occurs, a response to mismeasured data induces uncertainty in the output and subsequent indecision on corrective action. To attenuate the adverse effects arising from imperfect data, we can sometimes use the whole set of available information to:

- Cross-check the imperfect element against other relevant sources of information, and
- Gauge the extent to which the data may be subject to a given type of measurement error.

The weight associated with individual information variables should depend on how precisely those variables have been measured. A particularly adverse effect of errors in estimating the quality results is that of bias, which can be long-lasting and/or greater than what is generally accepted as error tolerances. Solution of the op risk database problem requires:

- Ensuring comprehensive coverage through organization
- Increasing frequency and accuracy of data collection
- Addressing data quality issues at every point of each trade
- Associating loss events to each type of identified op risk, and
- Recording the frequency of each op risk as well as its impact.

Data filtering is a challenge which, after being thoroughly studied, can be automatically performed using interactive knowledge artefacts (agents). Able solutions involve applying configurable filters both for input and for exception reports, assuring that a first class data validation process is in place, and monitoring all processes for early detection of op risks.

Results are significantly improved if we both plan and test *our* preparation to deal with operational risk issues, and data collection associated to them; establish clear responsibilities and accountabilities in terms of op risk information; and coordinate operational risk control with compliance requirements as well as cost control measures. A problem I have often encountered is that companies do not pay enough attention to:

- Tracking each operational risk event
- Identifying the legal issues connected to these events, or
- Maintaining a corporate memory facility (CMF).

Common reasons for being behind in operational risk tracking are: lack of strategic assessment, incomplete classification and identification of operational risks (see Chapter 2), insufficient definition of the different risk types, and a general weakness in databasing which may be due to legacy computer programs and the use of paleolithic computer technology. Other shortcomings manifest themselves from:

- Failures to report the frequency of op risks
- Failures to explore the later consequences of op risk, and
- Failures in implementing interactive datamining.

The latter case is widespread. It is particularly found among institutions that fail to appreciate that datamining has emerged as a class of analytical techniques that go beyond classical statistics. Its aim is that of examining large quantities of data that often involve multiple variables.

Challenges associated with datamining may be statistical in nature but they do go well beyond business statistics, targeting the inference of patterns from data. This calls for an inventory of tools and techniques that aim at examining large quantities of data in search of previously overlooked relationships, or even hints that prove to have specific value in problem solution.

As these issues demonstrate, the system analysis discussed in section 7.4 does not end with loss data and their study. A whole infrastructure has to be built. Under this modern business approach the better definition of datamining is the process of interactive analysis, testing, and extraction of information from databases for the purpose of discovering new and valuable:

- Patterns
- Rules, and
- Trends

from relationships existing, but not easily apparent, between data elements. Because of its potential, datamining is receiving widespread attention in finance and other branches of industry, while companies are increasingly investigating how best to exploit the potential of datamining technology to obtain competitive advantage.

Several credit institutions and other organizations are developing models to aid in analysis, testing, or prediction. Palo Alto Management, a consultancy, suggests that datamining is one of the fastest growing applications areas in the business intelligence market. It is also a multidisciplinary field, which draws from:

- Knowledge engineering
- Database management practices
- Data visualization tools
- Market research projects
- Pattern recognition
- Statistics, and other mathematical tools.

Current research into datamining helps in developing new algorithms, as well as in answering the basic question, i.e. how to perform this activity in the best possible way while keeping costs under check. Classification is one of the better ways of facing the datamining challenge within the realm of operational risk analysis. This is the reason so much attention has been paid to the classification/identification of operational risks in Chapter 2.

Practitioners sometimes complain that the multitude of datamining algorithms appears confusing. In reality, however, the underlying concepts are simple. They include taxonomy, distributions, clustering, pattern discovery, and modeling. Every one of these is vital to the able implementation of the loss distribution approach and of the scoreboard(s).

Clustering is concerned with partitioning data elements into homogeneous subsets. A cluster is a subset of data sharing one or more common characteristics that have been properly defined. This makes them in a way homogeneous for the project on hand. Datamining analytics help to:

- Uncover affinities among data consisting of one or more variables, and
- Understand the extent to which the presence of specified variables imply the presence of other variables across a data pattern.

Both points are important in tracking and analysing risk events. Let's remember, however, that datamining is not an end, but a means to an end. Its benefits accrue from the operational results and the assistance these provide in achieving a specific objective. The contribution of datamining is that of a discovery-driven approach, almost always with no a priori hypothesis stated for a particular problem under study.

7.7 Early findings with operational risk models, and the notion of model risk

It is reasonable to expect that increasing complexity in financial products and in banking at large boosts operational risks. Just as reasonable is the hypotheses that different business lines or channels will have different levels of operational risk. However, banks responding to the second consultative paper by the Basel Committee said they did not find significant differences between business lines. For instance,

- β for investment banking was not inherently more risky than β for retail banking (see section 7.3).

Subsequently, the Basel Committee has given itself the task of calibrating β for the standard approach. By contrast, with both the loss distribution approach and with scoreboard, credit institutions will be so-to-speak on their own in developing patterns for operational risk based on careful monitoring, calibration, and evaluation control.

These models help in a predictive sense but opinions among bankers are divided regarding the extent of this assistance. The British Bankers Association believes that past operational risk loss data does not enable prediction of future losses. Other organizational difficulties connected to the modeling endeavor we have been discussing include what to do with:

- Central functions
- Support activities
- Cost centers
- Profit centers
- Materiality, and
- Quality assurance.

Credit institutions should not believe that models are a kind of penicillin for operational risk control, or for any other activity. What the use of models does is provide a level ground for people assigned responsibilities for operational risk control, while also assuring better awareness about op risks, and a corporate memory facility to support future effort. Contrasted to the use of models, their development is more instrumental in terms of assistance, because it helps to:

- Clarify thinking
- Identify key variables
- Study their range of variation, and
- Pinpoint outliers.

Models should be used both in connection to normal testing and stress testing,[6] but we should also be aware that there is *model risk*. Model risk is a term that describes how different models can produce other than the intended results: for instance, different prices for the same financial instrument. Market-wide, these pricing differences have an effect on gains and losses.

Astute traders, with better models, can capitalize on mispricings in other traders' models which are less accurate than their own. The fact exists, however, that model failures can be significant when (1) only quantitative approaches are used for operational risk management and (2) the care exercised in model building (or model choice) is less than it should be. Model risk originates in:

- Hypotheses being made
- Insufficiency of data
- Algorithms being chosen, and the
- Way the model is being used.

One of the reasons for model risk is that, because they are usually built in an inflexible way, many models do not cope well with sudden alterations in relations among key market variables and factors characterizing financial instruments. Furthermore, Moody's Investors Service has conducted research indicating that models are not more accurate than analysts' opinions.

This conclusion is not at all surprising, since standard models for predicting credit quality typically contain less than five explanatory variables, while a top analyst may consider up to 1000 data points. An evident remark of course is that not everybody is a top analyst. Moody's thinks that models' benefits probably lie:

- More in performing a monitoring or warning function
- Rather than in arriving at a particular rating opinion.

What Moody's says about credit models is valuable also with market risk and operational risk models. The danger of overdependence on models is compounded by the fact that the financial industry has not yet succeeded in modeling operational risks in a highly dependable way. For instance, factors escaping modeling, at least so far, are mismanagement, and internal controls. There are also other reasons why models fail. At the risk of being repetitive, I bring them one more time to the reader's attention.

- Data is deficient, unreliable, or altogether non-existent.

In my experience, this happens in more than 95% of cases. Let's face it, too many banks still have a rather primitive database, with heterogeneous information elements which it is very difficult to exploit.

■ Assumptions and simplifications that abstract too much from the real world.

These typically concern hypotheses on market behavior and key product variables. Also, simplifications like linearities and the wide use of the normal distribution (see Chapter 8).

■ Management's misunderstanding or misinterpretation of the model's output.

This happens very often because senior management is not aware of the background factors and of what models do and do not provide. Model illiteracy sees to it that many managers do not appreciate the meaning of what they get in terms of model output.

■ The entity's IT infrastructure is a legacy loaded with applications that come from the IT equivalent of the Middle Ages.

A direct result of the so-called EDP-orientation is that the IT system does not work in real-time and does not use interactive datamining and ad hoc visualization. It is not for nothing that the abbreviation 'EDP' no longer means 'electronic data processing', but identifies emotionally disturbed people. Being stranded in this sort of backwater condition makes it impossible to establish a dynamic sensitivity to operational risks, to do stress testing, and to institute proactive op risk control solutions.

Let me conclude with this comment. Banks have to observe both qualitative and quantitative standards with AMA solutions. Qualitative standards start with an independent operational risk management function, including active involvement of board and senior management, and they extend all the way:

■ From reviews by internal and external auditors
■ To validation of metrics and models by auditors, as well as by supervisors.

Auditing must verify internal control processes (see Chapter 2), and pay particular attention to data flows. It must also assure that operational risk results, and their causes, are transparent and accessible. Also, that the op risk monitoring and documentation system is first class.

Quantitative standards for operational risk should be comparable to the Advanced IRB method for credit risk. They should include correlations, and show sufficient granularity. They should also have the ability to capture the tail of the distribution. Both internal and external operational risk data are important, and the same is true of scenario analysis and evaluation of control factors. Quantitative approaches must provide assurance that:

■ Expected losses in op risk are appropriately funded
■ Unexpected losses are modeled, and the bank provides a safety net, and

■ Risk mitigation, including insurance and cap on insurance, is thoroughly studied.

In the borderline between qualitative and quantitative standards for operational risk are boundary issues. For instance, cases where the boundary of op risk with credit risk and market risk is not clearly defined. Examples are:

■ Credit loss aggravated by faulty documentation
■ Market risk due to exposure that has not been immediately hedged.

A solution to boundary problems requires properly designed databases whose contents are enriched through steady monitoring and accurate data collection. A first class database solution is also necessary in order to develop and recognize empirical correlations.

Notes

1 This is the most important class.
2 Basel Committee on Banking Supervision, *Working Paper on the Regulatory Treatment of Operational Risk*, BIS, September 2001.
3 Basel Committee, *Regulatory Treatment of Operational Risk*.
4 D.N. Chorafas, *Stress Testing. Risk Management Strategies for Extreme Events*, Euromoney, London, 2002.
5 Chorafas, *Stress Testing*.
6 Chorafas, *Stress Testing*.

8 High frequency events, low frequency events and the Six Sigma method

8.1 Introduction

Chapter 7 has explained two of the three more advanced methods for operational risk control by the Basel Committee, which go beyond the basic and standard approaches. As the reader will recall, the loss distribution approach offers financial institutions the possibility of modeling their operational risk control based on their own loss data, under the supervision of the regulators.

The difference between loss distribution and those operational risk control approaches that lie lower in the food chain is that the former can allow many degrees of freedom on which a bank can capitalize. This issue of degrees of freedom provides a common ground between loss distribution and the scoreboard. This chapter explains a methodology and tools that can help in constructing a scoreboard eigenmodel beyond the matrix of loss distribution. The method I am advancing rests on two pillars:

1 A distinction between high frequency op risk events and low frequency events, which is necessary for planning purposes.

High frequency and low frequency events belong to different loss distributions. The way to bet is that high frequency operational risks tend to be low impact, though exceptions are always possible. The opposite is true of low frequency operational risk events. This chapter distinguishes between:

■ High frequency/low impact (HF/LI) events, and
■ Low frequency/high impact (LF/HI) events.

As Annette C. Austin, of ABN-Amro, told me: 'It is more easy to identify HF/LI events, than LF/HI events. Unexpected risks are usually the result of LF/HI events.' Austin also added that even for the same bank the pattern of HF/LI, LF/HI is not the same in all countries.

ABN-Amro operates in 48 countries. A pattern that prevails in the UK is not the same as that which characterizes operational risk in Romania. The principle with analytical studies is that the deeper we go in terms of focus and detail, the more careful we must be in regard to the frequencies and values assumed by the different factors we wish to control.

Let me add that HF/LI, LF/HI is a very recent classification which permits a more efficient way of attacking operational risk in its roots. It also provides means for controlling each distinct class of op risk events, and leads the user towards a methodology that might also be applicable with credit risk and market risk.

2 An efficient, statistics-based control method known as Six Sigma, which enables weakness in management control to be identified and redressed.

Six Sigma is above all a discipline, which has been successful *if* and *when* top management stands solidly behind it. This is the case study we will follow in sections 8.6 and 8.7. Taken individually, the tools included in Six Sigma are not new. What is new is their integration into a methodology that is used by the CEO and senior management to assure that they are in charge of operational risks.

Let me also add, in connection to the theme of this chapter and of Chapter 9, that the line dividing the scoreboard from loss distribution approach is not rigid. The difference largely lies in the methodology that is adopted and the tools used to obtain a more sophisticated solution, including:

- The frequencies associated to op risk loss events, and
- The necessary disciplinary action for operational risk control.

This chapter shows the method, describes the tools, and brings to the reader's attention the importance of discovery and its deliverables contrasted to the beaten path. Chapter 9 will present different applications, both less sophisticated, like templates, and more advanced. It will do so, most particularly, from the viewpoint of the contribution scoreboards might make to market discipline.

8.2 Understanding the concepts of high frequency and low frequency events

Figure 8.1 presents the pattern of a *normal distribution*. True enough, this is an approximation of events which happen in real life, where distributions may be skew, leptokyrtotic, platokyrtotic, chi-square, or have other characteristics like lognormal, Poisson, and so on. But even if it is an approximation, the normal distribution is widely used in finance, manufacturing, merchandising and scientific studies because:

- It constitutes a standard frame of reference, and
- It is endowed with rich tables enabling the analyst to make a great many tests.

To use a normal distribution we need metrics, or momenta. The first momentum of a normal distribution is the *mean*, identified by $\bar{x}$ when we talk of a sample, and by μ in case of the mean of a population. The former is called a *statistic*; the latter is known as a *parameter*. The second momentum is the *variance v*. The very often used *standard deviation* is the square root of the variance.

- *s* is employed to indicate the standard deviation of a sample.
- σ is the symbol of the standard deviation of a population.

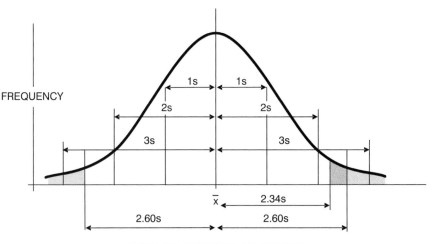

STANDARD DEVIATION FROM MEAN

Figure 8.1 The Bell-shaped curve of the normal distribution

The third momentum of a distribution is its *skewness*. The test for a skew distribution is that its mean and its *mode* do not coincide. The mode is the highest frequency in a distribution. Another statistic is the *median*: to the left and to the right of the median lie an equal number of measurements, or points. Still another statistic is the *mid-range*, half way between the highest and lowest measurement in a distribution.

In a normal, bell-shaped distribution, the mean, mode, median, and (theoretically only) mid-range are equal. This is not true of a skew distribution. The fourth momentum is its *kyrtosis*. We will not be concerned in this text with skewness and kyrtosis, though as experience is gained with high frequency and low frequency operational risk events they might become important metrics.[1]

The concept to retain from Figure 8.1 is the probability of events falling within 1, 2, and 3 standard deviations. Table 8.1 gives the probabilities associated to one-tailed and two-tailed distributions. We talk of two-tailed distributions when all extreme values, say beyond 3s – the outliers – are, for any reason, considered to be pertinent to the study or the test which we do.

This is not always the case. Often we are interested in extreme events represented only by the largest (or smallest) values in a distribution. In this case we are dealing with a one-tailed distribution. With value at risk (VAR), for example, the regulatory 99% level of confidence represents maximum amount of losses corresponding to a one-tailed normal distribution.

Taking into account the prevailing frequencies, it is evident that all operational risk events falling within $\bar{x} \pm 1s$ are high frequency compared to those towards the tails of the distribution. The same is true, albeit to a lesser degree, of events falling between $\bar{x} \pm 1s$ and $\bar{x} \pm 2s$. Beyond this, the frequency of operational risk events decreases, though when we talk of outliers we typically make reference to events which are:

■ Beyond $\bar{x} \pm 3s$
■ Or, even more so, beyond $\bar{x} \pm 5s$

With two-tailed distribution

$\bar{x} \pm 1s$	68.27% of the area under the curve
$\bar{x} \pm 2s$	95.45% of the area under the curve
$\bar{x} \pm 3s$	99.73% of the area under the curve

Also with two-tailed distribution

$\bar{x} \pm 1.96s$	95% of the area under the curve
$\bar{x} \pm 2.60s$	99% of the area under the curve

But with one-tailed distribution

$\bar{x} + 1.65s$	95% of the area under the curve
$\bar{x} + 2.34s$	99% of the area under the curve

The same statistics prevail with $\bar{x} - 1.65s$ and $\bar{x} - 2.34s$

Table 8.1 Area under the normal distribution curve for a given number of standard deviations

These outliers are very low frequency events, though somewhere out in the tail(s) there may be spikes of higher frequency (see Figure 6.4). The way to bet is that an operational event which is an outlier will, most likely, be of high impact. This lies behind the distinction made in the Introduction between:

- HF/LI, and
- LF/HI.

Outliers are not the only low frequency events fitting the above reference. Any operational risk with frequency beyond $\bar{x} \pm 1.96s$ for the two-tailed distribution; and $\bar{x} + 1.65s$ for the one-tailed distribution (or, correspondingly $\bar{x} - 1.65s$) is low frequency. Extreme events, however, are a special class to be watched very carefully.

Operational risk events, whether high frequency or low frequency, take place at any moment in the cycle of financial operations. An example of very frequent daily transactions with operational risk information is presented in Figure 8.2. 'In their *sundry losses* account, banks have extensive information on high frequency/low impact op risks,' according to Brandon Davies of Barclays Bank. These come from:

- Fraud,
- Errors in execution, and
- Other issues.

This op risk information is fairly well documented as it piggy-backs on other data, like accounting. It is also nearly free of cost. The challenge is to classify the operational risks embedded in it, and sort out sundry losses by class. More difficult to come by is information on low frequency/high impact operational risk events.

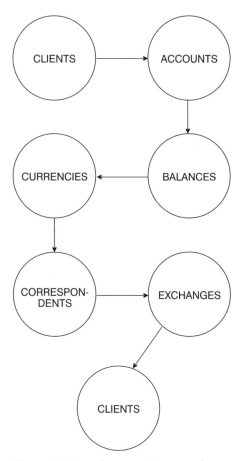

Figure 8.2 Intraday operations are always exposed to high frequency or low frequency operational risk events

The ability to handle statistically LF/HI items and their pattern is limited by lack of data. Hence the need for data analysis over several decades in conjunction with extreme value theory. We are not yet there, because the content of our databases is not what it should be, as explained in Chapter 7. And as Austin (above) has suggested, it is easier to identify HF/LI events than LF/HI events (see the Introduction).

As work along the HF/LI and LF/HI starts gaining momentum, the databases get richer, and experience on the analytics of operational risk accumulates, we will be confronted with a different type of challenges. The more astute analysts will want to know why, typically, operational risk losses are non-linear in terms of:

- Size
- Frequency, and
- Severity.

These will become very interesting studies giving the financial institutions that undertake them a competitive edge. For the time being, however, the priority is to establish a firm basis for data collection and for frequency-and-impact studies which permit analysis of real life events, like operational risk, by means of increasingly more powerful mathematical tools. This brings into the picture the issue of system design, which is the subject of section 8.4.

8.3   Characteristics of high frequency and low frequency events

As was explained in the previous section, some operational risks have high frequency but low impact (HF/LI). Others have low probabilities but potentially large financial impact (LF/HI). Examples of high impact are major errors and omissions, fraud in high value transactions, physical loss of securities, bankruptcy of IT supplier or outsourcer, and so on.

Some high impact operational risk events are extremely difficult to predict. An example is *Andersen Risk*, or the risk of deception. Because of risk migration and the specific nature of auditing, balance sheet evaluation and analysis may become highly unreliable. Conflicts of interest may make matters worse. Either case brings into perspective the risk of deception, which can have one or more origins:

- Incompetence
- Repeated errors
- Lack of information
- Lack of transparency, and
- Outright conflict of interest.

The Basel Committee advises that increased automation has transformed relatively low impact operational risk events to high impact events. The interruption of business processes because of an extended disruption of services is an example (see Chapter 5

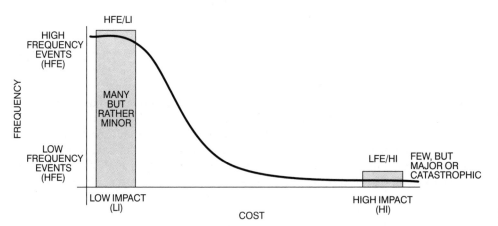

Figure 8.3 High frequency events and low frequency events are at the two ends of the distribution of operational risk

and Chapter 14). High frequency operational risk events, and those of low frequency, find themselves at the two ends of the distribution, in terms of impact, as shown in Figure 8.3.

With regard to frequency characteristics of operational risk events mentioned in section 8.2, the discussion on the normal distribution has documented that high frequency events occur within ±2 standard deviations from the mean. Low frequency events occur at the tails, or as outliers. *Spot* operational risk is typically of high frequency type. It occurs and it is recognized within a 1- to 5-day period. According to some estimates,

■ Spot events represent between 75% and 95% of the operational risk database.
■ Such events can be empirically observed, and they can be tracked with short time lag.
■ By contrast, low frequency op risks require a methodology for experimental analysis, as well as long-term observation and tracking.

Usually, though not always, low frequency events are forward operational risks. They often consist of residual high frequency events that went undetected, and grew over time. Sometimes the lead time to their painful discovery is quite long. Low frequency operational risk at Daiwa Bank (in its US operations), Sumitomo (the copper scandal), and Showa Shell took between 10 and 12 years to reach catastrophic proportions.

The Daiwa Bank, Barings and other similar examples suggest that it is wise to always remember that a high frequency, low impact event can become low frequency, high impact events over time. Nick Leeson's operational risk started with relatively minor misdemeanors but grew fast over 2 years. Improving an operational risk control system means looking proactively to minimize unexpected events, and the impact associated to them. The rule is that:

■ The older is the error,
■ The larger its potential impact and result.

Low frequency/high impact op risks, like trader malfeasance, might be externalized through innovative insurance policies with prompt pay-out features (see Part 3). This essentially means exchanging operational risk with credit risk. Alternatively, some years ago a French bank was saying that its policy was to keep in its safe the passports of its forex dealers.

It is better to be proactive and establish a system of forward-looking controls. However, low frequency operational risk problems have been addressed more in appearance than in fact. Particularly scant attention has been paid to their impact. To distinguish between high impact and low impact we must ask:

■ What's the product?
■ What's the process?
■ What's its specific nature?
■ What's its operational risk(s)?
■ What's the frequency of this op risk (or risks)?
■ What's their impact when they happen?

Timely corrective action is a critical variable. Typically, the cost is lower *if* the error is caught in time, particularly when the potential for damage is higher. That is why the preceding paragraphs have emphasized that the best strategy is that of projecting forward on operational risk. This requires:

■ Establishing the time horizon
■ Defining the set of market parameters
■ Examining the distribution of likely low frequency op risks
■ Examining the distribution of high frequency op risks, and
■ Having an effective mechanism for corrective action.

Can this be part of the scoreboard solution? The answer is: 'Yes!'; that's why I have included these two lists of bullet points. Though the exact definition of *scoreboard* has not been given by Basel, it is only normal to expect that the very interesting HF/LI, LF/HI approach needs a framework for its implementation – as well as control action, provided by Six Sigma (see sections 8.6 and 8.7 below).

Once the framework is in place, we can enrich it with analytics: for instance, calculating the effects of *volatility* in operational risk events within our enterprise and in its business environment. Equally important is to estimate, over time, the amount of operational risk events which are captured versus those that escape immediate attention and are discovered later on.

Both the frequency and the importance of transaction being executed, in money terms, influence the definition of low impact and high impact. Other factors, too, contribute in creating a system in which improvements in operational risk control can be effected by acting proactively to minimize unexpected losses from operational risk. Taking all these factors and risk characteristics into account, over a period of time we can create an *operational risk profile*, by type which has been classified and identified (see Chapter 2). Our goal should be:

■ To approach operational risk recognition with nearly 100% certainty, and
■ Apply statistical quality control charts to map the behavior of each identified op risk (more on this later).

In conclusion, the implementation of Basel's AMA methods, particularly loss distribution and scoreboard should be the pivot point for change in past practices where, to a large extent, operational risk problems have been addressed more in appearance than in fact. A documented analytical approach to operational risk control requires a thorough framework within which it will be exercised, as well as experimentation, including appropriate system design, as the following section documents.

8.4 Experimentation and system design for operational risk control

An experimental approach to operational risk control is not just the better alternative when we are faced with unknown factors. It is the only way. Indeed, this is a basic

Status	Severity	Tolerance
Catastrophic	Very high impact	Zero
Major	High impact	Extremely low
Minor	Low impact	Expressed through template[1]

1 See Chapter 9.

Table 8.2 A classification of operational risks by severity and tolerance

principle in all scientific disciplines. Operational risk control is an issue that can benefit greatly from involving both system design and thorough testing. Given that *data* is the No. 1 challenge, among the critical questions to be answered are:

- How reasonable do the numbers look?
- Can they stand comparison to real-life results?
- Which sort of system design is meaningful in the longer term?

Borrowing a leaf from science's book,[2] experimentation is an indivisible part of any sound methodology aimed at controlling operational risk. Experimental design and testing help us to be comfortable with the solution that we choose.

A major step in the experimental approach is the classification and identification of operational risks (discussed in Chapter 2) followed by the distribution of operational risks in terms of frequency and impact. All risks must be classified in terms of severity, financial impact, and tolerance. Table 8.2 provides an example. Tolerances must be specific by specialized functions such as:

- Legal
- Compliance, and
- Security.

Cross-function coordination should provide an enterprise-wide pattern. Thresholds that make operational risks change status are very important, and they should be clearly defined. An example of thresholds in terms of frequency and impact is provided in Figure 8.4.

Minute, detailed work along the notions outlined in the preceding paragraphs is the methodology applied to code cracking in military operations, to read the enemy's secret messages and information exchanges. Superior intelligence, however, has prerequisites. A control system must be characterized by simplicity, cost-effectiveness, and flexibility. All three require:

- Clear objectives
- Qualitative and quantitative approaches to evaluation, and
- The ability to compare alternatives and reach decisions.

Whether the operational risk control project focuses on high impact and low impact risks, or any other subject, a mature designer will take only small steps while

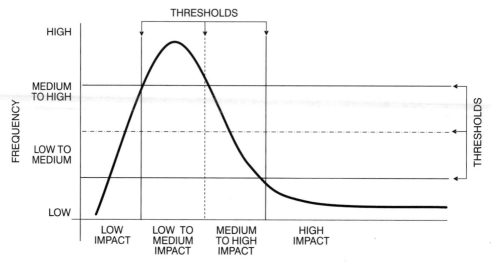

Figure 8.4 Thresholds in a frequency and impact characteristics curve

he investigates different possibilities. He will not implement a solution before making a prototype, obtaining results through testing, and examining gaps or inconsistencies. Systems designers who are worth their salt are:

■ Open to compromise on the detail,
■ But they would never compromise on the principle.

One of the principles in engineering design is *focus*. An operational risk model projected for a scoreboard solution must be focused in its design. Apart from the need for database support and algorithmic fitness, a great deal depends on answers to queries such as:

■ Who will use the model?
■ Under which conditions?
■ How accurate should it be?
■ Which type of test is appropriate?
■ Does the chosen level of confidence make sense?

If one were to sum up these five points in one sentence, this would read: Does the model and its results inspire confidence? Factual answers are important because the model output alone may not be convincing to the user – or the organization. The discipline and methodology of engineering design is the higher level reference.

In the 1980s and 1990s, when I was consultant to the board of the Union Bank of Switzerland, the bank had 35 computer-aided design (CAD) units in operation. Some of them were used for network design and maintenance. Others were implemented to automate office layout. During that same timeframe, in Tokyo, Nikko Securities was using CAD to design new financial instruments, and follow-up on them.

The use of engineering methods and tools in banking has given commendable results. Since the early 1980s Bankers Trust was talking about *bank engineering*. Once the discipline of engineering is admitted as being not only applicable but also desirable in a banking environment, system design becomes a culture – with plenty of benefits.

Let's also keep in mind that since 1996, with the Market Risk Amendment, the level of confidence, α, has become a stable issue in banking. This is an engineering tool widely used during World War II with the Manhattan Project, to promote high quality.

Figure 8.5 provides a bird's-eye view of the meaning of α, the confidence level. Operating characteristics (OC) curves, like the one in Figure 8.5, have been extensively used with the manufacturing of the atomic bomb as well as in aerospace projects. Originally implemented in the manufacturing industry, they assisted in defining the probability of acceptance of man-made goods by bringing into focus

- Producer's risk, the α, also known as Type I error, and
- Consumer's risk, β, the Type II error.

Notice that in an operating characteristics curve, consumer's risk, β, should not to be confused with volatility. The sense of it is that in spite of an inspection plan supposed to reject lots of lower quality than an established quality standard, some of them may filter through. An example from banking would be giving a loan to a party who would not qualify for it, because of nepotism, unreliable credit references, or other reasons.

By contrast, the producer's risk α corresponds to rejecting a lot that should have been accepted because of its quality characteristics. Translating into a credit institution's environment, this would mean rejecting a loan application that should

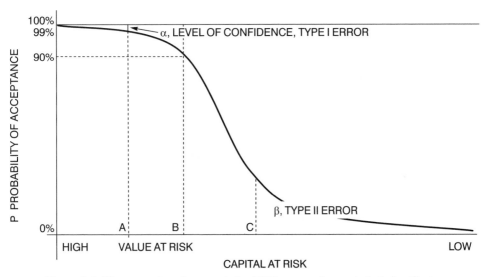

Figure 8.5 The operating characteristics (OC) curve of a statistical distribution

have been accepted. I had a professor of banking at UCLA who taught his students that a loans officer who rejects too many loan requests is as bad as one who is really poor in screening the loans.

In banking, operating characteristics curves have been employed with the risk adjusted returns on capital (RAROC) model, of the late 1980s, as well as with expert systems developed and used by the financial industry at around the same timeframe. Let's recall that the 1996 Market Risk Amendment by the Basel Committee stipulated that the level of confidence should be equal to 99%. As can be seen in Figure 8.5:

■ An $\alpha = 0.10$ (which corresponds to 90%) would give an estimate of value at risk (VAR) much less than an $\alpha = 0.01$.
■ The $\alpha = 0.10$ (Point B), however, will leave 10% of all cases out of this VAR measure, while with $\alpha = 0.01$ (Point A) the exception to computed VAR will be 1%.

All these concepts, though not the VAR model itself, are fully applicable with high frequency/low impact and low frequency/high impact operational risks – that's why I present them in this section. Supervisory authorities of G-10 countries look favorably to the development and use of operational risk models. As the directives coming out of Basel indicate, they believe that models should be developed for better management of operational risks – and they should enable a quantitative appreciation of risk by senior executives, and at board level.

8.5 Tools most useful in the analysis of operational risks

Like statistical quality control charts (see the following section), operational risk models can be instrumental in promoting internal control. The way the European Central Bank phrased its current policy: 'Measurement units and control procedures are two of the challenges lying ahead.' The pillars of measurement units are metrics and datastreams. Both must be reliable and this requires aggregating and consolidating data collection systems across business lines, while appreciating that business lines are not watertight in terms of information flows. Other requirements include:

■ Mapping business lines to risk-oriented regulatory definitions
■ Differentiating between risks which are HF/LI and those LF/HI
■ Projecting on how operational risk information will be interpreted by stakeholders, regulators, and credit rating agencies.

A prerequisite for effective op risk measurements is to analyse how to track progress towards uniform, comprehensive, and accurate measurement standards. Another prerequisite to operational risk analytics is the understanding, appreciation, and use of the appropriate tools. The following is a list of ten tools that I have found to be the most important for operational risk analysis and control – and therefore strongly advise they are used with the scoreboard method:

■ *Statistical distributions*: starting with the normal, and proceeding with lognormal, leptokyrtotic, Poisson, chi-square.

- *Classification studies* to help in identification of risks, and reflect their relative ranking through taxonomy
- *Bayesian probabilities*, leading to causal modeling, including cause and effect analysis.
- *Fuzzy engineering* to help in quantifying qualitative estimates of op risk frequency and severity.[3]
- *Genetic algorithms*, which assist in developing forward-looking operational risk data as well as in optimization.[4]
- *Extreme value theory* addressing maxima, minima, and the tail of operational risk distributions
- *Non-linearities*, to account for changes in trends and in frame of reference of operational risks
- *Experimental design*, including Latin squares, for the study of variance, as well as the use of control groups
- *Operating characteristics curves* to analyse the pattern of producer risk and consumer risk (see the previous section).
- *Quality control charts* by attributes and by variables, to plot op risk events as they happen (more on this in the next section).

Most of these tools can make a vital contribution to the identification, monitoring, and handling of high impact and low impact events, as well as in other operational risk studies. Exception reporting also helps, but it poses the challenge of capturing and interpreting outliers residing at the distribution's tails – therefore requiring the use of the aforementioned tools.

While accuracy of the systems and procedures we employ is only one dimension of overall performance, it is also a most crucial one to operational risk control, and a pivotal reference to the goodness of fit of end results. Therefore it requires special attention. A valid model for operational risk control will address at least five fundamental issues that arise in measuring accuracy of the system we are using:

- Defining *what* is measured, including the issue, its frequency, impact, datastream and the model which will use this data.
- Explaining *how* it must be measured, through which metrics and framework necessary to assure reliable data collection.
- Specifying *when* and *how* the data will be used to map observed HF/LI and LF/HI operational risks against limits and tolerances.
- Assuring continuity in the representation of the operational process, and the risks embedded into it, over a longer timeframe.
- Targeting corrective action aimed to assure that the operational risks we are after are steadily supervised and recorded.

Crucial to model accuracy is the type of errors being encountered and their frequency. These, and their likelihood, are best expressed through an operating characteristics curve, which has been explained above. In this and in many other projects where measurements play a most critical role in terms of accuracy and results, we typically encounter the two types of errors with which the reader is already familiar: α and β.

Enough about quantitative measurements; there are also qualitative ones. Take as an example option pricing. One of the cardinal principles in banking is that front desk and back office should be separated by a thick wall, in terms of responsibility. This is often violated through *outsourcing*, and *its* operational risk. For instance:

- Using brokers as consultants presents problems of conflicts of interest.
- Brokers have incentives to lean towards lower volatility estimates because they assist in making deals.

The price paid by NatWest Markets, the investment banking arm of National Westminster Bank, for mispricing its options is that it ceased to exist. In March 1997 the institution's controllers found a £50 million ($77 million) gap in its accounts which eventually grew to an alleged £300 million ($460 million).

After the announcement of such huge losses it was said that at NatWest Markets: Risk management did not have good enough computer models. This might be true, but it was not the only reason. The first and foremost reason for failure in pricing by NatWest Markets was the types of errors just mentioned, which can be plotted as Type 1 and Type II errors in an operating characteristics curve.

Prudence in product pricing tends to lead to less Type I errors than Type II. Analytical approaches should, however, target both types of errors, making them as small as possible. Larger sample sizes, both in absolute terms and as percentage of the population under study, help. It is above all advisable to be very prudent because, other things being equal, minimizing one type of error usually increases the other type of error – which is shown both in a practical sense and through statistical theory.

A snapshot of Type I and Type II errors associated to the pricing of options – a high impact operational risk – is given in Figure 8.6. Not only third party opinions, as in

ACTUAL VOLATILITY

	LOW	HIGH
ESTIMATED VOLATILITY — HIGH	CORRECT PREDICTION, PROPER ASSESSMENT	TYPE I ERROR, OPPORTUNITY COST POSSIBLY LEADING TO BANKRUPTCY
ESTIMATED VOLATILITY — LOW	TYPE II ERROR, OVERPRICING LEADING TO LOST SALES	CORRECT PREDICTION, PROPER ASSESSMENT

Figure 8.6 The pricing of options and op risk, Type I and Type II errors, operational risk measurements

this example on option pricing, but also strategic alliances and mergers increase operational risk. They do so because they make information less controllable as:

- They compound layers of bureaucracy, and
- Blur the company's responsibility lines.

In conclusion, solutions to be provided to the problem of measuring and controlling operational risk must be pragmatic. Their study should benefit from the best available tools. Financial institutions should maximize their operational risk activity by enabling interactive consultation between headquarters and operating units. This enables a better understanding of the types of operational risks, their frequencies, impact, possible limits and practical implications, which will in turn make feasible more rigorous op risk-based controls.

8.6   Using Six Sigma to improve management control over operations

Six Sigma is a management control methodology whose success rests, in large measure, on the exercise of discipline. Its tools are based on mathematical statistics and control charts. As such, it is an ideal solution for scoreboard approaches.

Six Sigma achieves results by reducing subjective errors, which are very often present in the assessment of problems. Its applications domain ranges from engineering and manufacturing, to finance and accounting.[5] For instance, in auditing, it helps auditors define a process where results are subpar and a concentrated effort must be made for improvements. Six Sigma tools help in:

- Measuring the process to determine current performance
- Analysing available information to pinpoint where things have gone wrong
- Instituting controls good enough to prevent future deviations and other mal-occurrences, and
- Improving the whole process to better its dependability and performance.

Sometimes senior management sets broader goals to be met through Six Sigma. 'Six Sigma is about developing tomorrow's managers,' says 3M Chairman and CEO W. James McNerney Jr. 'It gives them a shot to show what they can do.'[6] Companies should however be aware that Six Sigma is not the cure for all operational risks, neither is it waiving senior management's accountability. If anything, it makes it more visible.

There are two different ways to explain why Six Sigma can make a major contribution in operational risk control. It has been a deliberate choice to start with statistical quality control (SQC) charts that can serve as effective op risk tracking tools, and they should be looked at as the best currently available candidate for structuring the backbone of the *scoreboard* method.

For starters, a statistical quality control chart can be by *variables*, or by *attributes*. An SQC chart by variables has a central tendency (the *mean of means*, or $\bar{x}$) and upper and lower control limits. In its pure form, that is, in its original development, an SQC chart maps the critical variable measured by means of samples taken from a production process. Each sample has a mean $\bar{x}$. The central tendency of the SQC chart is the mean of these means, while each successive sample may be above or below that line $\bar{x}$.

'Nothing walks on a straight line,' said Dr Werner Heisenberg, the physicist. It is therefore proper to allow for variation, but within limits. A classical SQC chart has upper and lower tolerance limits (reflecting engineering specifications) and within them upper and lower quality control limits. As long as the sample measurements keep within these limits, the process is *in control*.

This concept of limits applies to many financial issues as well. For instance, the price of a barrel of oil may be targeted between $20 and $26, with $23 the mean value. Other commodities, too, are subject to targets or limits. Figure 8.7 shows that in the second quarter of 2000 spot prices for natural gas have escaped their traditional trading range, as they moved rapidly upwards.

A chart showing the trading range is not quite the same as a statistical quality control chart, but it is one familiar to bankers and as far as visualization is concerned

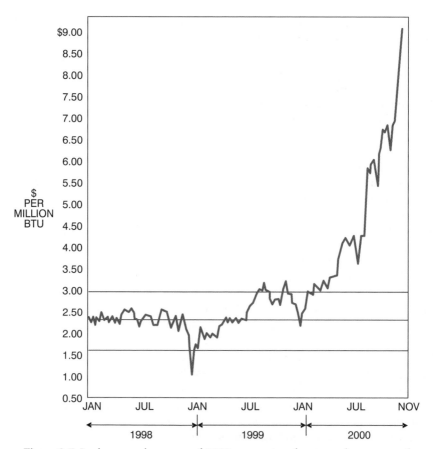

Figure 8.7 In the second quarter of 2000 spot prices for natural gas escaped their typical range and went out of control

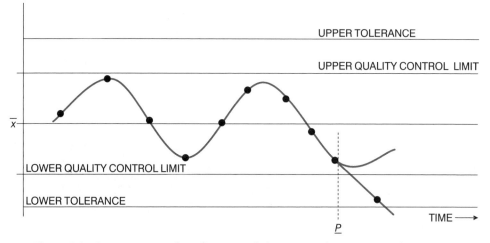

Figure 8.8 Using a statistical quality control chart to track currency exchange rates

the effect is nearly the same. That's why I chose it as a first example. Other examples are closer to the original concept of SQC charts. Figure 8.8 shows a statistical quality control chart designed to track currency exchange rates.

As it will be recalled, a couple of decades ago the European Common Market had established an exchange rate mechanism (ERM) with a currency exchange target and tolerances above and below that line. The central banks involved in this agreement:

- Supported a currency falling below the lower tolerance, and
- Saw to it that no currency broke the upper tolerance by strengthening against the others in 'the snake' in an inordinate way.

This and similar cases regarding tolerances can be followed effectively through a statistical quality control chart. Purposely, in Figure 8.8 both upper and lower tolerances *and* upper and lower control limits have been plotted. Statistical theory says that *if* there are three points in a row, *then* there is high probability a fourth one will follow in the same direction. Indeed, at point P there is a bifurcation.

- If the curve had a bend upwards, the process would have been in control.
- Since it continued downwards, the currency concerned had to be immediately supported or fall out of tolerance – as happened in the early 1990s with the British pound.

Other quality control charts are by *attributes*. Something either happens or it does not. These are most suited to low impact op risks. They help to bring op risk control tracking to each office, desk, and individual's level. An example is given in Figure 8.9. An extra reward from the implementation of quality control charts by variables and by attributes is the possibility of post-mortem evaluations. In my experience, post-mortems are most critical in:

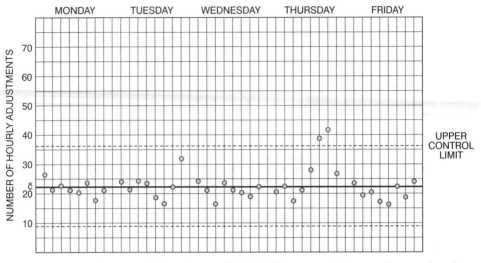

Figure 8.9 Quality control chart for number of defects per unit in a week on an hourly basis

- Building a risk awareness culture, and
- Providing consensus on operational risk control policies.

SQC charts and templates (see Chapter 9) are a support function permitting the matching of operational risks, people, and management control systems. After all, this is what operational risk control is all about.

In the following section we will follow a different approach in appreciating what can be achieved by the steady tracking of operational risk through mathematical statistics. This is an alternative and yet complementary method, and at the same time it goes to the heart of the cultural change targeted through Six Sigma.

8.7   The practical implementations of Six Sigma are convincing

Typically in business and industry, a distribution of events under measurement characterized by a large standard deviation stands for low quality. The opposite is true when the standard deviation of the distribution is small. Two normal distributions, for example, may have the same mean, but the standard deviation of the first is double that of the second. When this happens,

- The events (products, services) in the first distribution are low quality.
- Those in the second distribution are high quality compared to the first.

This can be appreciated in Figure 8.10 from a real life application at General Electric. Before Six Sigma was implemented, the expected value ($\bar{x}$, mean) of a distribution of goods was held at a reasonable distance from the customer's specification, but the standard deviation was large and with 3σ ($3s$ would have been more accurate) there

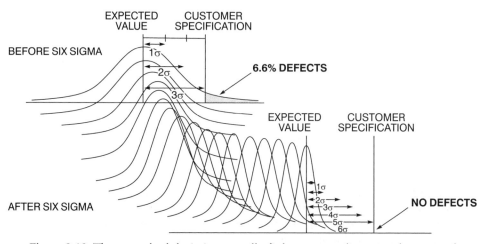

Figure 8.10 Three standard deviations usually fit between quality control target and customer specifications. But this is not enough (reproduced with permission of General Electric)

was 6.6% incidence of defects – that is, items that did not meet the specification, which can be seen as the tolerance in Figure 8.8.

Six Sigma, the methodology, changed all that. Quality improved greatly, and the standard deviation was halved. As a result, Six Sigma (6σ) separated the expected value – which in fact did not change – from the customer specification. There were no more defects. One might ask why accept the variation in the first place? The simple and straight-forward answer is: Because that's how natural and man-made systems behave.

- There are always tolerances, and
- There is in every case variation, even in the most tightly controlled processes.

Six Sigma's underlying control principles are much more general than the operational risk perspective, and its implementation gets increasingly enriched with mathematical and statistical tools. An example is General Electric's approach to quality control, not only in regard to the company's manufacturing divisions, but also at GE Capital.

GE Capital Six Sigma applications focus on financial services. A steady, unrelenting transition towards financial services has changed GE from a company that in 1980 derived 85% of its revenues from the sale of manufactured products to one that today is based 70% on the sale of services.

This planned, rapid transition has extended GE's market potential and enhanced its ability to bring value to its customers. But it has also required a deep cultural change – along with minute attention to operational risks – and Six Sigma has been instrumental in bringing both of them to life. The way GE has implemented them, the Six Sigma toolkits and methodology involve:

- Statistical quality control methods
- Experimental design to permit a rigorous test of hypothesis
- Chi-square testing to evaluate variance between two populations[7]
- A defect measurement method based on hard data
- A dashboard to map progress towards customer satisfaction (very important in banking)
- A Pareto diagram which exhibits relative frequency and/or size of events
- Root-cause analysis which targets original reasons for non-compliance or non-conformance
- Graphical tools for process mapping and interactive visualization.

GE Capital has derived very significant benefits from the implementation of Six Sigma. Its management says that the new methodology allows it to focus on quality, cost, op risks, and other root issues. In practical terms, it helps in reducing cycle time, swamping defects, and emphasizing the value of each individual contribution. The whole approach, and its implementation in financial operations, is guided by a systematic methodology:

- Utilizing training tools, and
- Doing a steady measurement of each individual performance.

Here is one example relating to marketing and sales. Business customers told GE Capital that for them a critical quality issue was how often a salesperson could answer their questions directly, without having to look into the matter later on and getting back to them with a certain delay. Adhering to the Six Sigma data-gathering discipline, each salesperson now keeps a meticulous diary, noting each time a customer asked him/her a question, and whether he or she was able to answer it immediately. Prior to Six Sigma immediate answers took place in only 50% of all cases. Therefore the effort was to deduce:

- Which types of questions salespeople are unprepared for
- What training would fill that gap, and
- Which people were best suited to the job of salesperson.

These are operational risk type problems. Their existence documents the fact that high quality of service and cost control correlate. Through Six Sigma, GE Capital Mortgage identified the branch that best handles the flow of customer calls. Then, management used that model to redesign the process in all other branches.

As Jack Welch, former CEO of GE, who turned Six Sigma into a fundamental methodology, put it: Customers once found the mortgage corporation inaccessible nearly 24% of the time. Now they have a 99% chance of speaking to a GE person on the first try. And since 40% of their calls result in business, the return for GE is already mounting into the millions.

J.P. Morgan Chase provides another example where Six Sigma's implementation led to commendable results. Both J.P. Morgan and Chase Manhattan were applying Six Sigma prior to their merger. After the merger, the applications got amplified. To bolster performance, the bank:

- Implemented Six Sigma in 300 projects where the main objective was that of squeezing costs out of every operation, and
- Put several of its channels under Six Sigma scrutiny. Applications range from distributing research results to selling derivatives.

Thousands of managers at JP Morgan Chase attended 'black belt' and 'green belt' classes to learn how to slash costs while increasing sales. Prior to the merger. Douglas A. Warner, then the JP Morgan Bank CEO, said these sessions helped to save $1.1 billion in 1999.[8]

The message the reader should take from these examples is that operational risk will not be controlled on its own accord. To bring it under lock and key, our culture, methodology, and tools must change. What is more the change has to be top-down with the board and the CEO:

- Taking the initiative, and
- Seeing that it seeps down the organization, to the lowest management level.

In conclusion, the methods and tools presented in this chapter are the *best scoreboard* solutions under today's technology. High frequency *vs* low frequency operational risk events, and the high impact *vs* low impact distinction enhance and strengthen the loss distribution approach, bringing it to a higher level of sophistication.

System design is necessary to provide the appropriate infrastructure. Statistical quality control and a broad range of other Six Sigma tools, particularly those targeting the control of defects[9], are the pillars of a methodology which ensures that senior management is in charge of operational risks.

Notes

1 D.N. Chorafas, *How to Understand and Use Mathematics for Derivatives, Volume 2 – Advanced Modelling Methods*, Euromoney, London, 1995.
2 D.N. Chorafas, *Modelling the Survival of Financial and Industrial Enterprises. Advantages, Challenges, and Problems with the Internal Rating-Based (IRB) Method*, Palgrave/Macmillan, London, 2002.
3 D.N. Chorafas, *Chaos Theory in the Financial Markets*, Probus, Chicago, 1994.
4 D.N. Chorafas, *Rocket Scientists in Banking*, Lafferty Publications, London and Dublin, 1995.
5 D.N. Chorafas, *Integrating ERP, CRM, Supply Chain Management and Smart Materials*, Auerbach, New York, 2001.
6 *BusinessWeek*, 22 July 2002.
7 D.N. Chorafas, *Statistical Processes and Reliability Engineering*, D. Van Nostrand, Princeton, NJ, 1960.
8 *BusinessWeek*, 18 September 2000.
9 D.N. Chorafas, *Integrating ERP, CRM, Supply Chain Management and Smart Materials*, Averbach, New York, 2001.

9 Market discipline, contrary opinion and scoreboard solutions

9.1 Introduction

'News,' said Lord Thompson, 'is what someone didn't want printed. The rest is advertising.' A prime mission, and responsibility, of the scoreboard approach should be to publish the operational risk news, the more so as there are no clear rules yet written for operational risk control – something comparable to the Code of Hammurabi for credit risk, published 3700 years ago.

Not only is the 'Code' missing, but also the regulation of, and capital allocation for, operational risk is very recent. It does not have roots. Chapter 1 has explained how it arose in 1999 and, by all likelihood, will be implemented in 2006. But Chapter 1 also brought to the reader's attention that the new capital adequacy framework by the Basel Committee rests on three pillars – and all three of them are important. Pillar 3 is *market discipline*.

To promote market discipline, banks must be transparent, avoid creative accounting, and have well-documented reserves. This applies to all three main exposures: credit risk, market risk, and operational risk. Transparency assures that the market is the criter; it also requires that the board and CEO provide regular public attestations as to:

- The soundness of the bank and of its assets
- The robustness of its systems, including management and information technology
- The existence of rigorous internal control, and
- Its ongoing exposure to credit, market, and operational risk.

It is beyond question that there must be strategic reserves to face imbalances in the banking book and trading book. The challenge is to provide the *evidence* about such reserves. To a large measure what Chapter 8 has outlined in connection to a sophisticated scoreboard – from high frequency/low frequency events to the implementation of Six Sigma – goes beyond capital allocation *per se* and has to do with market discipline.

Another important, but not thoroughly appreciated element, in market discipline and in operational risk control, is a culture permitting the development of dissent within the organization. Contrary opinion can be of great help in identifying and tracking credit risk, market risk, and operational risk. By contrast, a monolithic management culture is exposed to all types of risk. Dissent forces management to:

- Consider alternatives to op risk control
- Experiment with options, and
- Examine proactively results expected down the line.

The great leaders of industry have always encouraged diversity of opinion. They have promoted conflicting views among their immediate subordinates – and have wanted to see a dialog between different viewpoints, and therefore between conflicting judgments.

Effective decisions are not made by acclamation, and this is equally true of optimization of operational risk controls. Therefore, a scoreboard solution worth its salt should promote diversity of opinions up to the moment a decision is made on corrective action. It should establish criteria of relevance and define boundary conditions, but it should not lead to tunnel vision in operational risk control.

9.2 The Basel Committee on scoreboards and market discipline

According to a paper published by the Basel Committee in mid-2002, scoreboards provide means of translating *qualitative* assessments into *quantitative* metrics.[1] I would consider fuzzy engineering and the Delphi method as first class tools to do just that.[2] Basel advises the establishment of metrics that must give a relative ranking to different types of operational risk exposure. To be in charge of their operations risks banks should:

- Be productive in identifying indicators that may be predictive of future losses.
- Use as risk indicators statistics providing insight into the bank's risk position (the loss distribution being an example), and
- Establish thresholds and limits tied to risk indicators, alerting management to potential problem areas through steady tracking and visualization (see Chapter 8 on SQC charts).

Scoreboards, the Basel Committee says, may also be used to allocate economic capital to each business line. This can evidently be done with the standard approach (see Chapter 6) but only in a summary fashion, by pre-established groups of banking channels. Both the much greater detail and the duality of qualitative and quantitative characteristics should become available at scoreboard level.

Figure 9.1 provides a snapshot of what has been stated in the preceding paragraph, with an added reference to post-mortem verification. Borrowing a leaf from other regulatory disclosure requirements, such as credit risk, the following five points describe disclosures necessary for market discipline:[3]

- Past operational risks and their frequency
- Impact of each of these operational risk types
- Specific and general allowances made for control reasons
- Types of statistical methods used for quantitative disclosures
- Types of statistical methods used for qualitative disclosures.

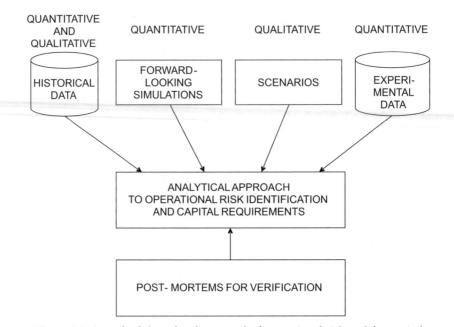

Figure 9.1 A methodology for the control of operational risk and for capital allocation

According to the new Basel directives, qualitative disclosures should be taken very seriously. All national regulators have the authority to conduct administrative proceedings that can result in censure, fines, issuance of cease-and-desist orders, suspension or expulsion of the bank or broker, its directors, officers, and employees. Correspondingly, also on the basis of extrapolation from Basel directives that focus on credit risk, quantitative disclosures for market discipline should be broken down by:

■ Aggregate amount of operational risk exposure
■ Specific types of operational risk exposure
■ Geographical distribution of such exposure
■ Industry/counterparty distribution of op risks including appropriate analyses.

An integral part of this quantitative evaluation is allowances for operational risk losses, recoveries, charge-offs, exposure covered by insurance contracts on-balance sheet, exposure covered through derivatives off-balance sheet, possible risk transfer through securitization similar to credit derivatives, identification of operational risk control enhancements and results being obtained.

All this is most pertinent to scoreboard solutions, because the majority of the issues outlined in the preceding paragraph are applicable only in connection to AMA. An example is the use of insurance as an operational risk mitigant. According to the Basel Committee, recognition of insurance instead of capital reserves for certain operational risks should be limited to those banks that use advanced measurement approaches.[4]

A scoreboard solution without embedded rules for post-mortems, as Figure 9.1 has suggested, would prove in the longer run to be substandard. We should always be ready to compare actual data with projections made on operational risks regarding frequency and impact, as well as to rethink our analysis of outliers. Not only are post-mortems crucial, but also the financial institution must make the results of operational risk post-mortems available:

- Externally to shareholders, and
- Internally to the jobholders.

That's market discipline. A good example here is the fact that more and more companies are undertaking to give their employees the same financial reports that they give their stockholders. One corporation, for example, has emphasized its annual 'Jobholders Meeting' in which management appears before the entire workforce and gives an account of its stewardship for the past year. Whether oral or written, such reports accomplish two results.

- They acknowledge the participation of the workforce in the enterprise, thereby enhancing their sense of dignity, and
- They convey an open, undistorted picture of the affairs of the institution and the problems it is facing, as well as its successes.

A basic notion that should become part of common consciousness is that no economy will produce the maximum benefits without an adequate system of incentives and rewards for all participants, and without market discipline. Key to both is accurate and dependable information – a reason why it is disquieting to see the fast rising number of proforma statements shown in Figure 9.2, which are themselves a sort of creative accounting with plenty of operational risk.

Regulators are trying to codify some norms for operational risk identification and reporting. In the UK the Financial Services Authority (FSA) has prepared an integrated prudential sourcebook which contains guidelines on op risks as contrasted to strict rules. Its implementation is projected for 1 January 2004. The contents include:

- Outsourcing
- Human resources
- Information technology
- Change management, and
- Business continuity.

A scoreboard's system design (see Chapter 8) should take full account of norms developed through such initiatives, even if their status is still that of guidelines. Beyond that, the design of a scoreboard should provide hard evidence on deliverables, accounting for the fact that internal and external auditors are the parties directly responsible for reports enhancing market discipline.

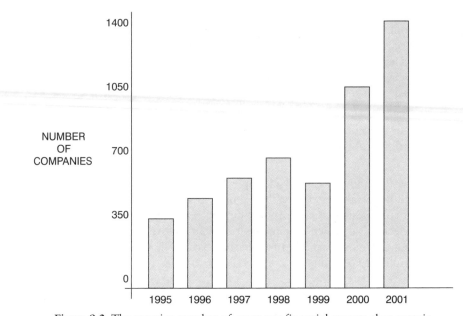

Figure 9.2 The growing number of company financial reports that contain proforma earnings. (*Source:* BIS, 72nd Annual Report, Basel, 2002)

■ Some regulators like the Fed, OCC, and FDIC, have their own examiners.
■ Others, like the FSA, are not resourced to do this, and they depend on the audit by chartered accountants.

In connection to this last point, there is a question of crossborder consistency. This, too, should be reflected in, and compensated by, the design of the scoreboard. To contribute to Pillar 3, external auditors must themselves be disciplined and they should use a normalized form of reporting on operational risk capital allocation by the entities they audit.

9.3   The use of templates with scoreboards

Reference has been made in Chapter 8 to the fact that there is no industry standard on what constitutes a scoreboard approach. Usually reference is made to a top-down method, which has a sound quantification basis, and for which historical data and datamining are very important. But the term scoreboard is not new. In the manufacturing industry it has been used for years to identify a methodology based on templates, able to:

■ Capture the profile of a process output, and
■ Represent the fitness of this production process within certain norms.

Scoreboards, in a template sense, are not terribly sophisticated, but they have been extensively used in risk control. They are essentially a system of mapping and assessment, which is easy to follow by production floor workers. In this sense, which fits well in an office environment in the financial industry, scoreboards could be distinguished into two groups:

- Lower end, and
- Higher end.

At the lower end, the scoreboard is a template, or family of templates, providing guidance on what falls within the norm(s). As such, it permits structuring of the control process regarding each specific operational risk. Its use should help to ensure that every office worker understands the error pattern, and each executive can immediately make a judgment.

An example from personal experience is given in Figure 9.3. It comes from the restructuring of warehousing operations with the objective of reducing the error rate in the expedition of lamps. In June, prior to the introduction of the new identification method, the error rate was high in all three warehouses: A, B, and C. But in three subsequent months, September, October, November, the error rate dropped significantly in warehouses A and B, where the new lamp identification method was introduced.[5]

- The average of results obtained in warehouses A and B became a template.
- The other 20 warehouses in which the new ID method was subsequently introduced had to perform, in terms of error reduction, as this template indicated or better.

As this example demonstrates, the objective of a template is that of fostering a consistent style of operational risk control for all departments and business units. The effective use of templates requires appreciating the risk impact of the events whose pattern is compared to that of the template acting as a control device. In simple, graphical terms, the template indicates:

- What is measured, and
- What is the acceptable/unacceptable op risk information.

What falls within the boundaries of the template (average error rate of A+B warehouses) is admissible in op risk control terms. What falls outside is not acceptable. The principle is that when control levels are standardized it is possible to overcome data incompatibility and provide for reconciliation within the operational system targeted by the template. Other uses of templates are:

- Building risk awareness culture, and
- Providing consensus on op risk policies.

It can be reasonably expected that the use of templates will increase as a result of continuing research by banks and professional organizations in principles, techniques, disclosure requirements, and visual presentation or operational risk information. Eventually, it might involve experimentation with forms of op risk statements that

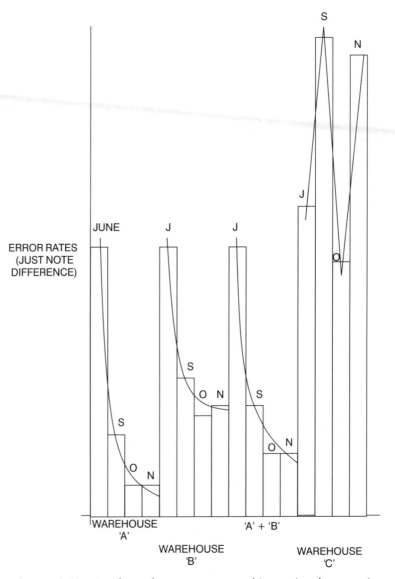

Figure 9.3 Hunting down the error sources and improving the system's accuracy

emphasize the reduction in the amount of exposure, and/or show the relationship of the individual worker to the operational risk profile of the company employing him or her.

Averages, trend lines, and histograms are the strength of templates. They help as a support function that reflects the profile of operational risks, the action of people, and the fitness of procedures within the perspective of a control system. Graphical presentation through templates is better than the so-called 'near misses' promoted by

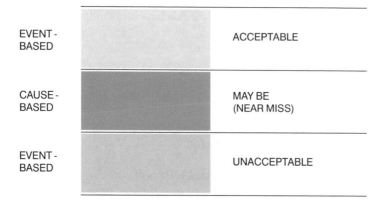

Figure 9.4 The establishment of early warning indicators is more complex with near misses

some national supervisors who still need to provide further guidance on this matter:

- What really constitutes a near miss?
- How do we quantify a near miss in practical terms?
- Should we establish a three-value control system: go/may be/no go, like the one shown in Figure 9.4?
- How can we motivate people to identify near misses?
- How do we integrate near misses into enterprise-wide operational risk management?

Another example of easy to understand and use templates are operating characteristics curves identifying acceptable α and β for each sampling plan. An operating characteristics curve is a high-end template – as discussed in Chapter 8. Though that presentation used only one operating characteristics curve, we can also have a family of them on the same template.

If we are able to determine capital charge based on loss data by business line, product or process within that line, and operational risk event, *then* we can develop and use OC curve templates for number of customer complaints, failures of account reconciliation, transaction amendments or cancellations, overrunning of limits, fraud incidents in a business unit, and so on. Operating characteristics curves are a very powerful tool indeed, which has not yet been used in the banking industry for effective and timely management control.

9.4 Developing more sophisticated scoreboard practices

Sophisticated scoreboard practices would go beyond the graphical presentation of templates, integrating with the bank's internal control to reflect each aspect of risk management, including monitoring and evaluation. An advanced modeling system for operational risk will have to be based on a fundamental study that addresses critical areas of management accountability in an effort to provide a comprehensive representation of op risk exposure. In order to calculate the value of each op risk control by the potential losses it guards against, this scoreboard study must:

- Require full and fast internal loss reporting
- Assure rigorous real-time data collection
- Support on-line modeling and datamining, and
- Steadily look after the validation of models.

Ideally, the fundamental study to which I refer will make it possible for the benefit of operational risk control improvements to be estimated against their costs. It will be rich in validation procedures, extend into stress testing, and pinpoint the personal responsibility of each party to operational risk events through a system of:

- Merits, and
- Demerits.

As has been made clear since Chapter 2, a thorough, well-documented classification of op risks is prerequisite to a fundamental study, not only because of the great diversity of operational risks but also for the reason that many of them tend to overlap with one another, thus making their tracking, monitoring, and control much more complex. Such a study should involve:

- Analysis of operational risk losses under normal conditions
- Worst case scenarios, including extreme events, and
- Estimation of residual risk values after a given type of control is chosen and implemented.

This implies the computation of value derived from control action plans, by measuring the efficiency of chosen control(s) against the operational risks being addressed, as well as ways and means for calculating costs *vs* the benefit of these controls. Contrary to standardized templates, advanced scoreboard solutions would be allocating resources on the basis of obtained benefit, and will pay great attention to whether or not benefits exceed incurred costs.

After the challenges of operational risk classification and identification are over, and management action has been outlined, cost-effectiveness of operational risk control becomes the salient problem. Because of diversity of operational risks, a thorough study of cost-effectiveness will not accept average figures, but focused estimates of:

- Risk likelihood
- Risk impact, and
- Cost of control.

Well-conducted studies will pay attention to likelihood and impact of each op risk under different scenarios, integrate actual event and loss data as they become available, include loss distributions, and incorporate event modeling. Take operational risk control with foreign exchange as an example. Foreign exchange trades have become commodity transactions, with:

■ High notional value
■ But little profit margin.

While the number of forex transactions routed through electronic platforms is growing, the bottom line from spot forex is not improving. Under this scenario, operational risks can be hard hitting. For instance:

■ Inconsistency in pricing spot forex via phone and the Web has lost clients, and
■ A relatively simple error such as transposing ask and bid can wipe out a month's profit.

That is not the sort of operational risk banks want to take. Other, less potent operational risk errors, too, have to be monitored and corrected. In the late 1970s Citibank dedicated a PDP 11 minicomputer to track foreign exchange operational risks. Every customer complaint was registered in that machine, which then:

■ Gave the forex department a deadline to fix the operational error, and
■ Applied a system of demerits (penalties), both because of the error itself and for any subsequent delays in providing a valid solution leading to error correction.

Interest rate derivatives provide another example of an operational risk control landscape. Fixed income modeling is an art few banks really master. Inability to bootstrap a yield curve can turn into a big money loser when the bank has an interest rate swaps book to price. Notice that both the forex and the interest rate examples are perceived as being market risks, but in reality they have an important operational risk component which requires a good deal of preparation to be overcome.

Part and parcel of this preparation is the planning method credited to Jean Monnet, a former banker widely accepted as the father of the European Union. Monnet said that you don't start planning at the beginning but at the end of the time period targeted for deliverables. Figure 9.5 makes this point: planning starts at t_5. The same figure also identifies, as an example, ten operational risks.

In each time period, t_1 to t_5 attention is paid to the op risks that require solution. Nearly all operational risks in this example show at the beginning and the end of the planning period, but they are individually distributed in the t_2, t_3, and t_4 periods of the objective timeframe. Throughout this exercise, care should be taken to account for damage control, including loss reduction, implicit in disaster recovery plans. Very helpful also is the identification of operational risk profiles and the issue of over- and under-controlled risks. A simple algorithm for operational risk self-assessment is:

Risk Impact = Probability • Financial Damage of Events

The financial damage should not be taken as standalone. The influence of operational risk on the institution's business line, including reputational issues, should

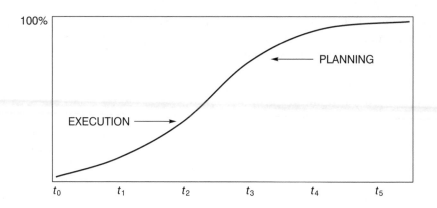

PROJECTED OPERATING RISK

Human Error	✓	✓		✓	✓
Link to Accounting	✓	✓			✓
Link to Internal Control	✓	✓			✓
Technology Failure	✓		✓	✓	✓
Defective Databases	✓	✓			✓
RT Deficiency	✓			✓	✓
Lack of Training	✓	✓	✓	✓	✓
Link to Counterparties	✓			✓	✓
Payment Faults				✓	✓
Supply Chain Faults	✓		✓	✓	✓

Figure 9.5 Using Jean Monnet's methods in identifying and correcting operational risks

be paid due attention. Equally important is to assess links between different operational risk controls and the type of events for which they have been instituted. For instance, all risks affected by the:

■ Same event, and
■ Same type of control.

A sophisticated scoreboard solution will also target operational risk trends, and whether gradually or discontinuously, they tend to increase over time. Some operational risks have the nasty habit of repeating themselves, leading to a leptokyrtotic distribution with fat tails. To study them we should simulate real life events by inserting a background probability of risks occurring even when controls are effective. Equally important is to simulate control failures, including:

- Those failing only once in a while
- Those staying failed after fixing, and
- Those slowly degrading over time.

In conclusion, what we would like to achieve with an advanced scoreboard solution is a system of traffic lights – green, amber, red – which can serve in channelling the attention of operational risk controllers. As Chapter 8 has shown, statistical quality control (SQC) charts can serve as effective tracking tools. An extra reward is the possibility of post-mortem evaluations based on SQC charts, which helps significantly in maintaining a policy of operational risk control.

9.5   Extreme value theory and genetic algorithms for operational risk control

The maximum and minimum values of a function $f(x)$, where x is a variable representing a given operational risk, are termed the extreme values of that function. It is assumed that the function and its derivatives are finite and continuous at all points. A continuous function has a maximum (minimum) value at a point where the value of $f(x)$ is greater (less) than all values in the immediate neighbourhood of the point.

A basic assumption with extreme value theory is that the curve corresponding to $f(x)$ is smooth and free of discontinuities or spikes (sharp points). This is not necessarily true of all functions $f(x)$ representing operational risks. If there are spikes, extreme value theory cannot be applied; it only deals in a meaningful sense with a smooth, continuous curve with maxima and minima. What is more, the maxima or minima of $f(x)$ can occur only at a stationary point that has a horizontal tangent.

- *If* the tangent slopes upwards at any point, *then* there are larger values of $f(x)$ immediately to the right of the point.
- *If* the tangent slopes downwards, *then* there are larger values of $f(x)$ immediately to the left of the point.

Neither of these cases is possible, by definition, at a point where $f(x)$ is a maximum (or minimum). The tangent can therefore only be horizontal at a maximum or minimum point. As a result, all maximum and minimum values of a function $f(x)$ are included among (temporarily) stationary values – which is another constraint in the use of extreme value theory in operational risk studies. The upside is that extreme value theory helps to:

- Identify turning points that could cause significant losses
- Evaluate historical data in narrative form, and
- Indicate where a process can break down and/or is out of control.

There is an increasing use of extreme value theory for simulation of the tail of a normal distribution, like the one we studied in Chapter 8. Some companies have also started to use extreme value theory in conjunction with scenario assessment of material process concentrations, regarding operational risk. This is, however, often done in a way that:

- Ignores actual material process concentrations in the bank, caused by total breakdowns, and
- Does not always concentrate on very low frequency but high impact events.

Also, some extreme value theory applications fail to ascertain a priori the smoothness and continuity of *f(x)*, or whether this function truly represents the level of control of individual process. Therefore, credit institutions have been examining the deliverables of other methods. As an alternative to extreme value theory some banks are now experimenting with genetic algorithms.

Genetic algorithms (GA) are stochastic systems effectively used for a simulated process of natural selection, particularly for reasons of optimization. Based on the process of biological evolution, they derive solutions to problems by carrying out an emulated evolutionary process on a population of possible choices or outcomes.

Genetic algorithms were developed as an alternative way for tackling minima/maxima, and optimization problems generally, with large search spaces. They have the advantage that, for most problems with a large search space, a good approximation to the optimum can be satisfactory. Their concept rests on that of Darwin's theory of evolution:

- Genetic operations between chromosomes eventually make fitter individuals more likely to survive.
- This is leading to the selection of the fittest, and the population of the species as a whole improves.

Studies involving genetic algorithms have prerequisites beyond the mathematical background briefly described in this section.[6] We have already spoken of the need for unambiguous classification and identification of operational risk (Chapter 2). Another prerequisite is the accurate definition of risk indicators. Their choice must meet criteria such as:

- Risk sensitivity
- Relative importance
- Guide to evolutionary action.

Risk sensitivity can be tested through analysis of variance (chi-square) and correlation between risk indicators and actual loss experience. For instance, some indicators associated with reconciliation of nostro accounts have higher correlation with loss experience than others. By contrast, risk indicators like client disputes have a rather low correlation with past direct monetary losses as contrasted with the deterioration of the client relationship.

Preferably, genetic algorithms should be used with high impact risks. The process characterizing their usage can be briefly described in three steps. First, generate at random a population of solutions, known in GA jargon as a family of chromosomes. Then, create a new population from the previous one by applying genetic operators to pairs of fittest chromosomes of the earlier population. The next step (or steps) is that of repeating step No. 2, until:

■ Either the fitness of the best solution has converged, or
■ A specified number of generations have been produced.

The *initialization* of the chromosomes determines random locations in the search space for the population to start the optimization process. Emulated natural selection flushes out the chromosomes to be recombined. A so-called *tournament selection* determines the chromosomes with the highest ability to solve a given problem (hence, the fittest) out of a number of randomly selected chromosomes from the population.

The motor power behind tournaments is mutations and recombinations. *Recombinations* exchange binary items between two chosen chromosomes. This is basically a *crossover. Mutations* introduce a small change to the chromosome. Usually, this is applied with a very low mutation probability, with each binary location in the chromosome flipped (0 to 1, or 1 to 0) according to this probability. There is also *cost function*, which computes the *fitness* of a chromosome.

In a nutshell, these are the basic concepts with genetic algorithms. The whole process is normally run a number of times, using a random number generator. The best solution in the final generation is taken as the acceptable approximation to the optimum for that problem that can be attained. Usually, this solution is represented as a fixed length binary string: 1001110 ... 00110. For a brief implementation example with genetic algorithms consider the values of the following sinusoidal coded in a binary string of 32 bits:

$$F(x) = x + |\sin 32x|$$

In a binary string of 32 bits, the exponent is 32. The mission is to look for *maximum*. The binary string is the genetic algorithm setting of a sinus function, shown in Figure 9.6. One of the key parameters in optimization through GA is population size. This is determined by the amount of binary digits in the string. The total population of a binary string can be encoded:

0000 00
0000 01
0000 10
.
.
.
1111 10
1111 11

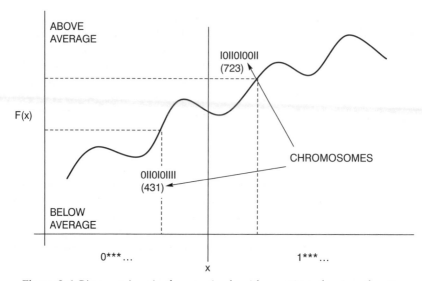

Figure 9.6 Binary strings in the genetic algorithm setting of a sinus function

A method for extreme value identification in connection to genetic algorithms is *hill climbing*, a term from John von Neumann's automata theory. Considering process values that progress in a continuous line, the genetic algorithm approach addresses functions that fluctuate, such as:

- Stock market values
- Credit rating systems
- Guaranteed fund approaches
- Risk and return with derivatives
- Operational risk controls.

When the value taken on by the population moves a little up or down, we talk of creeping. A rigorous optimization study will go well beyond creeping targeting minima or maxima associated to the behavior of the function under study. As has been already explained, we are not looking for perfection. By providing a good approximation, genetic algorithms are a powerful tool.

9.6 A common project on operational risk by a group of financial institutions

Within Chapter 6, reference was made to the ORX consortium on operational risk control (see section 6.5), which includes ABN-Amro, JP Morgan Chase, Deutsche Bank, BNP Paribas, Canadian Imperial Bank, and others, altogether a dozen. It also briefly described the specific aim of the project as one of establishing a methodology that helps to guarantee a level playing field across each member's business operations by sharing database resources, enhancing handholding, and developing a common

AMA method – probably loss distribution and bottom-up approach. Eventually the benefits are expected to cover several product lines:

- Corporate (wholesale) banking
- Retail banking
- Private banking
- Asset management, and
- Investment banking.

Among areas of common interest covered by this project, attention is also given to possible causes for contagion, spreading operational risks across related business lines. An interesting case is that of a process that may start as a non-op risk exposure – for instance a market crash where everybody tries to hide their market losses – thereafter turning into a high impact operational risk.

Another source of exposure under investigation is the op risk resulting from concentration of IT resources in one location. This particular problem is not new. Since the early 1970s banks have appreciated that the concentration of IT facilities introduces operational risks. In fact, in the early 1970s the Amsterdam–Rotterdam Bank built two computer centers, one near Amsterdam, the other to the south, more than 50 km away.

Overall, senior management backs this creative effort. At BNP Paribas, for example, the chairman issued a letter bringing to the attention of every manager in the organization the need to study and control operational risk. Top management's comprehension and support is particularly important in the case of operational risk data pooling aimed to organize a common database that preserves anonymity of the data originator. As I never tire repeating, the financial industry faces an acute need for robust and representative internal data on operational risk.

The banks of the ORX consortium have planned a historical observation period of three years. Concomitant to this goal is the ability to map losses by regulatory category, benefiting through a common regular validation of the complete operational risk measurement process. Another important aim is to establish a procedure for overriding data that, as is the case throughout the banking industry, are bound to be judgmental.

From what I have been able to learn, this is both good news and bad news associated with this common project. The good news is its concentration on the development of a rich database on operational risks, including causes and effects. This is indeed laudable. The bad news regards the model being chosen – a reincarnation of value at risk (VAR) for operational risk reasons. This is, in my judgment, is wrong:

- VAR has been written for some (not all) of the market risks.[7]

In fact, VAR can handle between one-third and two-thirds of the market risks faced by a financial institution, depending on the type of its business.

- Its extension into credit risk brought with it several serious problems.

I write this not as a critique of ORX but as a contribution to its efforts. (See also section 9.7 on the devil's advocate.)

- Such problems will be amplified by trying to fit VAR to op risks and vice versa.

Even leaving aside the many shortcomings of VAR, the undeniable fact is that models must be focused. They are not portable from one case or area of operation to another, like a sack of potatoes. Even the ability to test the hypothesis of VAR's portability is very limited, given that among the themes correctly examined by the ORX project is the fact that there exists little historical data in relation to operational risks.

Other themes featured in this common project include how to implement an Initial Capital Attribution (ICA), and what types of forward-looking data will be necessary to synthesize ICA. For evident reasons, the issue of ways and means of allocating capital to identified operational risks is a major goal of the project. At least according to one of the participating banks, this effort is based on an advanced method that rests on two pillars:

- The loss distribution approach, which is quantitative, and
- A scoreboard solution, which is mainly qualitative.

As BNP Paribas was to suggest during a London conference organized by IIR on 10 and 11 April 2002, the end solution should account for the fact that credit institutions are managed through a return-on-economic capital framework. A modified version of the matrix used for adjusting the allocation of economic capital (see Chapter 6) is shown in Figure 9.7. This matrix links corporate internal control to the internal control of the product, channel, or business unit under investigation. Each one of the banks chooses its own multipliers, f_i (i = 1 to 6).

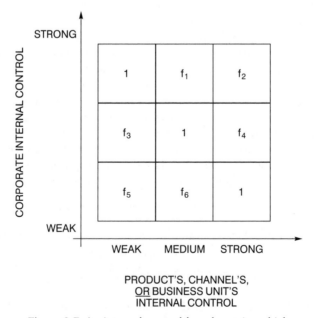

Figure 9.7 An internal control-based matrix, which might help in economic capital allocation to operational risk

- The use of strong, medium, and weak ratings is an indicative rating.
- This rating is also internal, because ratings by independent agencies do not reflect internal controls.

The inclusion of internal control characteristics in terms of a weak, medium, strong rating is, indeed, an interesting issue. Since 1999, many G-10 regulators require that certified public accountants audit the internal control system along with the bank's books.[8] The auditing firms resist this because, unlike their examination of the bank's books, which is quantitative, auditing internal controls is largely qualitative – and therefore subjective. There is not enough hard evidence to back up an opinion.

With the ORX project, however, we see that a group of banks has decided to make the status of their internal control part of self-rating for capital allocation to operation risks. In fact, according to the information provided at the aforementioned London conference, this is one of the main dimensions of the chosen approach. The ratings-based matrix used by this common project correlates two factors:

- Risk Control Self Assessment (RCSA) of the adequacy of existing internal controls, and
- Key risk indicators (KRIs), such as staff turnover, staff sicknesses, unsettled trades, customer complaints, and so on.

This is an interesting approach which forces management into clarifying the current quality of the company's internal environment. According to one of the project leaders, it promotes the use of forward-looking data. The role of the matrix advanced by this project is to help in summarizing forward-looking data in a single quantitative measure by means of an adjustment factor. This is expected to lead to the synthesis of allocation of economic capital along the loss distribution approach.

Loss severity is represented by a Poisson distribution and modeled through extreme value theory (see section 9.5). Different hypotheses concerning loss severity and loss frequency are used for:

- Expected, and
- Unexpected operational risks.

Severity and frequency modeling concentrates on both historical operational losses and potential losses. It is intended that adjustments for loss severity and loss frequency will follow the line of high frequency/low impact (HF/LI) events, and low frequency/high impact (LF/HI) events, discussed in Chapter 8.

It is also projected that adjustment factors will be specified by the business manager of the product line, in coordination with the corporate operational risk manager. The intention is to maintain operational risk measurement on the basis of a flexible combination of historical and forward-looking data, with different business lines given the flexibility to use sets of data and weights reflecting their own, true operational risk profile.

The method is interesting but it is not a foregone conclusion that it can or will fulfill another basic objective of this project: to reduce the capital reserves necessary for operational risk at the level of 20–30%. If this is achieved, it would amount to a

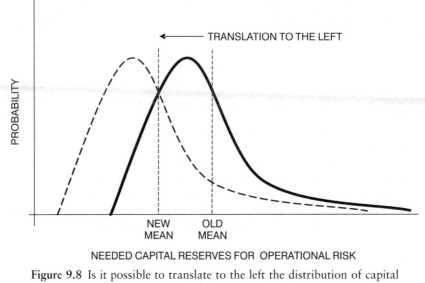

Figure 9.8 Is it possible to translate to the left the distribution of capital requirements for operational risk?

translation to the left of the log normal distribution curve, shown in Figure 9.8. For the time being, such translation to the left is only a hypothesis. Banks are hoping that AMA solutions for operational risk and internal ratings-based (IRB) methods for credit risk will reduce capital requirements. The keyword, until there is proof to the contrary, is 'hoping'.

9.7   A devil's advocate in operational risk management

Effective operational risk control must have some brilliant people assigned to the permanent doubting role of devil's advocate. Their mission should be to challenge possibly wrong hypotheses and assumptions – like the one in the last paragraph of section 9.6, and many others.

This role of the doubter is most important in every business activity, if we wish to avoid tunnel vision. It can apply all the way from market discipline to most types of risk control. 'I don't believe in the single god but believe in the single devil,' Professor Urs Birchler, of the Swiss National Bank told me, adding that: 'Market discipline does not bring us to paradise, but can preserve us from going to hell.'

Only wise people and well-managed institutions truly appreciate Birchler's words and therefore the need to challenge the obvious, to turn all stones in order to find where the scorpion hides. TIAA/CREF, America's largest pension fund, is the owner of more than 1% of New York Stock Exchange value. To help itself to manage its assets, TIAA/CREF monitors 25 governance issues:

- From board independence and diversity
- To the age of directors and their potential conflicts of interest.

Some 1500 companies making up its billions in equity investment undergo this test. Those falling short under a point system devised by the fund get inspection visits regardless of market value or performance. The budget behind this effort is a very nominal $1 million a year. The benefit is great, including:

■ Good-governance principles, and
■ Monitoring and encouragement of companies' management.

For the amount of assets managed by TIAA/CREF, $1 million a year is peanuts in comparison to the benefits from this close look at operational risk. But few financial institutions have taken this initiative, or have the courage to make this type of soul-searching investigation their policy.

No doubt, the job of the devil's advocate is neither easy nor linear. Take the scoreboard we have been examining as an example. Since most methods both concentrate on qualitative opinions and reflect quantitative estimates of past events, a devil's advocate will ask:

■ How valid are these qualitative opinions? Are they based on a significant sample of experts? Are they converging or diverging?
■ How reliable are the records of past events? Is the database covering at least 10 years? Is it being regularly updated? Are any errors or bias sneaking in?

A similar questioning attitude must be followed with the algorithms and heuristics chosen for operational risk control. I gave an example in section 9.6, by questioning the wisdom of employing still another reincarnation of VAR. One false step like that can invalidate a large-scale effort and its budget; and it is pity to take such a risk.

Neither is it true that better tools, like Monte Carlo simulation, will always give valid results. In a particular operational risk control project I have in mind, Monte Carlo was chosen as the method for simulation of some operational risks faced by the entity in the past years. The concept has been similar to that used with market risk. The problem is that:

■ The company did not have a statistically valid internal op risk database, and
■ External op risk loss databases were not found to fit or be reliable.

This is, indeed, a common downside, but the prospects improve if senior management sees this type of work as a learning process rather than as a final solution. And also *if* the board and the CEO appreciate the challenge of putting specific monetary values – down to dollars and pounds – on the impact of each operational risk, when it occurs.

As I had the chance to explain in the previous chapters, loss statistics help in these estimates, usually by taking account of means losses and percentiles, as well as by studying the shape of the loss distribution. But good enough percentiles, like $\alpha = 0.01$, and $\alpha = 0.001$ will tend to increase the required capital reserves for operational risks, rather than providing on a plate a cut of 20–30% on the standard op risk budget advanced by the Basel Committee.

Another major issue facing the devil's advocate is how well senior management accepts and absorbs criticism of the 'official line'. One of the basic reasons why companies mismanage their risks is that they don't care to keep open their communications channels at all times. Basically, this is itself an operational risk, and a vital one for that matter.

'What is important is to communicate even if something is simple,' said Dr Thomas Hess, director of research of Swiss Re. 'What is simple for us may not be so for the [product line] manager.' Quite frequently, communications are deficient because people are afraid of being wrong, or of expressing a contrary opinion. Therefore, they communicate only:

- What they know for certain, and
- What fits with senior management thinking.

By contrast, in operational risk management uncertainties are more crucial to communicate than certainties, because uncertainties are at the origins of risk. (A similar statement is valid with credit risk and market risk.) Analytics and modeling help in communications because they are instrumental in quantifying uncertainties by means of distributions. Currently available statistical tools help in explaining:

- What is known about a distribution, and
- The level of confidence at which inference is made.

Both narrowing down a distribution, that is, 'inference in the small', and exploring its outliers and its extreme values, therefore 'inference in the large', are extremely important for senior management decisions as well as for operational risk control purposes. Failure to take both approaches has given rise to the saying: 'The higher you are the flatter the distribution you perceive.'

Let me conclude with this thought. Lots of communications problems currently experienced by industry and finance come from the fact that the CEO is not properly challenged. He does not get a second opinion, let alone a contrary opinion, because people do not say what they really think.

Alfred Sloan, the legendary chief executive of General Motors, had a policy to handle the contrary opinion problem. When at board level everybody seemed to agree with everybody else, he adjourned the meeting and rescheduled it a fortnight later, asking that in the meantime members develop some dissent. *If* everybody agrees with everybody else, *then* there is no progress – but there is plenty of risk.

Notes

1 Basel Committee, *Second Practices for the Management and Supervision of Operational Risk*, BIS, Basel, July 2002.
2 Respectively see, D.N. Chorafas, *Chaos Theory in the Financial Markets*, Probus, Chicago, 1994; and D.N. Chorafas, *Rocket Scientists in Banking*, Lafferty Publications, London and Dublin, 1995.

3 Basel Committee, *Working Paper on Pillar 3 – Market Discipline*, BIS, Basel, September 2001.
4 Basel Committee, *Working Paper on the Regulatory Treatment of Operational Risk*, BIS, Basel, September 2001.
5 D.N. Chorafas, *Integrating ERP, CRM, Supply Chain Management and Smart Materials*, Auerbach, New York, 2001.
6 For a detailed discussion on genetic algorithms with practical implementation examples, see D.N. Chorafas, *Rocket Scientists in Banking*, Lafferty Publications, London and Dublin, 1995.
7 D.N. Chorafas, *Modelling the Survival of Financial and Industrial Enterprises. Advantages, Challenges, and Problems with the Internal Rating-Based (IRB) Method*, Palgrave/Macmillan, London, 2002.
8 D.N. Chorafas, *Implementing and Auditing the Internal Control System*, Macmillan, London, 2001.

Part 3

Control of technical risk and operational risk in the insurance industry

10 The science of insurance and the notion of technical risk

10.1 Introduction

The insurance industry has been chosen as a case study for operational risk identification, measurement, and control. The cases we will study in the five chapters of Part 3 originated from a variety of experiences and they address different operational risk types. Prior to looking at operational risk in the insurance industry, however, we should take a closer look at the *science of insurance*, and define the meaning of technical risk, which is, in a way, the counterpart of the credit risk taken with loans.

As Dr Thomas Hess, of Swiss Re, suggested, *technical risk*, or insurance risk is different from credit risk, market risk, and operational risk. Banks transact credit risks as intermediaries. Insurers take technical risks as part of their ongoing business. Depending on the line of business in which they are engaged, insurance companies are confronted with a variety of technical risk types:

- Life
- Non-life (which is a whole family of insurance risks)
- Third sector
- Other – marine and so on (see Chapter 13).

Insurance companies face expected risks and unexpected risks. In the latter category is included catastrophe risk, examples being events due to severe weather conditions, earthquakes and, more recently, terrorist acts. The technical risks insurance companies take morph into credit risks in case they default. As far as the survival of an insurance firm is concerned, a great deal depends on:

- How much technical risk the company assumes on its balance sheet
- How well the board and CEO manage this risk, and
- The evolution of investment positions over a number of years.

These three criteria are at the heart of technical risk models in insurance, as well as of evaluations done by reinsurance companies for protecting themselves. Many insurance companies, and most particularly reinsurers (see section 10.7) take all technical risks together and look at a joint distribution to compute *economic risk*.

- Economic risk will be covered through economic capital, in a way similar to that prevailing in the banking industry.

■ A significant difference with insurers is that the stress of technical risk on economic capital is long term.

The merging of financial instruments and insurance changes the perspective of technical risk at the frontline of the insurance industry. One of the policies insurers borrowed from bankers is securitization. They offer investors *event risk* oriented *securitized* instruments with their value linked to natural catastrophes. Hurricane *derivatives* are an example of catastrophe instruments which, through the capital markets, have gone public.

By all evidence, in the coming years we can expect a lot of insurance derivatives, whose market may overtake that of credit derivatives, altering the very sense of assumed technical risk. It is quite likely, though by no means certain, that technical risk transfer, through reinsurance and capital markets, will provide the model for policies insurers offer for operational risks.

Sections 10.2 to 10.4 deal with basic notions in insurance, to provide a common frame of reference. Section 10.5 examines the assets held by insurers; section 10.6 focuses on provisions; and the theme of section 10.7 is reinsurance.

10.2   The science of insurance

Insurance is the science of the unlikely. Risk coverage is usually given for improbable events. Understanding the frequency and severity of a potential claim is a prerequisite to sound insurance coverage. Better appreciation of risks invariably means including in our calculations not just expected risks that have a pattern, but also unexpected risk and extreme events – even the impossible.

From time to time, insurers are confronted with events that they would have qualified *ex ante* as being impossible. The use of passenger airliners as flying bombs crashing into high rising towers is an example. In consequence, 11 September 2001 (9/11) has led to a rigorous test of insurance hypotheses and mechanisms, as well as testing the insurers' adequacy of reserves and the notion of an insurer of last resort (see Chapter 14).

Is insurance a science? The answer is: 'Why not?' At the very least, it uses scientific tools like actuarial science (see section 10.4). It also features tolerances and limits (see Chapter 8). No science needs to be exact in order to feature tolerances and limits, yet both are scientific instruments. Insurance, and finance at large, are not exact sciences, but they are increasingly studied by means of analytics, and they apply scientific tools for risk management. It needs no explaining that insurance coverage cannot go beyond the ultimate insurable risk.

■ Insurance can only operate within the limits of insurability.
■ These limits are defined both by a finite insurance capacity and by other parameters.

The risks an insurance company confronts may be of a minute nature, but left unattended, they may one day balloon into something much bigger. These risks may be transferable, but also they might not lend themselves to transfer because the costs would be too high, or there is no market for them. Furthermore, uncertainty might be so great as to be unmanageable and, therefore, uninsurable.

Because insurance is a business in full evolution, a projection on its future should account for both its technical and operational risks, which are growing. Natural and man-made catastrophes are the high end of technical risk. As their frequency and magnitude increases, insurers have to decide whether catastrophe risk is sustainable within the confines of their industry.

Major catastrophes include: earthquakes in California, earthquakes and tsunami in Japan, tornadoes, hurricanes, and typhoons. These are natural catastrophes. By contrast, 9/11, asbestos, pollution, and others are man-made catastrophes. The pollution and asbestos claims (see Chapter 12) essentially rewrote the terms of engagement in the insurance industry, especially those emanating from the US because of the retroactive aspect of litigation.

When confronted with inordinate risks, insurers need a bigger party that can assume exposure associated with extreme events. This goes beyond the classical reinsurance processes, and therefore it leads to rethinking of the role the state might play as a potential *insurer of last resort*, which is a new concept.

For instance, while some of the cost of 9/11 will be compensated through insurance, when one or more companies are approaching the point of insolvency the government might lift them up. After 9/11 this happened with the air transport industry in the US; some carriers were helped by the injection of state funds but this did not save United Airlines from bankruptcy 15 months later. The use of taxpayers' money raises many questions which may revamp the science of insurance.

- Is the state a good insurer of last resort or do we need another system to complement current reinsurance solutions?
- How should the state, if and when acting as an insurer of last resort, complement the way a market functions?
- How far may state funds generate a call option, with a strike price to be set by the beneficiary in the form of insurance?
- Does it make sense, in a global market, for a single state to bail out companies with stakeholders in many different countries?

Other critical queries relate to *vulnerabilities* with or without acts of terrorism, but still involving extreme events. Vulnerabilities, and their likelihood, are an integral part of the science of insurance. They concern not only classical technical risks but also the effects of new technologies, environmental issues, and personal matters including longevity, accidents, retirement, unemployment, reorganization of the welfare state, as well as the push and pull factors that come with globalization, and are outlined in Figure 10.1.

The complexity of the pattern in Figure 10.1 is the best documentation of the need for analytics. An analytical approach to technical exposure will start with the classification of risks in the insurance business, using a methodology similar to that outlined in Chapter 2 for operational risk. From there, the study will try to derive limits to insurability. In *life insurance*, for example, critical factors are:

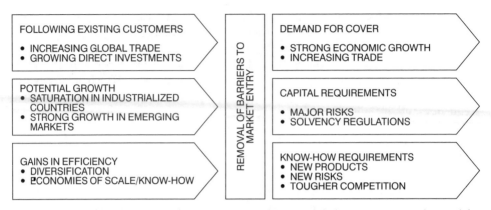

Figure 10.1 The driving forces of the insurance industry's globalization increase the need for able management of change. (*Source:* Swiss Re, *Sigma* No. 4/2000, reproduced with permission)

- Mortality risk
- Longevity risk, and
- Risk-related to guarantees.

Events within these classes of risk may be classified as high frequency/low impact (HF/LI) and low frequency/high impact (LF/HI), as we have already seen in Chapter 8 in connection to operational risk in banking. A similar statement is valid in connection to critical factors in non-life insurance, such as:

- Property risk
- Casualty risk by personal line (e.g. motors), and
- Casualty risk by commercial line (the liability side)

In non-life insurance, motor-related casualties are in the majority high frequency/ low impact. The exception is accumulation of problems. By contrast, commercial lines in the casualty-liability side tend to be low frequency/high impact (see also Chapter 11).

Beyond life insurance and non-life insurance comes third-sector insurance, which strictly speaking is neither life nor classical non-life. It targets personal disease, personal accident, and nursing care. This market is generally recognized as important, and it may be the only remaining lucrative market in our aging society.

As early starters, US insurers have enjoyed an almost exclusive dominance in the third-sector insurance market, which is considered to fall between life and non-life, a situation that has traditionally made market separation ambiguous. By its nature, third-sector insurance has also introduced new operational risks beyond those already known to exist in life and non-life insurance. Because they were the first to enter this line of business, American insurance firms have more experience with third-sector operational risks.

The frequency of events covered by insurance policies leads to claims. A forward approach to the computation of the aftermath of technical risk involves simulation.

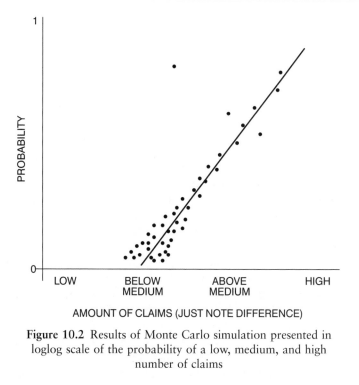

Figure 10.2 Results of Monte Carlo simulation presented in loglog scale of the probability of a low, medium, and high number of claims

Figure 10.2 shows the results of a Monte Carlo simulation of a low, medium, and high number of claims and their probability. Whether we talk of life, non-life, third sector insurance, or any other class, a basic principle in insurability is that all risk classes must be diversified. If they cannot be diversified, then they tend to go into the catastrophe category like earthquakes, which are an example of low frequency/high impact risk.

10.3 Definition of risk factors and their aftermath

Risk factors enter into the estimate of value and of the insurance premium. Therefore, the better risk factors are defined, the more protected is the insurer because it can manage technical risk in a documented and consistent way.

Risk factors should be subject to analysis and experimentation using a methodology that make underwriters comfortable in their decisions regarding *insurability* and the *pricing* of risk. In principle, insurance experts say, there is no limit to insurability for the whole industry. But there are limits for each single company because of polyvalent forms of technical risk which hit the bottom line. Examples are:

■ Hurricane Betsy
■ Hurricane Hugo

- The Piper Alpha oil platform disaster
- The *Exxon Valdez* oil spillage

as well as other events, such as the Perrier product contamination, Canary Wharf bombing, and the Twin Towers attack in New York, which represents an estimated $40–50 billion liability for its insurers. The crucial question is how much pain insurers and reinsurers can afford. 'Big individual (re-)insurers can absorb $1 billion to $2 billion of losses. Therefore, a $20 to $30 billion insurance loss, or even more, is insurable,' said Dr Hess.

Typically, an insurance contract will make exceptions to insurability. Technical risks which are uninsurable are Acts of God. In its core meaning, *Act of God* is an effect of natural forces so unexpected that no human foresight or skill could reasonably anticipate it. The term also has the wider meaning of any event that could not have been prevented by reasonable care on the part of anyone; such as the case of inevitable accident(s) due to a hurricane.

The examples presented in the preceding paragraphs were technical risks from the insurer's viewpoint. Technical risks may also be other companies' operational risks which were insured. Examples are: Natwest Markets' volatility smile, huge losses from Daiwa trading in New York, huge losses from UBS trading in Osaka, the Hunt-Bache cornering of the silver market, Sumitomo copper trading, BCCI money laundering activities, Kidder-Peabody failure of internal controls, Barings double books and trading in Osaka, and AIB/Allfirst failure in internal control – among others. To my knowledge none of these was insured, but this may be changing for future events.

Technical risks that have been insured, and those operational risks that *might* be insured in the future, are bringing up the issue of premium calculation policies and principles, including solvency margins and possible intra-group creation of capital (double gearing). Basic calculation principles established by regulators must be complied with irrespective of the method being used. This will leave out double gearing but will account for the entity's solvency margin and financial staying power.

Usually, although because of competition not always, insurance premiums are adjusted to improve the insurance industry's financial staying power. Competition kept insurance premiums down in 1999 and 2000 but in 2001, before 9/11, premiums were increased as the stock market's doldrums made it necessary for insurers to shore up their balance sheets, given:

- Weak investment returns, and
- Relatively heavy losses due to technical risk.

After 9/11 the premium increases were the result of a general consciousness that some years of above-average profitability were necessary to restore the insurance industry's financial health. The global distribution of 2000 total insurance premiums is shown in Figure 10.3. In a way, such statistics reflected both greater wealth and higher risk awareness.

Because of 9/11, insurance companies faced major claims. On 23 October 2001, Lloyd's of London indicated that it was confronted by a gross loss of £5.4 billion

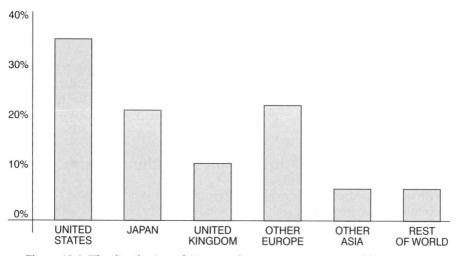

Figure 10.3 The distribution of 2000 total insurance premiums, of $2.4 trillion, reflects greater wealth and higher risk awareness. (*Source:* Statistics from Swiss Re, *Sigma*, No. 7/2001)

($8.3 billion) from the terrorist attacks in New York, labelled the most expensive event in Lloyd's 300-year history. Net cost estimates were more than 40% above those associated with the previous biggest catastrophe, America's Hurricane Hugo.

Lloyd's statistics were contained in a study by Standard & Poor's. While this study was done in collaboration between the two entities, Lloyd's said it was too soon to comment on fears expressed by S&P that some of its reinsurance claims might prove unrecoverable, thereby increasing its net exposure.

S&P, which maintained Lloyd's rating on credit watch with negative implications, suggested that exposure to the crisis placed a significant burden on the insurance market's liquidity. The independent rating agency also warned of a likely increase in the above £5.4 billion estimate, suggesting that on the balance of probabilities, the 9/11 costs are more likely to rise than fall, although it was not possible to put a high watermark number on it at that stage.

The California earthquake, whose damages may run up to $2 billion, was insured by Lloyd's and Berkshire. But even if current estimates put the 9/11 technical risk at between $40 billion and $50 billion, some experts think that eventually it may run upwards of $100 billion. Potential claims include:

- Compensation for wrongful death from relatives of those in the aircraft, and
- Compensation for injury or death from those on the ground.

Beyond this, spillover sees to it that suits could be levied against the architects, engineers, and builders for presumably faulty design and construction. As we will see in Chapter 13, mega-risk resulting not only from the event itself but also from spillover underlines the urgency of tort reform. For the purpose of this discussion, however, it is enough to bring to the reader's attention the fact that some technical risks may well prove to be unmanageable.

The premise behind prudential limits is that when risks are properly controlled they are insurable. Yet the question still remains about their joint effect down market, particularly in the aftermath of a huge catastrophe. Dr Thomas Hess advises that a discussion on limits and on insurability should not only look at insured risk(s), but also cover the assets and liabilities side (see section 10.5), most particularly the assets risk and associated credit risk and market risk, in conjunction with the technical risk being insured. This will give an integrative pattern for risk management.

10.4   Underwriting risk in insurance and the actuaries

As sections 10.2 and 10.3 have explained, technical risk is underwriting risk assumed by insurance companies. It roughly corresponds to credit risk taken with loans, and it includes all exposures related to premiums, hence the pricing of products, and the setting of adequate technical provisions to cover claims.

The management of underwriting risks relies on *actuarial calculations* for pricing the risks being taken, computing the technical provisions, and mitigating risks through reinsurance (see section 10.7). Within the perspective of high frequency/low impact and low frequency/high impact events, to which reference was made in section 10.2, technical provisions are the sum of:

- Estimates of uncured and unpaid claims
- Other expenses relating to these claims
- Unearned portion of premiums received, and
- Estimates of perceived deficiencies to these premiums.

The *actuary* responsible for these calculations is a professional experienced in quantitative methods, including not only mathematics and statistics but also demographics. The speciality of actuaries is computing the intrinsic value of money, analyzing the financial effects of contingent events, and designing financial security solutions to face them. Insurance and pensions are examples.

Legally binding clauses are necessary to assure what an insurance contract covers and what it does not cover. It is important to notice, however, that, as Figure 10.4 illustrates, this might allow for a gap in insurance coverage. If the worst comes to the worst, only those risks explicitly stated as being covered will be honoured by the insurance.

To reach conclusions about exposure and premiums, different calculations are necessary according to insurance branch, because of differences in risk profiles. The premiums are technical provisions that must be appropriate to meet liabilities arising out of insurance contracts. Such premiums constitute the majority of liabilities on an insurance company's balance sheet. They are:

- Nearly 80% of a life insurer's liabilities, and
- More than 50% of a non-life insurer's liabilities.

These are averages. The exact percentages vary between jurisdictions, insurance companies, accounting system being used, and the regulatory framework. Differences

Figure 10.4 What an insurance contract covers and what it does not cover does not add up to 100%

between companies are due to their risk profiles and provisioning policies, as well as their asset management practice.

Provisions are established by actuaries not only for known, and therefore expected risks, but also for unexpected risks embedded in obligations from insurance contracts. Several jurisdictions also require special provisions to be established for events of major impact, such as earthquakes.

- Such capital can be specifically earmarked, as in the case of equalization provisions.
- Both assets and liabilities must be considered, with many factors complicating their valuation.

For instance, an insurance policy might describe multiple amounts available at various times with the premium payments occurring throughout the term of the policy. Or, benefits and their timing might vary depending upon some outside index (more on this later). Furthermore, amounts and the timing of payments may be subject to a contingent event and its severity.

The result of litigation is one of the unknowns. Courts may retrospectively impose new liabilities on insured persons or entities, causing them to claim on their insurance contracts. Insurers are often exposed to a number of changes in circumstances through otherwise unrelated insurance contracts. It is therefore important to fully appreciate the extent to which the risks of loss on outstanding contracts are correlated within a given time horizon.

Not all insurers have the same time horizon. The same is true of banks. Among credit institutions, for example, Japanese and German banks have a longer time horizon, because they have given substantial credits to industry. American and British banks have a short time horizon by choice; Italian banks have a short time horizon because the regulators say so.

■ Insurers are obliged by the nature of their work to have a longer time horizon.
■ Therefore, the long term is part of the risks they are assuming.

As this example suggests, though they are both part of the financial industry, the challenges facing bankers and insurers are not the same. For instance, banks must guarantee liquidity of the market. This is not an objective of the insurance industry which, in order to survive and prosper, must concentrate on the application of sound actuarial standards.

But while in general actuarial methods and assumptions are mandated by the supervisors, in some jurisdictions policy provisions can differ. An example is the level of statutory compensation required in the event of injury caused by labor accidents. These vary from one jurisdiction to another. Accounting rules, too, tend to differ across jurisdictions, affecting the valuation of assets as well as the assumptions used in determining the amount of associated liability (see section 10.5).

At the same time, the tax laws differ by jurisdiction, which is quite significant to global insurers, because often provisions are a factor in determining a company's tax liabilities. A similar statement is valid in regard to the incidence of contingent events, with the longer-term horizon taken by insurers impacting on their performance.

The actuarial techniques being employed must account for all of the afore-mentioned factors – and many more: examples are risk factors like health conditions, mortality, theft, fire. Actuarial assumptions are based on these factors, as well as on the availability and quality of data in a way similar to the references made to operational risk events in Part 2.

Though, strictly speaking, it is not an actuarial duty to look after credit risk and market risk, their impact on the insurer's assets must be considered – particularly due to an insurance company's longer-term horizon. Classically, insurers took credit risk by buying corporate bonds and through private placements. In part, these were risks nobody else wanted to have, but they served the purpose of insurers:

■ By means of diversification, and
■ Through betting on an equity basis.

The amount of equity inventoried by insurers varies significantly from one firm to the other. Conservative companies keep it between 20 and 35% of their assets, usually near to the upper level when stock market bulls run the show, and at the lower end in a bear market. Insurers seeking capital growth and betting 50% or more of their portfolio on equities often get burned, as happened in 2000–2002 with British insurance companies.

Apart from the fact that they hope to get better return through equities, insurers comment that equities have the advantage of being liquid while the liability side of their loans is rather illiquid. Ironically, this led several insurers towards credit derivatives because, as one insurer I spoke to during my research put it: 'At least credit derivatives you can trade.' This argument however forgets the serious risks associated with credit derivatives, and most particularly the probability of default of corporates in the pool.

In conclusion, the management of risks faced by insurance companies is a major challenge that requires technology, methodology, and tools as well as highly trained actuaries and a firm hand at the steering wheel. Real-time data capture and interactive response to risk control issues is the only way to handle the growing amount of risk. Swiss Re, for example, knows its exposure at every hour of every day. This is necessary for the observance of limits on risk set by the board.

10.5   Assets held by insurers and their risks

Risk factors and their aftermath, as well as the assets held by the insurance firm, must be mapped into the company's accounting system. The International Accounting Standards Board (IASB) prepares a global standard for insurance contracts, including key issues in insurance and reinsurance. Both insurers and reinsurers in the European Union follow closely IASB's work because they are required to file in accordance with International Accounting Standards (IAS) by 2005.

IASB has split its work on insurance contracts into two phases. The first is a basic outline which will allow companies to continue preparing their accounts, as they do now, in compliance with local laws, with only a couple of exceptions. The second phase is the complete IAS standard which will probably come into force in 2006 or 2007, probably changing some of the notions brought forward in this section.

To complete this reference to accounting standards, it is necessary to note that in its late 2002 meeting the International Accounting Standards Board decided that *insurance risk* is risk other than financial risk, and it is significant only if there is a reasonable possibility that an event affecting the policyholder will cause an important change in the present value of the insurer's net cash flows arising from that contract. At that same meeting, a *reinsurance* contract has been defined as an insurance contract issued by one insurer (the reinsurer) to indemnify another insurer (the cedant) against losses on an insurance contract issued by the cedant.

In accounting terms, according to the new regulations offsetting reinsurance assets against the related direct insurance liabilities would be prohibited. When buying reinsurance, insurers will not be able to change the basis of measurement for the liabilities, such as switching from an undiscounted to a discounted basis. On catastrophe (CAT) bonds and other risk securitizations, IASB has tentatively taken the position of viewing each issue on its merits when deciding whether a deal meets the criteria for insurance.

As they come into the mainstream of the insurance business, the new accounting rules will definitely have an impact on technical provisions and the way insurers manage their assets. Today, the largest component of an insurance company's technical provisions is the money associated with its active policies. Frequently, these account:

- For nearly 70% of a life insurer's liabilities, and
- Some 85% of its technical provisions – a fact which reflects the long time horizon of the business.

In terms of liabilities, most claims do not occur until some time later, and for a life insurer the 'later' can be ten years or more down the line. The amount and timing of future claims has, however, to be estimated in advance, and this requires statistical methods. For this reason, in some jurisdictions these are known as *mathematical provisions*.

Part of the job of the actuary is to reconcile two different distributions of liabilities and assets (more on this later), while keeping an eye on profitability. In life insurance and other long-term policies, like disability, fixed premiums are paid in a level fashion and often they are front-end loaded. By contrast, the likelihood of claims is skewed toward the end of the coverage period, which essentially amounts to *prefunding*. Prefunding is less of an issue for non-life insurance because:

■ These policies are typically shorter-term policies, and
■ Insurance companies can increase premiums upon renewal.

Well-run life and non-life insurance have a healthy cash flow which must be invested to make possible the funding of liabilities and allow the firm a good profitability. Investment income is a support to underwriting results, which, at times and in some countries, may be negative, as shown in Table 10.1.

Chapter	Usual range of variation (%)
Loss ratio	56–86
Expense ratio	22–36
Underwriting result 100 – (a+b)	4–14
Investment yield	3–9
Asset leverage[a]	200–450
Net investment result	**12–25**
Other expenses/earnings	−12 to 2
Pre-tax profit margin	3–14
Tax rate	21–70
After tax profit margin	**1–11**
Solvency[b]	146–85
ROE	3–10

[a]Average invested assets in % of net premiums written (NPW).
[b]Average capital funds in % of net premiums written.

Table 10.1 Profitability analysis of major non-life insurers (1996–2000)

Table 10.1 presents figures from profitability analysis of major non-life insurers in the 1996–2000 timeframe. The third line gives the underwriting results, which in no way can be considered as brilliant. Essentially, the net investment results save the day. These come from money invested in bonds and equities and, increasingly so, in derivative financial products.

That investments made by insurance companies have credit risk and market risk does not need explaining. Both have the nasty habit of showing up at the most inopportune moment, turning an insurance company's capital adequacy ratio on its head. The way the industry defines it, the insurance capital adequacy ratio (ICAR) is:

■ Capital plus reserves
■ Divided by an actuarial assessment of capital required.

There is as well the American National Association of Insurance Commissioners (NAIC) capital model and other variants. Independent rating agencies have developed standards to judge the capital adequacy of insurance companies. An example is A.M. Best, which uses BCAR (Best Capital Adequacy Ratio). As José Sanchez-Crespo, of A.M. Best, suggested, his company's model was originally based on the NAIC model but then there have been improvements as well as a bifurcation in BCAR between:

■ A US domestic model which uses development triangles to adjust the baseline factors, and
■ An international model which relies on analyst judgment and inputs including inflation, legal environment, profitability, and reserve stability.

The following is BCAR's fundamental equation:

$$BCAR = \frac{\text{Adjusted surplus}}{\text{Net required capital}}$$

where:

$$NRC = \sqrt{B1^2 + B2^2 + B3^2 + 0.5B4^2 + (0.5B4 + B5^2) + B6^2} + B7$$

NRC = net required capital
B1 = bonds – default risk
B2 = equities
B2 = bonds – interest rate risk
B4 = credit
B5 = loss reserves
B6 = net written premium
B7 = off-balance sheet

Adjusted surplus is subject to several factors. The most important are: equity adjustments, debt adjustments, potential catastrophe losses, and future operating losses. The most important issue to remember is that an insurance company's capital adequacy ratio indicates whether its financial staying power makes it *secure* or *vulnerable*.

A.M. Best correlates its rating of an insurance company to the numerical value of BCAR. This is shown in Table 10.2. It is understood that the capital is invested in different forms of assets according to criteria established by insurance companies' boards and senior management.

The low inflation of 1997 to 2002 has meant only average yields on bonds, which have classically been staple assets for insurers and pension funds. Because bond yields

Rating	BCAR
A++	< 175
A+	160–175
A	145–159
A-	130–144
B++	115–129
B+	100–114
B, B-	80–99
C++, C+	60–79
C, C–	40–59

The cut-off rate between *secure* and *vulnerable* is in the 100–114 range.

Table 10.2 Rating expressed in function of best capital adequacy ratio (BCAR)

were so disappointing and stockmarkets were roaring, institutional investors went into shares in a big way in the late 1990s. Subsequently, they were hit by stockmarket crashes.

The 1990s have seen a pronounced trend to asset leverage, outstripping premium growth. Insurers have been obliged to increase their technical reserves because of the growing importance of the liability line of business, higher claims in some lines like medical care, and tort risk amplified through litigation (see Chapter 13). At year-end 2001, world-wide insurers held $11.5 trillion in assets, with life insurers accounting for 82% of the total. Geographically, 75% of assets holdings were concentrated in five countries: the US, Japan, the UK, Germany, and France.[1]

The changing pattern of asset allocation by insurance companies in the US and Europe is shown in Table 10.3. Because much money has moved into equities during the 1990s, and equities have plunged, experts think that many insurers' portfolios are now under water.

- A good deal of assets in equity had to be sold under distressed conditions.
- The result has been a dramatic erosion of the insurance industry's former financial strength.

According to a Fitch survey covering 75% of Germany's 118 life firms, at the end of 1999, the average capital-adequacy ratio was a 185%. By contrast, by the end of 2001, it was a weak 76%, and this position kept on deteriorating. In the first years of the twenty-first century, practically in all G-10 countries the insurance industry has been badly hit, largely because of:

- The mismanagement of its assets, and
- The assumption of unwarranted technical risks.

Asset classes	American insurers		European insurers	
	1992	2000	1992	2000
Bonds	62.9	53.0	36.2	35.0
Equity	11.6	30.0	23.4	37.1
Loans	15.6	8.9	22.6	12.1
Real Estate	2.5	1.0	9.0	5.0
Investment in Affiliates	-	-	2.5	3.8
Cash	4.6	3.3	2.1	1.0
Other	2.8	3.8	4.1	5.9

Source: Swiss Re, *Sigma*, No. 5/2002, Zurich

Table 10.3 The changing pattern of asset allocation (%) by US and European insurers

These events are not without precedence, all the way to failure of insurance companies. First Executive and First Capital Holdings failed in 1991 because of large concentrations of poorly performing junk bonds. Also in 1991, disastrous real estate investments triggered the insolvencies of Monarch Life and Mutual Benefit Life.

The insurance industry's regulators, too, must bear part of the blame. During the investigations into the failure of HIH Insurance, Australia's biggest-ever corporate collapse, it emerged that the group's liquidator had filed a A$5.6 billion ($3 billion) negligence suit against the government and the Australian Prudential Regulation Authority (Apra) for alleged negligence in performing duties as insurance regulator. The liquidator also began legal action against HIH's auditor and actuary – respectively, Arthur Andersen and David Slee Consulting – also for alleged negligence.[2]

10.6 The insurance of operational risk and its underwriting

Assets held by insurers may come under stress because of extending their line of business into new, so far unsettled product areas involving coverage of operational risk. This issue is treated to considerable extent in Chapter 11, in connection to op risk mitigation policies. This section and section 10.7 provide a first look, respectively through references to underwriting and reinsurance.

To improve underwriting results, at the inception of each policy the expected future premiums and investment income has to be actuarially above expected and unexpected future liabilities, in order to sustain financial staying power and leave a reasonable profit. An integrated profitability model is necessary, like the one shown in Figure 10.5, which is based on return on equity (ROE).

There are cases, however, where such computation is biased. One reason may be that the risk profile is volatile, and this has not been appropriately accounted for. Or, the calculations are inaccurate, because while insurance (like some other industry branches) is basing its technical risks on large numbers, the population to which

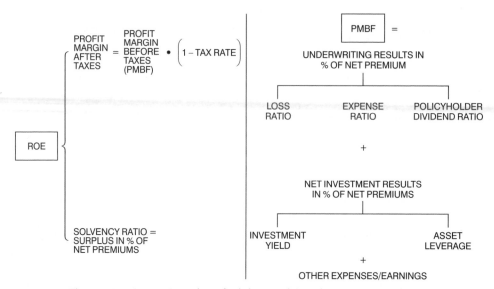

Figure 10.5 An integrated profitability model in the insurance industry

certain computations are applied is small. Credit institutions have a similar problem in wholesale banking.

An executive of an insurance company, speaking at a meeting in London, took as an example a contract of £1 million for which the risk was calculated as equal to less than 1%. For this reason, the insurer put aside £10 000. But the worst happened – the house burned down and left a gaping hole of £990 000 in the insurer's treasury.

The optional use of prefunding is another challenge. With prefunding insurance companies receive premiums that (hopefully) will exceed actual risk. But at later years in the insurance policy's life, the value of remaining premiums will tend to be less than residual expected exposure. Active policy provisions should be instituted to cover this deficit.

The computation of active policy provisions typically makes use of probability theory, and of time value of money – the actuaries' domain. Such calculations must address a number of contingencies and account for interrelationships that usually exist among risk factors. Assets backing these provisions have to be assessed in regard to:

■ Levels of credit
■ Interest rate risk
■ Reinvestment, and
■ Liquidity risk.

Asset and liability cash flows must be matched, and account taken of the fact nearly all the aforementioned activities involve operational risks. A similar statement is valid in connection to calculation of *claims provisions*, which are the largest component of technical provisions.

For non-life insurers the provision for outstanding claims is about 40% of the liabilities and some 70% of the technical provisions. The exact amount depends on the time horizon of the business, which may be medium-term as compared to the long-term of life insurers.

What about insurance policies issued to cover operational risks of other companies? Normally these should be short-term and involve carefully studied clauses. Models for claims provisions must be established for operational risk contracts. The way to bet is that those written for classical insurance contracts will not be valid.

- New statistical models will need to be developed, negotiated and tested.
- Given prevailing uncertainties in the op risk market, insurance policies should not be long-tailed.

When the settlement period can last many years, the likely result is a high amount of claims. Instead, contracts should specify that claims associated to operational risks are settled soon after being reported, but the total outstanding claim does not build up over time as happens for other types of claims that are not settled for years. The insurance industry can hardly afford another case of asbestos.

While experience with operational risk type of settlements is still thin, because very few such policies have been issued, it is quite likely that operational risk insurance policies will require provisions for incurred claims that have not been paid in full. Experts say these should be divided into two classes:

- Unpaid incurred claims, which have been reported but not yet settled.
- Incurred claims, which have not yet been reported and therefore are pending.

Different approaches are required for each class depending upon the characteristics of each type of operational risk being covered, and its associated claims. The case-by-case method, where an estimate is made for each known claim based on available facts, will in all likelihood eventually become the dominant method, but this is not easy in this decade because experience (and data) with operational risk coverage is still very thin.

The case-by-case method is used today with other types of insurance claims where, in some cases, it is difficult to assess the degree of liability and the amount payable – or there is a great deal of litigation. This approach employs the statistical method, based on a large number of similar types of claims, of the high frequency/low impact variety.

Experts believe that with operational risk coverage there may be, at all times, some incurred but not reported claims, suggesting that technical provisions must be established even for these. The amount of such unreported claims might vary by type of op risk, type of insurance company, type of policy servicing, and so on. It is therefore important to carefully keep claims records, including historical data, and choose a method that permits estimation of current amount outstanding.

Administrative expenses must be established for both high frequency and low frequency operational risks and their future claims. This can be done using patterns with other types of claims and a correction factor indicating that with op risks the insurance company may expect substantial fluctuations in the annual costs of insured events. Actuarial methods must be developed to deal with this probability.

In connection to coverage of operational risks, solutions must also be found to deal with *unearned premium provisions*. Most jurisdictions require insurance companies to reimburse policyholders if the policy is terminated before the end of the period for which premiums have been paid. Usually, the amount to be refunded is the pro-rata portion of the full premium, but sometimes this amount is reduced to account for expense incurred by the insurance company and its agents.

Even in jurisdictions where there is no requirement for reimbursement, actuarial models should reflect the need to establish a premium provision that accounts for premiums collected but not earned. Thinking by analogy, unearned premium provisions required for both life and non-life policies are making up about:

- 1% of the liabilities of a life insurer, and
- 5% of a property and casualty insurer's liabilities.

Finally, accounting for technical provisions should make sure that care is taken to cover new types of liabilities with respect to operational risks. Changes in the provisions from period to period have to be reflected in the profit and loss account of the insurer. If a policy was written, for instance, just prior to the balance sheet date, accounting provisions should ensure that premium income is spread over the life of the policy and not taken as profit immediately. This must reflect in an accurate way that there is a possibility of claims, and it should follow the new accounting rules by IASB (see section 10.5).

10.7   Services provided by reinsurance: a proxy for insurance of operational risk

Fundamentally, reinsurance is insurance for insurance companies, which pay a fee or premium to transfer certain risks to another underwriter. For example, an insurance firm may have accumulated a large exposure from its coverage of weather-related events. To limit this technical risk in its *book of business* it purchases reinsurance to protect itself in the event of a catastrophic loss in that area.

In several ways, as an exposure transfer mechanism reinsurance is critical to insurers because it allows them both to go after market share in a certain industry, which may mean concentration of risk, and to distribute or hedge their technical risks to avoid a catastrophic loss. (More about strategies to mitigate insurance risk in Chapter 11.) For good order, the use of reinsurance must be included in any performance evaluation because:

- It constitutes an alternative to further capital provisions, and
- There is potential exposure associated to both over- and under-reinsuring.

The essence of the first point above is that as an alternative to reinsurance (and other means to mitigate risk) provisions may be established taking into account the technical risk the insurance company has taken on, as a result of policies that it underwrites. The amount that companies are allowed to deduct from technical provisions to account for reinsurance varies between jurisdictions. It depends on:

- Statutory solvency requirements
- Practices established in the past, and
- Prevailing accounting rules.

Reinsurance is a good proxy of policies and practices, to be studied by companies seeking operational risk insurance. Like insurers, what essentially these companies are after is to transfer part of their exposure (in this case op risk) and thereby reduce their capital requirement. When – under conditions that we saw in Part 2 – regulators permit such capital reduction, the model that is built must account for:

- The actual nature of op risk transfer through (re)insurance contracts
- The credit risk that might be associated with the insurance counterparty, and
- Other relevant factors in connection to operational risk management.

This approach, too, is similar to that followed with reinsurance in domains where there is a background of considerable experience, which enables discussion on firm ground of the benefits that are obtained and the obligations resulting from a reinsurance strategy. Box 10.1 gives a snapshot of a guarantor or reinsurance view of capital.

Box 10.1   Guarantor or reinsurance view of return on capital: A = B + C

Where:
   A = Investor's Minimum Return, 10–15%
   B = Investor's Return to 'tied up' capital, 5–6%
   C = Percentage going to guarantor, 5–9%

Let me underline that while reinsurance provides an essential service to insurance companies in spreading risk, many experts believe that it is intrinsically different from primary insurance. Because they assume counterparty risk, insurers need means of assessing the capital adequacy of a reinsurer; and reinsurers must assess whether the insurer has done an adequate risk evaluation job.

Using this model as a proxy for insurance coverage of operational risk, we can see that the duality mentioned in the preceding paragraph will be one of the challenges of negotiating an insurance contract for op risk(s). Borrowing a leaf from the reinsurer's book, the following elements have to be brought to the reader's attention:

- A reinsurance contract is negotiated between peer organizations – the ceding insurance company and the reinsurer.
- Both parties are disposing financial means as well as legal and professional expertise in making appropriate evaluation of risks and benefits.

These two points encompass the relationship between a credit institution purchasing insurance for some of its operational risks and the insurer providing the coverage. In both the insurance/reinsurance and bank/insurance cases, supervisory activities must address issues connected to either and both parties and the commitments they make to one another.

Regulators regard financial failures associated to insurers (or reinsurers), and other hazards to the normal course of business, as a threat to stability, not only for reasons of solvency but also because of their potential impact on market confidence. Insurance and reinsurance are risk-spreading processes that, by definition, should know no boundaries but they should appreciate some basic rules:

- The strength of an insurance company is in the wide diversification of its liabilities and assets.
- The wider the pool of capital, and the greater the choice of companies to reinsure, the better the security.

In each country, and in practically each case, the supervisors are faced with a dual challenge: on one side protection of policyholders and public confidence, and on the other prevention of insurance and reinsurance failures against the multiple risks that are in their way. These two goals are difficult to separate – or, for that matter, to reconcile.

At the same time supervisors seek means of countering the effects on their home market of the danger of capital moving to offshore centers. This happens today with reinsurance; it will happen tomorrow with insurance for operational risks, the more so as many of the banks that will seek to buy op risk insurance will be global institutions.

Indeed, since the 1980s, to the supervisory concern stated in the preceding paragraphs has been added that of the world-wide nature of the insurance and reinsurance business. The irony is that in spite of globalization the national market is still geographically fragmented, while many entities, including supervisors, have difficulty in assessing the suitability of foreign reinsurers.

- There is much room for misunderstanding, and
- Systems of accounting and management are still different.

For several decades there has been a strong incentive for supervisors to require the creation of subsidiaries, or the placing of collateral against liabilities in special funds. In spite of the changing global economic environment, because of the aforementioned discrepancies insurance supervisors continue to wish (though they may not be fully satisfied) that foreign reinsurers meet their obligations, and they therefore seek:

- Either to find some means of direct control, or
- To achieve indirect control by maintaining strict requirements on the reinsurance programs of domestic insurers.

These are reasonable goals, which recognize that it is not possible to construct a regulatory regime on the basis of zero failures. That would demand measures that drive up costs to astronomical levels, swamp innovation, eliminate competition, and replace entrepreneurial decision-making with an irrational strait-jacket that makes compliance virtually impossible.

Trying to strike a balance between globalization and country-by-country regulation, the Comité Européene des Assurances (CEA) has proposed the introduction of a single passport for reinsurers, as a way of securing their world-wide mutual recognition, starting with recognition by all members states of the European Union (EU). According to this model, mutual recognition would be subsequently sought with American and other jurisdictions.

The goal of this proposed system of reinsurers recognition by insurance supervisors is to remove barriers, putting pure reinsurers on a par with insurers in terms of their ability to trade across borders and to set up branches. It is believed that this can simplify administrative arrangements for both supervisors and reinsurers as well as provide a guarantee of financial strength, transparency, and management quality in reinsurance companies operating across borders.

Should these goals be met, and this is not unlikely, there is no reason why the resulting system cannot also be used for the insurance of operational risks. Crossborder recognition is very important because for global companies many of the operational risks are crossborder and, in all likelihood, these will be among the first to be tested through an insurance-based scheme.

Notes

1 Swiss Re, *Sigma*, No. 5/2002, Zurich.
2 *Financial Times*, 14 November 2002.

11 The use of insurance policies to mitigate operational risk

11.1 Introduction

Insurance provides contingent capital. The basic reference in the context of using insurance in connection to operational risk is that the buyer substitutes a relatively small cost, the premium, for a larger but uncertain financial benefit: possible losses from the op risk being insured. The aim is to reduce economic impact of operational losses, in an integrative approach to operational risk management.

Rating agencies say that if an entity holds capital at $\alpha = 0.0003$, therefore at 99.97% level of confidence, this corresponds to about an AA rating in solvency terms. This statistic has been provided for insurers, but the type of coverage also plays a critical role. Fundamentally, it is easier to compute exposure when a policy assures:

- Organizational liability, personal liability, and property risks, rather than
- Unauthorized trading, and
- Operational risks novel to the insurance industry.

To my mind, buying insurance for unauthorized trading is an exercise that holds many surprises for the future. Still, as we have already seen in connection to banks adopting advanced method approaches, the Basel Committee is considering allowing insurance policies to act as mitigant to operational risk charges. Among the challenges in using insurance (or, alternatively, derivatives) as mitigant are:

- Type of coverage and payout
- Levels of coverage and associated triggers
- Incorporation of insurance policies into the capital allocation structure
- Resolution of issues involving litigation
- Delays in payment because of litigation procedures, and
- Some borderline cases involving credit risk *and* operational risk.

It is too early to comment on practical results of this approach. More certain is the fact that third party insurance helps in removing operational risk from the balance sheet, but at the same time it provides a potentially restrictive cover, and some uncertainty of payment. Self-insurance through captives results in distribution of operational risk across different business lines, but does not remove op risk from the consolidated balance sheet.

Securitization makes available potentially large limits in insurability of operational risk, but this is not yet a mature market. As a result, the issues may find no takers, and securities may be rated below A (see Chapter 12). As a Basel Committee document has suggested, 'Banks that use insurance should recognize that they might, in fact, be replacing with operational risk counterparty risk.' There are also questions relating to:

- Liquidity
- Loss adjustment
- Voidability
- Moral hazards
- Limits in product range, and
- Inclusion of insurance pay-outs in internal loss data.

Another challenge is payment lag, that is to say, the time it takes for an insurance company to pay damages associated to credit risk or operational risk. This is the regulators' largest reserve about op risk insurance, because the time lag to payment is as important as the surety of such payment. The latter might be put in doubt because of counterparty risk. Both may affect the bank's liquidity.

The time lag risk impacts much more on the smaller credit institution. Big banks may fund operational risk damages, and damage control activities, out of current cash flow. Small banks don't have that possibility, and though they paid their op risk premium to the insurer, they may find themselves against the wall when adversity hits.

However, the use of insurance as a means of operational risk transfer still has to be studied within the perspective of alternative risk transfer (ART). Operational risk mitigation is the subject of this chapter. At the same time, the wisdom of using insurance coverage should be examined in connection to how independent credit rating agencies look at the insurance industry at large, and at the insurability of new product lines (including op risk) in particular. This is the subject of Chapter 12.

11.2   Cost of equity, cost of debt, and cost of insurance

By creating a capital charge targeting operational risks facing entities under their authority, regulators opened up a new market. They also led the way towards integration between operational risk and other types of risk, while at the same time they raised questions regarding insurable perils and hazards. No opinion can be expressed on their frequency and impact prior to 5 or 6 years of somewhat wider insurance coverage, which means 2012 or thereafter.

The lack of precedents, and of statistics, in insurability of many operational risk types will be a problem for some time. Ambiguity is one of the basic factors that limit insurability. In many instances, the random variable describing a given operational risk has to be insured without the benefit of a probability distribution, because of:

- Absence of historical data, or
- Imperfect knowledge in this domain on the part of actuaries (see Chapter 10).

Because of these factors, the reader should appreciate that it is very difficult to calculate an insurance premium which protects the insurer from the exposure it is assuming, and at the same time is appealing to the insured.

- Worst-case scenarios have high premiums, and
- High premiums are unattractive to the insured.

This being said, there is no question that insurance for operational risk *is* an alternative whose cost should be taken into account for an objective evaluation, not just in absolute terms but also comparatively, in terms of returns, to:

- The cost of debt, and
- The cost of equity.

The *cost of debt* can be determined through the firm's current borrowing rate and interest rate mix. These reflect the expected return of debt holders. One way to compute the cost of debt is to first project the expected interest expense that a company expects to pay on its outstanding debt each year. This being done, the cost of debt is the discount rate that equates:

- To the current market value of debt,
- The present value of the stream of expected interest payments.

In a way similar to the cost of debt, which reflects the expected return to debtholders, the *cost of equity* maps the expected return to shareholders. Different models are available for this computation. One of them is the Capital Asset Pricing Model (CAPM), which calculates the cost of equity as the sum of:

- The risk-free interest rate (such as US Treasury Bonds), and
- The risk premium on the company's shares, projected in the coming years.

Expected risk premium is based on the sensitivity of a share's price to overall stock market movements. This approach has been consistently used by financial analysts, so that there is a body of knowledge in its regard. Therefore I employ it as part of the frame of reference in the cost of equity equation.

As the preceding paragraphs have shown, the *cost of insurance* is a different ball game. A good way of handling this issue is to define the cost of insurance as the entity's current insurance rate for its covered operational risks, measured as a percentage of reduction in operational risk capital requirement because of using insurance. The discount rate equates the present value of expected insurance premiums to the insurance value.[1]

Solving the cost of insurance puzzle is an urgent matter, because the number of experts who look at insurance coverage of operational risk as being both worth while and an important business line for insurers is growing. Swiss Re new markets, for example, offers several protection schemes for operational risk through insurance. One of them indemnifies only losses above a deductible of $50–100 million, but covers virtually any known risk, including:

- Unauthorized trading,[2]
- Professional indemnity,
- Employment liability, and
- Computer crime.

Note should also be taken of an eventual operational risk loss *equity put*. It enables its buyers to fund losses by issuing new securities at a pre-loss price. Other risks addressed by insurance or derivatives are: bandwidth price risk in emerging telecommunications markets, and water price risk in emerging water markets. These are basically market risks that can morph into operational risks.

A critical computation in this connection is to estimate the future stream of insurance premiums that the company is likely to pay, including those for operational risk. Different scenarios should be examined, for an alternative op risk transfer,

- From securitization,
- To a custom-made insurance policy underwritten by an insurer or reinsurer.

If insurance protection is provided by capital markets through securitization or derivatives, the insurance premium can be determined as the current trading price in over-the-counter trades. *If* it is to be obtained by means of an insurance contract, the current insurance premium may not be on hand, but it might be possible to bet on indicative quotes from insurance companies.

In deciding which strategy to follow, the reader should be aware of major differences between the three types of cost explained in this section. Two of them, cost of debt and cost of equity, are references to balance sheet capital. The securitization option is off-balance sheet (OBS) capital, accessible through derivatives or by means of transferring risks to other firms: the insurers and reinsurers. This transfer alters:

- The retained risk profile, and
- The capital structure of the entity.

By paying a premium to an insurance company, a firm can eliminate its exposure to some type of operational risk. The insured entity does not have to keep any paid-up capital or borrowed money to cover the insured operational risk, though it evidently has to pay the insurance premium.

In conclusion, the use of an insurance strategy for operational risk reasons requires understanding of the role of both on-balance sheet and off-balance sheet corporate capital. It also calls for an appreciation of the relevance of the approach to be chosen to the company's activities and its operational risks. The insurance option should be retained as an alternative, but it is most wise to remember that this is a field in the early stages of its development and one should not put all one's eggs in the same basket. (See also Chapter 12 on credit rating insurance companies.)

11.3 Operational risk securitization and moral hazard

Some of the proponents of the use of insurance as a means of mitigation of operational risk say that even if it has many uncertainties it is a better solution than doing nothing. This is not the right way of looking at the issue of capital allocation for operational risk because nobody ever said that a financial institution should do nothing. Well-managed companies examine their alternatives.

The four chapters of Part 2 have documented that between doing little or nothing and establishing an integrated control of operational risk commensurate with

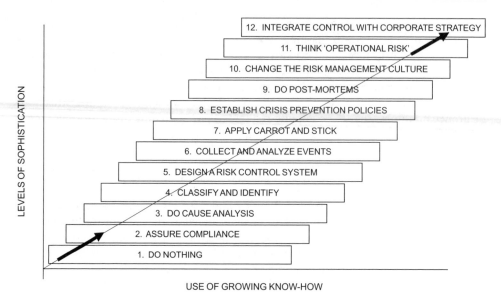

Figure 11.1 Stages of maturity in operational risk control

corporate strategy and regulatory requirements, there exist many intermediate levels. These are shown in Figure 11.1 in a way that graduates into an operational risk control methodology from compliance and cause and effect analysis (step 3) to the *think* operational risk level.

The salient problem in thinking operational risk, in terms of coverage through insurance and/or derivatives, is the lack of experience in doing so and the absence of reliable data, particularly, the lack of specific cases that can teach where and what can go wrong; or things can be twisted in a way that alters original intentions. As proxy to a case study on what could go wrong, I chose recent happenings with credit risk and its securitization.

According to a report in the *New York Times*, Citibank, a major lender to Enron, apparently protected itself from a significant portion of Enron's credit risk by passing it on to investors in credit-linked bonds. Citibank accomplished this risk transfer through an innovative transaction that *combines* credit derivatives and insurance with traditional securitization.[3]

Something comparable to this were the 1997/1998 J.P. Morgan *Bistro* transactions. At that time, this was seen as a new sort of synthetic securitization, the tip of the iceberg in a major trend in structured finance. The name of the game in both these examples is the increasing use of securitization to *manage risk* rather than to:

- Sell assets, or
- Raise funds.

J.P. Morgan Chase seems to have perfected the credit risk transfer method, by way of capital markets, with WorldCom. While experts at Wall Street have suggested that the bank's loans exposure to the defunct telecommunications company amounted to

$17 billion, which is what has been written in the press, J.P. Morgan Chase itself said that its loans exposure to WorldCom was only $20 million. Presumably nearly $17 billion were securitized and credit risk was assumed by investors.

Another way to look into capital markets and their instruments as risk transfer mechanisms is that this transformation has been the outgrowth of a new trend. This started in the mid- to late 1990s, and many analysts at Wall Street think that it will be gaining momentum in the coming years. It is not unlikely the operational risk transfer will add to its momentum *if* institutional investors and high net-worth individuals come to like it.

Will investors come round to buying securitized protection from unauthorized trading? For the time being, mainly the insurers have shown interest. Section 11.2 referred to a product by Swiss Re. This is not the only example. Following the trade-related losses at Barings, Sumitomo, and other entities, SVB, one of Lloyd's syndicates, began offering rogue trader insurance.

- This reimburses a firm for damages sustained from unauthorized trading.
- The basic condition is that such trading has been concealed from management's attention.

The first reported buyer of this new type of insurance-linked protection, to my knowledge, has been Chase Manhattan. It bought $300 million in rogue trader cover for a rumored annual premium of $2 million, or two-thirds of 1 percent. This is one of the best examples regarding early date (middle1990s) insurance coverage for operational risks faced by credit institutions.

While it is still too early to have a firm opinion about which way insurance coverage for op risk may go, and how extensive the range of op risk falling into the insurance net will be, a reasonable projection is that several issues may be tested for insurability creating a range within the broader definition of operational risk. Policies might, for instance, target exposure to loss resulting from inadequate or failed internal processes, people, and systems; or from external events.

For their own good, insurance companies should take notice that internal control failures, like the rogue trader paradigm, relate to human failure and, as such, they are dynamic. Other dynamic issues subject to insurance coverage connect to technology; for instance, the case of intruders. As Figure 11.2 shows, a study by Cornell University has documented that intruders use technology to increase the sophistication of their attack.

Participants in this study drew attention to another major risk associated with human failure: moral hazard. *Moral hazard* consists of actions of financial agents in minimizing their own risk and in maximizing their profits to the detriment of others. It is augmented by the fact that these economic agents don't bear the consequences of their actions due to occult, Mafia-type protection, nepotism, and other circumstances that prevent the assignment of full damages.

As with the different rescue plans by the International Monetary Fund, central banks (see also Chapter 14) or other parties, ex ante moral hazard makes sure that, because the risk is (so to speak) fully insured, the insured party has less incentive to prevent its occurrence. As a result, the probability of higher risk-taking starts to rise

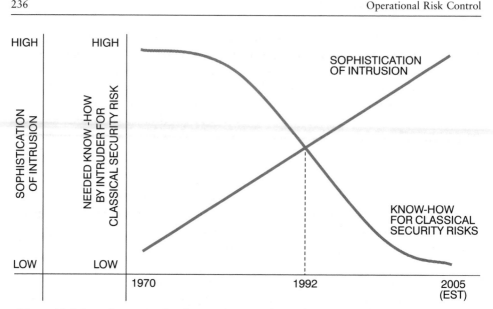

Figure 11.2 Intruders use technology to increase the sophistication of their attack. (Based on a study by Cornell University)

so that a premium that is held steady becomes less and less representative of real exposure:

- If the moral hazard cannot be properly contained, a risk may well become uninsurable.
- At the extreme, any insurance coverage obtained would have disastrous consequences, because the risk of accident will rise as a result of the availability of such insurance.

Indeed, the fact that liability insurance was banned in many western European countries up until the nineteenth century is a direct outcome of this moral hazard problem. With operational risks, new, more rigorous approaches are needed that allow insurers to fight against moral hazard in its different manifestations. For instance, a sort of partial insurance should:

- Keep the insured exposed to risk, and
- Oblige the insured to develop effective prevention measures.

There is also ex post moral hazard exemplified by the increase in claims against the insurance policy, beyond the services the claimant purchases when insured. In the case of medical coverage, for example, ex post moral hazard include excessive visits to doctors, too many medicines purchased, long hospital stays, and so on, which are at the roots of the ruin of social security.

In conclusion, the lack of precedence in operational risk coverage will be a problem for some time. As I have already brought to the reader's attention, one of the basic factors that limit insurability is ambiguity amplified by the absence of historical data.

Also, imperfect scientific knowledge makes it very difficult, if not outright impossible, to establish a pattern – and therefore to calculate accurate insurance premiums for operational risk events.

11.4   Advent of insurance-linked protection vehicles and underwriters risk

One of the key questions that will be posed with insurance coverage of operational risk, if it becomes popular, is how it should be treated from a financial reporting viewpoint. The answer to this is still pending, but a useful inference can be made through analogical reasoning from the *accounting status of derivatives*. Swiss Re suggests that regulators are currently addressing the issue of how an insurer's purchase of a derivative security to hedge its underwriting risk should be treated for accounting purposes.

Proponents of underwriting of contracts involving derivatives have asked the supervisory authorities to allow liberal underwriting accounting approaches, as long as the correlation between actual losses and the payoff of the derivative instrument is sufficient to keep basis risk below some acceptable threshold. Opponents argue that there must be actual indemnity because of significant correlation between:

- Actual losses, and
- Payoff of the derivative instruments.

Other experts, more neutral to both sides, say that for a derivative to be deemed effective, and therefore qualify for underlying accounting, it need only exhibit some positive correlation with the underlying risk.[4] Today, these regulatory issues concern primarily bankers and insurers. Tomorrow, they will be important to everybody, as all sorts of companies *and* investors will find themselves in a complex situation regarding tax issues and financial reporting at large. For this reason, it has been a deliberate choice to include in this text a brief appreciation of *insurance-linked securities* (ILS).

Let's start with a couple of definitions. Approaches involving the capital market in the insurance domain are also known as insurance-linked mechanisms for risk sharing. As the preceding sections demonstrated, to the insurers they present advantages because the capital market can be a great reinsurer, particularly for supercatastrophes. The problem is not in the design of these instruments, as there exist several types of them, but:

- In attracting investors from outside the insurance industry, and
- In providing ways and means for detection and management of trend-setters.

Early adopters typically include companies with institutional knowledge of insurance markets, investing in ILS because they offer a way to enter a line of business, or region, without building costly infrastructure. Ultimately, however, it will not be companies at large but focused investor populations, like institutional investors and high net-worth private individuals, who will contribute the most to the success of this market.

Insurers familiar with the benefits derived by involving the capital markets say that one of the attributes of insurance linked-securities is their liquidity, provided the secondary market for these assets is indeed active. In this case, investors can unwind their positions at relatively low cost. The opposite is also true. The absence of a liquid secondary market makes insurance-linked securities a non-attractive investment. This leads to a challenging problem:

- For the pricing and trading of ILSs to become appealing, more investors must become interested in them.
- Investors, however, would rather see more deals flow in exchanges – rather than OTC – before devoting time and effort to analysing the ILS.

Analysing risk and return with insurance-linked securities evidently involves the action by reinsurers and the rates which they apply. After all, the capital market's interest in ILS is in competition to the reinsurance industry. As Figure 11.3

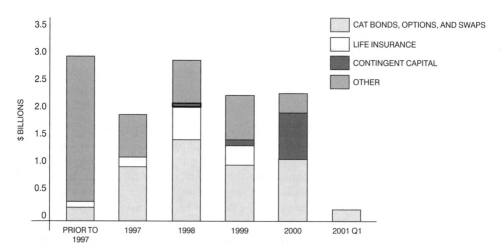

Figure 11.3 Statistics on catastrophe-linked securities in the mid-1990s to 2001 timeframe. (*Source:* Swiss Re, *Sigma* No. 3/2001, reproduced with permission)

documents, the issuance of catastrophe-linked securities stagnated after reinsurance rates fell in the late 1990s.

Another major factor in the acceptance of ILS is their design. The majority of catastrophe securitizations rely on one of three types of trigger: indemnity, index, and a physical criterion. *Indemnity* is the most popular form, used for more than half the total issuance. It employs settlements based on actual insurer losses. Critics say that while these deals have no basis risk, they do have the disadvantages of:

- Lengthy periods to settle claims, and
- Biased selection by the insurer; therefore moral hazard.

Index securitization is the second alternative, today representing about a quarter of all deals. It uses settlements based on industry losses reported by an independent agency, but has the disadvantage that such deals may pose substantial basis risk to the issuer. Different models exist for a *physical* criterion to settle claims. An example is the magnitude of earthquake activity in and around a given area as measured by a known, reliable authority specializing in this type of risk. This physical measure becomes key to determining payouts.

No doubt an important step towards a liquid market for insurance-linked securities is the establishment of benchmarks through which industry players can monitor the progress of an instrument and its underlier. This can be further assisted by the existence of stock market indices such as S&P 500, FTSE 100, and Nikkei 225, as well as benchmark securities like the 10-year Treasury bond.

Insurers work hard to make ILS acceptable. They suggest well-defined benchmarks will be instrumental in providing a foundation for capital market ILS solutions. They also seem to appreciate that the absence of a reliable benchmark will discourage investors from trading securitized insurance risks, including those of operational risk type. Which are the insurance-linked instruments that might attract the interest of capital markets in the coming years? Swiss Re suggests a number of them.[5] In alphabetic order, these are as follows.

Bank-funded life insurance takes the form of traditional financial reinsurance, where the reinsurer co-underwrites a book of life business by agreeing to pay a percentage of all future claims on a book of life business and receives in return the same percentage of premiums and investment earnings associated to that book. *Catastrophe bonds* (CAT bonds) are different.

- If no loss event occurs, investors receive return of principal and a stream of coupon payments.
- If a pre-defined catastrophic event takes place, investors suffer a loss of interest, principal, or both.

Catastrophe swaps is another way to transfer insurance risk. A series of fixed, predefined payments is exchanged for a series of floating payments whose values depend on the occurrence of an insured event. *Contingent capital* transactions take still another approach, providing the buyer with the right to issue and sell securities: equity, debt, or some hybrid products.

Exchange-traded catastrophe options are listed on the Chicago Board of Trade. They have the advantage of being publicly traded in a regulated exchange. So far, these have not been successful. Some experts, however, think exchange-traded instruments may eventually become a popular means of transferring insurance risk to capital markets. We shall see.

Another possibility is *industry loss warranties* (ILW). They resemble a catastrophe swap but are structured as a reinsurance transaction, with the risk transfer mechanism being a double trigger. This trigger is activated only if both insurance industry losses and actual losses incurred by the purchaser of the ILW exceed pre-established thresholds.

An alternative insurance-linked security is *life securitization*. In this transaction, an insurance company sells its rights to receive mortality and expense fees or policy acquisition expenses to a special purpose vehicle (SPV) which finances the purchase of these rights. The SPV does so by issuing securities to the capital markets.

In conclusion, catastrophe bonds, options, and swaps have existed for some time, but until recently they were a small amount compared to contingent capital. As we saw in Figure 11.3, they grew rapidly in 1997 and 1998 but then tapered off. This is indeed a complex market and much will be learned about it in the coming years. Therefore, in the mean time banks planning insurance coverage for operational risks, as well as insurers and reinsurers, should be very, very prudent.

11.5   Integrative approaches through alternative risk transfer

The examples presented in sections 11.3 to 11.5 of this chapter are in essence alternative risk transfer (ART) solutions. The concept of alternative risk transfer has existed, and it has been practised, since the 1980s. In principle, but only in principle, alternative risk transfer policies are followed when it is possible to quantify risk.

As we saw in the preceding sections, alternative risk transfer mechanisms usually bet on capital markets instruments for transfer of risk exposure, including catastrophe risk. For their part, the markets require some degree of certainty; with this, they are increasingly assuming risks whose cause and effect may not be as well established as with elder instruments. Table 11.1 provides a comparison between:

■ Classical insurance industry coverage, and
■ Insurance coverage involving the capital markets.

ART policies have been developed during the past few years but they still lag behind the classical insurance business by a wide margin. This is shown in Table 11.1. Some experts say that, after many years, the capital market will no doubt mature as an alternative risk transfer mechanism, even if this is not the case today. Other experts, however, take a wait-and-see attitude.

Alternative risk transfer is no monolithic solution. Its approaches can be polyvalent, but polyvalence has prerequisites and it comes at a price. A concept that might give insurance-linked operational risk coverage a boost is that of *finite-risk* reinsurance. This basically represents a combination of:

	Classical insurance industry coverage	Coverage involving the capital markets
History	300+ years	±10 years
Contracts	Trillions	About $100billion
Rating	AAA and AA insurers	No rating by independent agencies
Loss payments	Billions	?
Market continuity	Known	Unknown
Limits to exposure	Higher	Lower

Table 11.1 A comparison between the insurance industry and the capital market

- Risk transfer, and
- Risk financing.[6]

While it is based on the same instruments as traditional reinsurance, finite risk products put limits on exposure, which is attractive to the underwriter as well as to buyers of securitized instruments. An example mentioned in section 11.2 is that of a franchise of $50 million or $100 million, but limits may also be defined in a dynamic way in conjunction to some kind of specified event.

The target of such limits is to stabilize insurance/reinsurance costs connected to coverage of operational risk – while at the same time expanding underwriting capacity and smoothing fluctuation of results. Because of the nature of risks, however, effective limits should account for:

- The multiyear period of contracts
- Particular characteristics of each operational risk covered, and
- Possible sharing of financial results with the credit institution buying insurance for its op risks.

Extrapolating from other practices involving finite coverage insurance products, it can be seen as likely that an increasing number of offerings will be combined with more traditional type policies in blended covers. They will also account for response by regulators, public auditors, and tax authorities. For instance, regulators may refuse to recognize finite solutions as reinsurance unless they involve a substantial transfer of underwriting risk.

Chapter 10 referred to the fact that the level of acceptance of operational risk coverage by regulators, and other stakeholders, is far from being a foregone conclusion – let alone challenged in courts. Regarding the level of coverage, however, it is appropriate to notice that the classical insurers' channels don't give 100% risk protection either, though they do provide a range of choices for risk transfer.

Relatively popular in alternative risk transfer nowadays is the use of the derivative financial instruments by insurers and reinsurers. In Figure 11.4 the concept underpinning this statement is visualized through operating characteristics curves in a two-dimensional space, involving:

- Likelihood of an event, and
- Degree of insurance-based protection.

Basically, the level of coverage is a bilateral issue between insurer and insured. Beyond this come the regulators' concerns regarding alternative risk transfer at large, and other issues connected to operational risk. Among other reasons, concerns by supervisory authorities are propelled by:

- Complex voidance clauses, and
- Possible narrowly defined events.

Currently, different working groups address these issues, including a Basel Committee subgroup and the Property & Casualty Insurance Industry Working

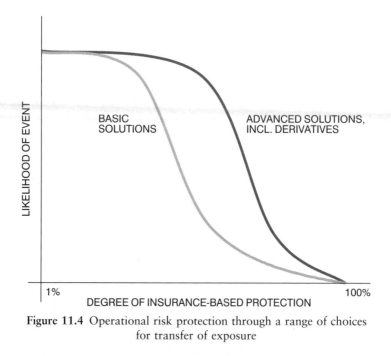

Figure 11.4 Operational risk protection through a range of choices for transfer of exposure

Group. If this work is successful in taking care of all stakeholder worries (regulators, insurers, and insured) it could make the insurance of operational risk a more strategic product than it currently is. The die, however, is not cast.

To be successful and long lasting, the work currently in progress for insurance coverage of operational risk must lead to a better definition and taxonomy of different types of exposure. This includes Pillar 1 charges, as well as a clarification of possible implications of Pillar 2 on insurance and, most importantly, the market discipline that is Pillar 3.

In summing up the concepts presented in this section, it can be stated that because they must account for different viewpoints, and regulatory issues, solutions will not be easy. Two fundamental principles of insurance are up for revaluation: the transfer of risk and sharing losses. But the ongoing work may reinforce the change that has taken place in the last 4–5 years, including:

- Greater attention to detail
- Wider coverage of risks, and
- Higher limits in alternative risk transfer.

We have gone a long way from the original concept underpinning what is today known as finite risk reinsurance. By several accounts, the more liberal approaches originated in the 1960s, when a lack of traditional insurance covers for oil exploration and drilling prompted the British insurers to develop some alternative solutions. The issues faced today are quite different – and so are the stakes – but there are also similarities between this past situation and insurance coverage of operational risk.

11.6   Frequency and impact of events in operational risk transfer through insurance

Like any other type of risk coverage, operational risk transfer using insurance indemnifies the credit institution from losses arising from a given type of op risk exposure. Also, as with all other types of insurance, before the firm can buy the insurance protection, it has to demonstrate that it has an *insurable* interest; and the insured entity can collect only *if* it actually incurs a loss.

Seen under this light, insurance-linked operational risk coverage is hedging. There exists, however, a major difference from one form of hedge to another – as well as between bilateral hedges and those made in capital markets. In the latter case,

- Hedges are not indemnification contracts, and
- Payments are made regardless of whether the firm incurs a loss.

Another major distinction between capital market-based hedges and the prevailing notion of insurance is that a company can purchase the hedge, such as a derivative, whether or not it is exposed to the underlying risk. If it is not exposed, then the hedge is really a speculation.

Speculation is precisely what has happened during the 1990s with derivatives at large, and it has accelerated to the point that four global banks – J.P. Morgan Chase, Deutsche Bank, Citigroup, and Bank of America (in that order of exposure) – hold among themselves more than $60 trillion in derivatives, in notional principal amount. Demodulated into toxic waste in case of global crisis, this represents an amount roughly equal to the US Gross National Product.[7]

The reader will appreciate that there are similarities between insurance for operational risk purposes and more classical hedges. For instance, like derivatives, insurance is off-balance sheet capital that covers the risks transferred by the firm. Like debt and equity, different insurance contracts can be constructed to address separate layers of risk:

- Exposure to risk comes by layers of insurance from high frequency events to low frequency but high impact events.
- Therefore, attention should be paid to excess-of-loss layers that cover low frequency events that can have a high loss impact.

Frequency and impact of operational risk events have a great deal to do with their insurability. They are necessary complements to the unambiguous identification of risk to be insured, and key to the correct pricing of the insurance contract.

Insurability also requires that the severity of the potential loss or the amount insured is not too small, because the transfer costs created by the operational risk sharing mechanism will be too high. At the other end of the scale are situations where the occurrence of events with huge financial consequences calls into doubt the wisdom of insuring them in the first place. After all those exceptional situations have been eliminated, it becomes feasible to define an operational risk insurance framework described in the frequency/impact event space.

Frequency and impact of operational risk events correlate to the concepts of limits and of finite risk, covered in the preceding sections. The same is true of the time dimension of operational risk insurance coverage. The best policy is that of making a distinction, which is practiced in reinsurance, between:

- Prospective contracts, which cover current and future underwriting years, and
- Retrospective contracts, where long settlement periods call for using the time value of money to price op risk insurance contracts.

Today, retrospective contracts are primarily found in long-tail business, such as occupational disability. Some experts think, however, that certain types of operational risks are also long-tail . Therefore, they can be better served and priced by means of retrospective contracts. The problem with operational risk insurance is that, unlike the coverage of disability, spikes may be hiding in the long tail.

Usually, loss portfolio transfers and insurance covers for adverse developments are retrospective in nature. That is, they relate to underwriting years in the past and, other things being equal, they require larger loss reserves. Precisely for the same reason of retrospective characteristics, insurance of some types of operational risk will quite likely resemble adverse development covers (ADCs). These provide covers for losses resulting from contracts concluded in the past whose aftermath, however, is felt in:

- The present, and
- The future.

For these reasons, to identify exposure associated with operational risk, and price appropriately contracts for insurance cover, estimates must be made regarding the frequency with which specific events occur and the extent of losses likely to be faced because of each of them. Classically these estimates use historical data of previous events and an analysis of what is likely to occur, but such data are not available with many types of op risks.

This may not inhibit alternative risk transfer *per se*, but it has an adverse impact on product pricing – and, therefore, the insurance company's bottom line. Depending on the frequency and impact of potential loss from operational risk events the conclusion may be reached that:

- Some op risks are not insurable,
- While others are not worth being insured.

Insurability of risks requires that the defined operational risk characteristics do exist, and losses have a stochastic character. At the same time, changes in supervisory and accounting regulations must be accounted for, as in the last analysis it may be found that extremely high impact op risk events are scarcely insurable even if they are low frequency. Some people question this statement saying that it is not true with earthquakes. Such argument forgets that:

- Earthquakes are natural events happening as one-offs.
- Risk from rogue traders and CEO malfeasance are man-made op risks, which sometimes, as in 2000–2002 become an industry trend.

Also, the challenge posed by statistics should never be underestimated. When the probability of the occurrence of certain operational risk events is very low, historical data would tend to be poor or even non-existent. Then, risk assessment and risk modeling may be nearly impossible – and the same is true of correct pricing for risk coverage.

11.7 Insurers who don't do their homework get burned

In has been a deliberate choice to bring to the reader's attention criteria of insurability which can turn an insured company's operational risk into the insurer's own technical risk. Any insurance contract that is long on hopes of getting new business but short on critical analysis, is a potential time bomb. To back-up this statement the present section presents some real life case studies, which complement those already discussed in Chapter 10.

In Britain, Norwich Union cut payouts to some policyholders as the markets where it had invested its assets, for greater return on equity, continued to fall. In the Netherlands, in 2002 Aegon issued the first profit warning in its history, after plunging stock markets and underwritten claims hurt performance. Many insurers do not heed the advice of Imam bin abi Taleb, who wrote in the sixth century AD: 'If God were to humiliate the human being he would deny him knowledge' – or the fruits of research. That's what doing one's homework is all about.

Among several German insurance companies that suffered, the example of two is outstanding. One is giant Allianz, which, in 2002, despite a still strong balance sheet saw its stock at a seven-year low – back to 1995 prices (more on this later). Another German insurer with big problems has been Familienfürsorge, which was forced into merger with HUK-Coburg, after admitting it could not meet obligations to policyholders.

Also hard hit have been two of the three major Swiss insurers. Zurich Financial Services, the embattled Swiss insurer lost a record $2 billion in the first half of 2002. In the aftermath, it was forced to restructure and raise $2.5 billion in fresh capital to save itself from bankruptcy. It also downsized to its core business after a disastrous foray into derivatives. To cut costs, the new management had to axe thousands of staffers as part of a $1 billion cost-savings plan. But is the reduction of headcount supposed to act as a wonder-drug for the ailing company?

Winterthur Insurance has also been on the sick list. Its parent, Crédit Suisse Group, was forced to inject $1.1 billion in new capital because of the markets' plunge. In musical chairs similar to those of Zurich Insurance, Winterthur's CEO was replaced, and a few months down the line the CEO of Crédit Suisse himself had to quit. What these examples have in common is they represent the fallout from management risk:

- From forays in commercial banking, in the case of Allianz
- To ill-defined 'financial services', which largely means high leveraging and bleeding with derivatives (in the case of Zurich).

Because when these decisions were taken they looked to be 'sure bets', but later on turned sour, insurers and reinsurers will be well advised to do a great deal of homework before jumping into operational risk coverage. Insurance companies are not, and should not think of themselves as being hedge funds ready to:

- Bet the shirt of their stakeholders in 'me to' market risks, and
- Play big in uncharted waters where they can sink with all their cargo.

There has been no lack of insurance company woes in the last year. On 14 August 2002, A.M. Best, the insurance industry's rating agency, downgraded eight British life companies, including well-known names like Scottish Assurance and Pearl Assurance. A.M. Best was concerned about the falling value of the assets that back their liabilities – therefore their readiness in meeting policyholder claims.

Not surprisingly the capitalization of insurance companies has greatly shrunk because they played it big in the stock market. At the London Stock Exchange the share price of Royal & Sun has fallen 70% in just one year – 2001; and it fell again in 2002, in the aftermath of revelations about potential losses with asbestos claims.

The risk from prolonged litigation has haunted insurers. On 13 September 2002, Allianz had to pump $750 million into Fireman's Fund, a US insurance subsidiary, to cover a surge in asbestos and other environmental claims (see Chapter 13). Earlier in 2002, the company's private-equity operation got burned when several investments, including planemaker Fairchild Dornier, failed.

Stock turmoil and a weak dollar reversed the growth in capital gains management. Funds managed for others by Allianz fell $42 billion, to $564 billion, in the first half of 2002. There has been more bad news for the German insurer. The worst case in its books has been Dresdner Bank, which lost $1 billion in the first half of 2002. Dresdner's corporate division was in trouble on two fronts:

- It has billions in bad debts, stemming from heavy loans to such companies as Kirch Media in Germany, WorldCom in the US, and a number of Latin American borrowers, and
- It came to the rescue of Dresdner Kleinwort Wasserstein (DKW), which bled money as trading revenues fell and it faced fees from mergers as well as acquisitions and the underwriting slump.

This is the downside of the merger between different sectors of the financial industry. Dresdner Bank had to nearly double its bad-loan provisions, to more than $1 billion. The acquisition of Dresdner Bank by the insurer proved to be a thorn in the side. Some experts said Allianz should never have bought Dresdner. Others suggested that it should sell or close DKW. In a nutshell:

- The insurer's strategy of building a global financial powerhouse has flopped,
- But its top management seems to be still committed to it, in spite of the bad news.

To make ends meet, on 18 September 2002 Allianz was selling off its stock portfolio, as Germany's Dax stock index crashed to a new five-year low.[8] The Dax was plunging towards the 3000 mark (when these lines were written, December 2002) compared to 8100 points in March 2000 and 5400 points in early 2002, but according to market analysts Allianz had to sell equities in its portfolio in order to save at least some of its core capital.

Other insurance companies, including Munich Re, were also selling their stock holdings, further contributing to the market meltdown. The panic button was hit by insurers because about 30% of the assets of Europe's insurance companies had been invested in the stock markets (see Chapter 10), and more than $165 billion of that money evaporated with the stock market crash.

The capitalization of major insurance companies themselves took a severe hit. The stock of Allianz, for instance, stood above 400 euro in 2000, but it fell below 100 euro in mid-September 2002, the lowest level in nine years, challenging the insurer's top management in regard to solvency.

Insurers in other continents did not fare that much better. AMP, a Sydney-based insurer and one of Australia's oldest companies, has been badly hit by its exposure to the falling UK stock market. In late September 2002 the difficulties at AMP's UK insurance division culminated in resignations of the Australian financial services group.

Like Zurich, AMP had branched into wider financial services outside its original charter. It owns Henderson Global Investors, the fund manager, and Pearl Life insurance. The parent company's shares almost halved in the late 2001 to late 2002 timeframe, hitting a low of A$11.25 on 23 September 2002, down from more than A$30 in mid-1998 shortly after the group demutualized and listed. The latest difficulties at Pearl only emerged after the Australian Securities and Investment Commission demanded clarification of statements about the insurer's capital adequacy buried in the back of a prospectus for an AMP capital raising.

11.8   Challenges with value accounting in the insurance business

Doing one's homework means several things at the same time. Stock market woes left aside, quite often companies forget that part and parcel of sound management is the prognostication of technical risk involved in future claims. The number of insurance companies that do not excel in this domain is in itself surprising.

In 1999, Korea Life Insurance, the country's biggest, with an 18% market share, was saved from bankruptcy with taxpayer's money. In 2002, the government was hoping to recover some of its money by selling 51% of it for $600 million. The suitor has been Hanwha Group, Korea's tenth largest chaebol. But according to published reports, Hanwha had several marks of 'distinction'.

- It did not report a profit in five years,
- Its debt equalled 232% of its equity, and

It was caught by regulators manipulating the books of three of its units.[9]

The irony, and the loophole, is that according to Korean law, this huge amount of 232% leverage would disqualify it from starting an insurance company, but not from buying one even if its finances are shaky, and policyholders of the insurers are at risk to lose their coverage and their nest egg too. Nobody can blame independent rating agencies for being vigilant to such happenings (see Chapter 12).

Experts say that a similar loophole may exist, with fair value accounting in certain forms of insurance. Theoretically, all stakeholders in the insurance business stand to profit from fair value accounting. But all practical aspects are not settled, including underwriting, pricing, and recognizing operational risk exposure.

Under fair value accounting, practically all assets and liabilities of an enterprise would be included in the balance sheet at their market value. This is the general rule. Each industry, however, faces problems of its own. For instance, in insurance there is an argument for recognizing unrealized profits on existing contracts at the time when the contracts are entered into.

Using the case of life insurance policies as a proxy, this would mean anticipating the expected profits to be earned over the total period of the contract. That's tough, because generally the *embedded value* of the contract can be over a period of 20–30 years. Fair estimates can only be made with the benefit of long experience – which is not the case with op risk.

Another issue under discussion with relevance to operational risk coverage is whether future profits on expected new business should be recognized. This represents the *appraisal value* of life insurance contracts and *renewal value* of non-life insurance contracts. Both issues relate to basic features characteristic of the insurance business, and both will have an impact on policies underwritten for operational risk.

To better appreciate the challenge associated to fair value accounting in insurance, we should briefly return back to basics. Typically, insurance companies give a commitment to policyholders to make agreed payments *if* a specific insured event occurs. As insurers provide cover, risks are transferred from policyholders to the insurance firm – a practice that is consistent with their core business.

- Insurers are responsible for a continuous provision of coverage over a specified period of time, and
- The provision of insurance protection covers the whole period set out in the insurance term.

The systematic assumption of risk is a stochastic process but timeframes vary. Life and health insurance contracts generally cover very long periods, over which the insurance firm does not have the right to cancel the contract. With property and casualty insurance, short duration contracts are more common. *If* the provision regarding *management intent* specified by Statement of Financial Accounting Standards 133 (which targets accounting for derivatives) is applied in connection to fair value accounting in insurance, *then*:

- The aforementioned long-term commitments will be carried at accrual value,
- While short term commitments, as well as the contents of the trading book, should be marked to market.

Not everybody, however, agrees with this approach, observing – not without reason – that an insurance contract resembles an all-or-nothing option, with the added complexity that life and health insurance contracts are long term. As it happens, with nearly all long-term financial instruments, there are no active markets for insurance/underwriting commitments that can be used as the basis for deriving fair values.

- Since it is not always possible to derive reliable fair values due to the uncertainties involved in assessing future cash flows,
- This poses the challenge of the reliability of the financial statements, because of the values they reflect.

While, when there is no recent trading information on fair value, marking to model can fill the gap, it is no less true that it is still early days for the whole concept of fair-value accounting. In fact, as Warren Buffett, best investor alive today, recently wrote in a seminal article, marking to model degenerates into marking-to-myth.[10] Some insurers indeed say that, for this reason, fair-value accounting of insurance contracts does not correspond to the currently applicable accounting treatment. They also add that insurance companies remain exposed to underwriting risks until such time as:

- The contract comes to an end, and
- Claims are discharged.

Exceptions made for value accounting of new contracts (or loans) have the nasty result of contradicting the more general basis of fair value accounting. The resulting challenge is one of comparability in consolidated financial reporting across different industries. For instance, companies in manufacturing industry, where sales are made before contractual delivery or fulfillment,

- Do not recognize profits when the contract is received.
- They do so over the period of project completion or after delivery of the finished product.

Another challenge lies in the fact that expenses relating directly to revenues should be included in the profit-and-loss account, in the corresponding periods. Extending this to insurance means that contracts should also be recognized over time as services are performed. Financial institutions are not allowed to recognize unearned interest on their financial transactions.

Still another concern of stakeholders, particularly investors and regulators, is that a recognition of profits on sales based on a fair-value approach, without fair values observable in deep and liquid markets, allows management the opportunity to massage reported earnings. This is particularly true if no proper rules are developed to provide reliable and comparable financial statements on a global basis – particularly so with instruments whose accounting does not benefit from tradition, the underwriting of operational risk being an example.

To avoid falling into a mess in the first place involves both rigorous research and stress testing. In 2000 FSA asked the British insurers under its authority to stress test their equity holdings, which is part of their economic capital. The stress threshold was set at 30% below market value and the results were comfortable. But then the stock market plunged, and several insurers were in trouble. They asked FSA to reduce the stress test margin, and permission was granted. The market dropped still more, and FSA had to ease the marking to market criteria, leading *The Economist* to question the wisdom of establishing benchmarks which later on will not be observed as adversity hits – yet, that's precisely the time when stress tests are most valuable.

In conclusion, not only the senior management of financial institutions must be keen on doing their homework, but also the rules have to be really international, covering a wide range of products, and not amenable to last-minute changes when adversity hits. Standards bodies and regulators should contribute the norms, and should observe them. They are all stakeholders in market discipline and the concept of compliance is applicable to everyone.

Notes

1 *Journal of Applied Corporate Finance*, 14/2, pp. 32–6, Winter 2002.
2 See also the reference to rogue trader insurance in section 11.3.
3 *Journal of Applied Corporate Finance*, 14/4, p. 25, Winter 2002.
4 *Sigma*, No. 3/2001, March 2001, Swiss Re, Zurich.
5 *Sigma*, No. 3/2001, March 2001, Swiss Re, Zurich.
6 *Sigma*, No. 5/1997, May 1997, Swiss Re, Zurich.
7 D.N. Chorafas, *Stress Testing. Risk Management Strategies for Extreme Events*, Euromoney, London, 2003.
8 *EIR*, 4 October 2002.
9 *BusinessWeek*, 16 September 2002.
10 Warren Buffet, 'Avoiding a Megacatastrophe', *Fortune*, 17 March 2003.

12 Role of rating agencies in the creditworthiness of insurance firms

12.1 Introduction

The more insurers expand their business frontier to include previously unfamiliar areas, the more important becomes the evaluation of their creditworthiness by independent agents, like well-established global rating agencies. Chapter 11 provided evidence to back this assertion, explaining why a measure of creditworthiness is particularly important as the scope of insurance operations is growing to encompass:

- Instruments for distributing risks, using the capital market, and
- Vehicles like alternative risk transfer solutions targeting operational risk.

Beyond this, the new capital adequacy framework by the Basel Committee on Banking Supervision has not only introduced operational risks beyond those classically associated to clearing, payments, and settlements, it has also brought the independent rating agencies into the picture in a big way. This is in connection to credit risk, but the reader will remember that insurance coverage is transforming operational risk into credit risk.

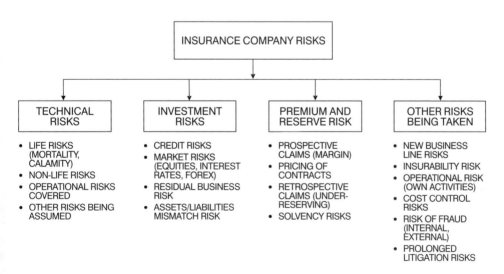

Figure 12.1 The array of risks demanding the attention of insurance companies

Because insurance companies have come forward offering to underwrite operational risks of credit institutions, they have become their partners in op risk control. But as Figure 12.1 shows, operational risks figure twice in the constellation of risks faced by insurers: They are technical risk (see Chapters 10 and 11) and part of other risks being taken. Insurers have to deal with operational risks from both sides:

- Both having these operational risks in their own back yard, since they are indivisible from their daily operations, and
- Insuring them, therefore being exposed to the probability of their happening somewhere else, with all this means in terms of adequacy of premiums and reserves.

For these reasons, Dr Thomas Hess of Swiss Re believes that insurers have to rethink and revamp their operational risk management. He considers risk control, in the whole range of activities shown in Figure 12.1, as a major operational risk for insurers and for all other financial firms. Insurers, he told me, should control assets and liabilities (A&L) in a proactive manner versus all their assured risks.

The insurers' management of assets and liabilities is a prime domain of interest of independent rating agencies. A&L testing is very important because major cases of business interruption, like 11 September 2001, can turn even the most carefully crafted balance of A&L *vs* assured risks on its head.

Regarding the adequacy of assets to meet assumed risks, Swiss Re is very careful in its portfolio management, paying particular emphasis to matching assets and liabilities with risks being assumed. If and when (or where) they don't match, insurers must make choices, often tough choices, regarding business products they support – to steer their portfolios. Then they should use financial instruments to reshape the risk position.

An example is to diversify the portfolio by getting into risks to which the insurer is unexposed. Prerequisite to this strategy, however, is top management's decision on what the company wants to achieve in terms of risk and return. Only after this is done in a comprehensive manner, can an insurer rationalize on what they really want to do. This is a strategy independent rating agencies appreciate because it strengthens the insurer's balance sheet.

For an insurance company fraud is also an item in the risk management list, particularly external fraud, which is a key source of losses in insurance. An example of operational risk relating to poor management is misjudging assumed risks because of not doing one's homework in a thorough and consistent manner (see Chapter 11). Consistency involves four basic steps.

- Risk selection
- Risk pricing
- Terms and conditions
- Reserving assets to meet assured risks.

According to Dr Hess, operational risks exist in every one of these steps. The risks to which an insurance company addresses itself might have been selected wrongly, or they may be priced inadequately given the amount of assumed exposure. The question of contractual clauses is also crucial. *If* the insurers can influence the contract, *then* they can do a lot in terms of risk management.

12.2   Independent rating agencies, their business and their role

The term 'nationally recognized statistical-rating organization' (NRSRO) was coined in 1975. At its peak, the US had eight such organizations, but industry consolidation has cut that to four. Initially, what is now called independent rating agencies started as publishers of financial data. The eldest on record, Poor's Publishing, was established in 1860. In 1941 it merged with Standard Statistics to form Standard and Poor's, now a division of McGraw–Hill.

Historically, the second on record is A.M. Best. Incorporated in 1899, it focused on specializing in information, and later on rating, for insurance industry. Moody's Investors Service was first established in 1900, ceased to exist during the market crash of 1907, and restarted its operations in 1909 – uninterrupted since then.

Other independent rating agencies came much later. IBCA was incorporated in 1978. In 1997 it merged with Fitch. Fitch Ratings is controlled by Fimalac, a French-capital holding. Other companies in the same holding are Duff & Phelps, Core Rating (specializing on corporate governance), and Thomson Bank Watch.

During the past two decades of the twentieth century, independent rating agencies have assumed increasing importance in rating companies and debt. The more markets globalized, the more independent rating became necessary. The 1999 new capital adequacy framework by the Basel Committee specifies that independent rating of creditworthiness is very important in capital allocation for credit risk.

The role of independent rating agencies fits between that of the regulators and the interests of the investing public. Regulators aim at orderly market behavior, market transparency, avoidance of systemic risk, and protection of investors, up to a point. But the explicit shareholder and bondholder protection is not part of their charter. Bondholder protection by means of credit risk grading is the work done by rating agencies, which address default probability of:

- Bonds
- Companies, and
- Sovereigns.

Regulators are increasingly interested in credit rating as attested through the new capital adequacy framework. In the G-10 countries the policy of regulators is that the market dictates the rating system. Independent rating agencies are the market's agent. In some developing countries, particularly in Latin America, rating has become obligatory. Major rating agencies now expect that this may also happen in Eastern Europe, though not necessarily in Asia.

Indirectly, rating agencies help regulators in doing their job, because they know that if they go too far in market control they can wipe out entrepreneurial activity. Hence it is better to do the needed credit risk evaluation by proxy, while at the same time providing a level field in creditworthiness evaluation, capitalizing on the global role played by independent rating agencies.

Not everything has gone smoothly with independent rating of creditworthiness. For instance, the US Congress raised concerns about credit rating agencies after Enron's 2001 failure, saying the agencies only reduced investment-grade ratings on the Houston energy-trading company's debt a few days before Enron went bankrupt. As a result of these concerns, a corporate-reform bill adopted in July 2002 ordered the US Securities and Exchange Commission to issue a report, in January 2003, on rating agencies. This is focusing on areas such as:

- Conflicts of interest, and
- Barriers to entry.

At a day-long meeting at the SEC in mid-November 2002, regulators acknowledged that designations of nationally recognized statistical-rating organizations seem to limit the number of credit-rating agencies and may be a barrier for entry by other firms. Therefore, the Securities and Exchange Commission began hearings on the part played by credit rating agencies in capital markets.

But entry into the independent credit rating domain, even if free for all, would not be without challenges. One of the problems for would-be NRSROs is that the designation hasn't been formally defined so that everybody knows what it means to be an NRSRO in terms of skills and obligations. In other terms,

- What it takes to become one, and
- What may be the formal appeals process for firms that are denied recognition.

Institutional investors and corporate-bond issuers at the aforementioned SEC meeting endorsed changes that would raise the number of rating agencies and shed more light on how credit analysts develop ratings. 'We would definitely advocate more NRSROs,' said Deborah Cunningham, of Pittsburgh-based Federated Investors. But in the opinion of Frank Fernandez, of the Securities Industry Association, building a reliable credit-rating business takes time, talent and money, and it is not clear whether investors want a panoply of ratings rather than reliance on a few proven providers.[1] For their part, rating agencies are refining their evaluation process to address new risks. Their measures include:

- Seeking additional disclosure, and
- Revising the way analysis of a business is incorporated in the consolidated rating of a parent.

They also are more careful in factoring the volatility of unregulated income streams into their rating, and in reflecting their propensity for expanding too fast. Since big name bankruptcies like Enron, Global Crossing, and WorldCom, regulators have uncovered the impact of deceptive trading, designed to inflate volumes and profits at corporate end, which unavoidably influence ratings. A good deal of doubt has been placed on their marking-to-market accounting which, for instance, considers up the value of a future contract (see Chapter 11).

The independent rating agencies themselves have been keen to improve their methods. An example is the use of what has become known as *interactive credit rating*, a two-way process based on:

■ Discovery, and
■ Communication.

To a large extent, communication includes confidential information, and personal meetings held with the rated company's senior management. Companies issue policies or issue debt, and independent agencies are asked to rate the firm and the debt. But while rating agencies may be commissioned by specific companies, in essence they believe that their ultimate client is the market.

Ratings influence in a significant way the interest companies have to pay for their debt. During the aforementioned mid-November 2002 hearings at the Securities and Exchange Commission, regarding nationally recognized statistical rating organizations, Standard & Poor's said the power and energy sector experienced its sharpest credit slide in decades, and more declines and possible defaults were anticipated, with the energy industry having more than $90 billion to refinance by 2006.

As the independent rating agencies continue to downgrade the credit of energy traders, each downgrade makes it more expensive for energy firms to obtain financing and continue operations (see Chapter 4). From 1997 to 2001, the debt to total capitalization ratio at energy traders rose from 53 to 60%, and cashflow coverage of total debt fell from 23 to 16%. Since late 1999, S&P began downgrading the energy traders. The real crisis began when, a couple of months prior to its bankruptcy, Enron revealed some of its financial statements had been built on financial trickery. The agencies downgraded its credit to junk.

12.3   Insurance companies and independent rating agencies

There is no lack of independent rating agencies in the world, but not all have the same standing. The four entities operating on a global scale are Standard & Poor's (S&P's), Moody's Investors Service, Fitch Ratings, and A.M. Best, which specializes in insurance. There are also smaller rating agencies rating public and private companies, sovereigns, bonds, asset-backed securities, commercial paper, and medium term notes.

The debt being rated may be corporate, municipal, government or other. The focal point is credit risk: the counterparty's ability to pay interest and repay the principal. Ratings are typically subject to revision as, over time, the credit quality of counterparties might change dramatically. Table 12.1 shows the levels of credit ratings by S&P's, Moody's and A.M. Best.

■ The rating system of A.M. Best has 11 graduations.
■ Those of S&P and Moody's have a scale of 20.

The granularity of these grading scales is part of the rating agencies' strength. It documents that the latter have a major role to play in the insurance industry now, when, in most markets, insurance companies encounter difficulties due to solvency problems that are a challenge to their creditworthiness. If *solvency* is expressed in average capital funds as percent on net premiums, then:

S&P's and other agencies	Moody's	A.M. Best	Credit message
AAA	Aaa	A++	Very high quality
AA+ AA AA–	Aa1 Aa2 Aa3	A+	High quality
A+ A A–	A1 A2 A3	A-	Good payment ability
BBB+ BBB BBB–	Baa1 Baa2 Baa3	B++	Adequate payment ability
BB+ BB BB–	Ba1 Ba2 Ba3	B B–	Uncertainty in payment ability
B+ B B-	B1 B2 B3	C++ C+	High risk operations
CCC+ CCC CCC–	Caa1 Caa2 Caa3	C	Vulnerability to default
CC C D	C	C– D	Bankruptcy likelihood or other major shortcoming

Table 12.1 Long-term senior debt rating by S&P's, Moody's, and A.M. Best

- Solvency ratios have declined in the past few years,
- Exits by insurance companies reduced capacity, and
- Non-life capital funds decreased by $90 billion in the aftermath of 9/11.

A perception of financial staying power in insurance, from outside the firm, is given in Figure 12.2, which is based on the result of a meeting with Swiss Re. Other sources indicate that among insurance companies underwriting results did not improve significantly, even if premiums increased after 9/11. At the same time,

- A sharp stock market decline hit hard the portfolio of insurance companies, and
- Default rates on corporate bonds rose from less than 1% in 1994–97 to 5% in 2000–2002.

As a result of these happenings, independent rating agencies downgraded insurance companies, informing investors on impending risks. One of the findings in my research has been that solvency is more important than liquidity in the insurance business.

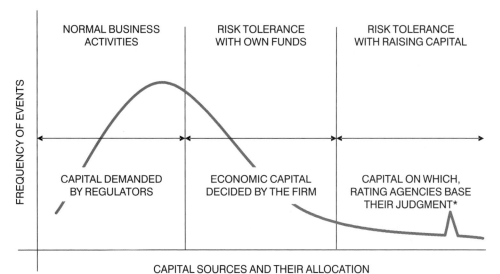

Figure 12.2 A view from Swiss Re of capital adequacy in insurance. (*This gives a perception of financial staying power from the outside)

'Our salient problem is not liquidity, but *solvency*,' said the director of research of a major insurer. To minimize credit risk this company's portfolio has 70% government bonds. Regulatory capital in insurance is:

■ 4–5% of assets in life insurance, and
■ 15% of revenue in non-life insurance.

Beyond this comes the insurance company's ability to raise funds in the capital market and through counterparties. Into this ability enters the evaluation algorithm of independent rating agencies, though the main object of analysis is the claims-paying ability of the firm. This is financial strength rating, and it has similarities with rating studies targeting the issuance of debt. According to A.M. Best, the criteria are:

■ Business profile
■ Management and strategy
■ Operating performance
■ Investment portfolio, and
■ Capitalization.

Business profile examines market position, competition, product mix, distribution channels, and geographical diversification. A management and strategy evaluation looks into overall corporate strategy, management experience, financial strategy, and acquisition or disinvestment strategy.

Operating performance targets the analysis of total bottom line results, as well as technical profitability in underwriting. What investment portfolio analysis is after has been discussed in Chapters 10 and 11. The study of an insurance company's capitalization looks into solvency, liquidity, reinsurance protection, and reserves.

The criteria used by Standard & Poor's and Moody's in rating insurance companies are shown in Box 12.1. These factors are always viewed and analysed within a given industry, level of market risk, and regulatory framework. Rating agencies are usually very careful in their evaluation of credit risk as they know that every time they assign a rating their name, credibility and integrity are on the line. The investment community would not permit slippage; its scrutiny of the ratings is almost constant. At the same time:

■ Rating agencies must cope with the fact that the demand for professional credit analysis has grown explosively, and
■ Globalization places particular strains on the rating process because it brings into the picture many unknowns having to do with different jurisdictions, regulations, and accounting standards.

Box 12.1   Criteria employed by Standard & Poor's and Moody's in rating insurance companies

Industry risk
Management and corporate strategy
Business review
Results from underwriting
Investment policy and results
Interest rate risk management
Capitalization
Liquidity
Capital and capital requirements

By Moody's
Competitive situation
Regulatory trends
Adequacy of equity capital
Investment risk
Profitability
Liquidity
Group interrelationships
Products and distribution channels
Quality of management and organization
   Other crucial criteria are:
   spread of risk
   loss reserves
   solvency margin
   reinsurance program

There is a difference in procedure between new ratings and the revision of old ones. First time ratings require fairly extensive work starting with preliminary discussion, following up with scheduled meetings and submitting advance background materials. This preparatory activity may take about a month and it is followed by:

- Analytical meetings with the rated company
- The agency's own credit analysis, and
- Rating committee meetings.

In all, some two or more months of work are necessary before the issuer and credit markets are informed of rating and its justifications. Rating reviews are needed if major changes occur in an issuer's near-term or long-term credit outlook. Rating agencies place the issuer's ratings under review, with contributing factors such as:

- Shifts in the industry
- Emerging technologies and their impact
- Government intervention
- Regulatory changes
- An evolution in macroeconomic variables.

All types of significant events are examined to determine the degree to which a key factor may or will affect the operating position of the company, and its future ability to meet its commitments. Default statistics are part of this picture and so is every other factor helpful in providing investors and issuers of debt with a factual and documented rating.

12.4 Qualitative and quantitative approaches to rating insurance companies

Commercial banks and insurers attract a great deal of interest in rating by independent rating agencies because, as shown in Figure 12.3, they muster among themselves about 50% of all financial institutions' assets (statistics based on American data). Other entities, too, are now rated by independent agencies. An example is not-for-profit foundations.[2]

The credit rating is typically a probability. It measures the likelihood that the issuer will default on the security over its life. This may depend on the instrument, the time horizon, the issuer's financial health, and willingness to perform. Such ratings incorporate an assessment of the expected loss should a default take place. In a way, the work of the analysts employed by the rating agencies is not very different from that of financial analysts addressing themselves to equities, but there is one major exception:

- Equity analysts approach their mission from the standpoint of shareholders.
- Rating specialists particularly look after the interests of bondholders and other lenders.

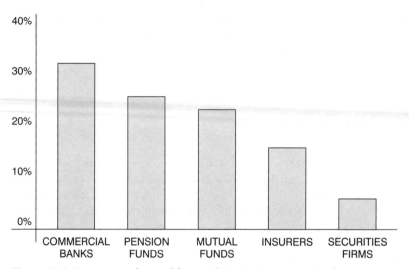

Figure 12.3 Percentage share of financial institutions assets in the US, 2001

As such, credit rating experts tend to have a longer time horizon than equity analysts as they investigate both business risk and financial risk, while they study the nature of each problem. Rating agencies meticulously collect annual and interim reports as well as other public data on issuers, recalculating this data to adjust for differing accounting methods and other factors. Let's keep all this in mind when we talk about how insurance companies are rated. A fine approach to credit rating will look at:

- Premium risk
- Reserve risk
- Credit risk by reinsurer
- Credit risk by bond underwriter
- Investment risk.

It will also use market profile criteria. At A.M. Best these include: competitive advantages or disadvantages, business mix and diversification, understanding the riskiness of business written, quality of distribution network, and peer-to-peer comparison. Much of this is qualitative information. Capital strength is quantitatively expressed in reserves, and retrocession/protection.

Ratings benefit from sensitivity analysis, including leading indicators of future balance sheet as shown in Figure 12.4. While it is very important, traditional solvency is not a sufficient measurement. A.M. Best looks at risk-adjusted capital structure, with capital strength evaluation involving:

- Best's Capital Adequacy Ratio (BCAR, see Chapter 10)
- Risk-Based Capital (RBC)
- Reinsurance Protection
- Reserve Adequacy, and
- Future Needs (growth, competitive positioning).

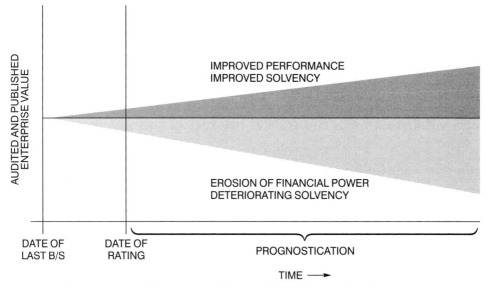

Figure 12.4 Analysis of financial strength, both historical and prospective

Operating performance is another major criterion, expressed in financial strategy, management quality, earnings generation (underwriting and total), investment philosophy, forward-looking earnings drivers, earnings measurements and targets, earnings quality (sustainability/volatility).

Whether the rating concerns an entity or an issue – and whether that entity and that issue is national or global – the rating is an opinion on *future ability* and legal obligations: for instance, the financial responsibility of an issuer to make timely payments on a given fixed income security; or the ability of an insurance company to honor the policies it has underwritten.

Gathering prospectuses, examining trust deeds, and indentures or other legal information relevant to particular securities or entities is only part of the problem. As we saw in section 12.3, valuable information is obtained through in-person meetings with company management which helps to understand current and upcoming challenges as well as strategies for the future.

A rating research team typically includes a lead analyst, who is a specialist in the issuer's industry, the director for the industry sector, country and regional specialists, accounting and other experts. In the insurance industry this work becomes increasingly complex because of the polyvalence of rated entities, as insurance companies compete more energetically, in more markets. An example is *Munich Re* which became:

■ A major life insurer, with 91.7% in Ergo
■ An asset manager, with $120 billion in its books
■ A banker, with 25.7% in Hypovereinsbank
■ A banker, with 10.4% in Commerzbank, and
■ A direct vendor of reinsurance to corporations.

Like any other insurer Munich Re is exposed to operational risk. One case alone, 11 September 2001, cost the company an estimated $1.9 billion. This is said to be the largest ever insurance loss. The challenge independent rating agencies face is to answer in a reliable way the query: Has the insurer the assets and solvency to absorb such shocks? Answers to such questions are usually confidential, based on selected criteria.

12.5   Information is the critical product of rating agencies

As section 12.4 has demonstrated, both qualification and quantification are integral parts of an analysis for credit rating. The evaluation of creditworthiness is not based on a pre-defined set of criteria, like ratios, which work in a mechanical way. It is the product of a comprehensive study of each individual entity, or debt issue, and it is expressed in a grading scale which includes measures of:

- Management skill
- Debt coverage
- Level of gearing
- Cash flow, and
- Risk control.

Credit rating is the output of experts who work as the distillers of information. This requires imagination, experience, and calculation. People have plenty of imagination but their ability to calculate is not outstanding. To counterbalance their limitations people group into teams, teams group into organizations, and organizations undertake analytical projects.

The rating agencies' teams must work diligently, but also have a questioning mind. This precondition leaves no room for bureaucracy. But as the case of Andersen, the auditors, has shown, it does not necessarily exclude conflict of interest. Time will tell. What can be stated for sure at this moment is that:

- Rating agencies cannot afford to let paperwork proliferate
- Or, clerical forces surpass productive agents in number.

This puts them at a different setting than bureaucracies where as much as half the cost of administering some companies can be charged against the processing of information, and the results are not necessarily good. The work done by rating agencies capitalizes on the fact that free markets require information in order to handle increased amounts of liabilities, and this process in itself generates more information that needs to be exploited.

Traditional information processes are the least satisfactory in respect to forecasting. Credit ratings are not a forecast, but transition matrices, and a steady upkeep makes them some kind of prognosticators. Modeling real life situations – in this case creditworthiness and its evolution – also helps.

- Models can comprehend a situation but they cannot conceive it.
- Experts must supplement the conceptual factors through simulation.

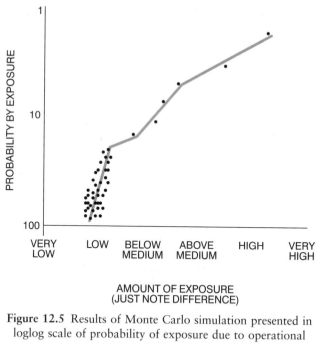

Figure 12.5 Results of Monte Carlo simulation presented in loglog scale of probability of exposure due to operational risks

Simulation is a working analogy. When analogous systems are constructed, or found to exist, then experimentation on one of them can lead to the investigation of others. Figure 12.5 presents the pattern resulting from Monte Carlo simulation, in logscale, of probability of exposure due to operational risks. The fine grain, 20-level classification of creditworthiness which was shown in Table 12.1, has precisely the objective of informing the reader on test results. Provided:

- Ratings have been constructed with due care, and
- Their accuracy has been thoroughly tested.

Under these conditions, models are very helpful in providing factual and documented results. One of them are the power curves used by Moody's as predictors of a company's default. Power curves are based on statistical inference. They reflect chosen critical factors that are able to tell how well a given organization manages its business. Examples are:

- Profitability
- Solvency
- Liquidity
- Assets, and
- Sales growth.

Through simulation we target a few, but focused answers from a large amount of data, or clearer answers from limited, sometimes fuzzy data. The former is known as *data reduction*; the latter as *data generation*. For a data reduction example take an earth satellite that is constantly beeping out information on conditions in space as it meets them in subsecond intervals. A computer absorbs this tremendous amount of information, collates it, processes it, and finally reduces it to a meaningful pattern.

For data generation, consider the computer at the missile test center. It receives rather limited information on the path of a fired missile and on the basis of this information forecasts its exact trajectory. That is, it generates data on the future behavior of the device, and if this behavior is forecast to be harmful in any respect to its creators, the computer would generate a signal that would cause the missile immediately to self-destruct in the air.

Credit rating involves both data reduction and data generation, which is also true of many other business activities. Research and analysis is instrumental in strengthening a company's balance sheet. An example of this proactive approach is that of operational risk valuation studies in ship insurance. The case study on Lloyd's in section 12.7 is based on a personal meeting with underwriter Peter Chrismas. I was impressed by the depth of his analysis (see sections 12.6 and 12.7).

The analysis done by Lloyd's hull insurers concentrates on management risk and technical risk. So do the credit ratings of insurance firms. In both cases, trend lines help. When they are well-documented, the results of analysis condense a long experience into a brief pattern. This is shown in Figure 12.6 through half a dozen characteristics curves whose cumulative effect defines estimated default frequency.

For practitioners, a pattern or a symbol is a most valuable snapshot. In terms of credit rating (see Table 12.1), the triple A (AAA or Aaa) represents gilt edge credit quality. To the professional, it means that the security ranks well above all other classes in margins of safety against default, even under severe economic conditions. By contrast, the C class indicates a very high level of credit risk.

Neither in the main grading classes nor the subclasses are ratings expected to go up and down with business cycles, supply and demand, or the last quarter's earnings report. While dramatic short-term events upset a rating, emphasis is placed on the longer term. The ratings in Table 12.1 are intended to measure long-term risk, hence the analytical focus is on fundamental factors that will drive each insurer's longer-term ability to meet their obligations.

As the preceding chapters brought to the reader's attention, algorithms expressing crucial variables are established and tested by mining rich databases that contain information permitting analysis of the pattern of defaults, and document behavior of underlying factors. Variation in one or more factors retained as crucial is used for experimentation. An example is the result of Monte Carlo simulation on probability of exposure due to operational risks, which we have seen in Figure 12.5.

Regulators look favorably on the development and use of credit risk models, as documented by the internal ratings-based (IRB) method by the Basel Committee, and its contribution to estimating capital requirements.[3] Credit risk models should also be developed for a better management of the financial institution, by enabling an appreciation of exposure due to credit risk, market risk, or operational risk at board level and by senior management.

Like market risk models and statistical quality control charts, credit risk models can be instrumental in promoting internal control. The same is true of operational risk models. As an executive of the European Central Bank was to say: 'Measurement units

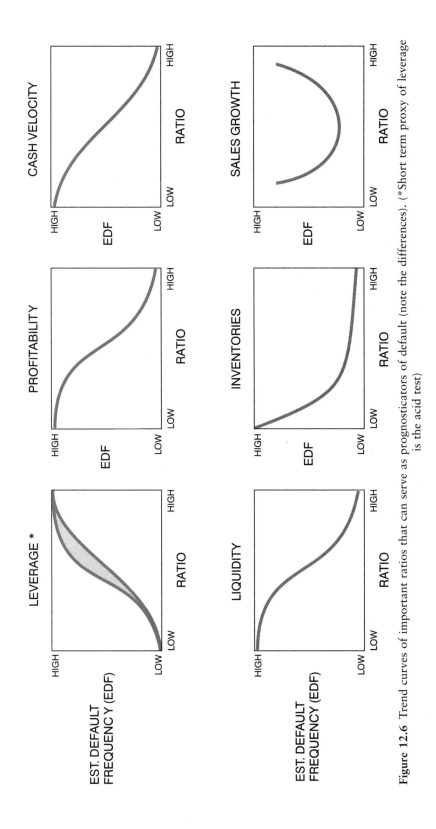

Figure 12.6 Trend curves of important ratios that can serve as prognosticators of default (note the differences). (*Short term proxy of leverage is the acid test)

and control procedures are two of the challenges lying ahead.' This is true all over business and industry. Section 12.6 takes the shipping business as a case study.

12.6   Analytical studies are the way of being in charge of risks

Just as banks must do appropriate research on credit rating prior to giving major loans, the best managed insurers must study what they can expect in terms of risk and return prior to underwriting a policy. It serves little to become an aggressive insurer without lots of homework to back up one's moves regarding:

- Risk being assumed, and
- The actuarial view of fair premium.

A good deal of the research associated with this homework is internal to the bank or the insurer. But, as banks gain from analysis done by independent rating agencies, insurers benefit from companies specializing in quality assurance. Veritas, the Norwegian certification agency, is a case in point.

Since the mid-1960s, nearly four decades ago, Veritas has been a leader in simulation (see section 12.5). Prior to that date its ship inspectors, like those of its competitors, were going through an itemized list of check-ups on a ship's seaworthiness (see section 12.7 for a list of crucial factors). This has been classically done on a standalone, item-by-item basis, but in a major leap forward in quality assurance Veritas developed a simulator which enabled it to:

- Take a holistic view of quality factors, leading to a factual and documented certification procedure.
- Develop a rich database on defects for all items in the analytical checklist, and their correlation.
- Experiment through simulation in order to uncover latent defects and focus on new leads, therefore making certification so much more effective.

Each of these three points is of capital importance to operational risk control. This is the way we should be working to improve our method and our deliverables. Yet many companies, including insurers, are slow to adapt to experimentation. This is counterproductive because it opens for them a mare's nest of surprises. By contrast, those who take research seriously hold the upper ground – as the following case study demonstrates.

In the late 1980s and early 1990s, London's Lloyd's has suffered some major setbacks because its risk and return evaluation was wanting.[4] But times have changed. Marine insurance, which is the subject of this and the following sections, has been traditionally dominated by Lloyd's syndicates. In 2000, out of a total market of £4.3 billion in gross premiums,

- Lloyd's had a share of £2.5 billion
- Other insurance companies, a little over £1.1 billion, and
- The Marine Protection & Indemnity (P&I) Clubs, nearly £600 million.[5]

The Marine P&I Clubs are mutual insurance associations of shipowners and charterers, originally founded in England in the nineteenth century. Today, in the liability sector they have a significant role, but the leading player is still Lloyd's in spite of the overall reduction in its syndicates from about 400 in 1991 to 86 in 2002 – following the crisis that hit Lloyd's in the early 1990s.

Other insurance companies, too, went through consolidation, examples being the 1996 merger of Royal Insurance and Sun Alliance; 1998 merger of Commercial Union, General Accident, and Norwich Union – followed in 2000 by the merger of the resulting entity with CGNU; as well as the takeovers. For instance, in 1986 Cornhill was taken over by Allianz; while in 1999 Guardian Royal Exchange was purchased by AXA.

The message to retain from these events is that they reduced the involvement of the London market in insurance. The consolidation at Lloyd's, however, proved to be much more radical than the aforementioned mergers and acquisitions. While many syndicates left, the remaining Lloyd's agents:

- Continued the concentration process,
- But also improved their risk management methods introducing urgently needed analytics.

To appreciate this change in culture and in management policy, it is helpful to recall that by 1990 – before the majority of huge losses struck – Lloyd's had evolved into a complex structure. The hubs were the 400 syndicates, each a relatively small unit managed by an active underwriter who was taking on insurance risks. In each syndicate, *managing agents* were:

- Establishing policy guidelines, and
- Supervising underwriting activities.

The capital required for the conduct of underwriting was provided by *names*. Till 1993, the names were the exclusive source of funds to Lloyd's, a tradition dating back to 1720 after a law enacted when the South Seas Bubble burst and many people, including the likes of Isaac Newton, lost lots of assets. As private individuals, the names were in fact the bottom of the food chain of Lloyd's underwriting, assigning the syndicates unlimited security. By contrast,

- Policy and the underwriting of huge risks was done by the managing agents and the lead underwriters.
- The losses that accumulated have shown that many agents and underwriters did not have their eyes wide open when taking risks.
- Lloyd's was underperforming other insurers, and large settlements acted as a substantial drag on the names' assets.

Over the years risk management had become lax and this led to the catastrophes which hit Lloyd's and the names a decade ago. In the aftermath, some of the consolidated syndicates got their act together and restructured their risk management. They instituted analytical studies, and investigated the roots of underwriting risk.

This is the subject of the case study presented in section 12.7, as it appeared to myself and Peter Chrismas, Hull Underwriter, Marine, Aviation Transport, and Sales Division, Lloyd's.

12.7 Operational risk with marine insurance underwriting: a case study

One of the underwriters' steady concerns is premiums or rates. In some markets, like energy, rates have increased dramatically in response to losses – 1000% on some lines in the 2000 to 2002 timeframe (see Chapter 4). Marine hull rates increased much less, though in 2001 they did grow by 20–30%, as high value risks with ferries, oil tankers, and container vessels, expanded. Even so, premiums have failed to adjust to meet risk increases while shipowners responded that they could not afford increased premiums because:

- There are more ships operating on slender margins, and
- Insurance is a large share of their operating costs.

Neither of these points contributes to risk reduction, just like a junk bond will not turn into AA rating because high interest rates ravage the company issuing it. Indeed, hull underwriters say that if policyholders want a quality product they must pay for it. Insurers cannot keep selling a product at a price that is not viable.

In the opinion of underwriter Christine Dandridge, for instance: 'If shipowners don't have the cash [to pay increased premiums], deductibles can be increased. This will change the loss frequency (distribution). Insurers will provide catastrophe cover only.'[6] According to other opinions, the quality of underwriting itself must improve. This is a basic objective of the work done by hull underwriter Peter Chrismas.

Basically, just like any other commodity, insurance rates are subject to supply and demand, and marine insurance has a cyclical nature. Players withdraw following losses, and reappear when profits show up, thereby fanning cycles. Hence, one of the problems with correctly pricing risk is the lack of logic characterizing providers of capital, who are no more the captive names – Lloyd's former financial strength.

Another factor to keep in perspective is that explained in section 12.6: the behavior of investors and underwriters has been classically characterized by too much 'seat of the pants' decision-making, calling into question the maintenance of viability of the marine insurance market. All this means that some branches of insurance, which is a medium- to long-term business, have been marred by short-term decisions:

- When there are profits, capital comes in and premiums fall.
- When there are losses, capital moves out and premiums rise.

But the likelihood of catastrophic events does not change because of this behavior by investors. What syndicates can do, and should do, is to significantly improve their own management, rigorously analyze their business, identify and classify the operational risk factors (see Chapter 2), and develop models that assist in improving the results by an order of magnitude. Box 12.2 shows 20 key factors entering the technical risk valuation model for ship insurance.

Box 12.2 Twenty key factors entering the op risk valuation model for ship insurance

- Ownership/management and ability to manage risk
- Current shipowner's credit rating
- Previous shipowner(s)
- Flag
- Type of ship
- Classification society
- Age of ship
- Main engine
- Power, in relation to size of ship
- Bedplate, crankshaft, etc. (relative to similar problems in similar vessels)
- Percentage of time within warranties (i.e. trade of the vessel)
- Past casualties (if any)
- Port state detention (if any)
- Cargo or passengers (certain trades/cargoes, such as logging, create greater risks)
- Service pattern (ports *vs* high seas)
- Liner trade or tramp
- Charter: spot or time
- Pollution at sea or harbor
- Risk scoring and audit trail
- Insured value

In No. 1 position in Box 12.2 is ownership/management. Experience suggests that the majority of casualties are due to human error and at its root is management risk. Its origins start at the top of the organization and the causes seep down all the way to the captain and the helping hands. While most accidents happen in entering and leaving ports, the direct responsibility of top management is always at stake. The principle is that:

- *If* the valuation by the owner is relatively low,
- *Then* there is something wrong in the way of personal accountability.

Flag is the No. 4 technical risk factor in the list presented in Box 12.2. Figure 12.7 shows much more than the fact that gross tonnage is unevenly distributed among 20 different flags from Panama to Great Britain. The family of curves distinguishes the age of ships. The Lloyd's study focused on six age brackets: 25+, 20–24, 15–19, 10–14, 5–9, 0–4, but Figure 12.7 shows only two age brackets: ships 9 years old or newer and the others.

An interesting documentation provided by the study of Peter Chrismas is that Panama not only has under its flag the largest share of global tonnage, about 22% of

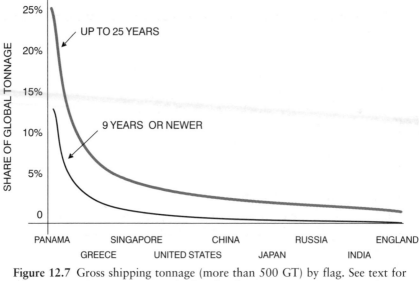

Figure 12.7 Gross shipping tonnage (more than 500 GT) by flag. See text for
further details

the total; it also has the newest fleet. Other things being equal, this is most significant
in terms of risks assumed by the insurance underwriter, because percentage of
casualties between age groups varies quite significantly.

Age of ship is the No. 7 risk factor in Box 12.2. Figure 12.8 shows that ships which
are up to 9 years old have a much smaller share of casualties than the rest. The share

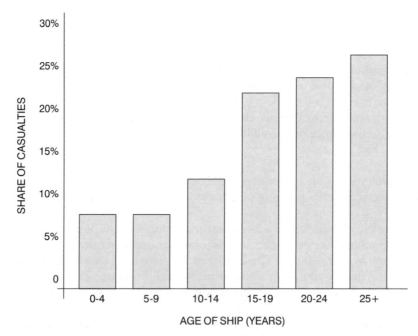

Figure 12.8 Percentage of shipping casualties by age group since 1994

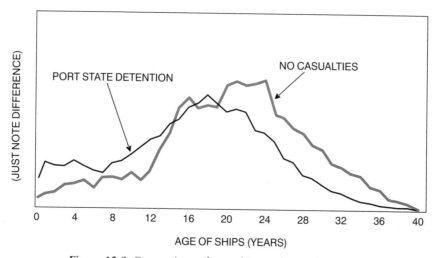

Figure 12.9 Comparison of casualties and port detentions

of casualties increases in the bracket of 10–14-year-old ships, then it jumps up with ships 15 years or older.

Interestingly, past the age of 25 the casualties curve bends, as shown in Figure 12.9. The same is true of the frequency of port state detention. Ships older than 25 years, which are museum pieces like the *Schiller* and *Gotthard* steamships on Lake Lucerne, are very carefully maintained by their owners. Therefore, their failure rate drops dramatically. The inverted U-curve provides food for thought.

Reliability studies have not yet entered ship insurance as a determinant factor, yet they can make a major contribution to insurability. To be effective, reliability should address both the drafting board of ships and their maintenance. Best results depend on engineers who have oriented their thinking toward sound fundamentals of reliable design.

- A system with a large number of simple items is preferred to one with a smaller number of complex items (see Chapter 5).
- Overall, reliability decreases sharply with increasing complexity; roughly, it is inversely proportional to the square number of components.
- Weak points in the system (like the hull of tankers) should be reinforced with built-in redundancy.
- Built-in absorbing points (limit switches, fuses, overload clutches) act as barriers to trouble.
- It is much more difficult, expensive, and time-consuming to increase the level of component reliability in the region of 99.9% than in the region of 99% or 90%.

Unnecessarily high reliability may be as bad in terms of final results as low reliability. The German V-2, in World War II, achieved what was then a high reliability of 78%. Three thousand were test-fired over a period of four years – but the greatly improved model was delivered too late to be of strategic value.

Chapter 5 has brought to the reader's attention the reliability equation, as well as mean time between failures (MTBF), mean time to repair (MTTR), and the concept of availability. It has also stressed the point that *if*, for example, a component must have a 95% chance of lasting 3 hours, *then* $\bar{T}$ for that component must exceed 58 hours. This means that reliability of individual components must be far greater than required reliability for the overall system. Statistical theory shows that if every component of a 500-component system is 99% reliable, the system will be only 1% reliable. This applies equally to ships, aircraft, and electronics.

A reliability study by Hughes Aircraft has shown that failures of particular airborne radar equipment closely approached reliability's negative exponential curve. Studies at Vitro Laboratories, based on a large number of shipboard electronic equipment failures, give a plot showing a $\bar{T}$ value of 165.8 hours and a corresponding 95% probability of about 8.4 hours.[7]

Regarding maintenance, a useful checklist comes from a survey conducted by Sandia Corporation, Albuquerque, New Mexico. Sandia studied suppliers' plants to determine whether or not manufacturing processes were adequate to assure a product of satisfactory quality and reliability. Reasons believed responsible for processing failure are listed in Table 12.2 in decreasing order of occurrence, not necessarily in order of importance. Percentages figures refer to observed infractions as compared with total situations where infractions were possible.

Reliability should be the *alter ego* of hull and machinery insurance. As these examples help to demonstrate, underwriting is not a matter of black and white but shades of grey. Because shipowners operate in a commercial environment they are faced with compromises. Therefore, through analytical studies, insurance underwriters must address the likelihood of catastrophes due to technical risks:

- Appreciating how good ship owners manage *their* risk
- Mining databases, using statistical evidence, and doing reliability studies, and
- Thinking quite a lot on how different risks relate to one another.

Test equipment or gauges not regularly compared with standard	72%
Inadequate identification of control of material in process	52%
Inadequate inspection records and reports (including information on process improvements)	36%
Sampling plans not adequate – plans not statistically sound, or plans that did not allow for human judgment error	25%
Lack of materials-testing for conformity and acceptance	25%
Materials used before certification was available	25%
Inadequate inspection instructions – important characteristics not inspected or improperly inspected	18%
No regular use of inspection reports to improve process	18%
Production personnel inspecting their own work – lack of separate inspection	14%

Table 12.2 Where to look for unreliability

Analytical studies are important not only to sharpen the underwriter's judgment and protect the investors, but also because of the trend to securitization of ship insurance and the role capital markets would play. Reliability studies in shipping may well be the counterpart of credit rating. As Peter Chrismas was to suggest, in future ship owners will be faced with a two-tier market:

■ Big operators, who will most likely transfer risk in different fashions, such as alternative risk transfer (see Chapter 11), and
■ The smaller to medium-size companies, which will continue to buy insurance in the traditional fashion.

The role of the broker, too, will change. He will become a consultant for a range of maritime requirements, including insurance. Also, in all likelihood, marine insurance companies will act as aggregators of risk and they will securitize their products.

For all the reasons outlined in this section, not only insurers but also shipowners should get busy with analytics. Successful securitization requires first class professionals, plenty of reliable statistics, powerful mathematical models, and a significant amount of experimentation.

In conclusion, like so many other insurance underwriting sectors, marine insurance is essentially applying knowledge, statistical evidence, prognostication of events, and common sense. The problem with common sense is that it so widely distributed that each one of us has very little.

Notes

1 *Wall Street Journal*, 18 November 2002.
2 D.N. Chorafas, *The Management of Philanthropy in the 21st Century*, Institutional Investor, New York, 2002.
3 D.N. Chorafas, *Modelling the Survival of Financial and Industrial Enterprises. Advantages, Challenges, and Problems with the Internal Rating-Based (IRB) Method*, Palgrave/Macmillan, London, 2002.
4 D.N. Chorafas, *Managing Credit Risk, Volume 2 – The Lessons of VAR Failures and Imprudent Exposure*, Euromoney, London, 2000.
5 *Sigma*, No. 3/2002, March 2002, Swiss Re, Zurich.
6 *Insurance Times*, 14 November 2002.
7 D.N. Chorafas, *What You Should Know About Designing for Reliability*, Product Engineering, 10 November 1958. The statistics don't change because 45 years have gone by – and it is surprising such studies have not yet found their way into shipping.

13 Tort is technical and operational risk of insurers

13.1 Introduction

Tort means any private or civil wrong, including damage or prejudice for which damages may be claimed – other than breach of contract. All injuries done to another person or legal entity are torts, unless there is some justification recognized by law. Because tort litigation can cripple companies, tort reform has been a continuing policy issue for the past ten years or so.

- Insurers, many businesses, non-trial lawyers, and certain consumer groups are for reform.
- Trial lawyers, labor, and opposing business groups are defending the status quo in tort legislation.

As a legal issue, tort is operational risk. The twist is that in many old and new tort events, experts find it difficult to distinguish clearly between those cases that have scientific foundation, and those cases that have none. Yet settlements in hundreds of billions of dollars have taken place for tobacco and asbestos (see sections 13.4 and 13.5) – and bigger ones may be coming with 9/11.

At root, the law of tort overlaps to some extent other branches of the law; for instance the law of contract. The concepts of *tort* and *contract*, as we now understand them, would have conveyed little of their meaning to the early lawyers who thought in terms of *actions* rather than in terms of *substantive rights*.

- The early remedies for tort were chiefly trespass upon the case followed, generally, by limited action.[1]
- The early remedies for breach of contract were actions of debt, of covenant, and detinue, which was very similar to debt but also closely related to tort.

Because many cases involving tort are open to class action, and juries are inclined to award tens and hundreds of millions or even billions of dollars in settlements, I strongly recommend using drills in connection to the evaluation of tort liability, as well as of the financial aftermath of major changes in legislation and regulation. Had Sealed Air done such a drill, it might not have had to pay a third of its equity as settlement (see section 13.4).

The case of *asbestos* as king-size operational risk documents the wisdom of being very, very careful. Through many lawsuits, asbestos litigation has led to the bankruptcy of more than 70 firms. The number of jobs lost due to these lawsuits is thought to be 60 000, and according to some estimates the cost of associated court actions could reach $200 billion.

Asbestos litigation is one of the best examples not only of tort, but also on its spillover. Slowly, such litigation has spread from firms involved directly in the mining of asbestos or the manufacture of and sale of asbestos-based products, to others that had only some dealings with asbestos producers, and therefore peripheral involvement.

Interests embedded in current tort legislation see to it that change in the letter of the law will not come easily. Often, the results of a major change – legislative, judicial or regulatory – are not possible to predict because the consequences are not transparent when such change is contemplated. Yet under conditions of historical precedence or hypothetical statements about the after-effect of critical change(s), analytical studies can be instrumental in revealing the more likely outcome.

An example where tort reform was enacted because of an expected torrent of litigation has been liability for year 2000 (Y2K) problems (see section 13.3). This was preceded by challenging studies evaluating extreme versus normal conditions; the spikes to be expected from the former documented the wisdom of legislative change by the US Congress.

13.2 Why tort reform is necessary

Because our society is litigation prone, and the probability of court action has significantly increased over time, tort reform is necessary to tame lawsuit abuse. As Chapter 3 documented, legal risk is operational risk; lawsuit abuse is its spike considered by experts to be as great a threat to investors as the accounting practices of the once mighty Houston energy trader Enron. During the year 2000 election campaign, the then aspirant George W. Bush vowed to push through Congress legislation that would:

- Cut excessive legal fees
- Punish frivolous litigation
- Deter bad-faith lawsuits, and
- Force losers to pay, under certain circumstances.

But two years down the line, by January 2003, lawyers and analysts suggest that only piecemeal reforms have a chance of passage through Congress. One necessary measure, the same experts say, should aim to limit the number, and impede the progress, of class action lawsuits. This can be done by forcing them out of state courts and into the federal system, which has tougher standards. In February 2002 the US Chamber of Commerce called for the passage of such legislation, saying that abusive and frivolous lawsuits:

- Impede job creation, and
- Stunt economic growth.

However, people and companies opposed to tort reform counterattack by asking for a different measure, which will increase operational risk by extending litigation to an area that has been so far immune, namely allowing patients to sue health maintenance organizations for coverage decisions.

Those in favour of tort reform speak of a sound measure the Bush Administration has taken, which amounts to a major civil justice reform in American history. This is the establishment of a government fund to compensate the victims of the events of 11 September 2001 at the Twin Towers and the Pentagon (section 13.5 describes the second implementation of this concept). This fund has been a unique experiment in victim compensation. Rather than leaving victims to the vagaries of the much maligned system of tort; or personal injury law, which could easily have bankrupted defendants such as airlines, airports, and others targeted with liability, the government set up a social insurance fund. To claim from it, victims must give up the right to sue.

Some experts suggest that this US government-sponsored fund reflects an implicit recognition of the flaws of civil litigation, which is intolerably slow and capricious; it cheats some of the victims; and feeds the greed of others. Over and above that, critics maintain, current tort legislation is inefficient, too often enriching lawyers at the expense of their own clients.

Many people now say that the events of 9/11 provided trial lawyers with the opportunity to find new ills, and causes of action. Others are producing documentation that with both new and old tort events, even the experts find it difficult to distinguish too clearly between ills that have scientific foundation and those that have none – while the tort roster continues to grow.

In the case of 9/11, for example, potential litigation includes wrongful death claims from those in the aircraft, and injury or death claims from those on the ground. Potential spillover could see suits levied against the architects, engineers, and builders for presumably faulty design and construction (see also Chapter 14 on operational risk from terrorism).

The list of injured parties seeking compensation may not end there. Other suits could include hundreds of thousands of people exposed to concrete dust, possibly laced with some asbestos. It is therefore understandable that the events of 9/11 galvanized, in some quarters, opposition to the current law, and led to determination to push for tort reform through legislation.

One particular subject on which worst case drills for tort reform should concentrate is that an explosion of liability from an event the size of 9/11, which is affecting so many people, is essentially uninsurable. Until mega-risk of these proportions came into the picture the insurance industry worked on the premise that liability risk is inherently insurable – but the conditions seem to have changed.

The hypothesis of insurability remains valid if, and only if, tort awards and settlements are of manageable proportions, and they exhibit a low correlation among themselves. While there is really no clear line between big risk and mega-risk, as I have outlined in Chapter 10, losses of $1 billion to $2 billion seem to be insurable by a single company, or an order of magnitude bigger than that by the insurance industry in unison. By contrast, losses of tens or hundreds of billions of dollars are not.

The experts opinion can be summarized as follows. A California earthquake, whose damages may run up to $2 billion was insured in the past by Lloyd's and more recently by Berkshire. However, prior to 9/11 Warren Buffett, CEO of Berkshire, said that when the current policy expired he was not going to renew it, because insurance premiums have dropped significantly and the earthquake is not aware of that fact.

Buffet's justification for insuring a mega-risk, like the California earthquake, has been that, in a worst case scenario, the catastrophe would represent 1–2% of Berkshire assets. But what company would insure a potential risk of awards and settlements of $100 billion, which may represent all of its assets?

In a way fairly similar to the 2002 drill by the Group of Seven involving a worst case scenario among financial institutions, a worst case evaluation drill should not be limited to financial and other property damage, including life. It should examine from all possible angles the aftermath of a supercatastrophe, big ticket events as well as a concentration of more mundane disparate events.

■ It must address multiple injuries on multiple policies from a large scale action, and
■ It should examine innovative lawsuits, when there is no legal precedence or precedential value other than the wave of liability losses for insurers.

Analytical studies along the lines I am suggesting must reflect the likelihood that events involving a concentration of claims can lead to mega-risk equivalents. That's what the manufacturers of vaccines have examined in establishing their agenda for tort reform, while medical laboratories also have a special list. In 2001, in France, doctors refused to perform diagnosis of malfunctions in the unborn because they were sued for huge compensation by children born with malfunctions that had not been detected in the womb. Eventually, this case was settled by new legislation that put major restrictions on some claims.

One of the key advantages of worst case analyses is, precisely, the ability to study not only the likely magnitude of a catastrophe but also the advisable number and nature of legal restrictions in order to keep operational risk under control and the insurance industry on its feet.

13.3 Learning from the precedent of Y2K tort

This short section seeks to substantiate the thesis for tort reform advanced in section 13.2, through the example of year 2000 (Y2K) claims and potential claims that never fully materialized. Prior to reform in the US, concerning this specific Y2K problem, Andrew Grove, Intel's chairman, had predicted that:

■ America would be tied down in a sea of litigation, and
■ Year 2000 litigation would put the asbestos litigation in the shade.

An example of the fear inspired by the first of these points was the fact that in the United States some big system integrators kept away from projects for fear they would be held liable for unresolved problems, long after the projects were over, because of Y2K.

Added to that has been the fact that exposure to Year 2000 problems was a very opaque operational risk. Some companies attempted to factor it into their legal risk exposure, with varying degree of success. Both rating agencies and insurance firms worked along that line, but the results were not convincing. Insurers were worried that defendant industries might seek to force them to:

■ Cover their legal fees, and
■ Pay damages awarded by courts.

If the US tort legislation relating to Y2K had not changed in time, Y2K cost to the insurance industry could have been, indeed, catastrophic. The Independent Insurance Agents of America estimated that they could reach $65 billion.[2] Therefore, insurance companies moved quickly to prevent Y2K-related suits.

Some of the insurers I know revised their policies, to exclude Y2K claims on the ground that Y2K perils were not known to exist when the policies were written. As a result, insurers said, premiums had not been collected for such coverage. Shipowner's insurance went through the same procedure. An example is Clause 3–24a of Norwegian marine insurance, which governed the shipowner's insurance cover. This has been a safety regulation obliging the assured to guarantee that manufacturers of:

■ Computers
■ Electrical equipment, and
■ Electronic equipment

on board ships have given a written confirmation of Y2K compliance. Short of this, the shipowner should itself assure compliance because, otherwise, the insurer explicitly stated that it would decline to cover losses arising from non-compliance with clause 3–24a – on grounds that the insured's failure to take needed Y2K steps would amount to gross negligence.

At about the same time, the Association of British Insurers (ABI), which represents more than 95% of the UK's insurance industry, announced that insurers would exclude year 2000 problems from policies. The reason given was that insurance is designed to cover what is basically an unforeseeable event. By contrast,

■ The millennium problem was known and foreseeable
■ It was manageable, though many insured companies had chosen to ignore it.

I see these three examples, the American, Norwegian, and British, as good precedents for other tort problems. The sense derived from these and similar cases is that tort is manageable (see also section 13.7) provided that either the legislation does not allow excesses in compensation, or the proper measures are taken in time.

Proactive action requires insight and foresight. A methodology of successive steps in setting up and maintaining a tort control program is shown in Figure 13.1. Notice that both the Norwegian marine insurance and ABI acted proactively. They redefined insurance policies and events covered by insurance on the ground that the wide public attention drawn to Y2K meant that it was no longer unforeseeable – and therefore gross negligence was involved at the insured entity's side if it failed in compliance and in taking needed control action.

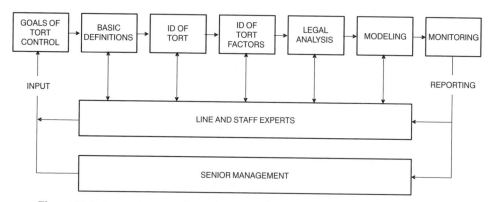

Figure 13.1 Successive steps in setting up and maintaining a tort control program

13.4   Compensation for claims: a case study with asbestos

Both mega-risks of the 9/11 variety and a concentration of claims amplified by class actions, which are followed by very liberal settlements, have turned the classical way of calculating insurance premiums on its head. In spite of all the talk about globalization, old formulas need to be rigorously revised. How deep this revision should be depends to a significant extent on the jurisdiction under which cases are tried if they come to court.

As I already mentioned in connection to legal risk, in England decisions on compensation for victims of asbestos are set by judges. Typically they run at the level of £50 000 to £60 000 ($75 000 to $90 000). In the US they are decided by juries, and can run at hundreds of millions of dollars. The most recent case on tobacco in the US was set at the unrealistic level of $28 billion – a high multiple of the capitalization of Philip Morris.

Even a third of the capitalization of a company paid for asbestos compensation is a scary statistic. On 29 November 2002, Sealed Air, a maker of bubble wrap, agreed to pay one-third of its then market value, some $730 million, in cash and shares to a trust fund being created to benefit asbestos victims, out of the bankruptcy of W.R. Grace, the chemicals company. The irony is that Sealed Air never produced, marketed, or sold asbestos.

The litigation against Sealed Air is a good example on tort spillover because it came by way of an acquisition structured to avoid this type of legal problem. In 1998 the firm paid $5 billion for a division of W.R. Grace that made plastic shrink-wrap for meat and fish in grocery stores – but never used asbestos. The gateway for asbestos defendants was that Sealed Air got from Grace an indemnity against any possible asbestos litigation, but that guarantee disappeared in April 2001, when Grace declared bankruptcy. A year later, lawyers for asbestos victims found the loophole and sued, arguing that:

- Sealed Air's acquisition had been fraudulent, and
- The firm had brought Grace's legal liabilities with its operations.

The cost of settlement for a crime it did not commit has been devastating to Sealed Air. Neither is this the only case of peripheral asbestos damage. Crown Cork & Seal, for example, was overwhelmed by suits tied to a firm it owned briefly in 1963, when asbestos was still the material of choice, and long before any health hazards were widely known.

There is another irony in this Sealed Air story. In July 2002, as asbestos litigation against the company built up steam, the market penalized its equity, which plunged from $40 to $14. After the settlement was announced, in spite of giving one-third of the equity away, its share price rose by 40%. That increased equivalently the value of the 9 million shares put in the trust for asbestos victims under the settlement.

With dilution of equity of the magnitude we have just seen, and the golden horde of settlements for asbestos victims and their lawyers, there is no surprise that asbestos has come to scare investors and shred share prices. In late July 2002, Saint-Gobain's shares fell 20% after the glass and building materials group announced a first semester of 2002 provision of €50 million to meet potential claims. Both the extraordinary reserves and the big drop in Saint-Gobain's equity price in the aftermath of the market news is a consequence of the fact the company cannot rely only on its insurance because of the emergence of a new class of bulk claims which has increased the level of claimants to 60 000. In fact, Saint-Gobain said that it was to set aside a further €50 million, while leaving open the possibility that claims could stretch into the future.

The problems faced by Asea Brown Boveri (ABB), the Swiss-Swedish engineering group, which has large-scale operations in Europe, the US, and Asia, have been amplified by mounting asbestos losses in the US. To these has been added the failure to get a suspension to additional compensation claims, for which ABB had appealed to the US Supreme Court.

ABB attempted to limit future asbestos liabilities by seeking bankruptcy protection for Combustion Engineering, its troubled US subsidiary which in the 1950s used to be an engineering powerhouse. US lawyers, including those behind the year 2002 appeal to the US Supreme Court, said flaws in the legal system meant some states would allow alleged victims to sue the parent company regardless of any bankruptcy by its local subsidiary.[3]

In connection to the operational risk that hit Combustion Engineering, a West Virginia court case has revealed how weak-willed companies can be when taking on litigants. ABB seized on the idea of isolating its US subsidiary, possibly via Chapter 11, as if bankruptcy were a magic solution. Because ABB faced its own severe financial problems, the move has not only shown how desperate the parent company was, but also the fact that it did not do its homework.

Since Combustion Engineering is virtually bankrupt and US juries tend to grant huge compensations, ABB would have had to throw more money into the bottomless pit to appease claimants. But there was not much money around, and the company's bondholders and shareholders felt the pinch.

- ABB's bonds were quoted below 50 cents to the dollar.
- This indicated ABB's equity was virtually worthless.

By the end of 2002, ABB had net debt at 1.5 billion, and another $3.7 billion of debt maturing in 2003. Therefore, unless Combustion Engineering could be fully isolated, the only hope of ABB, by putting it into Chapter 11, was to win a stay of execution. Asbestos was not the only cause of the company's downfall, but it made a bad case even worse.

For bondholders of ABB, the troubles had started well before the asbestos case hit. In the week of 25 March 2002, ABB had to negotiate new terms on $3 billion loans, including higher interest payments from Libor plus 60 basis points, with banks also receiving a 40 basis points arrangement fee. Citigroup and Crédit Suisse First Boston, which had underwritten the original loan, were the renegotiators of new terms. But the market was not convinced. Both Moody's, which rated ABB A3, and Standard & Poor's, which rated it A+, expressed concerns. Traders said:

- Credit derivatives for ABB were trading at a spread of 450–500 basis points over Libor,
- Analysis observed that such an important spread is more in line with a B rated credit, below junk status.

Not surprisingly, the equity markets took notice. ABB's capitalization collapsed from $39.8 billion in February 2000 to just $1 billion on 22 October 2002, when the company's stock reached a low point. This, in spite of the fact that its four main divisions – automation technology, utilities, power technology, and industries – constituted Europe's second biggest engineering group. There was also the inevitable warning on profits which contributed to cutting ABB's share price by nearly two-thirds (see also section 13.7 on ABB).

If an insurance company had underwritten the asbestos problems of ABB, its equity would have taken the same beating in the capital market as that received by the engineering group. In fact, insurance stocks were not at all immune to market blues (as we saw in Chapter 12), and asbestos hit them strongly (see section 13.5). Insurance stocks have been particularly weak because of fears that the almost relentless slide in equity markets will leave insurance companies:

- Highly exposed in capital terms, and
- This will trigger forced selling.

As Murphy's law suggests, "If something can go wrong, it will." Whether we talk of asbestos, tobacco or other claims that develop into mega-risks, it is important to do stress testing and run worst case scenarios,[4] in an effort to challenge the obvious and flush out ahead of time what can go wrong, where, when, and how. When it comes to premiums, insurance coverage, and capital adequacy, the time for half-measures and postponements has definitely passed. It is not the old risks which should frighten insurers. It is the new and unknown, and mega-compensations which are part of them.

13.5 Asbestos claims have been a nightmare to the insurance industry

A.M. Best has estimated that the insurance industry may ultimately face up to $121 billion in asbestos and environmental (A&E) losses, adding that commercial insurers, and to a lesser extent reinsurers, remain underfunded by approximately 50% with regard to reserves for ultimate, undiscounted A&E liabilities. Both the "A" and "E" type losses are heavy. Even if environmental payouts are declining, they still represent more than 50% of A&E settlements.

In the UK, confirmation of the rumoured £200 million ($310 million) rights issue from British Insurance reminded the market of the need for more fund-raising in the sector. In September 2002, Royal & Sun Alliance was expected to tap its shareholders for about £1 billion ($1.55 billion), but in October of that same year its equity lost nearly 8% in one day due to a persistent rumour that Royal & Sun was exposed to major asbestos claims.

Both the companies facing legal risk because of asbestos, tobacco, or other 'popular' reasons for litigation, and their insurers, are scared of human ingenuity in bringing to the public eye, for exploitation, operational risks not identified when a product or process was originally designed and implemented (see the case of Crown Court and Sealed Air in section 13.4).

Royal & Sun Alliance had also been sued by defunct engineering firm Turner & Newall on behalf of former T&N employees who were said to be covered by an employer's liability policy in effect from 1969 to the end of 1977. That news, together with reports that Swedish engineering groups Atlas Copco, Trellebord, and Sandvik had also been named in asbestos-related lawsuits, sent European share prices tumbling at the beginning of November 2002.

In the US, a study by A.M. Best notes that asbestos loss reserves jumped 24% in one year alone: 2001. Best attributes this significant rise in asbestos losses actions propelled by payments that increased 13%, or more than $200 million over that same year, by defendants and insurers. That trend is compounded by:

- Bankruptcy filings by major asbestos producers
- Proliferation of lawsuits filed on behalf of peripheral defendants
- Collapse of several settlements and payments schemes
- Packaging of numerous asymptotic plaintiffs with a handful of seriously ill plaintiffs, and
- Rise in number of asbestos practices among plaintiff attorneys.

Asbestos compensation has become a perpetual motion machine. With the increase in number of lawyers specializing in asbestos claims the aftermath of asbestos-related compensation turned to the worst in the fourth quarter of 2002. Insurers and industrial groups in the US and Europe found themselves obliged to add to reserves as they were getting deeper into litigation.

This new surge in potential asbestos losses was highlighted by the US insurer Chubb, which in late October 2002 announced that it had added $625 million in reserves for asbestos-related litigation. The move resulted in Chubb having a $242 million net loss for the third quarter of 2002. Interestingly, the insurer boosted its asbestos reserves after embarking on a study of reserve adequacy.

The Chubb study was announced weeks after St Paul Companies agreed to pay over $987 million to settle asbestos claims from policyholder MacArthur, a former distributor of asbestos products and third-party claimant. This settlement raised the possibility of a wider range of companies filing asbestos claims against carriers. In fact, MacArthur, and its Western MacArthur unit, filed a lawsuit against Hartford Accident & Indemnity for the period 1967–76. Hartford said that MacArthur's policy limits were exhausted in 1987.

Some insurers found it difficult to survive. New Jersey-based non-life group Highlands Insurance filed for Chapter 11 bankruptcy protection months after it adopted a plan to cease writing of new and renewal business, and run off its insurance operations. Highlands was spun-off by Halliburton, the oil-services firm, in 1996, and it has seen its financial condition deteriorate over the past several years.

Continued underwriting losses and additions to asbestos and environmental reserves gave Highland a net loss of $342 million in 2001, following a loss of over $106 million in 2000. In its filing, the company listed negative surplus of $180 million with assets of $1.64 billion and liabilities of $1.82 billion as of 30 June 2002.

In Germany, Allianz added $750 million to asbestos reserves of its US unit Fireman's Fund Insurance; Munich Re added $370 million in asbestos reserves for American Re-Insurance as part of a recent $2 billion capital infusion for its subsidiary. To survive, even rich companies like the German insurers and reinsurers will have to watch their assets, liabilities, and risks much more closely than they have done so far.

On 14 November 2002 Allianz also blamed huge losses on loans to South American and German companies for a record amount of red ink. The company said steep increases in provisions for asbestos and floor-related insurance claims, and continuing stock market volatility, were also major contributors to a 2002 third-quarter loss of €2.5 billion – which turned a €1.6 billion profit for the first half of 2002 into a €900 million torrent of red ink for the first nine months of the year.

In an attempt to improve its capital strength, Allianz has been considering plans to raise about €2 billion through two bond issues. Neither is asbestos the only bottomless hole. Banking, particularly the Dresdner Bank and its DRW subsidiary, contributed losses of €972 million (see Chapter 12). Companies which thought the go-go 1990s of easy money would never end are now deeply regretting their foray outside their core business.

To face the mounting financial and operational risk challenges, the German insurance industry is setting up an organization, known as Protector, to take over the obligations of life firms that get into trouble. Some experts think that 30% of insurance companies could disappear in the next 3–5 years, through mergers or by ceasing to write new business.[5] This projection reflects the fact that according to many analysts several German life insurance groups are sitting on hidden losses after tumbling stock markets wiped out their reserves. This has fuelled worries about their:

- Capital adequacy, and
- Financial health.

A sign of the insurance industry's woes came in mid-November 2002, as AMB Generali, Germany's third biggest insurer, warned it would miss its 2002 profit target after massive writedowns on equity investments forced it into the red in the third quarter of the year. For its part, Goldman Sachs warned that the life assurance industry faced a radical shake up, estimating that between 25 and 30 insurance groups could have difficulty meeting capital adequacy requirements.

Fitch Ratings has also highlighted the dramatic decline in the capital strength of life insurance companies. Indeed, growing fears of a possible insolvency in the insurance sector led Germany's financial regulator to put about 20 companies on a special watch list. Concern also prompted the big insurers to agree to back an industry pool that would bale out smaller rivals if they were unable to pay the 3.25% guaranteed rate of return to their policyholders.

13.6   Challenges facing major financial institutions and their daily business

Nobody today would really like to be in the shoes of Citigroup, the largest US financial company, with about $1 trillion in assets. As 2002 came to an end, Citigroup faced a potential triple risk: Big payouts over lawsuits, stiff fines imposed by regulators and legal authorities, and a regulatory crackdown, including tighter supervision, which the financial institution tried to avoid by dividing its Salomon Smith Barney subsidiary into a Salomon investment bank and Smith Barney broker – endowing the latter with an independent financial analysis unit.

'Regulators may feel that Citigroup has to slow down and apply better risk management, rather than continuing to build their empire,' said David Hendler, an analysts with Credit Sights.[6] Serious damage could come from Citigroup's links with Enron, including the special purpose vehicles (SPVs) deals, Citi's and J.P. Morgan Chase's offshore transactions intended to beautify the telecoms market appearance, and the *prepays* – the alchemy which turned Enron's debt into assets. Experts said that Citigroup's liability could hinge on whether it knew it was doing something wrong.

- Senate investigators alleged that $4.8 billion in Citi transactions with Enron were shams and that the bank knowingly assisted the energy company in deceiving investors and the public.
- Neither was Citigroup alone. J.P. Morgan Chase had another $3.7 billion out of a total of $8.5 billion in dubious deals with Enron.

Pension holders have been suing both Citi and J.P. Morgan Chase over these Enron deals. In parallel to this action, a major bondholders' suit alleged Citi and other banks did not show proper due diligence before selling them $11 billion worth of WorldCom bonds. These have been suits that fall in the junction between tort and breach of contract, containing elements of both as well as of operational risk.

At Wall Street, analysts said that it was not unreasonable for Citigroup to set aside $1.5 billion in the fourth quarter of 2002, to settle claims that it misled customers with biased stock research – an operational risk; and also, to cover different loans losses, which represent credit risk. Citigroup's provisions included a $400 million payment to settle regulatory probes into Wall Street's conflicts of interest in stock research and funds for related lawsuits.

Citi was the first of several banks taking action after a 20 December 2002 announcement of a $1.4 billion settlement over research conflicts between state and federal securities firms. Bank of America also announced setting aside $1.2 billion in reserves for the fourth quarter of 2002, but mainly for loans losses.

Bloomberg Professional suggested that Citigroup faced at least 62 lawsuits tied to its research practices, according to regulatory filings.[7] The charge which it took was expected to reduce its fourth quarter 2002 earnings by 29 cents a share. On the upside, it created a legal reserve which gave investors some confidence that the credit institution was taking care of its operational risks and other exposures.

Some analysts commented that all these extra reserves may not ultimately be enough to cover the entire cost of settling private litigation – which is part of the financial industry's operational risk. In the 1990s, for instance, Prudential Securities ended up paying 300% over its originally estimated liability to settle regulatory charges and investor lawsuits – to the tune of $8 billion.

Experts say that we will be hearing much more about court action involving due diligence in the years to come, because new financial instruments open a landscape where court cases involving tort relating to due diligence can prosper. The Internet at large, and more specifically electronic banking, provide examples of other operational risks which have developed during the past few years.

The Internet, and on-line banking generally, brought many challenges to financial institutions in connection to existing legal frameworks as well as regulatory rules originally designed to address issues affecting the physical world. Beyond this, not only all the consequences of new technology but also new laws and regulations have not been interpreted by the courts in a way to create crossborder jurisprudence. Here are some of the issues affecting the developing e-banking delivery channels:

- On-line offerings may be considered solicitations, which in some countries are not permitted by the law
- Relationships created with customers in different jurisdictions may become legally unstable, and
- Regulations applying to Internet banking are different than those addressing traditional delivery mechanisms, affecting products with multi-channel delivery.

Core to all these issues is the fact that on-line financial services exist in a global and, therefore, multijurisdictional world. Legal problems surfacing on the Internet do so not because there is no law, but because it is not clear about which country's laws apply in every specific case, as well as what should be done when there are legal contradictions from state to state.

Here are examples of British laws that are not valid in the countries of continental Europe: Bills of Exchange Act 1882, Copyright Act 1911, Companies Act 1985, Consumer Credit Act 1974, Patents Act 1977, Unfair Contract Terms Act 1977, Forgery and Counterfeiting Act 1981, Consumer Protection Act 1987, Control and Misleading Advertisements Regulation 1988, Copyright Designs and Patents Act 1988, Trade Marks Act 1994, Data Protection Act 1984 & 1998, Contracts Protection Act 1990, Electronic Communications Act 2000, Regulation of Investigatory Powers Act 2000, Unfair Terms in Consumer Contracts Regulations 2001.

Apart from legal incompatibilities from state to state, new laws and regulations are necessary to cover issues specific to on-line banking, as current regulations leave many loopholes. For instance, credit risk assumed by a bank, and the way it is managed, can be affected by Internet banking activities in different ways:

- Remote communication can make it much more difficult to assess creditworthiness of existing and potential customers
- The Internet can allow banks to expand very rapidly, leading to weakened internal control, and
- There is a tendency to pay higher rates on e-banking deposits squeezing profit margin, as well as grant sub-prime credits leading to heightened credit risk.

Legal and regulatory solutions to be provided at the junction of tort and breach of contract must take a system view. Otherwise they can be neither effective nor consistent. Figure 13.2 provides an answer to this challenge, starting with the product, proceeding to the processes of production and delivery (which may be on-line or brick and mortar), and following up with the three main components of the dual delivery channels: people, technology, and methodology.

Another example of a challenge, brought to the foreground by technology and globalization, which currently confronts financial institutions, is liquidity risk precipitated by adverse information about a bank. True or false, such information can be easily disseminated over the Internet through bulletin boards and news groups,

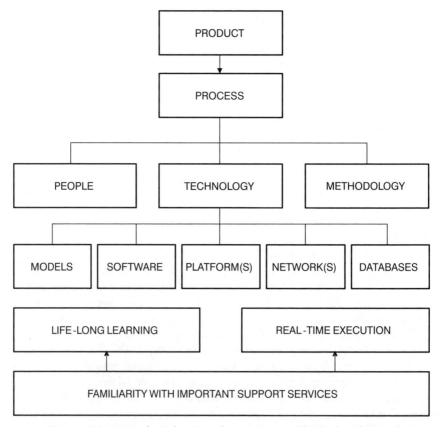

Figure 13.2 An analytical approach to operational risk identification

causing depositors to withdraw their funds in large number at any time of the day, thereby creating a tort with respect to the financial institution.

New technology and the rapid dissemination of information also tend to increase deposit volatility as customers get into the habit of maintaining accounts on the basis of interest rates and/or better contractual terms. Therefore, it is necessary to exercise a more accurate monitoring of liquidity than in the past. Changes in the composition of deposits and loans must now be managed dynamically, in real time. This is doable, but few banks have the technology and the skills to execute it in an able manner.

13.7   Tort exposure and management risk correlate

To a significant extent, tort is management risk and vice versa – management risk is at the origin of many cases of tort. Because of this, the two notions have a great deal in common, and the same is true of their effects. This can be shown through a couple of examples involving due diligence on management's behalf.

- The fall of Martin Ebner's hedge funds because of wrong betting, and
- The Swissair meltdown, in the aftermath of a long list of poor managerial decisions.

By practically every account, Martin Ebner, one of Switzerland's wealthiest investors, went through the 1990s at the helm of one of Europe's top hedge funds. But on 1 August 2002 he was forced to sell his four quoted investment funds and liquidate part of his sizeable stakes in several of Switzerland's best-known blue chip stocks.

- Ebner quit the hedge funds game after losing more than 5 billion Swiss francs (CHF) ($3.4 billion) from the collapse in equities on which he was betting, the foremost being Crédit Suisse and ABB.
- Sizeable stakes were part of Ebner's strategy. He had made his fortune by taking large stakes in a few big Swiss companies during the bull market, but the bears unravelled his investments edifice.

During his years of might, Ebner championed shareholder rights and scored victories connected to executive performance. A recent one has been the ousting of Percy Barnevik at Asea Brown Boveri. His influence however meant bigger shareholdings and board membership, and this ultimately compromised his ability to make a swift exit from his investments as arbitrageurs should do.

The cost of being deeply involved in management problems and internal musical chairs in companies in which his money was invested has been red ink. It amounted to estimated losses of around CHF 800 million in 2002 alone. At Crédit Suisse, where he supported Lukas Muhlemann, the former CEO, the loss on his investment stood at an estimated CHF 4 billion.

Ebner concentrated on agitating the Swiss business elite. The aftermath of this has been that his Swiss financials funds lost 53% of their value over one year (mid-2001 to mid-2002), which compares poorly with a sector loss of 37%. The irony here is that in the leveraged bond blood bath of 1994, when the Fed increased interest rates in six successive steps, Ebner prided himself on having lost much less than other hedge funds, as for instance Steinhart's.

None of Ebner's investors who lost a fortune have as yet gone to court for negligence, or for his mixing of investment and king-making. This would have amplified the financial woes, as his decision to sell control of his four quoted investment funds, known as the *Visions* – Pharma Vision, BK Vision, Stillhalter Vision, and Spezialitäten Vision – and substantially reduce his stake in Crédit Suisse (his biggest single investment) followed speculation that he was under financial pressure after sharp falls in equity markets.

From the start of 2002 to disinvestment, the market value of the four quoted investment vehicles of BZ Group, Ebner's private investment company, has fallen from CHF 3.6 billion to 3 billion. The market value of Crédit Suisse, in which Ebner had a nearly 10% stake until shortly before disinvestment, in July 2002, has fallen by CHF 54 billion since the end of 2000. ABB, in which Ebner retained a 9.7% stake, has seen its market value drop by CHF 40 billion over the same period.

The sale of the four companies to the Zurich Kantonalbank, for an undisclosed sum, had been prompted by BZ Group's unwillingness to continue supporting the share prices of Crédit Suisse and ABB.[8] There was also a cross-leverage. Swiss bankers said Credit Suisse, one of the country's two big banks, had increased its exposure to BZ Group by extending additional credit.

UBS, too, was involved in financing Martin Ebner, but it started to withdraw in 2001, and completed its exit earlier in 2002 – just in time. While the management of *Visions* failed to support the interests of its investors, UBS has been a better judge of risk and return. It pulled out of what was becoming a major exposure, and therefore it saved itself from navigating in a sea of red ink.

The operational risk connected to the Swissair meltdown was not too different in terms of lack of due diligence, as far as investors interests were concerned. Swissair used to be the flower of the air transport industry, but then its management made a series of blunders. When this happens stockholders pay the price, while the senior brass itself opens its golden parachute.

The blunders started with the failure of the contemplated merger between Swissair, KLM, SAS, and Austrian Airlines. This would have created a global aircarrier, with each of the first three entities taking a 30% equity in the new concern, and the balance going to Austrian Airlines. Egos rather than financial hurdles stood in the way, and the merger did not go through.

Subsequent to that, as if to demonstrate the cost of management risk, the Swissair directors and CEO miscalculated their options. Since getting money from the banks was no problem, they went on a shopping spree with deep pockets. The AOM, Air Liberté, and Sabena investments were the worst of a series of false steps that dragged down a once-proud airline. Until the late 1990s Swissair was one of the most admired carriers, famous for punctuality and superior in-flight service.

- It was financially stable, a microcosm of the country whose flag was displayed on its airliners' tails
- It was also operationally solid, reliable, orderly and successful – an emblem of dependability.

All that became a thing of the past. By mid-2001 Swissair was struggling to avoid going bust. In 2000 its losses were CHF 2.9 billion ($2.0 billion), and as the business forecast became bleaker, its debts of CHF 7.8 billion reached more than six times the value of its equity. A leverage of 600% is unheard off for a maturing industry like the airlines. Neither was the future looking much better.

Global alliances might have been an option, but they did not get off the ground. As we saw, the deals with SAS, KLM, and Australian Airlines fell through, Singapore Airlines deserted the Global Excellence alliance, and Delta Air Lines abandoned the Atlantic Excellence. Neither did Swissair's top management show an excellence of its own.

One of Swissair's major problems has been that it was based in a high-cost country and, because Switzerland was not a member of the European Union, its airline did not have the freedom to expand alone in Europe. This, plus mismanagement, led to the AOM, Air Liberté, and Sabena blunders under the banner of the Qualiflyer Group. Other small carriers with which Swissair sought links were LOT Polish Airlines, LTU in Germany, and TAP, Portugal's flag carrier. It also hooked up with South African Airways.

Money turned to dust in those airlines in which Swissair acquired equity, while its management was left with the hope that the other partners would probably become customers for Swissair's catering and other aviation-service subsidiaries, which was non-core business and small fry. Altogether Swissair spent more than $1 billion on different stakes, on top of a similar amount building up its catering operation to make it appealing to its partners. In effect, Swissair was buying customers for the aviation-service businesses it also had to acquire.

All this flawed strategy was chosen without due regard for the fact that nearly all the airlines Swissair was buying into were in deep difficulties. They had hopelessly big losses and little freedom to cut costs, because continental European labor laws do not allow hire and fire. Management incompetence saw to it that the commitments were made without an exit strategy. Then the flag carrier went bust, leaving its stakeholders high and dry in a deal that involved management risk and tort.

Notes

1 P.H. Winfield, *A Textbook of the Law of Tort*, Sweet & Maxwell, London, 1943.
2 *Herald Tribune*, 4 May 1998.
3 *Financial Times*, 23 October 2002.
4 D.N. Chorafas, *Stress Testing. Risk Management Strategies for Extreme Events*, Euromoney, London, 2003.
5 *The Economist*, 16 November 2002.
6 *BusinessWeek*, 5–12 August 2002.
7 *Bloomberg Professional*, 23 December 2002.
8 *Financial Times*, 1 August 2002.

14 The challenge of terrorism and insurer of last resort

14.1 Introduction

According to A.M. Best, insurance contracts related to terrorist acts, in the way they are underwritten today, did not exist before 11 September 2001. Acts of terrorism were covered under standard property/casualty policies, but the clauses of these policies did not specifically exclude losses resulting from terrorism as contrasted to acts of war.[1]

'Whether or not terrorism is an insurable risk is debatable,' says A.M. Best, from a credit rating agency's viewpoint. Some insurers, however, have shown appetite for terrorism exposure. American International Group (AIG) is the leader in a co-insurance program for aviation war risk and hijacking liability. Among other participants in this type of exposure are ACE, AXA, Chubb, and GE Frankona.

Also, five big European insurers and reinsurers – Allianz, Hannover Re, Scor, Swiss Re and Zurich Financial – collaborate in funding a new entity known as Risk Insurance and Reinsurance Luxembourg. The capital of this new company is €500 million, and the goal is to provide property coverage against terrorist acts – which is a policy of high exposure.

Because of *business disruption*, perils to human life, and likely huge physical damages, terrorist acts have changed the insurance landscape. They call for rethinking conditions and clauses of insurability; updating the definition of technical and operational risk; identifying hidden exposures; pricing these policies; and focusing on perils that should be excluded. Risks associated to terrorist acts make it necessary to develop refined pricing methods by:

- Operational risk type
- Extreme event
- Risk expectancy
- Risk impact
- Country, city, neighbourhood
- Loss experience.

Terrorist acts magnify the sense of business interruption as a major operational risk for all companies. Loss of life and loss of property aside, terrorist acts are underlining the aftermath of business disruption on the economy as a whole, and most particularly on insurers and reinsurers. For the latter, business interruption has a double impact.

- It is a technical risk because they insure their clients against the perils of business interruption (see section 14.2), and
- It is an operational risk, because insurers and reinsurers themselves are subject to business interruption.

The risk of business disruption should be examined in its broader concept. A seminar on 5 December 2002 at MIT on supply chain response to terrorism emphasized the need to plan for the *unexpected*. The likelihood of large-scale terrorist acts, MIT says, should lead supply chain managers to adjust relations with their business partners, contend with transportation difficulties, and amend inventory management strategies. In doing so, they must provide valid answers to three key challenges:

- Defining the possible collaborative avenues between the public and private sector
- Managing supply chains under increased uncertainty due to business disruption
- Preparing for another attack, ensuring that supply lines are maintained while controlling inventory costs.

As a result of the events of 11 September 2001, threat scenarios currently being made by insurers differ substantially from those of the past, when terrorism was usually part of the standard fire and business interruption policy. Rarely if ever an additional premium was calculated for terrorist acts. This lack of special attention to extreme events associated to terrorism reflected a risk management assessment that this type of loss was only of really minor importance as far as frequency and severity were concerned. However, after 9/11 such estimates have been fundamentally revised with classical measures of loss severity like:

- Probable Maximum Loss (PML), and
- Estimated Maximum Loss (EML)

being brought to the drafting board for revision. PML and EML quantify maximum loss under normal conditions, assuming not total loss of a building or plant but a partial one, often offset to some extent by preventive measures. This has become inadequate, and with it the notion that acts of terrorism are definitely insurable.

The huge amount of losses that may be associated to terrorist acts themselves, and to business disruption resulting from them, challenges this concept of insurability. It brings into the picture the need for an *insurer of last resort* (see section 14.6) – similar to the one already existing as lender of last resort, which dates back to the late eighteenth century. Historical evidence indicates the concept of lender of last resort dates back to 1797, when Francis Baring described in these terms the Bank of England. A century later, the Bank of England obliged, saving his institution from bankruptcy – but it did not repeat the gesture in 1995, and Barings failed.

14.2   Business disruption resulting from 9/11

The concept of business disruption and the risks it represents were introduced in Chapter 5 in connection to technology. During the events of 9/11 at the World Trade Center, the worst losses were suffered by financial services companies like Cantor Fitzgerald, which lost 700 of its people. Morgan Stanley had more than 3000 staff at work in the south tower, but was able to evacuate all but just under 40 before the tower collapsed.

Communications companies, too, lost staff. In spite of that, they struggled with the feat of keeping their networks running, while coping with destroyed facilities and record call volumes. According to some accounts, in the aftermath of 9/11 as many as 25 000 technology and communications workers world-wide have been contracted by companies working to repair or restore their telecommunications facilities. There have also been reports of some companies putting personal computers in apartments in New Jersey, trying to remain operational through temporary solutions.

Some companies headquartered in adjoining buildings to the Twin Towers said their operations have not been affected, even though they could not access their offices. An example is American Express whose global headquarters were in the World Financial Center, too close to the World Trade Center and therefore inaccessible for security reasons. To avoid business disruption, American Express capitalized on its operations located world-wide, shifting resources to assure that services could run uninterrupted.

From Cantor Fitzgerald to American Express, there is a sea of difference in terms of business interruption due to the same terrorist act. Therefore, to develop new risk management concepts to cover the threat of terrorism we must ascertain which high impact terrorism risks are insurable at all. In the general case a likely answer is Yes in the case of American Express, but the answer may be No in the case of Cantor Fitzgerald. Also, No in concentration of risk – like insuring many tenants in a skyscraper. As is the practice in the insurance industry, the insurability of risks must be assessed according to their:

■ Ease of quantification and qualification
■ Lack of correlation with other risks and among themselves
■ Mutually shared interest of insured entities in the risks being insured, and
■ Economic feasibility of placing them under guarantee.

As 9/11 shows, the risk of terrorism does not conform with these criteria taken in unison. Equally important is the fact that, as opposed to natural catastrophes (see section 14.3), historical data and statistics give little or no indication of the frequency and severity of future losses from terrorism. What we all seem to know so far is that terrorism is uncorrelated with other risks, and some experts say that even of this we cannot be 100% sure.

Since it is difficult to balance the risk due to the severity of loss resulting from terrorism, and the coordinated attack at several locations, the economic viability of insurance is questionable. To learn more about risk and return, the insurance industry must develop models able to estimate the severity of loss resulting from the new perspective of terrorism risks at large, and of business disruption in particular. This requires a new perspective of quantifying the risks and the crucial conditions for making terrorism risks insurable. It also calls for testing innovative solutions such as:

- Forms of insurance like finite risk
- Pools of insurers working in a way similar to syndicated loans, and
- The use of capital markets to achieve a broad risk spread.

As we will see in section 14.6, in all likelihood, the government will also be called upon to act as reinsurer of last resort, particularly so if insurers and reinsurers were required to provide terrorism cover at a regulated price. The issue of a *regulated price* is controversial because it means free markets do not work any more. In this case, short of government support, terrorism would trigger a wave of bankruptcies in the insurance industry.

All this is written in the understanding that claims for contingent business interruption from 9/11 have raised very complex coverage issues. Some claims were being filed by companies hundreds and thousands of miles from New York City. These and other events bring forward questions about the conflict between:

- The underwriters' intent, including premium charged, and
- The customer's alleged understanding of the policy's coverage.

Because of the complexity of some of the issues, and the billions of dollars at stake, the way to bet is that some of these claims will be decided in the courts. They will also raise soul-searching questions in insurers' boardrooms, as directors and CEOs have to ask themselves if their company can afford to write any form of terrorism coverage given the uncertainties and unpredictability of what location, form, magnitude, and intensity future terrorist acts will have. Classical principles in the insurance industry have been:

- *If* a risk cannot be assessed, *then* it is uninsurable, and
- *If* limits of insurability have been reached for a single event, *then* they will be most probably exceeded in case of major catastrophes.

Insurers and reinsurers cannot afford to discount estimates that business interruption losses following 9/11 could reach 25% of all insured losses, while other projections suggest that exposure to that risk remains largely unknown. Some experts say that it might be worse than this 25% guestimate, because many losses relating to 9/11 cannot be properly assessed and court action will be largely based on other party's guestimates.

As one of the research meetings pointed out, after 9/11 insurers and reinsurers have concluded that when it comes to terrorism, the existing alternative risk-spreading mechanisms must respect several principles, some of which are contradictory; for instance, assuring a consumer access to terrorism insurance at affordable cost *and* protecting the survivability of insurance companies. A corollary to this is that policymakers have to decide:

- How to spread losses across the insurance industry, and
- Whether to spread them across an even wider base, including governments.

Those who look favourably at the message conveyed by the second point here, say that the primary driving force behind the government's decision to enter into terrorism reinsurance should be to safeguard the economy's access to needed insurance protection. At the same time, measures must be taken to avoid bureaucracy and therefore protect the taxpayers from inefficiency and excessive costs.

Experts opposed to government intervention as reinsurer of last resort point out that alternative risk transfer (ART) instruments could do the risk spreading job. This may be true up to a point, but it is unwise to disregard credit risk associated to ART-type solutions (see Chapter 11).

Indeed, an area raising concern when it comes to mega-risks is that risk transfer instruments may handle the insurer's technical risk at the cost of growing credit risk. *If* alternative risk transfer instruments are extended to include terrorism-linked insurance risks, *then* they will become the alter-ego of default swaps and collateralized debt obligations that enable banks to transfer credit risks to other entities, including insurance companies, as buyers of these derivatives instruments.

The statement made in the preceding paragraph points to an inherent contradiction in ART-type solutions. It is also wise to account for the fact that this market would eventually taper off. According to the IMF, between 1997 and 2001, the amount of outstanding obligations of these instruments increased by about nine-fold to an estimated US$ 1.6 trillion.

- *If* the bigger risk of terrorist acts and business disruption is added to this securitized market,
- *Then* we might see extreme events in credit risk, at a time when altogether credit risk is deteriorating.

It should escape nobody's attention that some man-made catastrophes can easily become far more expensive than natural catastrophes. Because much less risk diversification across lines is possible with terrorist acts, single events can greatly affect many lines of business leading, at the same time, to dramatic results on the insurance industry's balance sheet.

14.3   Learning from technical limits with insurance of natural catastrophes

The hardest hit insurers and reinsurers because of 9/11 were Lloyd's, Berkshire, Swiss Re and Munich Re, beyond $2 billion each; Allianz, with about $1.3 billion; St Paul, Nissan, AIG, Zurich, XLCapital, Ace, Chubb, Taisei, GE Reinsurance, AXA, and Citigroup, each from $500 million to nearly $1 billion. With the next events the names may change, but the underlying issue does not:

- Man-made catastrophes now compete with natural catastrophes on which is more expensive.

To better appreciate the extent and impact of man-made catastrophes at large, and specifically of terrorism, it is wise to compare them to the impact of natural catastrophes. Prior to 9/11 only one event, Hurricane Andrew in 1992, tested the functionality and survivability of the insurance system to a very high impact. Hurricanes are a known risk. By contrast, the 9/11 case involved not only an unprecedented sum that insurers had to pay out, it was also a new kind of risk that highlighted some of the vulnerabilities and limitations of insurance systems. In so doing:

- It raised general questions about the limits of insurability, and
- Led to a debate on the role and responsibilities of the insurance sector in a service economy.

Beyond considerations of general suffering, and the loss of thousands of lives, as we saw in section 14.2 the insurance and reinsurance industries had to rethink the severity of future technical risks and operational risks as well. As we have seen, experts suggest that the costs for insurers world-wide from 9/11 could amount to approximately $40–50 billion. As a comparison, Hurricane Andrew caused losses of $19.6 billion.

Which other events of the past decade or so belong to the huge impact class, beyond the level of $4 billion? After Andrew, in line of importance these events are: the Northridge earthquake at $16.3 billion; Typoon Mireille, $7.1 billion; Windstorm Daria, $6.1 billion; Windstorm Lothar, $6.0 billion; Hurricane Hugo, $5.8 billion; Windstorm Vivian, $4.2 billion; Typhoon Bart, also $4.2 billion. Including Andrew, their total cost is $69.3 billion – but it has been spread over a decade.

Natural catastrophes, as these instances document, would not be eclipsed from the risk and return screen because of 9/11. Not only are they here to stay, but also climate change is translated into an increase in the number of natural catastrophes, including tropical and extratropical storms, landslides, temporary flooding of coastal regions, a growing frequency and intensity of river floods, tidal waves, heatwaves, droughts, and increasing spread of tropical infectious diseases.

Just as an example along this frame of reference, a simulation done in late 2002 in Hamburg on a supercomputer suggests that the 2002 floods in the Dresden area may not be an exceptional event but a precursor of annual catastrophes as the Elbe recovers its former bed. A similar study in France raised the likelihood that 3.5 million people may have to leave their homes, or accept that they are flooded two or three times per year. Both these projections are based on climate change.

Such events evidently lead to a rise in potential claims. Some European insurance companies predict that the current expected losses per year will quite likely double as a result of European winter storms. Many statements made after research into the consequences of climate change refer to greenhouse effect and project a high impact period which is expected to occur in the next 50–100 years.

- This longer timeframe goes against most insurers culture.
- Even with life and health insurance the planning horizons usually are 5, 10 or 20 years, with 30 years an outlier.

In my judgment, to a considerable extent this perceived discrepancy between 'the insurers' culture' and 'real life' is a misconception. Contrary to terrorist acts, effects of climatic changes will not suddenly take place but will increase gradually over the next years and decades, albeit with some spikes. Therefore, there is plenty of reason to study measures focusing on:

- Customers
- Products
- Contracts, and
- Premiums.

One of the important but not appreciated technical and operational risks in insurance is that clauses of premiums and contracts show a long time-lag between the day they are drawn up and the effect of actions taken to take hold of environmental and other risks or suffer the consequences. Hence the need to simulate different thresholds, starting with the nature, degree, and likelihood of climate change, and concluding with net insured loss. This requires a systems approach (see Chapter 5).

Figure 14.1 is a modified diagram of a solution advanced by German insurers. The eight building blocks in this figure are largely self-explanatory. A projection of climatic change and its aftermath is the starting point, followed by the rethinking of existing contractual clauses with the aim to reduce insured losses: for instance, through the introduction, or increase, of deductibles in a way to downsize loss potential.

- Deductibles can be effective in the event of an increasing frequency of catastrophic events and/or their intensity.
- But in the longer term, a sophisticated premium policy is necessary, and this requires thorough experimentation.

In connection to natural catastrophes, for instance, the simulator must take building type and locality into account for homeowner's insurance. The result will be a personalized insurance policy client-by-client, rather than indiscriminately increasing premiums at national level. Flat premium increases are essentially subsidising those who face extreme risks by taxing those who don't.

A similar statement is valid in connection to the risk of terrorism. The methodology in Figure 14.1 can be applied to advantage, because it identifies the crucial issues affecting insurers and reinsurers. What I would advise in this case is an extension of this methodology to cover credit risk and market risk associated to derivatives products addressing extreme events caused by terrorism. The fact that counterparties may suffer a double blow because of deteriorating financial markets should be included in the simulator.

It is also most advisable to add some incentives to the insurance policies. A merit pricing system might for instance follow the one used in motor insurance. Unknown risk factors such as local conditions, the state of a building, and superstructures can be included in the premium, while the merits clauses encourage the policyholder to take all necessary precautions in a similar way to Y2K insurance (see Chapter 13).

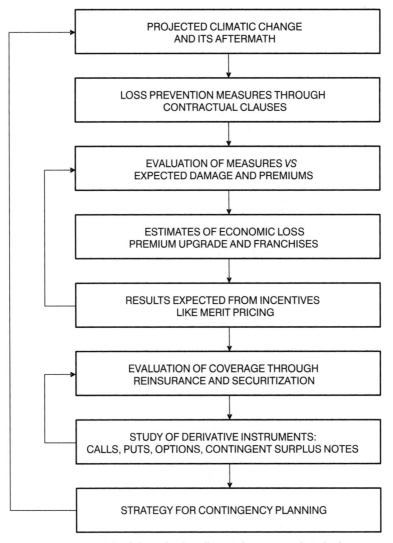

Figure 14.1 A methodology for handling risk associated with climatic change

Another lesson that can be learned from insurance associated to climatic change is the increasing importance of contingency reserves. Part of such reserves should exist in the insurance company, while it should be possible to mobilize the other part without delay. An example is equity put options, contingent surplus notes, and securitization. Many factors need to be analysed and the best ones selected in the context of:

■ Strategic alignment
■ Type of insured events

- Clauses in policies, and
- Dynamic premiums.

Weather derivatives constitute a precedent.[2] They also attest that financial instruments are in full evolution. The hypothesis made in the mid-1990s that if an investor can buy a derivatives contract based on an index, then why not do so with the underlying probability of an earthquake or hurricane, proved right. Since 1997 investors have been able to buy or sell a contract whose value depended entirely on:

- Fluctuations in temperature, or
- Accumulations of rain or snow.

Some weather derivatives pay out if the amount of rainfall at a specified location ranged between 30 and 50 centimetres from 1 November through 31 March. By writing such contracts insurers have helped themselves by providing for future claims by policyholders. The uncertainty of terrorist acts makes simulation a more complex exercise, but it is doable.

The careful reader will note that, whichever the purpose, insurance contracts have to be based on rigorous analytics and mathematical modeling. If they are not resting on analysis, they will not attract institutional investors. Mortgage-backed financing (MBF) provides an example. Without option adjusted spread, MBF would not have become part of the business of custom-packaging securities sold to institutional investors.

A similar statement is valid about CAT securitization. Regulators have kept an open mind about catastrophe derivatives. In research I did in the late 1990s, an executive of the German Federal Banking Supervisory Board was to suggest: 'It is a good idea to introduce catastrophe derivatives, to spread insurance risk to the investor. But it is very important to study the risks involved, and this needs long time series.' This is precisely the issue the securitization of insurance addressing terrorist acts cannot yet handle.

14.4   Policies for rethinking insurability of operational risks

In a nutshell, the message the previous section brought to the reader's attention is that risk analysis and premium calculation can no more be based on a lower loss severity and national level tariffs that assume an average threshold for everybody. They have to account for loss distribution and they must be personalized to allow insurers and reinsurers to estimate their maximum exposure by major counterparty or group of counterparties. Scenario analysis can assist the methodology of risk pricing in providing links between:

- Underwriting
- Investment risk
- Terrorist risk, and
- Other operational risks.

The pricing methodology should consider: higher and lower population densities; concentrations of exposed insured assets; growth of insured values locally, nationally, and world-wide; novel forms of risks being assumed; and the morphing of old risks. It should also include and identify preventive measures, risk control incentives, and the rethinking of deductibles.

The type of study we have seen in Chapter 13 in connection to hull insurance is a model for the pricing methodology, including both the work done by Peter Chrismas and the value added reference to reliability. Another value differentiation is a risk analysis process to determine required capital, like the one followed today by independent rating agencies. An example based on A.M. Best references is given in Figure 14.2.

An integral credit rating process, and its required capital perspective, can help senior management's hand in deciding which technical risk and operational risk exposure to assume, and which to leave to competitors. Behind this statement is the understanding that, together with the airline industry, the insurance industry has arguably been the one most significantly affected by the terrorist acts of 11 September 2001.

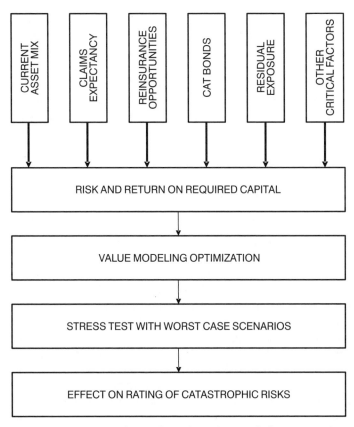

Figure 14.2 A simulation for risk analysis including required capital is the key to credit rating

Not only the impact of catastrophic events has dire financial consequences for individual affected insurance companies, but also, as we have seen in section 14.2, the industry as a whole felt the aftermath and it had to rethink its pricing mechanisms in a fundamental way. This is precisely what is targeted by the simulation suggested in Figure 14.2:

■ Immediately adapting insurance activities in the aftermath of every catastrophic event, and
■ Reallocating resources to limit (or expand) insurance coverage as experience with such events accumulates.

Research, analysis, and simulation are a good paradigm for what needs to be done to successfully attack technical and operational risks affecting every insurer. Catastrophic events are so much more serious when response to op risk challenges is too static, or too lifeless, to reflect what happens. The best solution is that of an adaptive system able to self-organize in response to interactions among economic agents to which it addresses itself.

Terrorism the way it manifested itself on 9/11 is not the only form of what to expect in the future. Examples of other forms of terrorist activity seen in recent years include hijacking and dynamiting of airplanes, PanAm type in-flight risks, bombs in the underground in France, suicide bombers in Israel, car bombs in Spain, the Oklahoma City bomb attack, chemical attacks in Japan, and many other ways in which terrorism is morphing.

Because people are ingenious and new forms of terrorism are unpredictable, insurers have to be flexible in their studies. This has happened in the past. Originally, fire insurance covered fire and explosion damage regardless of its cause. Exceptions were civil war, civil commotion, and war between states. As already mentioned,

■ Because terrorism was not mentioned in war exclusion clauses, in most jurisdictions it was covered.
■ However, Israel, South Africa, Spain, and the UK have had special regulations and pool solutions, some with government support.

The rethinking of insurability has to be both wide and deep. Risk coverage is usually sold under specified circumstances for suffered losses due to *ex ante* defined events. However, the preceding paragraphs have underlined that understanding the frequency and severity of potential claims, and when and how the losses that arise from an insured event are to be compensated, is a necessary precondition for sound insurance contracts. To do so, insurance companies must work diligently.

Scoreboard solutions can help, most particularly the high frequency/low impact and low frequency/high impact approach outlined in Chapter 8. Experimentation and system design for operational risk control as outlined in that same chapter (section 8.4) is fully applicable to the methodology I am suggesting here. The same is true of practical applications of Six Sigma to assure the board and CEO are truly in charge of underwriting.

Management of both insurance companies and of entities seeking insurance should appreciate that the knowledge base supporting the world of risk analysis and risk control keeps expanding rapidly. Advances in mathematical tools have made it possible to construct models that are significantly more sophisticated than what was available just a few years ago. We now have the technology to deal with instruments that are subject to:

- Time varying volatility
- Poisson distribution jumps
- Time and state dependent correlations, and more.

The use of increasingly more powerful tools is necessary because innovation in the real world is proceeding at a remarkable pace. New classes of securities are transforming the derivatives landscape – the securitization of complex and risky insurance coverage being one of them.

In conclusion, it helps not at all just to admit terrorism is a huge technical risk for insurers, and operational risk for everybody, if we do not restructure our methods and renew our tools to be able to deal with the challenge. To do so, insurance companies must change their culture. They should also work diligently to obtain:

- Timely and accurate information
- Efficient methods for computation, experimentation and projection, and
- Improved understanding of why, when, where, and how certain events happen.

These are basic prerequisites. Short of them it will be impossible to establish sound insurance contracts for mega-risks, let alone to manage them. The methodology which I am suggesting is valid not only for acts of terrorism which has been the focal point of this chapter, but also for all types of *operational risks* insurers currently underwrite, or plan to underwrite – rogue traders and CEO malfeasance being examples.

14.5   Benefits catastrophe bonds might provide

The type of system-analytical approach I am suggesting is made even more urgent by the fact that, eventually, insurance contracts for technical and operational risks at large may be securitized along the model of catastrophe bond (CAT bond) transactions.[3] These were first introduced in 1997, by a special purpose vehicle (SPV) owned and established by the United Services Automobile Association (USAA) which floated a $477 million bond with an exposure period of one year.

Securitization, however, does not solve every problem and growing risks have seen to it that during the past few years some insurers have exited the market. Examples are CNA from international reinsurance; Hartford, also from international reinsurance; XL Capital/NAC Re, from pooled aviation (Bermuda) and medical stop-loss reinsurance; St Paul from medical malpractice and several reinsurance lines; Zurich Financial spun off its reinsurance, renamed Converium; while Copenhagen Re, Overseas Partners, and Scandinavian Re also had second thoughts.

- As a number of players exited insurance and reinsurance, there has been a shrinkage of capacity.
- This has been counterbalanced by CAT bonds which entered the capital markets' main stream in six short years.

By means of catastrophe-linked bonds, capital market investors are now providing the insurance and reinsurance industries with an additional $1 billion of capacity per year. Insurers worked hard to see that happen. As an example, the majority of CAT bond transactions have been rated (see Chapter 13), which added to the investors' comfort with insurance-linked securities.

One of the issues worth keeping in mind is that in a precedent, which can be helpful with operational risks bonds, the rating of CAT bonds by independent rating agencies is not linked to credit risk, but to the underlying *insurance risk*. It is likely that the securitization of terrorist risk coverage, if and when it happens, will follow a similar path.

- Classical credit rating gives an indication of the likelihood of a default triggered, for instance, by the lack of financial staying power.
- The risk related to a CAT bond is narrowly defined as that of an insured catastrophe loss of a given size occurring, or not incurring.

A point of interest to the eventual offering of operational risk bonds, is that CAT bonds involve a considerable amount of risk transfer. Therefore, most have below-investment-grade ratings. The exception is that early issues, mainly in the period prior to March 1998, were rated investment-grade mainly because they offered some or full protection of principal.

- Prior to March 1998, 26% of CAT bonds were AAA, 9% BBB, 58% BB (junk bonds), and 7% were not rated.
- A year later (prior to March 1999) only 6% were AAA or AA, 21% A, 64% BB, 2% B, and 8% non-rated.
- By 2001, there have been no AAA, AA or A CAT bonds, 4% were BBB, 94% BB, and 2% non-rated.

Clearly there has been a rapid trend toward greater risk transfer, resulting in lower-rated bonds. Maturities also changed. Prior to March 1998, most of the CAT bonds had short maturities (no longer than 12 months), reflecting the fact that conventional reinsurance rates are usually fixed for one year. But since then CAT bonds have been issued with longer-term maturities. By January 2002:

- 38% were short term
- 9% between 1 and 2 years
- 31% between 2 and 3 years
- 11% between 3 and 4 years, and
- 11% over 4 years.

Another interesting statistic is that over 85% of these securities are sold in the US capital market, and this for several reasons. The American capital market is the largest in the world; the US financial landscape is also the largest in terms of both insurance and reinsurance premiums; the market for insurance-linked risk effectively originated with the catastrophe-linked options and futures introduced by the Chicago Board of Trade (CBOT) in 1992; and there has been openness to financial innovations in the US capital market.

Globalization, however, alters this frame of reference and it also poses some interesting questions in terms of capital market response in the different G-10 countries. Another intriguing query is what sort of information will be necessary for an effective securitization of operational risk at large, and of terrorism risk in particular. The answer is polyvalent and it includes:

- Op risk identification
- Impact of each op risk type
- Frequency of each op risk type
- Evidence on op risk management capability, and
- Documentation on precedence.

Transparency is critical. Statistics must come in a factual and documented manner from company reports, certified financial accounts, operational accounts, statutory reporting, security rating agencies, and other market players providing reliable information. Unavoidably gossip, too, will be part of the picture.

Lack of transparency as well as obsolescence and/or unreliability of information would severely damage the securitization of operational risk. The management of op risk databases will pose major challenges as the volume of operational risk information continues to grow – while the data itself is confusing, mostly out of date, and there are no easy ways of establishing what is true and what is false.

The role of insurers and reinsurers and their capital adequacy needs rethinking, because many of them will act as interfaces between operational risk securitization and its appeal to the capital market, in a way similar to what they now do with CAT. There will, also, be sidelines. For instance, Swiss Re and the American International Group (AIG) are in the business of providing their corporate clients with *contingent capital* – such as sub debt and equity lines of credit – while the capital market is attracted by more classical forms of catastrophe-linked bonds.

14.6   Lloyd's record losses with 9/11: a prognosticator of future red ink?

On 10 April 2002, Lloyd's broke with 300 years of tradition by announcing a move to annual reporting. It also revealed record £3.11 billion ($4.81 billion) losses following the 11 September 2001 terrorist attacks in the United States. Lloyd's reforms included another novelty, by proposing to scrap the existing system of 'names' (that is, investors who underwrite risk on an unlimited liability basis, see Chapter 12).

At Lloyd's terrorist events had a major financial impact as, after 11 September 2001, the insurer made cash calls on its members, totalling £1.34 billion ($1.88 billion). The news also painted a gloomy retroactive picture for 2000 and 2001 by making reference to a torrent of red ink. Christopher Stockwell, of the Lloyd's Names Association, called the results 'appalling'.[4]

Aside from the huge liability for 9/11, Lloyd's faced other losses totalling £371 million ($519.5 million) stemming from exceptional catastrophes in 2001, including the Petrobras oil rig disaster off the Brazilian coast, the attack on Air Lanka airplanes in Sri Lanka, Tropical Storm Alison in the US, and the Toulouse factory explosion in France. Lloyd's chief executive Nick Prettejohn said: 'We have paid a heavy penalty for the poor businesses in the market. Our bottom quartile of syndicates was responsible for two-thirds of our losses from 1999 to 2001.'[5]

There have also been a couple of other significant events in Lloyd's long history. In terms of financial reporting Lloyd's usually publishes accounts three years in arrears. However, in early April 2002 it announced 2001 figures, saying the decision to report on an annual basis was in line with proposed reforms to modernize the global insurance market. The careful reader should notice, however, that this global insurance market last made a profit in 1996.

Lloyd's market needed to reform if it was to retain its position as a global insurance center. As for the 9/11 losses, insurance experts said they are staggering, but they are only part of other losses adding up to much higher figures. Also announced in April 2002, Lloyd's 85 syndicates posted losses of up to £1.9 billion ($2.66 billion) for 1999, compared with Lloyd's £1.67 billion ($2.4 billion) loss forecast a few months earlier, in November 2001.

At Lloyd's, as elsewhere, the terrorist attacks have led to a shift in conception of the risks modern societies face as well as of the sheer magnitude of a potential insured loss. The aftermath has been rising prices of catastrophe covers, as shown in Figure 14.3 reflecting the fact that the newly shaped landscape involved extraordinary cumulative consequences.

The silver lining has been a more general level of understanding about insurance and the complexity of managing and transferring risks. Insurers and reinsurers came to appreciate this process is not always as well developed as it should be. Therefore, they started to realize the importance of:

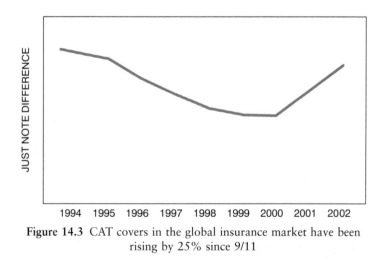

Figure 14.3 CAT covers in the global insurance market have been rising by 25% since 9/11

- Creating new knowledge, and
- Further the understanding of extreme events.

Both are instrumental to the comprehension of risk management. As cannot be repeated too often, experimentation is not just the better approach, it is the only approach possible when faced with new risks as well as old ones which change their pattern.

Lloyd's huge losses brought to the reader's attention in the opening paragraphs of this section were not just one entity's misfortunes, as it might appear to be at first glance. The reason why they have been included in this text is that they mirror what has happened in the insurance industry at large. The crucial question then becomes: Can the events we have just reviewed be a prognostication of future red ink? And *if* this happens:

- Will the insurance industry be able to fulfill its conceptual obligations regarding mega-risk losses?
- Is global insurance diversification work, with loss spread widely between insurers and reinsurers, the answer?
- Or will the revealed weaknesses in the insurance industry regarding extreme events cover lead to deeper structural change than presently thought?

One of the worries expressed by insurers in regard to the last query lies in the fact of capital depletion (among insurers and reinsurers) because of the dual impact of

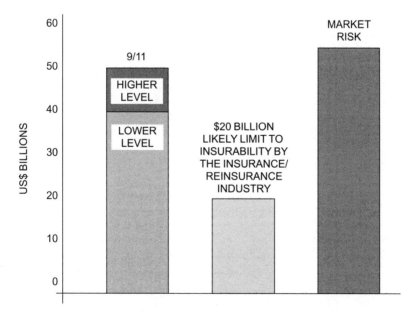

Figure 14.4 Capital depletion among insurers has been greater on the market risk side, compared to 9/11. (Statistics from the Geneva Association, General Information No. 173, October 2002)

huge losses due to technical risk and of even larger losses due to market risk hitting the insurers portfolio, and therefore their assets. As Figure 14.4 shows,

■ During the 2001–2002 timeframe the market risk at $53 billion to $55 billion has been higher than the presently conceived cost of technical risk relating to 9/11.
■ Against this huge depletion of assets, there has been in 2001 and 2002 a relatively meager inflow of new capital at the level of $31 billion; two-thirds of it in 2001.

One of the reasons capital depletion is a worry is that the high water mark of technical risk and operational risk is so unpredictable. Take the case of ports and airports as an example. There are 18.5 million containers that arrive in the US every year by truck, railcar, and sea. These containers constitute an economic lifeline, but also a major operational risk. Statistics indicated that:

■ Only 5% of vehicles crossing in from Canada or Mexico are physically inspected.
■ At 361 coastal and inland ports, through which 95% of US international trade flows, just one or two of every 100 inbound containers are ever opened.

All this is fertile ground for terrorists seeking to transport biological weapons, lethal chemicals, or home-made nuclear weapons. The port of entry could be a tempting target for an attack. Therefore, ports and airports present an operational national security risk. What is more, the control of this operational risk is diffused between port authorities, airport authorities, and half-a-dozen federal agencies, including Customs, Coast Guard, Drug Enforcement Agency, Attorney General, and the Treasury – though this may change with the new home security agency.

To be in charge of risk involved in a complex situation like the one just described, not only port/airport authorities and insurers have to learn how to assess and manage the new risks, but also financial analysts and rating agencies have to be educated as to the extremely high and unpredictable loss potential. To do their homework, insurers and reinsurers have to look very carefully into:

■ Coverage, clauses and wordings, updating the definition of risk, insured perils and excluded perils
■ Limits traditionally established to restrict the scope of covers that have become obsolete,
■ Pricing risk exposures adjusted to technical risk and operational risk by type, country, loss experience, and prognostication.

No doubt, a crucial role will be played by astute risk management, using scenarios, statistical inference, and stress testing connected to extreme events, including terrorist attacks. This means, however, that there is a crying need for enhancing the analysts' skills to investigate for correlation between business lines, scrutinize underwriting and operational risks, develop alternative risk transfer products, and address capital requirements for unexpected catastrophe events well before these take place. As we have seen, simulations and drills can be instrumental in assuring an insurer's and reinsurer's solvency.

14.6   Governments as insurers of last resort: a precedent with deposit insurance

A critical message the preceding sections conveyed is the urgent need to improve risk management in order to solve the uninsurability problem. A methodological way to do so is to understand the frequency, severity, and exposure to potential claims, secure adequate financial staying power, and price insurance coverage in a factual and documented way. Hard work, not miracles, should be the means of finding valid solutions to insurability.

In parallel to this, insurance and reinsurance companies should create a better public understanding about the role and the importance of their business for the modern economy. This means bringing into the picture the insurability or lack of it of extreme events, like terrorism risk, and therefore the need for assessment of public sector intervention.

An integral part of this argument is the fact that one of the responsibilities of the state in an economy is to provide internal and external stability. Therefore, protection is required against risks associated with events that exceed the private sector's capacity to be in charge – but this must be done without creating conditions of moral hazard (see Chapter 11).

Bank bailouts provide a precedent. The Introduction to this chapter made reference to the origin of the term 'insurer of last resort'; the very first 'last resort' bailout on record was done nearly twenty centuries ago by the Roman emperor Tiberius, in 33 AD. The Roman banking system had failed as a result of fraud, defaults, liquidity crisis, sinking of uninsured cargoes, and a slave revolt. The state felt that it had to act. In their modern sense, the way we know them today, the so-called government safety nets were really invented in the twentieth century, and with them (at least in some countries) bank bailouts at taxpayers' expense become rather commonplace. Fitch Ratings says that only one out of five banks that fail go bankrupt. The other four simply get bailed out. Bailout policies became more controversial as:

■ The externalities associated with the failure of a single bank increased, and
■ Moral hazard and the penalization of taxpayers grew with the amount of money spent on bailouts.

In a similar way to bank bailouts, because the cost to insurers from the events of 11 September 2001 has been so high, the US taxpayer is called into the picture as potential insurer of last resort. This has already happened with government support for airlines, on the grounds that the US transport system will otherwise be crippled.

Similarly, with insurance companies the public risks seeing the insurance policies it has against extreme events like terrorism cancelled. If this happens, it will indeed be a most critical problem for the economy and all of its agents.

But is the US government's pledge to absorb the losses insurers would face from future acts of terrorism, in order to persuade the industry to continue offering policies, a rational one? On 24 October 2001, some 6 weeks after 9/11, Treasury Secretary Paul O'Neill warned that many businesses might find it impossible to renew their policies against terrorism at the end of 2001,

- Either because insurers would refuse to take the risk,
- Or because premiums were so high.

What has happened since then in no way substantiated what O'Neill told the US Senate Banking Committee: 'The economy is facing a temporary, but critical, market problem in the provision of terrorism risk insurance.'[6] However, O'Neill's remarks had followed an October 15 proposal by president George W. Bush about propping up the insurance industry to the tune of as much as $229 billion over three years with this scenario:

- The first year, the government would pay 80% of claims on the first $20 billion in damages, and 90% on the next $80 billion.
- But in years two and three, insurers would be responsible for larger shares of the cost, with the industry's exposure capped at $70 billion.

'This plan can be sold on Capitol Hill as short-term emergency relief, just like food and blankets for flood victims,' said analyst Steve Blumenthal of Schwab Capital Markets. But others were not so sure. As New Jersey senator Jon Corzine, formerly CEO of Goldman Sachs, suggested: 'It just strikes me that this exposure is very, very high.'

The counterproposal to blanket coverage has been to let the Federal Deposit Insurance Corporation (FDIC) handle the claims. Since FDIC's institution after the Great Depression, individual banks have over the years paid small premiums that cover all banks' depositors against potential losses. FDIC, like any good insurance plan, spreads risks instead of ducking them. There is also a precedent in France, where natural catastrophes are handled through this type of contribution to a fund by insurance companies.

Given the FDIC's success, a deposit insurance restructured in a way commensurate with assumed risk by insurers and reinsurers looks like being the better solution. Let's recall, however, that with the exception of the US, deposit insurance necessary to prevent runs on the bank typically focuses on small deposits.

There exist different schemes of deposit insurance. In the United States credit institutions contribute proactively to the FDIC fund a small share of their income, and for every individual bank depositor FDIC pays up to $100 000 in the event that the bank fails. This is not the case in Switzerland, where up to CHF 30 000 ($20 000) in deposits is privately guaranteed by the Swiss Bankers Association (SBA).

- Unlike FDIC, SBA will collect the funds after the fact.
- It will have priority in the liquidation of assets, and
- It will ask other banks to contribute money, if necessary.

Solutions able to address huge losses, like those associated to terrorism, may make necessary both an ex ante and a post mortem approach. Nevertheless, whichever its exact rescue operation might be, deposit insurance will have to be characterized by caps on the guaranteed amount. Also, the capital for deposit insurance has to be permanent, available at the time of insolvency, and accessible in the jurisdiction of liquidation.

These conditions are difficult to meet in a globalized insurance industry, as they are difficult to meet in globalized retail banking. Therefore in the latter case several regulators now prefer locally incorporated subsidiaries of global banks subject to the law of the land.

There are also other requirements important to both an insurance solution for risks associated to global catastrophes, including terrorism, and to global banking. These are best expressed by the results of a meeting of representatives of supervisors and legal experts of G-10 central banks on 14 December 2001 at the Basel Committee headquarters.

The focus of that meeting was on banking activities and on the possibilities of preventing the global financial system from being misused to support terrorist activities. The participants agreed this cannot be achieved unless financial service providers have in place effective *know your customer* (KYC) and *customer due diligence* (CDD) policies and procedures. Similar concepts should apply with insurance coverage addressing supercatastrophes – as well as reinsurance. The insurer of last resort should thoroughly know its *global* 'customers' and exercise due diligence in covering, at least partly, extraordinary claims.

Notes

1 A.M. Best, Special Report, September 2002, Oldwich, NJ, USA.
2 D.N. Chorafas, *Credit Derivatives and the Management of Risk*, New York Institute of Finance, New York, 2000.
3 D.N. Chorafas, *Credit Derivatives and the Management of Risk*, New York Institute of Finance, New York, 2000.
4 *Financial Times*, April 2002.
5 *The Daily Telegraph*, 11 April, 2002.
6 *The Daily Telegraph*, 26 October, 2001.

Part 4

The importance of cost-consciousness in operational risk control

15 Deficient cost control is the result of management risk

15.1 Introduction

Poor management, high overhead, and lousy cost controls correlate among themselves and with operational risk. Runaway costs are an operational risk that can morph into credit risk and market risk, as this chapter demonstrates through examples from the banking industry. Credit institutions that are not in control of their costs are usually characterized by weak management and a steady drift in their financial staying power.

Costs tend to grow over time, and this is particularly true of overhead. Overhead means bureaucracy. As an opening salvo, let's look at the case of IBM. The company, which was very efficient in the 1950s and 1960s, drifted in the 1970s, and was well on its way to extinction in the late 1980s/early 1990s. By early 1993, IBM was collapsing under the weight of its own bureaucracy. Some 26%, or more than one out of four of its 90 000 employees in the Europe, Middle East, and Africa (EMEA) area of operations were riding desks, operating in 'support' rather than frontline functions.

If this happened in a company whose computer solutions were expected to wipe out paperwork and bring efficiency to its customers, think about companies where paperwork is core business. Bureaucracy is acting as a substantial drag to efficiency. It also breeds operational risk because much of its strength lies in an informal system of political alliances that does not permit any challenge to, let alone an attempt to correct, what is going wrong. The origins of operational risk cannot be taken care of:

■ When management is more interested in pushing paper than in taking action,
■ Or the executives are hanging on by their fingertips and are afraid to step on each other's toes.

This book has given plenty of evidence that only rigorous studies supported by top management and the will to challenge the 'obvious' can bend the operational risk curve. Figure 15.1 offers a three-dimensional frame of reference for operational risk studies, which I found quite useful in judging op risk control approaches and their likely effectiveness. At the top is *cost* under a dual perspective.

■ Cost of overhead and of dead wood.
■ Cost of the operational risk control solution itself.

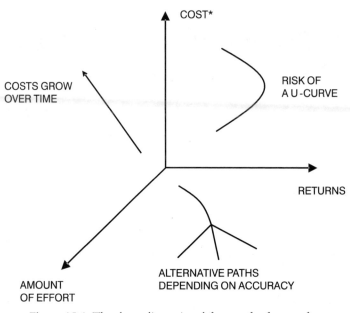

Figure 15.1 The three-dimensional frame of reference for operational risk studies. (*Many banks have identified the cost of operational risk analysis as equal to the Y2K problem)

Speaking from personal experience, a number of companies have no idea what their costs are, which is evidently silly. While operational risk must be controlled in a rigorous and determined manner, both cost and return on investment should be taken into account. As Figure 15.1 shows, their relationship is not characterized by a straight line but by a U-curve. Throwing money at the problem solves nothing. Optimization is, therefore, absolutely necessary.

What I have said in the preceding paragraph is that much more true as the overall cost of operational risk control will, in all likelihood, end by being quite high. The exact level is only an educated guess, and it will no doubt depend on several factors. An estimate I have heard from several banks – and one that does not look unreasonable – is that the cost of operational risk analysis and the necessary action for an effective control system will roughly equal that of the year 2000 (Y2K) problem.

15.2   The low cost producer holds the upper ground

Whether its line of business is in finance, manufacturing or merchandising, no company can escape the golden rule that its profitability and its long-term survival depends on its ability to be a low cost producer. In 1979, Chrysler had to sell 2.3 million cars and trucks to break even, and it was selling 1 million. The company went bankrupt, saved at the eleventh hour by a loan by the US taxpayer.

But by 1982 Chrysler's new management reduced the break-even point to less than half – just 1.1 million cars and trucks. It also increased its auto market share through a hard sales drive. With sales reaching 1.4 million units, Chrysler became profitable, repaid the government's 2 billion dollars loan, and returned good value for its shareholders – until a change in management ran the company down once again. There is no better documentation that high costs are part and parcel of management risk than Chrysler's example.

A similar principle is valid in banking, particularly so because in a credit institution's non-interest budget between 70 and 75% of all costs are human costs. Beyond that, 66% of all human costs are managerial and professional costs, even if the managerial and professional personnel is less than a third a bank's employment. As these statistics show:

- Roughly 50% of all non-money costs are at managerial/professional level, and
- That's where a focused study on cost control should start, rather than at rank and file.

Costs matter. Every cost item counts, and personnel costs should be at the top of priorities. Quoting from an article in *BusinessWeek*: 'In Germany, Citibank Privatkunden boasted a cost–income ratio of just 44 percent in the first nine months of 2002, 40 percent to 50 percent below those of big private banks retail operations.'[1] (See also Table 15.1.)

When greater management efficiency achieves 40–50% savings in overhead, compared to costs of competitors, then there is money to invest in effective control of operational costs. At the same time, however, it is a fallacy to think that 'more money' will solve the operational risk control challenge. As I never tire repeating, throwing money at the problem does not solve it: it only makes it worse.

A bank cannot be an employment outfit trying to solve social problems single-handed. That is not its mission. The bank has a responsibility to shareholders as well as to customers. If it is overmanned, and its non-interest budget is overfat, then it has

Bank	Overhead (%)
Royal Bank of Scotland	43.7
LloydsTSB	46.3
Barclays	51.5
HSBC	56.8
Commerzbank	57.8
BBVA	57.9
Crédit Agricole	57.3
BNP Paribas	63.4
UBS	75.5
Deutsche Bank	83.7

Source: BusinessWeek, 29 July 2002

Table 15.1 Major differences in overhead of banks

to slim down. Otherwise, it will not perform its duties in an able manner, and therefore it will not survive.

In the highly competitive market developed by deregulation, globalization, and technology, a great deal depends on management's determination to offset labor cost pressures. Specific cases of how a company deals with its labor cost problems are instructive. It is not easy to be ahead of the curve. In spite of the significant personnel reductions by investment banks in 2001–2002, many among them remain overstaffed because their business has fallen.

Among investment banks, Dresdner Kleinwort Wasserstein (DKW) is an example. Crédit Suisse First Boston is another. Both have been hit by rising labor costs, and this has been an issue that concerned not only their shareholders but also analysts looking into such labor cost problems – which have often been a reason for bearishness on a stock. Excuses for high labor costs can always be found. Some companies have been citing higher costs because of tasks associated with the Internet, intranet, enterprise software, and others requiring technology experts.

Now for the intriguing part: many companies responded to cost pressures by implementing a 5–10% or more across-the-board employee reduction. 'Across the board' is the wrong solution. Cutting the fat with a sharp knife is necessary, but it has to be precise – often by exiting one or more product lines and chopping off its payroll, top to bottom. When I am confronted with cost control problems, I look at two patterns:

- One *inside* the organization, over a period of 15–20 years.
- The other in comparison to an industry standard, or at least industry average and spread.

Study and comparison of similar chapters in internal costs can speak volumes on how well the company is managed at the cost control end. If the credit institution operates globally, it is revealing to compare the cost control performance of one location against another. As is not always appreciated, significant differences can exist within the same bank in different countries. For instance, the overhead of Allied Irish Banks has been:

- 50% in its AIB Irish operations
- 54% in its AIB British operations
- 64% in its AIB Allfirst in the United States.[2]

The external comparison pattern evaluates cost performance of the company under examination against its peers. In my experience, this can reveal a horror story of costs that have gone out of control. An example is given in Table 15.1. Between Royal Bank of Scotland, the best in the sample, and Deutsche Bank, the difference is nearly 1:2. There is no reason for such discrepancy, except that management makes the difference, though some other conditions also carry weight. For instance, in Germany bank personnel are paid more than people working in other sectors of the economy, as shown in Figure 15.2.

Management lax in cost control should remember that pre-tax profits and the cost of doing business correlate. This is documented in Table 15.2, which compares the

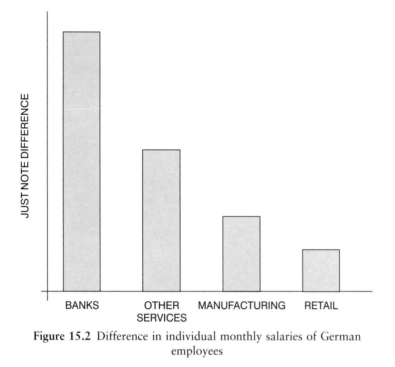

Figure 15.2 Difference in individual monthly salaries of German employees

results of six different investment banks. Look at 'profit per employee' as the most significant figure. Between the best and the worst performer, at the time these statistics were made available, the difference is nearly 1:22.

Frederick Winslow Taylor, the father of scientific management, once said that *if* the difference in productivity exceeds a ratio of 1:2.2 *then* there is something wrong with management. Just to pre-empt a possible criticism of the table let me add that one might think the 1987 statistics are obsolete. Not so. Big differences exist all the time, year-after-year. Only the names of mismanaged banks change.

	1987 pre-tax profits ($m)	Profits per employee ($000)
Lazard Freres	134	183.5
Morgan Stanley	364	56.0
Salomon Brothers	225	37.5
First Boston	120	22.0
Merrill Lynch	391	9.0
Paine Webber	110	8.5

Source: BusinessWeek, 30 May 1988

Table 15.2 Earnings per employee among investments banks

Experts suggest that in 2002 Citigroup has been the best cost-cutter in the industry. Other banks have laid off thousands of people but still carry more fat than the passenger list of a cruise liner. This is poison when a financial institution is operating at less than maximum capacity, while its headquarters is still overfat and overloaded with unnecessary costs.

In other industries, too, significant differences exist in cost performance. An example from airlines, a service industry, is presented in Table 15.3. In this sample, the

Airline	Cost per seat mile (US cents)
Southwest	7.7
America West	8.8
Continental	9.7
Northwest	10.0
Alaska	10.0
Delta	10.3
American	11.1
United	11.4
US Airways	12.5

Table 15.3 Airlines that want to survive cut costs (November 2001 statistics)

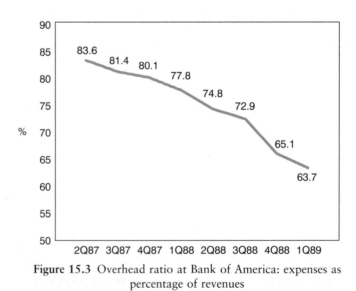

Figure 15.3 Overhead ratio at Bank of America: expenses as percentage of revenues

best is Southwest Airlines. The worst case is US Airways, which has gone bankrupt. It is appropriate to take notice that the correction of a cost situation that has gone out of control is a rewarding exercise. An example is given in Figure 15.3 with Bank of America. In the mid-1980s its overhead had run wild – equal to the worst case in Table 15.1. Then, over a period of less than two years, a new management was able to trim the overhead by nearly 25%.

15.3   Alert companies are in charge of their risks and of their costs: Berkshire and TIAA

What cost-restructuring can produce in terms of economic accomplishments, in the absence of any cost of inflation pressures, is still not well known. But some of the more astute analysts are stating that the consciousness that costs matter has been a fundamental reason for the success of some companies in riding the wave of bad market news in the 2000–2002 timeframe.

Indeed, it has been widely known for over a decade that the banking industry needs to consolidate as the demographic profile of the United States and of Europe creates excess capacity. Consolidation is not only done through mergers. Banks that aim to survive shrink their costs and make their operations more efficient. They are also using technology to reduce working capital.

It comes as no surprise that in every sector of industry this process has become a major stockmarket theme, though many companies pay it only lip service. Financial analysts think that a process of sharp cost-cutting and consolidation should characterize all sectors of the economy: from banking and retailing to even government itself. This section presents two of the best examples of today in senior management efficiency.

The first example is Berkshire Hawthorn. Its overhead ratio is 1/250 of that of most mutual funds, and its after-tax cost of running the business has come down to 0.5 of one basis point of capitalization. By contrast, many mutual funds are at the level of 100 to 125 basis points relative to capitalization. The difference is by no means a matter of 'luck'.

More than 40 000 people work for Berkshire, but the group is run by only 12 people at headquarters. This is one of the best examples of a truly efficient management operation. 'We hope to grow a lot. However, we don't hope to grow at headquarters,' says CEO Warren Buffett. His very small headquarters staff is motivated and works diligently, with bureaucracy being a dirty word.

The careful reader would contrast this culture to that of many financial institutions, as well as plenty of other organizations that are *Fat Cat* companies. Their inefficiency can be easily detected by their runaway overhead; section 15.2 presented several examples. *Cost-conscious* companies have a different pattern. They are thrifty on overhead because they understand that fat cats don't survive.

Another excellent example of overhead efficiency is TIAA. The Carnegie Foundation for the Advancement of Teaching established the Teachers Insurance and Annuities Association (TIAA) in 1915, with an endowment of $15 million. Subsequently, TIAA created the College Retirement and Equity Fund (CREF) investing in securities. Today, TIAA–CREF owns about 1% of all US stocks. It is also a very efficient organization, with an unusually low overhead:

- 0.25% for TIAA
- 0.40% for CREF

As the Berkshire and TIAA examples document, cost control is a culture. Mere lip service to the reduction of overhead leads nowhere. Compared to the examples I have just presented, even after a supposedly radical downsizing, many banks remain overstaffed because they have failed in taking a factual and documented view of what is really necessary. They have also been unable to conduct a qualitative and quantitative analysis of *their* cost factors.

The quantitative expression of cost factors and their appropriate allocation is an integral part of cost control. As basic cost accounting theory teaches, a number of decisions are necessary to properly divide costs into fixed, semivariable, and variable. The fixed costs and some of the semivariables are joint costs incurred in one area for the benefit of many others – provided that there is such benefit.

This is not the usual case. High overhead is organizational fat that goes undetected, or at least uncontrolled. There are two ways to cut it down. The one is the CEO's initiative and decision to stick to a low overhead diet. Berkshire and TIAA are examples. The other is a meticulous standard cost study. That's where Taylor and the Galbraiths have made their contribution.

The first consistent effort to measure the results of labor was directed at the production floor. Known as time study, it started with F.W. Taylor at Bethlehem Steel just prior to World War I. The so-called scientific management (of labor) continued with the motion study developed by the Galbraiths during the inter-war years. Time and motion approaches are not necessarily applicable to management, though standard cost tables (like MTM) and the ratio delay study (of post World War II years) might be.[3]

As far as the financial industry is concerned, Taylor's contribution is a milestone, not because of the mechanics of his time study but for the reason that no other effort in modern business history inspired such strongly held views and left such a legacy. 'Work better for more pay' was Taylor's credo. To many who like to take it easy, he was a dangerous radical intent on upsetting the equilibrium of the factory, which was at the time low wages for low output.

Perhaps the fact that there were no moderate opinions of Taylor had to do with his own temperament. 'A man of immense spirit, intelligence, and tenacity, he managed to alienate, or at least irritate, almost everyone, including many of his own circle of admirers,' says Robert Kanigel.[4]

- Rational inquiry into all aspects of industrial productivity is a necessary precursor for automation and modern business practices.
- The cornerstone is analysis focusing on both ideas and actions, packaging them and projecting into the future.

Quantification is still a valid approach to labor productivity, but due to the increasing automation of the production process its impact has shrunk to the benefit of a joint qualification and quantification approach. Most importantly, the intellectual nature of financial work does not lend itself to quantitative measurements of the sort the foregoing paragraphs have suggested.

- By contrast, a ratio delay study can indicate whether or not a person is busy.
- Cost comparisons, like those presented in section 15.2, will provide an indicator of competitiveness in the job being done.
- Quality control will tell a good deal about the quality of a person's work and the imagination he or she applies in the business.

The first two bullet points explain why a standard cost system is important. The third point brings qualification into the predominantly quantitative characteristics of the first two. An example on how to apply management control is Six Sigma (see Chapter 8). All three approaches are vital to a system solution, and therefore they should attract the attention of management.

In spite of a great deal of talk about better performance, and its impact on shareholder value, few financial institutions have established a performance measurement system based on standard costs. Based on research findings, Figure 15.4 provides some interesting statistics. What is important to keep in mind is that unless we can measure the variable we are after – whether this is operational risk, a cost factor, or anything else – we will not be able to control it.

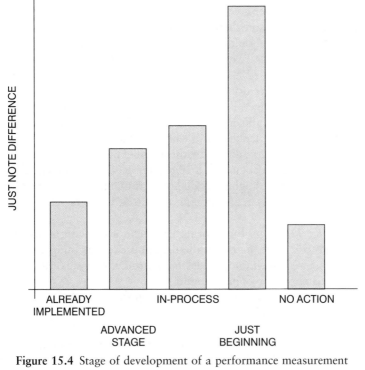

Figure 15.4 Stage of development of a performance measurement system

15.4   An example of controllable technology spending

Without standards against which to gauge our performance, there can be no documented opinion regarding how well or how badly we are doing in our job. Every well-managed company should look at the overhead of Berkshire and TIAA as the strategic frame of reference – while standard costs assist in providing the tactical framework for cost control and overhead expense. An equally important standard is to require managers to spell out return on investment (ROI) on the expenditures they ask for.

The calculation of an objective return on investment must take into account not only costs, including administrative costs, but also the risks being taken with the investment. Risks are always present, including operational risks. With financial investments, for example, risk increases as the instrument in which a company or a person is investing assets becomes more complex or, alternatively, includes a number of unknowns that have not been appropriately researched.

- Complexity means there are a greater number of unknowns.
- In practice, every time the term 'enhanced' is used by investment advisors, risk goes up.

For instance an 'enhanced' fixed income portfolio may have junk bonds in it. It is enhanced in the sense its average interest rate is higher, but also it represents more exposure of which the investor is not always aware. While all bonds have credit risk; junk bonds have much higher credit risk than others. All bonds also have interest rate risk, which is market risk, and there are operational risks in their handling.

Return on investment should also be key to budgetary appropriations for information technology. The reader will recall from Chapter 5 that well-managed banks have established a 20–22% return on IT investments. *If* this is documented when budgetary appropriations are done *then*, and only then, the IT budget may go up to 22–25% of non-interest budget. For instance, in their time of glory both Bankers Trust and the Mellon Bank had established a policy of 20–22%, or better, ROI. How has this return on investment been calculated and what was the overall policy?

'We are bankers,' said George di Nardo, the member of the executive board at Mellon responsible for IT. 'If we can document a 20 percent ROI, we would not hesitate to put more money in technology.' Higher productivity at managerial and professional level was one of the lucrative ways to gain greater return. At Bankers Trust:

- There was an *R&D budget* for information technology with no quantitative ROI target attached to it – but marketing had to approve this budget.
- Every other expense in technology was *an investment* with quantitative return, ROI being calculated chapter by chapter, and
- Every project of over $500 000 was audited post mortem in terms of obtained return on investment results.

This is a much better solution than a usually superficial feasibility study on new technology, which is largely guesswork and provides non-controllable deliverables. At both Bankers Trust and the Mellon Bank, return on investment criteria changed the way top management looked at information technology, its deliverables, and its costs. The policy at Bankers Trust was that for every payroll dollar the bank saved from the use of state of the art IT, it invested 40 cents in technology. This left 60 cents in profits.

How are IT costs being controlled? In many cases in which I have been personally involved in IT restructuring, cost-effectiveness has been the rule. There is much that can be achieved by scrutinizing every expense, zero budgeting being a good method. This means putting on active status every IT expense chapter and every development project.

Bank-to-bank, and bank-to-outsourcer comparisons help. In one IT restructuring project I had found that the cost of in-house software developments varied between 1 and 10 depending on the policies followed at subsidiary level and the quality of project management (see also section 15.5). Other things being equal, banks that run an efficient IT are those which:

■ Have made an accurate calculation of costs pertaining to computer and communications services, and
■ Are running their IT end-to-end, as profit center, billing the end-user.

Costing and billing are an integral part of controlling expenditures associated to banking services. This statement is just as valid of costing the services themselves, as it is of tracking computer costs all the way to banking products and into product pricing. Alert companies are in charge of their costs.

One of the global banks to which I was consultant to the board, developed a first class network, which worked round the clock at 99.9% reliability (see Chapter 5). The problem, however, was cost. The user departments billed for the network's services rebelled against the bills they got. Costs had to come down.

A study was done to establish competitive prices, in collaboration with AT&T, British Telecom, Sprint, and a couple of other phone companies. The board decided that the network bills should be set at 10% below the average of these five tariffs simulated to reflect the pattern of the bank's operations. Costs had to be cut near to the scalp. This was done through computer aided design (CAD) for network maintenance. The challenge was met.[5]

One cannot blame the user departments for pressing for lower costs. As profit margins come under increasing pressure from competition, fees and service charges are becoming more important as sources of revenue. If those fees are to contribute to the bottom line, they must be rationally calculated to cover costs and leave a profit – yet they should not be as high as to be non-competitive. The answer is tough internal cost control, while assuring the bank's technology has an impact on customers,

■ Giving much more timely information about the customer's overall relationship with the bank
■ Identifying business opportunities that may be hidden, and
■ Permitting risk to be managed more effectively any time, at any place, for any transaction.

This process calls for firm foundations. Realistic pricing, based on comprehensive cost analysis can be a major factor in assuring that fee income covers all costs and contributes to the bank's bottom line. Controlling costs, however, should never be used as a reason for lax operational risk control – or, more generally, for substandard global risk management.

Behind advanced IT initiatives lies the fact that all resources at the bank's arsenal must be integrated and support one another. In this, databases play a pivot role (see Chapter 5). One of the patchworks tried in the past, with no results worth mentioning, has been the building of data warehouses, a superstructure on multiple, heterogeneous, and overlapping databases aimed at pulling management data together. This is creating redundancies, delays, and lots of errors, which lead to:

- Non-competitive response to customer requirements, and
- Increase in the operational risk being assumed.

In contrast to such patchworks and substandard systems, competitive approaches require an integrated approach, able to take information about a whole range of transaction types and exploit it in real-time. Integrative solutions and interactive computational finance help to develop patterns of *risk profiles* right across a broad range of instruments and clients.

The reason why I emphasize these issues in a chapter of cost control is that, in my experience, in the majority of cases the true role of modern information technology has not been fully understood. Only the best managed companies are in charge both of their *risks* and of their *costs*. They build an integrated technology architecture, at affordable cost, to cover all the instruments which the bank trades and all the processes serving these instruments.

In conclusion, any-to-any real-time solutions change the way the bank views its business. But there is a strong need for reengineering with both quality and cost control targets. This requires rethinking the way of doing IT operations, along the lines suggested in this section.

15.5   Isaac Newton appreciated that throwing money at the problem leads nowhere

In banking, advanced technology solutions are inseparable from *rocket science*, which is a culture and an investigative attitude – not just mathematical skills and tools. Isaac Newton was the first rocket scientist on record. By becoming the Warden of the Royal Mint, he transferred his skills from mathematical analysis, the study of gravity, and optics, to economics and finance.

History books say that Newton's involvement in economics was in conjunction with the efforts by Charles Montagu, the Chancellor of the Exchequer, to redress British finances and introduce a new currency. Montagu wanted this new currency to be much better controlled than the old. He saw this as an urgent task because:

- The element of trust in the old coinage had been eroded, and
- Commerce was breaking down because of lack of business confidence.

Old coins recalled and melted down actually weighted only 54% of their legal weight because of chippers and counterfeiters, and the troubles were much broader than fraud. Therefore, there was an urgent need to reconstruct the entire financial infrastructure of England, and only the best minds could measure up to this job.

Newton's contribution to the British Treasury proved to be invaluable, largely thanks to his conceptual and analytical skills which he had already demonstrated through his work in mathematics and physics. At the time of his death, his library contained 31 volumes on economics (an impressive number in the early eighteenth century) which evidence suggests were among the most used books in his collection.

A pragmatic approach to economics was only one of his endeavors. Immediately after being appointed Warden at the Royal Mint (and before becoming Master), Isaac Newton concerned himself with how to increase the efficiency of the minting process. He carefully watched each step and carried out a time and motion study, well before F.W. Taylor did so (see sections 15.2 and 15.3). Newton:

- Calculated where and how improvements could be made, and
- Analyzed the process of minting in every detail so that he could materialize such improvements.

This is precisely what needs to be done for operational risk control reasons, as well as for cost control in business today. The answer is not in spending more money, but in planning meticulously how it is spent and what is the ROI. Notice as well that on repeated occasions Newton applied his mathematical skills to cost analysis, and this led him to clash with greedy government contractors.

Quoting from Michael White's biography of Newton: 'Long years of study and practical work at a quite different furnace had enabled Newton to calculate that one troy ounce of alloy for the production of coins could be produced at a cost of 7½d. So when the financiers . . . submitted tender of 12½d. per pound, Newton called their bluff and forced them down.'[6]

This is precisely what banks need in running their technology in an efficient manner. Spending large sums of money on information technology without bothering about return on investment has become a tradition for many banks. Only among well-managed institutions does the board ask about benefits that will be derived. Long-term, quite large IT projects continue to be implemented as an act of faith rather than as critically assessed investment factors. This is done even when:

- Cost/benefit analyses are not positive,
- Or, large capital expenditures have to be done.

Parkinson's law dominates the IT appropriations. There are surveys which claim that 65% of large companies are still unable to quantify the contribution of information technology to their business. Most board members and CEOs intuitively believe their investment in IT is 'absolutely necessary'. Neither, until very recently, have financial institutions paid due attention to the operational risks associated to information technology – their own and that of their business partners.

Yet, as Chapter 5 documented, operational risks are pervasive in IT and related activities, such as conversion procedures like restructuring the entity's risks archives. Restructuring requires shutting down the bank's customer systems for a long weekend to cut over, involving millions of customer accounts. Another fallacy is that of believing they can seamlessly replace some of the heterogeneous legacy procedures through a job done piecemeal, without an overall strategic plan that includes:

■ Training on a modern, competitive IT culture, and
■ A new architecture that capitalizes on the latest technological advances.

Beyond these two points, what surprises me is that many banks are not quite aware of operational risks associated with this piecemeal transition. The costs, too, can be important. The bill to a London clearing bank which did this changeover has been over £100 million ($155 million), and this is not a worst case scenario.

While changeovers are necessary to capitalize on the rapid evolution of IT and also, if not primarily, because of the business challenges in the twenty-first century, the cultural change and the architectural solution should come before anything else. Part of the cultural change is aligning information technology investments with business strategy. Among tier-1 banks this has more or less taken place. Another challenge is that of rapidly realigning IT investments and solutions when the business changes quite unexpectedly.

■ Clear-sighted industry leaders see this fast adaptation as their salient problem.
■ Achieving a low latency level to keep IT investments and strategies aligned is what competitiveness is all about.

This challenge cannot be faced by a fat IT budget. The answer is *vision* and *hard work* to achieve zero latency, which allows an organization to direct its product development, marketing and IT money more efficiently. An example on return on investment in the manufacturing industry is the profits coming from a tightly linked Internet sales and on-line inventory management,

■ Enriched with agents and sophisticated software for on-the-fly product personalization, and
■ Targeting competitive advantages, typically associated with firms able to hold the high ground.

Another example on IT ROI is using technology to keep down the cost of distribution. The real cost of distribution includes much more than pre distribution costs. Any major distribution decision can affect the cost of doing business upstream, at R&D level, and also relate to other cost issues. All of the following elements may prove critical in evaluating the impact of alternative distribution approaches on total costs:

■ Warehousing
■ Inventories
■ Inventory obsolescence
■ Supply chain alternatives
■ Cost concessions
■ Channels of distribution

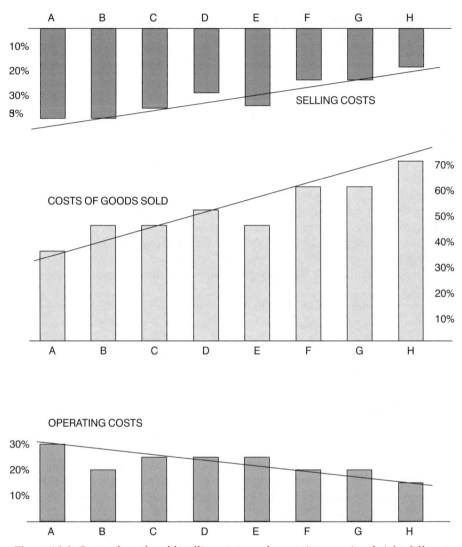

Figure 15.5 Costs of goods sold, selling costs, and operating margin of eight different computer manufacturers

- Alternative transportation facilities
- Maintenance of supply chain links.

Runaway costs of goods sold hit the bottom line, as many companies found to their expense. The example in Figure 15.5 is that of eight computer manufacturers with varying degrees of success in controlling their costs. 'A' is the best performer and has the lowest costs of goods sold, which allows it to put more money in sales, improve its market share, and still end up with the best profit figures in the sample.

This new consciousness starts seeping down organizations in different industry branches. According to some estimates, between 5 and 10% of Fortune 500 companies already have in place mechanisms that allow them to re-engineer their cost structure, and revamp their information technology, to take advantage of more efficient solutions. There may also well be another 15–20% that understands the need to do so, rethinking their processes.

15.6 Putting into action a costing and pricing mechanism for operational risk control

In this section, I take software development projects as a proxy for operational risk control projects, because that is where significant experience exists today. What is being written about cases of cost control with software projects is widely applicable and its underlying principles can help with operational risk projects as well.

For starters, once project deliverables, skills, timetables, and costs have been established, it is a simple matter to elaborate a time and expense plan for user-oriented software products and their maintenance. The difficult part is in deciding how to recover these costs through the *pricing* mechanism of the programming product (see also section 15.4).

Though it is not without its challenges, development work – meaning new programming products – is much easier to cost and price than software *maintenance*. If for no other reasons, this is true because the term 'maintenance' is used to mean different things to different people and different projects. In my book, software maintenance may be necessary because of either of three reasons:

■ The law has changed
■ There are mistakes in the programming product, or
■ The user department requires greater (or different) functionality.

If there are programming errors, then IT should absorb the cost of maintenance, writing it against its profit and loss. By contrast, in the other two cases costs should be chargeable to the user department. For this reason, the *cost and time* estimate must be approved by the user,

■ It should be an integral part of the costing and debiting procedures, and
■ The user must have the right to challenge the cost estimate, prior to giving approval (see the example on costing network services in section 15.4).

Hardware and software costing/billing procedures should be defined through formal procedural steps. This is an organizational challenge. To assign factual and documented costs to software development and maintenance, the systems and programming department must have in place a planning and control system. The same is true with operational risk projects. Planning should take several factors into account:

■ The job itself and its importance
■ The timetable for deliverables
■ Skill: knowledge engineers, analysts and programmers

- Salaries applicable to the above classes of people
- Overhead, including supervision and quality control
- Machine time to be allocated per activity within each project

Control is basically a comparison of total planned man-hours with actual man-hours, estimating how much time and cost will be required for job completion. This is a core activity in project management, with quality of deliverables being the other critical component. By relating total direct expenses to project milestones, we position ourselves in terms of costing a programming product. This process is portable to projects for operational risk control.

A costing structure can in no way be insensitive to the profitability resulting from the project. If it were, it would be short-lived and incapable of dealing with the most intricate aspects of management control. Failure to provide this correlation between costing and benefit from deliverables is at the origin of the fact that so many senior bank executives are generally disappointed with the return on their investments in technology, when they see that:

- Their company has not been able to use technology to achieve lasting competitive advantage over their principal competitors, and
- IT expenditures have failed to reduce operating costs in line with expectations, or as promised when the IT budget was authorized.

This should not happen with operational risk control projects. Let's keep in mind as well that – whether with new software development or op risk control – the cost of developing a certain product cannot be recovered as long as this product is not yet in production. Only when end-users are in the picture from the start of the project, as they should be, they are not so averse to paying some upfront costs to get the service into operation.

There is another positive side to this issue of end-user coinvolvement. Several financial institutions have found, by experience, that by demonstrating the functionality of properly identifying new programming products through prototyping, user level requirements for product development are better understood – and the resulting specifications are more accurate.

- The prototype is, so to speak, an artefact able to convey a message about its functionality, and it is immediately available for testing.
- Shells available for rapid prototyping have permitted investment banks to be way ahead of their competitors in IT deliverables.

Let's now bring this experience into operational risk control projects. To start with, as the preceding sections have outlined, a key to a solid procedure is the establishment of a budget with time, quantity, and quality of deliverables included. This budget will turn into a development costs fund, recovering expenses, including interest, during production time. Development and production should be based on an initially agreed upon timeframe.

In a real-life project on operational risk control, a costing application made along these lines calculated unit costs by analyzing the effect of various pricing alternatives.

This provided significant insight into cost structures, some of which had escaped management attention.

- Management policies required to allocate operational risk control charges to each unit and product line.
- Other applications areas, such as the distribution of op risk related systems support costs were facilitated by using a similar approach.

With hindsight, it is interesting in this connection that because there were several parameters and standards to understand, several tests were conducted for profiling purposes. Attention was also paid to tools and norms, allowing measurement of the performance of operational risk controls on an experimental basis. This made it possible to:

- Find glitches before they occurred, and
- Institute measures that kept deliverables from op risk control at an acceptable level.

The result of the approach outlined here has been that the cost of each op risk control project could be thoroughly scrutinized and compared to benefits from deliverables. Using budget and expense matrices, management could also make available to itself a plan-*vs*-actual evaluation. Simulation also went forward comparing operational risk control costs with projected savings, through *what if* scenarios – with various pricing alternatives.

Projections on savings from operational risk control, by business unit, and charged prices were seen as two interrelated processes. Once the total budgeted costs for operational risk projects were calculated, the prior year's saving for each op risk control activity were entered and cost/benefit estimates analyzed. The same experience also demonstrated that, short of a flat order by the board and CEO to do op risk control projects, selling such projects down the line was very much a marketing job.

Marketing is always based on product appeal and prices. Therefore, able costing and savings estimates are in reality an integral part of the bank's longer-term operational risk control effort. But while flat orders from the top of the organization can enable the starting of an op risk control project from scratch, continuing dependence on flat orders destabilizes the organization.

Notes

1 *BusinessWeek*, 7 December 2002.
2 *Financial Times*, 1 August 2002.
3 D.N. Chorafas, *Bank Profitability*, Butterworths, London, 1989.
4 Robert Kanigel, *The One Best Way, Frederick Winslow Taylor and the Enigma of Efficiency*, Viking, New York, 2002.
5 D.N. Chorafas and Heinrich Stainmann, *Intelligent Networks*, CRC Press, Boca Raton, FL, 1990.
6 Michael White, *Isaac Newton*, Fourth Estate, London, 1998.

16 Cost control is indivisible from operational risk management

16.1 Introduction

Chapter 15 has shown that though cost, including overhead, may not be viewed as a salient operational risk factor it does require senior management's attention. Cost control is a persistent and important issue. One of the domains where run-away cost is a prognosticator of op risk is in the back office, where lie the origins of the classical operational risk types. Another case is that of inefficiency in managerial and professional activities, all the way down to clerical and secretarial functions.

This chapter brings to the reader's attention three strategic issues underpinning runaway costs: The failure to appreciate the difference between the cost of being in business, and the cost of staying in business; the spoilage of a company's assets because of excessive compensation not related to performance, including executive options; and merger for merger's sake, which is the philosophy of the cancer cell.

All three issues have a great deal to do with inefficiency. As another example, one of the reasons why commercial paper and different forms of asset-backed financing have, to a significant extent, replaced classical bank loans is the inefficiency of the banking system. The total cost of intermediating a security over the life of an asset is:

- Under 50 basis points in capital market operations
- But over 200 basis points in banking intermediation.[1]

Because there is no reason to believe that people working in the capital markets are that much more smart and hardworking than bankers, the only reasonable conclusion for this huge difference is that banks are poor at cost control. They are also constrained by labor regulations unfavorable to them. When in the early 1990s Bank of America closed down its operations in Equador, it had to pay its 49 employees 6 years of salary.

At first sight, this may seem as an issue outside the scope of this book. In reality it is part of it, because what Bank of America faced in Equador and elsewhere is legal risk that, in all likelihood, has not been appropriately studied – including the exit clauses – before entering that market. And legal risk is an operational risk. In most financial institutions, the conventional wisdom has been that the reduction of the bank's cost structure is a one-time procedure.

- Dispensable managers are let go
- Superfluous branches are closed, and that is that.

That's false. Cost control is a way of thinking, and therefore a *process*, not a one-time event. Therefore, well-managed companies are steadily examining their business policies and procedures to find ways to cut the roots of sprawling costs. The core issue is not so much that costs have to be reduced, but that cost control should be a virtuous cycle.

As a way of thinking, cost control helps banks maintain their profitability even when business is flat or intensely competitive. That is why it is most important to make virtually every cost, including labor, more variable than in the past. This is helped by the fact that technology is giving timely access to the knowledge and information institutions needed to reduce working capital throughout the economic system. But there are several misconceptions associated to cost management.

16.2   The cost of staying in business

Like any other company, a credit institution must serve its own survival; this means it must operate at a profit. Profit performs a function essential to the success of any industrial and post-industrial society, and *profitability* must be the criterion of responsible business decisions. Not only does the survival of a bank depend upon its economic performance, but also the overriding demand of society is for economic performance.

To keep its resources intact, the financial institution must be able to cover costs out of current business. This goes beyond the cost of doing business, because financial and industrial activity focuses in the future. Two top measures to be taken by management are to:

- Shrink the cost base and make operations more efficient, and
- Pay a great deal of attention to the cost of *staying in business*.

To appreciate the meaning of the second point, it is appropriate to recall that, classically, banks look at their budget as divided into two parts: the interest budget (roughly two-thirds of the total), and the non-interest budget. The latter should take care not only of expenses associated to ongoing operations, but also of expenses necessary for the longer-term survival of the enterprise.

- The *cost of doing* business practically includes all day-to-day operational costs.
- The cost of *staying in business* is money invested in research and development (R&D), and generally activities that guarantee a place in the market in the future.

Since banking has become an industry it is very important that it takes care of its R&D budget, and the projects to be planned, financed, and controlled – as well as their deliverables. This applies not only to the development of new products and services, but also to projects aimed to control credit risk, market risk, and operational risk. *Risk management* is part of the cost of staying in business.

The structure of a post-industrial economy is radically different from that of a trading economy. While a *trading* economy focuses on the past, with the difference between past cost and current revenue a profit, an industrial economy focuses on the future and must cover out of its current revenue not only current cost of doing business and future cost of staying in business, but also:

- An indirect share of losses of unsuccessful enterprises, and
- A reasonable share of society's non-economic burden, which, because of demographic and other reasons, increases over time.

This suggests that the modern enterprise owes some additional duties to its stakeholders, including the society of which it is a part. These duties, though often not represented in the average balance sheet, are necessary charges against current operations.

For instance, an indirect share of losses from unsuccessful enterprises shows itself through increase in government taxation, reduction in market potential, excessive requests of labor unions, or special governmental regulations. In fact, the *dry holes*, the competitive failures in a free enterprise system, are wastes that any individual enterprise might avoid, but a society of enterprises cannot avoid entirely. They even perform a necessary function: that of keeping the economy's valves open.

- It is not by eliminating competition that the social waste of failure can be avoided.
- Competition and failure are the ways by which elements of risk in an advanced economy can be explored.

It should also be appreciated that a going enterprise bears, again out of its current activities, a share of social costs that do not pertain to its own economic process: schools, hospitals, universities, foundations, etc. This is a form of social responsibility that has become a 'must'.

Then, we must not forget that out of its current revenues the enterprise must maximize its profits, reinvest some of these profits in its transformation process – in the form of capital expenditures – and pay dividends to its stockholders. Only if the enterprise can cover all these costs in an able manner,

- Will it preserve its own resources, and
- Will it contribute to the economic growth of its society.

In pre-industrial economies the product risks were mostly physical. Today, physical risks are always present, but the modern company is also subject to growing economic risks, from marketability of products to control of risks associated to after-sales responsibilities. In banking, an after-sales responsibility is what to do with accumulated 'toxic waste' from derivative instruments and non-performing loans.

At one end of the spectrum, product risk stems from unforeseeable shifts in demand. It may be a change in fashion, or an ingeniously improved product marketed by competitors. Product risk can be controlled, in an industrial economy, only when it operates under extreme scarcity conditions; when any product is eagerly bought at any price. This happened in the post-World War II years, but it is not the case with our economy.

Tools like *market research* and analysis help to decrease product risk by foreseeing the economic future of one's products. Through R&D a firm may develop new and better products, and hold its share in an expanding market. To minimize product risk, management must answer, in an effective manner, the questions: *when*, *what*, and *how*.

- When, what, and how are crucial queries for an economy to expand and improve, but still more is required in a post-industrial economy.
- This 'more' is rigorous risk control because the New Economy prospers by taking major risks, and by managing change.

All societies change, but change in pre-industrial economies was mostly the effect of outside forces: wars, conquests, explorations. Quite different is the change to which the post-industrial economy is subject. This change is self-generated, built in the productive system, and it is part of the cost of staying in business – hence the emphasis on:

- Research and development, and
- Enterprise risk management.

Modern organizations (states, enterprises, societies, associations) are either expanding or contracting, increasing their economic resources or using them up. Therefore, expansion is the key need of the modern industrial economy.

Classical economists knew of only one way to increase economic production: the employment of existing resources for the activity they were best fitted for. The resources themselves were considered God-given and unchangeable. Marx and his followers understood that expansion is not only desirable but also necessary to the new industrial economy. Yet, they saw only one possibility of expansion: expansion into new territory through exporting the 'proletarian revolution'. So, the misconception developed that expansion was impossible except at somebody's expense.

Examined under the light of the situation as presented at the beginning of the twenty-first century, both doctrines are utterly wrong. What is basically new about the post-industrial system is its power to expand at nobody's expense: the application of technology results in an actual transformation:

- Of old and fully utilized resources,
- Into bigger and more productive ones.

Modern technology has shown that the best way to increase productivity is by an improvement in the method and in the system, by which the same resources employed in the same activity or a new one are made capable of producing more and better products – the agent being the innovator. This is the cost of staying in business.

16.3   Operational risk control and the administrative budget

Section 16.2 brought to the reader's attention that the cost of staying in business should not be confused with the cost of doing business. Both have to be covered out of the current non-interest budget, and operational risk is part of both of them:

- Research necessary to identify operational risk and develop the control framework is part of the cost of staying in business.
- By contrast, the steady exercise of day-to-day operational risk control is part of the classical administrative budget, hence of the cost of doing business.

Let me repeat this point. The development of new models, methods, and systems for operational risk identification and control must be financed by the R&D budget – which is also part of the non-interest budget, but quite distinct from money allocated to day-to-day administration. The steady exercise of op risk controls, however, is part of normal administrative chores.

The problem in this connection is that when normal administrative costs, often referred to as operating costs, get out of control, as so often happens, they leave precious little to be invested into the mission of staying in business. Only top-tier management appreciates the fine print behind this issue, and takes the measures necessary to keep normal administrative costs under control.

A different way of stating the need to keep a sharp watch on every dollar or pound spent in current administrative costs is that while in the banking industry cost control has become a major theme the effort surrounding it is often misdirected. Cost control attracts too much lip service and very little real action. Even cost-cutting that concentrates on headcount is overwhelmingly directed to rank and file, rather than taking a system-wide view.

This chase after headcount at the bottom of the organizational pyramid leads to several distortions, wild outsourcing being one of them.[2] At the risk of being repetitive, here is the case of a British investment bank which outsourced its networks, including the local area network (LAN) in its trading room, in order to reduce the headcount. The system specialists who ran the LAN:

- Were hired by the insourcer
- Continued working on the bank's premises, and
- Were billed by the insourcer to the bank at much higher price than their original wages.

While reducing the headcount is important, it is much less important than the factual and documented definition of what cost-restructuring is and is not, as well as what it can produce by way of accomplishments. The consciousness that *costs matter* is part of systems thinking.

The statement made in the last sentence is polyvalent. It includes cultural issues as well as technical questions such as: At what level of performance do managers and professionals release the best of their capabilities? Can the current IT structure support this level of performance or is it the bottleneck? More precisely:

- What is the higher level of performance from human resources and IT systems needed to be ahead of competition?
- What kind of incentives can help *our* bank reach the level that we target? (See also section 16.5 on executive options.)

Depending on the size and diversity of our bank's operations, the demands posed upon the human capital vary – and the same should be true of incentives permitting strategic and tactical goals set by the board and the chief executive officer to be reached or exceeded.

Big egos and 'me-too' approaches blur the strategic moves. They lead to actions that have nothing to do with rationality. For instance, it has been widely known for more than a decade that the banking industry needs to consolidate, but big egos have seen to it that consolidation has been often confused with costly mergers and acquisitions that are empty of deliverables, if not outright counterproductive (see section 16.4).

While management's attention is distracted, and the operating budget is drained by issues that contribute little to the bottom line, other crucial issues get scant attention. An example I never tire of repeating is enterprise risk management, which is pivotal to sound corporate governance.

Running a company today is simpler and more complex at the same time, compared to the immediate post-World War II years. Communications and IT make the management task easier, helping to produce a higher level of performance than in older times *if*, and only if, they are properly designed and implemented.

At the same time, the process of company management has become more complex, driving the need for services and system solutions to address fast developing market requirements throughout the world.

- New technologies must be supported at high performance levels, washing away the constraints of legacy systems, and
- Senior management must be endowed with means of increasing insight and foresight, necessary for the control of a myriad of risks.

Risks are costs with the potential to be three orders of magnitude higher than savings from the reduction of rank and file headcount on which so many companies concentrate. At the same time, if we use advanced methods, models, and technology to cut the cost of risk, we cannot remain indifferent to other costs. Chapter 15 has already brought to the reader's attention that *all* costs must be slashed.

In my experience I have often found the effort to reduce the intrinsic cost of credit risk, market risk, and operational risk wanting. This is partly due to the fact that only the best management companies look at risk as a major cost item. The others simply hope that divine providence will turn the risks they have taken their way. Real life does not work like that.

Sometimes miracles happen, but this is very rare indeed. For instance, on 19 December 2002 a judge in the United States reduced the $28 billion in compensation Phillip Morris was condemned to pay tobacco victims to $28 million. The difference in the cost of this particular legal risk is three orders of magnitude, but then the original $28 billion was just crazy. Some sort of 'miracle' had to happen.

The only way to keep costs under control is to watch after them very carefully. Much can be learned from the manufacturing industry on how to use technology in controlling costs. Take as an example the case of components manufacturing. Today, components comprise over 70% of the cost of a typical electronic subassembly. The cost associated with them can be reduced by using a component information system.

- Making on-line datamining available to the entire enterprise, from the very start of the design process, and
- Supporting through merits and demerits normalization and reuse of preferred components by design engineers.

Able technological solutions address a myriad of problems, from attacking productivity bottlenecks, to reducing process errors, and decreasing design cycle time. Also, since on-line processing provides an audit trail, it is easier to control the merging together of information from various runs which were previously standalone.

By comparison, batch handling, which is still practised by the majority of financial institutions, and other legacy IT tools and methods, provide no history or revision mechanism for individual runtimes and their integration into an enterprise management system. Yet, if we wish to cut cost and control risks, we must support managers, traders, loans officers, and everybody else with a real-time roadmap – as well as tools to help them quickly learn what is happening with transactions and process flows as they evolve.

From Chapter 5 the reader should be aware that real-time solutions, database mining, and interactive knowledge artefacts provide a mechanism to monitor and regulate the status of ongoing trades and other transactions, including operational risk control. This is achieved by making possible closer collaboration among geographically dispersed teams while continuing to improve efficiency and communication.

In conclusion, in terms of cost control and operational risk control, heightened accessibility over data and processes is especially important. Control action becomes so much more efficient if it is possible to investigate cause and effect, as suggested in Figure 16.1.

A basic principle in any business is that of being alert. When the entity's dimensions are small, management (perhaps just one individual) can size up risks and opportunities by keeping their eyes wide open. This is not sufficient with big firms. Because many deals are worked on by business units, which reside in different places, interactive computational finance is a 'must'. For this reason, its development is part of staying in business.

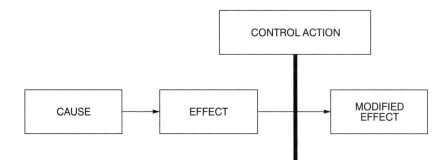

Figure 16.1 Cause and effect before and after operational risk control

16.4   Are mergers and disinvestments a good way to cut costs?

Mergers among credit institutions, for reasons of economies of scale, big egos, or any other, are a vast subject, and, with one exception, are not the theme of this book. The exception is mergers of a specific division belonging to different financial entities, which then becomes their *insourcer*. An example is the merger of mortgage divisions of three major German banks for cost cutting reasons. In early November 2001 Commerzbank, Deutsche Bank, and Dresdner Bank announced the merger of their mortgage banking operations, in a move which created Germany's biggest property lender. Based on the merged operations of three major credit institutions, the assets of the new entity stood at more than $215 billion. The combined activity represented an estimated 25% of domestic market share. The move came as Germany's big commercial banks stepped up cost cuts and shed jobs at a time of falling profits, and pressures for consolidation among Germany's Hypotheken (mortgage) banks, which have been hit by:

- Shrinking margins, and
- Heavy loan losses after a frenzy of lending in eastern Germany in the early 1990s and beyond.

The jointly owned unit essentially serves as an insourcer of the mortgage banking operations of each of its three parent credit institutions. Though insourcing and outsourcing is not a theme of this book, a couple of words help to put this and similar mergers for reasons of economies of scale into perspective.

Outsourcing is a delegation of authority but not of responsibility. The responsibility rests with the outsourcer, even if by assuming the authority the insourcer also has its own share of responsibility. Beyond this, as John Hasson, director of information technology and treasury operations at Abbey National Bank, aptly says: 'I am comfortable with outsourcing as much as I convince myself that what I outsource is a commodity. But I don't like to see outsourcing becoming an accounting device.' In fact, Abbey National looked at outsourcing its back office operations but did not like what it saw. 'What you outsource is high volume,' Hasson said. 'Because we don't have high volume in the investment banking business, it did not make sense to outsource that service.' Mortgages however do have high volume, so from that viewpoint the action of the three German banks made sense.

In different terms outsourcing the mortgage portfolio of three major credit institutions satisfies the prerequisite of mass production – hence, the commodity argument – but what about other conditions? A problem that comes up immediately is joint management of the common subsidiary; another problem is that of unavoidable confidentiality issues.

There is always a difference between good intentions and obtained results. Expected returns and real returns may deviate substantially, as Figure 16.2 suggests. An example is COVISINT, the procurement subsidiary by General Motors, Ford, and Daimler–Chrysler launched in February 2000, which never really got off the ground.[3]

A similar statement is valid regarding the good initial intentions associated to disinvestments, and the results obtained a few years down the line. Disinvestment, like mergers, is an activity involving an inordinate amount of operational risk because,

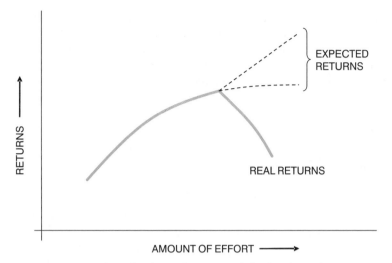

Figure 16.2 The risk of overshooting and the bending of returns

most often, the functionality of different departments finding themselves at the borderline has to be cut down the middle. For different reasons, part of the cost associated to mergers and acquisitions is an increase in operational risk.

Is this higher operational risk cost compensated by extraordinary benefits? The best way to answer this query is through practical examples. In November 1997, the acquisition of BZW's European equities and corporate financing business by Crédit Suisse First Boston (CSFB) from Barclays, seemed to be fulfilling the latter's ambition to become Europe's investment banking powerhouse. At least this was the plan.

In a transaction described by financial analysts as 'brilliant' for the buyer and awful for the vendor, CSFB paid £100 million ($155 million) for the BZW operations, which was 33% less than the division's book value. On paper, the BZW purchase created a third home market for CSFB in the UK. It also gave it BZW's businesses and clients access to the US market.

On Barclays' side, the advantage of this deal was closing down the costs of BZW, its investment banking subsidiary. In February 1998 Barclays admitted that it had paid at least £688 million ($1.1 billion) to leave the big league of investment banking business. What remained from BZW has been downsized into a medium-size investment operation known as Barclays Capital.

Barclays Capital started by employing about 3500 staff, 800 of them in the United States. The new unit chose to specialize in challenging the logic that was driving the rapid consolidation of investment banking. It did not arrange new share issues, trade shares, or offer advice on mergers and acquisitions. Its operations centered in:

- Foreign-exchange trading, and
- Bonds denominated in sterling.

Originally, Barclays Capital also included some traditional banking businesses into which Barclays wanted to inject investment banking expertise, such as financing big infrastructure projects and providing loans for less creditworthy companies. In a matter of a few years, however, Barclays Capital grew and expanded into new fields like investment advice in deals involving deleveraging and outsourcing.

What did the enlarged CSFB get for its money? It did not really become a major force in UK corporate broking, or in mergers and acquisitions – at least not in a way that it could truly compete with the three largest US investment banks: Goldman Sachs, Morgan Stanley Dean Witter and Merrill Lynch. These are the three big ones that dominate the:

- Global equity capital markets, and
- Investment banking services.

The acquisition of BZW by CSFB did not enable the latter to dethrone any of the big three and take its place. Instead, according to some accounts, over and above the price it paid for the acquisition of BZW operations in the UK and the US, Crédit Suisse First Boston spent $300 million to lure back a team of 40 bond traders headed to Barclays. The extra cost of personnel is one of the operational risks being assumed in acquisitions.

What about the profits? The good news is that in 2000, CSFB earned $358 million for underwriting $5.4 billion of technology IPOs. This represented the combined operations from the existing base and the acquisition. The bad news is that staffers in the CSFB technology group keep about 50% of net fees they generate. Essentially, it is they who profited from CSFB's acquisition of BZW. The very bad news is that in 2001 and 2002, this market nearly disappeared.

Neither did the enlarged CSFB benefit from a stronger UK and US presence than European rivals, like (the then competitors) SBC Warburg Dillon Reed, UBS Phillips and Drew, ABN–Amro Rothschild, Deutsche Morgan Grenfell, and Dresdner Kleinwort Benson. Yet, CSFB could capitalize on the fact that BZW:

- Was adviser and broker to 150 UK companies, including 22 of the FTSE 100
- Was Number 2 underwriter of UK equity, and
- Ranked second in UK equity trading.

This is one more piece of evidence that few mergers and acquisitions reach the objective they have originally set themselves. This is not finger-pointing to a couple of investment banks but a general observation. A recent article in *The Economist* said that: 'Investment banks are among the worst-managed institutions on the planet because they are built on a loose confederation of franchises and outsize egos. Once you start counting conflicts of interest within them, you soon run out of fingers.'[4] Management risk is inherent in such a situation.

Another blunder has been the $12 billion spent in year 2000 by Crédit Suisse First Boston to purchase rival Donaldson, Lufkin & Jenrette (DLJ) in the United States. By 2002, fewer than half of DLJ's 2000 bankers remained at CSFB – and, apart from that, the business benefits have been minimal. By contrast, the $12 billion spent on DLJ depleted the reserves of Crédit Suisse and, combined with problems at Winterthur, left the bank in a difficult condition in 2002.

16.5   Why fat executive options work against shareholder value

In the aftermath of the various scandals surrounding overblown executive options, legal experts suggested that this has become a case study in the mismanagement of morality – an operational risk. According to some estimates, in 2002 alone corporate scandals, options being one of them, have cost investors a cool $200 billion.[5] Among the hardest hit investors were the pension funds.

In his book *Take On The Street* Arthur Levitt, Jr says that when he became chairman of the Securities & Exchange Commission, in mid-1993, he found a controversy raging over whether companies should treat stock options as expense against earnings on their income statements. This would have been similar to the way they treat salaries, bonuses, and other forms of compensation.

- The Financial Accounting Standards Board (FASB) said they should expense options.
- But corporations insisted they should not, since no money actually flowed from the company's treasury.

Correctly, the FASB argued that options involved real costs to shareholders. Therefore, in June 1993, it voted unanimously to seek opinion on a rule that would make companies put a fair value on their stock option grants, and record that number as an expense. The pressure against expensing options, Levitt suggests, came from everywhere: big companies and small start-ups, particularly those from Silicon Valley.

Both the big boys and the small fry were large campaign contributors to politicians. The core of the matter was that by saying non-expensed stock options were essential, companies were arguing, in effect, that transparent financial statements should be secondary to personal, political and short-term economic goals. This turned prudential cost management on its head.

- CEOs and chief financial officers were also fighting for accounting and reporting standards that let them understate expenses and exaggerate profits.
- The auditors went along. They did not rally to the cause of protecting investors, but supported the demands of their corporate clients all the way.

Non-expensing fat options which stole the equity of shareholders was not the only gimmick. Arthur Levitt suggests that over the years a succession of SEC chief accountants – Walter Schuetze, Mike Sutton, Lynn Turner – warned him that they were seeing a marked increase in manipulated corporate financial numbers.

A common creative accounting manipulation – an operational risk *par excellence* – was to push ordinary expenses into the category of one-time or non-recurring costs – like WorldCom did in a big way. Other companies added these expenses back into their earnings and called the result *pro forma*. This was against the rules of the generally accepted accounting principles (GAAP), which required that such expenses be properly subtracted from earnings.

In some quarters, people did not hesitate to talk of corporate crime. In late October 2003 Canada signalled a tough line against that sort of operational risk, charging four former executives of bankrupt entertainment company Livent with defrauding investors and creditors of about C$ 500 million (US$ 315 million).

The charges followed a four-year police investigation covering alleged accounting irregularities between 1989 and 1998. This has been the first significant accounting fraud charges brought by the Canadian authorities since the series of US corporate scandals erupted in 2001. The Royal Canadian Mounted Police said the Livent's two founders, along with two other executives,

- Falsified the company's financial statements, and
- Misrepresented its financial health to investors.

Livent once was the largest live theatre company in North America, with venues in Toronto, Vancouver, New York, and Chicago. It collapsed in 1998 unleashing a number of lawsuits. The company's former chief executive and president have also been indicted in the United States on charges of conspiracy and securities fraud in connection with Livent's collapse. Management risk, deceit, and absence of cost consciousness morph in many ways:

- From the softer approach of stock options
- To the hard one of manipulation of financial statements – an outright fraud.

The pattern of taking money out of the shareholders' pockets did not take long to develop. Companies were playing with their earnings until they arrived at the best possible number that could have a big market impact. Earnings press releases revealed only the good news, and auditors whitewashed the corporate accounts in spite of the trickery.

The numbers game became a policy. From 1997 through 2000, 700 companies would find flaws in past financial statements and restate their earnings. By comparison, only three companies restated in 1981.[6] This is the depth of degradation which business morals can reach, and fat executive options played a central role in keeping the fraud off the radar screen.

When they were originally offered by start-up companies in order to attract some of the best young graduates, options were intended to give a sense of ownership to executives and professionals. This was a good strategy. Eventually, however, they became overexploited for all types of incentives for 'better performance'; then they drifted to a level that had little or nothing to do with performance itself. Analysts at Wall Street calculated that:

- In the general case, options take a cut of 10% of annual company profits.
- For technology companies this rises to between 20 and 25% – and it can go up to 50%, as in the case of Intel.

In other terms, shareholders take all the risks but they gain only three-quarters of the profits, or even less than that. This sort of heavy decreaming has become very similar to the policy followed by hedge funds which take 20–30% of profits, while their investors assume all the risks.

There is no denying that many companies, particularly technology outfits, have got away with shareholder assets by using options as free money, which does not appear on income statements. Siebel Systems, a software firm, provides an example. In 2001, Siebel had income of $254.6 million, or 56 cents per share. Counting all options in the share count, that shrank to 33 cents a share, about 40% lower.

- *If* Siebel had expensed options, then it would have reported a $467 million loss, or $1.02 a share,
- This and other examples from expensing options speak volumes of disappearing shareholder value, turning the income statement on its head.

Experts say that misleading accounting for stock options has concealed a tremendous transfer of wealth from shareholders and their companies to managers and professionals.[7] One way to measure the cost of stock options is to assign a value to options at the time when they are granted. Another, simpler one used by government statisticians is to count the net proceeds of exercised stock options as wages paid by companies.

The latter method has the advantage of measuring actual cash going to managers and other employees. An executive who exercises 1000 stock options with a difference of $100 between the market price and the exercise price and then sells the shares walks away with $100 000 in cash. In many cases, the company opts to buy back those shares and thereby effectively pays out the $100 000 to the executive. According to this accounting model, the effective wealth transfer from options has been very significant and shareholders paid for it.

16.6   What it means to be in charge of re-engineering

All of the different forms of creative accounting are operational risks. They are no innovation of financial services but, rather, a misrepresentation of facts and figures. The massive and unwarranted granting of executive options falls into this class. The same is true, in terms of shareholders' misinformation, of more than half the reasons given for mergers and acquisitions. Statistics show that:

- Two-thirds of mergers have been failures, and
- Less than one out of five mergers and major acquisitions could be regarded as a success.

If mergers and acquisitions are not the wonderdrug for high costs and other business ills, *then* what might be the solution? The answer is being an innovative but also very low cost producer of financial services. This is the subject of the present section.

In the first decade of the twenty-first century no bank can place itself beyond the bounds of a free market's checks and balances. There is no financial market that is a certain company's personal fiefdom, as the reader will recall from the discussion so far. Highly competitive environments are known to reward the low cost producers and distributors of services, equipped with:

- A top performance product, and
- A well-thought-out strategic plan.

Only those companies satisfying these criteria can survive, because survival in a highly competitive market means steady innovation with products offered at an affordable price. As we saw in section 16.2, innovation constitutes the cost of staying in business and is the basis of an entity's present and future profitability.

Innovation and efficiency correlate. One of the sources of investment profits on which Henry Kravis and George Roberts counted was increased efficiency. Their rule has been that every big company is hidebound by excess overhead, bureaucracy, and pay not based on merits. At most of the companies KKR had acquired, headquarters staffs were too large. 'I called them people who report to people,' Kravis often remarked. 'Companies build up layers and layers of fat.'

Therefore, the virtues of cost-cutting became almost a theological point for Henry Kravis. It has also been a strategy for acquisitions that can be expressed in one simple sentence: 'Pursue big-name clients but keep your own overhead small.' Safeway is a case in point, and a good example of a company's inbred inefficiency, which acts like a cancer.

As Kravis and Roberts dug into the Safeway finances, they found confidential figures that were the grocery chain's secret shame, and the delight of their analysts. As it happens with so many commercial banks and investment banks, while overall Safeway was profitable, huge chunks of its territory were operating deep in the red. The supermarket chain was pursuing a strategy common to many big companies:

- Quietly draining cash from its strong business, and
- Subsidising other inefficient operations that were never dropped.

Unwillingness to chop off dead wood is a management weakness, therefore an operational risk. It is also a miscalculation based on the hope that some miraculous turnaround will bring short-term gains, even if this happens at the expense of long-term survival. The problem with the status quo, which is galvanising the base and does away with tough decisions, is that senior management misguides itself into thinking it can have its pie and eat it too.

Few in management have heard or, if they have, really appreciated, the wisdom of H.J. Stern, who in his retirement from the helm advised the investment banker he called in-house to sell his firm: 'A company isn't like an oil well where all you have to do is hold a pan out and collect the oil. It's like a violin. And I'm not sure my sons have what it takes to play the violin.'

Neither are there many boards who know how to play the violin. A testament to this is provided by the straits in which the automobile industry found itself in the late 1980s/early 1990s, a process which continues into the twenty-first century. Coping with a major downturn has been hard for Detroit's big car makers. GM, Ford, and Chrysler plunged into losses time and again, in recent years, even as sales boomed. This profitless prosperity:

- Drained their treasury, and
- Drew attention to their liabilities, such as their underfunded pension and other worker benefits plans.

On account of these woes, the independent rating agencies downgraded the debt of Ford and General Motors almost to junk, unheard of for big companies in a mature industry. This made it costlier for them to raise capital, creating a credit risk which morphed into operational risk, and the other way around. Behind each case has been management's inability to come up from under.

Experts suggest that such persistent depression hitting big, mature companies is the outward manifestation of management risk. Some companies, like General Electric, have escaped by re-engineering themselves. Others persisted in the drift. The results coming out of huge bureaucracies contrast to those achieved by successful entrepreneurs. Many people erroneously think that all turnaround specialists have really done is to take over companies, but they forget that none of these deals became successful:

■ By warming executive armchairs
■ Or by exercising some magic.

Most of the companies taken over by experts in business re-engineering had major problems, and all required innovative financing structures as well as an efficiency principle well-embedded at top management level. Each turnaround has taken a lot of time, thought, and effort to bring about.

The financial track record of Kravis and Roberts, for example, did not just happen. It took a lot of work, worry, thought, planning – and luck. In many cases the old management said that it was undermined in its efforts. But careful analysis documents that this is far from the truth. The old management undermined itself by:

■ Not staying up on market developments
■ Not reading reports critical of the way things were going, and
■ Not looking after efficiency at every line of operation, as well as at headquarters.

It takes very intelligent and sensitive people to run a modern company. And it is wrong to believe that the outside world does not know the difference regarding the fairest and best way to handle problems. 'A person without problems is decadent,' one of my professors taught his students at UCLA. Therefore, management should not complain that it has problems. Instead, it should be keen to:

■ Set effective business strategies
■ Assure they are properly executed
■ Invite contrary opinion
■ Re-engineer and restructure
■ Analyze and monitor financial reports, and
■ Pride itself on a rigorous financial discipline.

In conclusion, organizations unable to reinvent themselves, and steadily improve their efficiency, are self-destructive. As the discrepancy between their profit-making and money-losing activities mounts, raiders move in chop the management, take over the firm and turn it around – or cut it to pieces and sell it, when profits from the pieces are greater than from the company kept as one unit.

16.7   Establishing and sustaining a transnational advantage

In a globalized economy, being an innovator and low cost producer of products and services can make the difference between success and failure. But while this is vital, it is not enough. To sustain a competitive advantage in a transnational industry, such as banking, computers, communications, and software, a firm must sell to all significant country markets. Particularly important are markets that contain advanced and demanding buyers because they stimulate further innovative thinking:

- Mastering sophisticated markets helps management understand the most important customer needs.
- In turn, these create pressures that push towards rapid process in innovative and, up to a point, profitable services.

This is a matter of steady transition. The principle is always that transition comes with costs, but failure to make the transition results in a much higher cost. An enterprise can go out of business and die if it cannot make changes, and the same is true of any organization, including entities of national interest (like social security and the health service), and empires.

The rapid evolution in demand is a basic reason why nations with sophisticated clients are those where leading international competitors are based, making it all the more challenging to beat them at their home base. In banking, for example, access to the world's best markets is necessary to sustain competitive advantages.

In finance, as well as in manufacturing and merchandising, the most rewarding form of loyalty to domestic suppliers is to confront them in no uncertain terms with the need for innovation and cost control. Also, with a stringent requirement for matching their foreign competitors in high quality of deliverables in order to retain the business relationship.

- No source of supply should be guaranteed the business.
- Unless the business partner is taking aggressive action to innovate, upgrade quality, and cut costs, supporting domestic suppliers is nobody's ultimate gain.

A similar statement is valid in terms of operational risk control. Any company aspiring to competitive advantage must be aware of all important R&D work going on in the world that is related to its business. This is as true of banking as it is of any firm operating in a competitive industry and seeking market advantages.

Whether in banking or in the peak technology sectors of manufacturing, management must meet head-on the best rivals in the market, in order to sustain and upgrade the company's edge. This is the concept of leadership and, as such, it contrasts to the conditions found in many firms where managers:

- Misperceive the true basis of competitive advantage, and
- Become preoccupied with their own turf rather than with their company's profits and its survival.

Time and again, an industry's leaders are those who have a broad view of competition in which change and innovation is integral to competitive success. They work hard to improve that state of mind and keep ahead of the curve in their business environment. They also encourage internal competition, sometimes through painful new policies.

Basically, this is what globalization is all about. Those who revolt against globalization do so because they are against change, when change eats into their old way of doing things – the status quo. This is true whether the status quo represents fat and unsustainable social benefits; big, inflationary government spending; early retirement with comfortable revenue; or greater effort and more imagination in the work one is doing.

Mid-November 2002, *The Economist* ran a survey which showed that in France a mere 37% of the 55–64 age group are in the labor market.[8] This compares very poorly with 70% in Switzerland, and is part of the exorbitant French social costs. No wonder that for every €100 ($100) every French employee takes home, a French employer still has to shell out €288, compared to half that amount in other countries. In Britain the pay out corresponds to €166.

Huge handouts and the preservation of the status quo are not the stuff out of which competitive strategies are made. Competitive strategies require change and innovation brought about by leaders who think in transnational terms. Competitive strategies also call for long-range plans able to enhance and extend the current position by:

- Engaging the competitors in their own ground
- Inspiring their organizations to meet new challenges, and
- Serving current market needs cost-effectively, while keeping on progressing.

Whether in finance or in any other sector of the economy industry leaders always find ways of overcoming constraints and demolish roadblocks that limit innovation or present obstacles to change. They facilitate the transfer of skills and pay particular attention to the need to grow their human and financial resources while watching the costs. Globalization has not done away with this need. If anything, it brought it into focus.

This is true of all industries, independently of how wealthy an entrepreneur or his or her company may be. The movie industry is global. Steven Spielberg, the film director and producer, according to an article in *Business Week*, gets deeply involved with money matters – especially budgets. That's rare in an industry where $100 million budgets are becoming commonplace and talented directors have severely damaged their careers with profligate spending.

Family training seems to have played a major role. His father was vice president/ manufacturing of Univac, the computer company, and taught his son the value of money. As a boy, Spielberg learned that he had to watch the bottom line. To this day, Steven Spielberg is always on the lookout for ways to hold costs down.

No cost savings seems to be too small for Spielberg or too big. Just weeks before shooting one of his movies was to begin, he called up demanding that the producer cut $20 million out of the already trimmed-down $56 million budget. 'He told me, "Honey, that film isn't getting made until it has a '3' in front of its budget, so get cutting",' said Debbie Allen, the producer.[9] I would like to see board members tell exactly the same thing to the CEO and the executive vice presidents. No cost savings should be too small or too big in a financial institution.

16.8   Capitalizing on the evolving role of financial instruments

Fundamentally, the business of banking is that of buying and selling time. This is precisely what credit institutions do by taking deposits and giving loans; also, through trading. However, the instruments they are using are changing over time.

'Clothes and automobiles change every year,' said Paul M. Mazur of Lehman Brothers, 'but because the currency remains the same in appearance, though its value steadily declines, most people believe that finance does not change. Actually, debt financing changes like everything else. We have to find new models in financing, just as in clothes and automobiles, if we want to stay on top. We must remain inventive architects of the money business.'[10]

Paul Mazur's statement was made four decades ago, but his words were prophetic. Figure 16.3 shows in a nutshell how and why during the past 40 years industrial development has accelerated, particularly in the financial sector. This evolutionary process is propelled by the cost of staying in business, whose vital importance to company survival has been underlined in section 16.2.

In principle, the more wealthy and more sophisticated are the customers the greater are their requirements for financial innovation and quality of deliverables. A thorough study I did with one of the leading financial institutions in terms of asset management led to the 1‰ rule. Out of a total of, say, 1 000 000 customers,

- The top segment of 1000 customers, the 1‰, posed very sophisticated requirements.
- The next 1% of customers, or 10 000, presented significant demands.
- The following 5% of customers, the next 50 000, had to be satisfied with a great deal of effort.

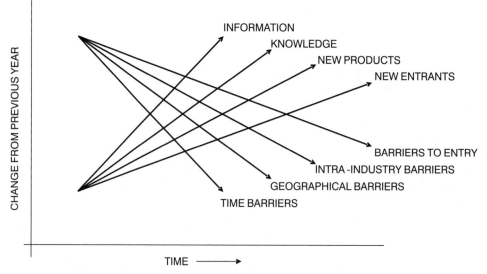

Figure 16.3 Background reasons why industrial development has accelerated – particularly in finance

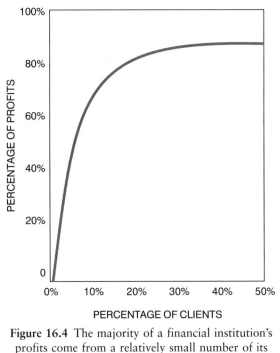

Figure 16.4 The majority of a financial institution's profits come from a relatively small number of its clients

Both innovation and quality of deliverables were at the top of the list of requirements of these three populations, but at different thresholds. Demands posed by the next 10% also gave rise to a good deal of effort, while the balance of 84% of customers was handled through already established products and procedures in a satisfactory way.

Profits for the financial institution followed the inverse line of these percentages. The largest profile – at the level of 20% of total profits – came from the top 1% of the institution's clients. The top 10% of clients roughly accounted for 60% of profits, and the 20% for nearly 85%. This follows closely enough Pareto's law, creating the power curve in Figure 16.4.

The top percentage of customers was largely composed of big international companies, institutional investors, and high net worth individuals. All three classes posed significant demands in customer handling, financial analysis, new instruments, and (in the majority) real-time reporting. A particular demand has been the level of handholding, which is not unreasonable.

Low frequency but high impact (LF/HI, see Chapter 8) operational risk lies in this area of the power curve. By contrast, the way to bet is that the balance of the customer population will more or less feature high frequency, low impact operational risk – though there may always be exceptions. There are several reasons for this statement and they converge towards two groups:

- The unknowns, which are always embedded in new instruments, and
- Risk inherent in high stakes, which may be credit, market, and operational exposures.

Bankers and investors careless enough to forget about the risks they are taking get obliterated. Without first class risk management companies go bust because the financial world is one of instability, not of equilibrium. To cope with this fact we have to change our culture, upgrade our tools and methods, and become much more alert to our risks. The drama in this connection is that, while in their heads people suspect change is inevitable, in their hearts they want precious little to change – and companies are made up of people.

Notes

1 B. Caouette, E.I. Altman, P. Navayanan, *Managing Credit Risk*, Wiley, New York, 1998.
2 D.N. Chorafas, *Outsourcing, Insourcing and IT for Enterprise Management*, Macmillan/Palgrave, London, 2003.
3 D.N. Chorafas, *Internet Supply Chain. Its Impact on Accounting and Logistics*, Macmillan, London, 2001.
4 *The Economist*, 16 November 2002.
5 CNN, Friday 18 November 2002.
6 *BusinessWeek*, 30 September 2002.
7 *BusinessWeek*, 4 November 2002.
8 *The Economist*, 16 November 2002.
9 *BusinessWeek*, 13 July 1998.
10 Joseph Wechsberg, *The Merchant Bankers*, Pocket Books/Simon and Schuster, New York, 1966.

Index